# The Intracoastal Waterway Chartbook

Chesapeake Bay
Cape Charles
VIRGINIA
Norfolk
Albemarle Sound
NORTH CAROLINA
Cape Hatteras
Pamlico Sound
Cape Lookout
Wilmington
SOUTH CAROLINA
Cape Fear
Georgetown
Charleston
GEORGIA
Port Royal
Beaufort
Savannah
Brunswick
Atlantic Ocean
Jacksonville
FLORIDA
Cape Canaveral
Tampa
West Palm Beach
Fort Lauderdale
Miami
Bahama Islands
Florida Keys
Intracoastal Waterway

# The Intracoastal Waterway Chartbook

## NORFOLK TO MIAMI

Chart Editors:
## JOHN AND LESLIE KETTLEWELL

Seven Seas Press
Camden, Maine

Published by Seven Seas Press

10 9 8 7 6 5 4 3 2 1

Copyright © 1991 by Seven Seas Press, an imprint of TAB BOOKS. TAB BOOKS is a division of McGraw-Hill, Inc.

All rights reserved. The publisher takes no responsibility for the use of any of the materials or methods described in this book, nor for the products thereof. Printed in the United States of America.

Library of Congress Cataloging-in-Publication Data

Kettlewell, John.
   The intracoastal waterway chartbook, Norfolk to Miami / John and Leslie Kettlewell.
     p.   cm.
   Includes index.
   ISBN 0-915160-65-X
   1. Intracoastal waterways—South Atlantic States—Maps.
2. Atlantic Intracoastal Waterway—Maps.  3. Boats and boating—
Maps.   I. Kettlewell, Leslie.  II. Title.
G1286.P53.K4  1991  <G&M>
623.89'22348—dc20                                90-24194
                                                            CIP
                                                            MAP

TAB BOOKS offers software for sale. For information and a catalog, please contact TAB Software Department, Blue Ridge Summit, PA 17294-0850.

Questions regarding the content of this book should be addressed to:

Seven Seas Press/International Marine Publishing
P.O. Box 220
Camden, ME 04843

Typeset by Typeworks, Belfast, ME
Printed by Arcata Kingsport, Kingsport, TN
Design by Dawn Peterson

# CONTENTS

| | |
|---|---|
| Preface | v |
| Introduction | vi |
| Inside Out | ix |
| Instructions | x |
| The Intracoastal Waterway: Norfolk to Miami | 1–194 |
| Inlets | 195–217, 219–220 |
|     Beaufort, NC | 195 |
|     Southport, NC | 196 |
|     Georgetown—Winyah Bay, SC | 197–198 |
|     Charleston, SC | 199 |
|     St. Helena Sound, SC | 200–201 |
|     Port Royal Sound, SC | 202–203 |
|     Hilton Head, SC | 204 |
|     Savannah River, SC/GA | 205–206 |
|     St. Catherines Sound, GA | 207 |
|     Sapelo Sound, GA | 208 |
|     St. Simons Sound, GA | 209 |
|     St. Marys River Entrance, GA/FL | 210 |
|     St. John River Entrance, FL | 211–212 |
|     Cape Canaveral Barge Canal, FL | 213–216 |
|     Cape Canaveral Entrance, FL | 217 |
|     Miami Inlet–Government Cut, FL | 219–220 |
| New River, Fort Lauderdale, FL | 218 |
| Miami River, FL | 221 |
| Coconut Grove, FL | 222 |
| Great Dismal Swamp Canal Route 2 | 223–232 |
| Umbrella Cut Alternate Route, GA | 233–234 |
| Appendix A   Bridges (Under 65 Feet) and Locks on the Intracoastal Waterway | 235 |
| Appendix B   General Pilotage | 239 |
| Appendix C   Pilotage Notes for Individual Charts | 240 |
| Appendix D   Mileage Tables and Conversion Tables | 245 |
| Appendix E   NOAA Chart Cross-Reference and Notice to Mariners Information | 249 |
| Appendix F   Facilities Listings | 250 |
| Index | 256 |

# PREFACE

I sit in the cockpit watching the sun set behind the drowned trees of the Alligator River. The smoke from our grill wafts astern over the mirror-like water, disturbed only by the gentle ripples of another cruiser dropping the hook. Several boats gather at anchor, creating a small community in the primordial wilderness of the Alligator-Pungo swamp. Quiet domestic sounds drift in the evening air, punctuated by birdcalls and the furtive rustling noises made by wildlife ashore.

Sipping a cocktail, I chart our southerly progress and wonder what the next misty morning will bring on the Alligator-Pungo Canal. If only we had a compact chart book that was accurate, complete, and easy to use in the cockpit! Why do all of the available charts for the Waterway require three hands and many square feet of plotting area? Why can't the pages be arranged in a simple sequential order? Why do we need to spend so much money on charts to cover the Waterway from Norfolk to Miami?

This chart atlas is an answer to these questions, posed by hundreds of boaters on the Intracoastal Waterway and at boat shows all over the country. It was designed in the cockpit to be used on the water by real people. Send us a postcard from Miami or Norfolk and tell us how it worked!

# INTRODUCTION

The Intracoastal Waterway charted here is 1,090 miles of "toll-free canal" from Norfolk, Virginia to Miami, Florida. Distances are measured in statute miles on the Waterway and are marked every five miles on the charts. To convert statute miles to nautical miles, see Appendix D, which also contains useful distance tables for both inside and outside routes.

The average auxiliary sailboat should travel at least 50 statute miles in a full day, with most of it under power. An extra-fast day might see 80 miles pass under the keel, but frequent delays at locks, fuel stops, and bridge openings keep the average lower. It is impossible to estimate an average speed for motor vessels, as they often cannot go full speed. There are many "speed zones," especially south of St. Lucie in Florida, and this, in combination with the need to refuel more often in fast boats, slows even the fastest boats to averages near 10 knots.

This brings up the touchy subject of excessive wake. Many areas not actually designated as "speed zones" could benefit from less wake. The Alligator-Pungo Canal is lined with debris cleared from the water. We've seen this junk wash back in as an enormous wake scours the banks. Many people have docks near the Waterway and do not appreciate their boats being slammed against pilings and planking. In some cases wakes roll right over private lawns and into houses close to the water.

Wake problems can be alleviated with proper passing techniques. Incidentally, this is no longer a sail-versus-power problem, since many trawler yachts proceed at a rather stately pace and are frequently passed by faster boats. First, I'll commit heresy by telling you to ignore most horn signals! Very few boaters know the proper signals, but they can easily imitate the wrong signal. Whenever I hear a horn from behind I pull over to starboard, which is usually the request regardless of the signal. If the passing boat slows before he reaches my stern, I too slow to near idle and let him pass swiftly. He then checks to make sure we are clear of his wake before accelerating back to cruising speed. We can turn sharply into his passing wake if we deem it necessary.

The horn signals you should listen to come from the commercial operators. You will often encounter a huge tug pushing or pulling a string of barges hundreds of feet long. These guys don't have much room to maneuver, and they love it if you contact them on VHF Channel 13. Ask the skipper where you can go to best allow him through. He'll often say something like "Roger, skipper, that's two blasts," meaning he's passing you on the port side. This way everyone avoids horn blasting and really knows what's going on. One blast would be the signal for him passing you to starboard. At turning points in the channel, tows will often need the whole width of the Intracoastal. The operative rule of the road is to give way to anybody bigger than you and congratulate yourself on being so polite.

The VHF radio is almost indispensable. In addition to vessel-to-vessel communications, you can talk to most bridges and locks on VHF Channel 13 or 16. Again, this avoids confusing whistle blowing and establishes what is going on if there is a delay. A good handheld VHF that can be recharged at night is more useful than one down below, out of earshot. When in doubt about a bridge's restricted hours, you can often call ahead or ask a boat coming the other way. Lock tenders can tell you which side to tie up to and where you can wait while another group locks through. We check the weather channels at various times during the day, especially if thunderstorms may be brewing.

If you can't raise the bridge on VHF, the proper signal is one prolonged blast on your horn followed quickly by one short blast. Please don't annoy the bridge tender by signalling before you get there or before the bridge's assigned opening time. If he's going to open you'll get the same signal in return. If he can't open or has to close quickly you'll get 5 short blasts, which is also the danger signal if anyone is in trouble. When in great distress and approaching a bridge that you need open in a hurry, try the danger signal. The bridge should open, but don't count on it. I think this ploy has been tried too many times by boats who shouldn't have, ruining it for the rest of us. Try to relax and enjoy the leisurely pace of Intracoastal cruising. The bridge tenders are just following rules and regulations and will often let you through when they shouldn't.

Approach all bridges cautiously, as there is often a stiff current running through the constricted channel beneath the bridge. Try to gauge the current before committing yourself. It often takes a few minutes for the bridge to open, so keep a safe distance until you can go through. In two of our scariest boating experiences, we were swept down on slow opening bridges by a nasty current in a narrow channel. Be prepared to turn completely around into the current to wait out delays.

Increasingly, we see restricted opening times on bridges all along the Waterway, especially in Florida. Some bridges open only once an hour for pleasure craft; others don't open at all at certain times of day (usually rush hours). It's a good idea to plan your day's run in advance so as to better your chances of getting through on time. Be conservative in your speed estimates; you can lose 15 minutes at a bridge due to water- or land-traffic problems. Check Appendix A for full information on all bridges, remembering how rapidly these regulations change.

This talk of bridges would be misleading were we not to mention how easy it is to get through most of them. Many times the bridge tender has had the span up before we've gotten there, and we've not even touched the throttle. Often the tender will wait to let the last, slow straggler through before the restricted time begins. We've heard of bridge operators helping boaters in distress and relaying messages for them. When you raise all of these bridges you feel that you're finally getting your money's worth from your tax dollars!

There is one lock in Great Bridge, Virginia, on the main route, and two locks on the Dismal Swamp Canal. The Great Bridge lock is easy to negotiate, with only a foot or two of depth change. The lockmasters monitor VHF 13 and will change the traffic lights to green when you can enter. The proper horn signal is two long and two short blasts for opening a lock. If there are boats coming the other way, you may have to wait up to a half-hour for lockage. We usually tie up to the dolphins or bulkhead outside the locks while waiting. The rise and fall is greater in the Dismal Swamp locks, and the walls somewhat rougher. Be prepared with bow and stern lines at least 30 feet long, plenty of fenders on both sides, and a stout fender board properly placed. Never move into or out of a lock until the lockmaster tells you to, and proceed at dead-slow idle speed.

The controlling depth in the Dismal Swamp Canal is about 6 feet, and everyone bumps a few floating logs or old stumps on the way through. The ancient canal is lined with large trees overhanging the water, so watch your masthead or tuna tower carefully. Here you are totally sheltered in an idyllic woodland setting while gliding along in your oceangoing home. A new Dismal Swamp Canal Visitor's Center, opened in 1989, offers 150 feet of free overnight dockage. Located 5 miles north of the South Mills locks, this is an ideal spot to stay while in the canal. We've marked the location on page 226. Due to restricted opening times for the locks, you should plan your trip carefully if you plan on doing the entire canal in one day. We know of only one good anchorage between Elizabeth City and South Mills, a quiet spot near statute mile 44, behind Goat Island. Approach the 6-foot spot carefully (as marked on the chart), making your turn near marker 11.

Elizabeth City is famous for its fabulous welcome to passing boaters. Free dockage is offered right on the downtown waterfront. You will be greeted by a welcoming committee complete with fresh roses and maps of the area. We particularly enjoy using the courtesy bicycles for exploring the picturesque old town. You can get most supplies here and enjoy the evening cocktail hour on the docks while trading Waterway wisdom with new friends.

Most of the Waterway can handle a draft of at least 6 feet, and we talked to a boat that made it through drawing 7½ feet. Almost everyone goes aground at some point due to inattention or confusion. The greater your draft, the more often you'll be in the mud. Usually you can work the keel free by backing and filling under power. In a sailboat you can raise sail to heel the boat and reduce your draft (if you don't have a winged keel). Obviously, you must be more careful in a twin-screw powerboat, as the props will be the first thing to hit. Several companies have erected prominent billboards advertising prop and strut repairs right on the Waterway.

A quick mention should be made of the floating debris problem. These inland waters are surrounded by trees and sprinkled with old docks and pilings, and this stuff gets adrift and inevitably ends up in front of your boat from time to time. We always hit something each day on the water but find our full-keeled sailboat sheds the offending items before they can do any damage. Many power vessels and some sailboats with exposed props come to grief, providing a steady source of income to marine businesses along the Waterway. The only answer is to slow down and be vigilant, or put your insurance agent at the helm.

Give most Waterway markers a wide berth, as they often sit on shoals. They may have marked deep water several years ago, but continual shoaling has left many markers high and dry at low tide. If you see a cattle egret wading next to a mark, watch out! Tiny "Mexican hat"–shaped buoys sometimes mark the channel near inlets or side canals. These buoys are impossible to identify and difficult to see until you're right on top of them. We get so used to looking at tall daymarks we find ourselves confused by the sudden appearance of a fleet of minuscule floating marks. The obvious solution is to study the upcoming waterway on your charts so you know what to expect. Pay particular attention to channel junctions, where several sets of conflicting marks may not readily explain themselves.

An odd phenomenon I've noticed on our boat is the Waterway Rhythm Syndrome. After a few days on the water you begin to settle into a routine. We set the throttle to 2000 rpm and go, go, go until we drop the hook for the night. The smooth water glides under our hull endlessly as we tick off the miles on our charts. Suddenly the side channel to our overnight stop comes up and we blast along at 2000 rpm between cattails and old stumps until we come to an inconvenient stop in the mud. Another common scenario sees us arriving at a bridge a little early, only to discover that a 3-knot current is the cause of our excess speed. Our wild crash turn just in the nick of time entertains the bridge tender but annoys the flotilla that has been nipping at our heels. We've had a wild few minutes when a group of sailboats all piled up behind a slow opening bridge, and none of us could stem the current in reverse. When we got sorted out we were all facing the direction from which we had come just to maintain position in the strong current. Try to anticipate upcoming hazards that will alter your normal routine. Enjoy the gentle rhythms of the Waterway, but be prepared for the contrasts.

Overhead clearance is limited by several 65-foot fixed bridges and a 56-foot span on the Julia Tuttle Causeway in Miami. If you are close to these limits, approach the bridges with extreme caution. Most of the Waterway is tidal, and water levels can fluctuate more than usual during times of extreme weather. Most fixed bridges and many opening bridges have a clearance gauge at the bulkhead below the bridge, but these are notoriously inaccurate and always seem to be obscured by green slime. We've seen more than one boat tickle the underside of a bridge with its VHF antenna.

Most Waterway navigation is simple, consisting of proceeding from one mark to the next using "eyeball navigation." Some stretches require the plotting of an occasional compass course. When visibility is poor or marks are far apart, you might have to make timed runs on plotted courses. We've encountered sudden, blinding thunderstorms while crossing Albemarle and Pamlico Sounds. In these conditions you can make good use of an entire navigational arsenal, including Loran, radar, compass, and depth sounder. A sounder easily visible from the helm is a comfort for those with deeper draft.

Sailing on the Waterway can be frustrating, though boats have negotiated its entire length with no engine at all. (One of the earlier such voyages, made in a small catboat, is recounted with charm in a book titled *The Boy, Me, and the Cat*. If you can find a copy, it makes wonderful background reading for a trip on the ICW.) We find the use of a roller-furling jib quite helpful at times. The main can be set in some of the more open stretches and will ease the motion when a chop kicks up. We've had beautiful sails across Albemarle and Pamlico sounds, up or down the Neuse River, and even in the Indian River in Florida. With the motor ticking over, we're ready for quick maneuvering should it be necessary. You should never attempt to sail under an opening bridge, and we don't attempt it with fixed bridges either. Sometimes at the critical moment under the span you find your sails blanketed by the bridge structure. If the current is against you, some fast engine starting will be in order.

No pleasure boat should travel after dark if at all possible. You'll see commercial vessels pass by utilizing huge spotlights, but don't emulate them. They have a tremendous knowledge of the local waters and can withstand the occasional grounding better than you. The lighted marks are far apart and often difficult to identify, while the channels are twisting and shoal. We struggled from Wrightsville Beach to Masonboro one night and lived to tell about it, but I would not do it again. We had to weave from one side of the channel to the other using the depth sounder to tell us when to turn. Our speed made good was probably near two knots. Plan to stop by 4:00 PM or 5:00 PM, and stick to your schedule. If we arrive early we use the time for exploring on foot or by dinghy.

There are hundreds of fabulous gunkholes all along the Intracoastal, and only Florida has significant restrictions on anchoring out. For some reason, more and more towns in Florida look upon the traveling boater as a vagabond who will dirty their waterfront, ruin their view, and pollute their waters. If you are the type who does these things you'll find less and less tolerance among cruisers and officials. The vast majority of Waterway travelers are law-abiding, quiet, and neat — probably more so than the average citizen living ashore. We find the boating community as a whole to be tremendously honest and considerate of their fellow travelers on this vessel we know as Earth.

We anchor out most of the time unless we are south of Palm Beach. From Palm Beach to Miami there are few good anchorages where you will be welcome. This area is lined with beautiful estates and high-rises. Side canals are filled with marinas and private docks. Many of the commercial marinas are surprisingly reasonable and will welcome the visiting boater. We take advantage of this and stock up our larder or wander ashore to visit the sights. Here you can wash down the boat, take a long, hot shower, and see a movie after dinner. Enjoy civilization while you have the chance.

When leaving the marked Waterway in search of an anchorage, proceed cautiously. Many side channels have silted in and are full of debris or even old, sunken vessels. The bottom is generally gooey black mud, and the holding is excellent. A power washdown pump for the anchor and chain can make morning chores more enjoyable, though we've always managed with a mop and bucket. Be sure you are well outside the channel and showing a proper anchor light. A light near deck level is better than the masthead type, which is above normal sight lines. Most of our anchorages have been peaceful, sheltered, and idyllic. We feel safe from all normal storms and enjoy the wild solitude of anchoring out.

The ICW can be used all year, though most boats make the trip in the fall and spring. Southbound, leaving Norfolk in October is ideal. By November frosts will be quite frequent north of South Carolina, and in December it will be cold as far south as the Florida border. January and February bring occasional winter storms as far south as Miami. Even in the middle of the winter, however, temperatures through most of Florida will rise to 70 or 75 degrees in the daytime. South of Vero Beach you're likely to get temperatures in the 80s even in February.

The pattern reverses itself as you head north in the spring. It is best to stay below Charleston until May. Reaching Norfolk in late May or early June, you'll find warm days and mild evenings. By June, hot weather prevails all along the Waterway. We made it to Norfolk on June 12th one year only to find temperatures over 100 degrees! It was so hot one of the bridges refused to open until sprayed with water. Our ideal schedule would be to hit New England by the first half of June, when the northern weather finally stabilizes.

Most winter northers won't bother you much in the protected channels of the ICW. Headed south, you'll have the storm at your back, pushing you along. Sailboats can then sail down stretches they would normally power through. The cold, rain, and wind will last just a few days, reminding you why you're headed south. Trying to head north into the teeth of one of these storms can be wet and miserable in some of the more open sections. Several bridges may not be open if the winds get strong enough. Before starting out, you should call ahead if in doubt as to storm conditions. Beware of the possibility of unusually high and low tides in certain areas. After heavy rains, expect to see large amounts of flotsam in the water.

The havoc wreaked by Hurricane Hugo was a grim reminder of the vulnerability of certain portions of the Waterway to violent storms. The Ben Sawyer Bridge near Charleston was actually ripped loose from its mounts and had to be welded in place as a temporary fix. It will be years before many marinas in the Charleston area regain their former operating status. We monitor the VHF weather stations every day and plot the progress of approaching storms on a small-scale (large-area) chart. Hurricane season is June through October, with the most dangerous months being August and September. While the area covered in this book is likely to be hit by several severe storms each year, it offers many places to hide from the weather. There are literally thousands of protected hurricane holes just off the Intracoastal.

Our basic hurricane and storm strategy is to avoid all marinas and popular harbors. We head inland as far as possible, anchoring far up some winding creek surrounded by soft marshland. We put big anchors in the mud and ashore or tie off to sturdy-looking trees. Most problems are caused by chafe on the lines. Heavy, clear PVC water tubing around critical portions of the lines prevent chafe as well as anything. I carry 10 or 20 feet of this stuff in a cockpit locker. Get a size big enough to slide over your lines easily, so you don't have to split it. Keep abreast of the latest hurricane reports, and prepare early when one threatens. Television reports are often the most up to date but will scare you with their pictures of death and destruction. Keep in mind that news is packaged to sell, and these reports focus on the worst that has happened.

What are the highlights of a trip along the ICW? This is a very subjective topic, so the best we can offer is our highly biased opinions. The northernmost section, from Norfolk to Beaufort, North Carolina via the Dismal Swamp Canal, is the epitome of inland cruising. You find canals, locks, bridges, open sounds, wild swamps, lonely anchorages, and sleepy towns with an air of America's past. Each day brings a new terrain and a new Waterway experience. Beaufort, North Carolina, has a fascinating maritime museum, a friendly waterfront, and wild horses on the beach. St. Augustine, Florida is the oldest city in the U.S. and boasts a Spanish fort and a French patisserie. Miami is a big city right on the beach. Here you can catch a flight, go to the boat show in February, stock up for crossing the Gulf Stream, have a Reuben at Wolfie's deli or stone crabs at Joe's. These places are great, but our favorite spots are the unknown bends and creeks where the sun sets over waving grasslands and the egrets step gingerly along the water's edge. Blue herons glide overhead, and we whisper in the cockpit to preserve the silence. We hope you find your own idyllic anchorage on these charts.

# INSIDE OUT

Most sailboats and many large powerboats like to combine ocean runs with their Intracoastal trip. We almost always take a hop "outside" if weather permits. Outside there is no shelter from the full force of the Atlantic Ocean, and many inlets can be rough or dangerous when an onshore sea piles up against an outgoing current. Even the "all weather" inlets should be avoided in strong onshore winds. Study your charts carefully, as the inlets are often protected by long submerged jetties extending well out to sea. Shoals may surround the marked entrance channels, causing large areas of breaking seas in heavy weather. If it is very calm (glassy smooth) you might try one of the smaller inlets by following a local dragger through the ever-shifting channels. When the chart shows no buoys for an inlet, you know it demands "local knowledge." Such an inlet can be tempting in settled weather, but be prepared to retreat if you can't sort out the buoyage. Beware of big swells from some distant storm breaking heavily even though the local weather may be calm.

Heading south, your first chance to jump outside is at Southport, North Carolina. It is not worth venturing outside north of Frying Pan Shoals, as you would have to go all the way out to the Gulf Stream before heading back in. Winyah Bay is the next really good entrance, followed by Charleston, then Port Royal Sound. After that you have Hilton Head and the Savannah River right next to each other. St. Simons Sound is next, with the St. Marys River right on the Georgia-Florida border. Florida's best inlets are the St. Johns River, Cape Canaveral, Ft. Pierce, Palm Beach (Lake Worth), Ft. Lauderdale, and Miami. The Cape Florida and Biscayne channels are good jumping off spots for Bahamas-bound cruisers.

All of these inlets are included in this atlas, and we've also included several inlets we consider less safe in bad weather. These include St. Helena Sound, St. Catherines Sound, and Sapelo Sound. Though many boats use these inlets, and they are well marked, they should be attempted only with favorable wind and tide conditions. Be sure to obtain the necessary offshore charts before venturing outside.

Boats can benefit in both speed and reduced frustration by heading outside south of Ft. Pierce or Palm Beach. Southeastern Florida is chock-full of restricted bridges and wake-throwing speedboats, and powerboats will be annoyed by the frequent "No Wake" signs enforced by a vigilant Florida Marine Patrol. These factors can make the inside trip miserable. Some boats can't clear the 56-foot Julia Tuttle Causeway in Miami and have to go outside. Southbound, we've jumped outside as far north as Cape Canaveral, where we caught a cold front and rode the strong northwest winds all the way to Miami. It was a thrilling moonlit sleighride less than a mile off the beach to windward. Be careful not to get out into the Gulf Stream if headed south, but use it for a 2- to 3-knot boost in speed when headed north.

The Gulf Stream from Florida north to Beaufort, North Carolina provides a ride not to be missed. With favorable winds and current, we've averaged 7 to 10 knots the whole way in a 37-foot sailboat. Be ready to abandon the conveyor belt if a norther brews up in the states, however, because northerly winds against the Gulf Stream create square waves with pits between them. When caught out in something like this, you'll understand the origins of the Bermuda Triangle legend.

With good forecasts you should have a marvelous outside trip. We find the Florida television stations offer the best weather forecasts in the country, including lengthy discussions of the weather systems and their effects on the long-term outlook. Floridians love to hear how superior their weather is!

The outside option can add variety to your trip. You'll have dolphins riding your bow wave under big blue skies filled with puffy white clouds, and when you go back inside you'll appreciate the winding, sheltered creeks of the Waterway that much more. It is a pleasure that is missed by many who travel the ICW.

# INSTRUCTIONS

Though we hope the use of this chartbook is self-explanatory, a few hints may be in order. The charts are arranged in geographic order starting with Norfolk, Virginia on page 1, proceeding south down the Intracoastal Waterway to Miami, Florida on page 192, and continuing to Key Biscayne and the Florida Channel on pages 193 and 194. The Dismal Swamp Canal, which is the principal alternate route you will encounter on the Waterway, is covered on pages 223 through 232, and details of many inlets, rivers, and other alternate routes appear on pages 195 through 222 and 233 through 234. The table of contents and index should help you locate particular places. Several appendices include further information as provided on the NOAA charts and in other government publications, and addresses for the Coast Guard's *Local Notices to Mariners*. By subscribing to these Notices you can keep the charts in this book up to date. An appendix lists the government chart number and edition used to create each chart page in the book.

Each chart page carries notations of interest. Statute mile designations are prominently marked in the border, along with marks for the location of each opening bridge and lock. To find the operating characteristics of a particular bridge, refer to the matching mile designation in Appendix A. Please note that bridge regulations are constantly changing and may differ from those published here. We have included listings for several high-level fixed bridges that have recently replaced opening bridges. Some of these changes have not yet appeared on the government charts.

An ideal companion volume to these charts would be *The Intracoastal Waterway, Norfolk to Miami: A Cockpit Guide*, written by Jan and Bill Moeller and available from International Marine Publishing Company, nautical bookstores, and many of the chandleries near and on the Waterway. For quick cross-references, refer to the statute-mile markers on the charts. If you are planning an offshore trip you will need to obtain the proper charts to join our inlet charts. NOAA charts may be ordered directly from:

Distribution Branch
N/CG33
National Ocean Service
Riverdale, MD 20737-1199
(301) 436-6990

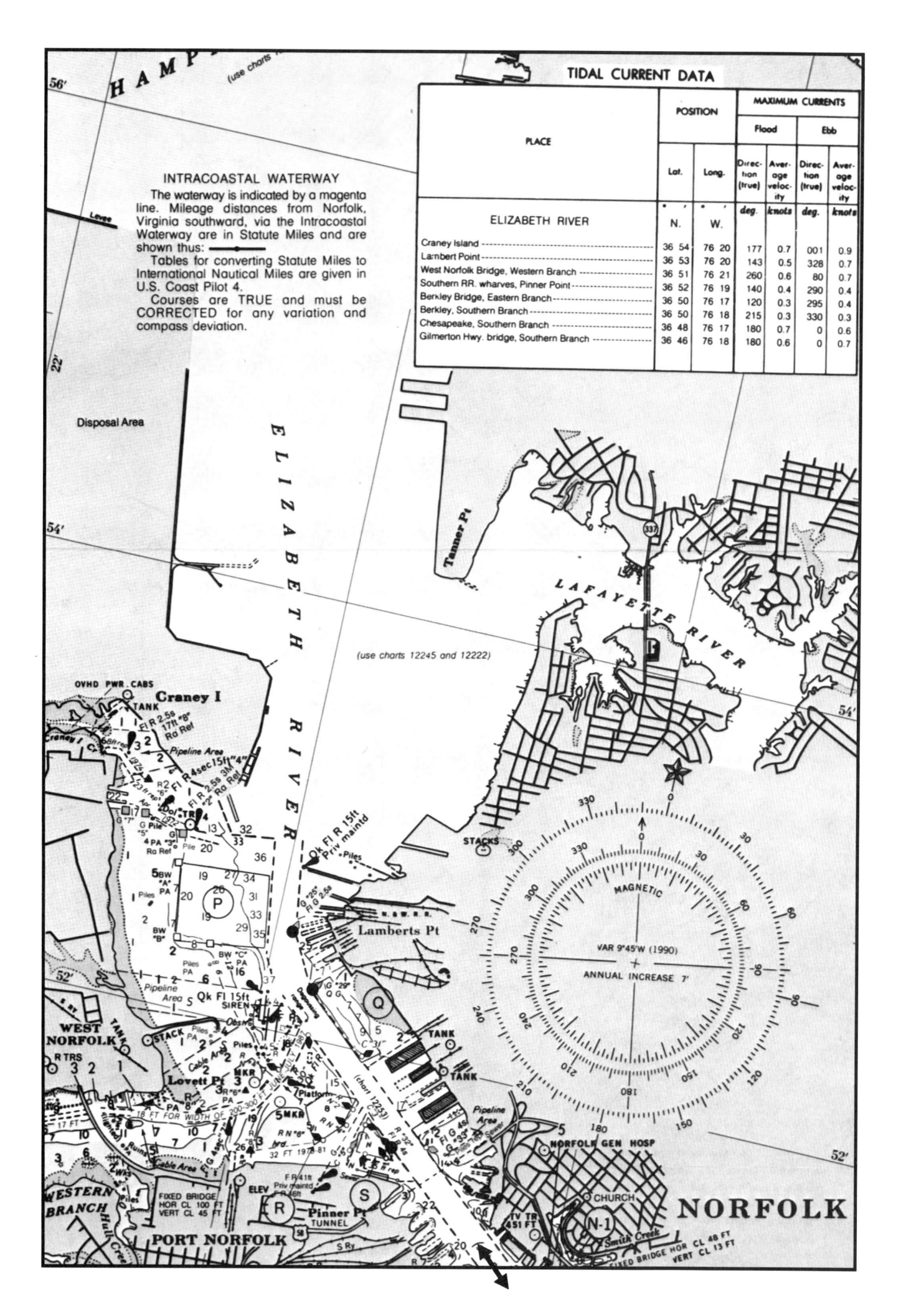

## INTRACOASTAL WATERWAY

The waterway is indicated by a magenta line. Mileage distances from Norfolk, Virginia southward, via the Intracoastal Waterway are in Statute Miles and are shown thus:

Tables for converting Statute Miles to International Nautical Miles are given in U.S. Coast Pilot 4.

Courses are TRUE and must be CORRECTED for any variation and compass deviation.

### TIDAL CURRENT DATA

| PLACE | POSITION Lat. N. ° ′ | POSITION Long. W. ° ′ | Flood Direction (true) deg. | Flood Average velocity knots | Ebb Direction (true) deg. | Ebb Average velocity knots |
|---|---|---|---|---|---|---|
| **ELIZABETH RIVER** | | | | | | |
| Craney Island | 36 54 | 76 20 | 177 | 0.7 | 001 | 0.9 |
| Lambert Point | 36 53 | 76 20 | 143 | 0.5 | 328 | 0.7 |
| West Norfolk Bridge, Western Branch | 36 51 | 76 21 | 260 | 0.6 | 80 | 0.7 |
| Southern RR. wharves, Pinner Point | 36 52 | 76 19 | 140 | 0.4 | 290 | 0.4 |
| Berkley Bridge, Eastern Branch | 36 50 | 76 17 | 120 | 0.3 | 295 | 0.4 |
| Berkley, Southern Branch | 36 50 | 76 18 | 215 | 0.3 | 330 | 0.3 |
| Chesapeake, Southern Branch | 36 48 | 76 17 | 180 | 0.7 | 0 | 0.6 |
| Gilmerton Hwy. bridge, Southern Branch | 36 46 | 76 18 | 180 | 0.6 | 0 | 0.7 |

VAR 9°45′W (1990)
ANNUAL INCREASE 7′

NORFOLK

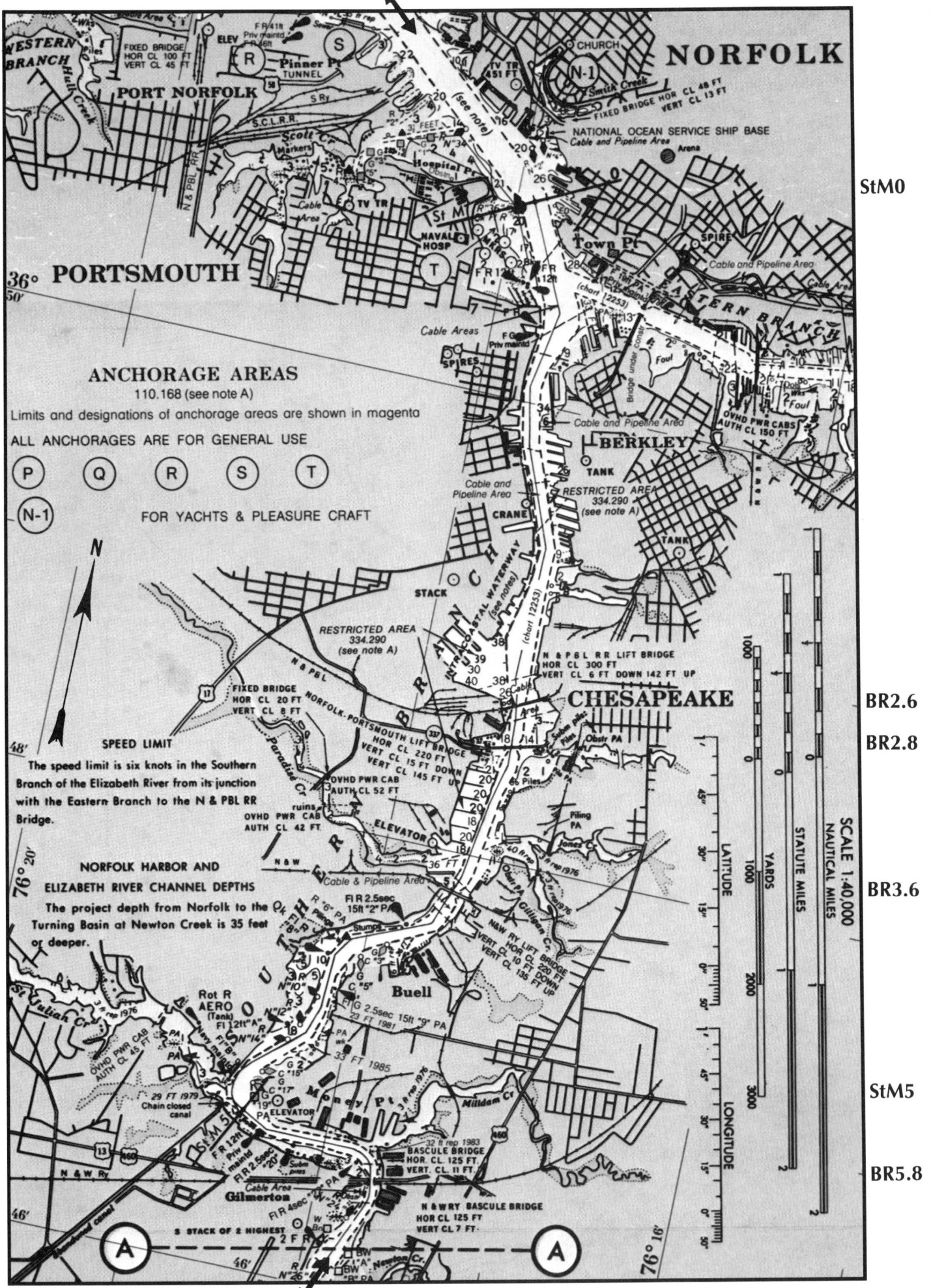

# NORFOLK

**PORT NORFOLK**

**PORTSMOUTH**

**BERKLEY**

**CHESAPEAKE**

## ANCHORAGE AREAS
110.168 (see note A)

Limits and designations of anchorage areas are shown in magenta

ALL ANCHORAGES ARE FOR GENERAL USE

(P) (Q) (R) (S) (T)

(N-1)   FOR YACHTS & PLEASURE CRAFT

### SPEED LIMIT
The speed limit is six knots in the Southern Branch of the Elizabeth River from its junction with the Eastern Branch to the N & PBL RR Bridge.

### NORFOLK HARBOR AND ELIZABETH RIVER CHANNEL DEPTHS
The project depth from Norfolk to the Turning Basin at Newton Creek is 35 feet or deeper.

SCALE 1:40,000

StM0

BR2.6
BR2.8

BR3.6

StM5

BR5.8

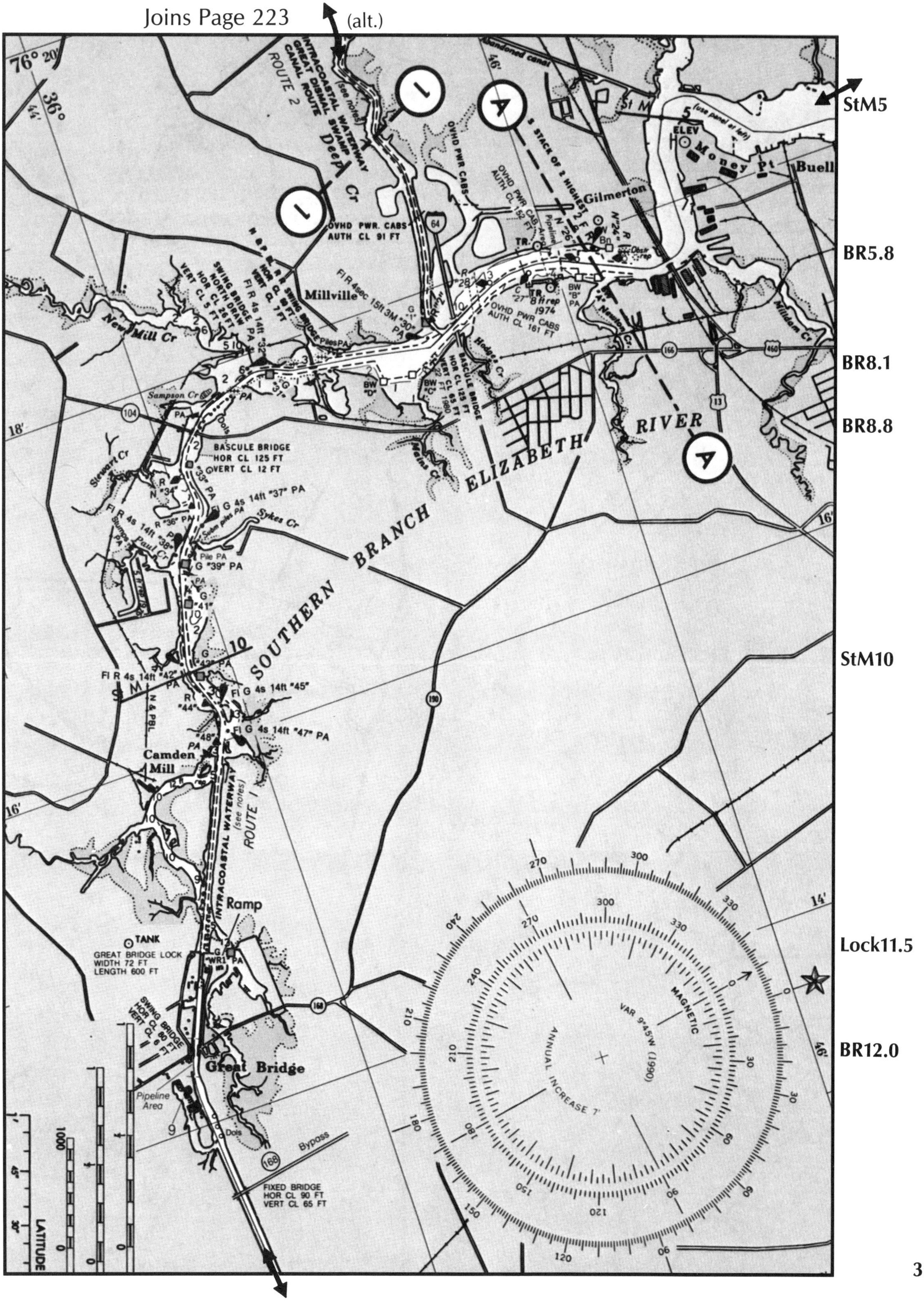

Joins Page 223
(alt.)
StM5
BR5.8
BR8.1
BR8.8
StM10
Lock11.5
BR12.0
INTRACOASTAL WATERWAY GREAT DISMAL SWAMP CANAL ROUTE
ROUTE 2
Deep Cr
OVHD PWR. CABS AUTH CL 91 FT
Millville
New Mill Cr
Gilmerton
Money Pt
Buell
SOUTHERN BRANCH ELIZABETH RIVER
BASCULE BRIDGE HOR CL 125 FT VERT CL 12 FT
Sampson Cr
Stewart Cr
Sykes Cr
Paul Cr
Camden Mill
INTRACOASTAL WATERWAY
ROUTE 1
Ramp
TANK
GREAT BRIDGE LOCK WIDTH 72 FT LENGTH 600 FT
Great Bridge
Pipeline Area
Bypass
FIXED BRIDGE HOR CL 90 FT VERT CL 65 FT
VAR 9°45'W (1990)
ANNUAL INCREASE 7'
MAGNETIC
LATITUDE

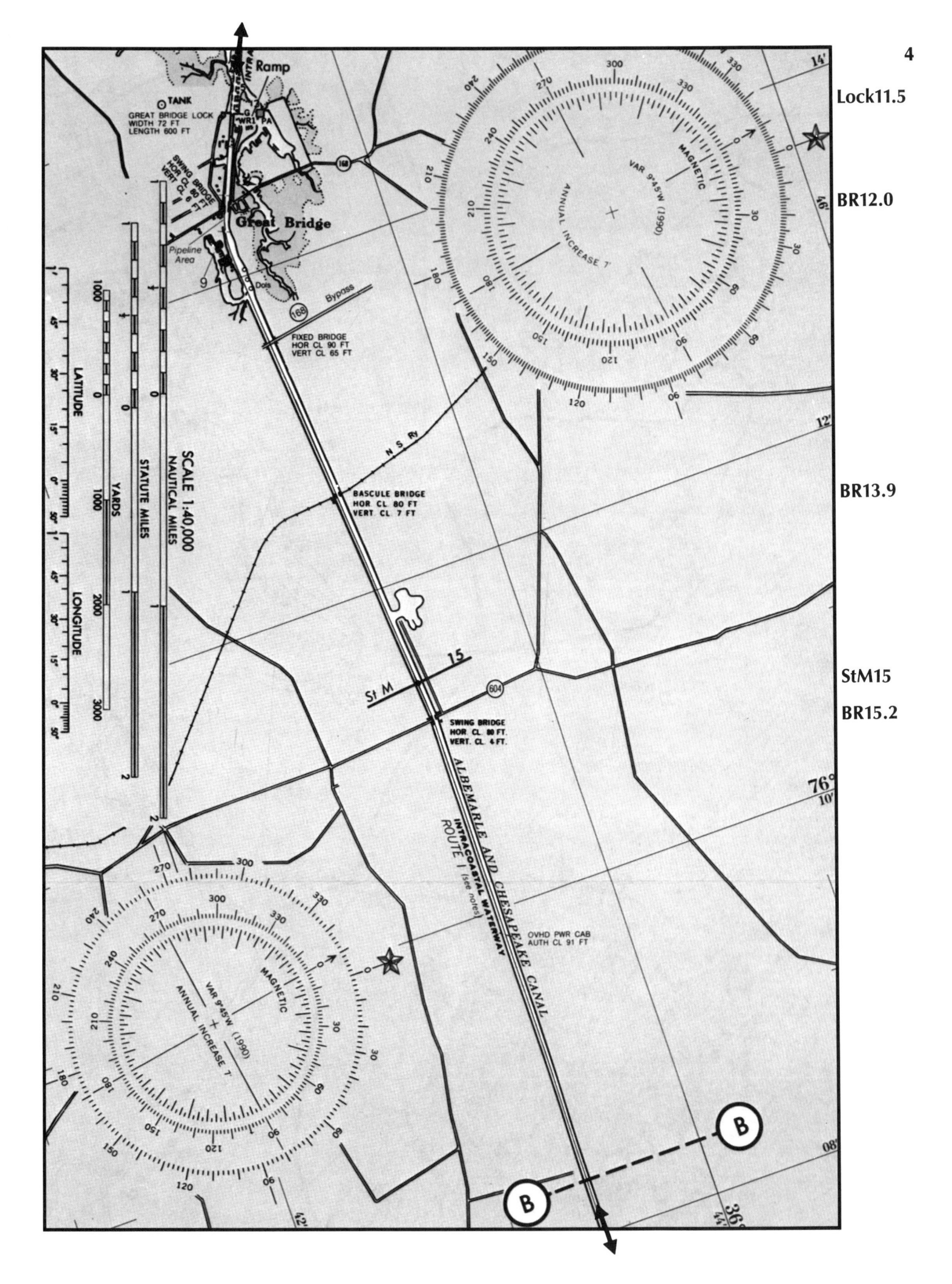

4

Lock11.5

BR12.0

BR13.9

StM15

BR15.2

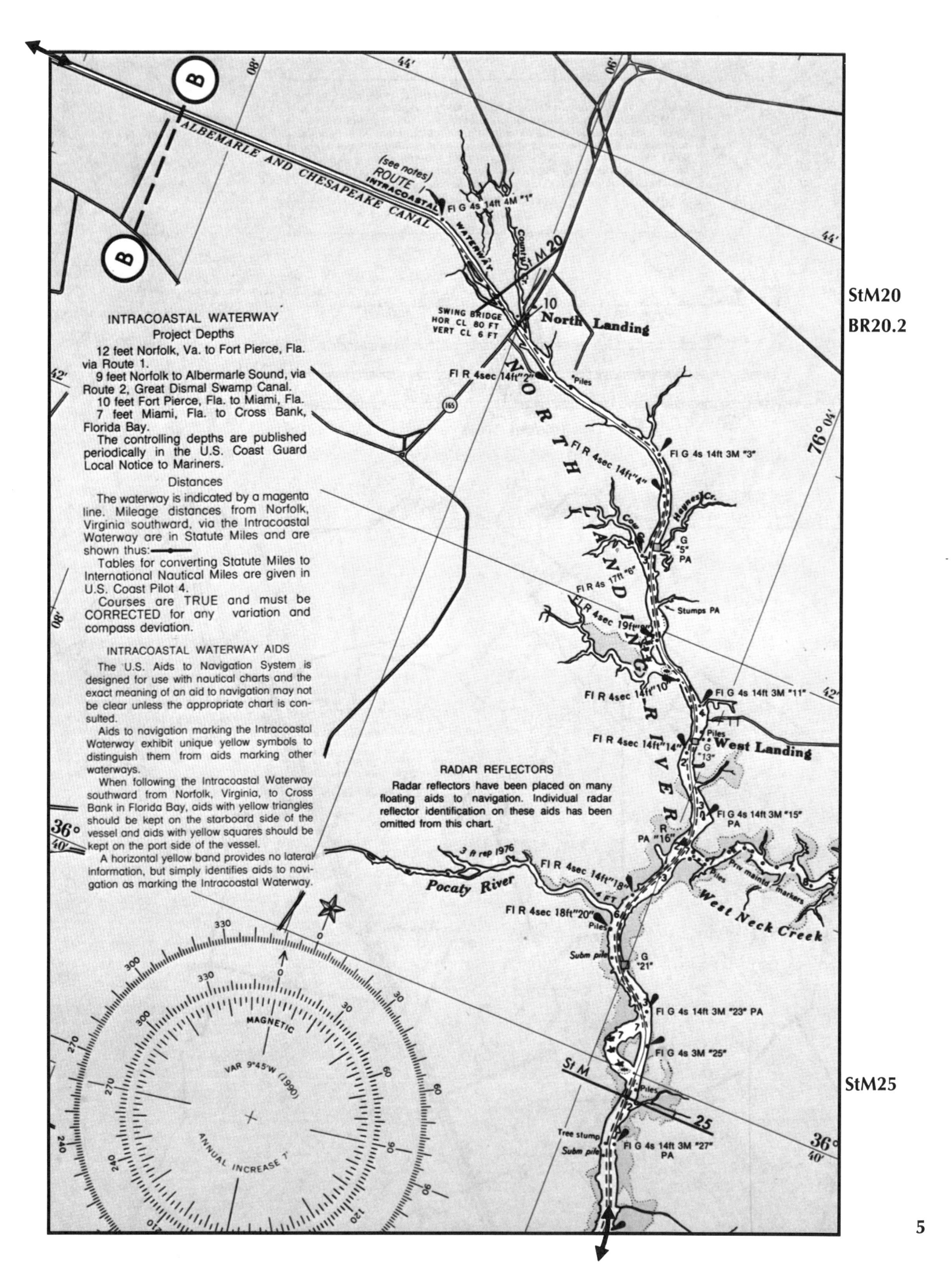

## INTRACOASTAL WATERWAY
### Project Depths
12 feet Norfolk, Va. to Fort Pierce, Fla. via Route 1.
9 feet Norfolk to Albermarle Sound, via Route 2, Great Dismal Swamp Canal.
10 feet Fort Pierce, Fla. to Miami, Fla.
7 feet Miami, Fla. to Cross Bank, Florida Bay.
The controlling depths are published periodically in the U.S. Coast Guard Local Notice to Mariners.

### Distances
The waterway is indicated by a magenta line. Mileage distances from Norfolk, Virginia southward, via the Intracoastal Waterway are in Statute Miles and are shown thus:———
Tables for converting Statute Miles to International Nautical Miles are given in U.S. Coast Pilot 4.
Courses are TRUE and must be CORRECTED for any variation and compass deviation.

### INTRACOASTAL WATERWAY AIDS
The U.S. Aids to Navigation System is designed for use with nautical charts and the exact meaning of an aid to navigation may not be clear unless the appropriate chart is consulted.
Aids to navigation marking the Intracoastal Waterway exhibit unique yellow symbols to distinguish them from aids marking other waterways.
When following the Intracoastal Waterway southward from Norfolk, Virginia, to Cross Bank in Florida Bay, aids with yellow triangles should be kept on the starboard side of the vessel and aids with yellow squares should be kept on the port side of the vessel.
A horizontal yellow band provides no lateral information, but simply identifies aids to navigation as marking the Intracoastal Waterway.

### RADAR REFLECTORS
Radar reflectors have been placed on many floating aids to navigation. Individual radar reflector identification on these aids has been omitted from this chart.

StM20
BR20.2

StM25

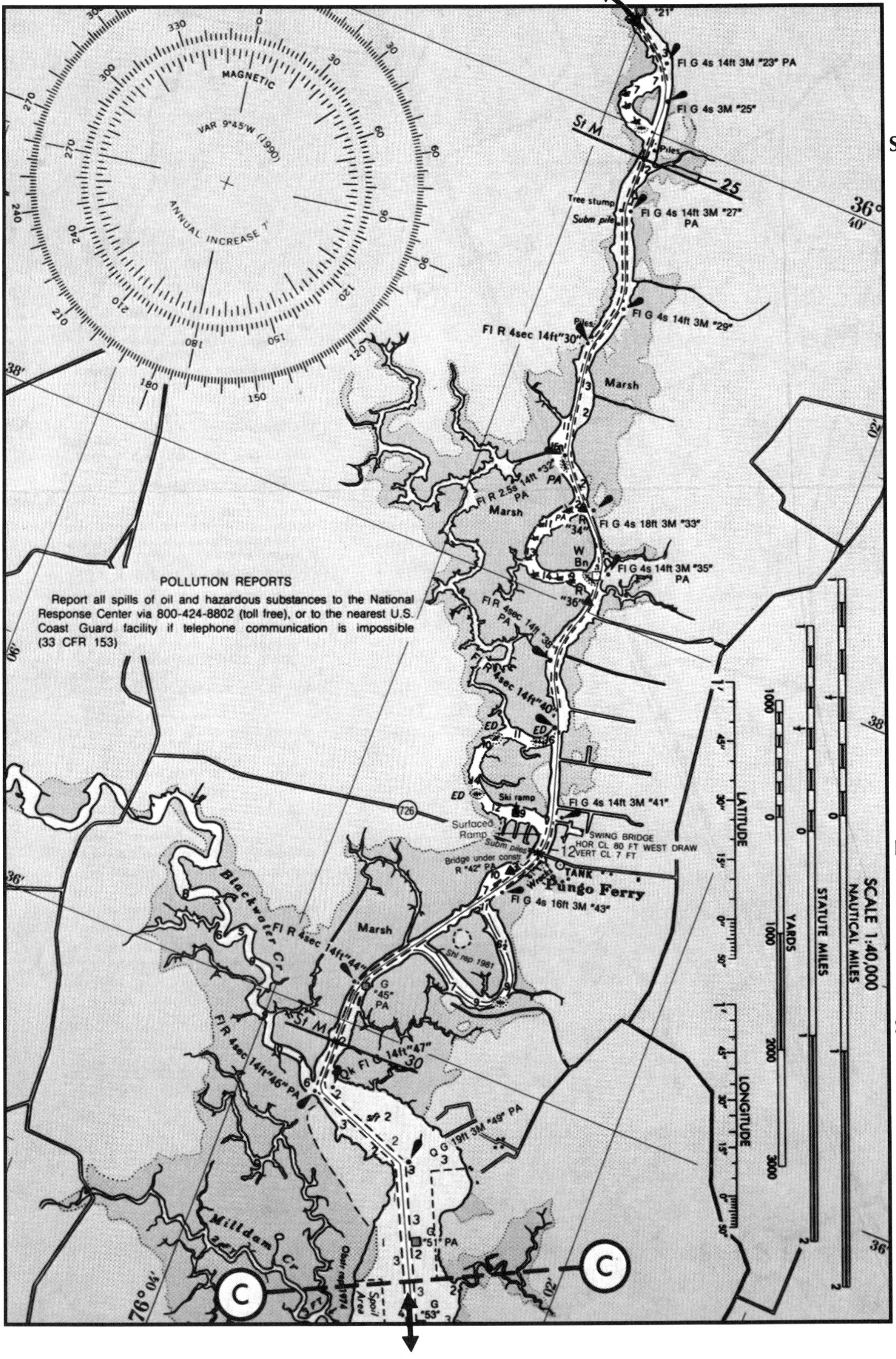


StM25

BR28.3

StM30

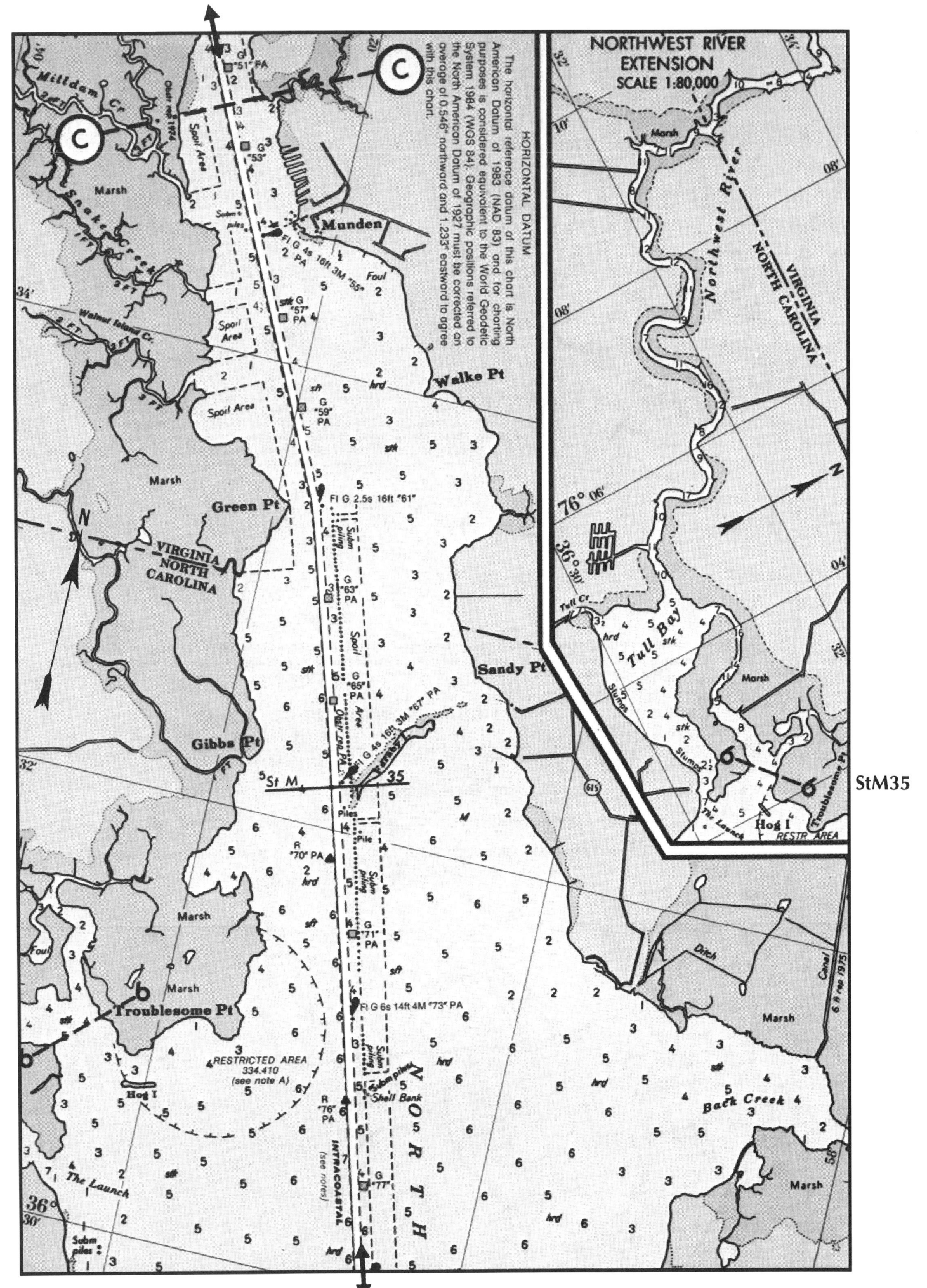

## NORTHWEST RIVER EXTENSION
### SCALE 1:80,000

**HORIZONTAL DATUM**

The horizontal reference datum of this chart is North American Datum of 1983 (NAD 83) and for charting purposes is considered equivalent to the World Geodetic System 1984 (WGS 84). Geographic positions referred to the North American Datum of 1927 must be corrected an average of 0.546" northward and 1.233" eastward to agree with this chart.

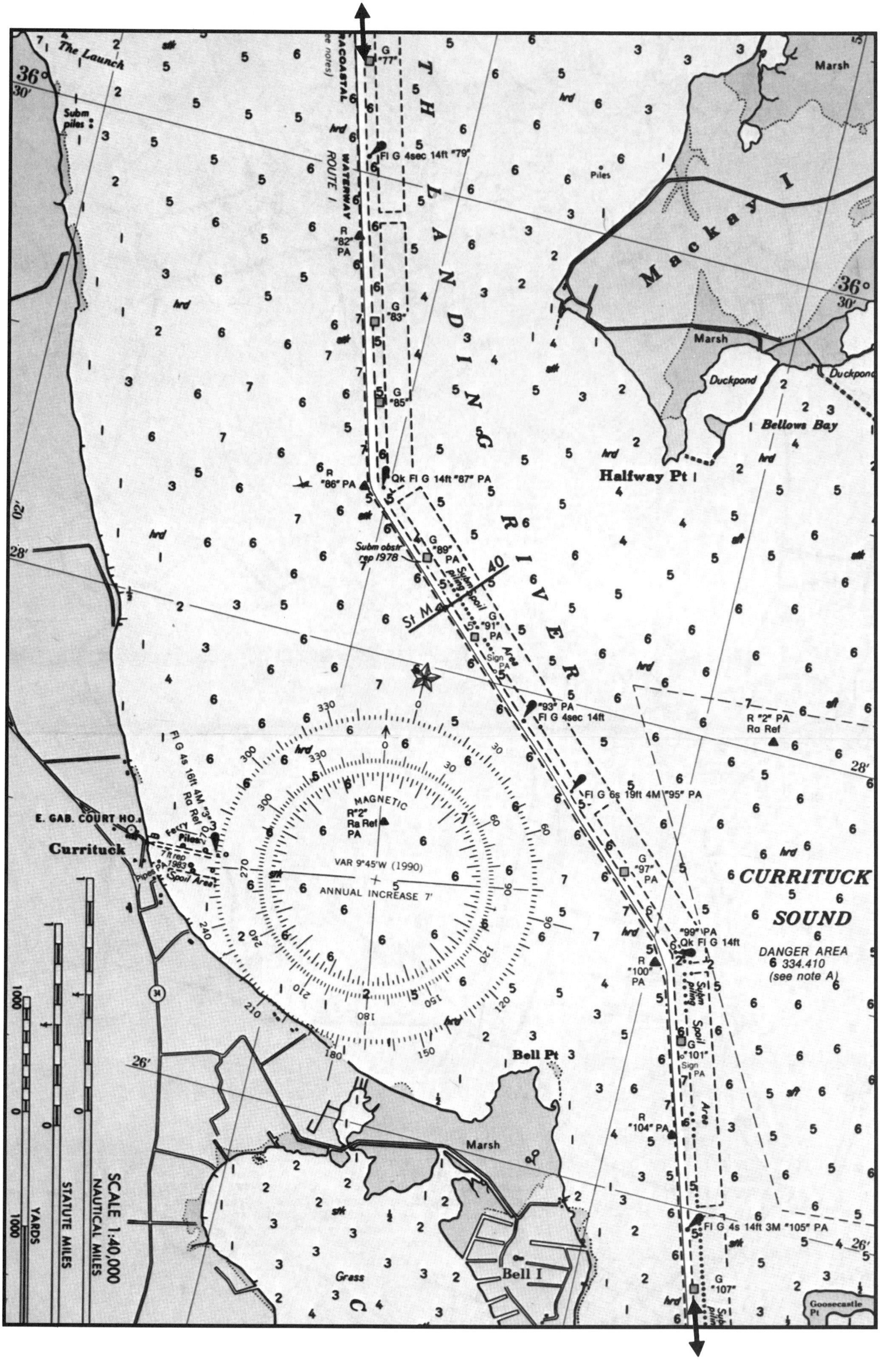
The Launch
Subm piles
Piles
Mackay I
Marsh
Duckpond
Bellows Bay
Halfway Pt
NORTH LANDING RIVER
INTRACOASTAL WATERWAY ROUTE 1
G "77"
Fl G 4sec 14ft "79"
R "82" PA
G "83"
G "85"
Qk Fl G 14ft "87" PA
R "86" PA
Subm obstr rep 1978
G "89" PA
St M 40
G "91" PA
Sign PA
Spoil Area
"93" PA
Fl G 4sec 14ft
Fl G 6s 19ft 4M "95" PA
G "97" PA
"99" PA
Qk Fl G 14ft
R "100" PA
G "101"
R "104" PA
Fl G 4s 14ft 3M "105" PA
G "107"
R "2" PA
Ra Ref
CURRITUCK SOUND
DANGER AREA
334.410
(see note A)
E. GAB. COURT HO.
Currituck
Fl G 4s 16ft 4M "3" Ra Ref
Ferry
Piles
7 ft rep 1983
Pipes
Spoil Area
MAGNETIC
R "2" Ra Ref PA
VAR 9°45'W (1990)
ANNUAL INCREASE 7'
Bell Pt
Marsh
Bell I
Grass
Goosecastle Pt
36° 30'
28'
26'
02'
SCALE 1:40,000
NAUTICAL MILES
STATUTE MILES
YARDS

StM40

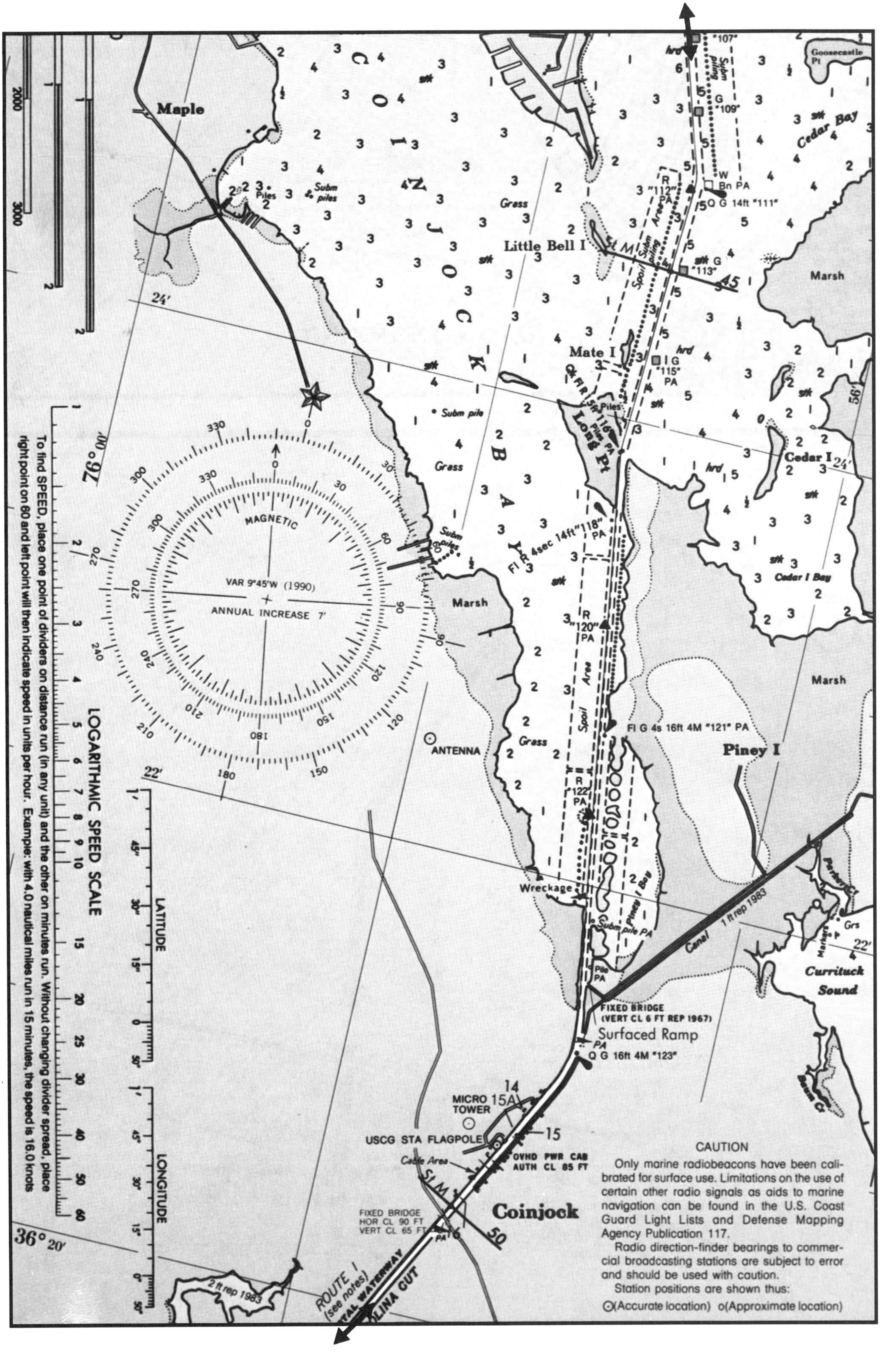

Maple
Little Bell I
Mate I
Long Pt
Cedar Bay
Goosecastle Pt
Cedar I
Cedar I Bay
Marsh
Piney I
Piney I Bay
Currituck Sound
Coinjock
Grass
Subm piles
Subm pile
Spoil Area
Subm piling
Fl R 4sec 14ft "118" PA
Fl G 4s 16ft 4M "121" PA
Q G 14ft "111"
Q G 16ft 4M "123"
FIXED BRIDGE (VERT CL 6 FT REP 1967)
Surfaced Ramp
Canal 1 ft rep 1983
Wreckage
ANTENNA
MICRO TOWER
USCG STA FLAGPOLE
OVHD PWR CAB AUTH CL 85 FT
Cable Area
FIXED BRIDGE HOR CL 90 FT VERT CL 65 FT
2 ft rep 1983
ROUTE 1 (see notes)
MAGNETIC
VAR 9°45'W (1990)
ANNUAL INCREASE 7'
LOGARITHMIC SPEED SCALE
To find SPEED, place one point of dividers on distance run (in any unit) and the other on minutes run. Without changing divider spread, place right point on 60 and left point will then indicate speed in units per hour. Example: with 4.0 nautical miles run in 15 minutes, the speed is 16.0 knots
LATITUDE
LONGITUDE
76°00'
36°20'
CAUTION
Only marine radiobeacons have been calibrated for surface use. Limitations on the use of certain other radio signals as aids to marine navigation can be found in the U.S. Coast Guard Light Lists and Defense Mapping Agency Publication 117.
Radio direction-finder bearings to commercial broadcasting stations are subject to error and should be used with caution.
Station positions are shown thus:
⊙(Accurate location) o(Approximate location)


StM45

StM50

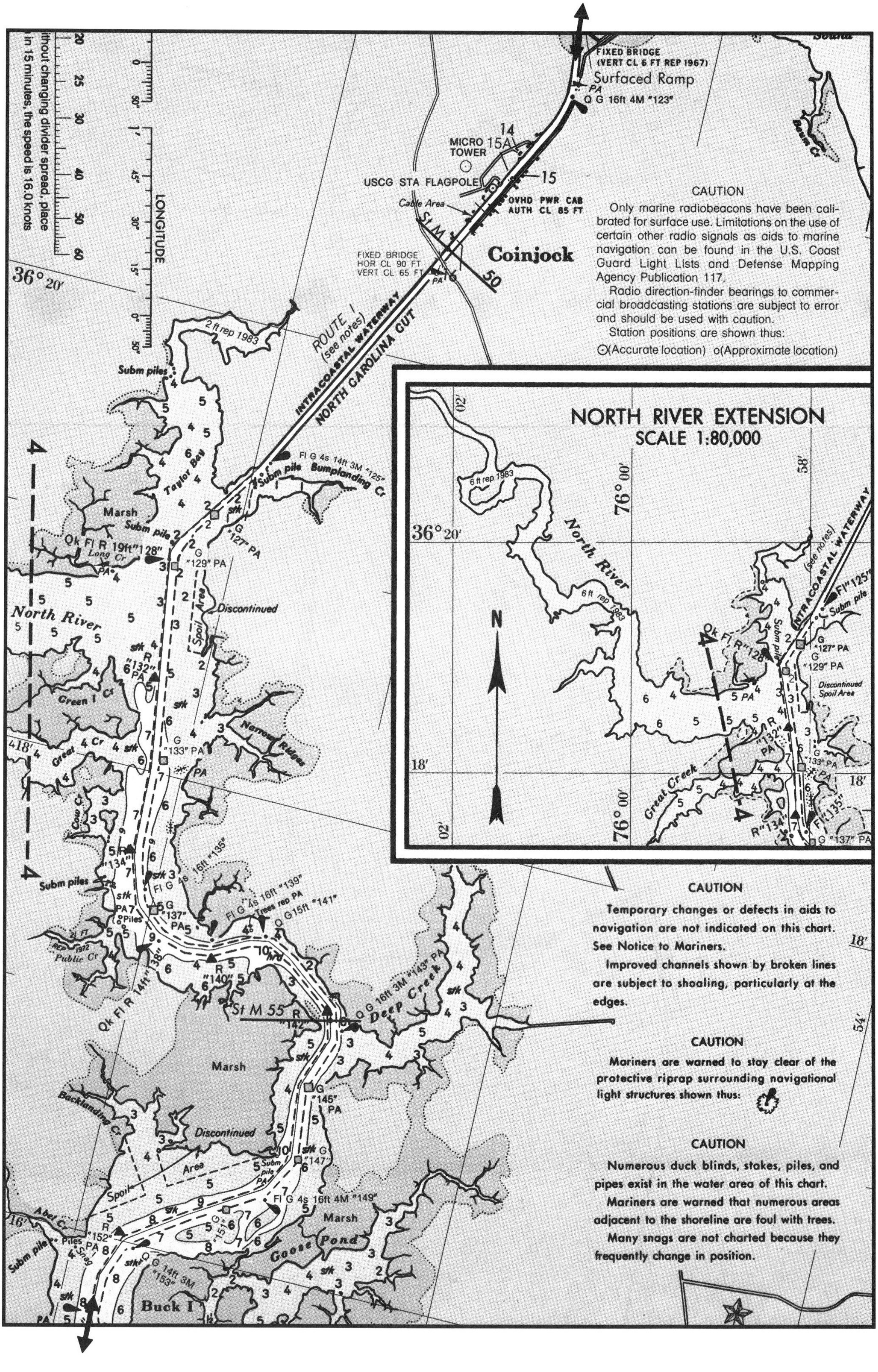
FIXED BRIDGE
(VERT CL 6 FT REP 1967)
Surfaced Ramp
Q G 16ft 4M "123"
MICRO TOWER
USCG STA FLAGPOLE
Cable Area
OVHD PWR CAB AUTH CL 85 FT
FIXED BRIDGE HOR CL 90 FT VERT CL 65 FT
Coinjock
St M 50
CAUTION
Only marine radiobeacons have been calibrated for surface use. Limitations on the use of certain other radio signals as aids to marine navigation can be found in the U.S. Coast Guard Light Lists and Defense Mapping Agency Publication 117.
Radio direction-finder bearings to commercial broadcasting stations are subject to error and should be used with caution.
Station positions are shown thus:
(Accurate location) o(Approximate location)
LONGITUDE
Without changing divider spread, place in 15 minutes, the speed is 16.0 knots
36° 20′
ROUTE 1 (see notes)
INTRACOASTAL WATERWAY
NORTH CAROLINA CUT
2 ft rep 1983
Subm piles
Taylor Bay
Marsh
Subm pile
Bumplanding Cr
Fl G 4s 14ft 3M "125"
Qk Fl R 19ft "128"
Long Cr
North River
Spoil Area
Discontinued
Green I Cr
Great Cr
Narrow Ridge
Cow Cr
Public Cr
Qk Fl R 14ft "138"
Fl G 4s 16ft "135"
Fl G 4s 16ft "139"
Trees rep PA
Q G 15ft "141"
Q G 16ft 3M "143" PA
Deep Creek
St M 55
Marsh
Backlanding Cr
Discontinued
Spoil Area
Abel Cr
Fl G 4s 16ft 4M "149"
Marsh
Goose Pond
Q G 14ft 3M "153"
Buck I
NORTH RIVER EXTENSION
SCALE 1:80,000
6 ft rep 1983
North River
76° 00′
36° 20′
Great Creek
INTRACOASTAL WATERWAY
Discontinued Spoil Area
CAUTION
Temporary changes or defects in aids to navigation are not indicated on this chart. See Notice to Mariners.
Improved channels shown by broken lines are subject to shoaling, particularly at the edges.
CAUTION
Mariners are warned to stay clear of the protective riprap surrounding navigational light structures shown thus:
CAUTION
Numerous duck blinds, stakes, piles, and pipes exist in the water area of this chart.
Mariners are warned that numerous areas adjacent to the shoreline are foul with trees.
Many snags are not charted because they frequently change in position.

StM50

StM55

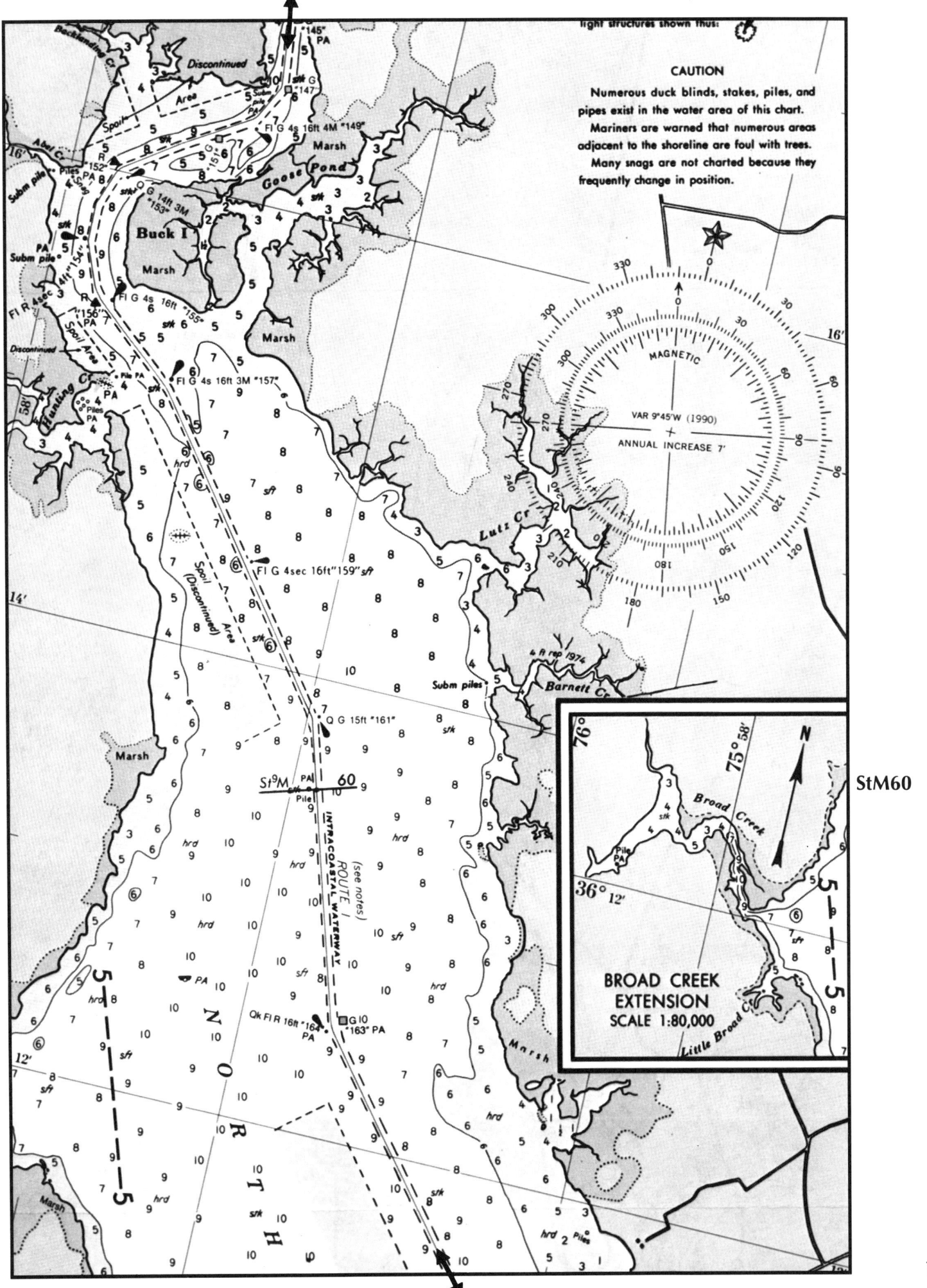

## CAUTION

Numerous duck blinds, stakes, piles, and pipes exist in the water area of this chart.

Mariners are warned that numerous areas adjacent to the shoreline are foul with trees.

Many snags are not charted because they frequently change in position.

**BROAD CREEK EXTENSION**
SCALE 1:80,000

StM60

StM60

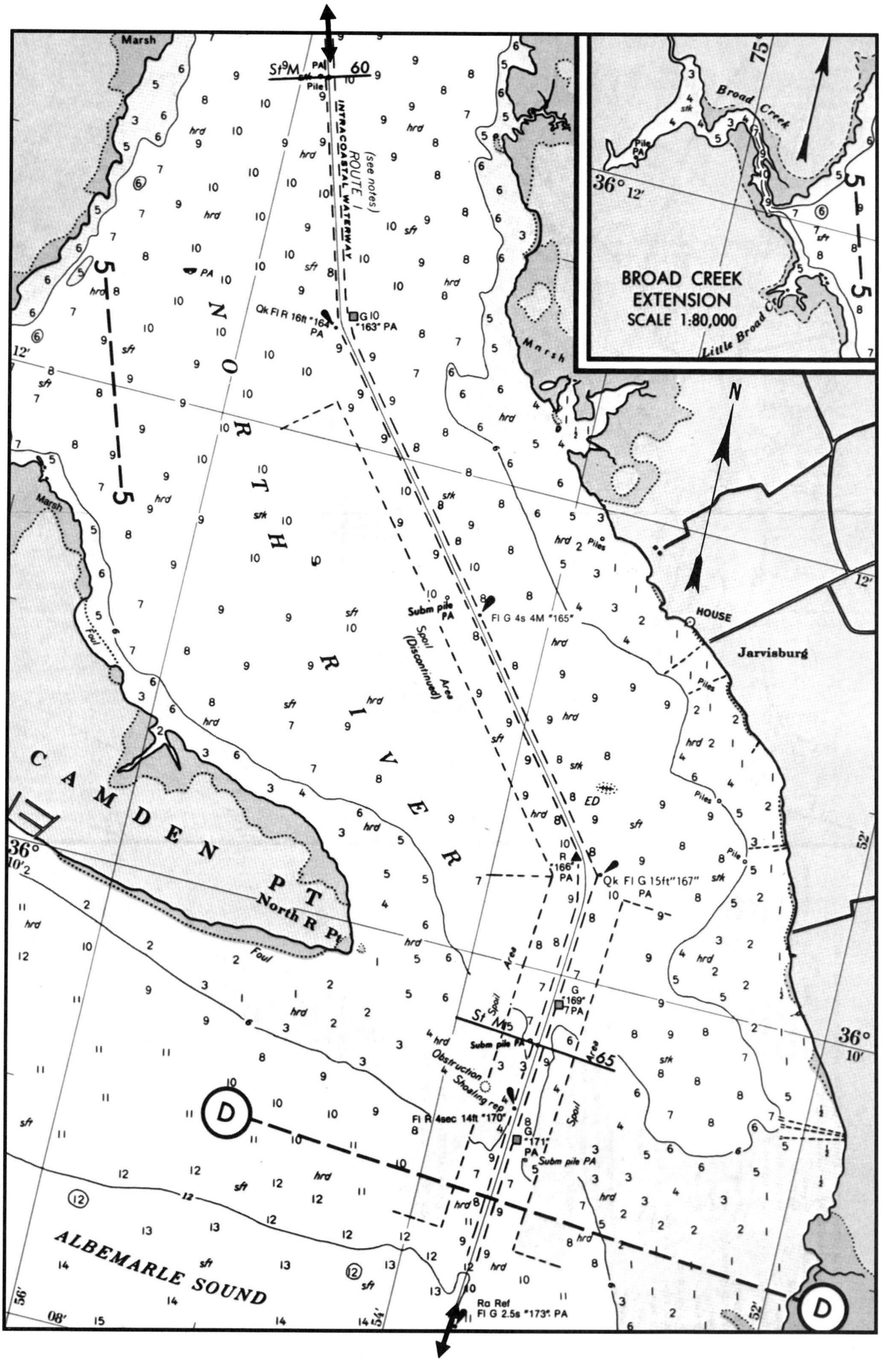
BROAD CREEK
EXTENSION
SCALE 1:80,000
Broad Creek
Little Broad Cr.
Pile PA
36° 12′
75
N O R T H R I V E R
C A M D E N P T
North R Pt
ALBEMARLE SOUND
INTRACOASTAL WATERWAY
ROUTE I
(see notes)
St M 60
St M 65
Qk Fl R 16ft "164" PA
G 10 "163" PA
Fl G 4s 4M "165"
Subm pile PA
Spoil Area (Discontinued)
R "166" PA
Qk Fl G 15ft "167" PA
G "169" 7 PA
Obstruction & Shoaling rep
Fl R 4sec 14ft "170"
G "171" PA
Subm pile PA
Ra Ref
Fl G 2.5s "173" PA
Spoil Area
HOUSE
Jarvisburg
Marsh
Piles
Pile
Foul
ED
D
36° 10′
12′
52′
54′
56′
08′

StM65

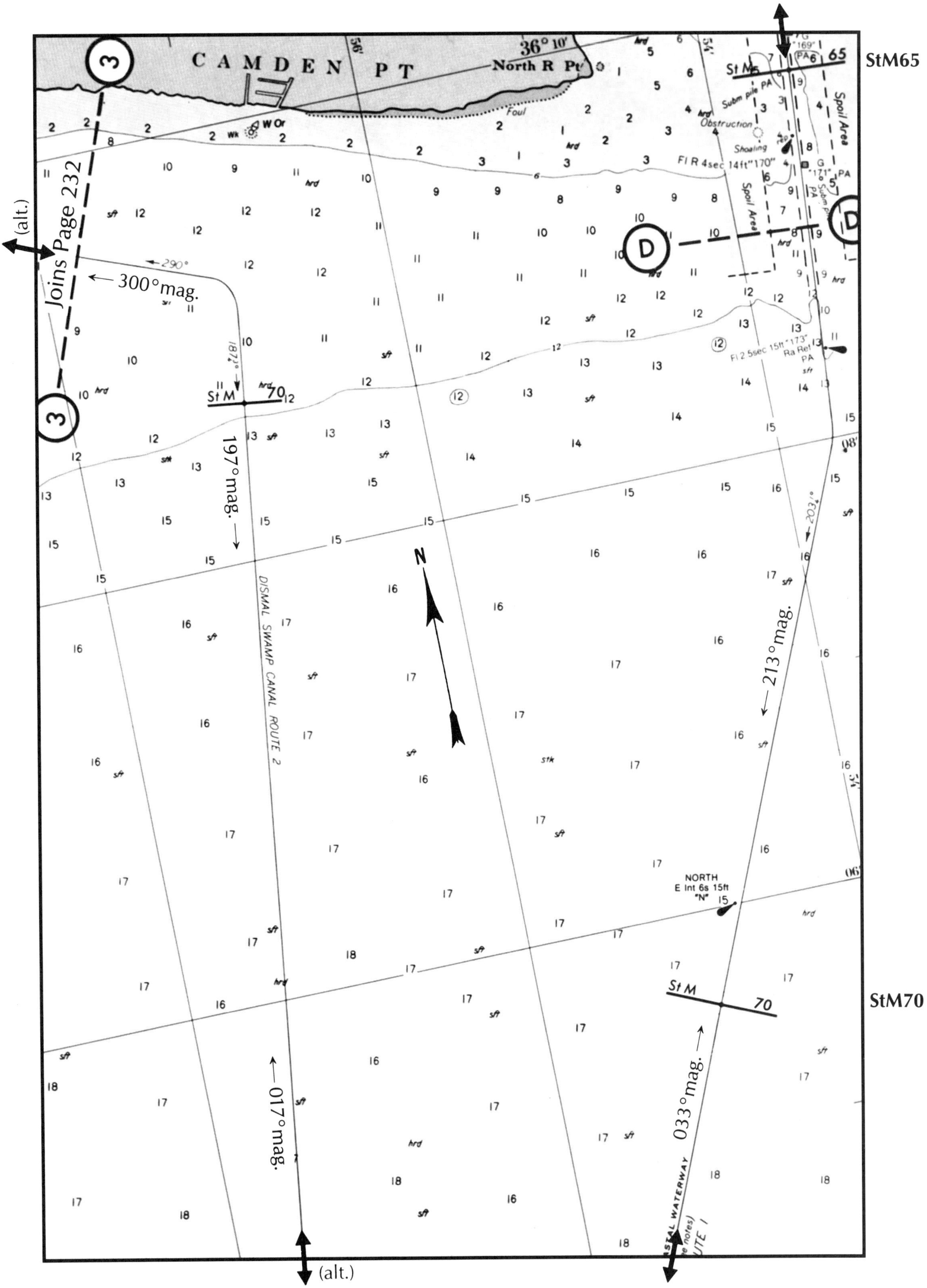
CAMDEN PT
North R Pt
36° 10'
56'
54'
W Or
Wk
Foul
Obstruction
Shoaling
Subm pile PA
Spoil Area
Fl R 4sec 14ft "170"
G "171" PA
"169" PA
Fl 2.5sec 15ft "173" Ra Ref
NORTH
E Int 6s 15ft
"N"
DISMAL SWAMP CANAL ROUTE 2
St M 65
St M 70
StM65
StM70
Joins Page 232
(alt.)
300°mag.
290°
187°
197°mag.
203°
213°mag.
017°mag.
033°mag.
N
08'
06'

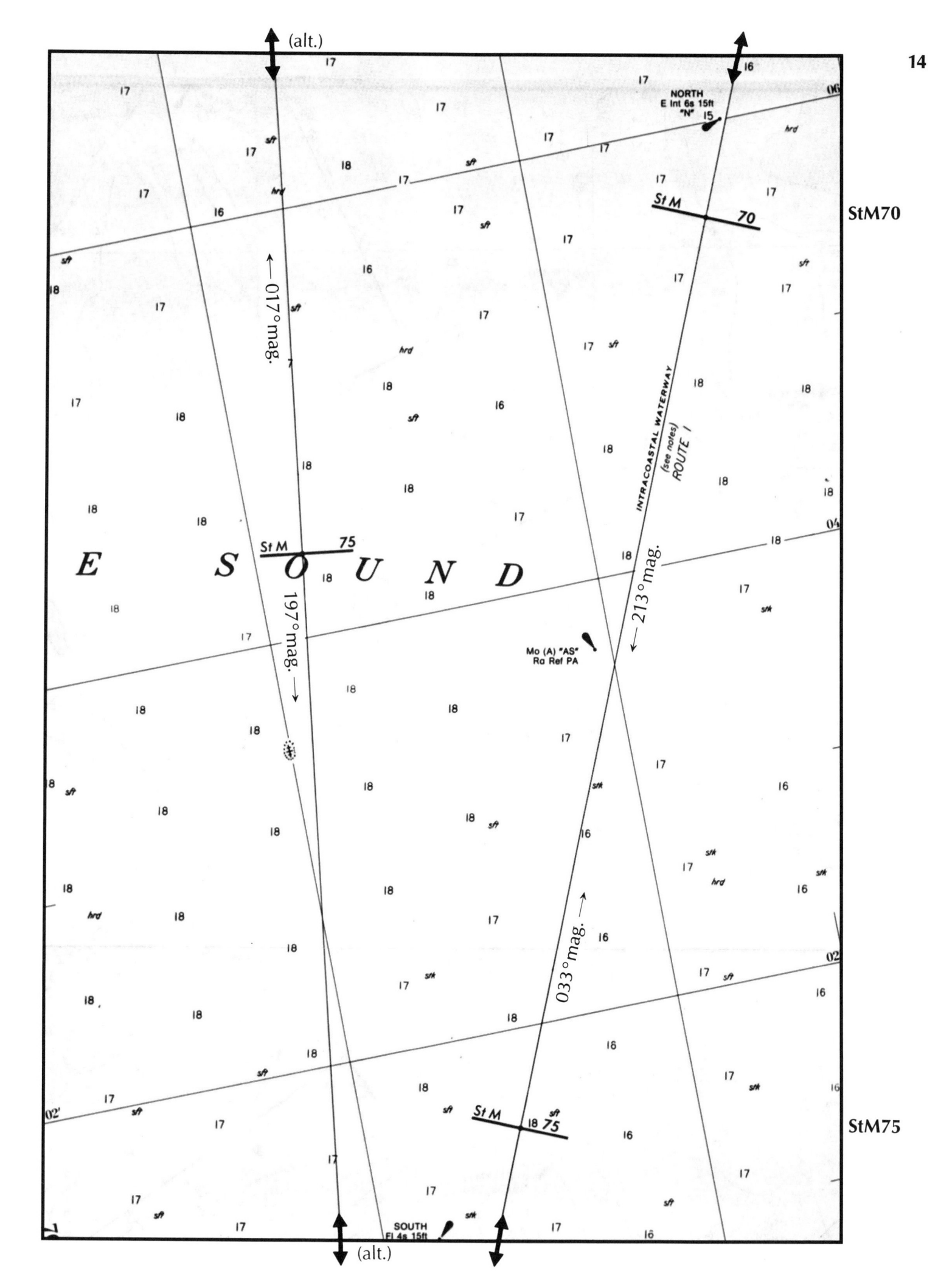

**StM70**

**E SOUND**

StM 70
StM 75
StM 75

NORTH
E Int 6s 15ft
"N" 15

Mo (A) "AS"
Ra Ref PA

SOUTH
Fl 4s 15ft

← 017° mag.
197° mag. →
← 213° mag.
033° mag. →

INTRACOASTAL WATERWAY
(see notes)
ROUTE 1

(alt.)
(alt.)

**StM75**

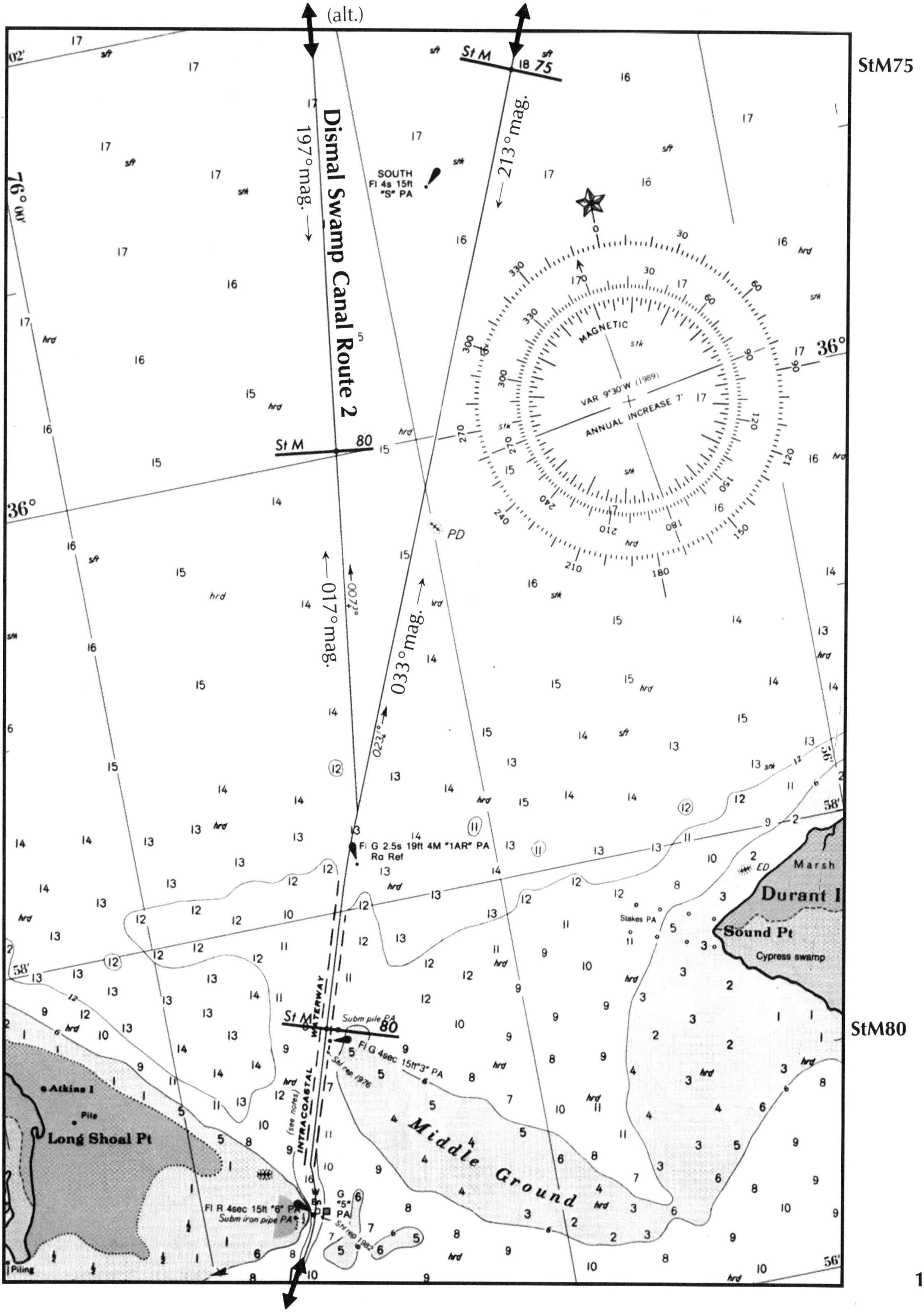
(alt.)
StM75
StM80
Dismal Swamp Canal Route 2
197°mag. →
← 213°mag.
←017°mag.
033°mag. →
SOUTH
Fl 4s 15ft
"S" PA
MAGNETIC
VAR 9°30'W (1989)
ANNUAL INCREASE 7'
Fl G 2.5s 19ft 4M "1AR" PA
Ra Ref
Fl G 4sec 15ft "3" PA
Subm pile PA
INTRACOASTAL WATERWAY
(see notes)
Fl R 4sec 15ft "6" PA
Subm iron pipe PA
G "5" PA
Middle Ground
Durant I
Marsh
Sound Pt
Cypress swamp
Stakes PA
Atkins I
Pile
Long Shoal Pt
Piling
76°00'
36°
58'
56'

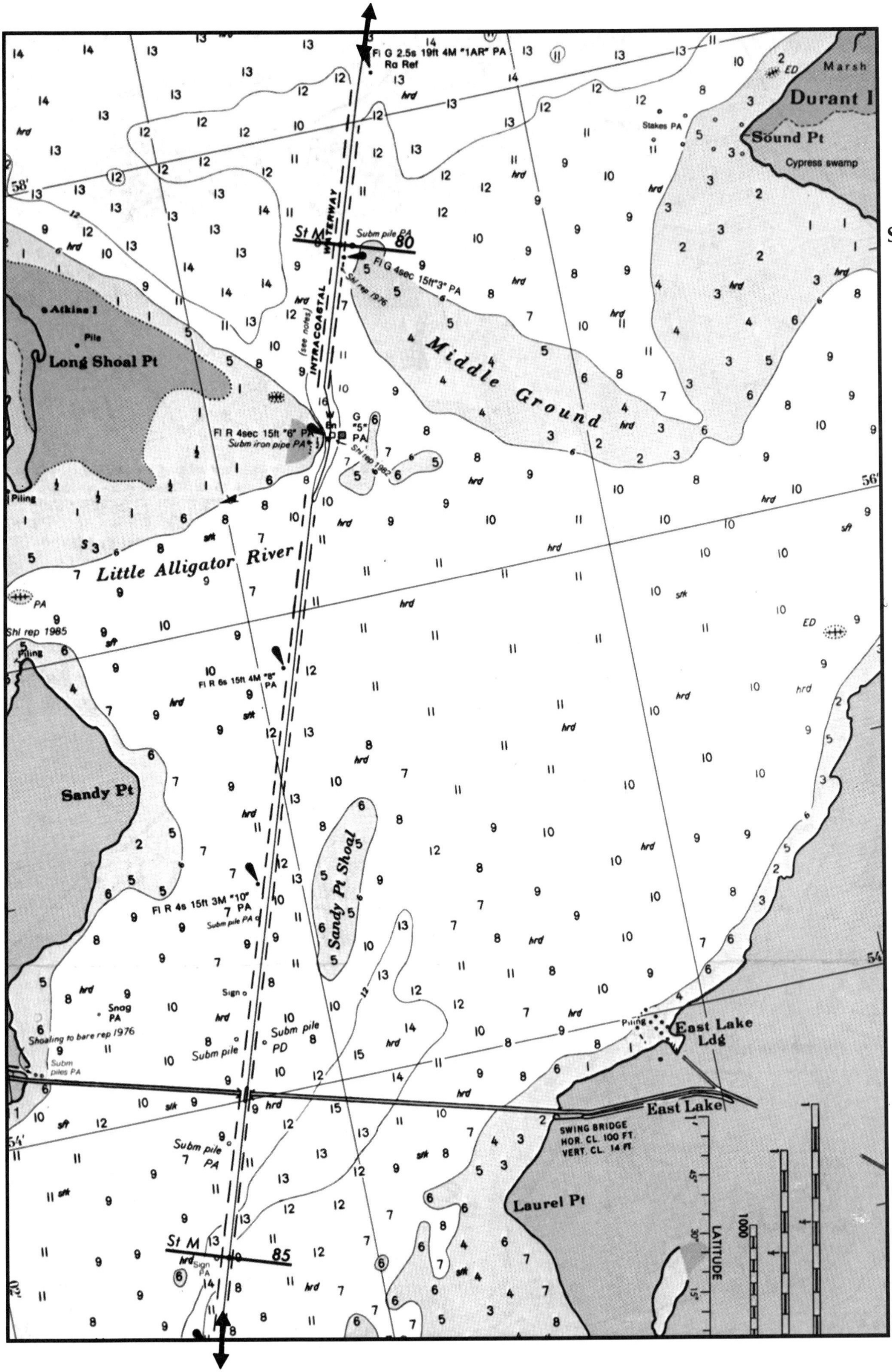


StM80

BR84.2

StM85

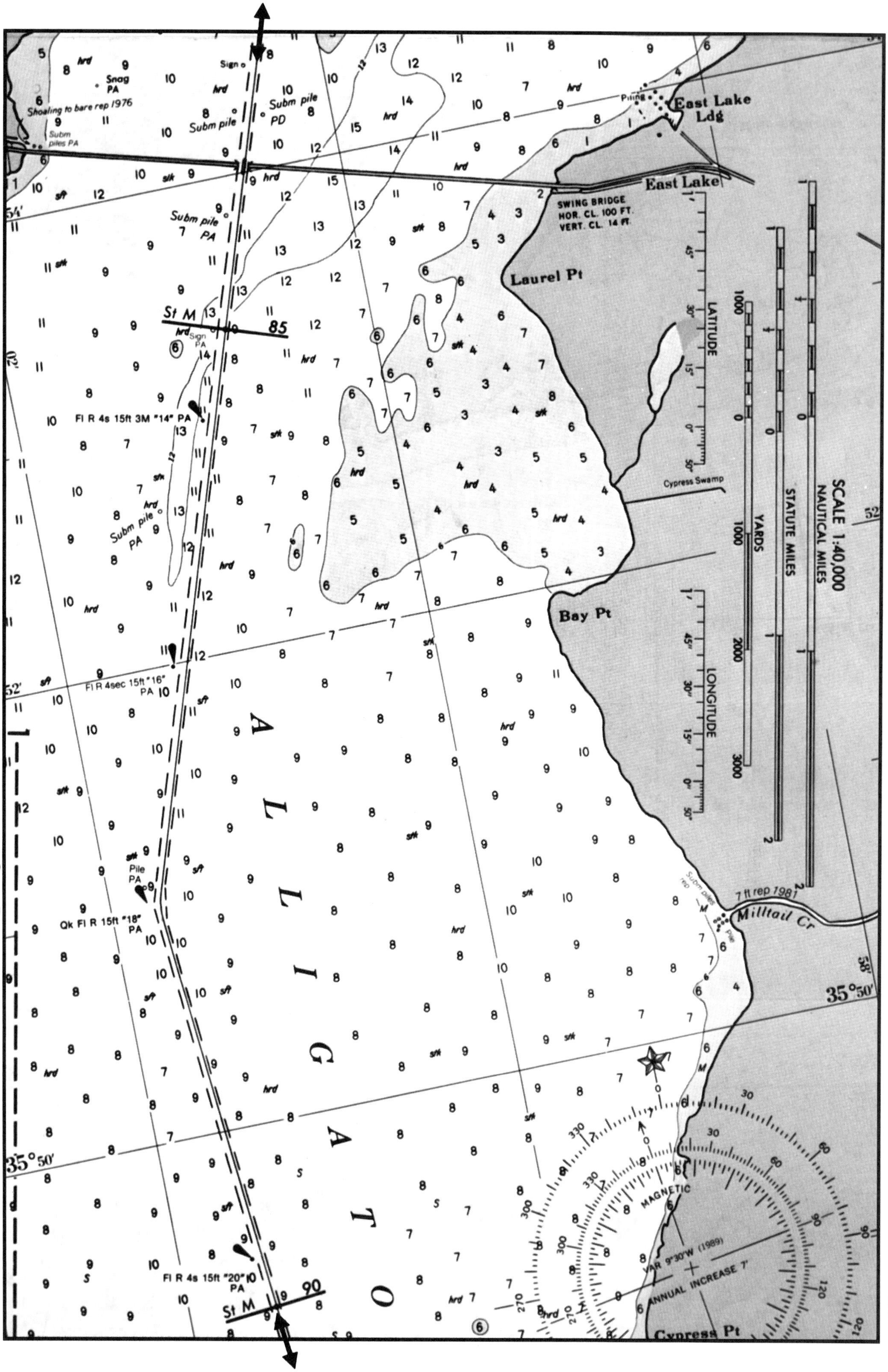


See Page 22

BR84.2

StM85

StM90

18

StM90

ORR RIVER

Cypress Pt
Cypress swamp

Catfish Pt
Clabber Pt
Cypress swamp

Stumpy Pt

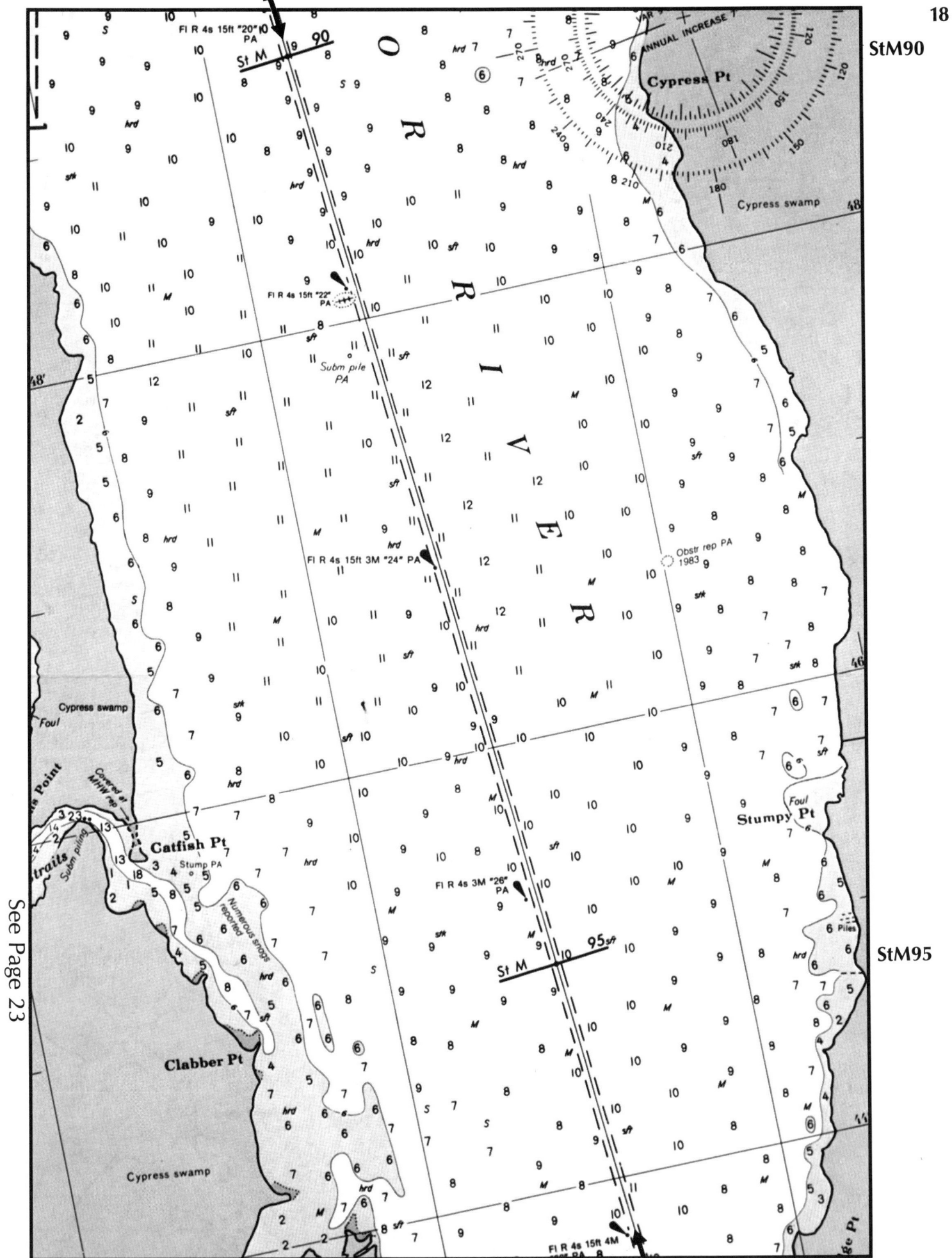

StM95

See Page 23

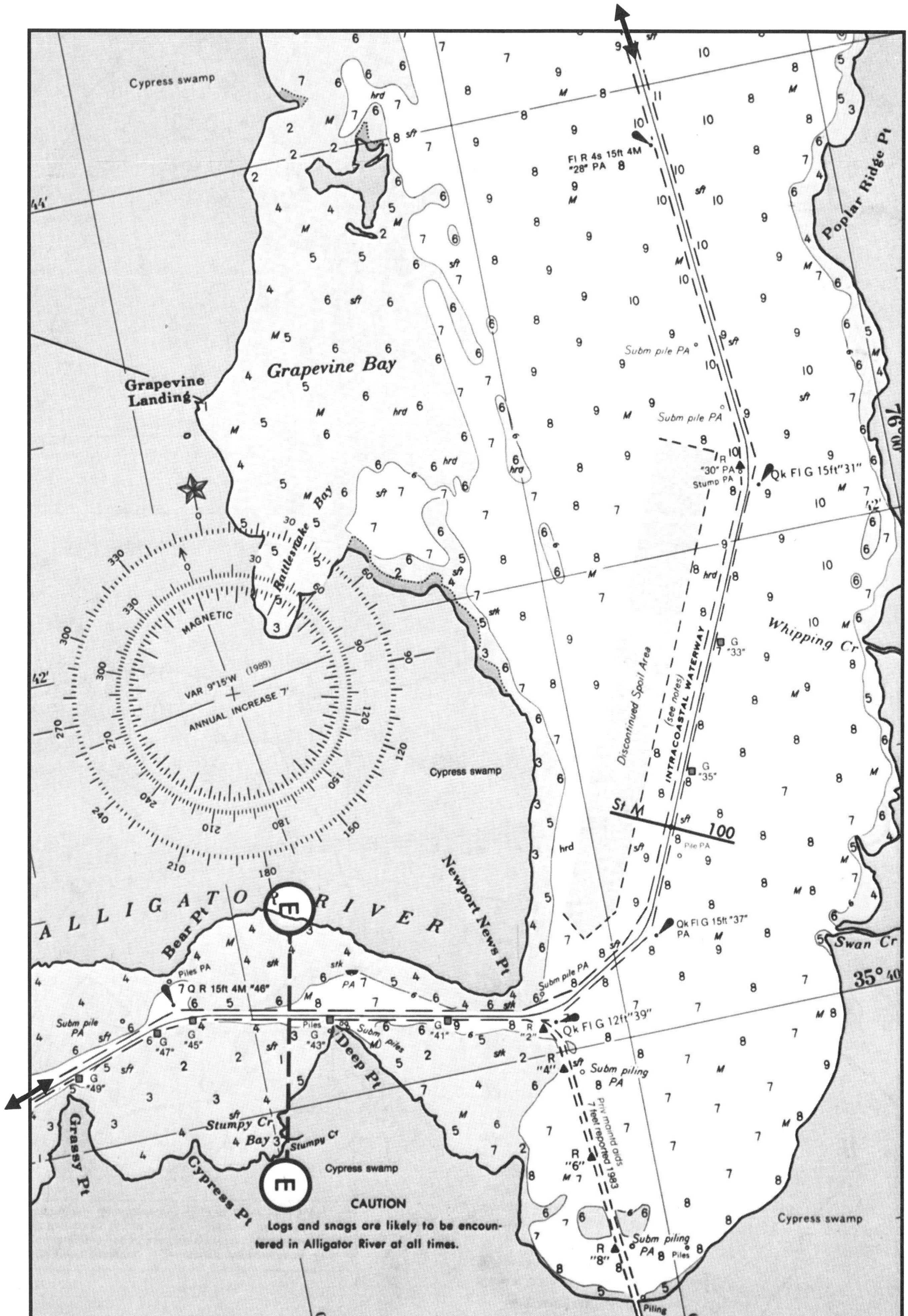
Cypress swamp
Grapevine Bay
Grapevine Landing
Rattlesnake Bay
Poplar Ridge Pt
Fl R 4s 15ft 4M "28" PA
Subm pile PA
"30" PA
Stump PA
Qk Fl G 15ft "31"
MAGNETIC
VAR 9°15'W (1989)
ANNUAL INCREASE 7'
Whipping Cr
Discontinued Spoil Area
(see notes)
INTRACOASTAL WATERWAY
"33"
"35"
St M 100
Pile PA
Cypress swamp
Newport News Pt
ALLIGATOR RIVER
Bear Pt
Qk Fl G 15ft "37" PA
Swan Cr
Piles PA
7 Q R 15ft 4M "46"
Subm pile PA
Subm piles
Piles
"47"
"45"
"43"
"41"
"2"
Qk Fl G 12ft "39"
Deep Pt
"4"
Subm piling PA
"49"
Grassy Pt
Stumpy Cr
Bay
Stumpy Cr
Cypress Pt
Cypress swamp
"6"
Priv maintd aids
7 feet reported 1983
Subm piling PA
Piles
"8"
Piling
Cypress swamp
CAUTION
Logs and snags are likely to be encountered in Alligator River at all times.

StM100

# NOTE C

## CAUTION
## ALLIGATOR RIVER-PUNGO RIVER CANAL

Both sides of the canal are foul with debris, snags, submerged stumps, and continuous bank erosion is caused by passing boats and tows. Corps of Engineers controlling dimensions, published in the U.S. Coast Guard Local Notices to Mariners, are generally for less than the 90-foot project width; consequently, navigation near mid-channel is recommended unless otherwise specified in the U.S. Coast Guard Local Notices to Mariners. Mariners are

## ALLIGATOR RIVER EXTENSION
SCALE 1:80,000

## CAUTION
Logs and snags are likely to be encountered in Alligator River at all times.

## CAUTION
Temporary changes or defects in aids to navigation are not indicated on this chart. See Notice to Mariners.

Improved channels shown by broken lines are subject to shoaling, particularly at the edges.

## CAUTION
Small craft should stay clear of large commercial and government vessels even if small craft have the right-of-way.

All craft should avoid areas where the skin divers flag, a red square with a diagonal white stripe, is displayed.

To find SPEED, place one point of dividers on distance, right point on 60 and left point will then indicate speed

INTRACOASTAL WATERWAY
ALLIGATOR RIVER - PUNGO RIVER CANAL (see notes)

VAR 9°15'W (1989)
ANNUAL INCREASE 7'
MAGNETIC

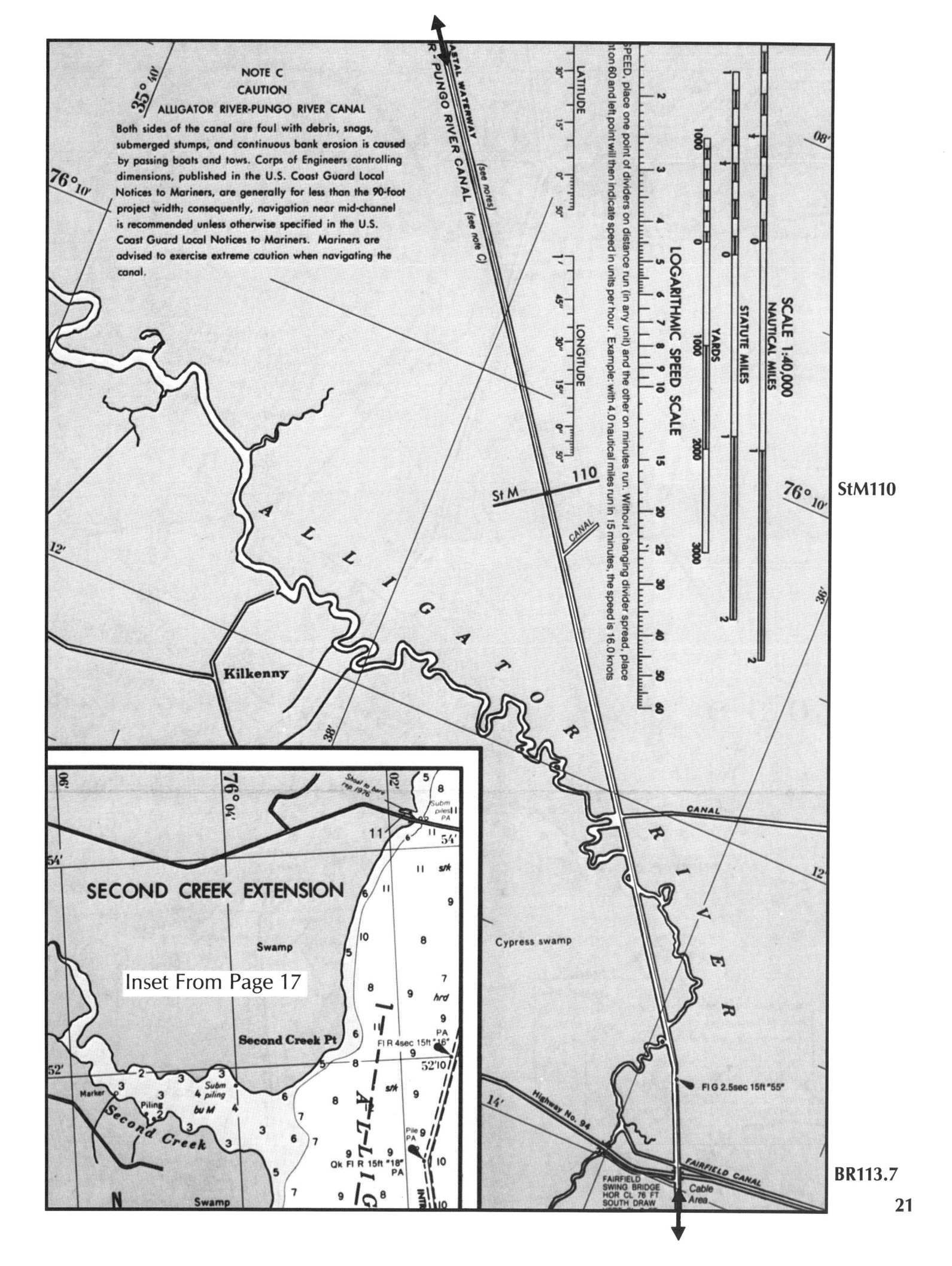

## NOTE C
### CAUTION
### ALLIGATOR RIVER-PUNGO RIVER CANAL

Both sides of the canal are foul with debris, snags, submerged stumps, and continuous bank erosion is caused by passing boats and tows. Corps of Engineers controlling dimensions, published in the U.S. Coast Guard Local Notices to Mariners, are generally for less than the 90-foot project width; consequently, navigation near mid-channel is recommended unless otherwise specified in the U.S. Coast Guard Local Notices to Mariners. Mariners are advised to exercise extreme caution when navigating the canal.

SCALE 1:40,000

**SECOND CREEK EXTENSION**

Inset From Page 17

StM110

BR113.7

**22**

## SECOND CREEK EXTENSION

Inset From Page 17

Swamp

Second Creek Pt

52'

Marker

Piling

Second Creek

Subm
4 piling
bu M

Swamp

N

Goose Cr

5

35°50'

Swamp

76°06'

48'

06'

18'

### SCALE 1:80,000
#### NAUTICAL MILES
0    1    2    3

#### STATUTE MILES
1    0    1    2    3

#### YARDS
1000    0    1000    2000    3000    4000    5000

Shoal to here
rep 1976

76°00'

02'

Subm
piles
PA

54'

11

Subm piles
PA

stk

A L L I G A T O R   R I V E R

stk

Second Creek Pt    Fl R 4sec 15ft "16"
PA

52'10'

stk

Pile
PA

Qk Fl R 15ft "18"
PA

hrd

CONTINUED ON PANEL ABOVE

INTRACOASTAL WATERWAY

Fl R 4s 15ft "20"
PA

hrd

stk

M

48'

02'

hrd

### CAUTION

Only marine radiobeacons have been calibrated for surface use. Limitations on the use of certain other radio signals as aids to marine navigation can be found in the U.S. Coast Guard Light Lists and Defense Mapping Agency Publication 117.

Radio direction-finder bearings to commercial broadcasting stations are subject to error and should be used with caution.

Station positions are shown thus:

⊙(Accurate location)  o(Approximate location)

### RULES OF THE ROAD
#### (ABRIDGED)

Motorless craft have the right-of-way in almost all cases. Sailing vessels and motorboats less than sixty-five feet in length, shall not hamper, in a narrow channel, the safe passage of a vessel which can navigate only inside that channel.

A motorboat being overtaken has the right-of-way.

Motorboats approaching head to head or nearly so should pass port to port.

When motorboats approach each other at right angles or

CANAL

R I V E R

12'

Cypress swamp

14'

Highway No. 94

Fl G 2.5sec 15ft "55"

FAIRFIELD CANAL

FAIRFIELD
SWING BRIDGE
HOR CL 76 FT
SOUTH DRAW
VERT CL 7 FT

Cable
Area

14'

Fl G 4s 15ft 4M "57"

St M    115

Cypress swamp

16'

16'

54'

CANAL

**BR113.7**

**StM115**

### INTRACOASTAL WATERWAY

#### Project Depth

12 feet Norfolk, Va. to Fort Pierce, Fla. via Route 1.

9 feet Norfolk to Albemarle Sound via Route 2 (Dismal Swamp Canal) to junction with Route 1.

10 feet Fort Pierce, Fla. Miami, Fla.

channel.
A motorboat being overtaken has the right-of-way.
Motorboats approaching head to head or nearly so should pass port to port.
When motorboats approach each other at right angles or obliquely, the boat on the right has the right-of-way in most cases.
Motorboats must keep to the right in narrow channels, when safe and practicable.
Mariners are urged to become familiar with the complete text of the Rules of the Road in U.S. Coast Guard publication "Navigation Rules".

7 feet Norfolk to Albemarle Sound via Route 2 (Dismal Swamp Canal) to junction with Route 1.
10 feet Fort Pierce, Fla. Miami, Fla.
7 feet Miami, Fla. to Cross Bank Florida Bay.
The controlling depths are published periodically in the U.S. Coast Guard Local Notice to Mariners.

### Distances

The Waterway is indicated by a magenta line. Mileage distances along the Waterway are in Statute Miles, southward from Norfolk, Virginia, and indicated thus: ———
Tables for converting Statute Miles to International Nautical Miles are given in U.S. Coast Pilot 4.
Courses are TRUE and must be CORRECTED for any variation and compass deviation.

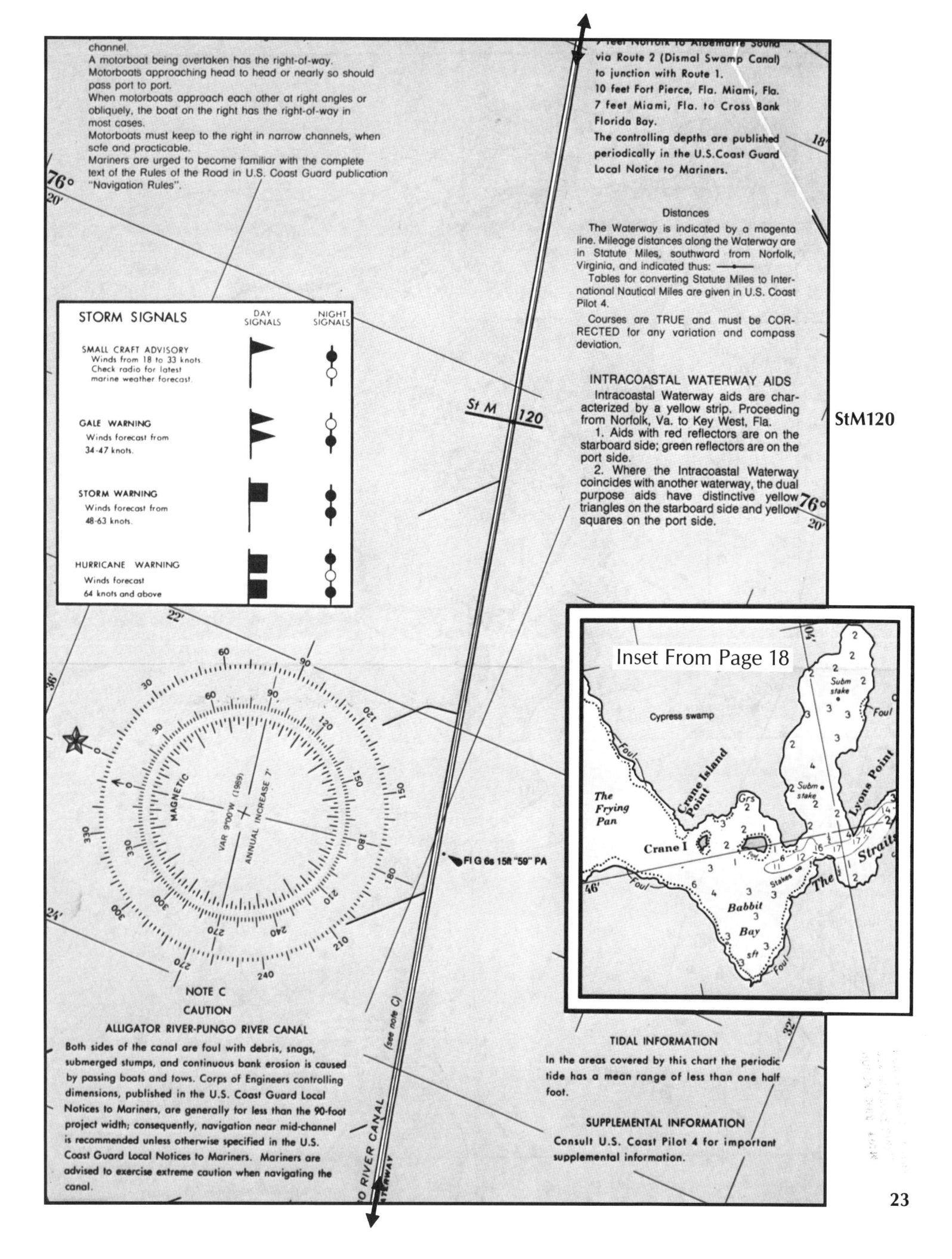

### INTRACOASTAL WATERWAY AIDS

Intracoastal Waterway aids are characterized by a yellow strip. Proceeding from Norfolk, Va. to Key West, Fla.
1. Aids with red reflectors are on the starboard side; green reflectors are on the port side.
2. Where the Intracoastal Waterway coincides with another waterway, the dual purpose aids have distinctive yellow triangles on the starboard side and yellow squares on the port side.

### STORM SIGNALS

| | DAY SIGNALS | NIGHT SIGNALS |
|---|---|---|
| SMALL CRAFT ADVISORY Winds from 18 to 33 knots. Check radio for latest marine weather forecast. | ▼ | ● ○ |
| GALE WARNING Winds forecast from 34-47 knots. | ▼▼ | ○ ● |
| STORM WARNING Winds forecast from 48-63 knots. | ■ | ● ● |
| HURRICANE WARNING Winds forecast 64 knots and above | ■ ■ | ● ○ ● |

### NOTE C
### CAUTION
### ALLIGATOR RIVER-PUNGO RIVER CANAL

Both sides of the canal are foul with debris, snags, submerged stumps, and continuous bank erosion is caused by passing boats and tows. Corps of Engineers controlling dimensions, published in the U.S. Coast Guard Local Notices to Mariners, are generally for less than the 90-foot project width; consequently, navigation near mid-channel is recommended unless otherwise specified in the U.S. Coast Guard Local Notices to Mariners. Mariners are advised to exercise extreme caution when navigating the canal.

Inset From Page 18

### TIDAL INFORMATION

In the areas covered by this chart the periodic tide has a mean range of less than one half foot.

### SUPPLEMENTAL INFORMATION

Consult U.S. Coast Pilot 4 for important supplemental information.

Caution: Wilkerson Bridge reported up to 2 feet below authorized clearance.

StM130

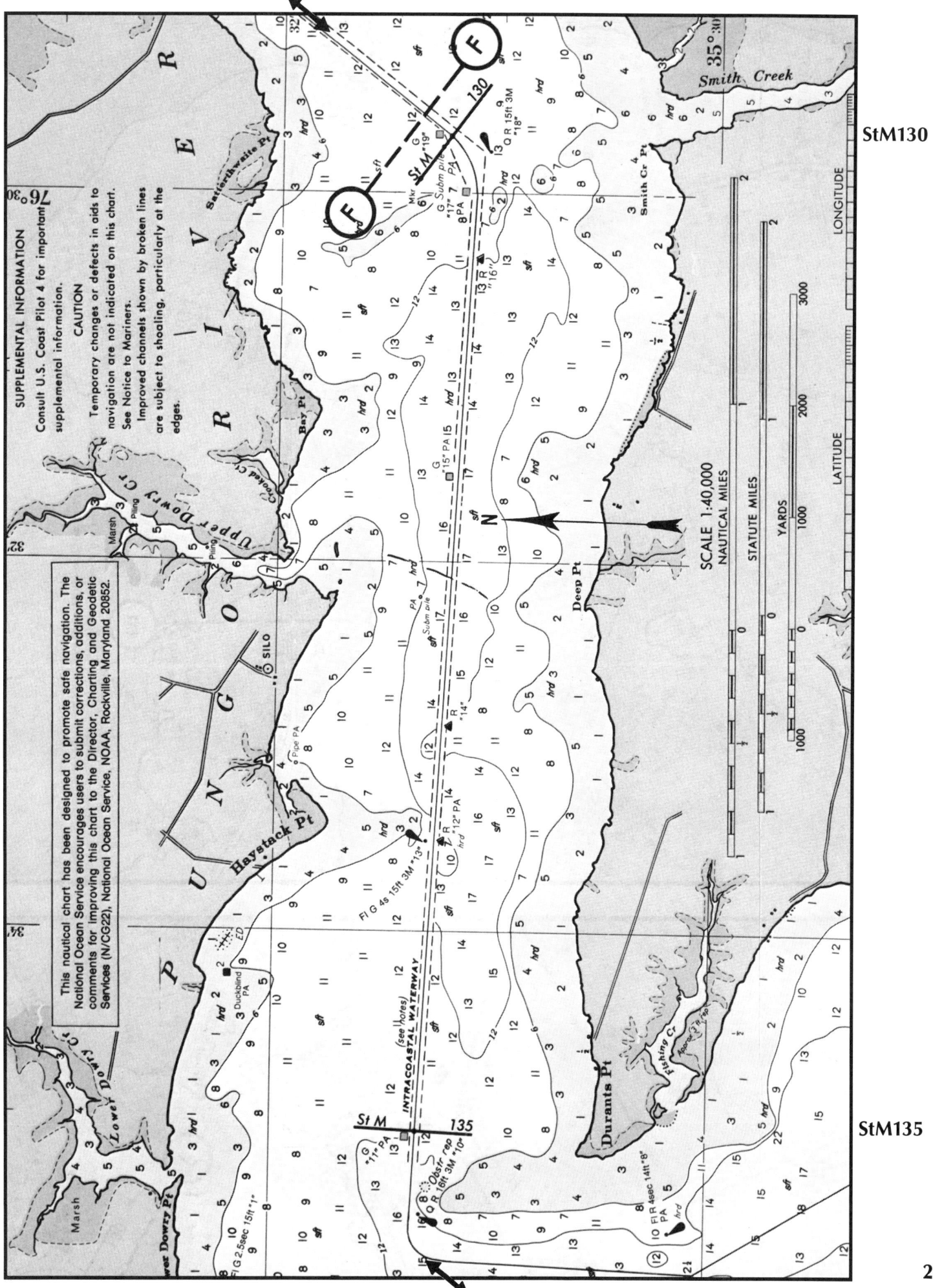

StM135

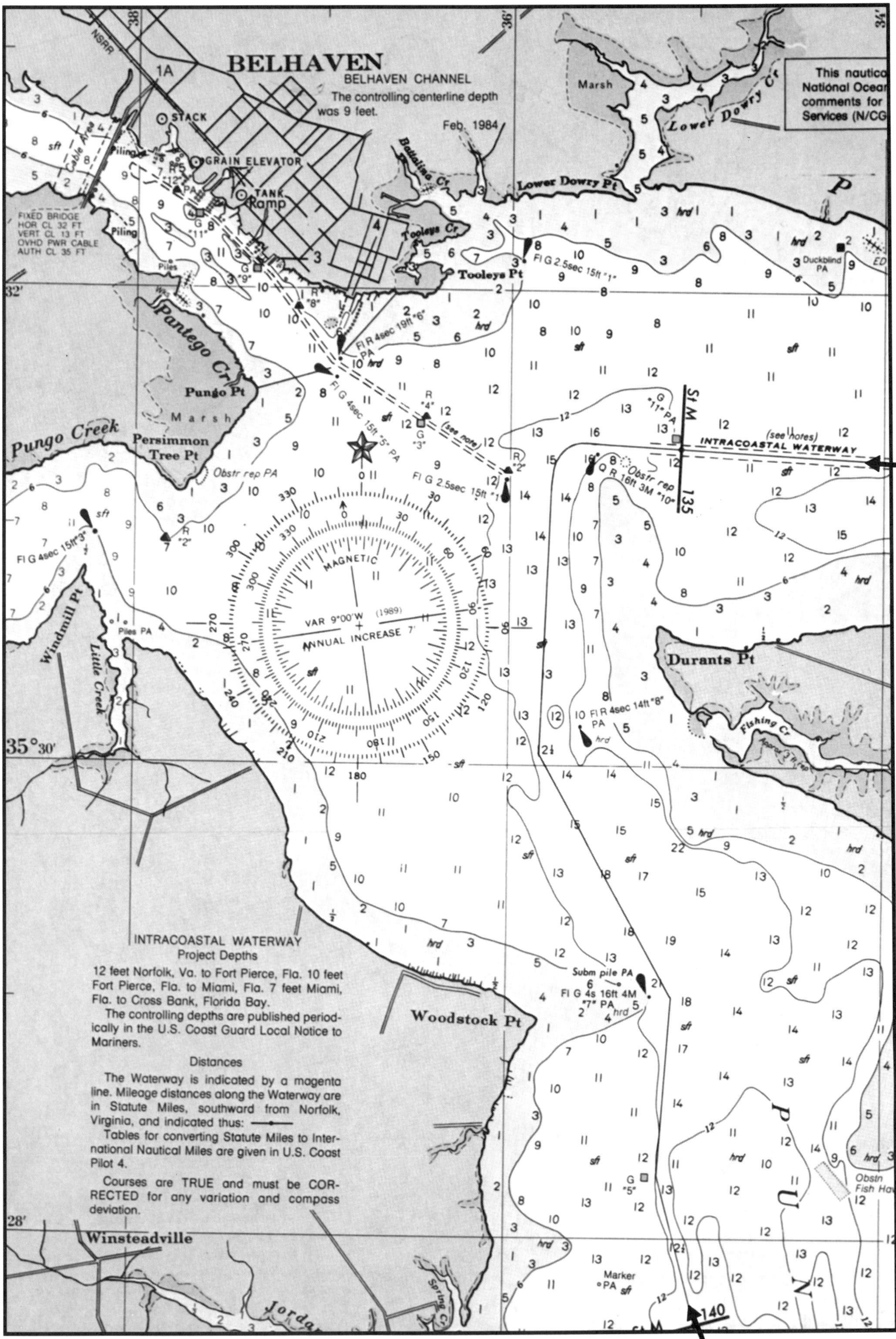

26

**BELHAVEN**

BELHAVEN CHANNEL
The controlling centerline depth
was 9 feet.
Feb. 1984

Marsh

Lower Dowry Cr

Lower Dowry Pt

Duckblind PA

This nautica
National Ocean
comments for
Services (N/CG

STACK

GRAIN ELEVATOR

TANK
Ramp

FIXED BRIDGE
HOR CL 32 FT
VERT CL 13 FT
OVHD PWR CABLE
AUTH CL 35 FT

Piling

Cable A

Piles

Tooleys Cr

Tooleys Pt

Fl G 2.5sec 15ft "1"

Pantego Cr

Pungo Pt

Marsh

Persimmon
Tree Pt

Pungo Creek

Fl R 4sec 19ft "6"
PA

R "4"

G "3"

(see note)

R "2"

Fl G 4sec 15ft "5" PA

Obstr rep PA

Fl G 2.5sec 15ft "1"

StM

INTRACOASTAL WATERWAY (see notes)

StM 135

Obstr rep
Q R 16ft 3M "10"

Fl G 4sec 15ft "3"

R "2"

MAGNETIC

VAR 9°00'W (1989)
ANNUAL INCREASE 7'

Windmill Pt

Piles PA

Little Creek

35°30'

Durants Pt

Fishing Cr

(12) 10 Fl R 4sec 14ft "8"
PA

INTRACOASTAL WATERWAY
Project Depths

12 feet Norfolk, Va. to Fort Pierce, Fla. 10 feet
Fort Pierce, Fla. to Miami, Fla. 7 feet Miami,
Fla. to Cross Bank, Florida Bay.

The controlling depths are published periodically in the U.S. Coast Guard Local Notice to
Mariners.

Distances

The Waterway is indicated by a magenta
line. Mileage distances along the Waterway are
in Statute Miles, southward from Norfolk,
Virginia, and indicated thus: ———

Tables for converting Statute Miles to International Nautical Miles are given in U.S. Coast
Pilot 4.

Courses are TRUE and must be COR-
RECTED for any variation and compass
deviation.

Woodstock Pt

Subm pile PA

Fl G 4s 16ft 4M
"7" PA

Obstn
Fish Hav

P U N

Winsteadville

Marker
PA sft

28'

Jordan

StM140

StM135

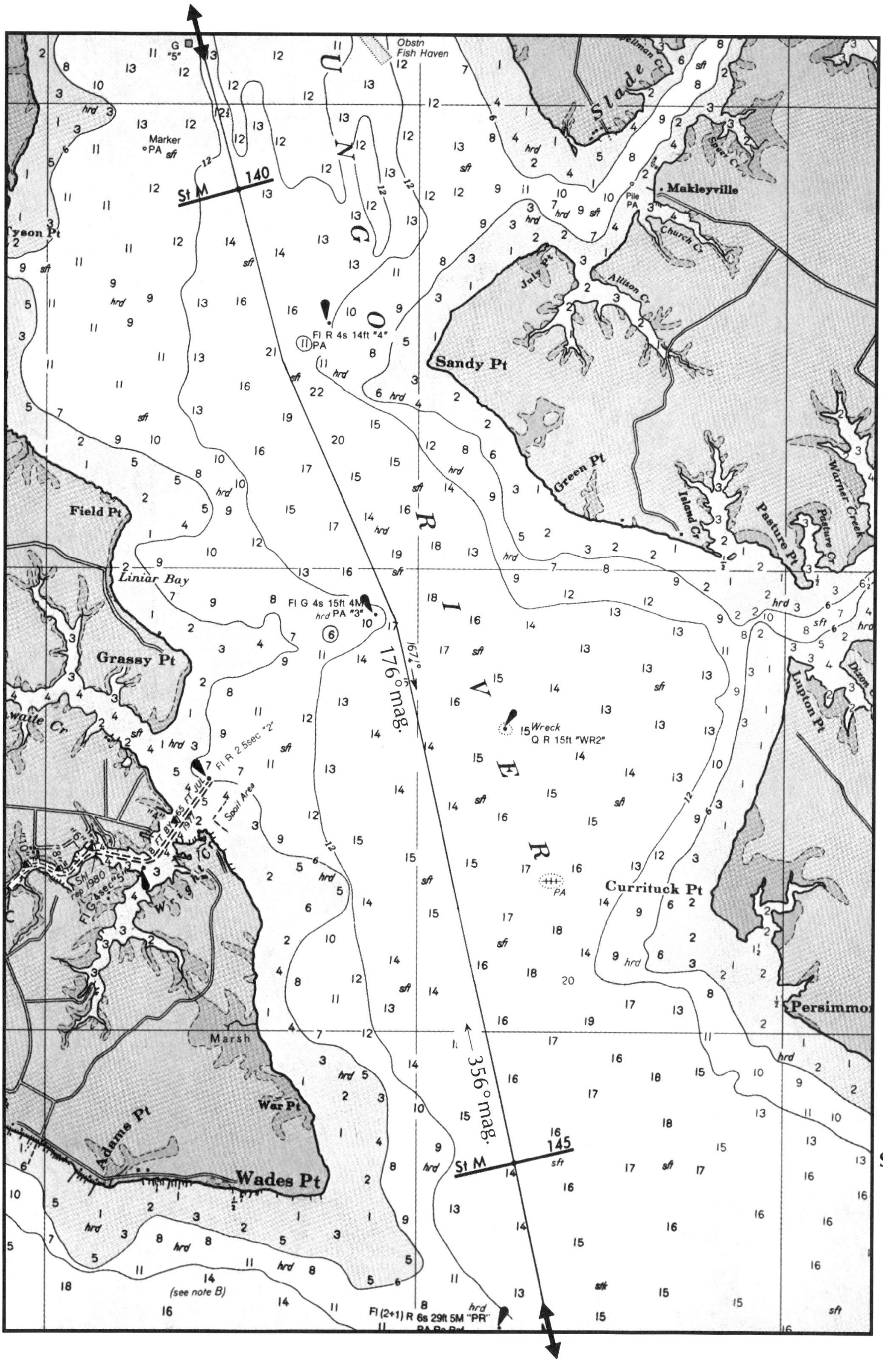


StM140

StM145

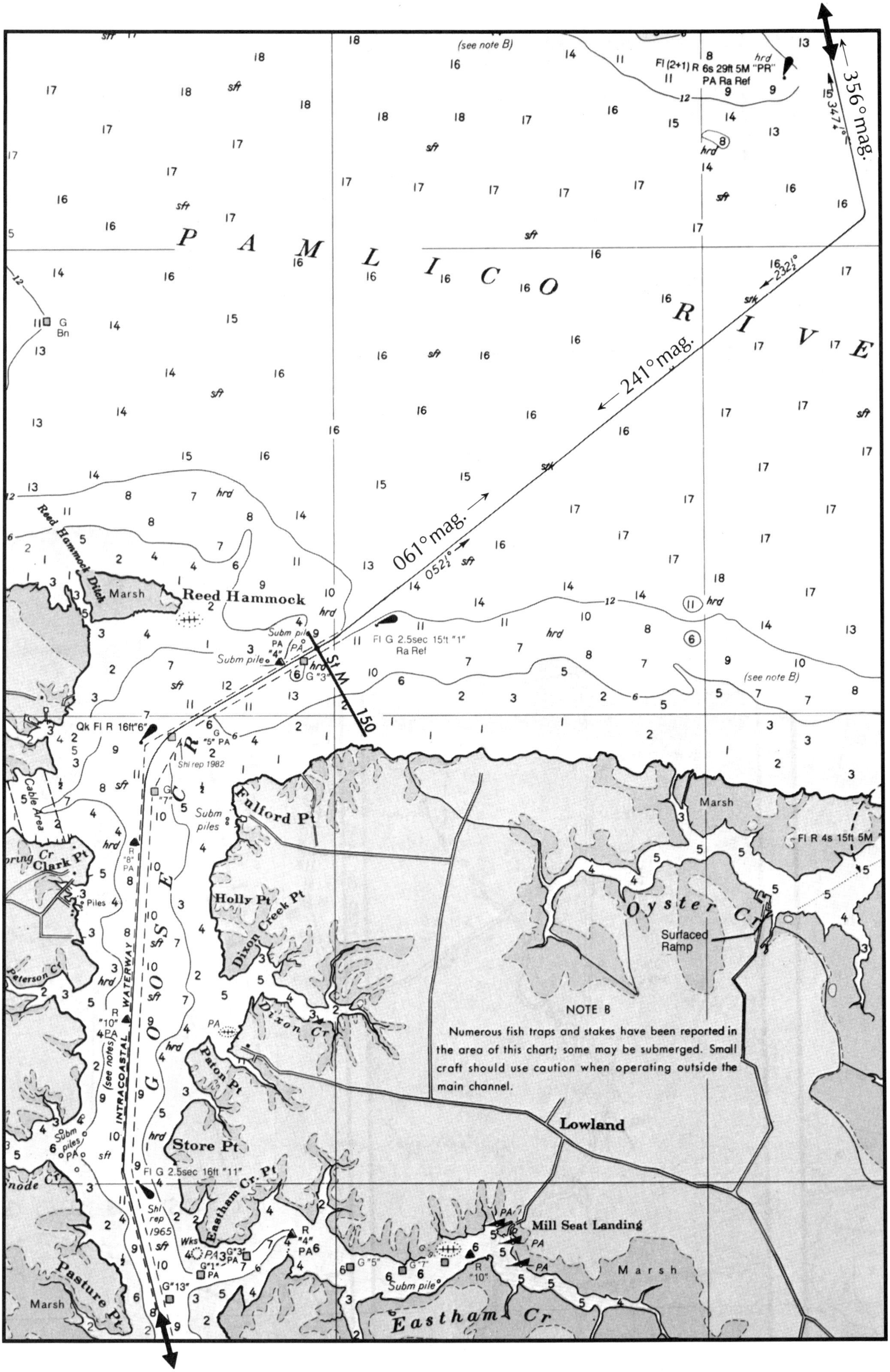
PAMLICO RIVER
356° mag.
241° mag.
061° mag.
StM 150
Fl (2+1) R 6s 29ft 5M "PR"
PA Ra Ref
Fl G 2.5sec 15ft "1"
Ra Ref
Qk Fl R 16ft "6"
Fl G 2.5sec 16ft "11"
Fl R 4s 15ft 5M
Reed Hammock
Reed Hammock Ditch
Marsh
GOOSE CR
INTRACOASTAL WATERWAY
(see notes)
Fulford Pt
Clark Pt
Holly Pt
Dixon Creek Pt
Dixon Cr
Paton Pt
Store Pt
Eastham Cr. Pt
Eastham Cr
Pasture Pt
Cable Area
Oyster Cr
Surfaced Ramp
Lowland
Mill Seat Landing
Subm piles
Shl rep 1982
Shl rep 1965
NOTE B
Numerous fish traps and stakes have been reported in the area of this chart; some may be submerged. Small craft should use caution when operating outside the main channel.
(see note B)

StM150

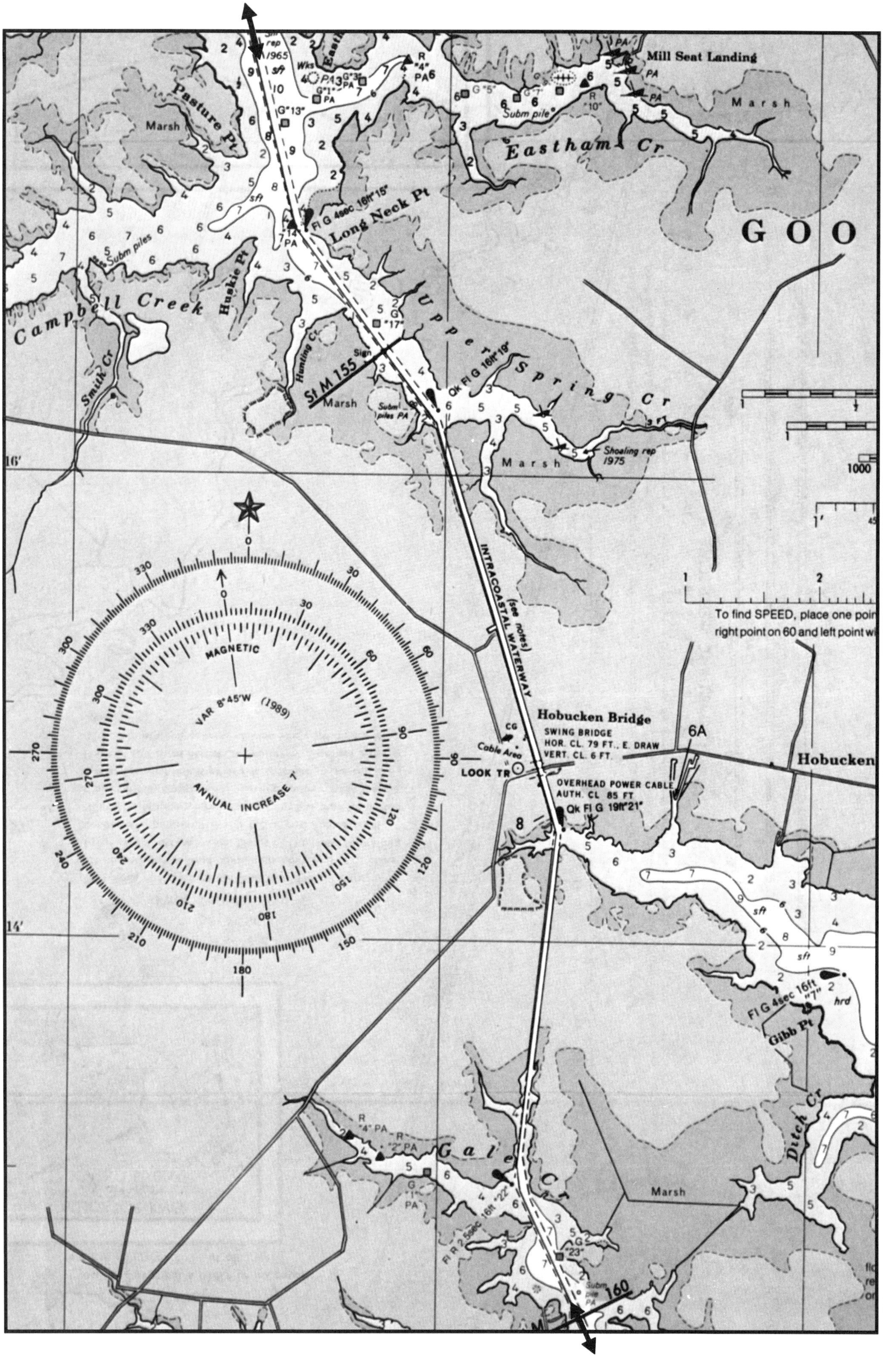


StM155

BR157.2

StM160

StM160

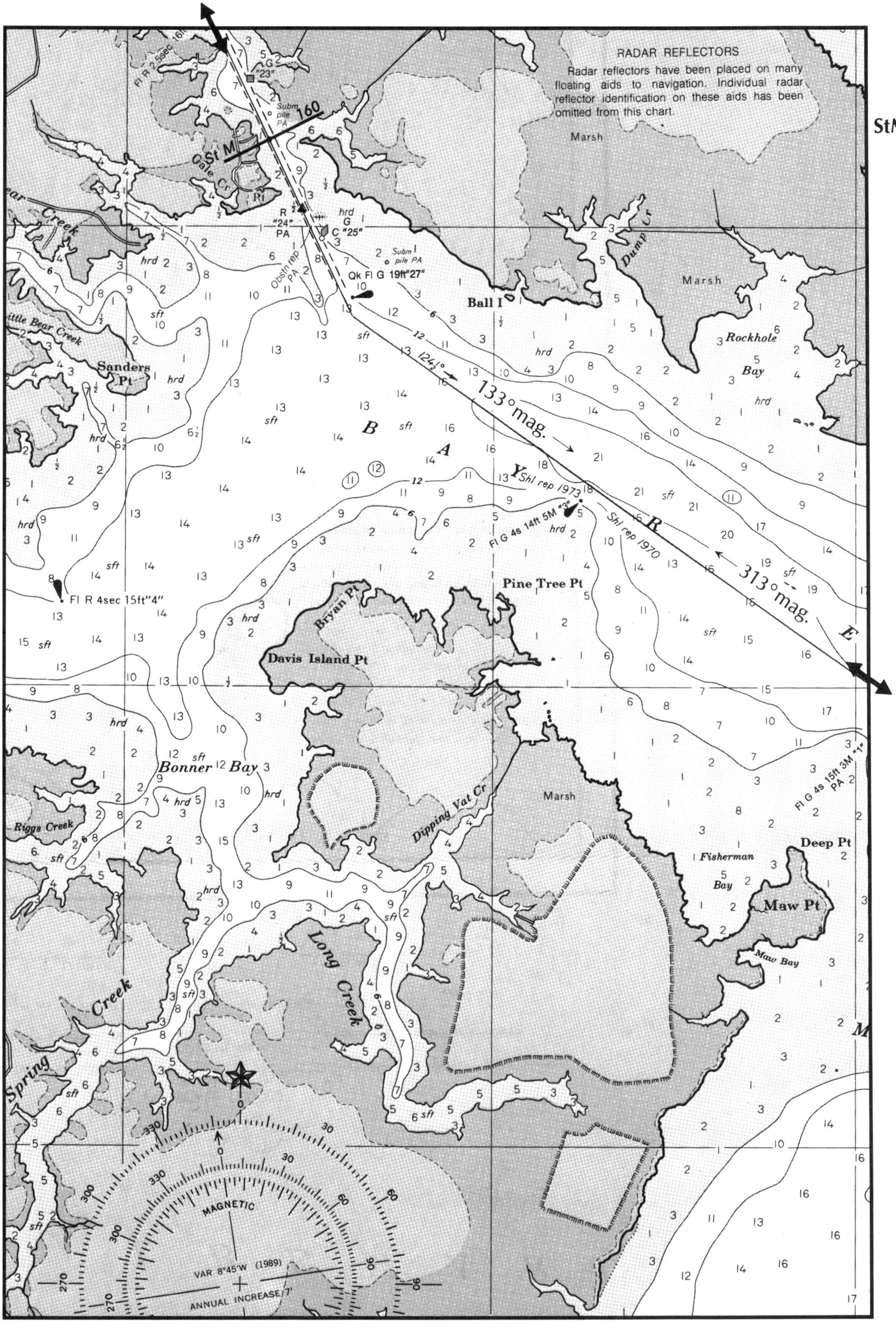
RADAR REFLECTORS
Radar reflectors have been placed on many floating aids to navigation. Individual radar reflector identification on these aids has been omitted from this chart.
Marsh
St M 160
Gale Cr
Pt
"23"
Fl R 2.5sec 16ft
R "24" PA
G C "25"
Qk Fl G 19ft"27"
Obstn rep PA
Subm pile PA
Ball I
Dump Cr
Rockhole Bay
Little Bear Creek
Bear Creek
Sanders Pt
124½°
133° mag.
313° mag.
B A Y R E
Shl rep 1973
Shl rep 1970
Fl G 4s 14ft 5M "3"
Pine Tree Pt
Fl R 4sec 15ft"4"
Davis Island Pt
Bryan Pt
Bonner Bay
Riggs Creek
Dipping Vat Cr
Fl G 4s 15ft 3M "1" PA
Deep Pt
Fisherman Bay
Maw Pt
Maw Bay
Long Creek
Spring Creek
MAGNETIC
VAR 8°45'W (1989)
ANNUAL INCREASE 7'

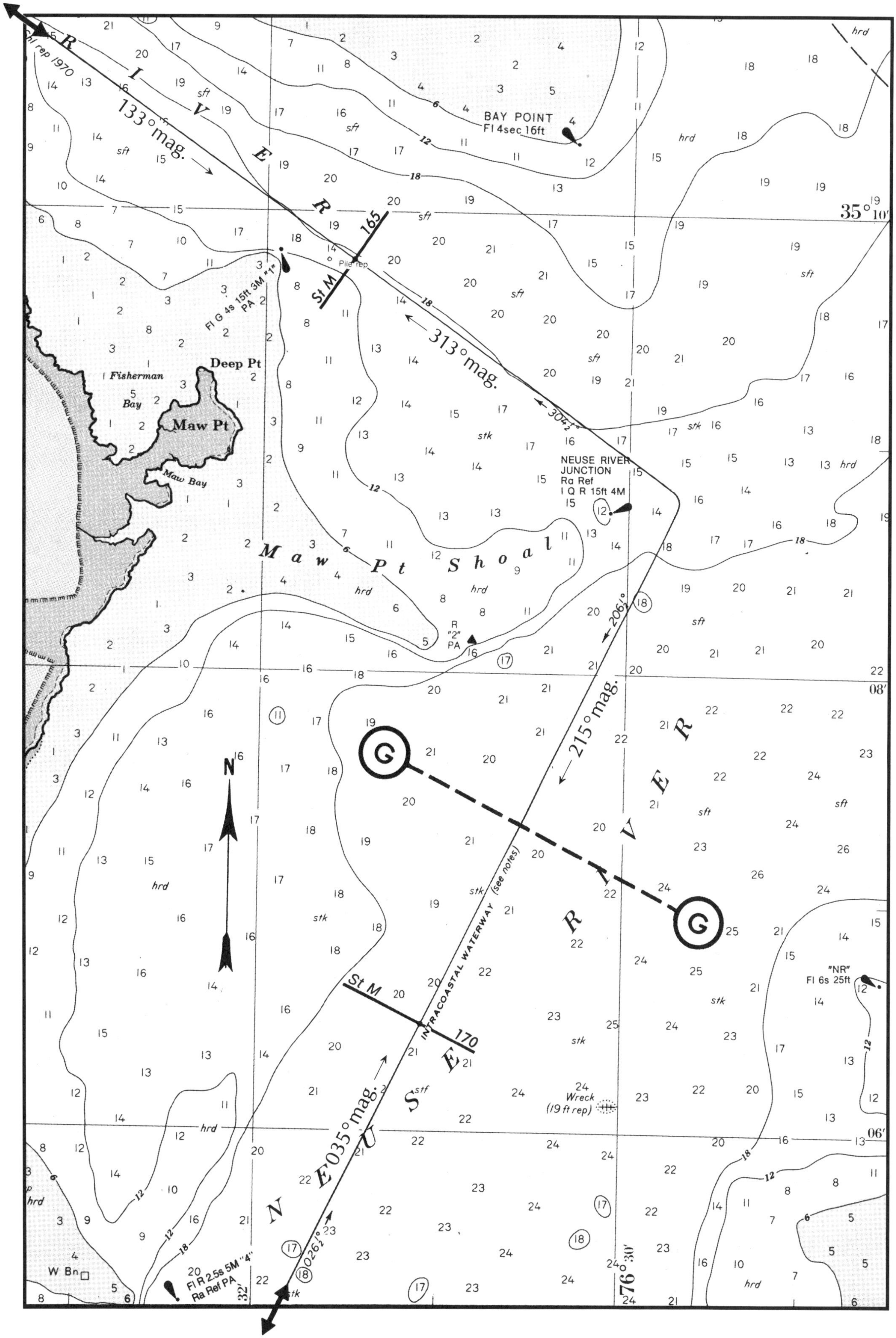


StM165

StM170

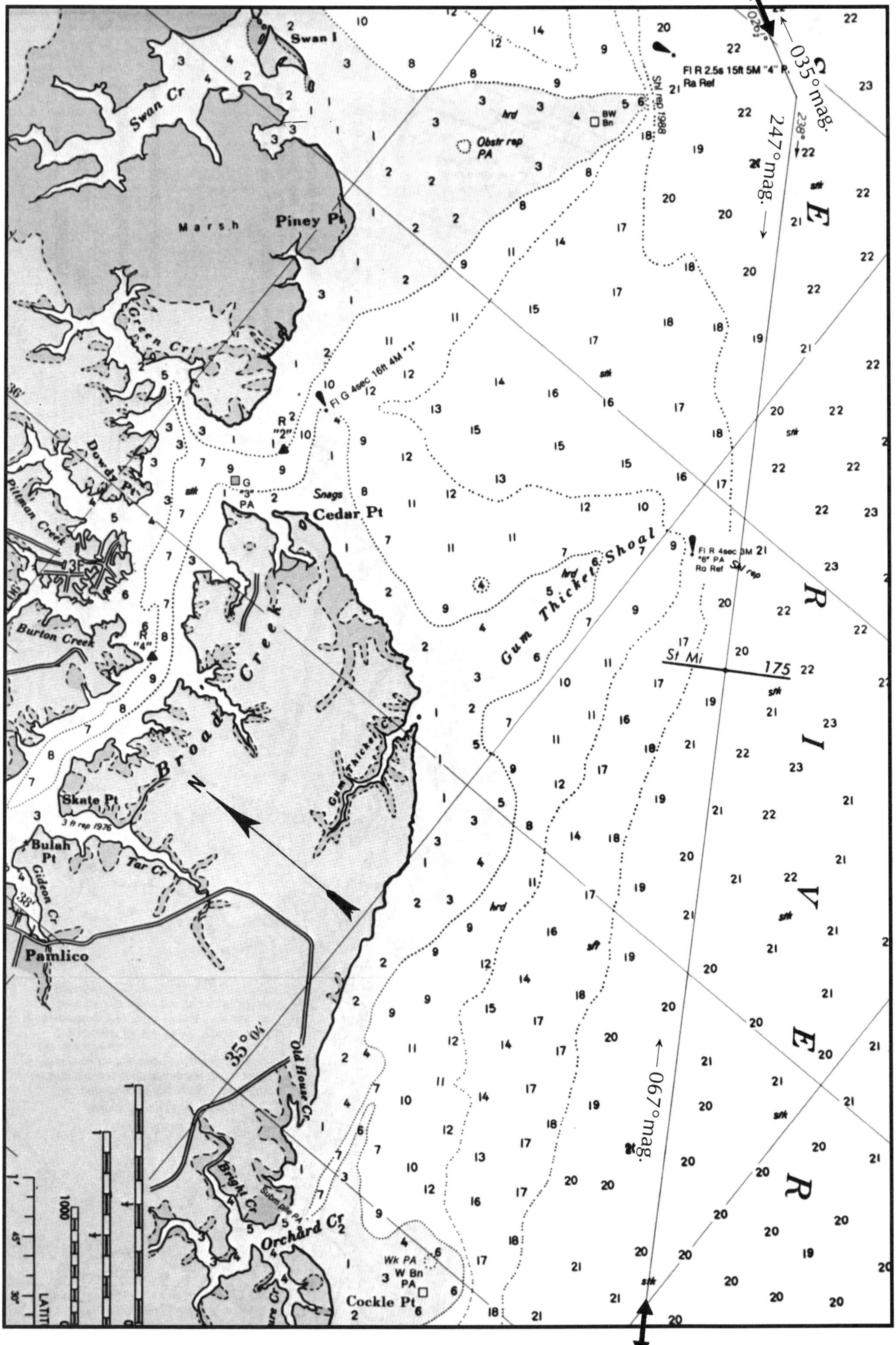

StM175
035°mag.
247°mag.
067°mag.
238°
St Mi 175
R I V E R
Swan I
Swan Cr
Marsh
Piney Pt
Green Cr
Dowdy Pt
Pittman Creek
Burton Creek
Cedar Pt
Snags
Broad Creek
Gum Thicket Cr
Gum Thicket Shoal
Skate Pt
3 ft rep 1976
Bulah Pt
Tar Cr
Gideon Cr
Pamlico
35°04'
Old House Cr
Bright Cr
Orchard Cr
Cockle Pt
Fl R 2.5s 15ft 5M "4" P
Ra Ref
Fl G 4sec 16ft 4M "1"
Fl R 4sec 3M 21 "6" PA Ra Ref
Obstr rep PA
BW Bn
W Bn PA
Wk PA
Subm pile PA
R "2"
R "4"
G "3" PA
Stl rep 1988
Stl rep

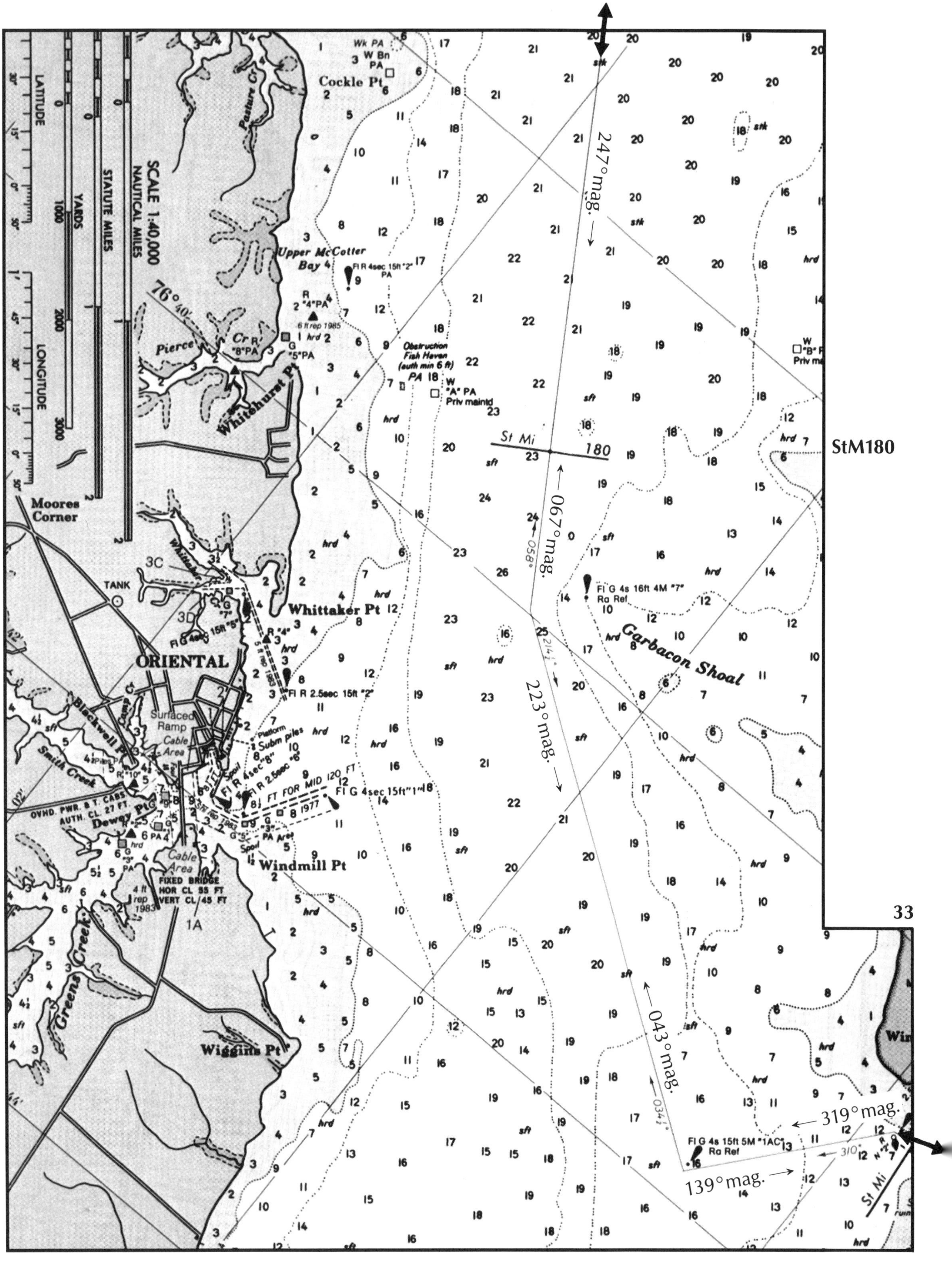

SCALE 1:40,000
NAUTICAL MILES
STATUTE MILES
YARDS
LATITUDE
LONGITUDE
76° 40'
Cockle Pt
Pasture Cr
Upper McCotter Bay
Pierce Cr
Whitehurst Pt
Moores Corner
TANK
Whittaker Cr
Whittaker Pt
ORIENTAL
Camp Cr
Blackwell Pt
Smith Creek
Dewey Pt
Surfaced Ramp
Cable Area
OVHD. PWR. & T. CABS AUTH. CL. 27 FT.
FIXED BRIDGE HOR CL 55 FT VERT CL 45 FT
Windmill Pt
Greens Creek
Wiggins Pt
Obstruction Fish Haven (auth min 6 ft) PA
W "A" PA Priv maintd
W "B" PA Priv maintd
Fl G 4s 16ft 4M "7" Ra Ref
Fl G 4s 15ft 5M "1AC" Ra Ref
Fl R 4sec 15ft "2" PA
Fl R 2.5sec 15ft "2"
Fl G 4sec 15ft "1"
Garbacon Shoal
St Mi 180
StM180
247° mag.
067° mag.
223° mag.
043° mag.
319° mag.
139° mag.
058°
214½°
034½°
310°
3C
3D
1A
33

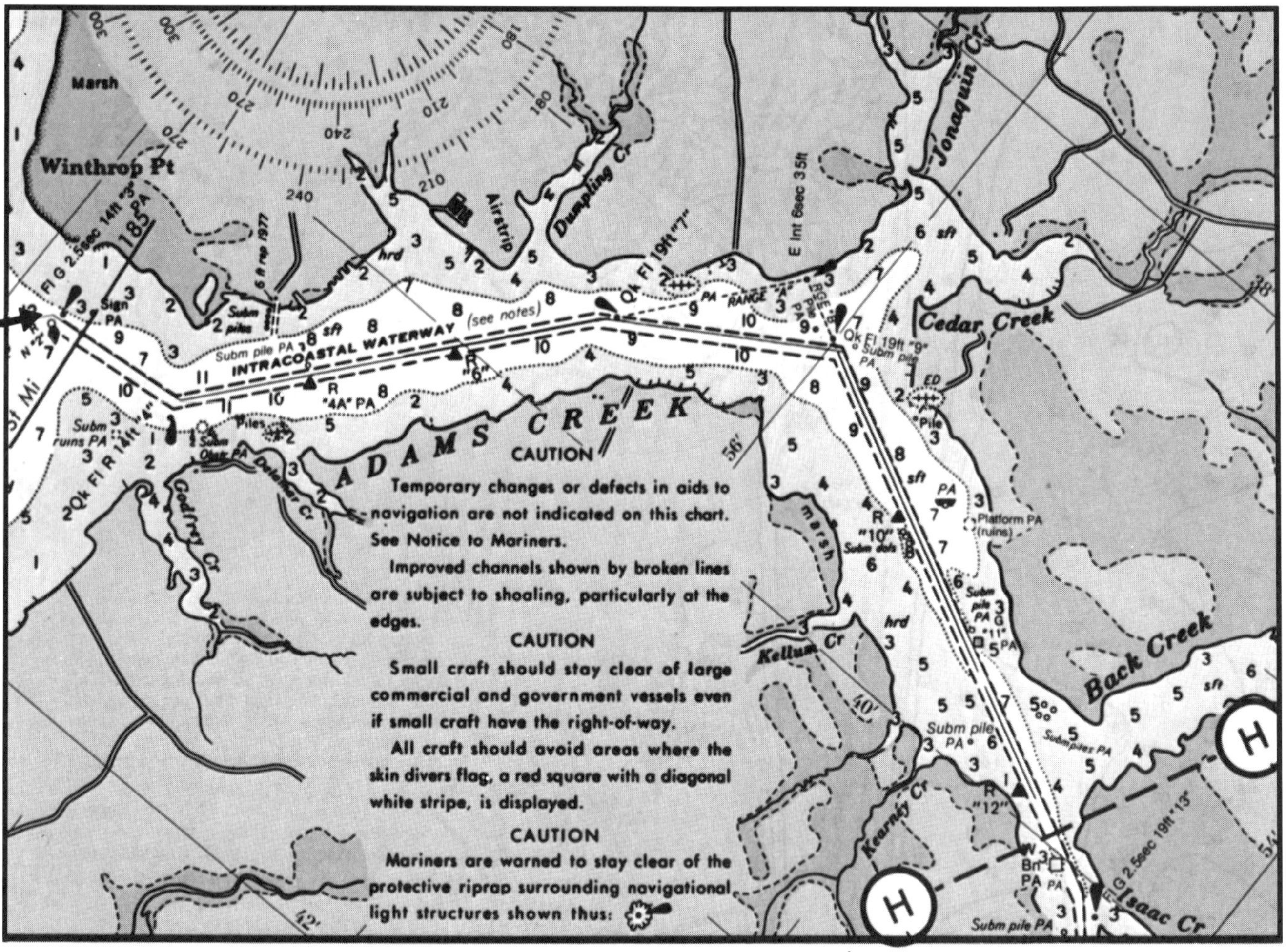

34

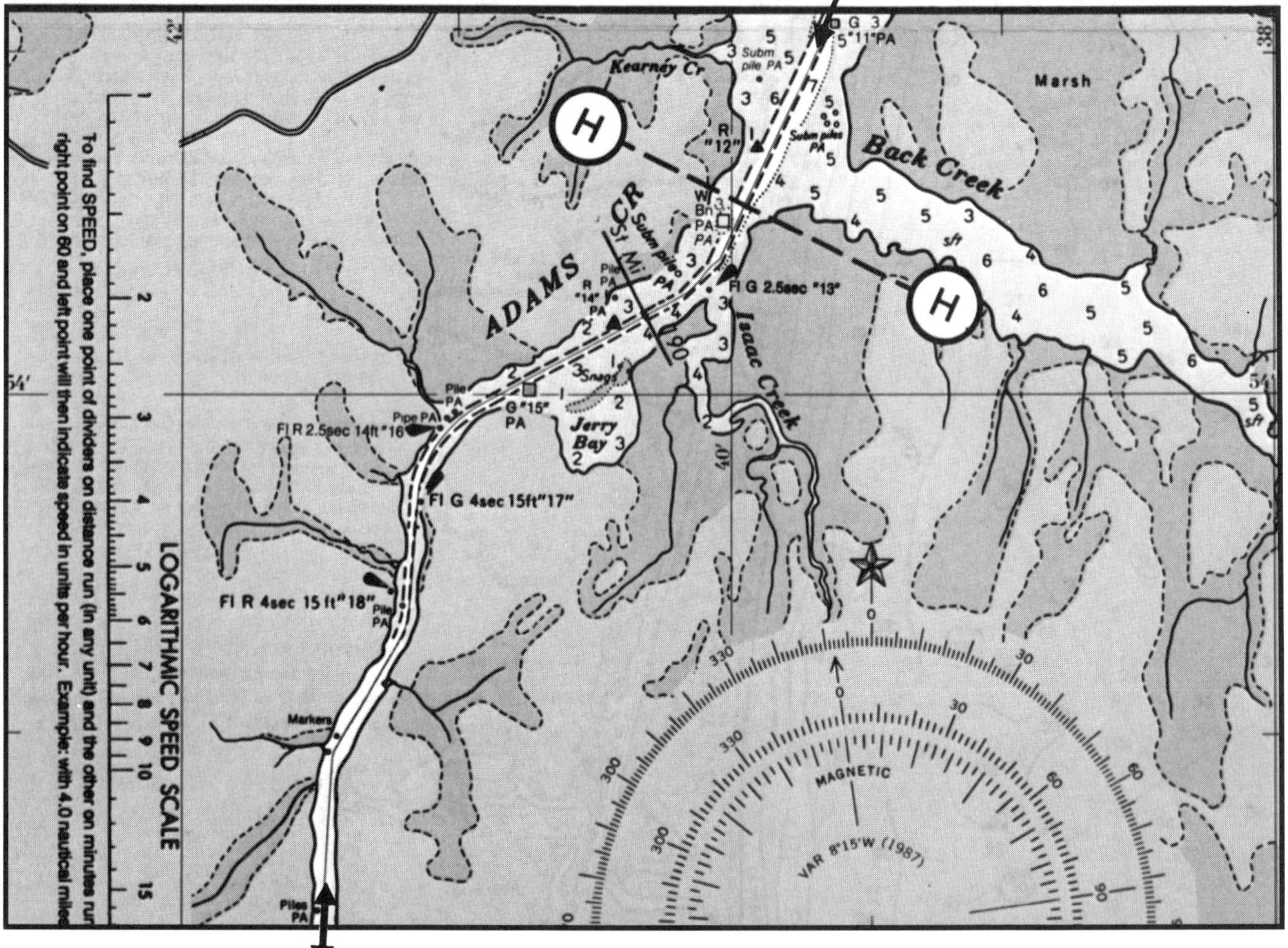

StM195

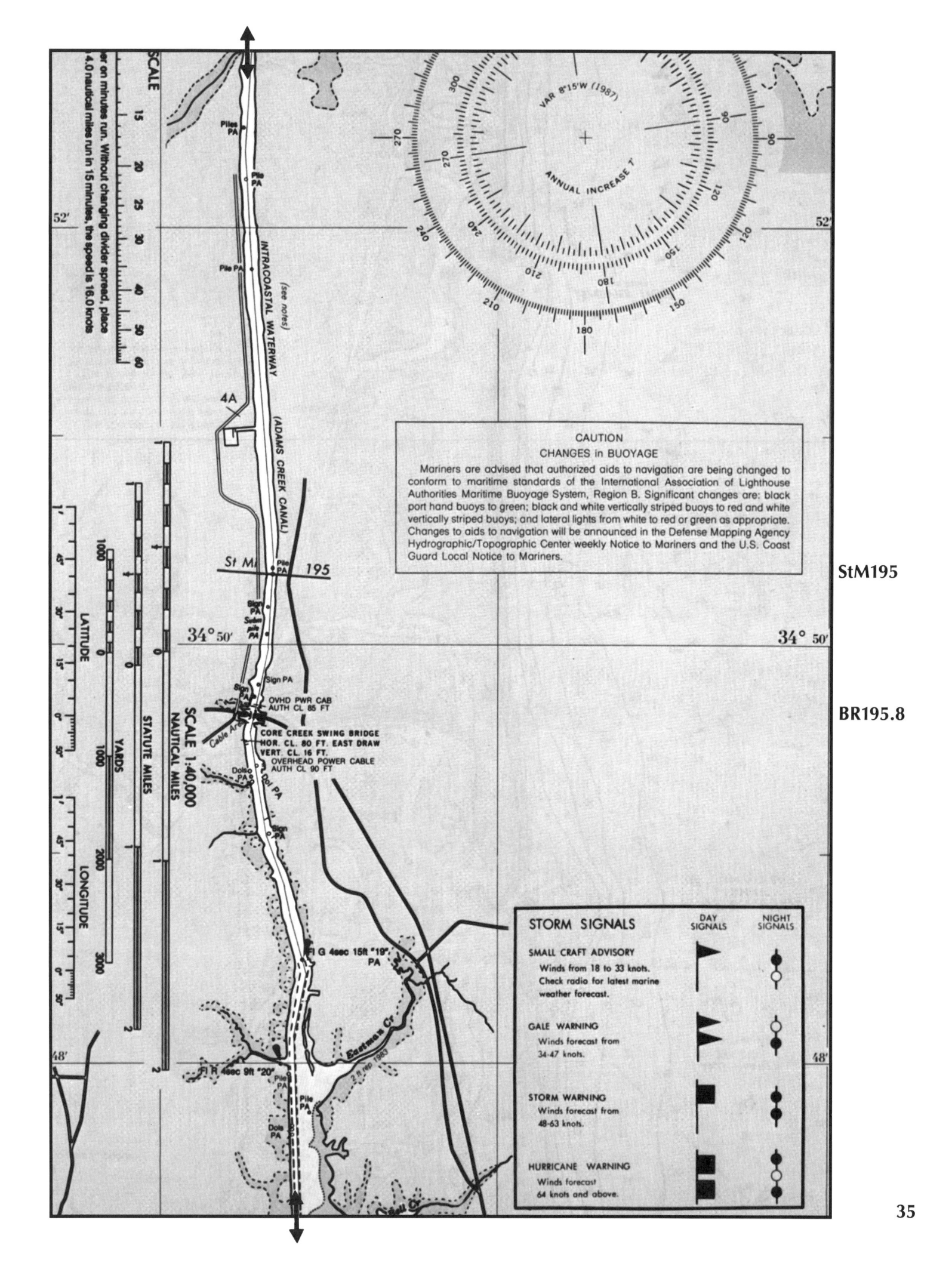

BR195.8

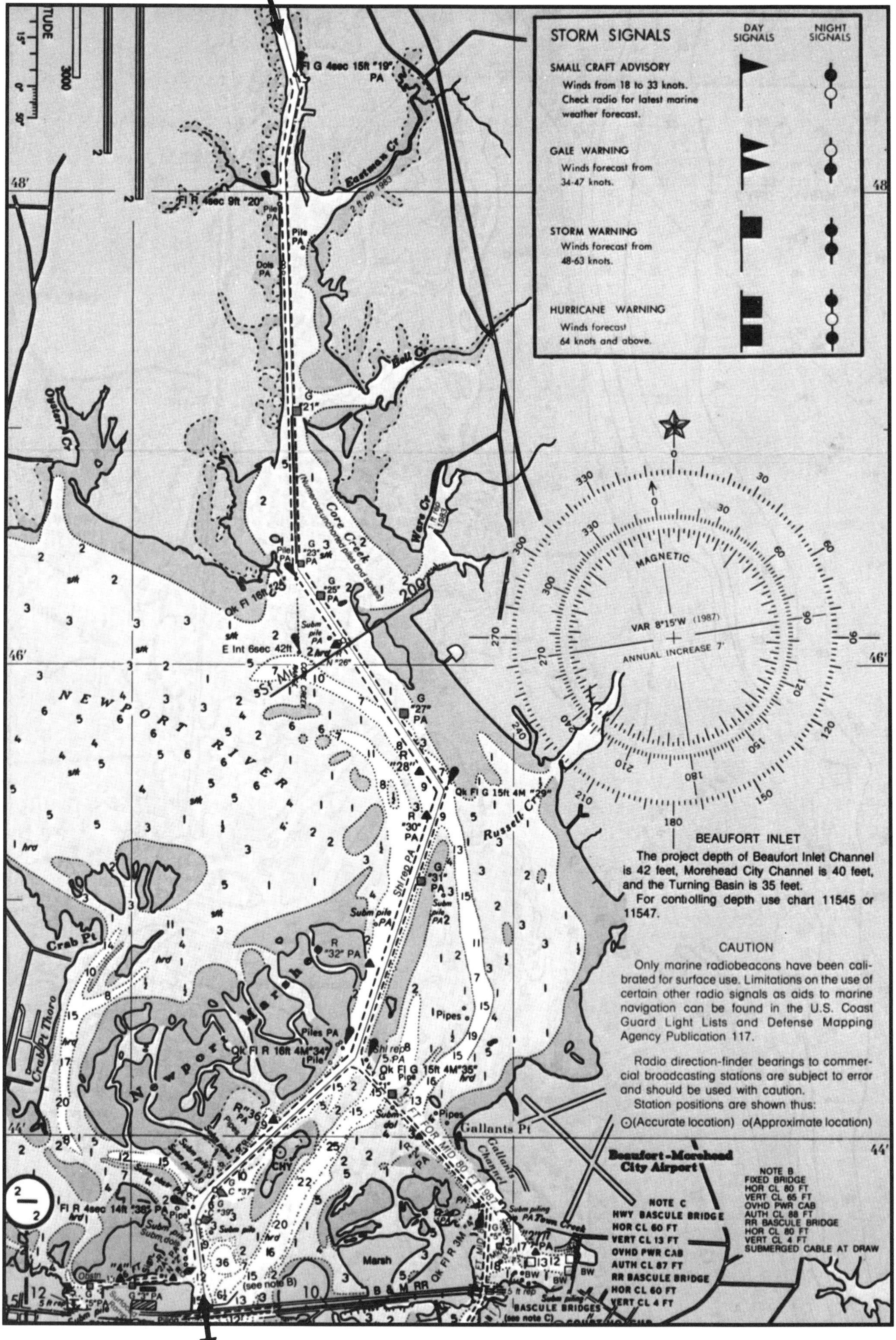

36

## STORM SIGNALS

| | DAY SIGNALS | NIGHT SIGNALS |
|---|---|---|

**SMALL CRAFT ADVISORY**
Winds from 18 to 33 knots. Check radio for latest marine weather forecast.

**GALE WARNING**
Winds forecast from 34-47 knots.

**STORM WARNING**
Winds forecast from 48-63 knots.

**HURRICANE WARNING**
Winds forecast 64 knots and above.

MAGNETIC

VAR 8°15'W (1987)

ANNUAL INCREASE 7'

### BEAUFORT INLET

The project depth of Beaufort Inlet Channel is 42 feet, Morehead City Channel is 40 feet, and the Turning Basin is 35 feet.

For controlling depth use chart 11545 or 11547.

### CAUTION

Only marine radiobeacons have been calibrated for surface use. Limitations on the use of certain other radio signals as aids to marine navigation can be found in the U.S. Coast Guard Light Lists and Defense Mapping Agency Publication 117.

Radio direction-finder bearings to commercial broadcasting stations are subject to error and should be used with caution.

Station positions are shown thus:

⊙(Accurate location)  o(Approximate location)

**Beaufort-Morehead City Airport**

**NOTE C**
HWY BASCULE BRIDGE
HOR CL 60 FT
VERT CL 13 FT
OVHD PWR CAB
AUTH CL 87 FT
RR BASCULE BRIDGE
HOR CL 60 FT
VERT CL 4 FT

**NOTE B**
FIXED BRIDGE
HOR CL 80 FT
VERT CL 65 FT
OVHD PWR CAB
AUTH CL 88 FT
RR BASCULE BRIDGE
HOR CL 80 FT
VERT CL 4 FT
SUBMERGED CABLE AT DRAW

BASCULE BRIDGES (see note C)

*Chart labels:*
NEWPORT RIVER · Core Creek · Eastman Cr · Bell Cr · Ware Cr · Russell Cr · Oyster Cr · Crab Pt · Newport Marsh · Gallants Pt · Gallants Channel · Marsh · Crab Pt Thoro

Fl G 4sec 15ft "19" PA
Fl R 4sec 9ft "20"
Qk Fl 16ft "25"
E Int 6sec 42ft
Qk Fl G 15ft 4M "29"
Qk Fl R 16ft 4M "34"
Qk Fl G 15ft 4M "35"
Fl R 4sec 14ft "38" PA

48'   46'   44'

StM200

BR203.8

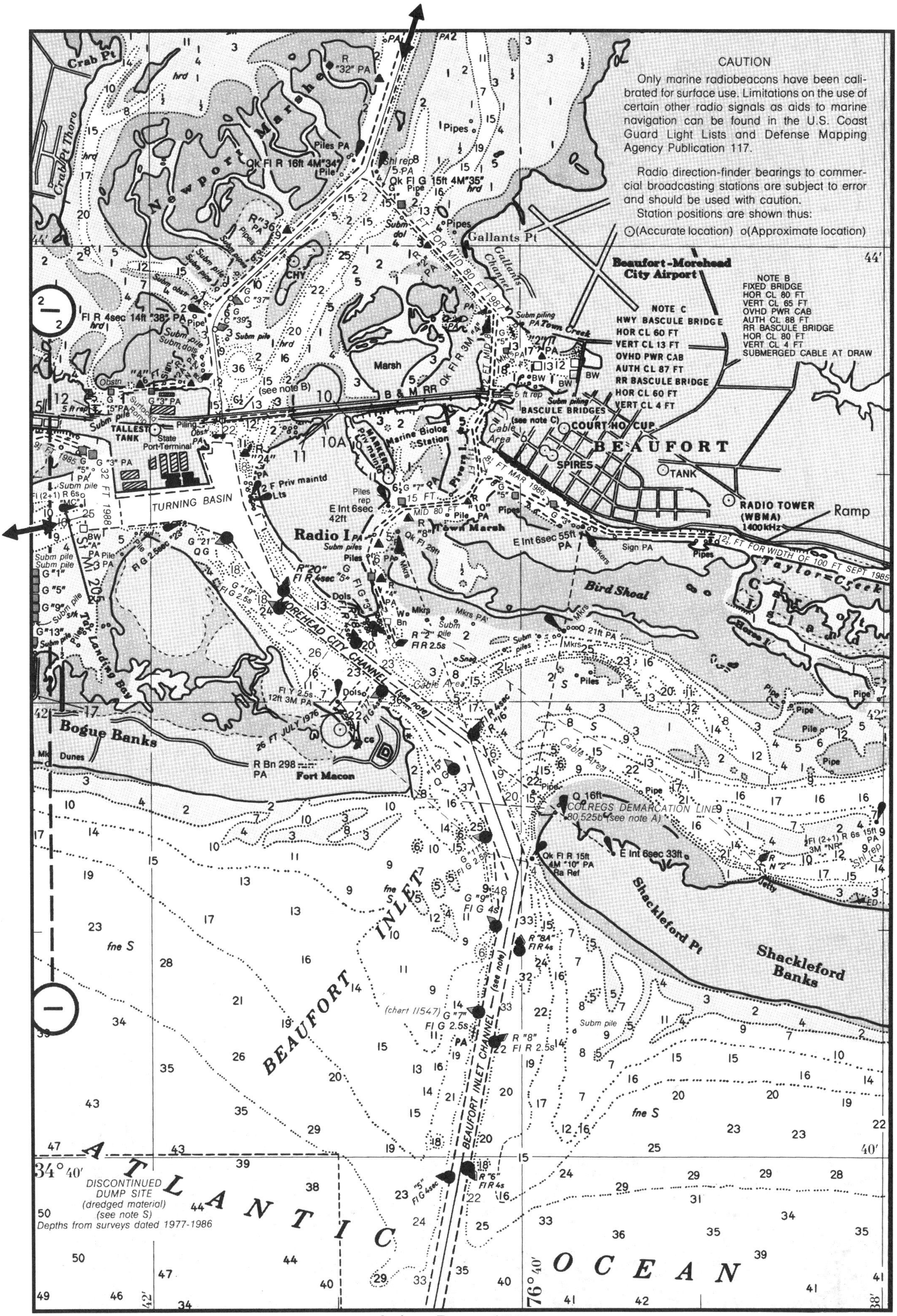


BR203.8

StM205

Joins Page 195

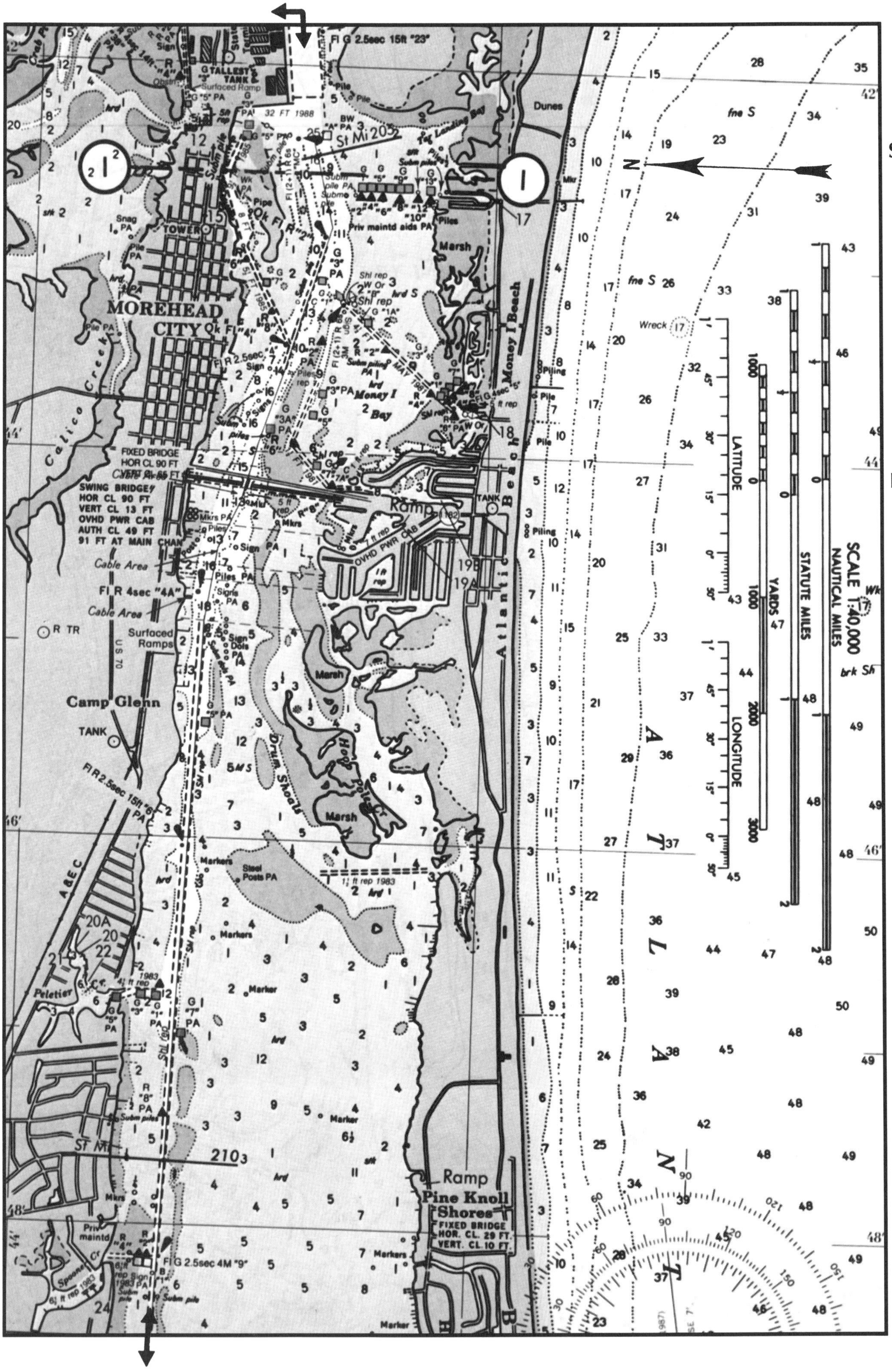


StM205

BR206.7

StM210

StM215

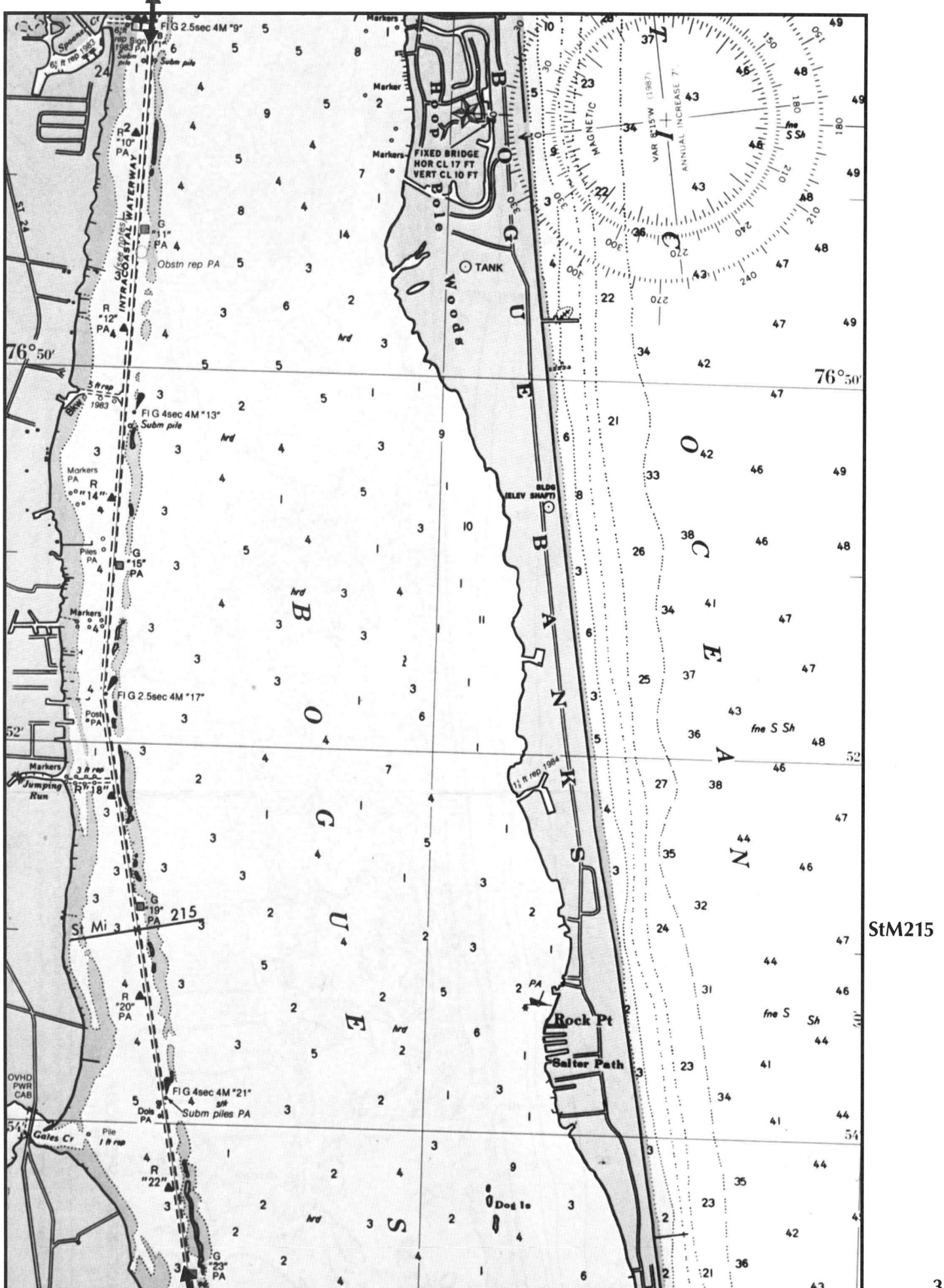

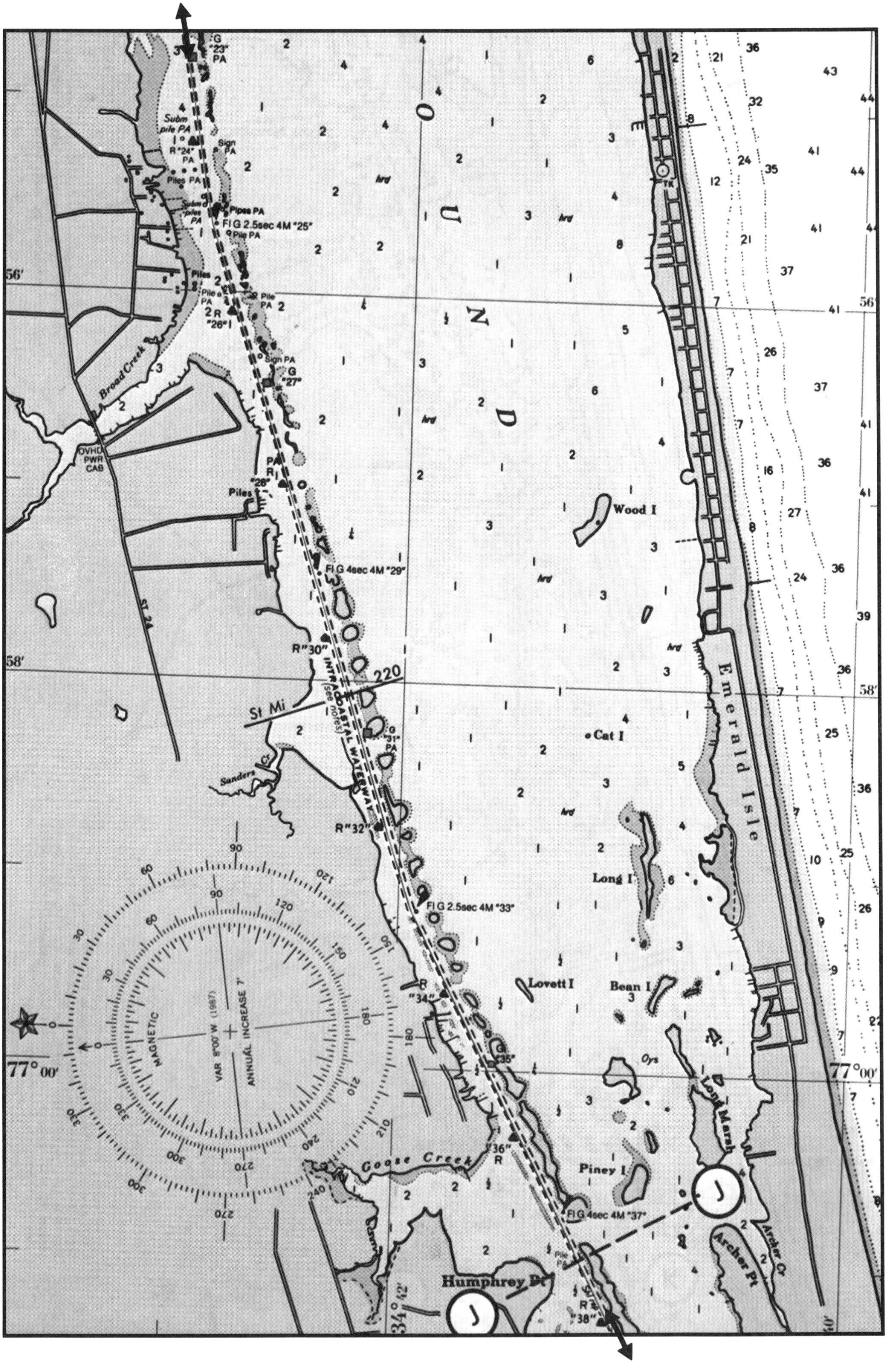
Emerald Isle
Wood I
Cat I
Long I
Lovett I
Bean I
Piney I
Long Marsh
Archer Pt
Archer Cr
Humphrey Pt
Broad Creek
Goose Creek
Sanders Cr
INTRACOASTAL WATERWAY (see notes)
St Mi
220
ST 24
OVHD PWR CAB
Fl G 2.5sec 4M "25"
Fl G 4sec 4M "29"
Fl G 2.5sec 4M "33"
Fl G 4sec 4M "37"
R "30"
R "32"
VAR 8°00' W (1987)
ANNUAL INCREASE 7'
MAGNETIC
77°00'
34°42'
56'
58'

StM220

StM225

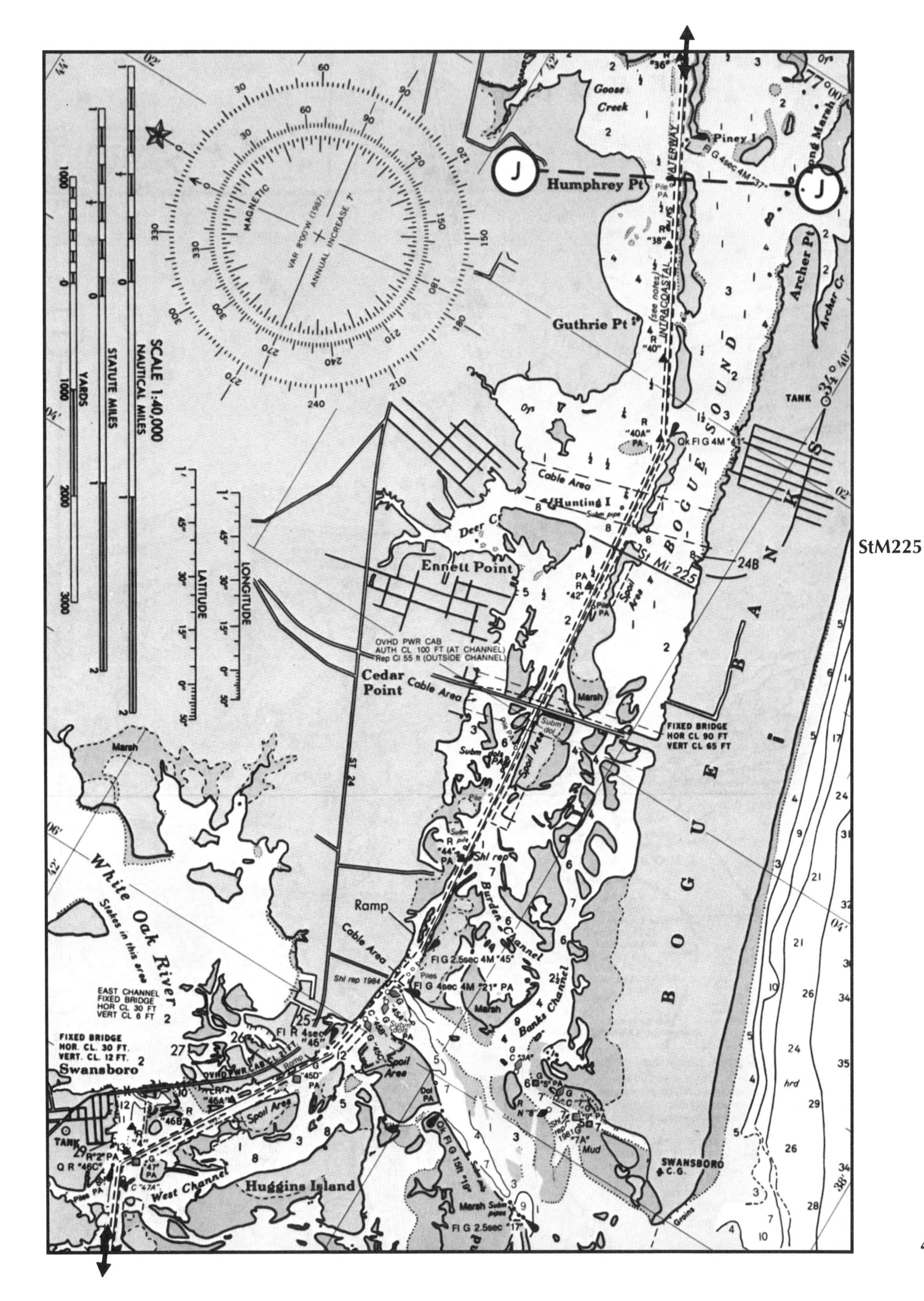

41

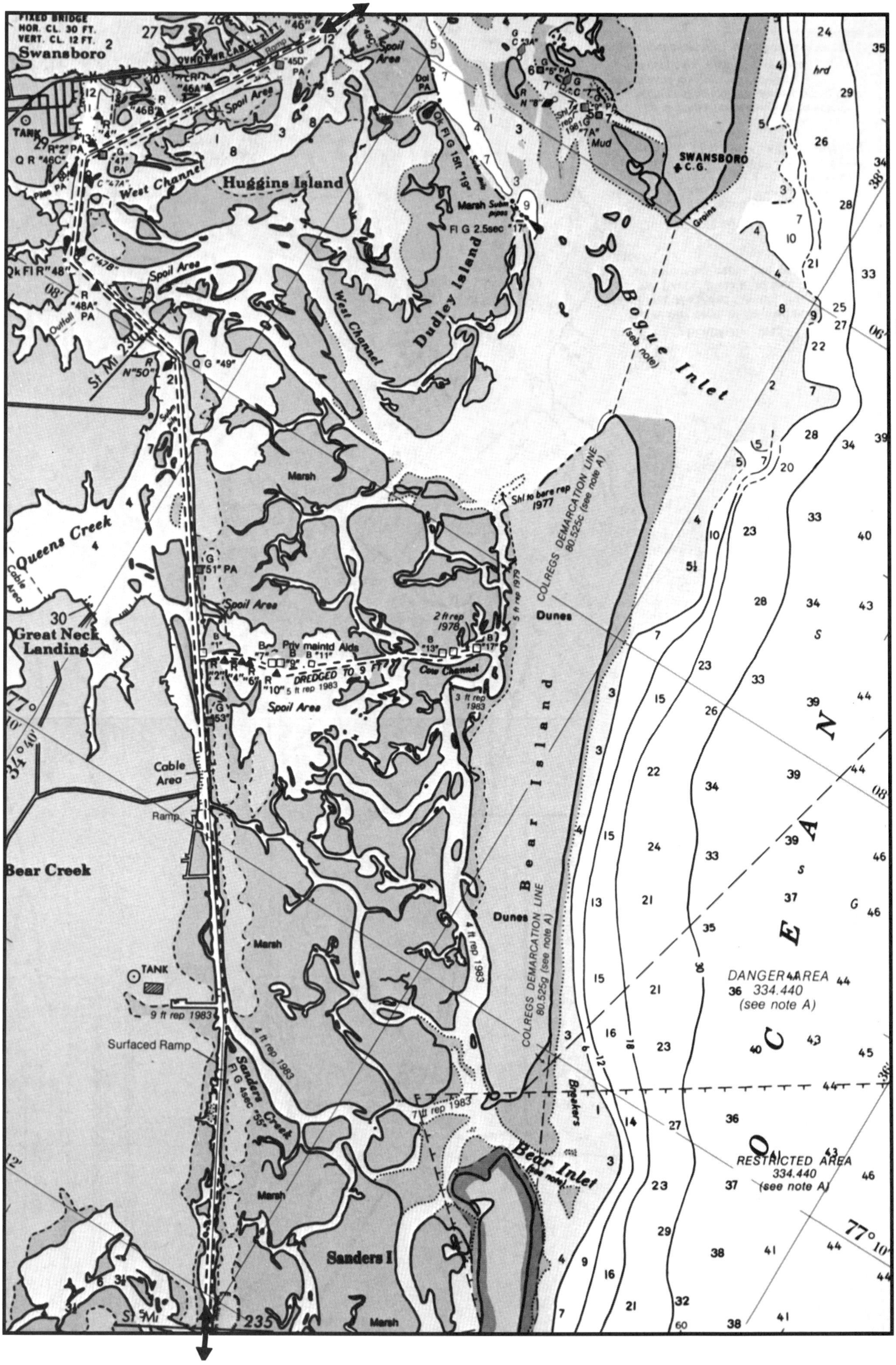


StM230

StM235

## CAUTION
### Entrances and Channels

The channels at the entrances to the inlets and the channels to the Intracoastal Waterway on this chart are subject to continuous change.

The buoys in the New Topsail Inlet, Masonboro Inlet and Bogue Inlet are not charted because they are frequently shifted in position.

## INTRACOASTAL WATERWAY
### Project Depths

12 feet Norfolk, Va. to Fort Pierce, Fla. 10 feet Fort Pierce, Fla. to Miami, Fla. 7 feet Miami, Fla. to Cross Bank, Florida Bay.

The controlling depths are published periodically in the U.S. Coast Guard Local Notice to Mariners.

### Distances

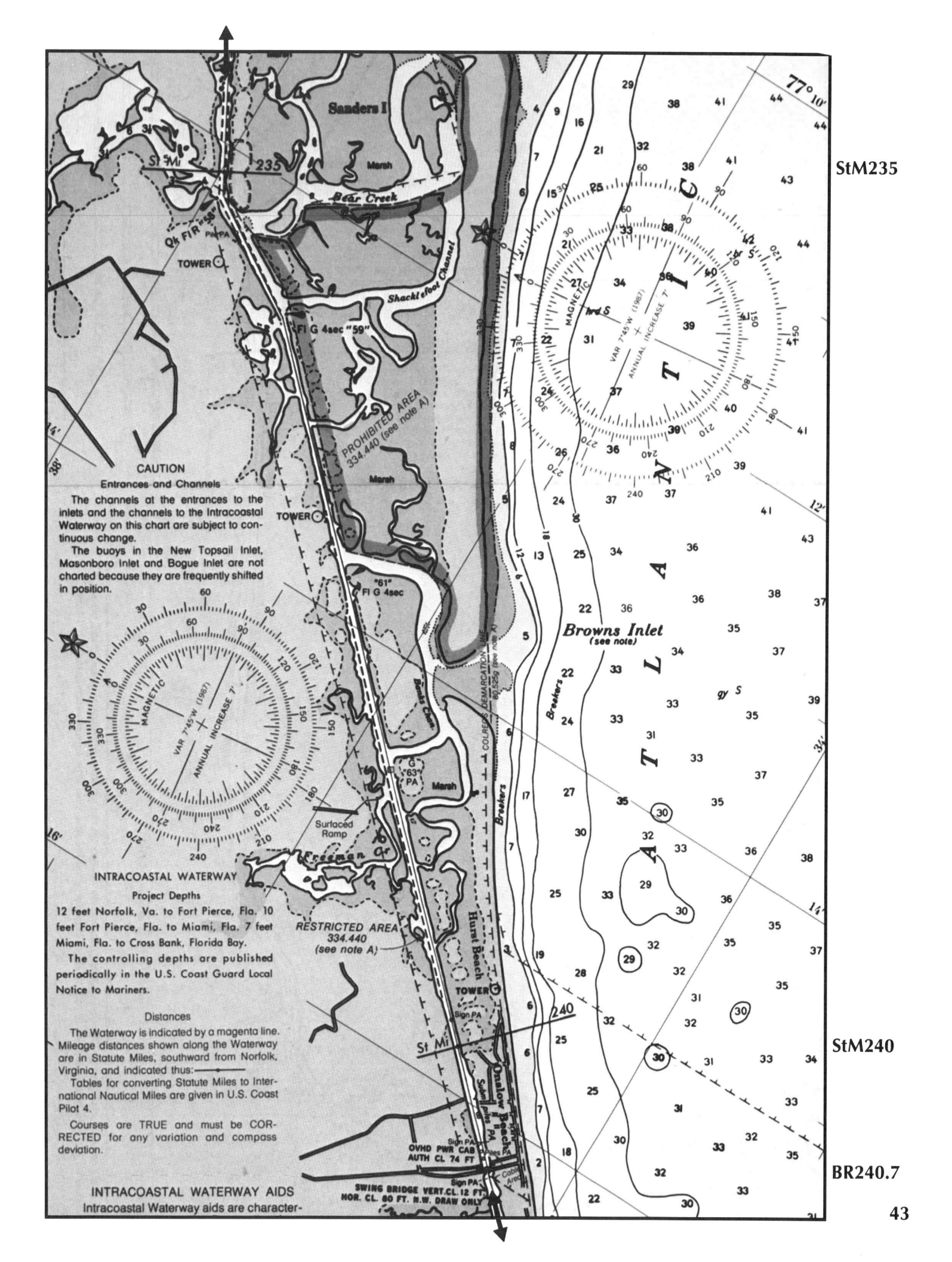

The Waterway is indicated by a magenta line. Mileage distances shown along the Waterway are in Statute Miles, southward from Norfolk, Virginia, and indicated thus:———

Tables for converting Statute Miles to International Nautical Miles are given in U.S. Coast Pilot 4.

Courses are TRUE and must be CORRECTED for any variation and compass deviation.

## INTRACOASTAL WATERWAY AIDS

Intracoastal Waterway aids are character-

StM235

StM240

BR240.7

43

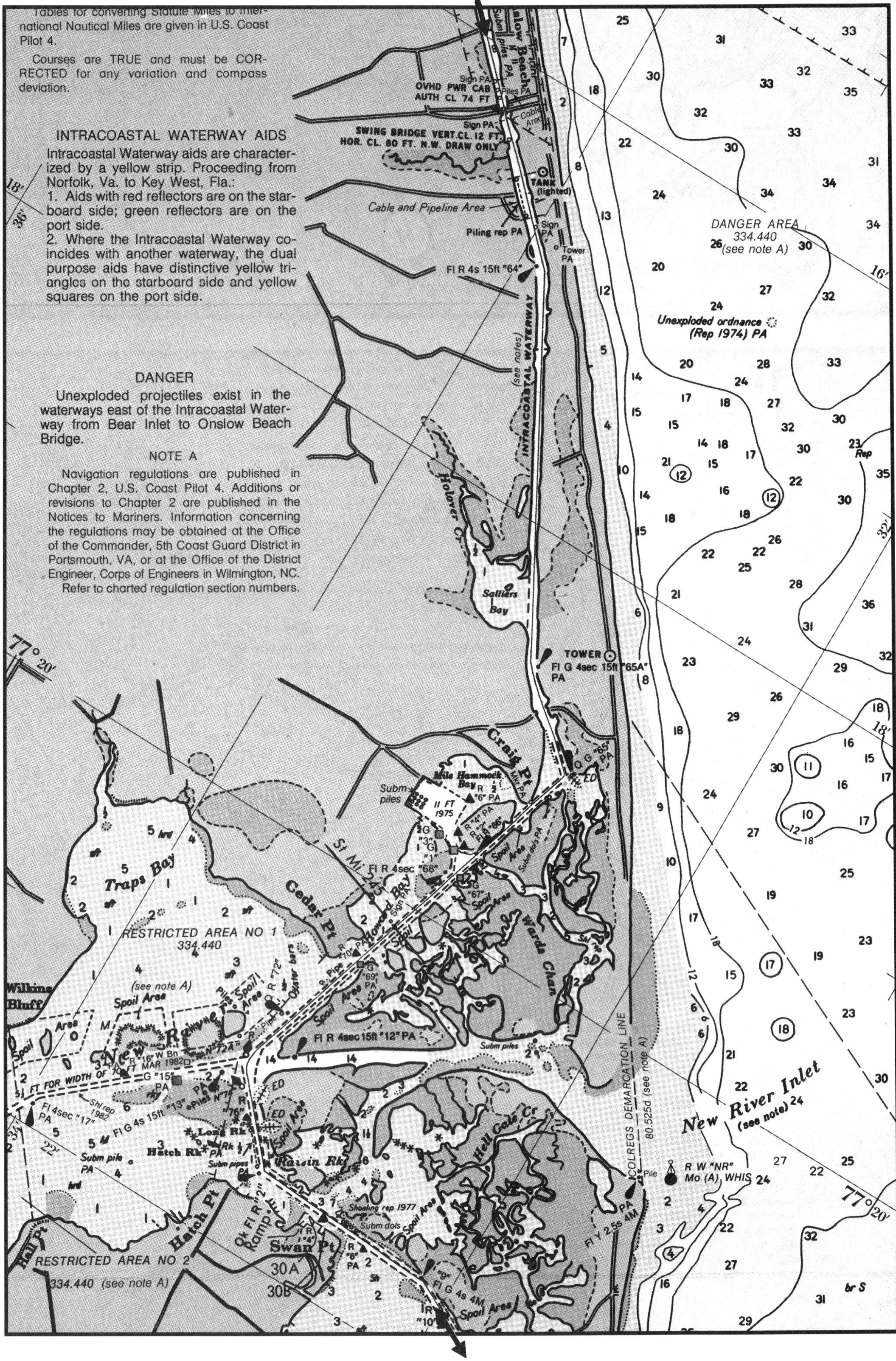


BR240.7

StM245

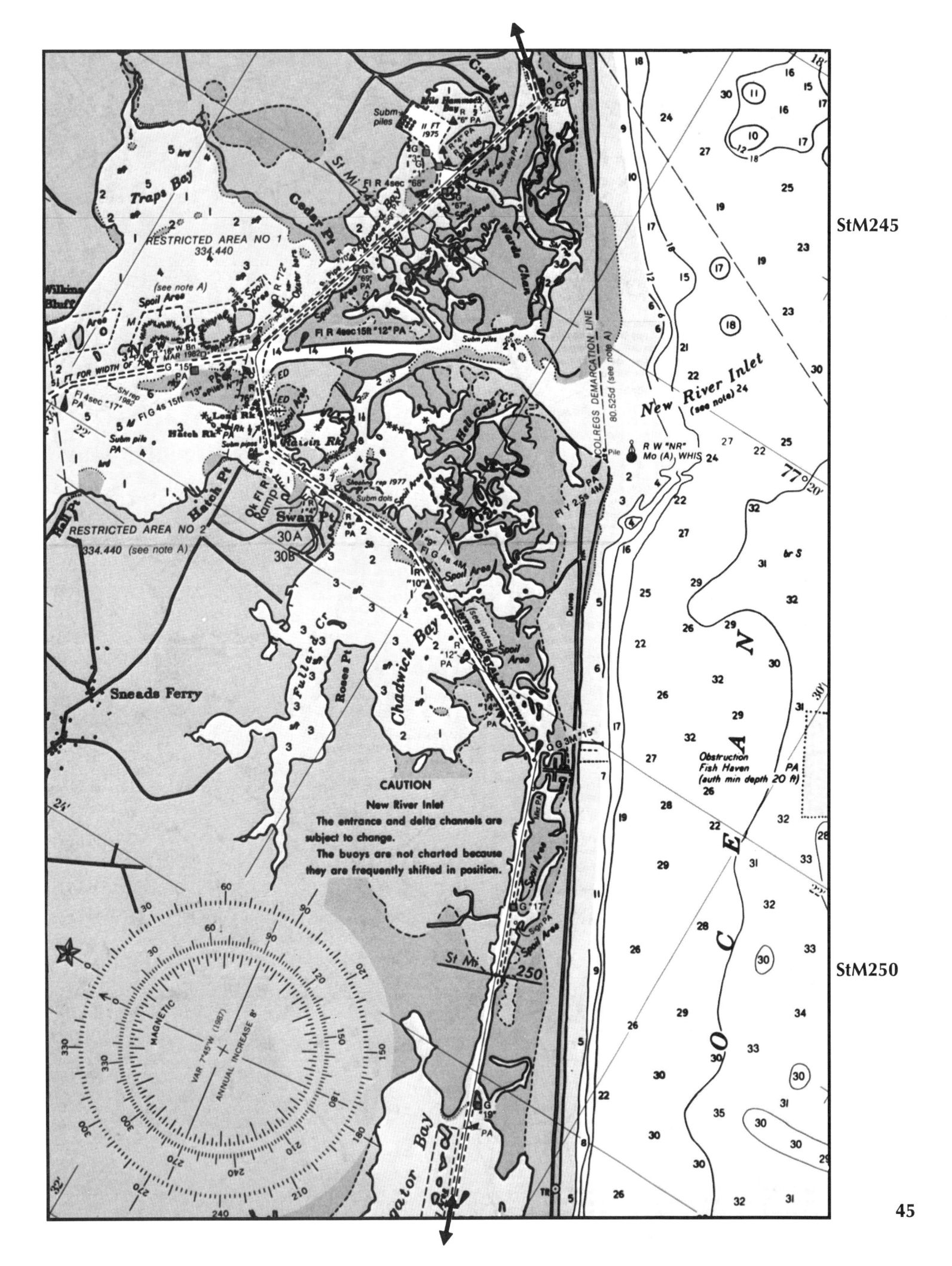

**CAUTION**

New River Inlet

The entrance and delta channels are subject to change.

The buoys are not charted because they are frequently shifted in position.

StM245

StM250

45

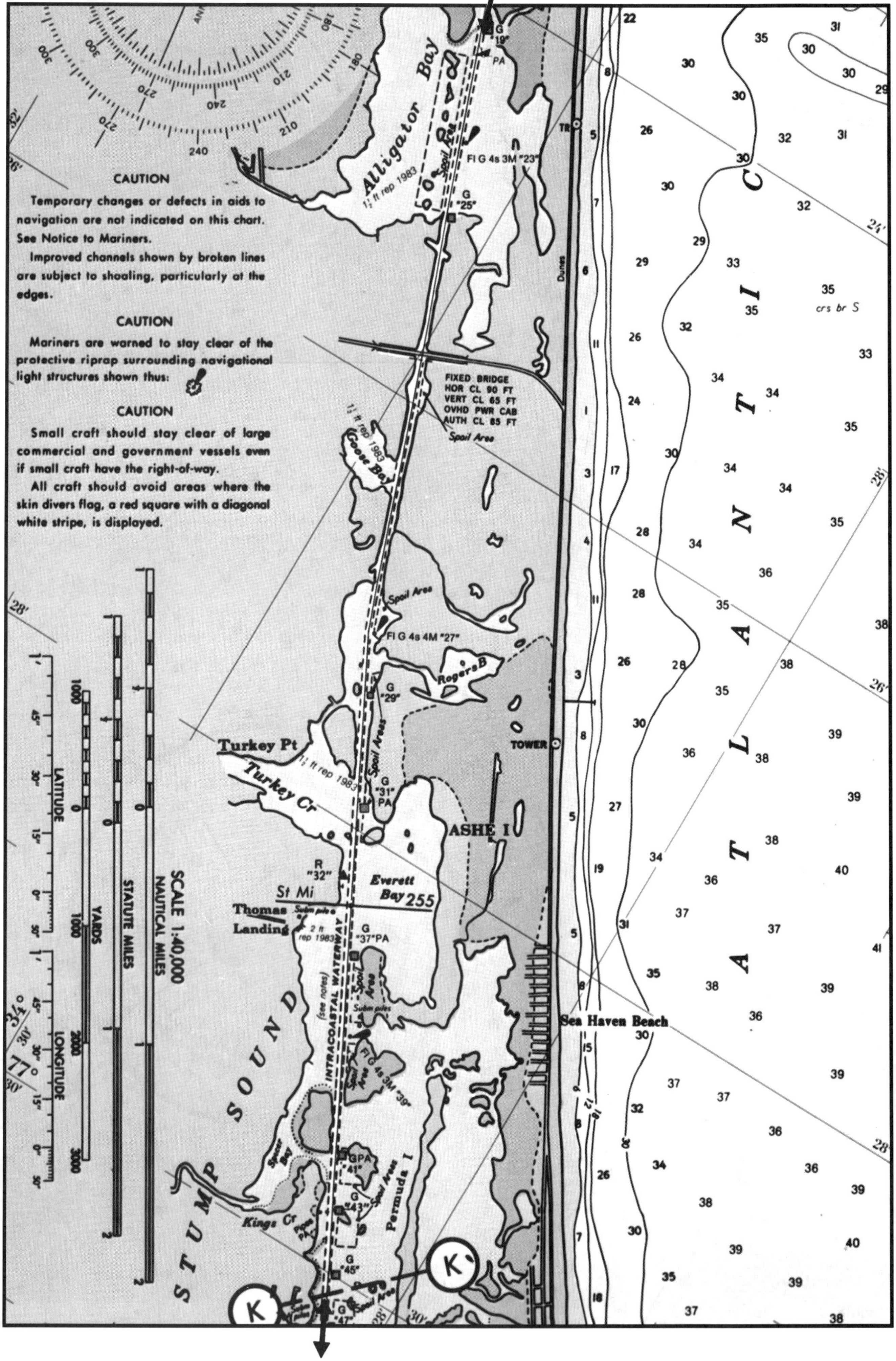
CAUTION
Temporary changes or defects in aids to navigation are not indicated on this chart. See Notice to Mariners.
Improved channels shown by broken lines are subject to shoaling, particularly at the edges.
CAUTION
Mariners are warned to stay clear of the protective riprap surrounding navigational light structures shown thus:
CAUTION
Small craft should stay clear of large commercial and government vessels even if small craft have the right-of-way.
All craft should avoid areas where the skin divers flag, a red square with a diagonal white stripe, is displayed.
SCALE 1:40,000
NAUTICAL MILES
STATUTE MILES
YARDS
LATITUDE
LONGITUDE
Alligator Bay
Goose Bay
Rogers B
Turkey Pt
Turkey Cr
ASHE I
Everett Bay
St Mi 255
Thomas Landing
INTRACOASTAL WATERWAY
STUMP SOUND
Kings Cr
Permuda I
Sea Haven Beach
TOWER
Dunes
FIXED BRIDGE
HOR CL 90 FT
VERT CL 65 FT
OVHD PWR CAB
AUTH CL 85 FT
Spoil Area
Fl G 4s 3M "23"
Fl G 4s 4M "27"
Fl G 4s 3M "39"
ATLANTIC
crs br S

StM255

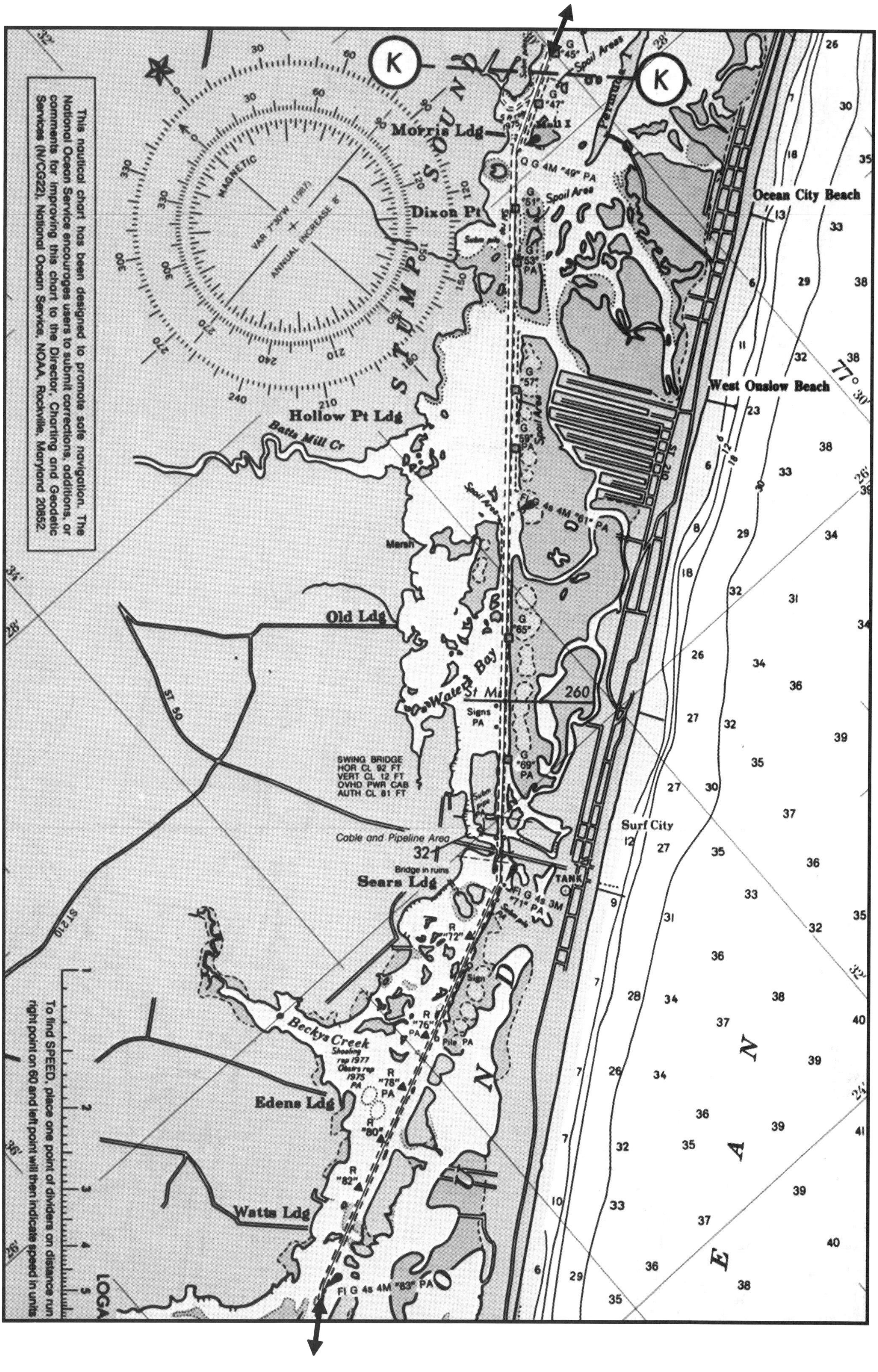


StM260

BR260.7

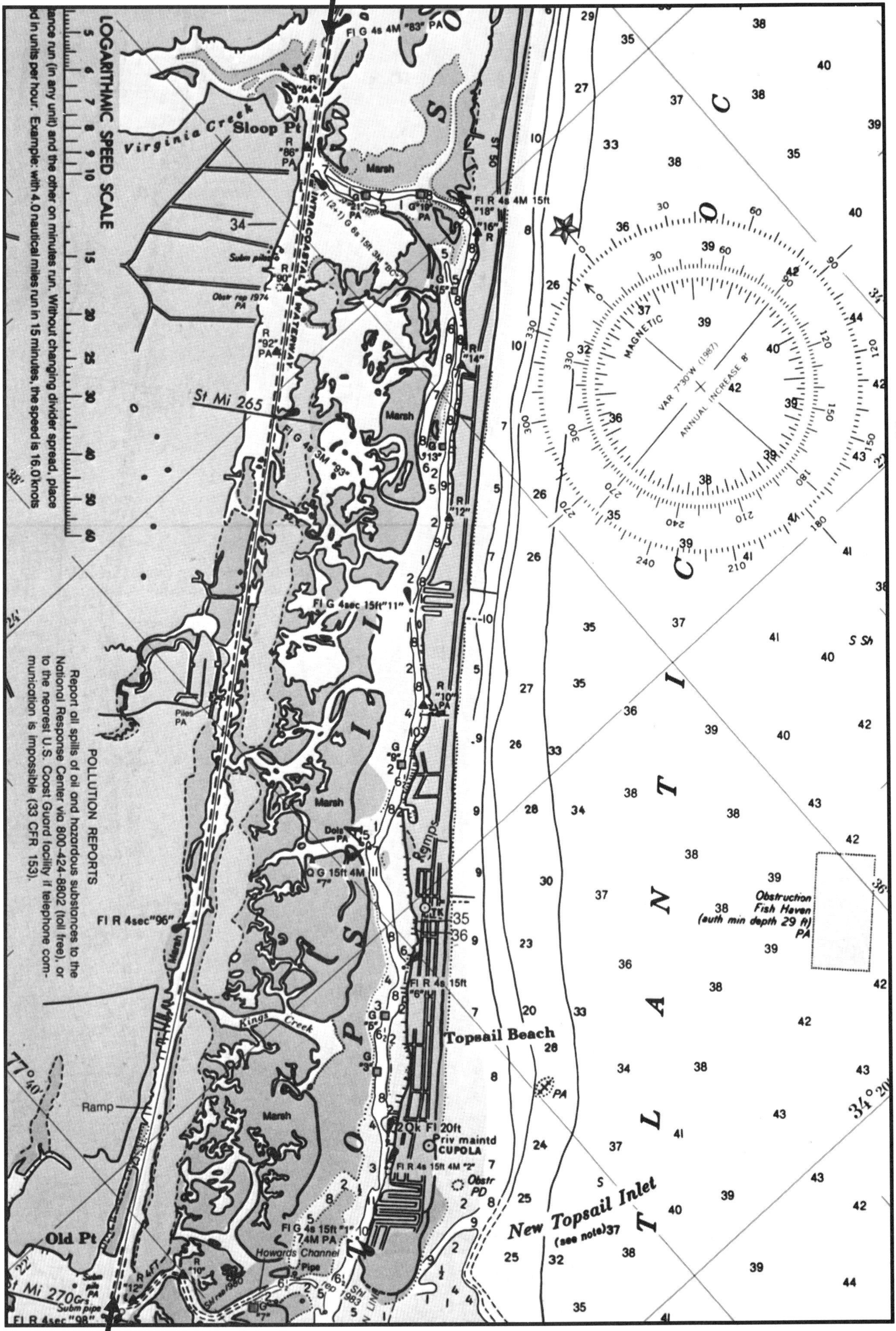


StM265

StM270

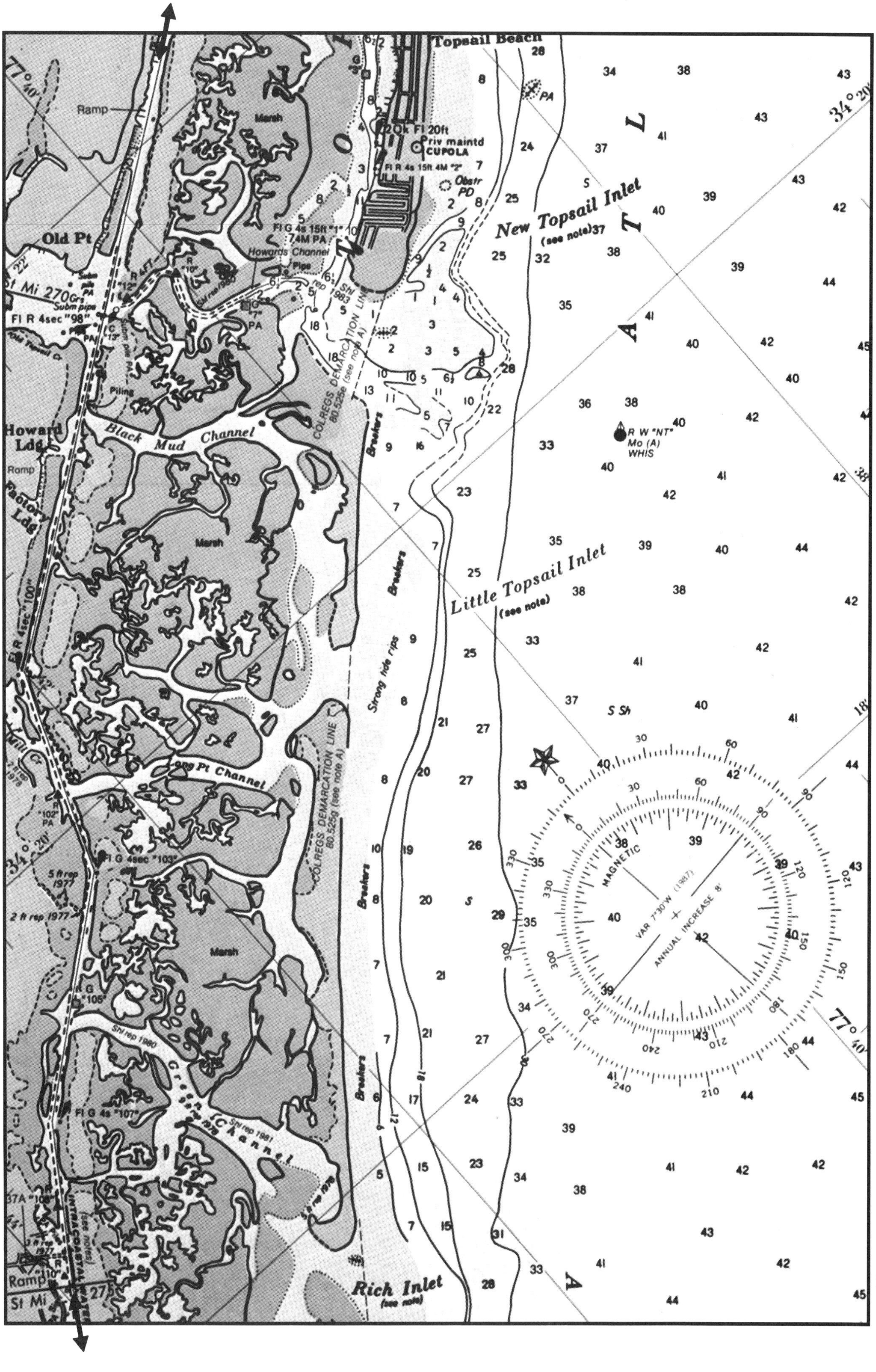


StM270

StM275

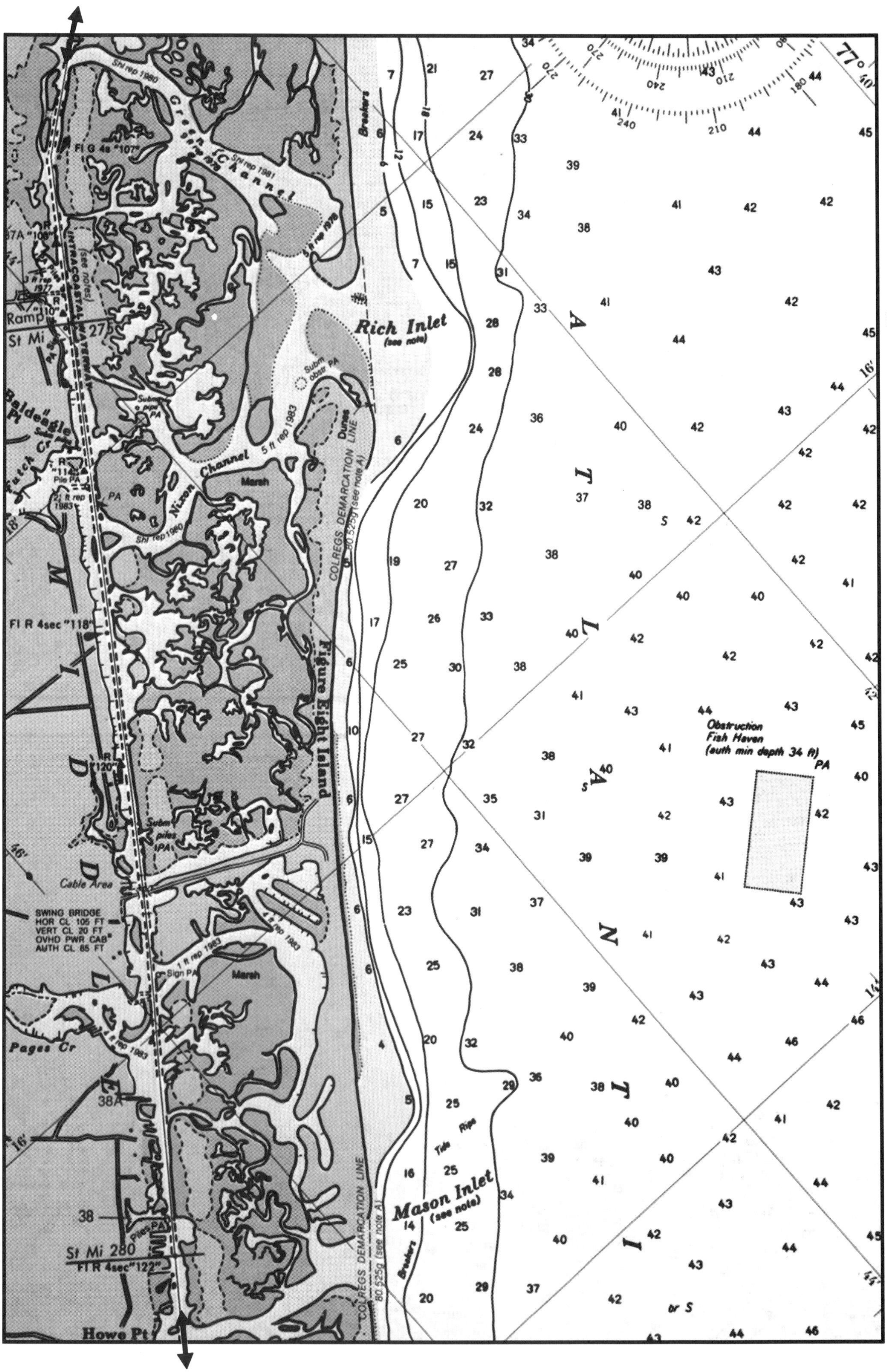


StM275

BR278.1

StM280

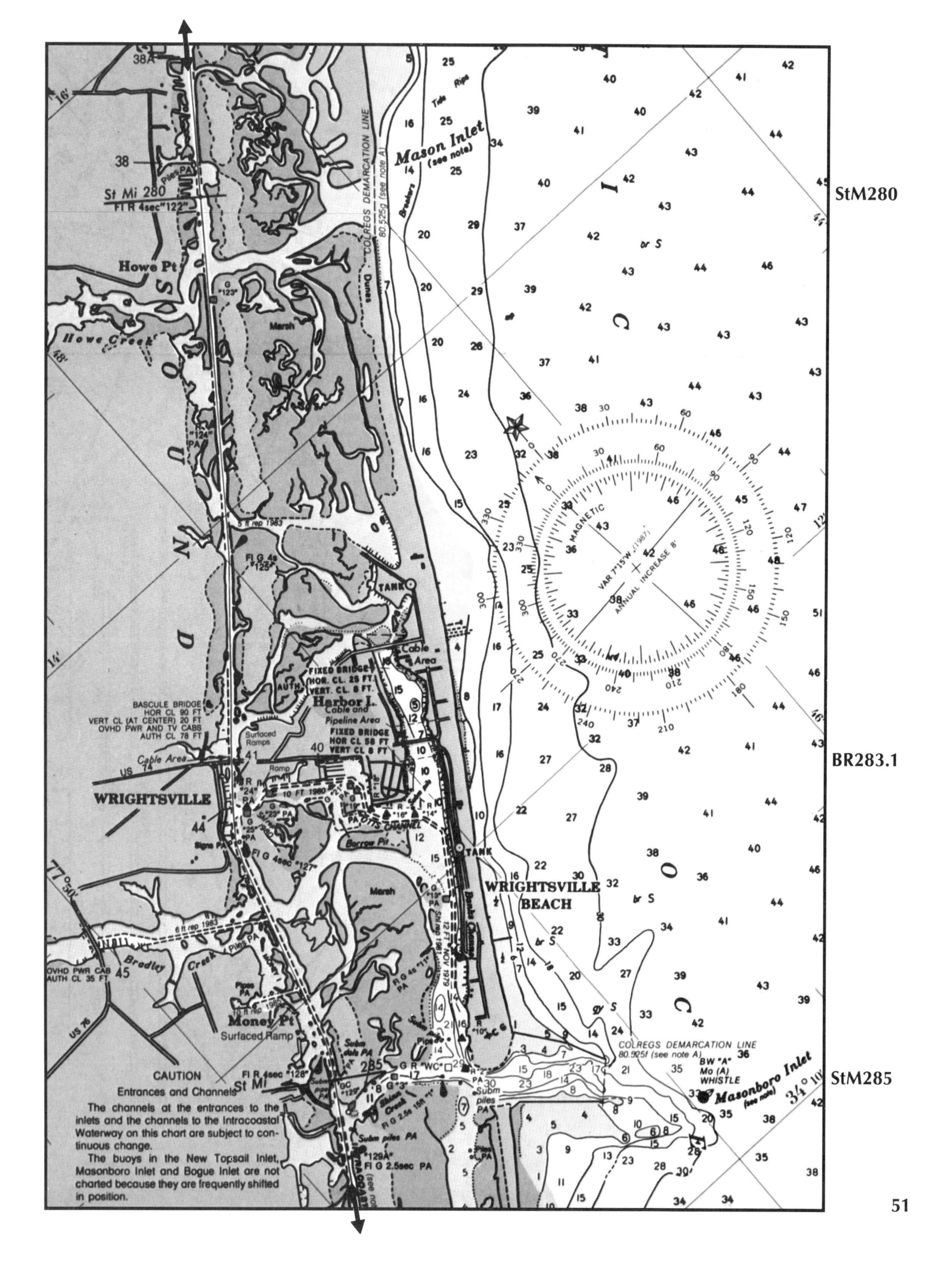

## CAUTION
Entrances and Channels

The channels at the entrances to the inlets and the channels to the Intracoastal Waterway on this chart are subject to continuous change.

The buoys in the New Topsail Inlet, Masonboro Inlet and Bogue Inlet are not charted because they are frequently shifted in position.

StM280

BR283.1

StM285

51

StM285

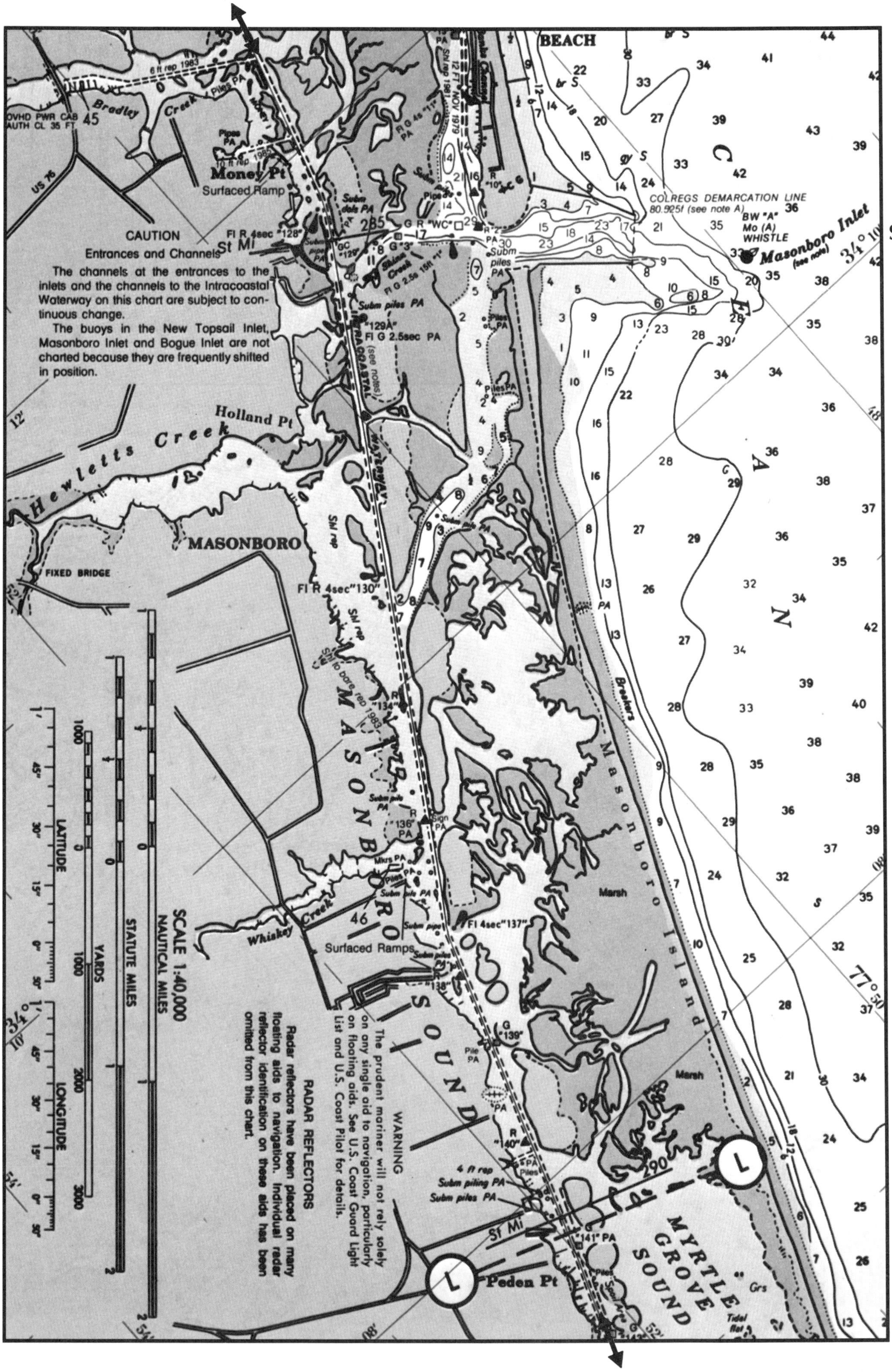


StM290

StM290

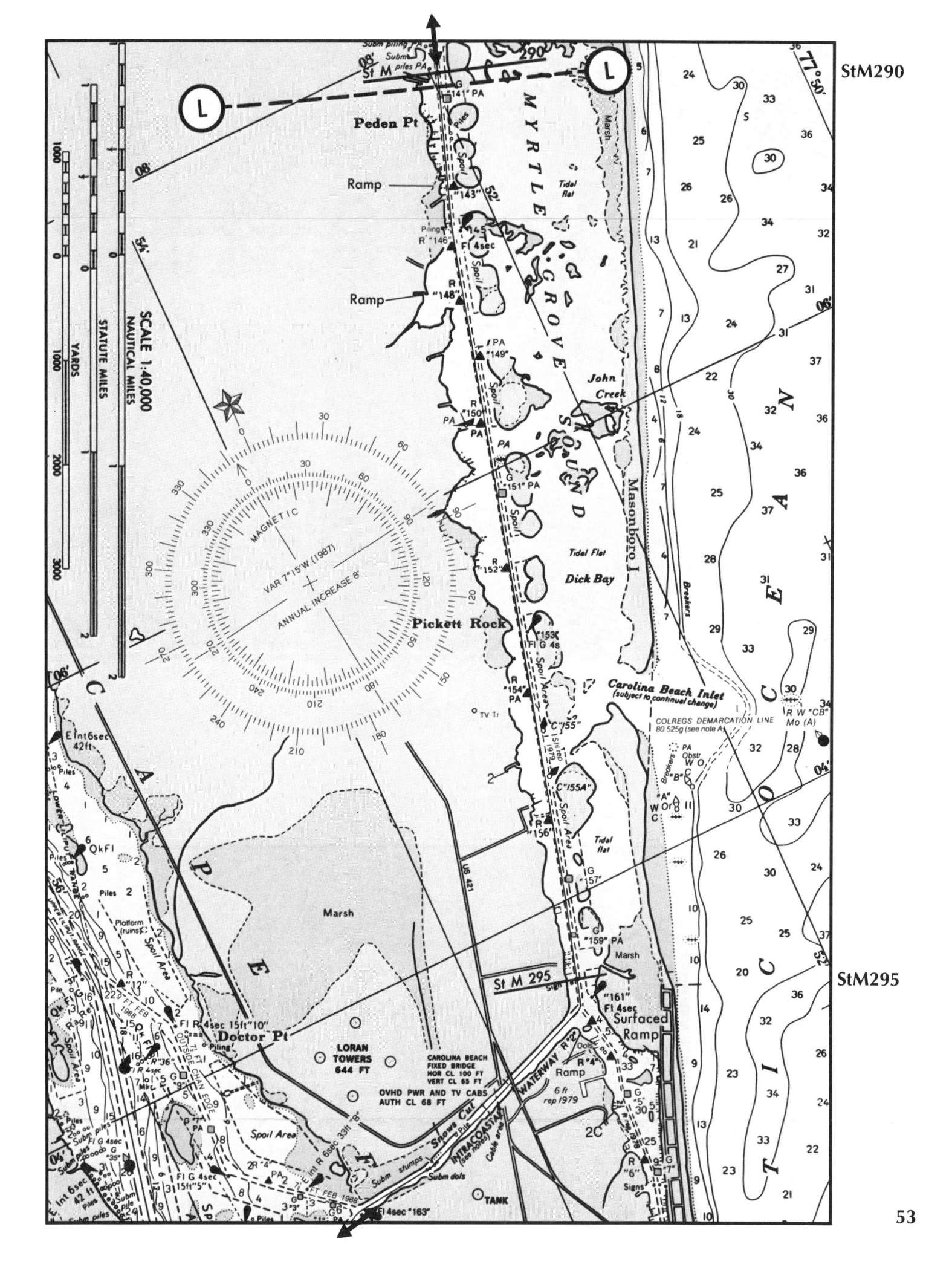

StM295

54

StM295

StM300

St M 295

St M 300

Doctor Pt

LORAN TOWERS 644 FT

CAROLINA BEACH FIXED BRIDGE
HOR CL 100 FT
VERT CL 65 FT
OVHD PWR AND TV CABS
AUTH CL 68 FT

Shows Cut

INTRACOASTAL (see note)

WATERWAY

Surfaced Ramp

"161" Fl 4sec

Ramp
6 ft rep 1979

Spoil Area

Subm stumps
Subm dols

Cable area

TANK

Orton Pt

Submpiles

Fl G 4sec

E Int 6sec 42 ft

Qk Fl R 20ft "B"

Qk Fl "A"

E Int 6sec "A"
E Int 6sec

Qk Fl R "34"

R "170" PA

R "172"

R "174" PA

R"32" Sign
Fl R 4sec

R "176" PA

LOWER MIDNIGHT CHANNEL RANGE

Fl 4sec "163"

6 ft rep 1975

G "165" PA

G "167" PA

TANK

Carolina Beach

Ditch

Ditch

R

Obstr

Spoil Area

Wilmington Beach

Andersons Landing

Ruins of Old Brunswick
Fl G 4s "31"

Snag PA

Fl 4sec "177"

Subm Obstr PA

Qk Fl

Pipe

Piles

Spoil Area

Wharf No 3

G "25"

QC "19"

G "17"

Fl R 4sec "16"

Fl R 4s "14"

St M 300

Subm pile Platform

Qk Fl G "27" PA

RESTRICTED AREA
334.450
(see note A)

Fl R 2.5sec "12"

"10"
Fl R 4sec

Wharf No 2

Subm pipe

Fl R 4sec "8"

Subm pipe

Ditch

MICRO TR

TANK

Ruins

Foul

Spoil Area

Kure Beach

Peters Pt.

Reaves Pt

Fl G 4sec "5"

Fl (2+1) R 6s "13"

Fl G 2.5sec "1" PA

G "3"

Fl G 4s "25"

Qk Fl G "24"

Fl R 4s "2"

Fl G 4sec

Marsh

Marsh

Subm pile Platform

Piles

Pipe

Pipeline

Ramp
RA DOMES

US 421

Pipeline

Spoil Area

Pipeline

Marsh

34°00'

34°00'

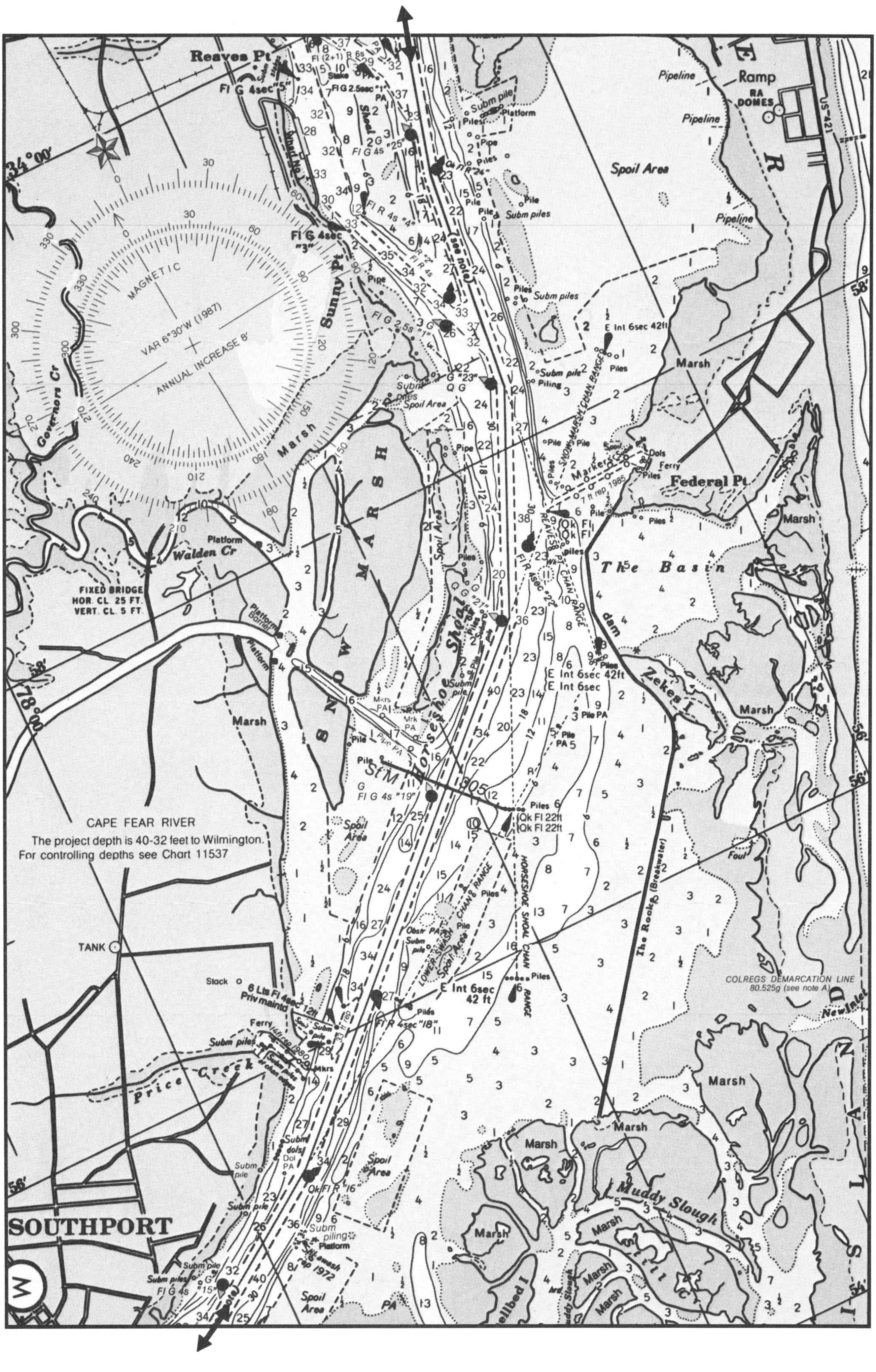

Reaves Pt
Sunny Pt
Governors Cr
Walden Cr
FIXED BRIDGE
HOR. CL. 25 FT.
VERT. CL. 5 FT.
MAGNETIC
VAR 6°30'W (1987)
ANNUAL INCREASE 8'
SNOWS MARSH
Horseshoe Shoal
Marsh
Spoil Area
Pipeline
Ramp
RA DOMES
Federal Pt
The Basin
Zekes I
The Rocks (Breakwater)
CAPE FEAR RIVER
The project depth is 40-32 feet to Wilmington.
For controlling depths see Chart 11537
TANK
Stack
Price Creek
SOUTHPORT
Muddy Slough
COLREGS DEMARCATION LINE
80.525g (see note A)
New Inlet
Subm piles
Platform
Ferry


StM305

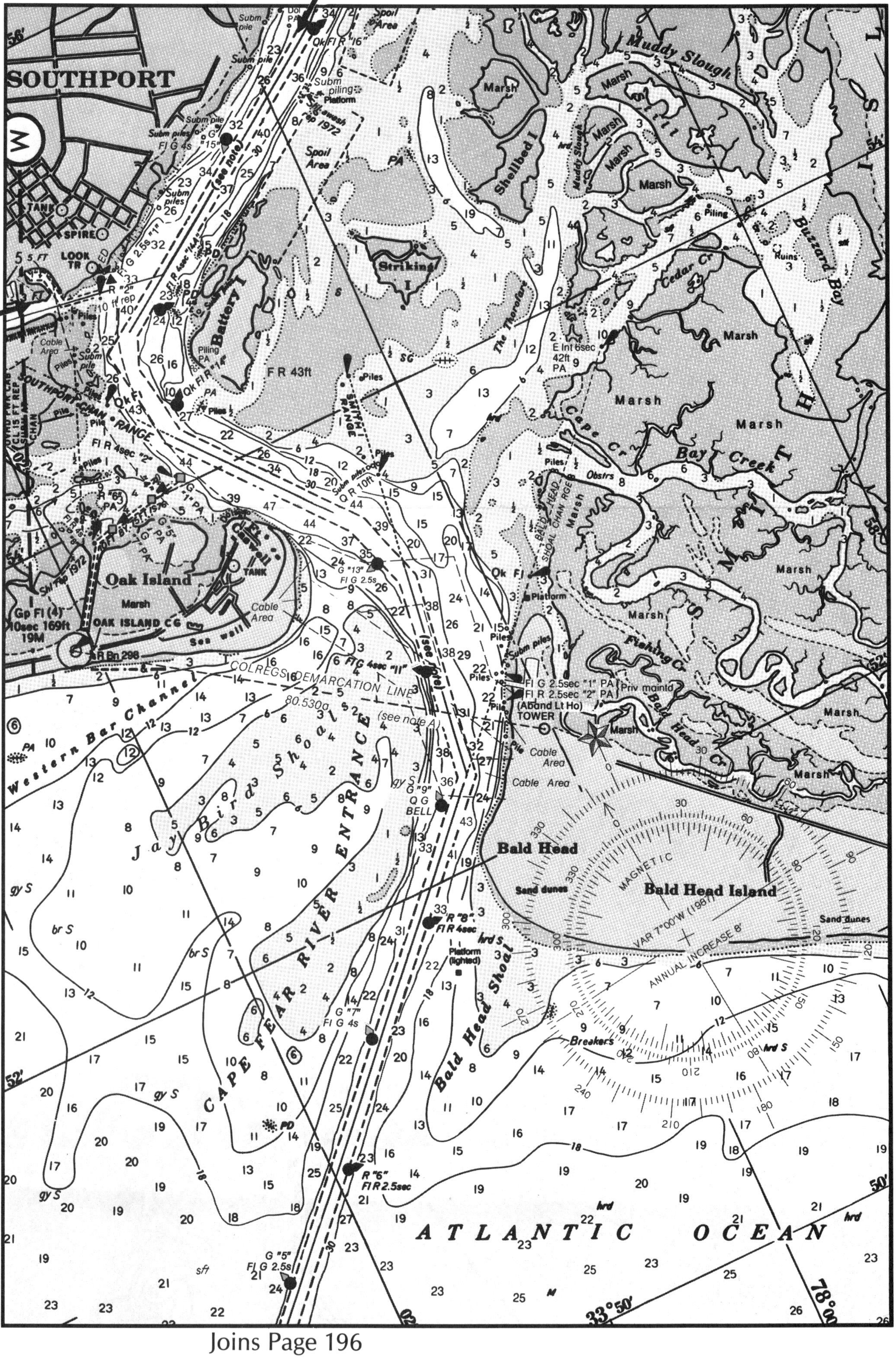

56

SOUTHPORT

W

TANK
SPIRE

LOOK TR

Battery I

Striking I

Shellbed I

Muddy Slough

Marsh

Marsh

Marsh

Marsh

Buzzard Bay

Ruins

Cedar Cr

Marsh

Marsh

Marsh

Bay Creek

Marsh

Marsh

Marsh

The Thorofare

Cape Cr

SMITH RANGE

SOUTHPORT CHAN RANGE

Oak Island

Marsh

OAK ISLAND CG

Gp Fl (4)
10sec 169ft
19M

Sea wall

Cable Area

COLREGS DEMARCATION LINE
80.530a

Western Bar Channel

Jay Bird Shoal

CAPE FEAR RIVER ENTRANCE

Bald Head Shoal

Fishing Cr

Bald Head Cr

Bald Head

Bald Head Island

Sand dunes

Sand dunes

MAGNETIC

VAR 7°00'W (1981)
ANNUAL INCREASE 8'

Breakers

TOWER
(Aband Lt Ho)

Cable Area

Cable Area

Platform
(lighted)

ATLANTIC OCEAN

33°50'

78°00'

Joins Page 196

StM310

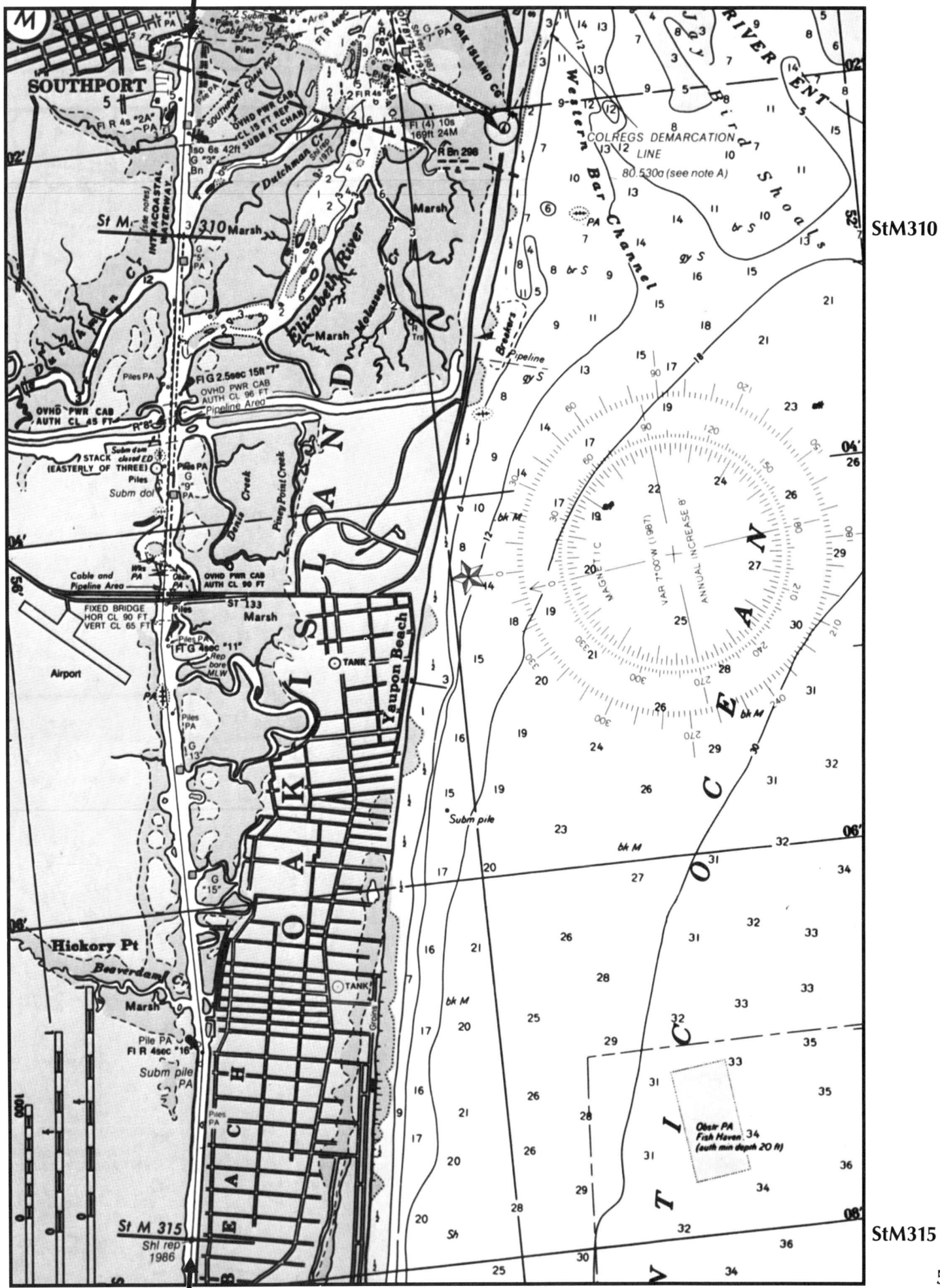

StM315

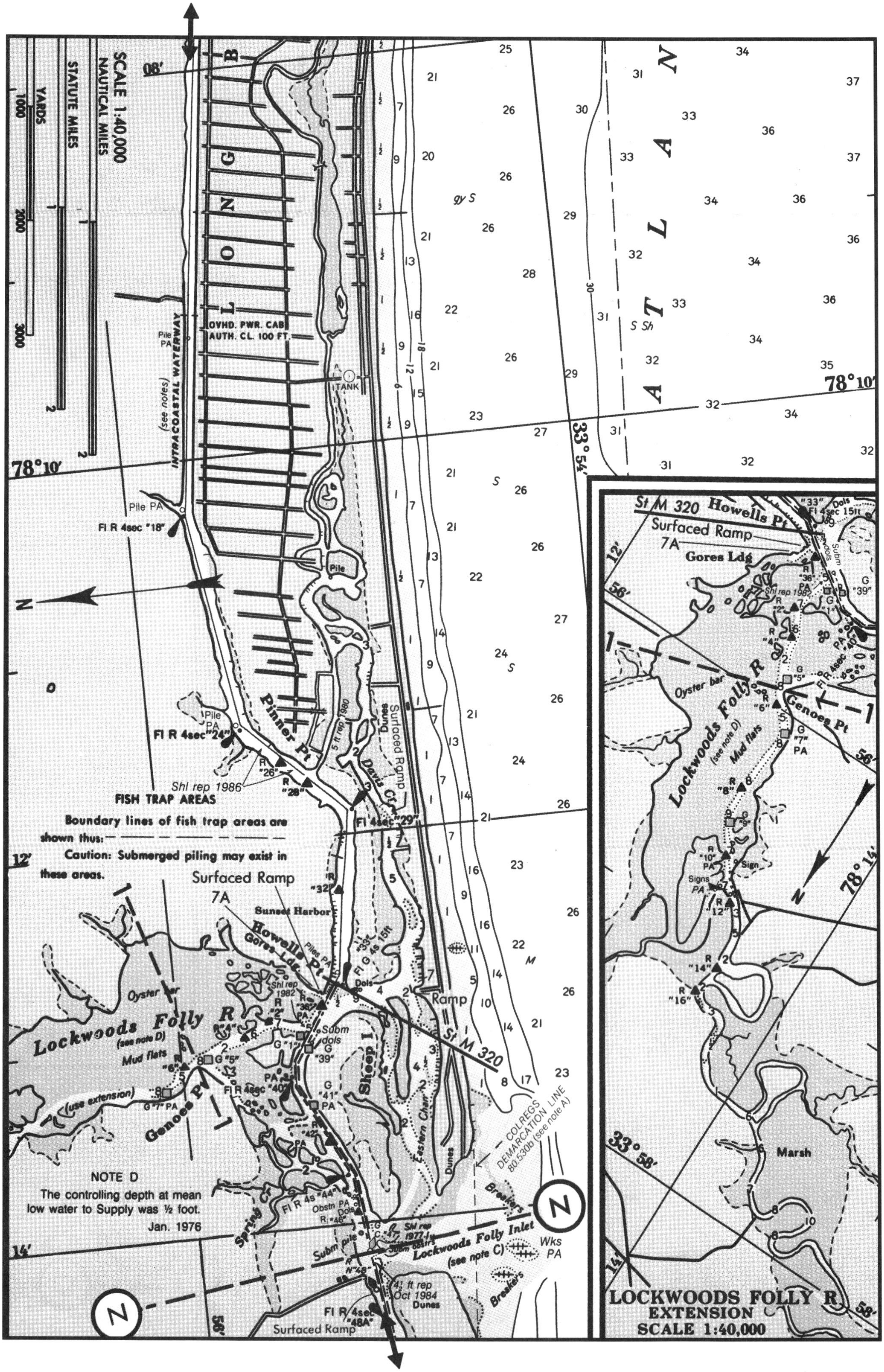
SCALE 1:40,000
NAUTICAL MILES
STATUTE MILES
YARDS
LONG B
ATLAN
INTRACOASTAL WATERWAY (see notes)
OVHD. PWR. CAB AUTH. CL. 100 FT.
FISH TRAP AREAS
Boundary lines of fish trap areas are shown thus:
Caution: Submerged piling may exist in these areas.
Surfaced Ramp
7A
Sunset Harbor
Howells Pt
Gores Ldg
Pinner Pt
Davis Cr
St M 320
Lockwoods Folly R
(see note D)
Mud flats
Oyster bar
Genoes Pt
Sheep I
Eastern Chan
Spring Cr
Lockwoods Folly Inlet
(see note C)
Breakers
COLREGS DEMARCATION LINE 80.530b (see note A)
NOTE D
The controlling depth at mean low water to Supply was ½ foot.
Jan. 1976
Shl rep 1986
Shl rep 1982
4' ft rep Oct 1984
Dunes
Fl R 4sec "18"
Fl R 4sec "24"
Fl 4sec "29"
Fl G 4s 15ft
Fl R 4sec "48A"
LOCKWOODS FOLLY R EXTENSION
SCALE 1:40,000
Marsh

StM320

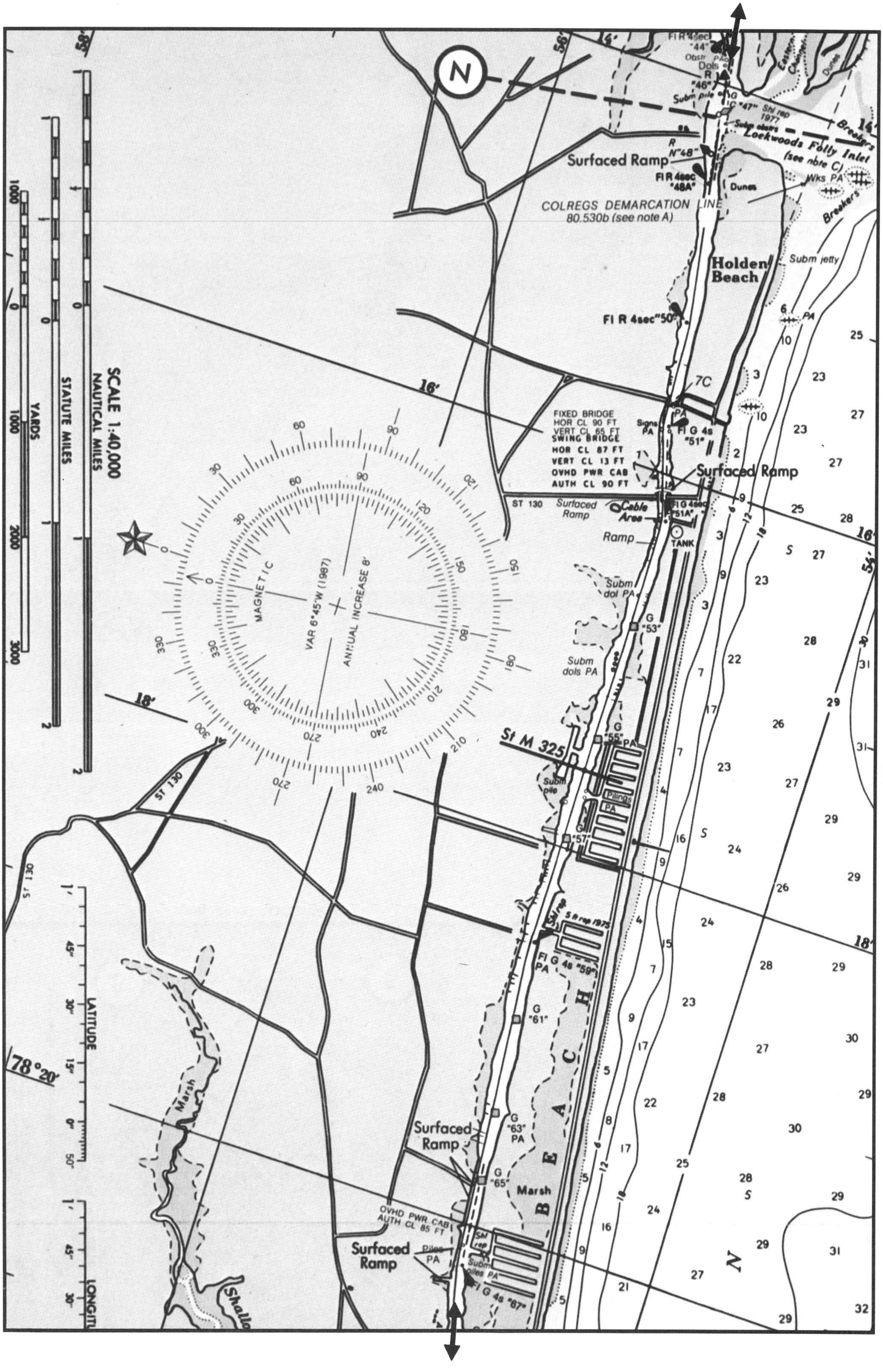

BR323.6

StM325

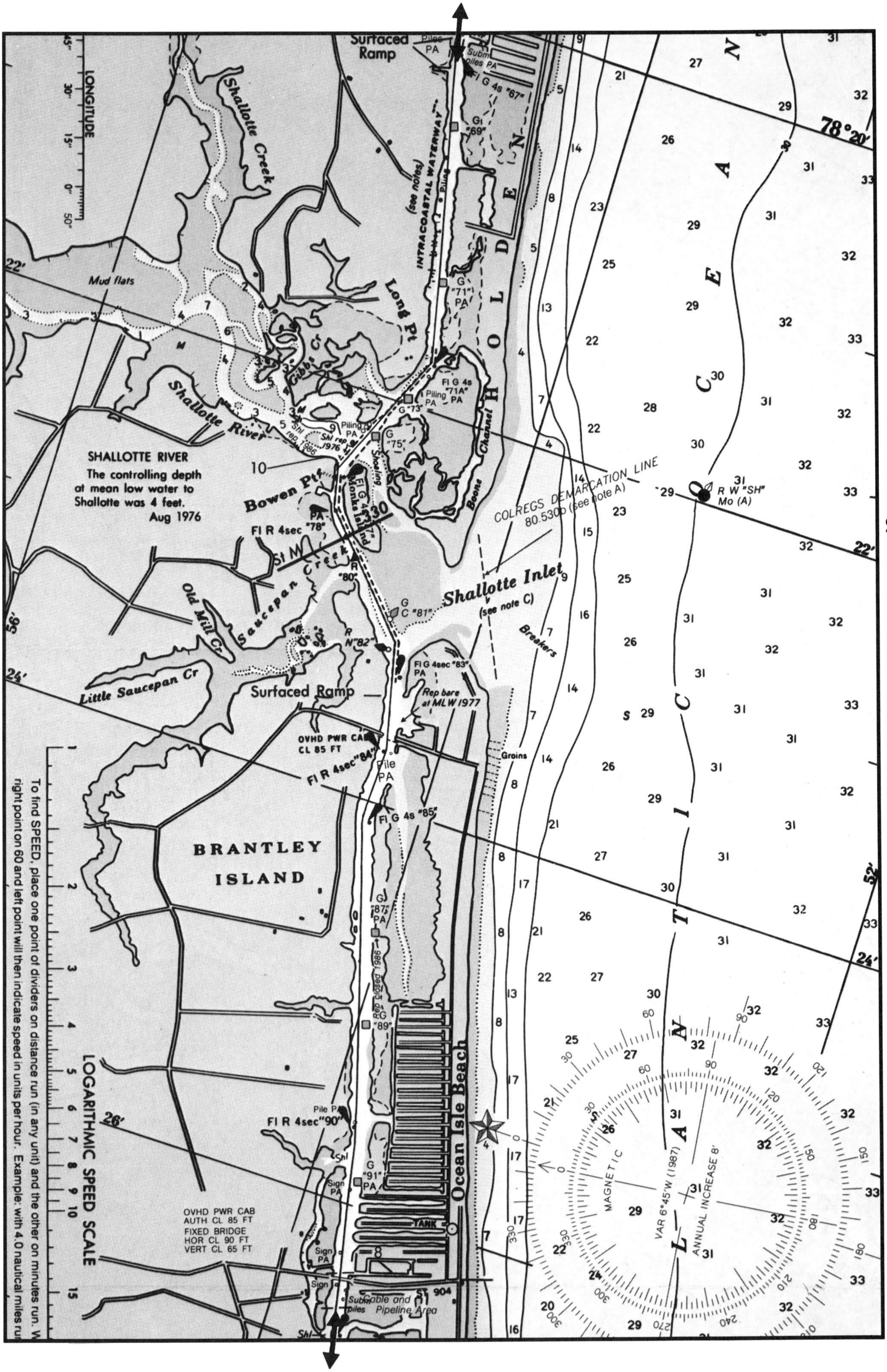
Ocean Isle Beach
BRANTLEY ISLAND
HOLDEN
ATLANTIC OCEAN
Shallotte Inlet
(see note C)
Shallotte River
Shallotte Creek
Saucepan Creek
Little Saucepan Cr
Old Mill Cr.
Gibbs Cr.
Long Pt
Bowen Pt
Monks Island
Boone Channel
INTRACOASTAL WATERWAY (see notes)
Mud flats
Breakers
Groins
Shoaling
Surfaced Ramp
Rep bare at MLW 1977
SHALLOTTE RIVER
The controlling depth at mean low water to Shallotte was 4 feet.
Aug 1976
COLREGS DEMARCATION LINE
80.530D (see note A)
R W "SH" Mo (A)
Fl R 4sec "78"
Fl R 4sec "84"
Fl R 4sec "90"
Fl G 4s "85"
Fl G 4sec "83"
Fl G 4s "71A"
Fl G 4s "67"
OVHD PWR CAB CL 85 FT
OVHD PWR CAB AUTH CL 85 FT
FIXED BRIDGE HOR CL 90 FT VERT CL 65 FT
Cable and Pipeline Area
StM 330
MAGNETIC
VAR 6°45'W (1987)
ANNUAL INCREASE 8'
78°20'
LOGARITHMIC SPEED SCALE
To find SPEED, place one point of dividers on distance run (in any unit) and the other on minutes run. With right point on 60 and left point will then indicate speed in units per hour. Example: with 4.0 nautical miles run
LONGITUDE

StM330

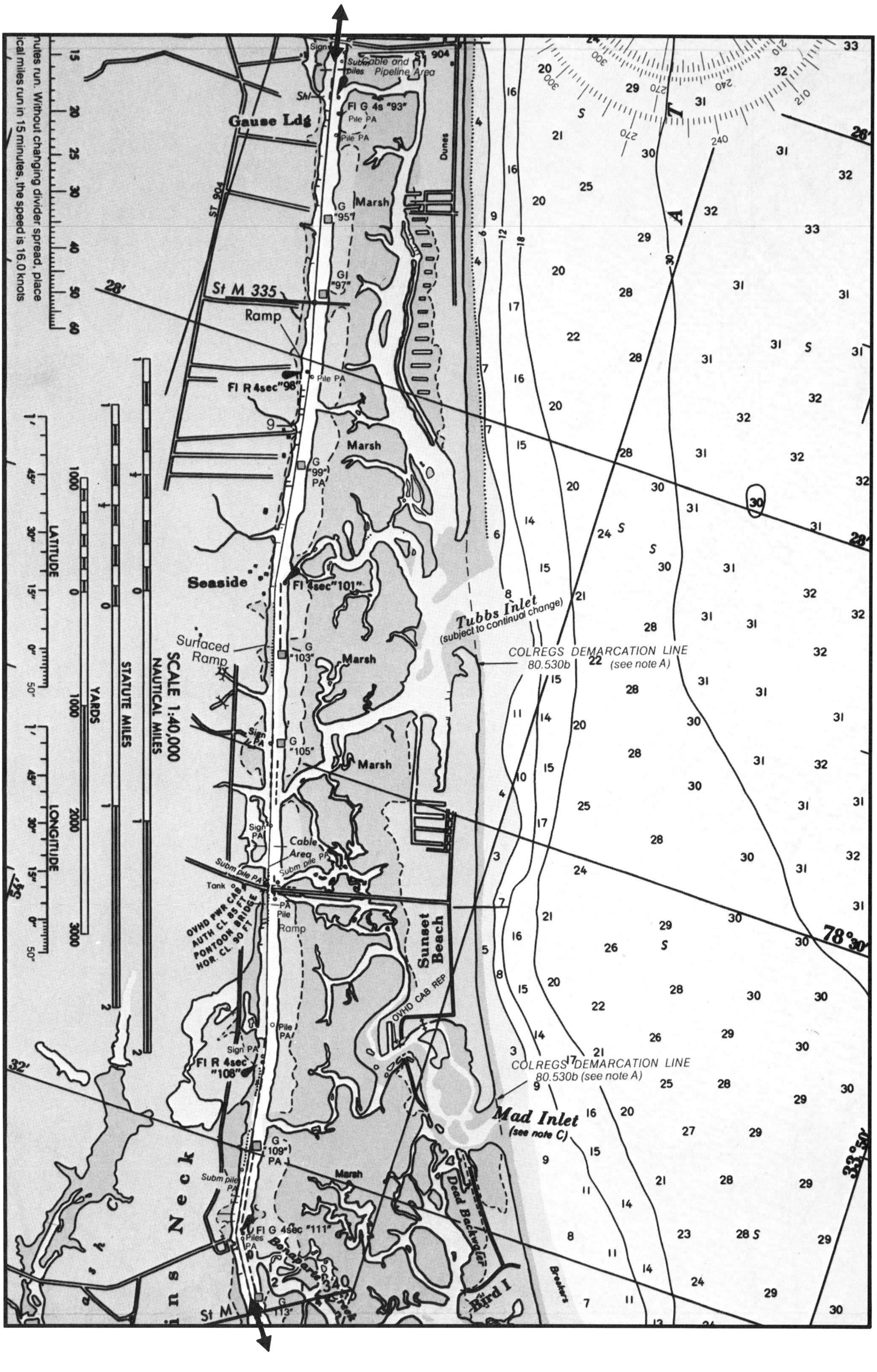


StM335

BR337.9

StM340

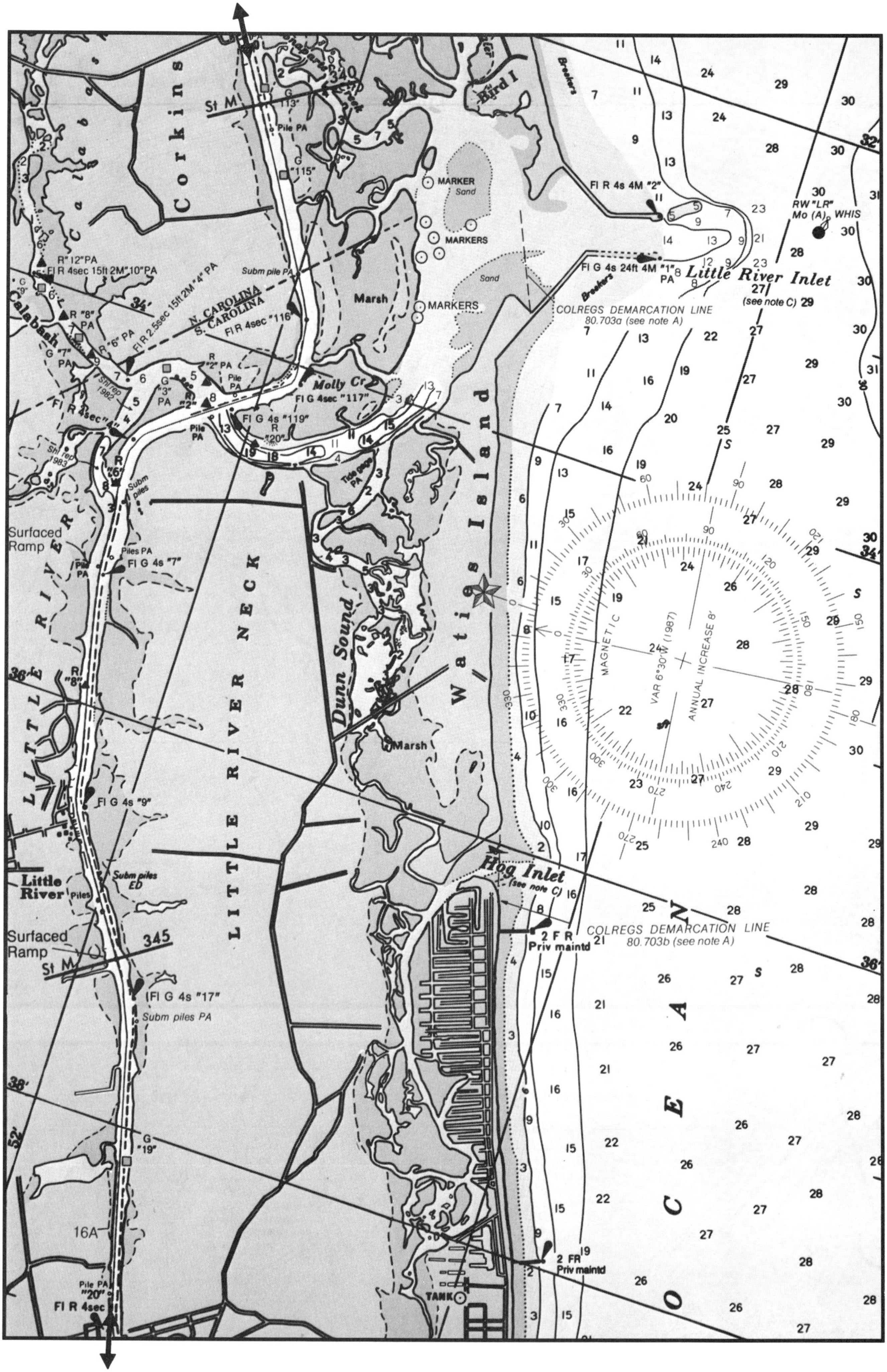

62

StM340

StM345

Corkins

Calabash

N. CAROLINA
S. CAROLINA

Marsh

MARKER
Sand

MARKERS

MARKERS

Sand

Bird I

Breakers

Fl R 4s 4M "2"

Fl G 4s 24ft 4M "1"
PA

Little River Inlet
(see note C)

RW "LR"
Mo (A) WHIS

COLREGS DEMARCATION LINE
80.703a (see note A)

Molly Cr

Fl G 4sec "117"

Fl G 4s "119"
R "20"

Subm pile PA

R "12" PA
Fl R 4sec 15ft 2M "10" PA

R "8" PA

Fl R 2.5sec 15ft 2M "4" PA

Fl R 4sec "116"

R "6" PA

R "2" PA
Pile PA

G "3" PA

G "2"

Fl R 4sec "1"

R "6"

Subm
piles

L I T T L E   R I V E R

Surfaced
Ramp

Fl G 4s "7"

R "8"

Fl G 4s "9"

Little
River

Subm piles
ED

Piles

Surfaced
Ramp
St M

Fl G 4s "17"

Subm piles PA

G "19"

16A

Pile PA "20"
Fl R 4sec

L I T T L E   R I V E R   N E C K

Dunn Sound

W a t i e s   I s l a n d

Marsh

Hog Inlet
(see note C)

2 F R
Priv maintd

COLREGS DEMARCATION LINE
80.703b (see note A)

2 FR
Priv maintd

TANK

O C E A N

MAGNETIC
VAR 6°30'W (1987)
ANNUAL INCREASE 8'

St M

34'

345

BR347.3

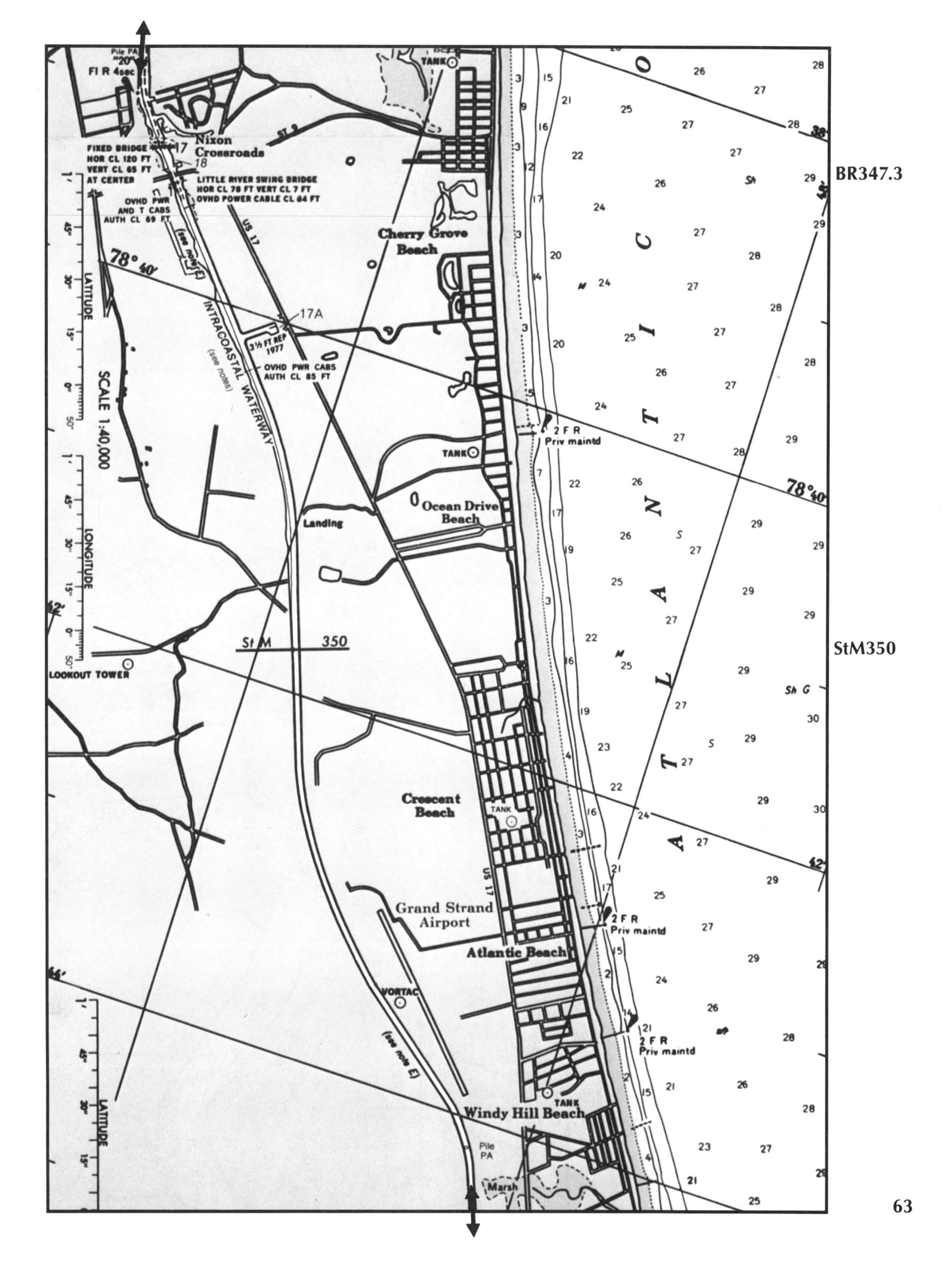

StM350

63

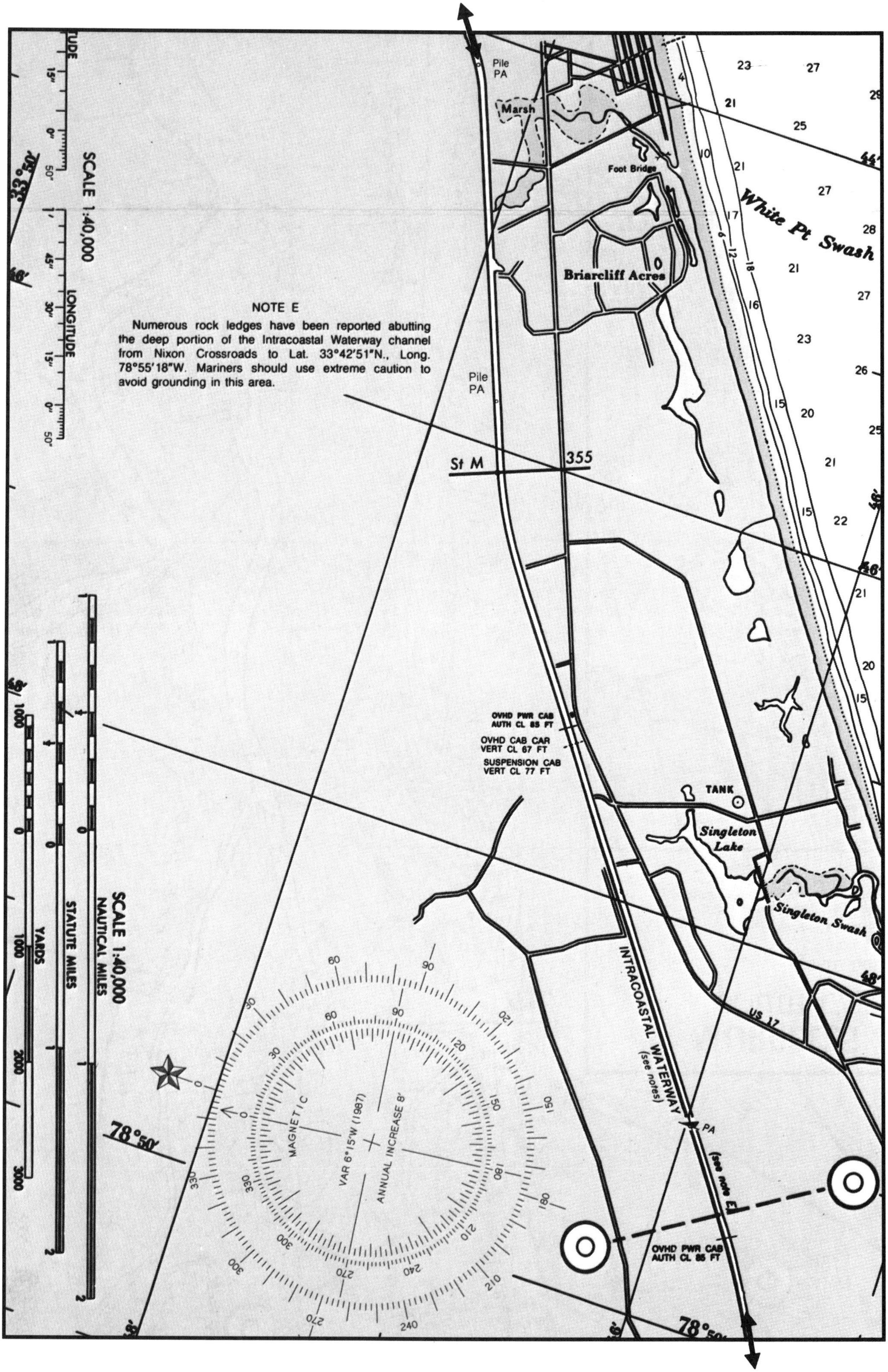

**NOTE E**

Numerous rock ledges have been reported abutting the deep portion of the Intracoastal Waterway channel from Nixon Crossroads to Lat. 33°42'51"N., Long. 78°55'18"W. Mariners should use extreme caution to avoid grounding in this area.

SCALE 1:40,000

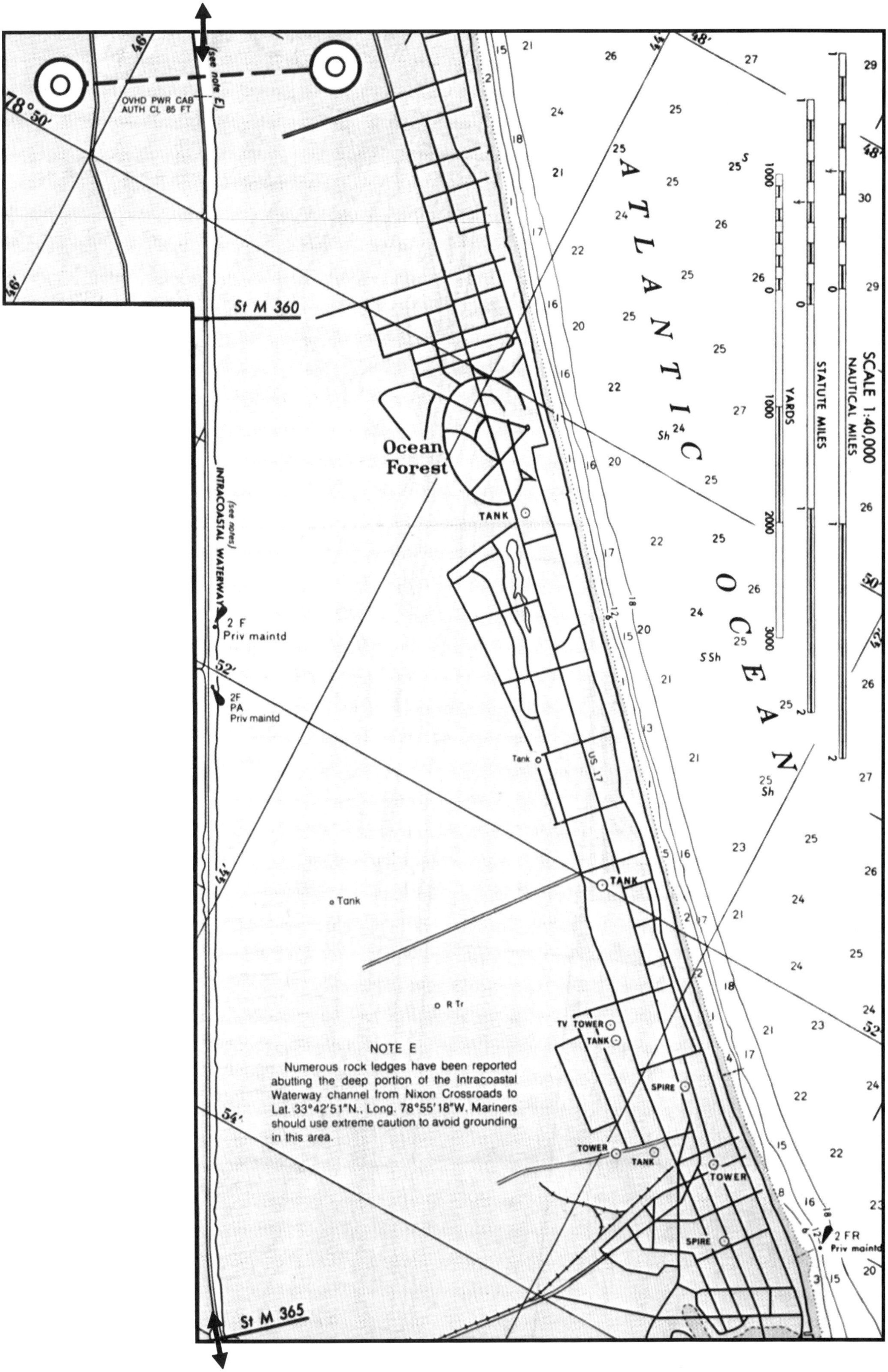

StM360
StM365

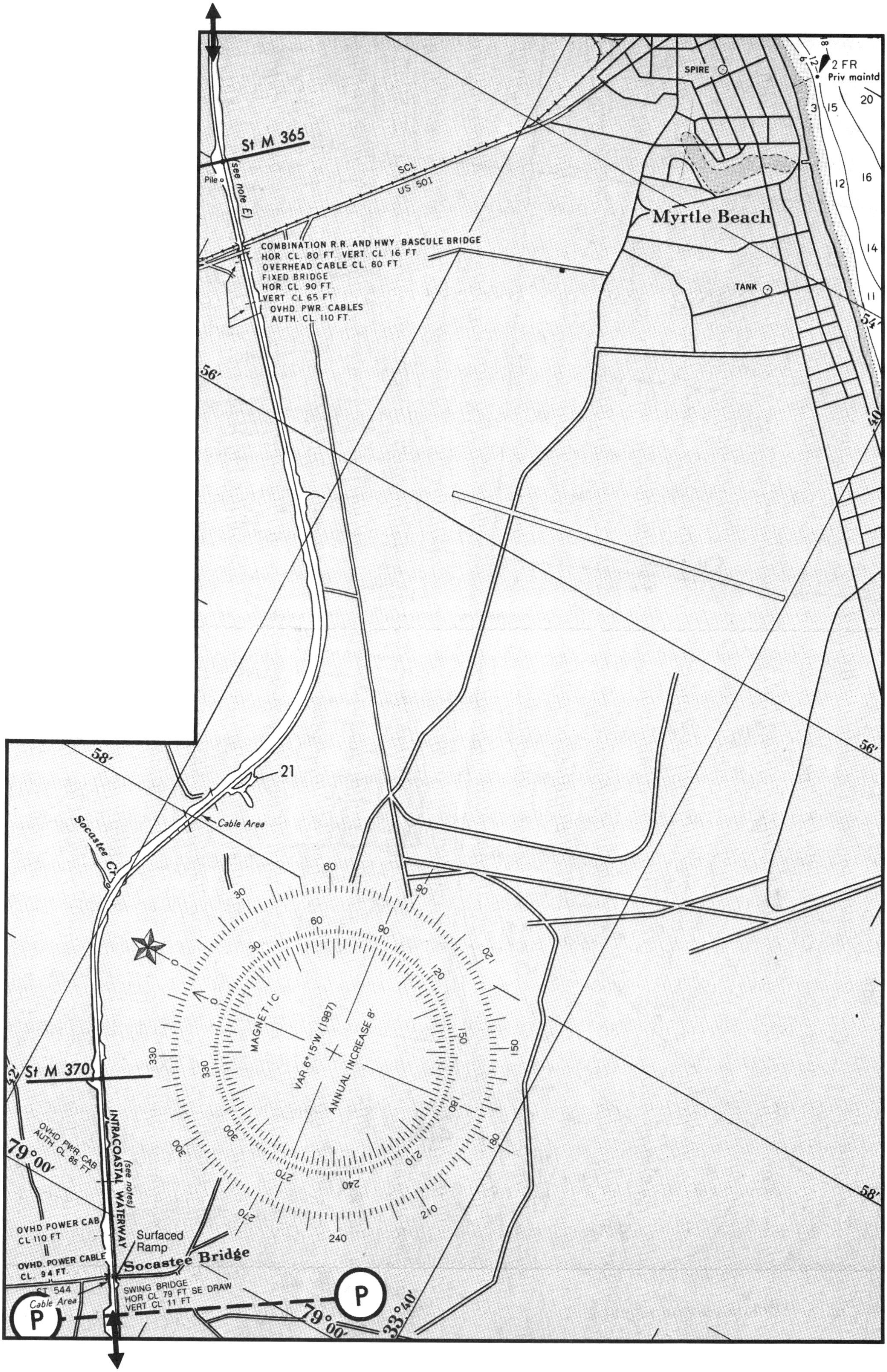

66

SPIRE

2 FR
Priv maintd

20

StM365

St M 365

3  15

Pile

see note E)

SCL

US 501

12  16

Myrtle Beach

BR365.4

COMBINATION R.R. AND HWY. BASCULE BRIDGE
HOR. CL. 80 FT. VERT. CL. 16 FT.
OVERHEAD CABLE CL. 80 FT.
FIXED BRIDGE
HOR. CL. 90 FT.
VERT. CL 65 FT.
OVHD. PWR. CABLES
AUTH. CL 110 FT.

TANK

14

11

54

56'

50

56'

58'

21

Socastee Cr

Cable Area

60

90

60

90

30

30

MAGNETIC

VAR 6°15'W (1987)

ANNUAL INCREASE 8'

120

20

StM370

St M 370

150

50

330

330

180

300

210

300

79°00'

OVHD PWR CAB
AUTH CL 85 FT

INTRACOASTAL WATERWAY

(see notes)

270

240

270

210

58'

OVHD POWER CAB
CL 110 FT

Surfaced
Ramp

240

OVHD. POWER CABLE
CL. 94 FT.

Socastee Bridge

BR371.0

St 544

Cable Area

SWING BRIDGE
HOR CL 79 FT SE DRAW
VERT CL 11 FT

P

P

79°00'

33°40'

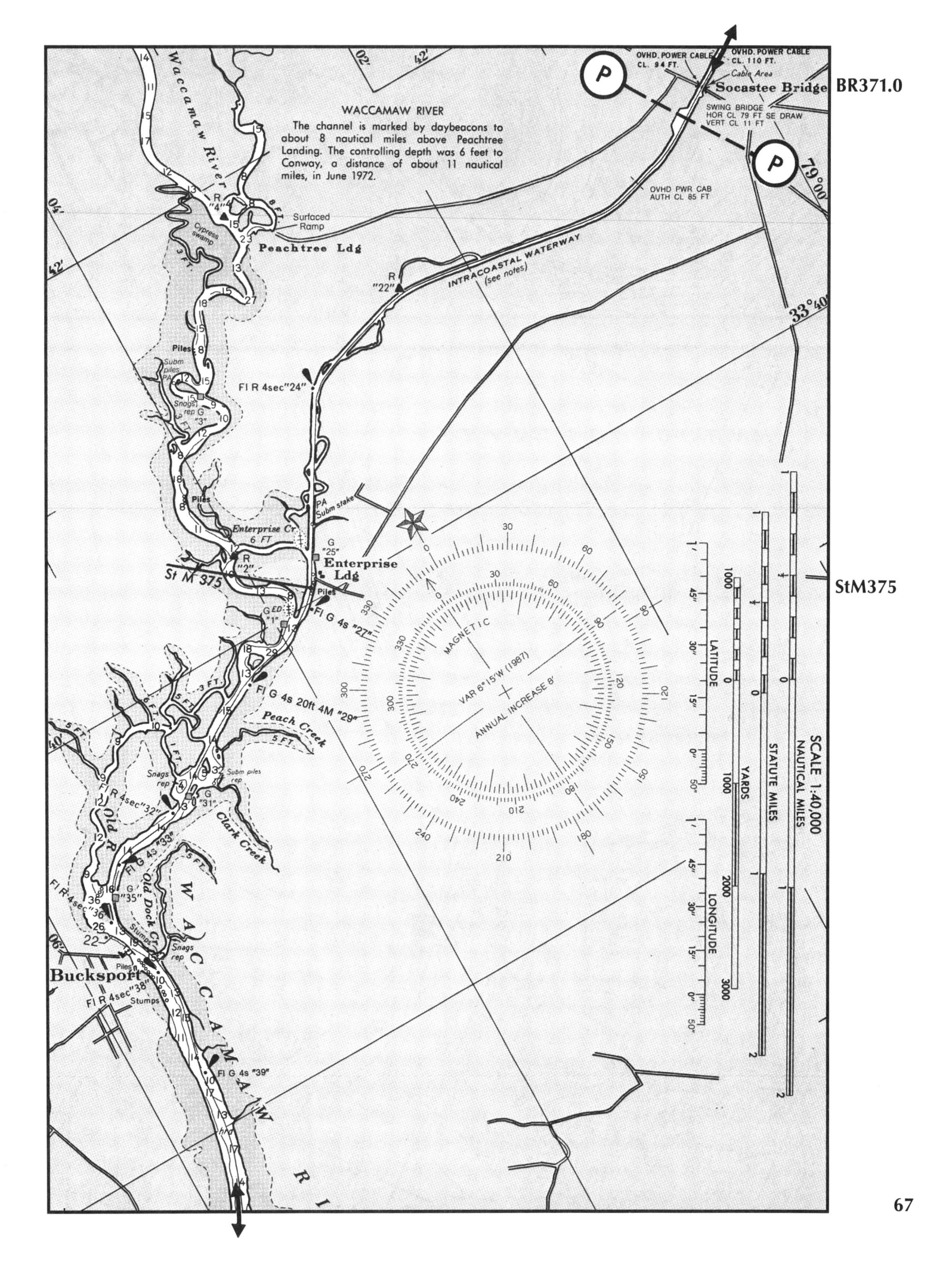

## WACCAMAW RIVER

The channel is marked by daybeacons to about 8 nautical miles above Peachtree Landing. The controlling depth was 6 feet to Conway, a distance of about 11 nautical miles, in June 1972.

BR371.0

Socastee Bridge

StM375

SCALE 1:40,000

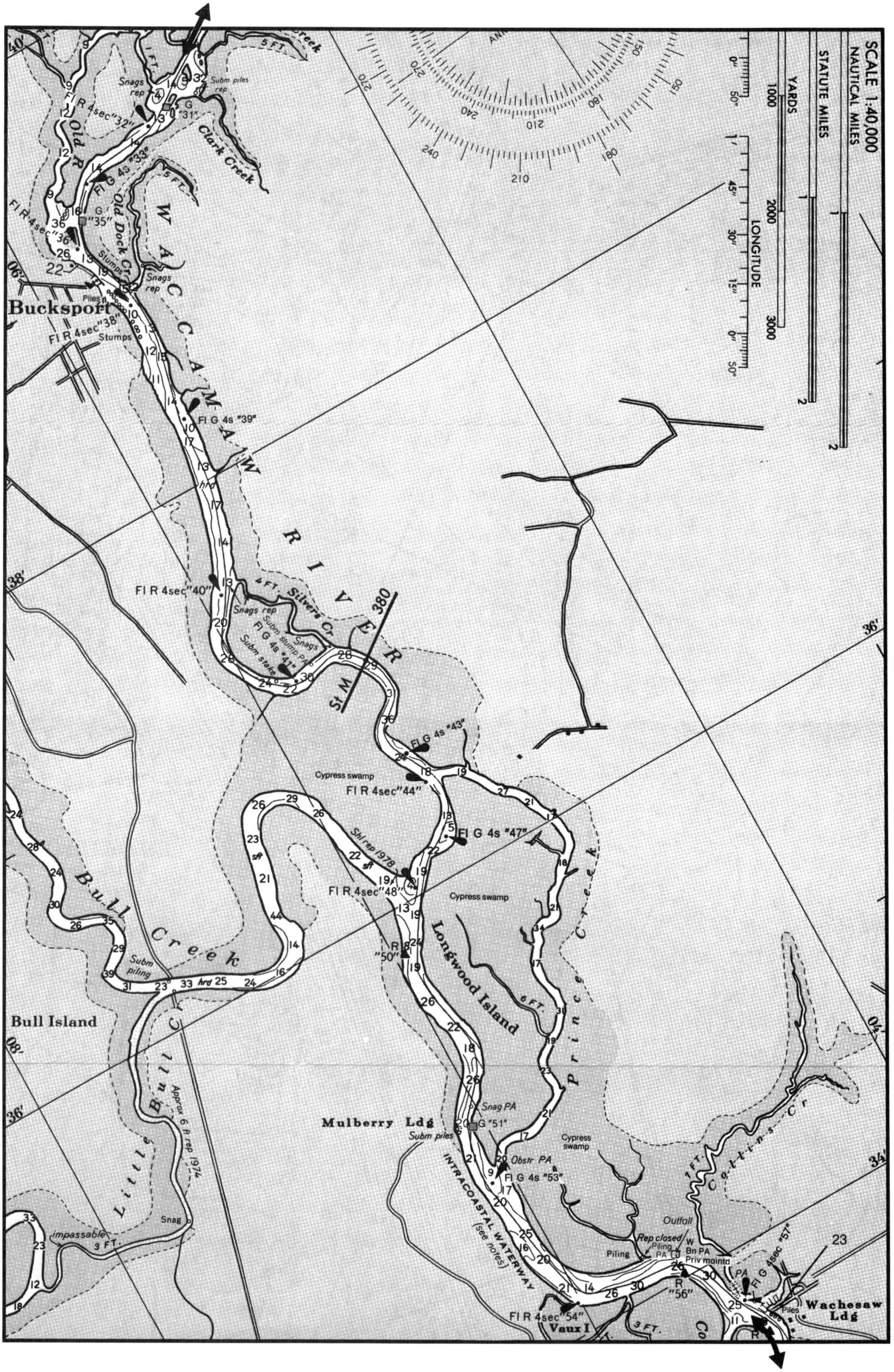
SCALE 1:40,000
NAUTICAL MILES
STATUTE MILES
YARDS
LONGITUDE
Bucksport
Fl R 4sec "38"
Old Dock Cr
Clark Creek
Old R
Fl G 4s "33"
Fl R 4sec "32"
Fl R 4sec "36"
Fl G 4s "39"
W A C C A M A W
R I V E R
Fl R 4sec "40"
Silvers Cr
Fl G 4s "41"
StM 380
Fl G 4s "43"
Cypress swamp
Fl R 4sec "44"
Fl G 4s "47"
Shl rep 1978
Fl R 4sec "48"
Bull Creek
Longwood Island
Prince Creek
Bull Island
Little Bull Cr
Approx 6 ft rep 1974
Mulberry Ldg
Subm piles
G "51"
Snag PA
Obstr PA
Fl G 4s "53"
INTRACOASTAL WATERWAY
(see notes)
Cottins Cr
Rep closed
Piling
W Bn PA Priv maintd
R "56"
Fl R 4sec "54"
Vaux I
Fl G 4sec "57"
Wachesaw Ldg

StM380

StM385

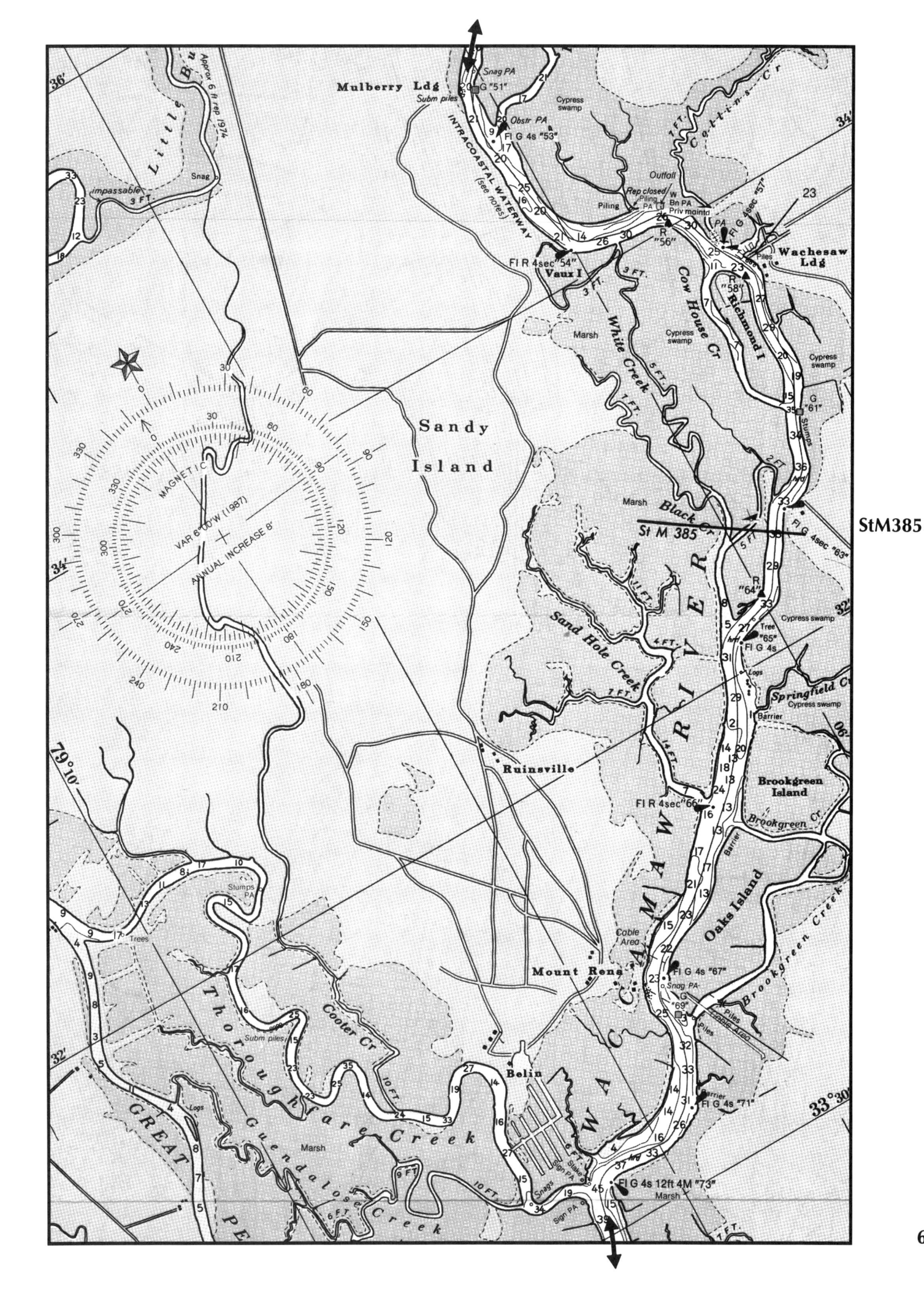

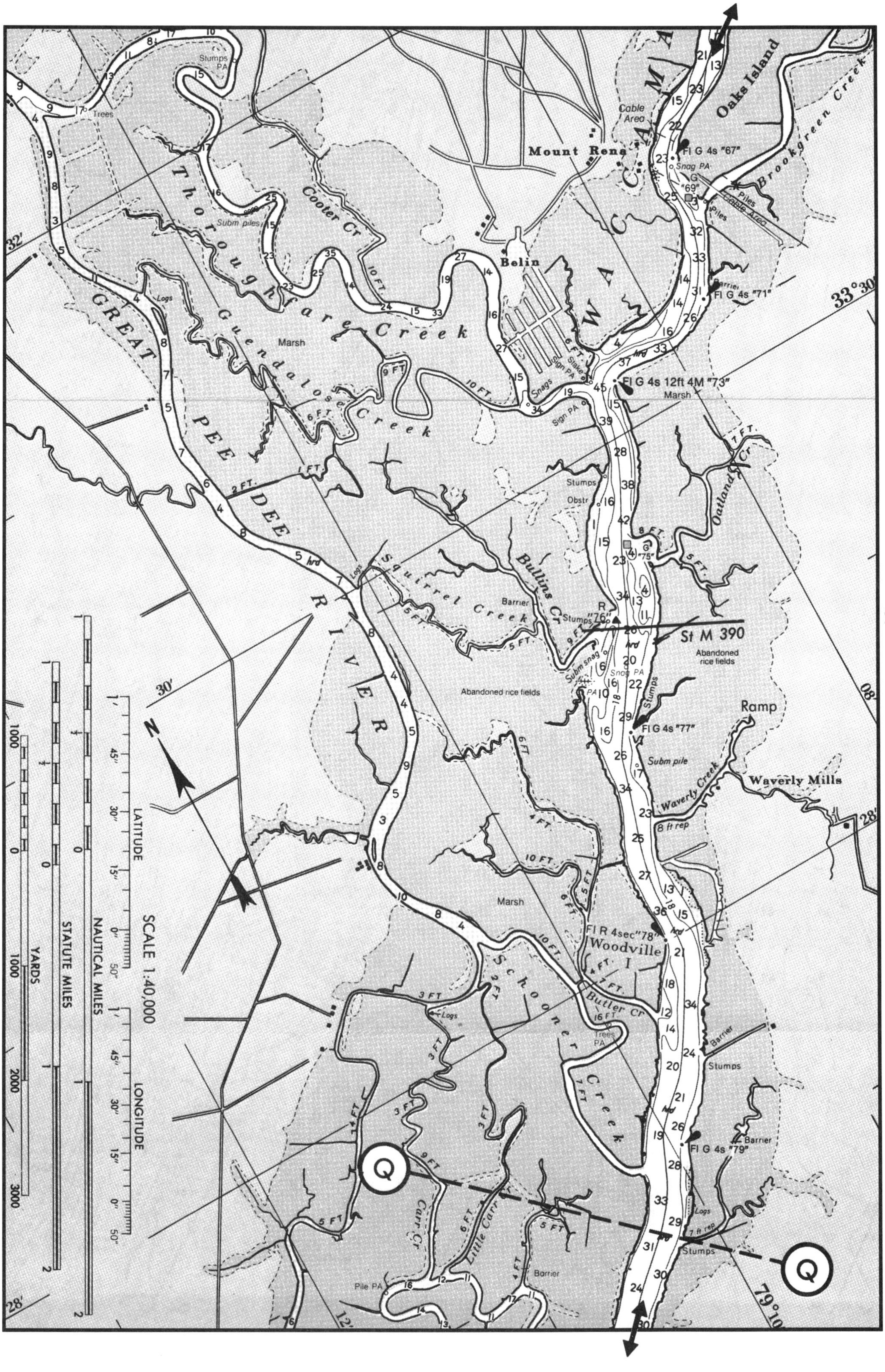
Oaks Island
Brookgreen Creek
Mount Rena
Cable Area
Fl G 4s "67"
Snag PA
G "69"
Piles
Cable Area
Belin
Fl G 4s "71"
33°30'
Thoroughfare Creek
Cooter Cr
Subm piles
Guendalose Creek
GREAT PEE DEE RIVER
Marsh
Logs
Trees
Stumps PA
Fl G 4s 12ft 4M "73"
Sign PA
Snags
Stake
Oatland Cr
Stumps
Obstr
"75"
Bullins Cr
Squirrel Creek
Barrier
R "76"
St M 390
Abandoned rice fields
Subm snag
Snag PA
Fl G 4s "77"
Ramp
Subm pile
Waverly Creek
Waverly Mills
8 ft rep
Marsh
Fl R 4sec "78"
Woodville I
Butler Cr
Schooner Creek
Fl G 4s "79"
Little Carr Cr
Carr Cr
Pile PA
Logs
7 ft rep
79°10'
SCALE 1:40,000
LATITUDE
LONGITUDE
NAUTICAL MILES
STATUTE MILES
YARDS
N

StM390

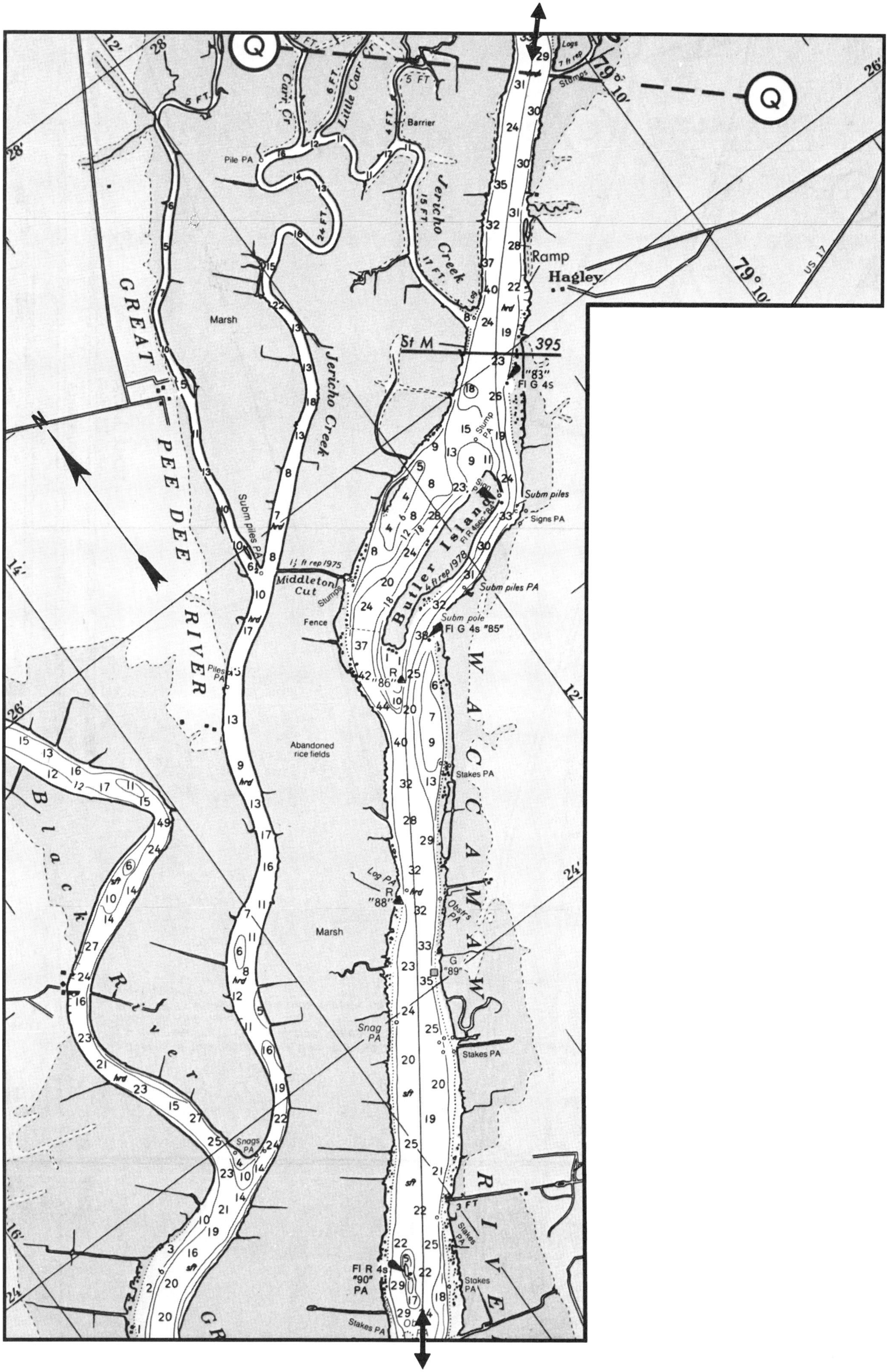
St M 395
Hagley
Ramp
Jericho Creek
Little Carr
Carr Cr
Barrier
Pile PA
Marsh
GREAT PEE DEE RIVER
Butler Island
Middleton Cut
Fence
Abandoned rice fields
Black River
WACCAMAW RIVER
"83" Fl G 4s
Fl G 4s "85"
"86"
R "88"
G "89"
Fl R 4s "90" PA
Subm piles
Signs PA
Subm piles PA
Subm pole
Stakes PA
Snag PA
Snags PA
Log PA
Obstrs PA
US 17
79° 10'

StM395

72

StM400

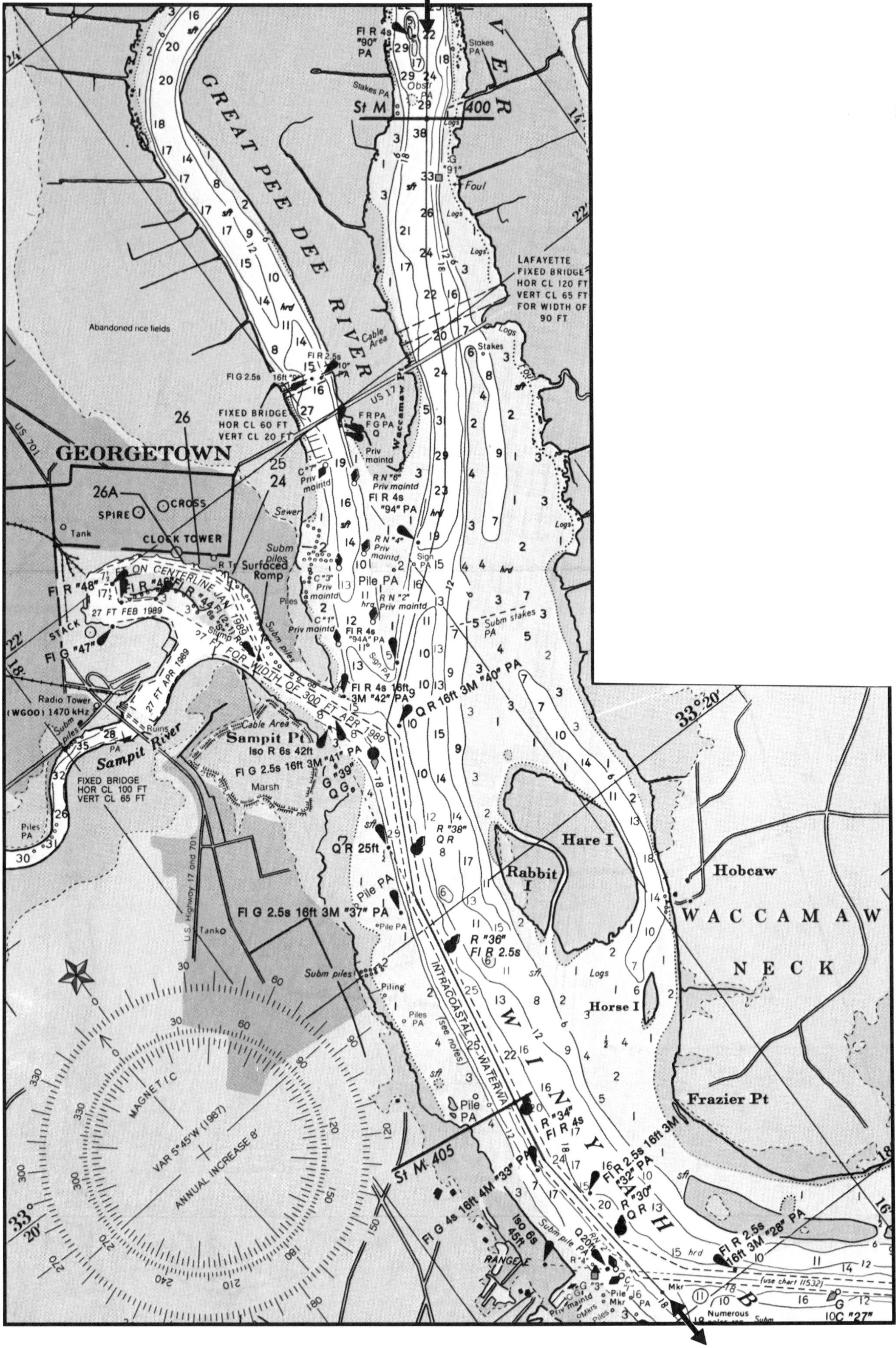

StM405

GREAT PEE DEE RIVER

Fl R 4s "90" PA

St M 400

G "91"

Foul

Logs

Logs

Logs

LAFAYETTE FIXED BRIDGE
HOR CL 120 FT
VERT CL 65 FT
FOR WIDTH OF 90 FT

Cable Area

Stakes PA

Obstr PA

Stakes PA

Fl R 2.5s "10" PA

Fl G 2.5s 16ft PA

US 17

Waccamaw P

FIXED BRIDGE
HOR CL 60 FT
VERT CL 20 FT

F R PA
F G PA
Q

Priv maintd

C "7" Priv maintd

R N "6" Priv maintd
Fl R 4s "94" PA

R N "4" Priv maintd

Sign PA

GEORGETOWN

26

25
24

26A
SPIRE

CROSS

CLOCK TOWER

Tank

R Tr

Submd piles
Surfaced Ramp

Piles

Sewer

C "3" Priv maintd

C "2" Priv maintd

C "1" Priv maintd

Pile PA

R N "2" Priv maintd

Subm stakes PA

12 Fl R 4s "94A" PA

Sign PA

Fl R 4s 16ft 3M "42" PA

Q R 16ft 3M "40" PA

Fl R "48"

Fl R "46"

Fl R "44"

ON CENTERLINE JAN 1989

27 FT FEB 1989

STACK

Fl G "47"

Radio Tower (WGOO) 1470 kHz

Subm piles

Ruins

FOR WIDTH OF 300 FT APR 1989

27 FT APR 1989

Cable Area

Sampit River

Sampit Pt
Iso R 6s 42ft

Fl G 2.5s 16ft 3M "41" PA

Marsh

G "39"
Q G

Q R 25ft

Pile PA

33°20'

Hare I

Rabbit I

Hobcaw

WACCAMAW

NECK

FIXED BRIDGE
HOR CL 100 FT
VERT CL 65 FT

Piles PA

Fl G 2.5s 16ft 3M "37" PA

Subm piles

Piling

Pile PA

Piles PA

INTRACOASTAL WATERWAY (see notes)

R "38"
Q R

R "36"
Fl R 2.5s

Horse I

Frazier Pt

StM405

U.S. Highway 17 and 701

Tank

MAGNETIC

VAR 5°45'W (1987)

ANNUAL INCREASE 8'

330

300

270

240

210

180

150

120

90

60

30

Pile PA

R "34"
Fl R 4s

St M 405

Fl R 4s 16ft 4M "33"

W I N Y A H

R "32" PA

Fl R 2.5s 16ft 3M "32" PA

R "30"
Q R

R "28" PA
Fl R 2.5s 16ft 3M "28" PA

RANGE E

Fl G 4s 16ft 3M "33"

RANGE

R N "2"
Q

Pile Mkr

Priv maintd Mkrs

Piles

Mkr

Numerous Subm piles

(use chart 11532)

G "27"

33°20'

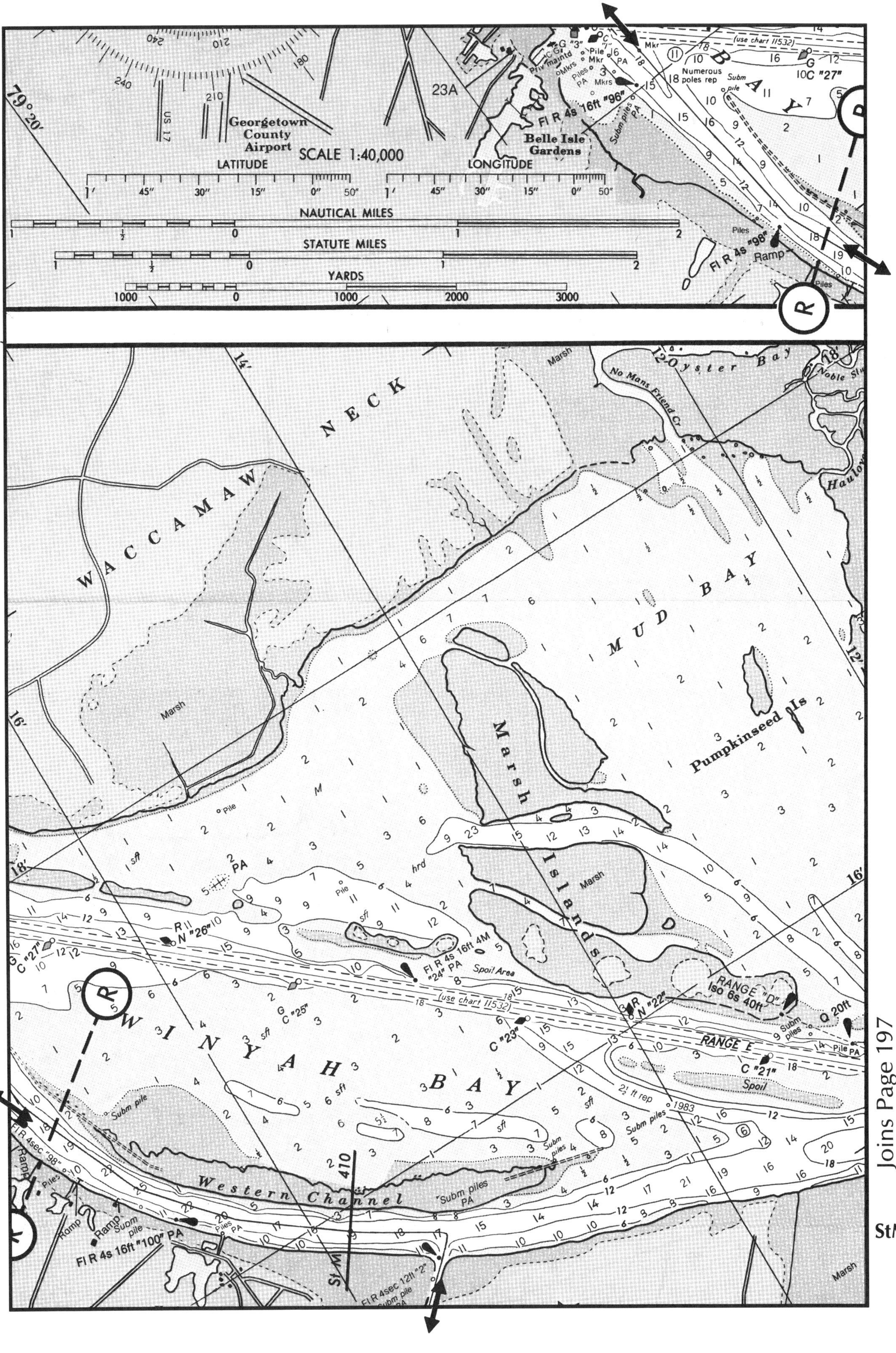


Joins Page 197

StM410

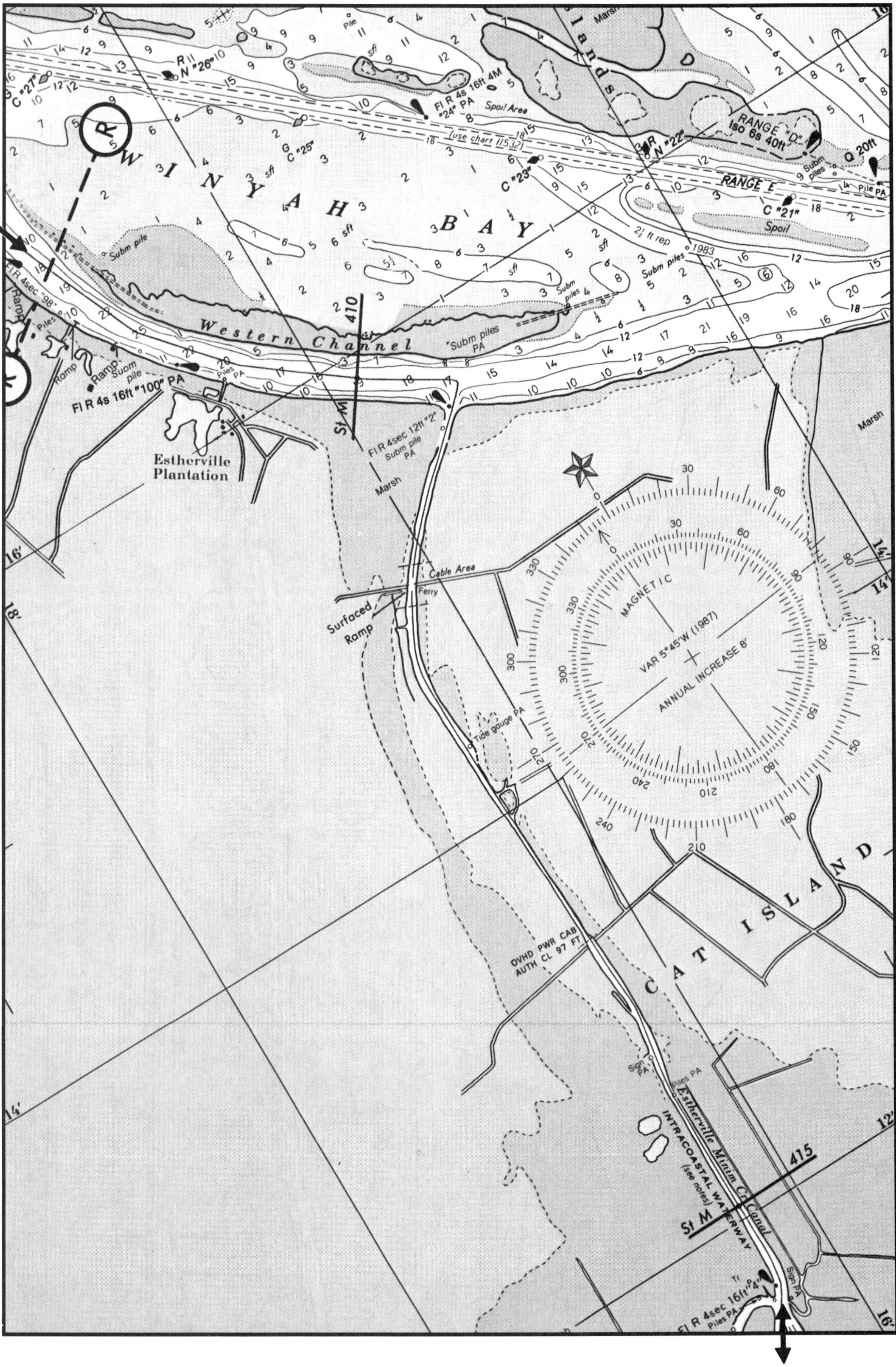


StM410

StM415

Joins Page 197

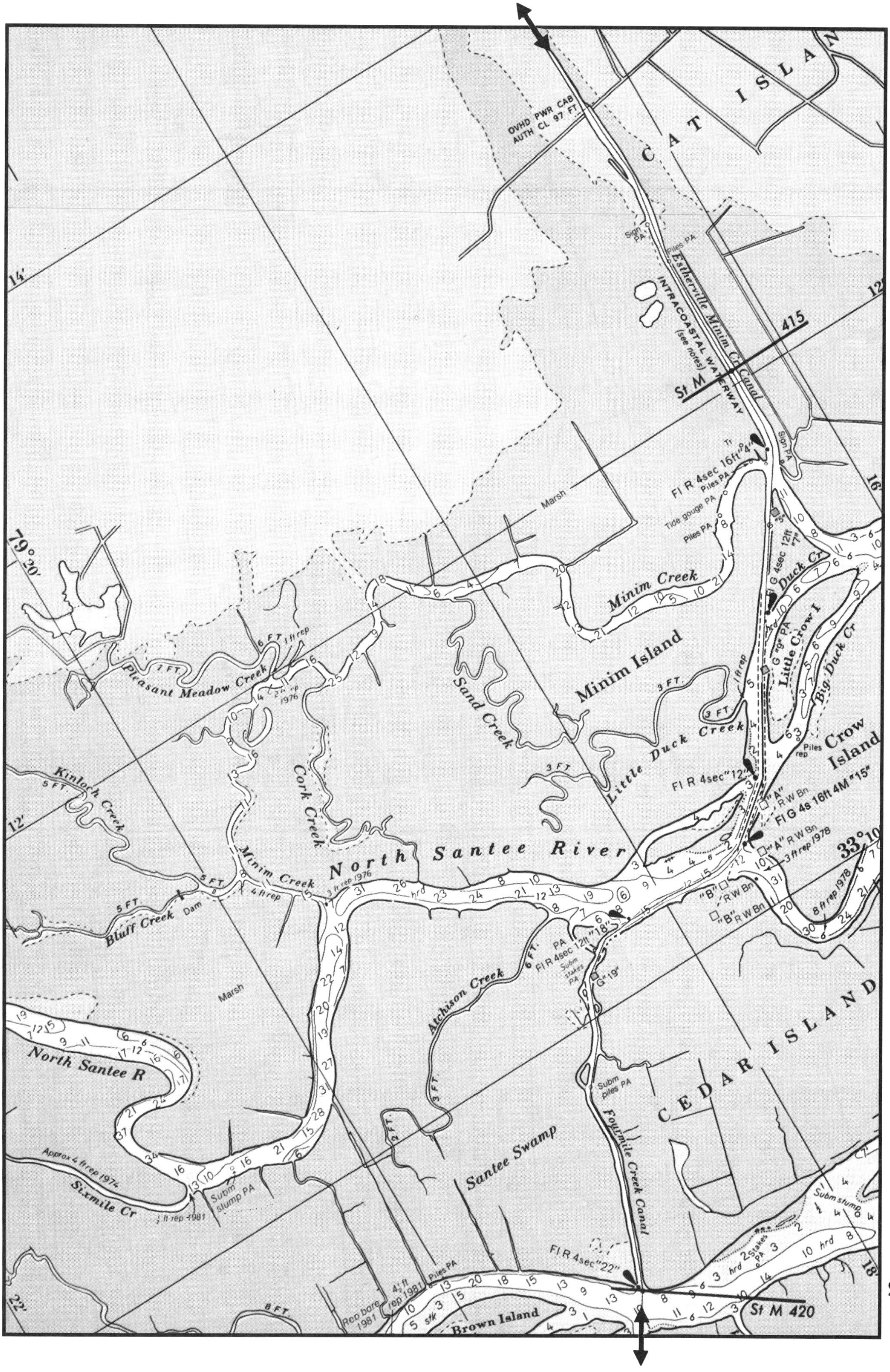


StM415

StM420

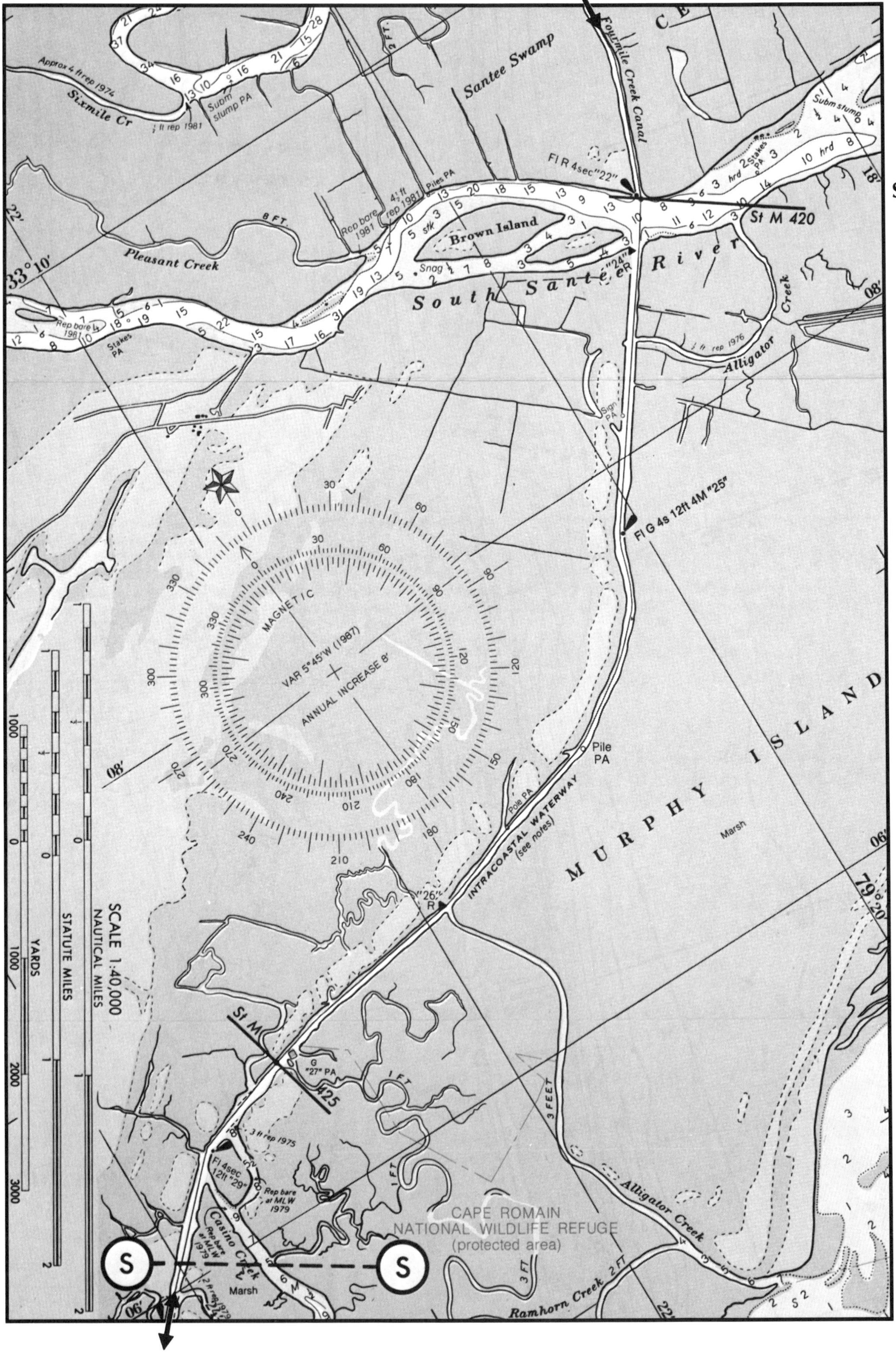


StM420

StM425

StM425

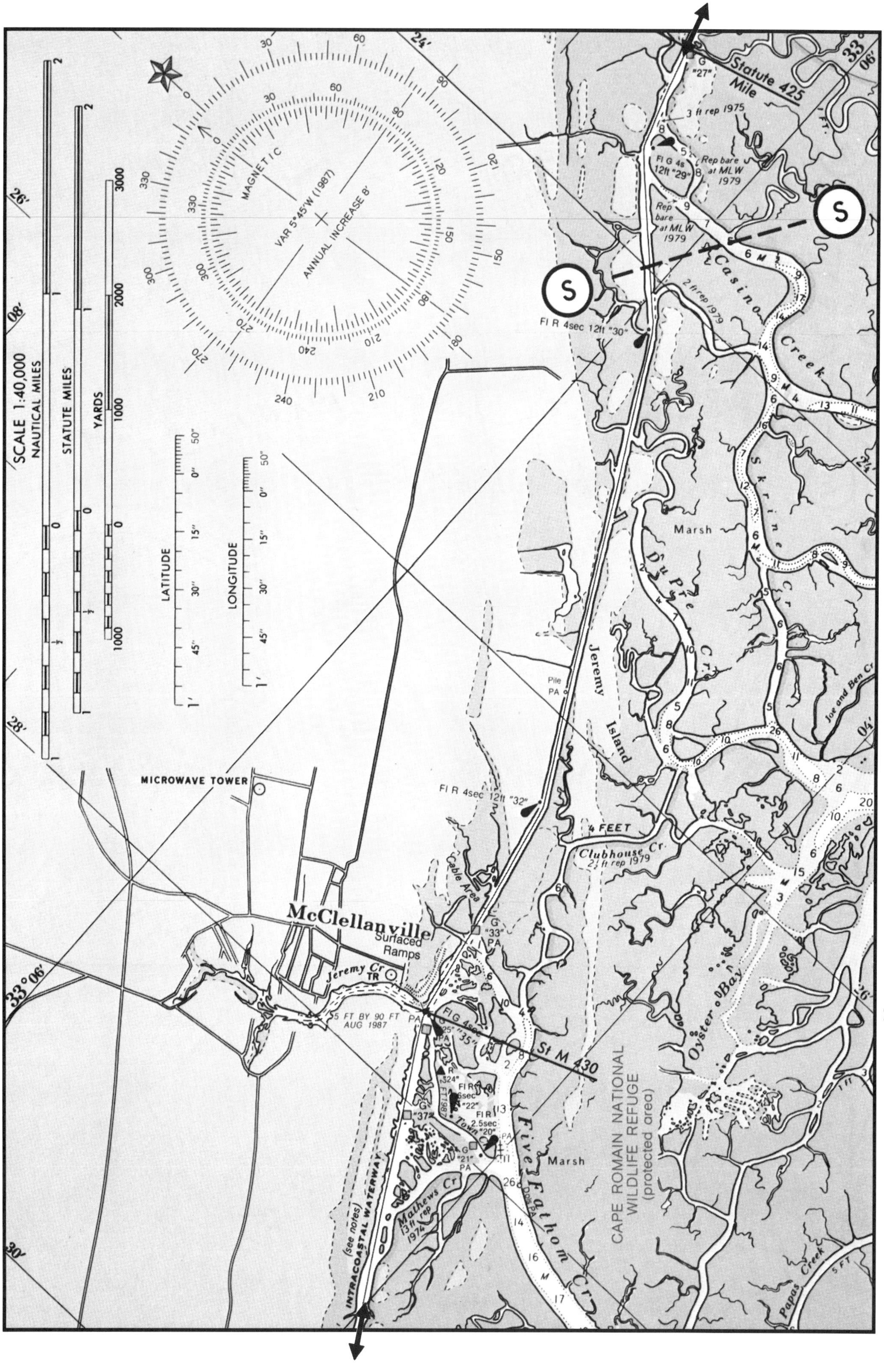


StM430

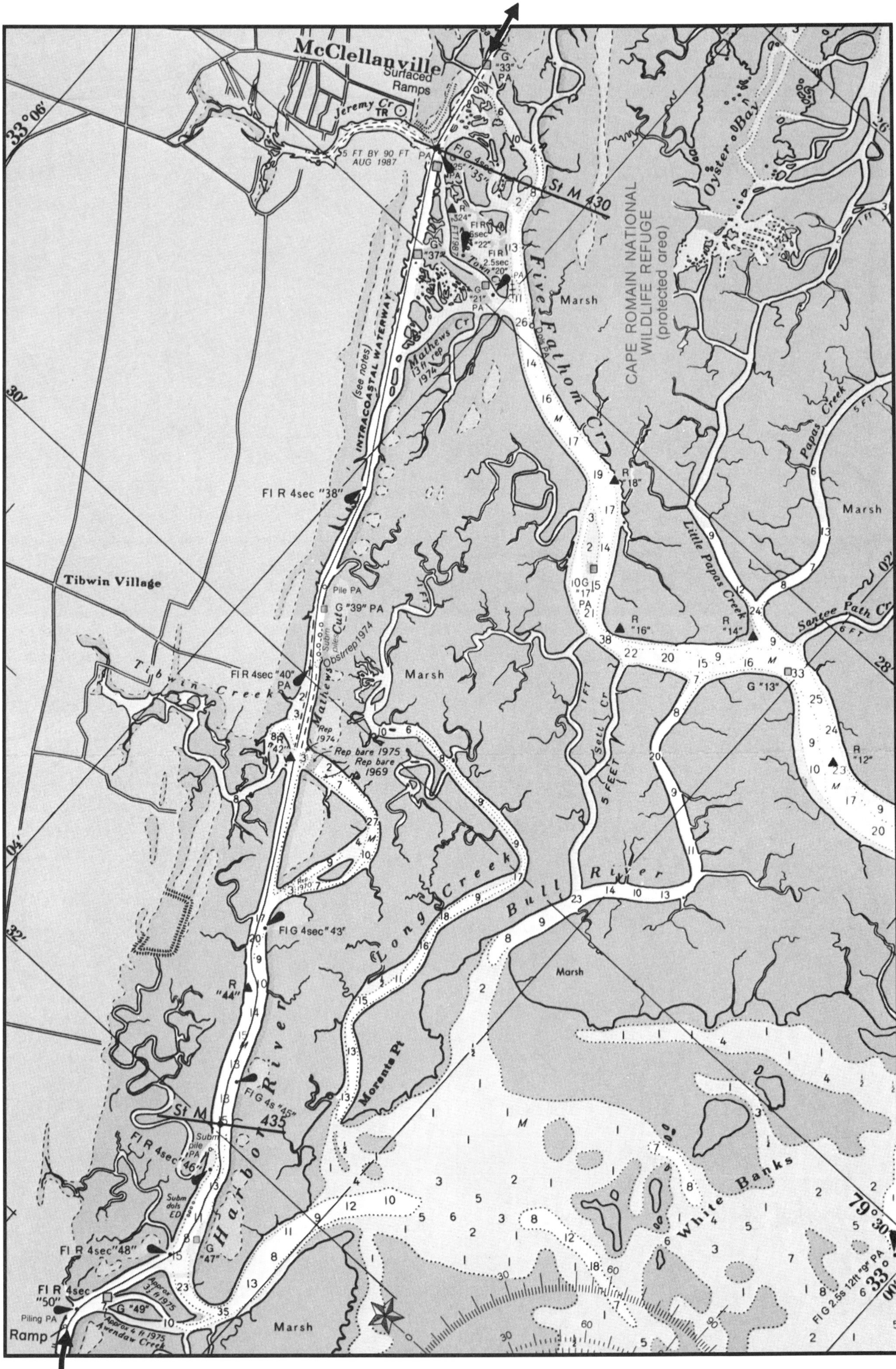

StM430

StM435

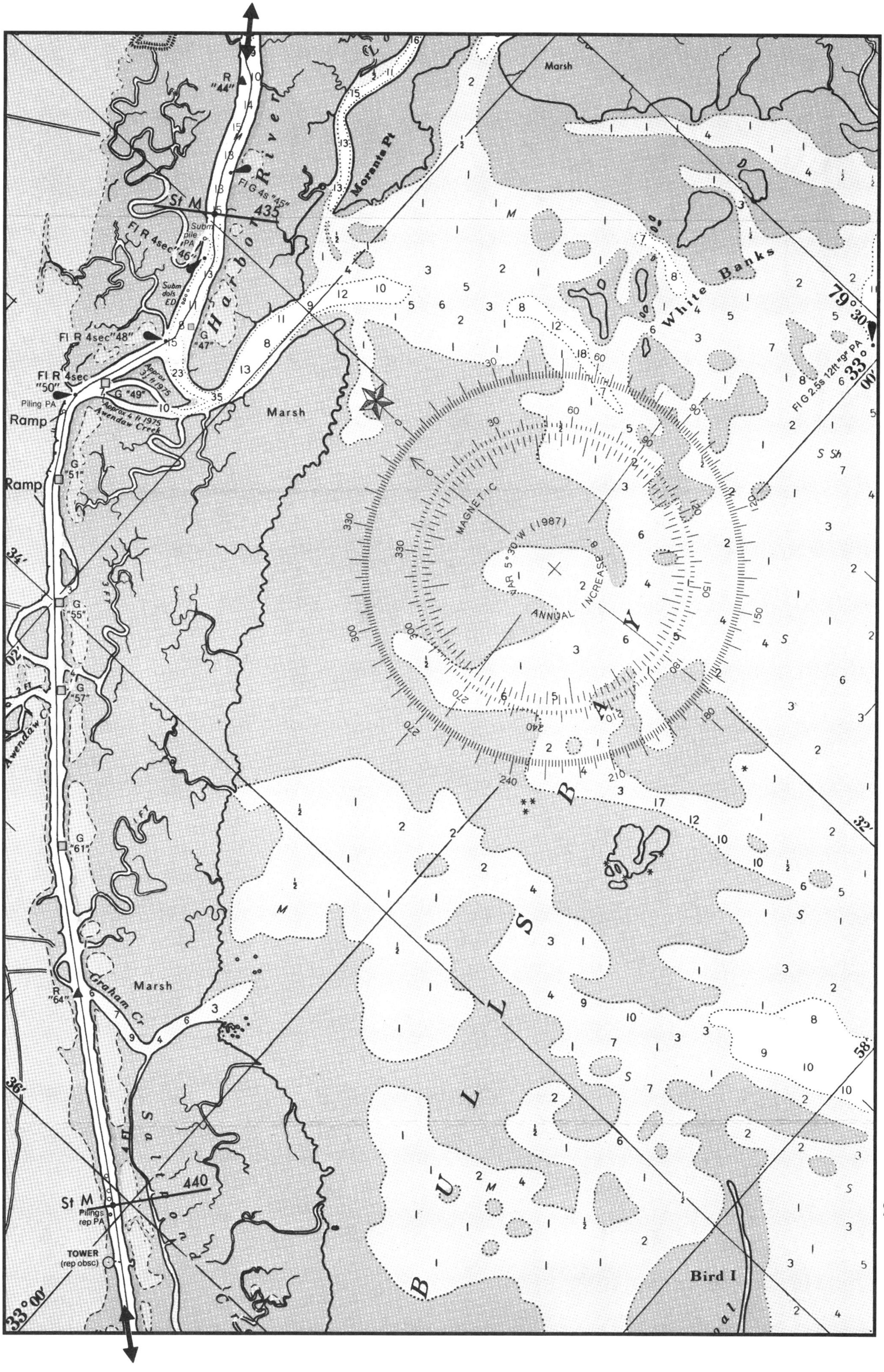
Harbor River
Moranta Pt
Marsh
White Banks
St M
435
440
Fl G 4s "45"
Fl R 4sec "46"
Fl R 4sec "48"
Fl R 4sec "50"
R "44"
G "47"
G "49"
G "51"
G "55"
G "57"
G "61"
R "64"
Subm pile PA
Subm dols ED
Piling PA
Ramp
Approx 3½ ft 1975
Approx 4 ft 1975
Awendaw Creek
Awendaw Cr
Graham Cr
Pilings rep PA
TOWER (rep obsc)
Fl G 2.5s 12ft "gr" PA
MAGNETIC
VAR 5°30'W (1987)
ANNUAL INCREASE 8'
BULLS BAY
Bird I
79°30'
33°00'

StM440

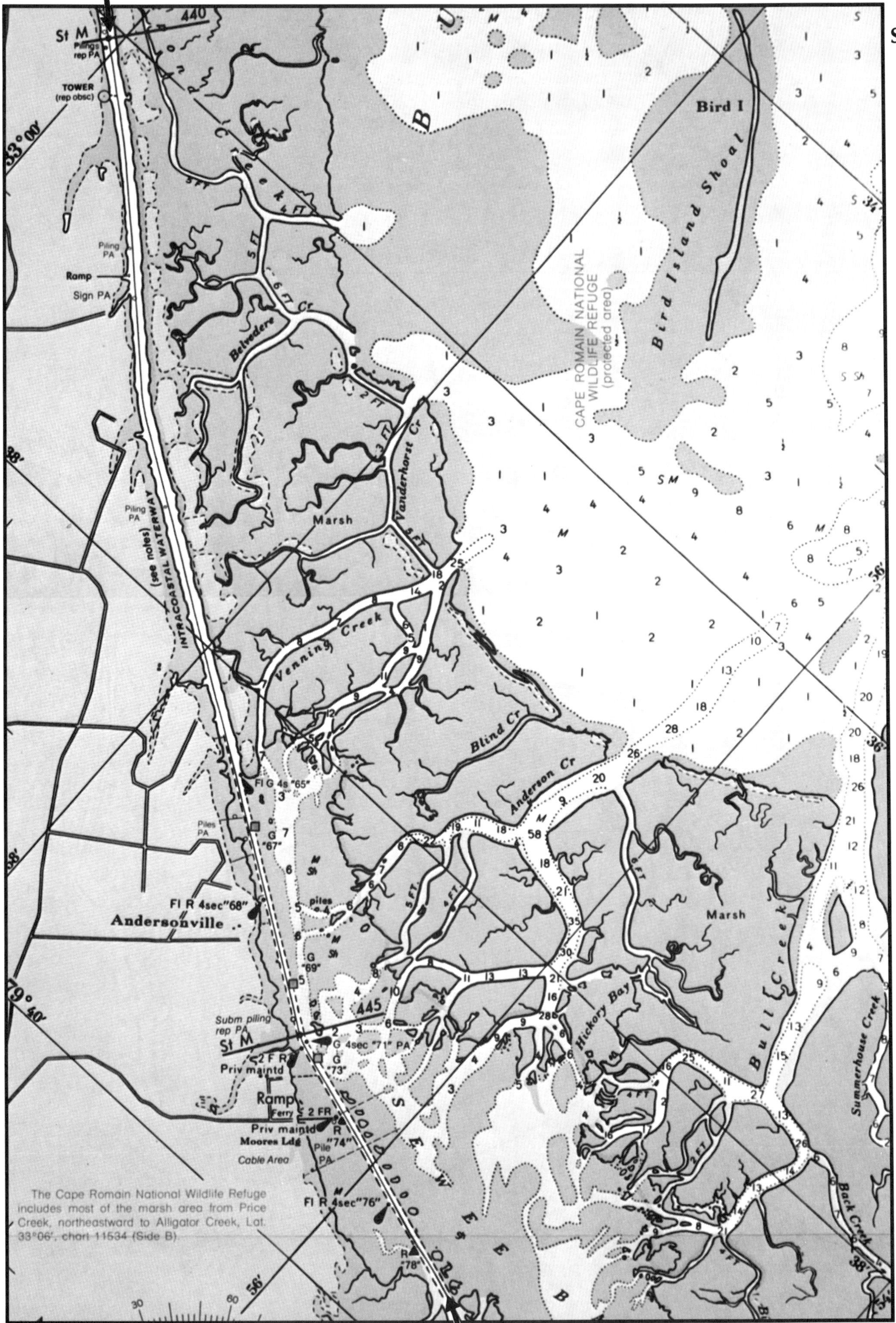


StM445

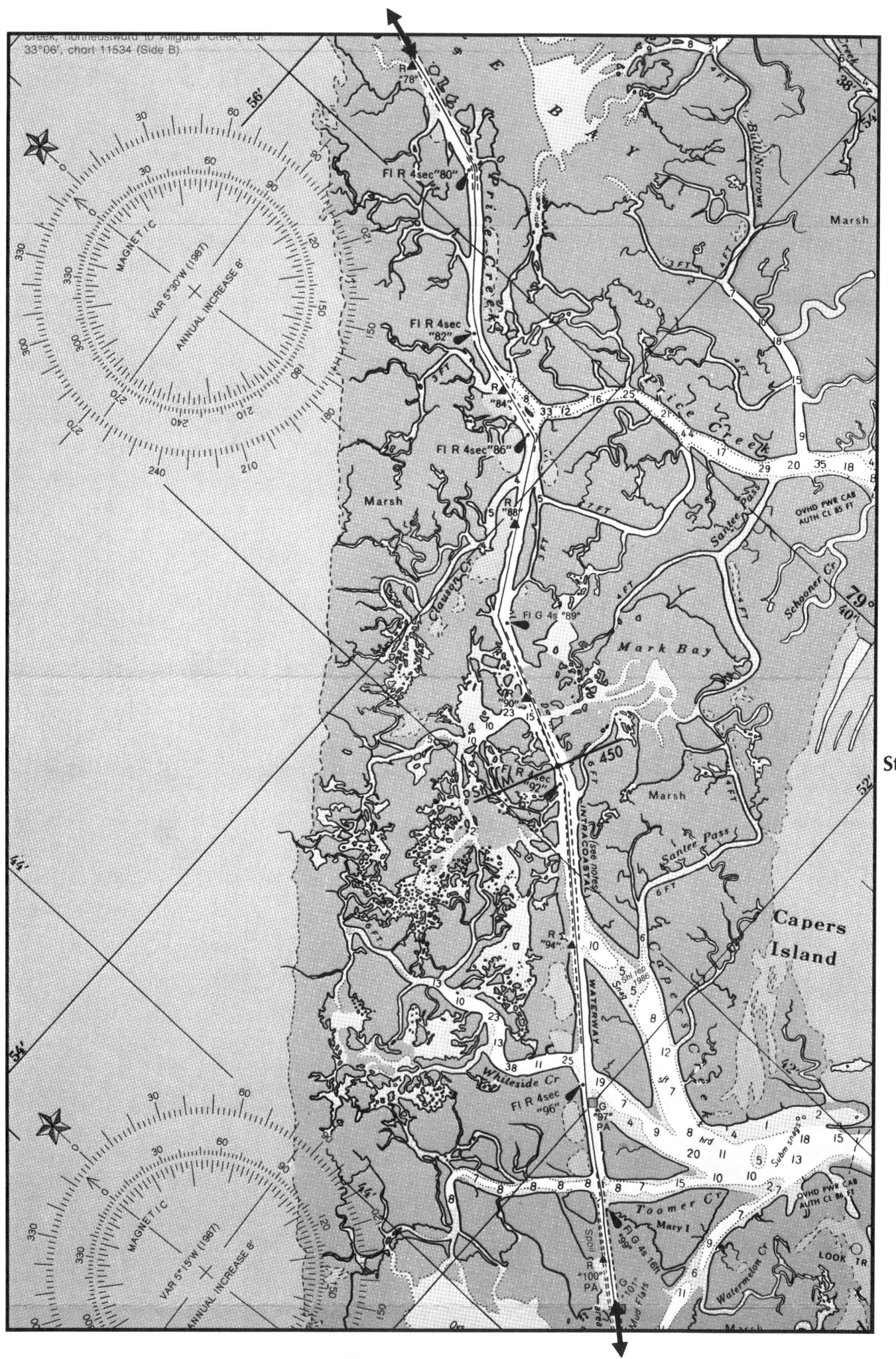

StM450

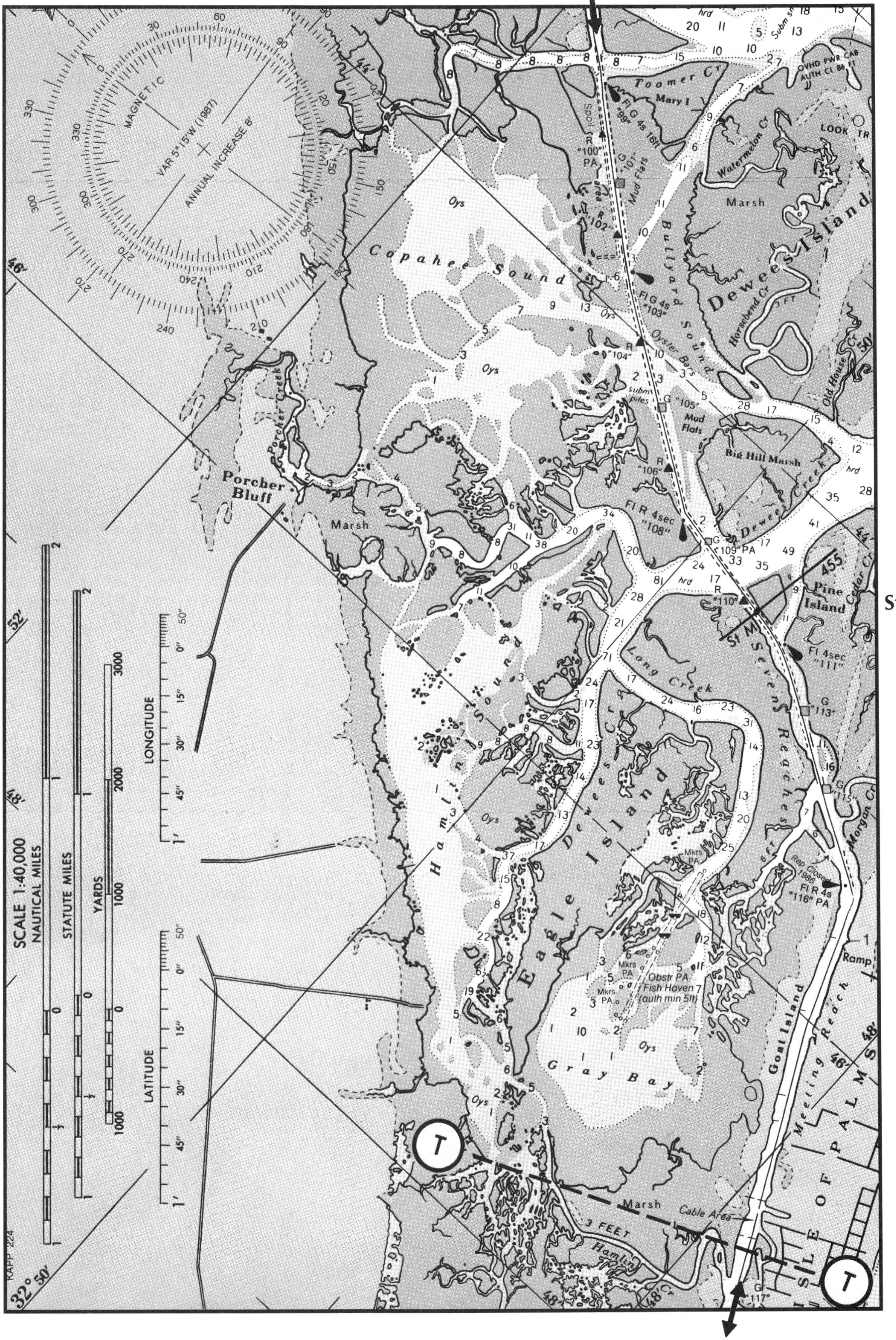
SCALE 1:40,000
NAUTICAL MILES
STATUTE MILES
YARDS
LATITUDE
LONGITUDE
VAR 5°15'W (1987)
ANNUAL INCREASE 8'
MAGNETIC
KAPP 224
Copahee Sound
Dewees Island
Bullyard Sound
Eagle Island
Hamlin Sound
Gray Bay
Porcher Bluff
Porcher Creek
Toomer Cr
Mary I
Watermelon Cr
Horsebend Cr
Old House Cr
Big Hill Marsh
Dewees Creek
Dewees Cr
Pine Island
Cedar Cr
Long Creek
St M Sevens Reaches
Goat Island
Meeting Reach
ISLE OF PALMS
Morgan Cr
Hamlin Cr
Cable Area
3 FEET
Marsh
Mud Flats
Oyster Bars
Oys
OVHD PWR CAB AUTH CL 86 FT
LOOK TR
Obstr PA Fish Haven 7 (auth min 5ft)
Rep Closed 1986
Fl R 4s "116" PA
Fl 4sec "111"
Fl R 4sec "108"
Fl G 4s "103"
Fl G 4s 16ft "99"
455

StM455

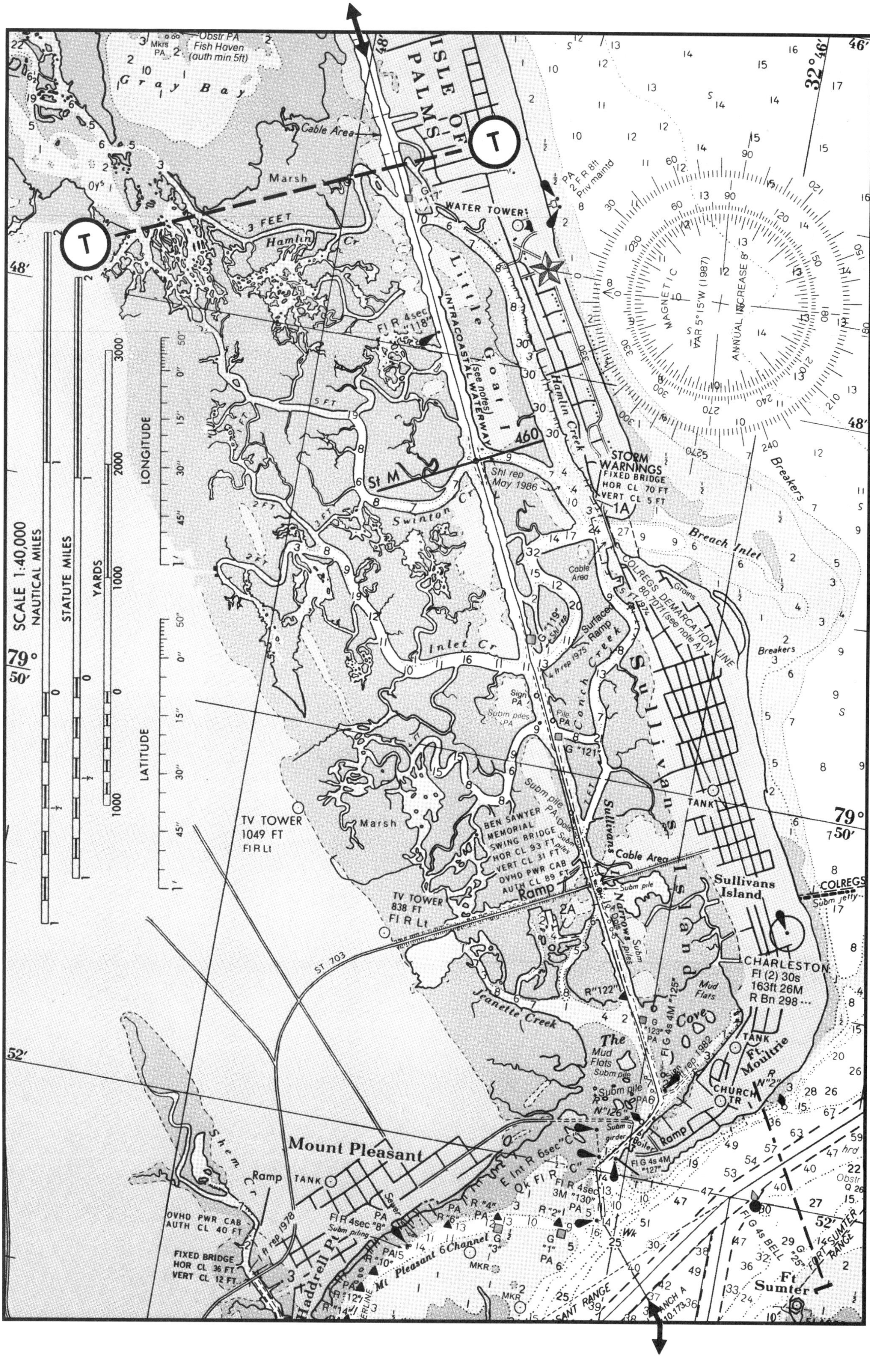


StM460

BR462.2

Joins Page 199

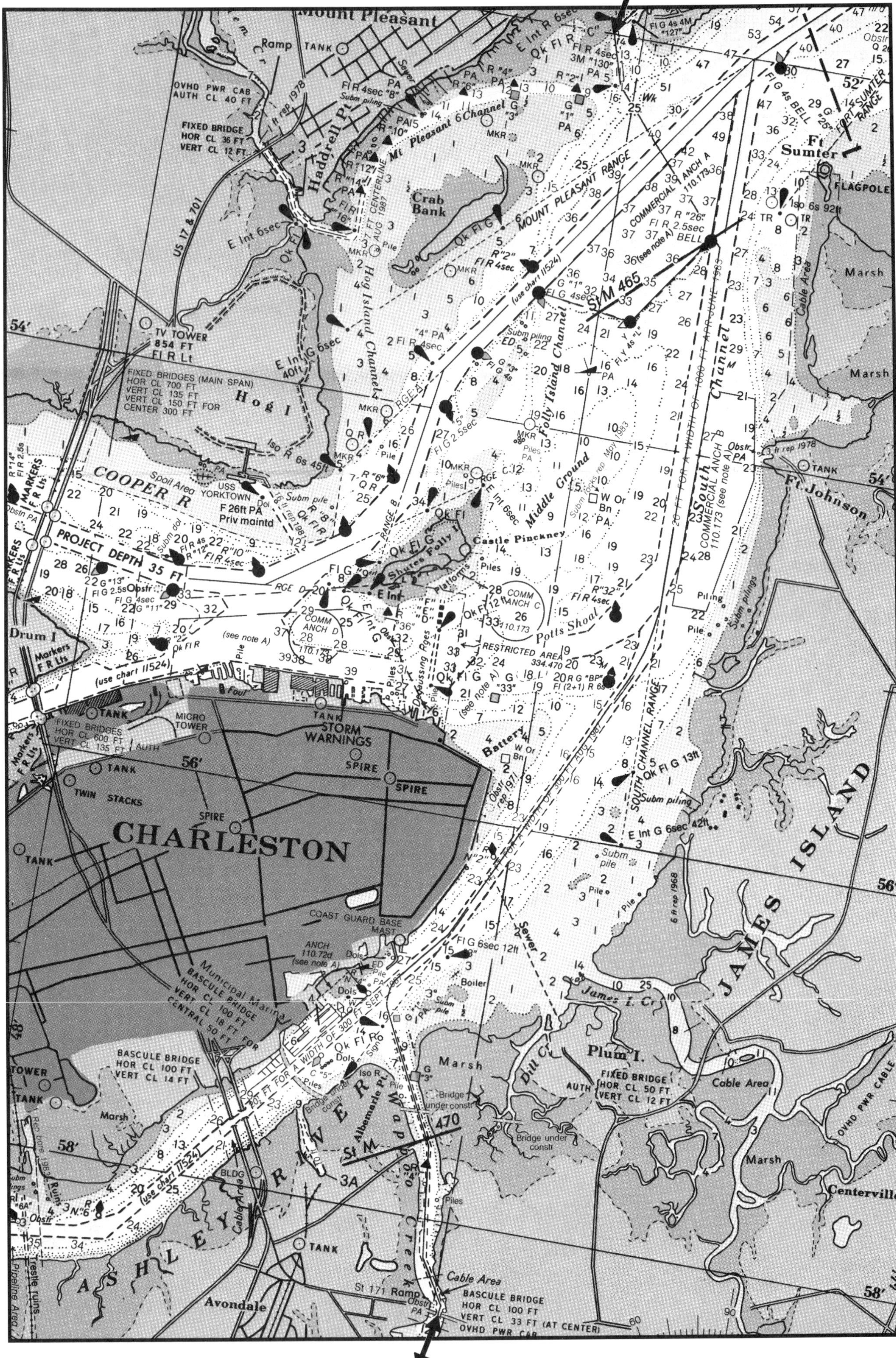


StM465

StM470

BR470.8

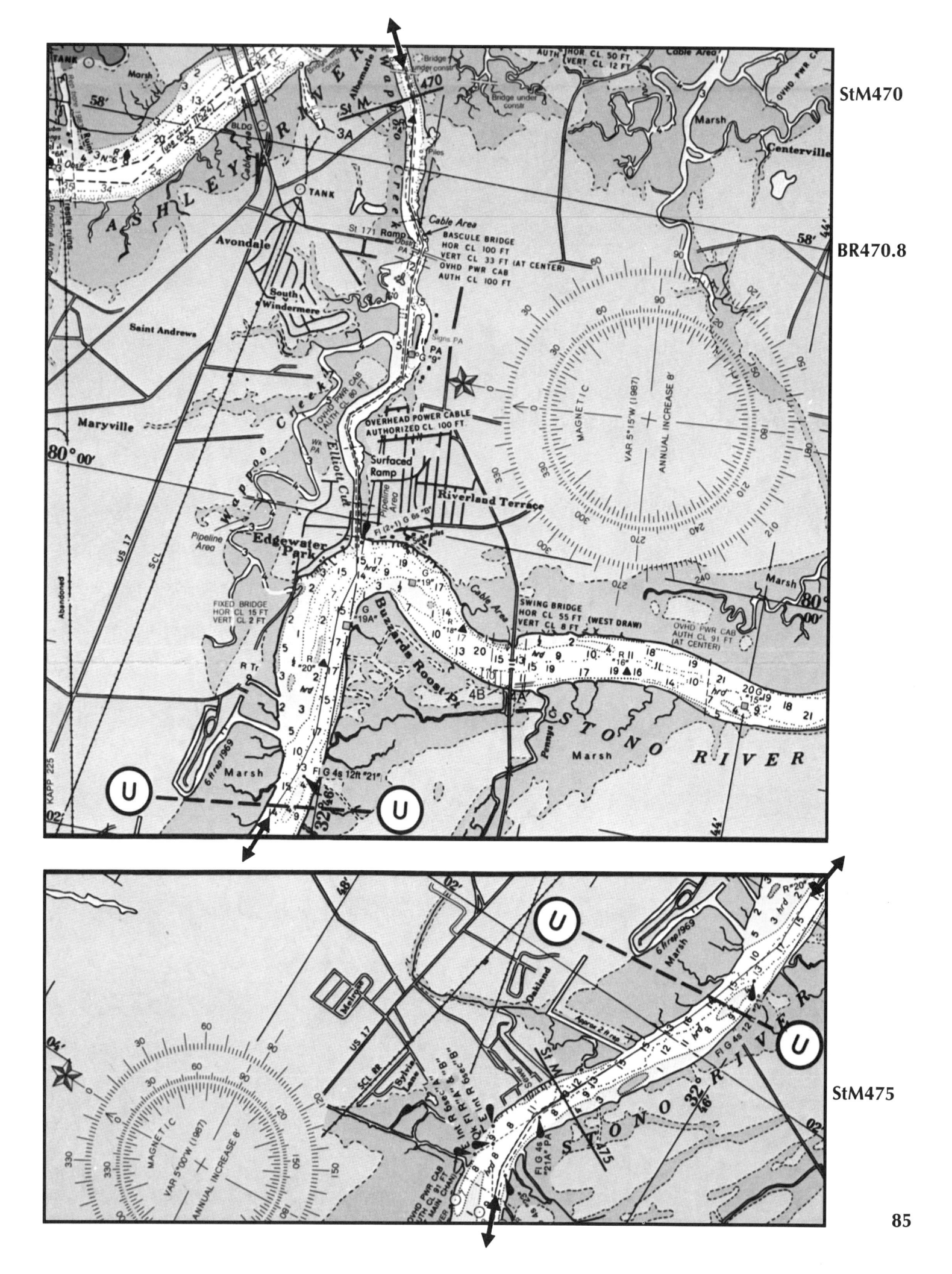

StM470

BR470.8

StM475

85

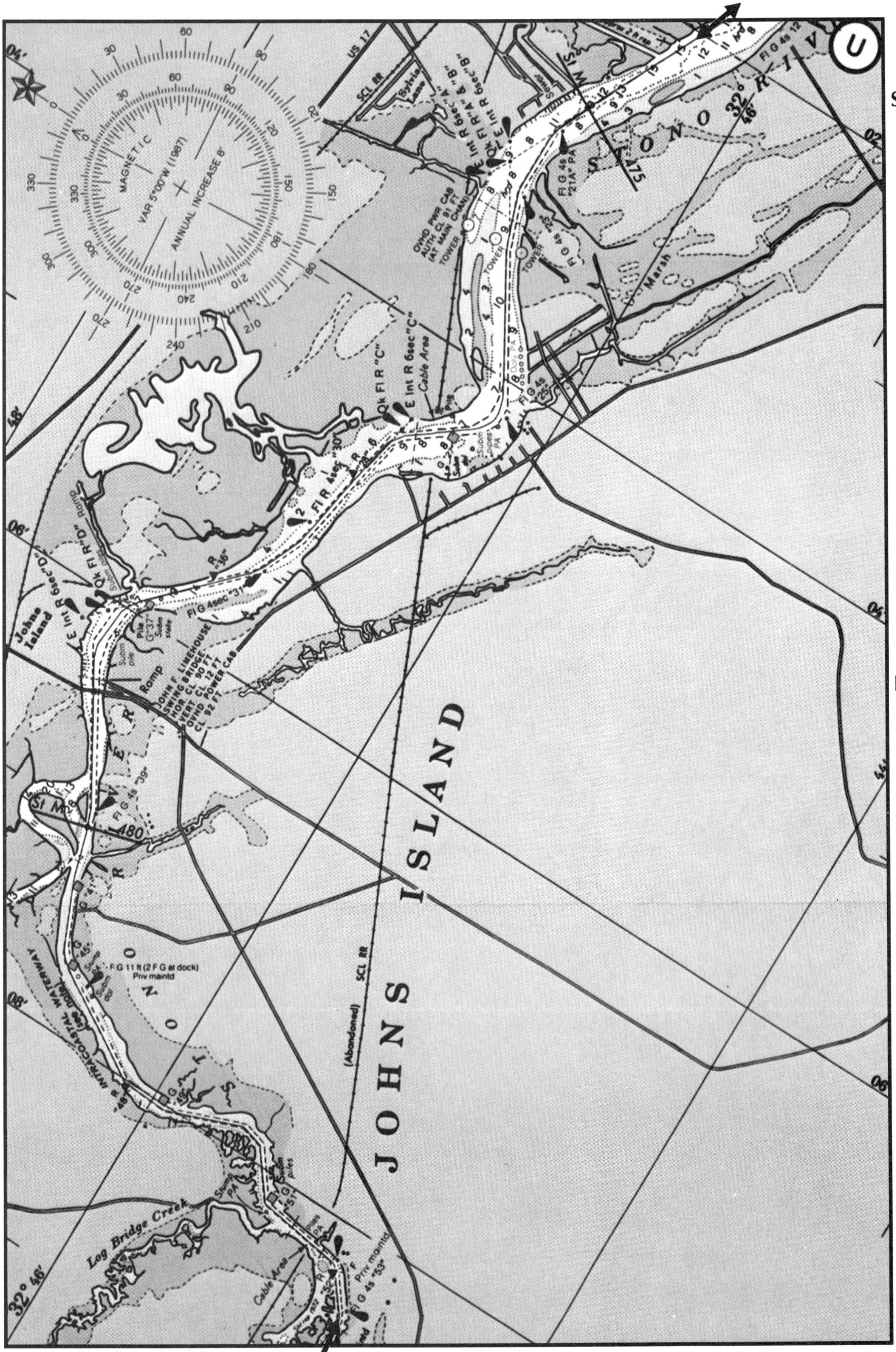


StM475

BR479.3

StM480

StM485

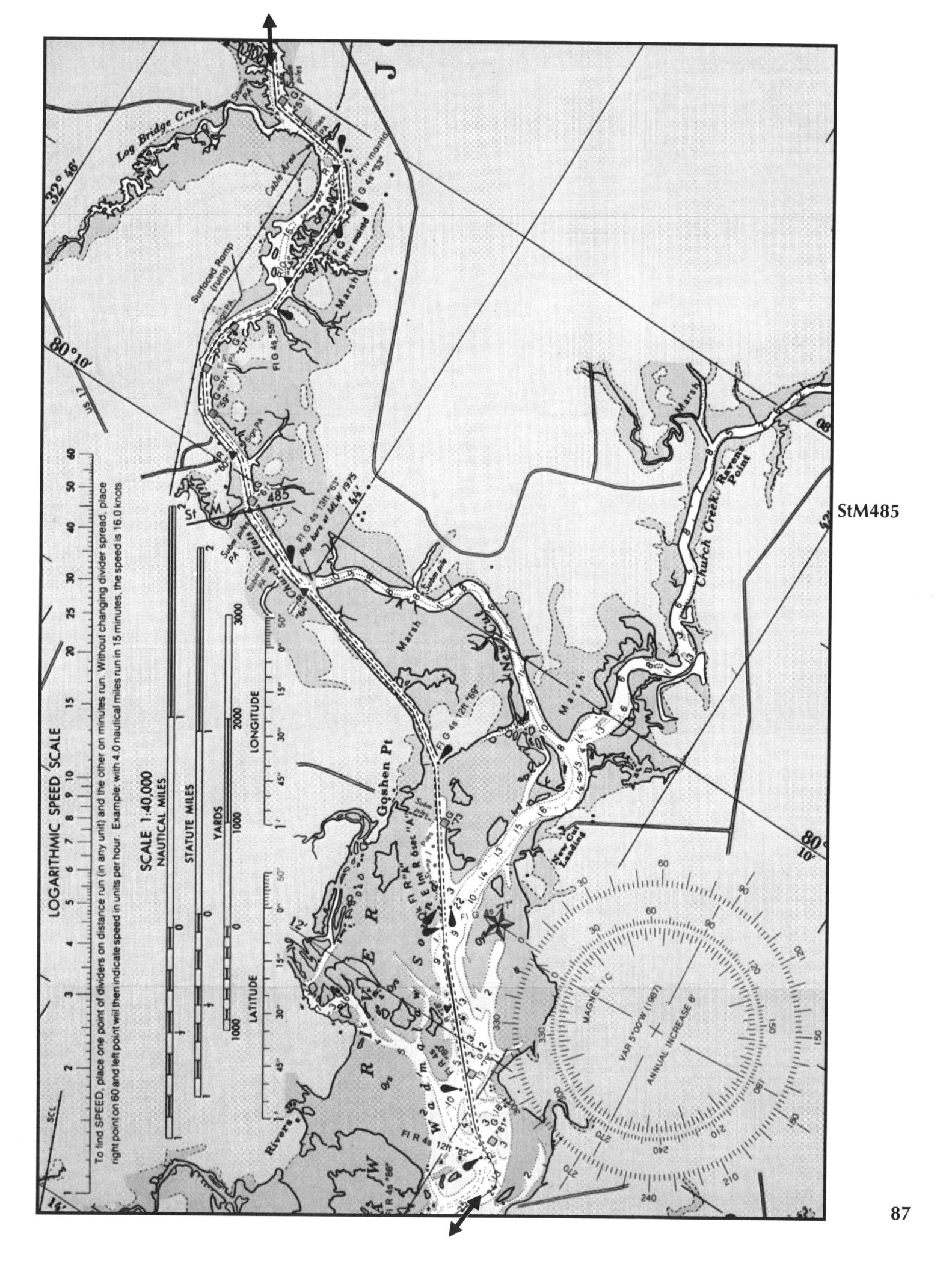

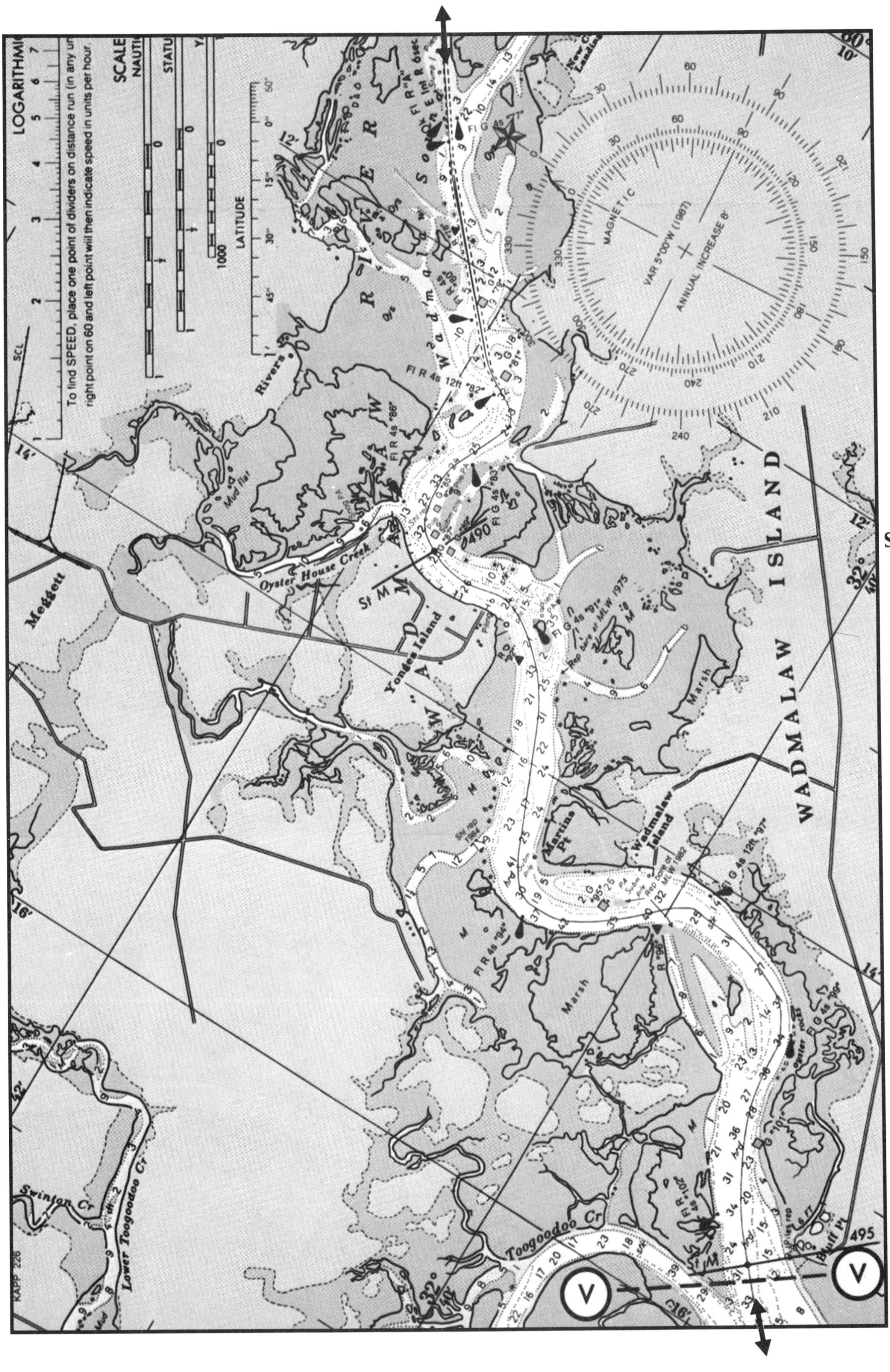


StM490

StM495

StM495

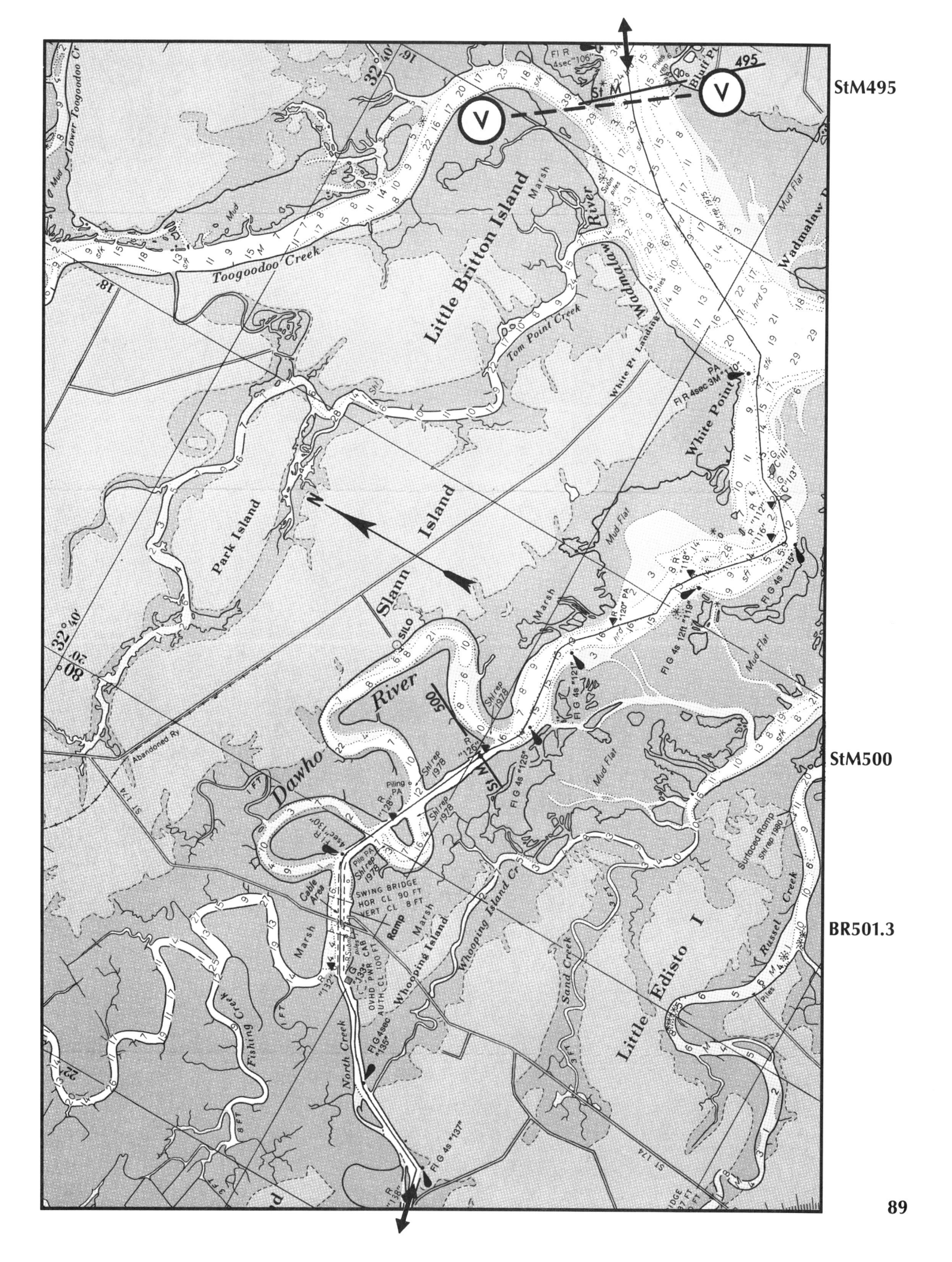

StM500

BR501.3

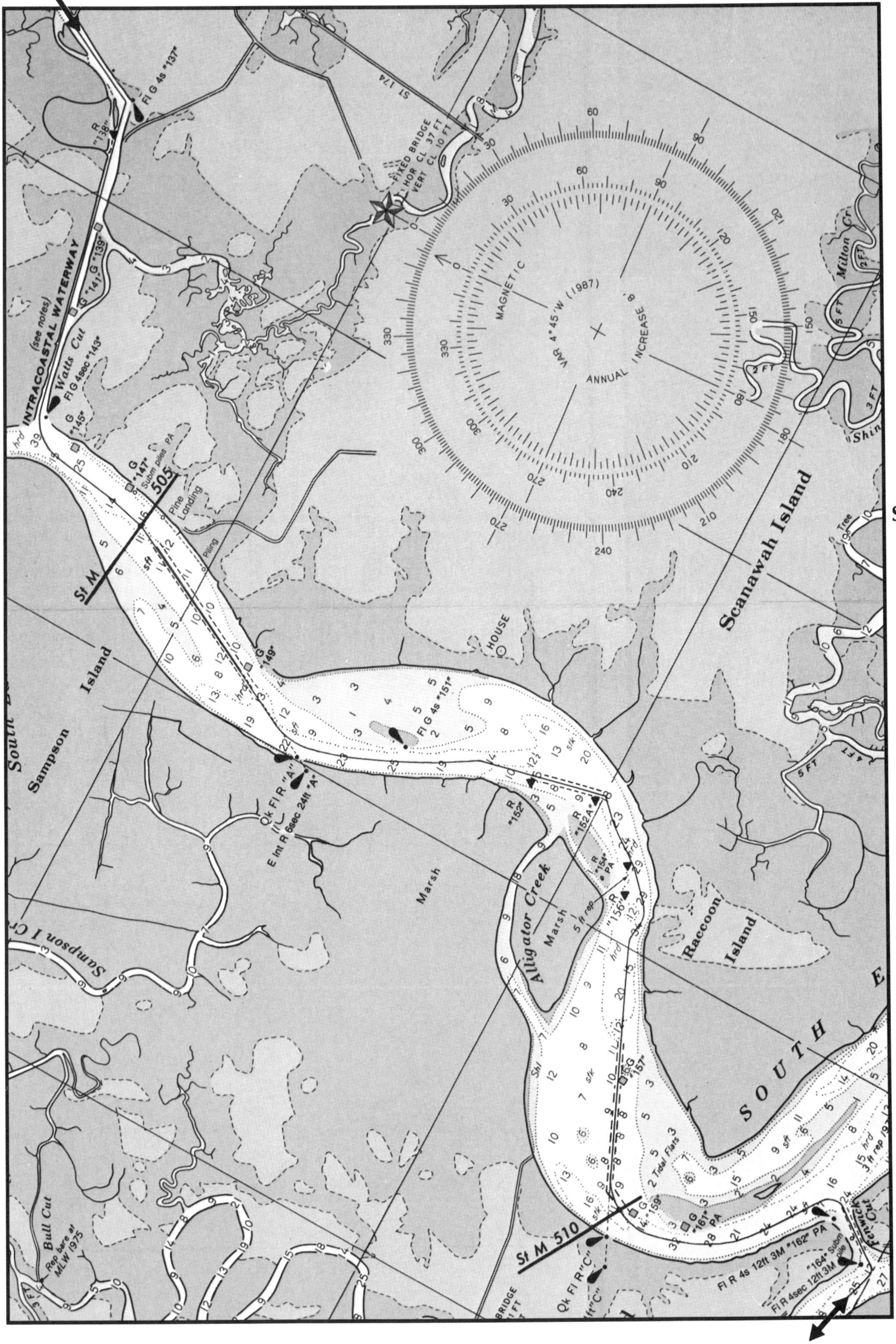

INTRACOASTAL WATERWAY
(see notes)
Watts Cut
Fl G 4sec "143"
G "145"
G "141" G "139"
Fl G 4s "137"
R "138"
G "147" Subm piles PA
505
St M
Pine Landing
Piling
G "149"
Fl G 4s "151"
Qk Fl R "A"
E Int R 6sec 24ft "A"
R "152"
R "152A"
R "154" PA
R "156"
5 ft rep
Sampson Island
Sampson I Cr
South
Marsh
Alligator Creek
Marsh
Raccoon Island
Scanawah Island
SOUTH E
HOUSE
FIXED BRIDGE HOR CL 37 FT VERT CL 10 FT
ST 174
VAR 4°45'W (1987)
ANNUAL INCREASE 8'
MAGNETIC
Milton Cr
Shin
Tree
G "157"
G "159"
G "161" PA
2 Tidal Flats 3
St M 510
Qk Fl R "C"
Fl R 4s 12ft 3M "162" PA
"164" Subm pile
Fl R 4sec 12ft 3M
Fenwick Cut
Bull Cut
Rep bare at MLW 1975
BRIDGE


StM505
StM510

StM510

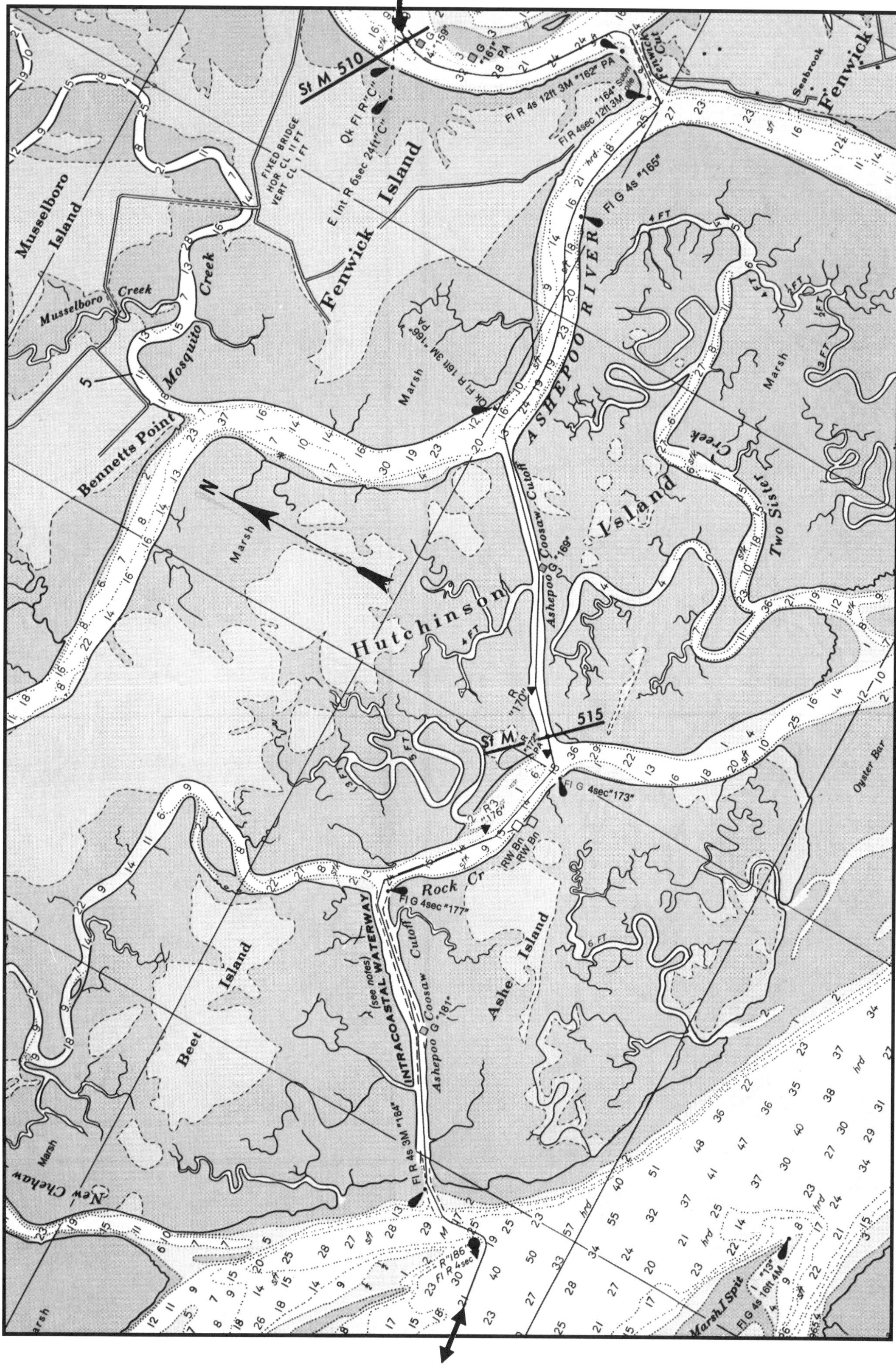


StM515

Joins Page 200

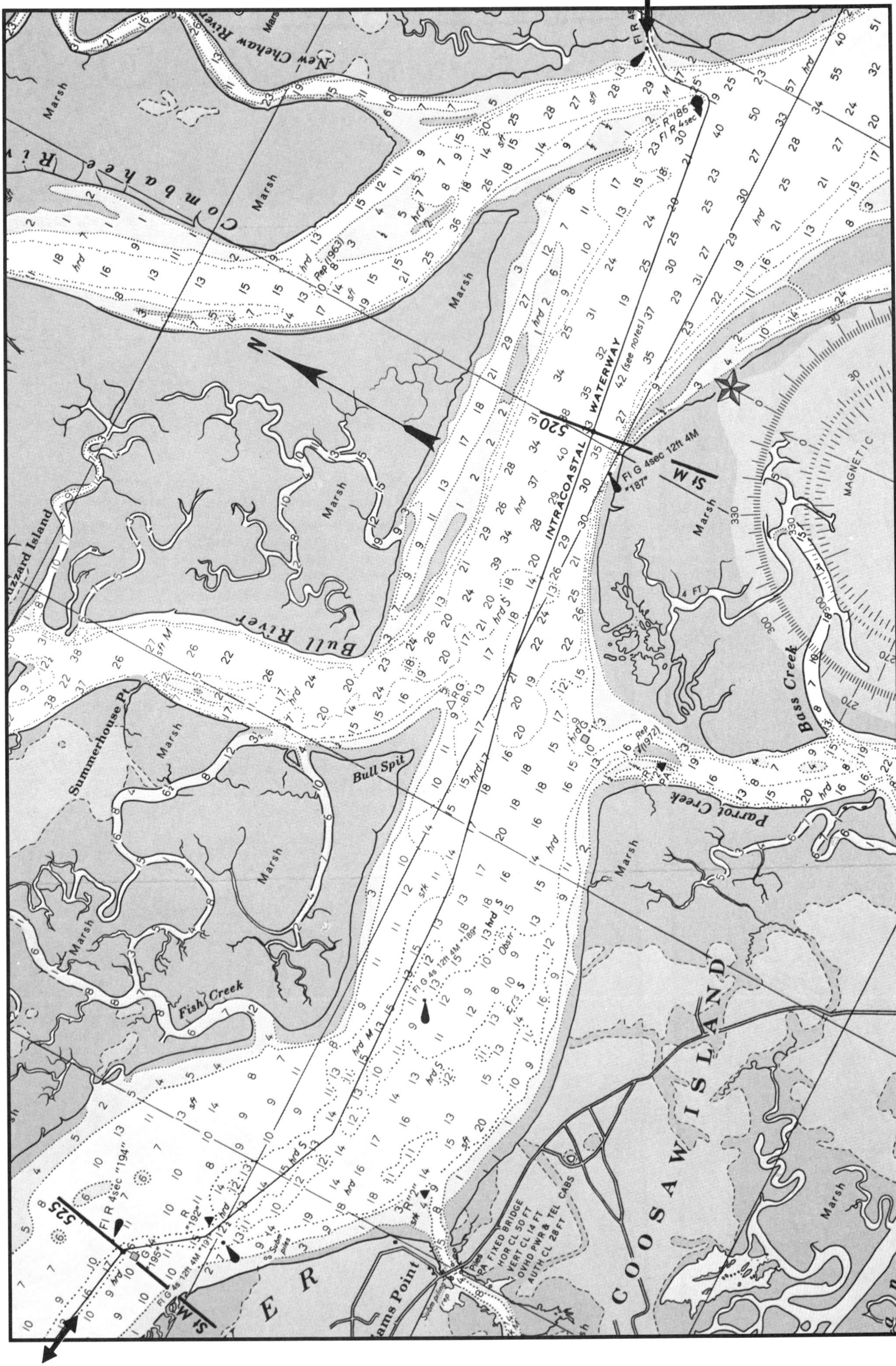


StM520

StM525

StM525

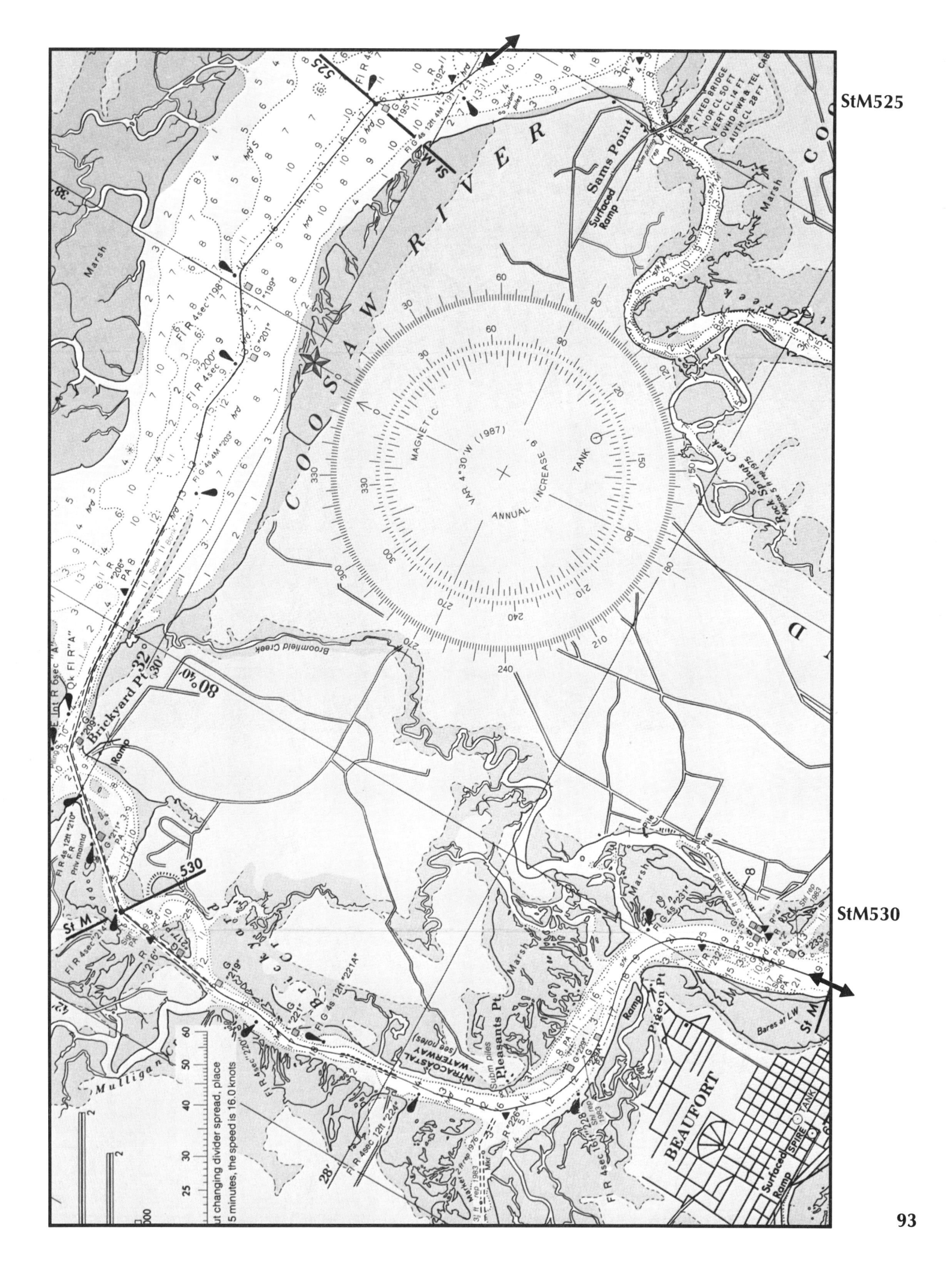

StM530

93

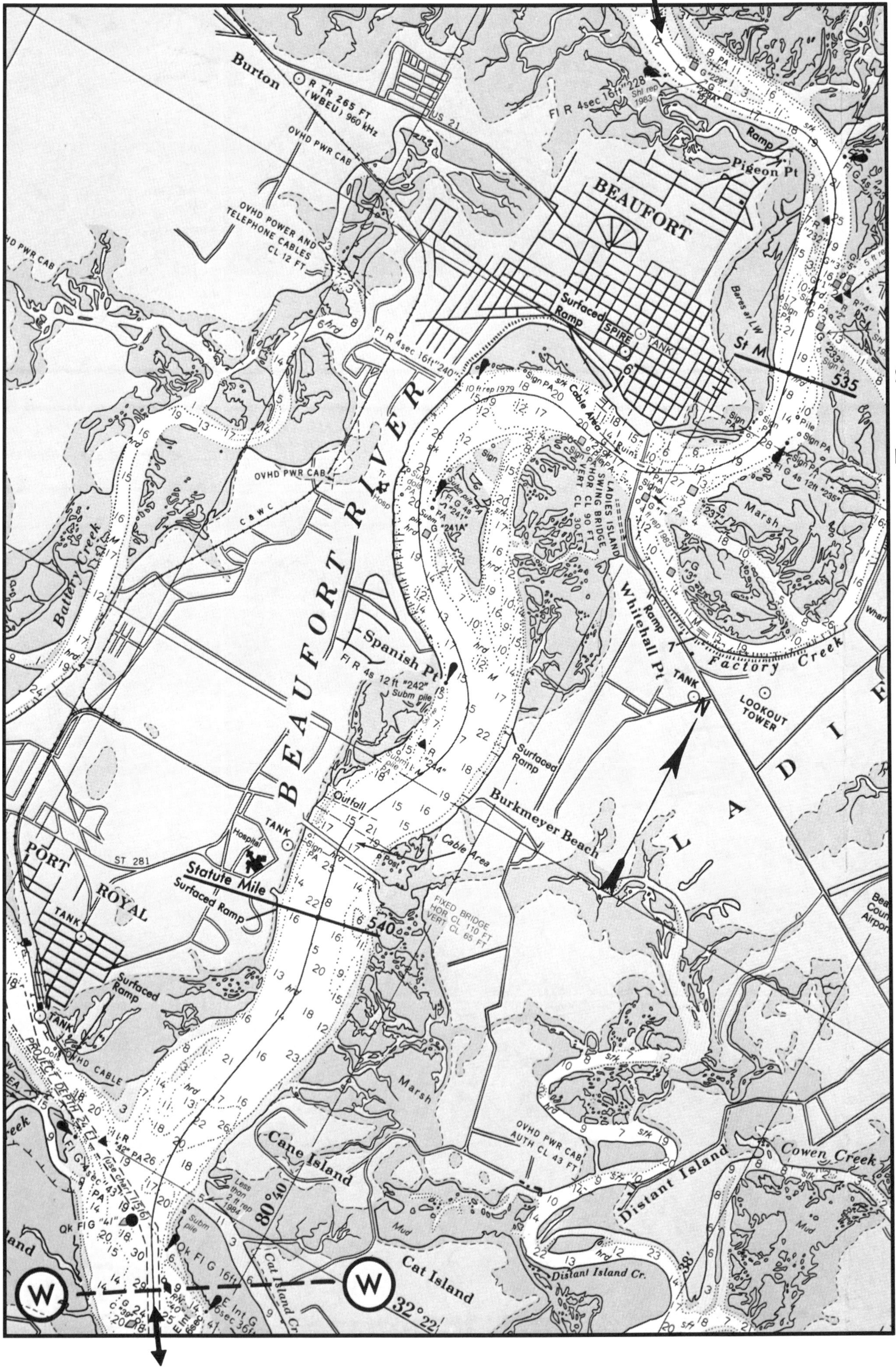


StM535

BR536.0

StM540

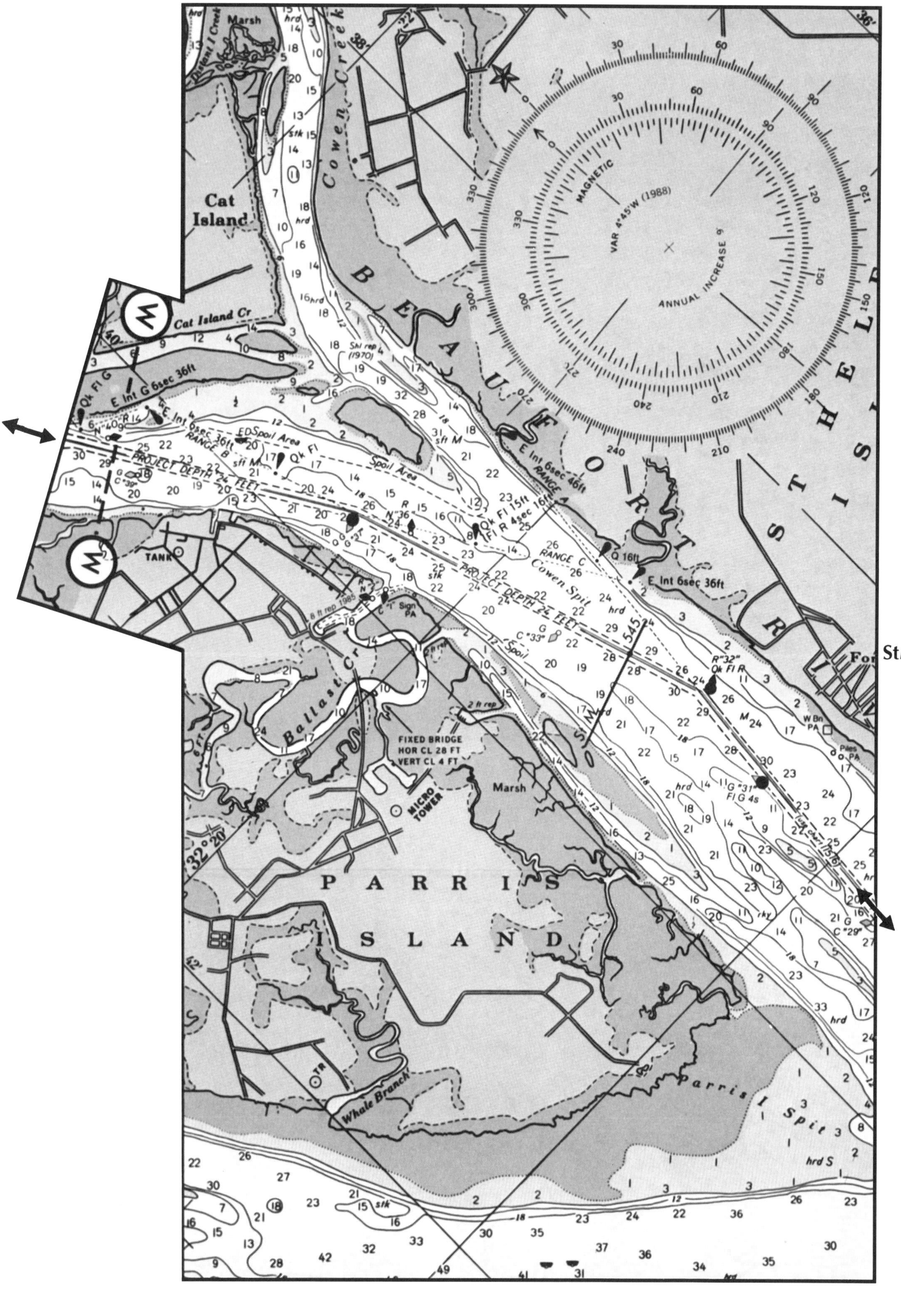
Cat Island
Cat Island Cr
Cowen Creek
B E A U F O R T
P A R R I S
I S L A N D
Ballast Cr
Whale Branch
Parris I Spit
Cowen Spit
FIXED BRIDGE
HOR CL 28 FT
VERT CL 4 FT
MICRO TOWER
TANK
Marsh
PROJECT DEPTH 24 FEET
RANGE A
RANGE B
RANGE C
Spoil Area
E Int 6sec 36ft
E Int 6sec 46ft
Qk Fl 15ft
Fl R 4sec 16ft
Q 16ft
G "31"
Fl G 4s
R "32"
Qk Fl R
VAR 4°45'W (1988)
ANNUAL INCREASE 9'
MAGNETIC
545

StM545

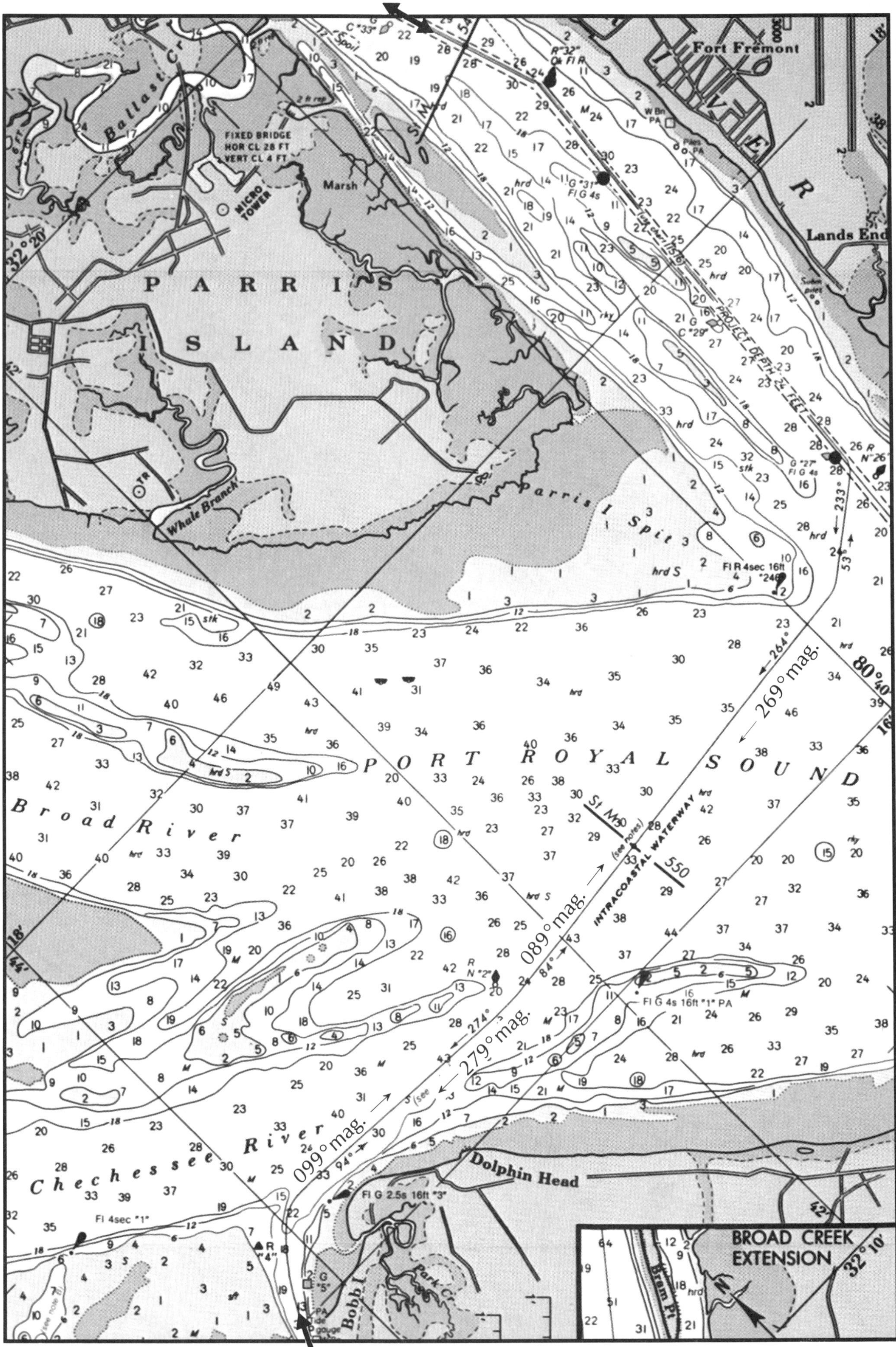

96
StM545

Joins Page 202

StM550

Fort Frémont
Lands End

BALLAST Cr.

FIXED BRIDGE
HOR CL 28 FT
VERT CL 4 FT

MICRO TOWER

Marsh

P A R R I S   I S L A N D

Whale Branch

Parris I Spit

hrd S

Fl R 4sec 16ft "248"

C "33"
R "32" Qk Fl R
M 24
W Bn PA
G "31" Fl G 4s
C "29"
PROJECT DEPTH 27 TO 28 FEET
G "27" Fl G 4s
R N "26"

233°
53°

P O R T   R O Y A L   S O U N D

269° mag.
264° mag.
80°40'

B r o a d   R i v e r

St M30
(see notes)
INTRACOASTAL WATERWAY
550

089° mag.

R N "2"
B4°
274° mag.
279° mag.

Fl G 4s 16ft "1" PA

C h e c h e s s e e   R i v e r

099° mag.
94°

Dolphin Head

Fl 4sec "1"

R "4"

Fl G 2.5s 16ft "3"

G "5"

Bobb I.
Park Cr.

BROAD CREEK
EXTENSION

Bram Pt.

32°20'

32°10'

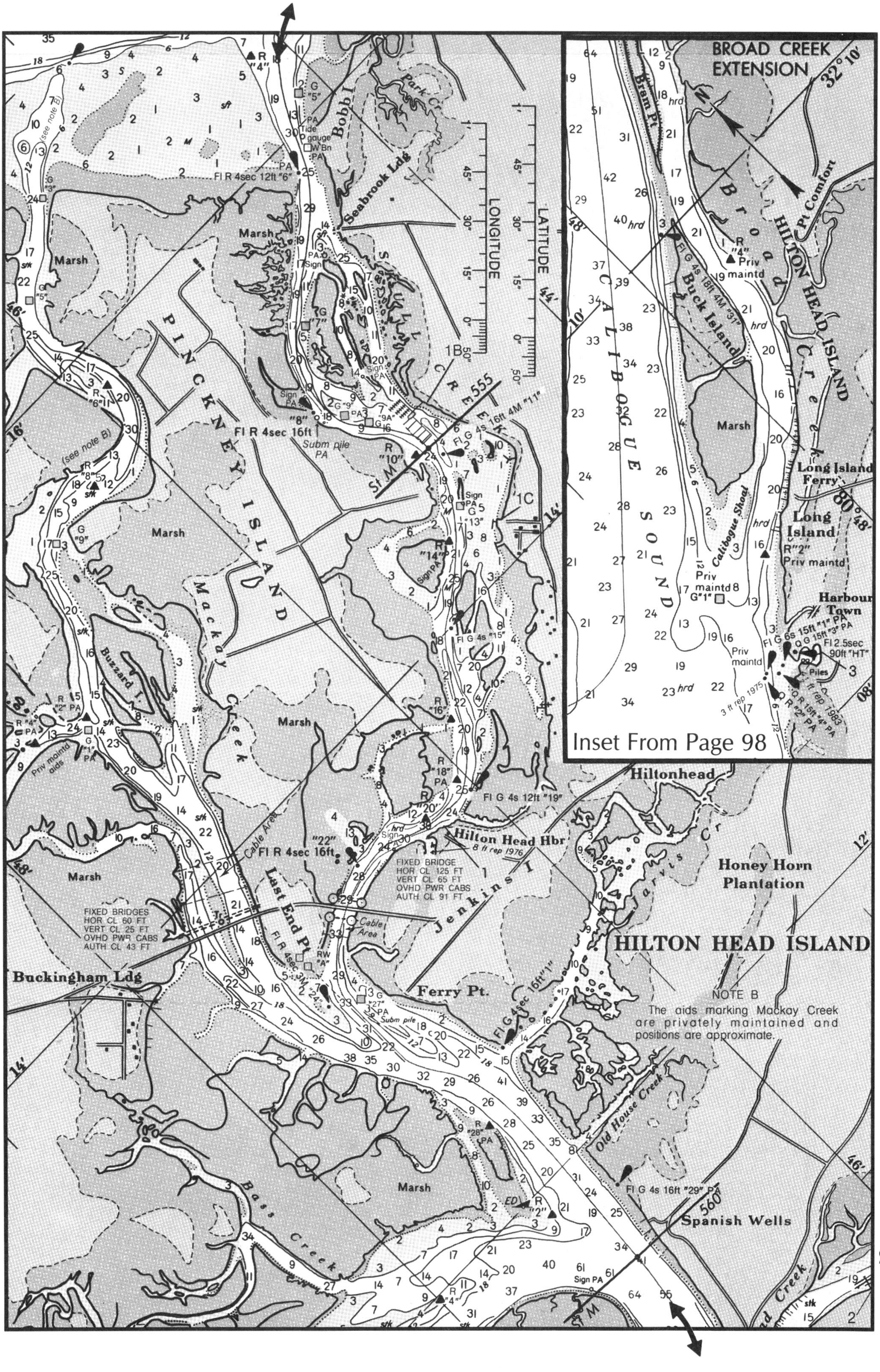


StM555

StM560

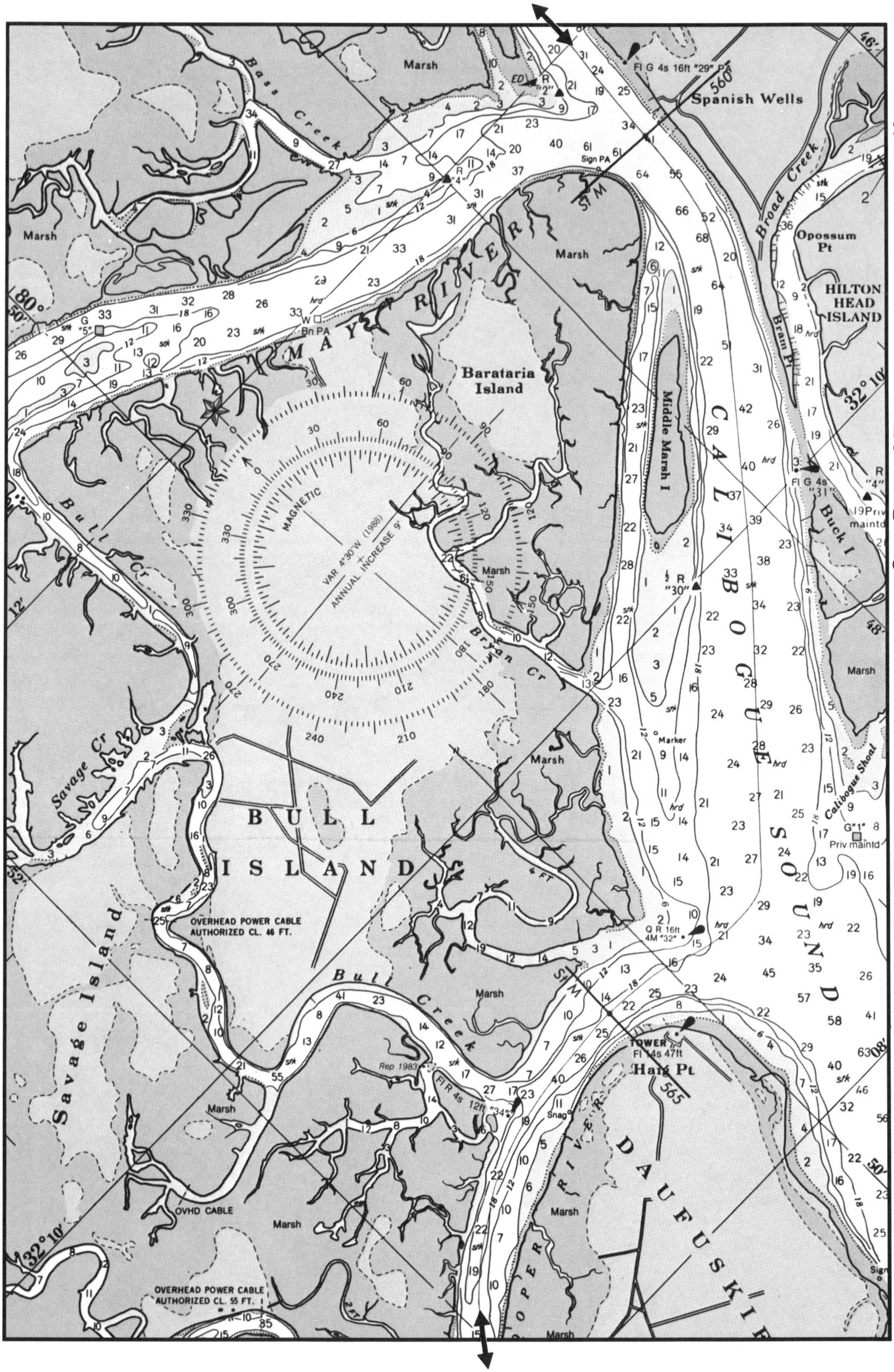


StM560

See Page 97

Joins Page 204

StM565

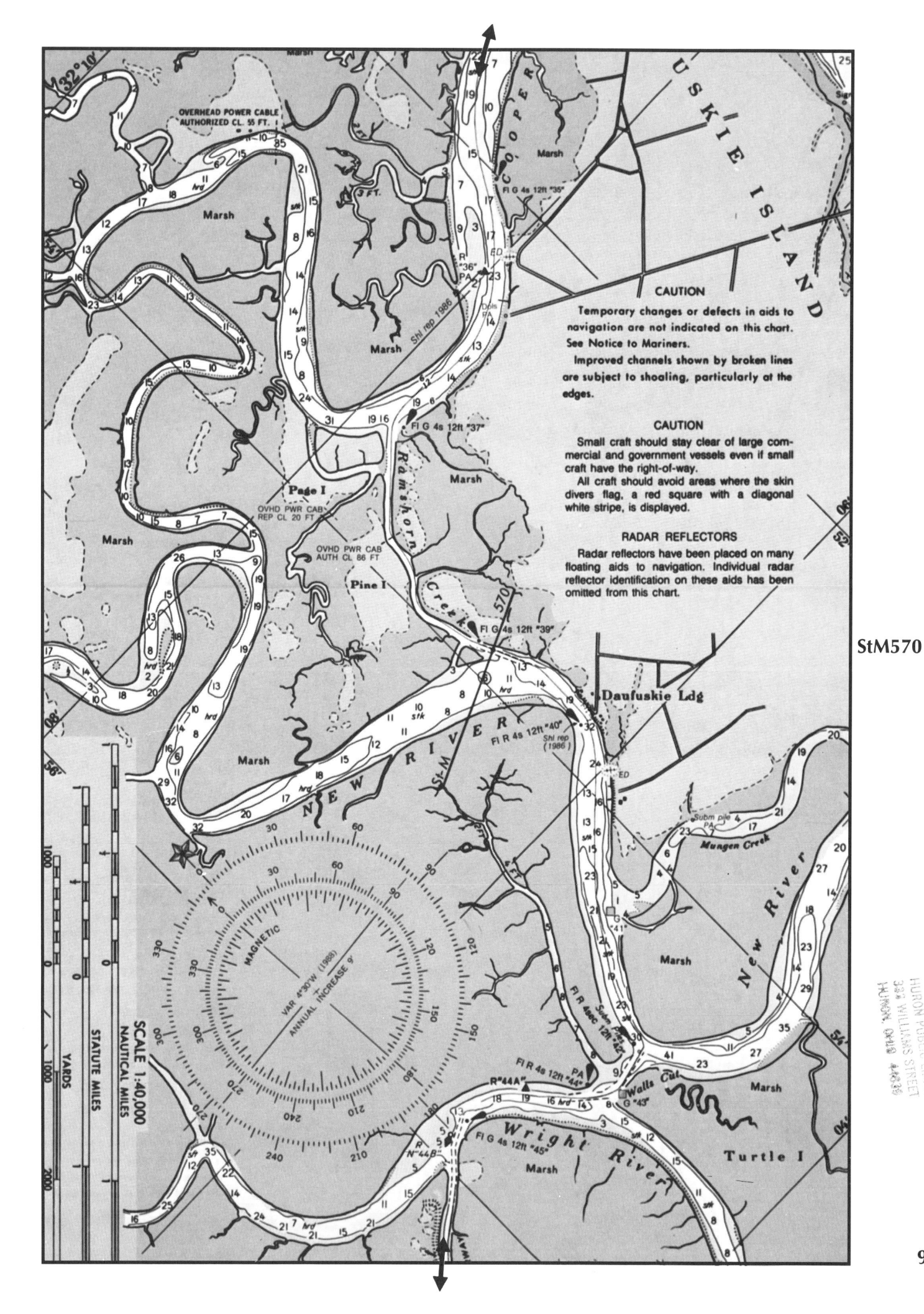

## CAUTION

Temporary changes or defects in aids to navigation are not indicated on this chart. See Notice to Mariners.

Improved channels shown by broken lines are subject to shoaling, particularly at the edges.

## CAUTION

Small craft should stay clear of large commercial and government vessels even if small craft have the right-of-way.

All craft should avoid areas where the skin divers flag, a red square with a diagonal white stripe, is displayed.

## RADAR REFLECTORS

Radar reflectors have been placed on many floating aids to navigation. Individual radar reflector identification on these aids has been omitted from this chart.

StM570

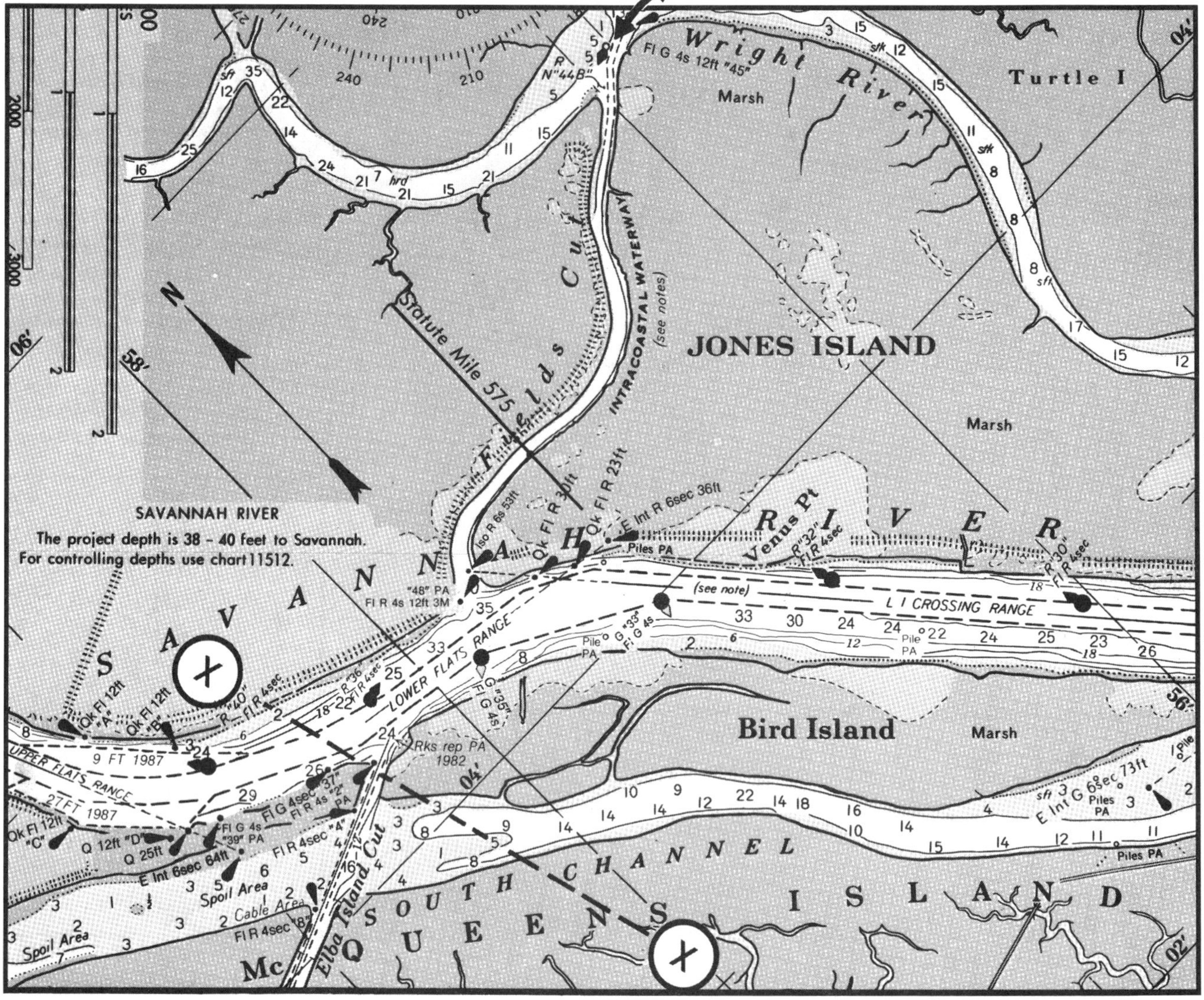


StM575

Joins Page 205

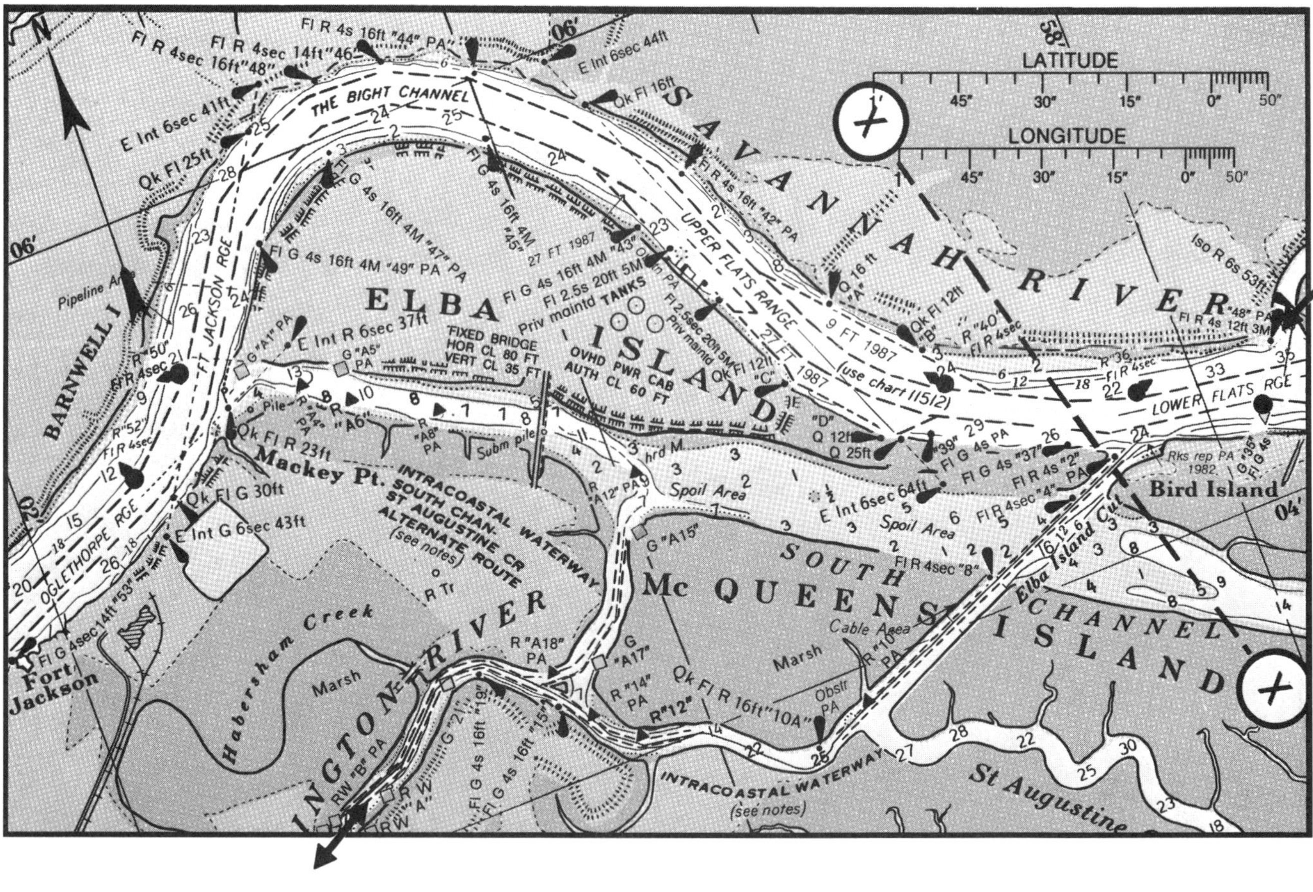

BR579.9
StM580

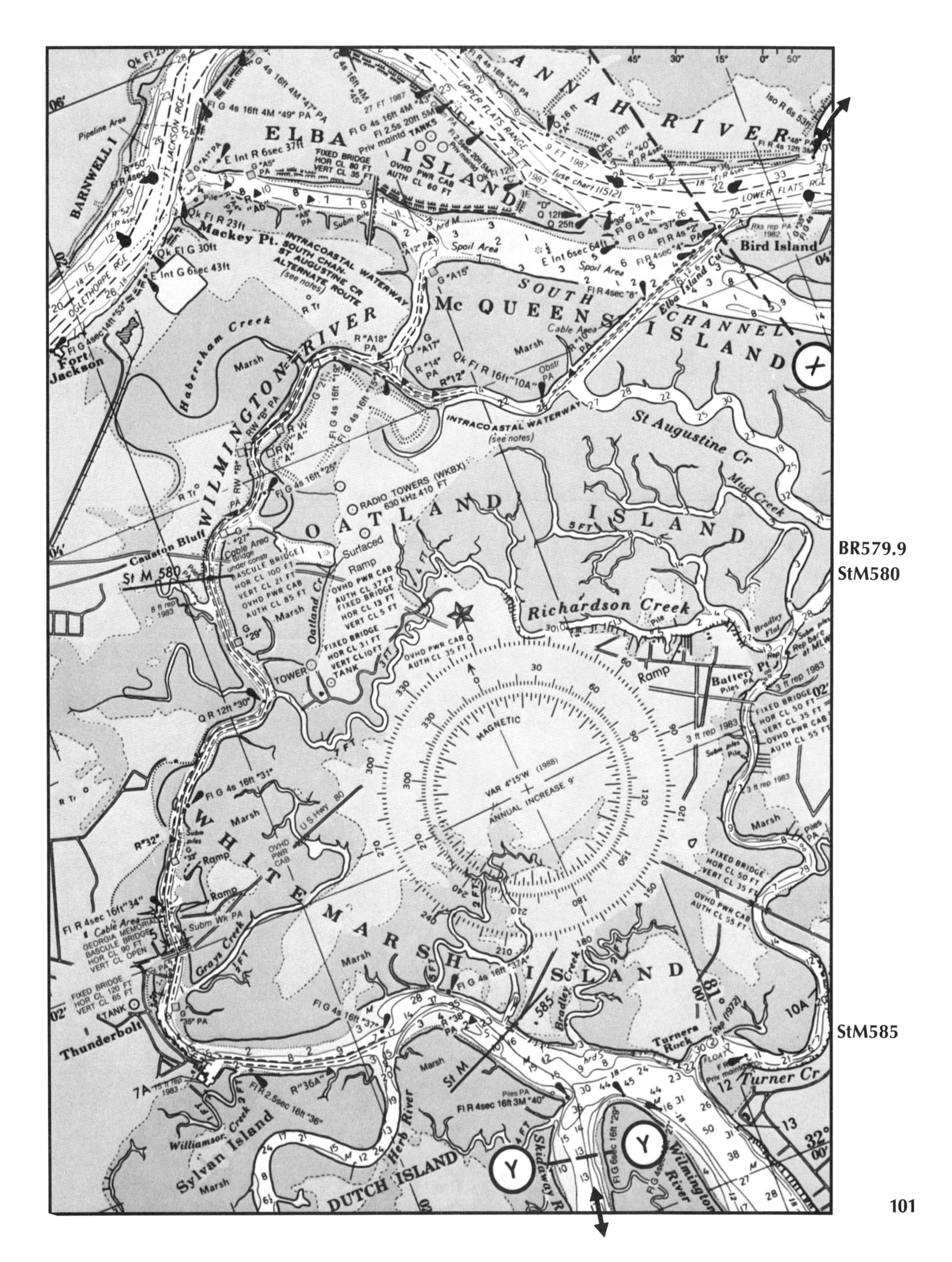

StM585

101

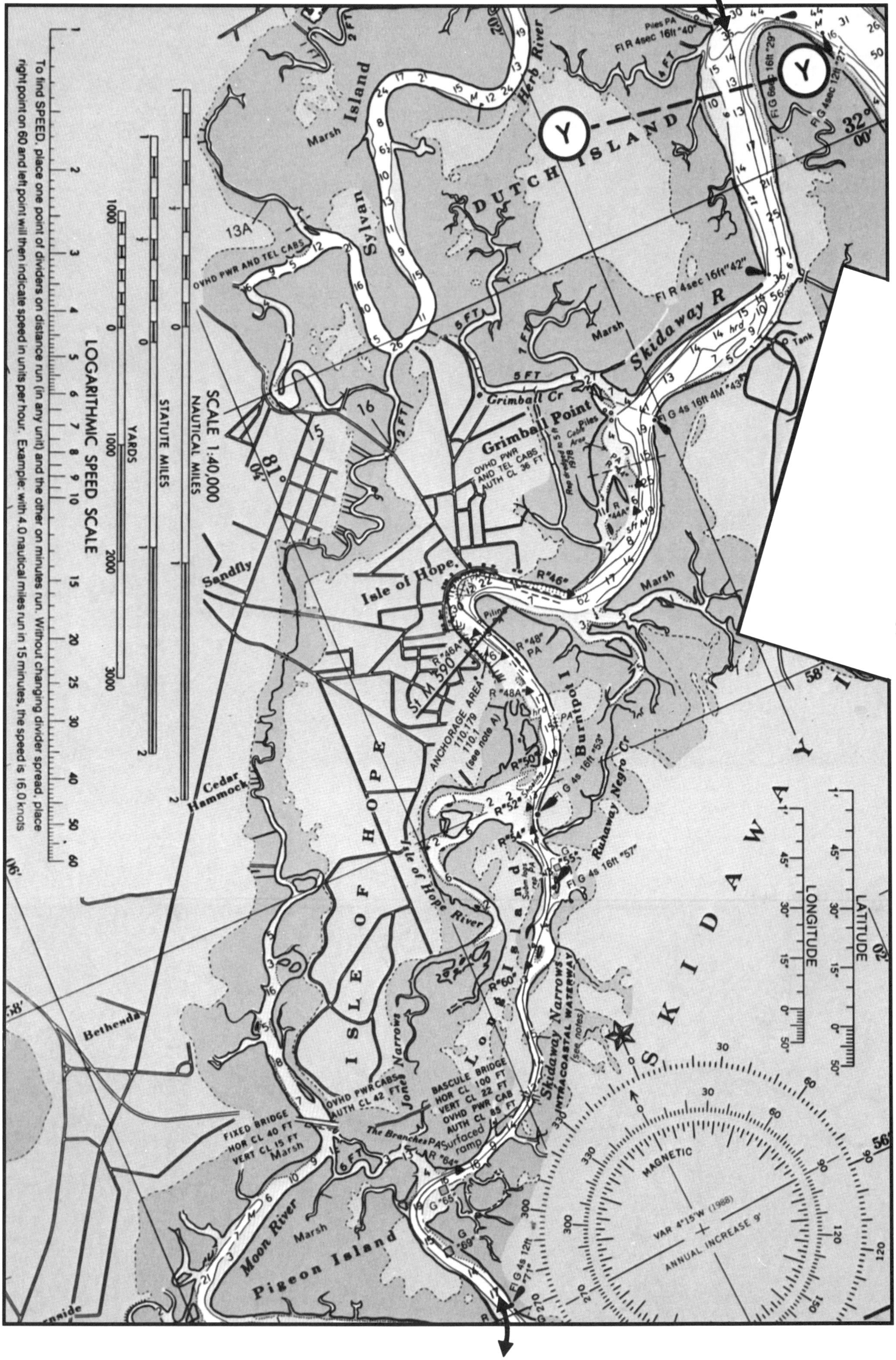


StM590

BR592.8

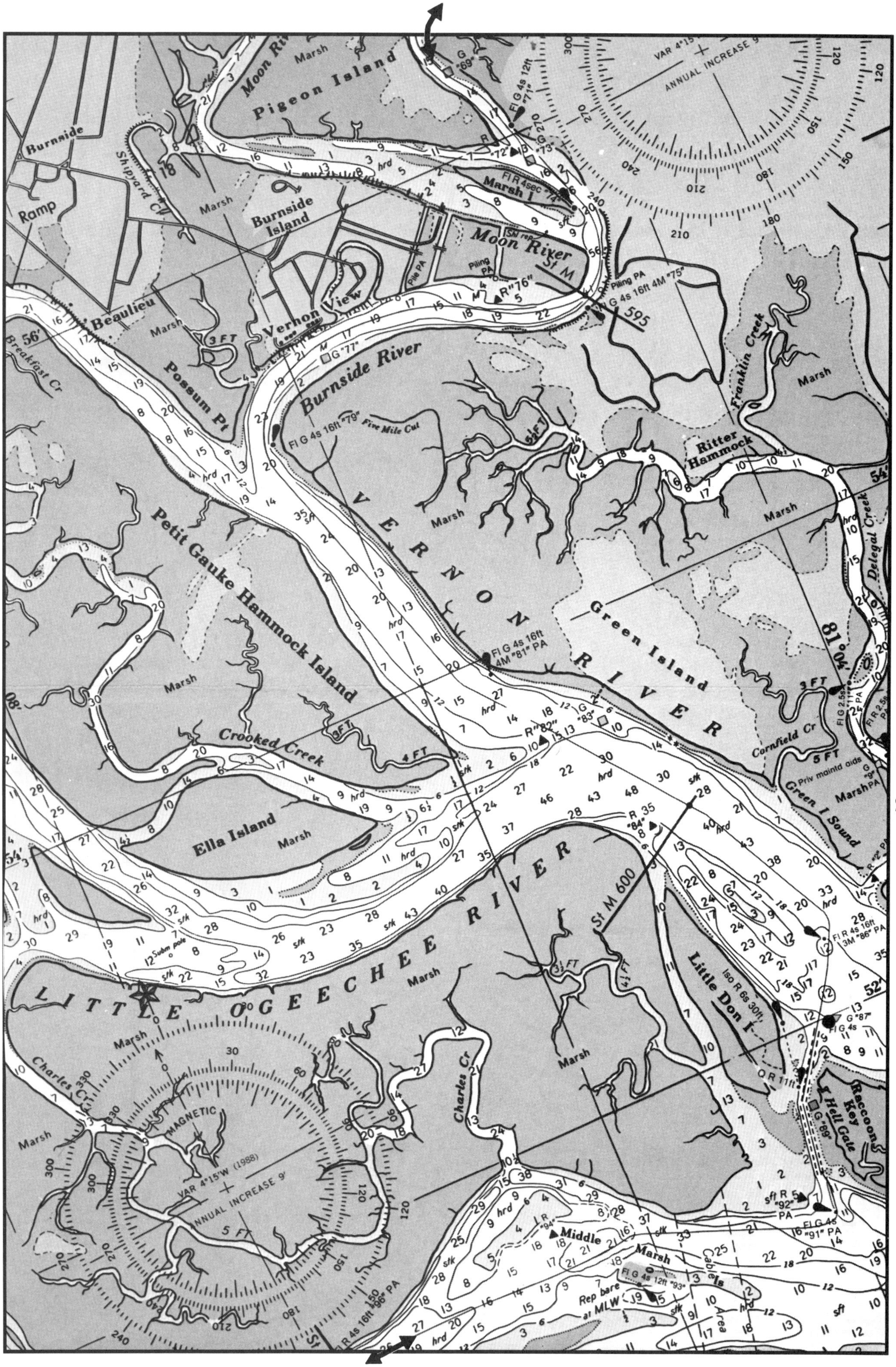


StM595

StM600

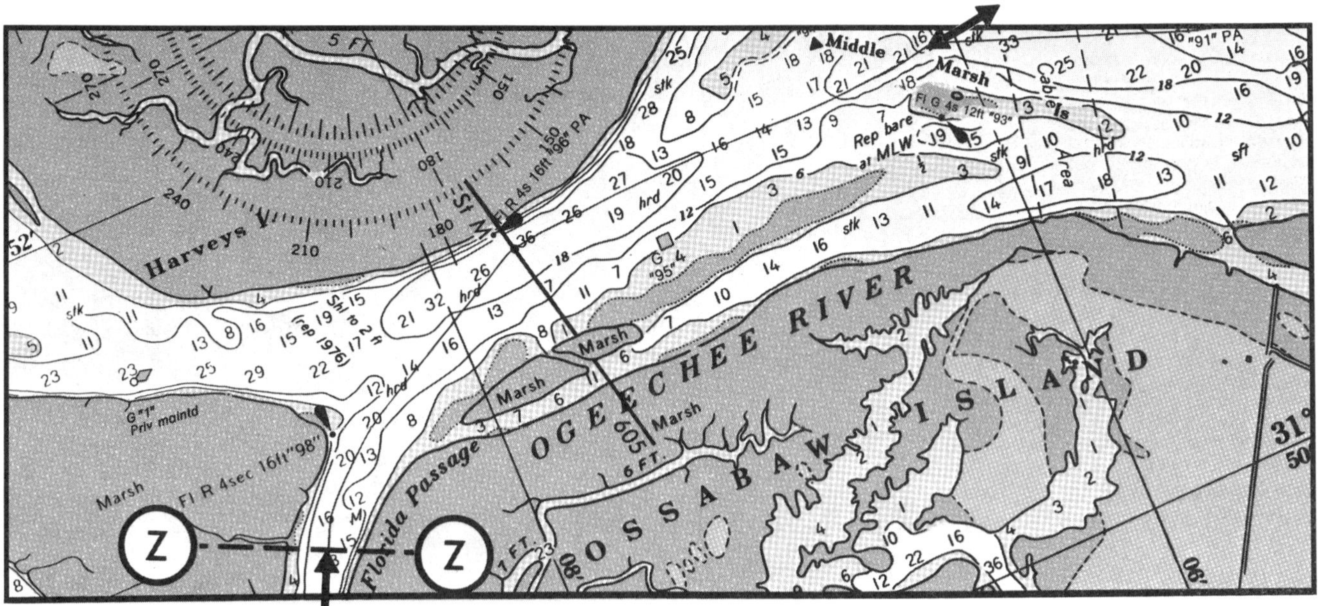


StM605

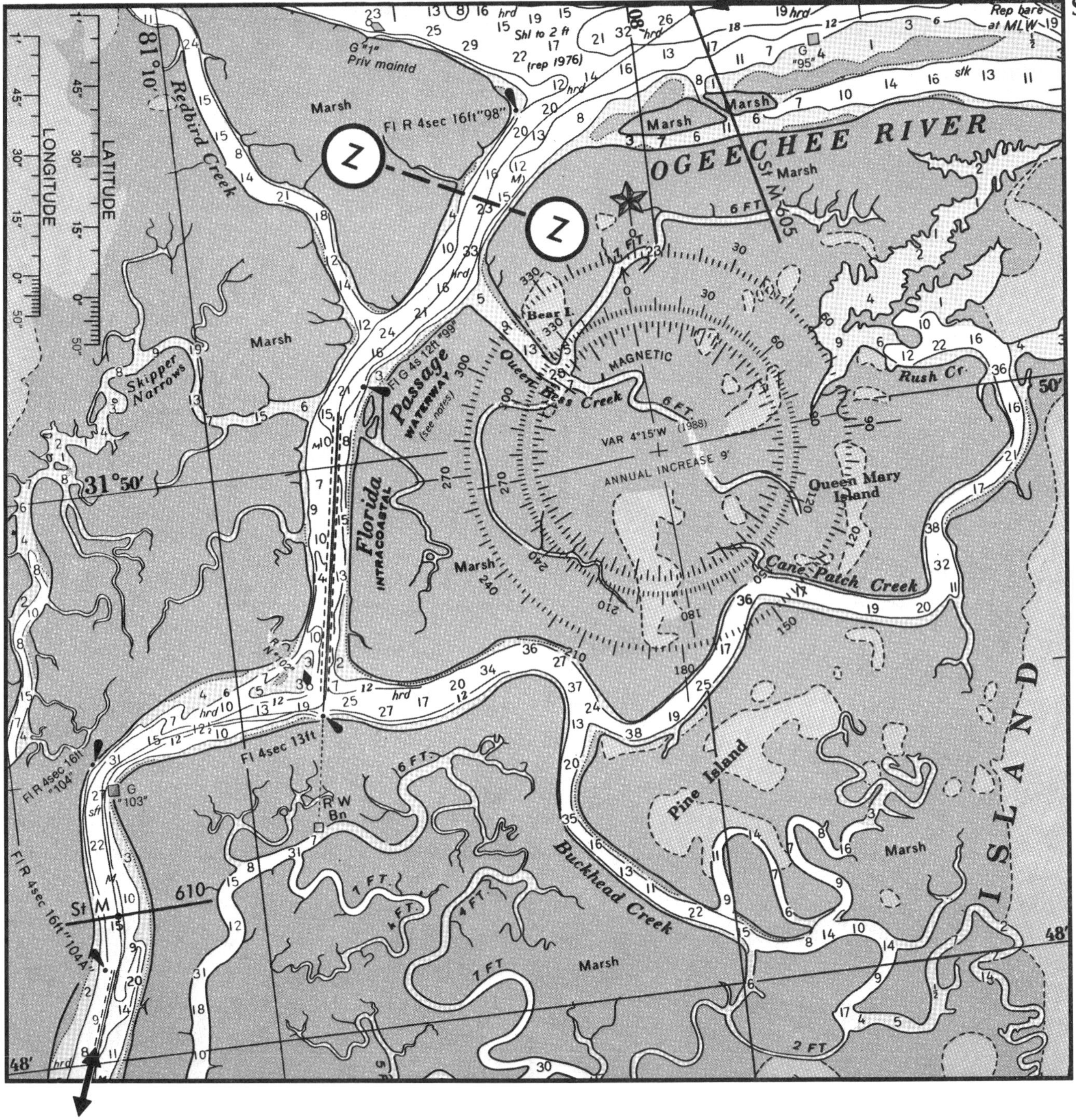


StM605

StM610

105

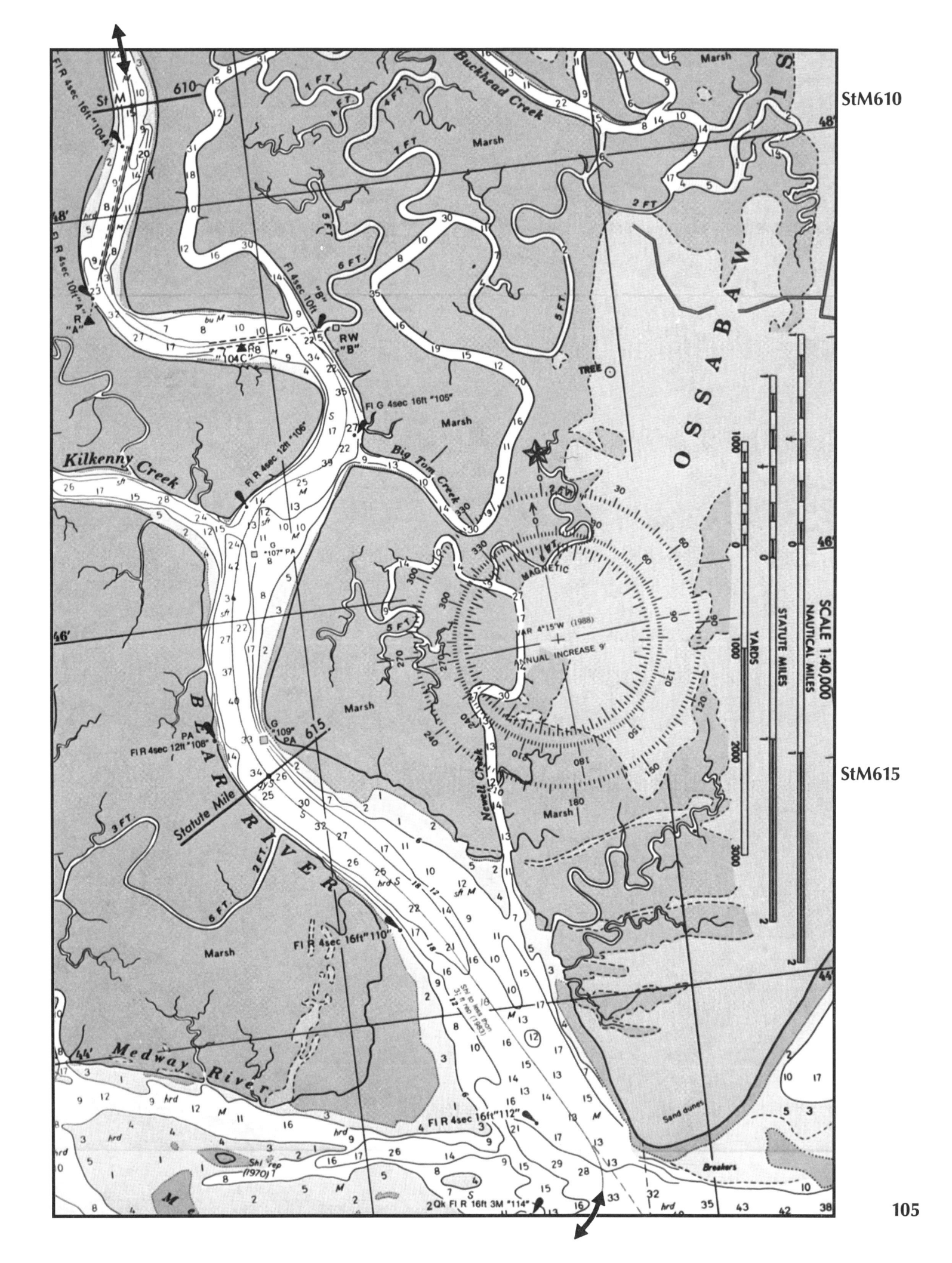

## INTRACOASTAL WATERWAY AIDS

Intracoastal Waterway aids are characterized by a yellow strip. Proceeding from Norfolk, Va., to Key West, Fla.:

1. Aids with red reflectors are on the starboard side; green reflectors are on the port side.
2. Where the Intracoastal Waterway coincides with another waterway, the dual purpose aids have distinctive yellow triangles on the starboard side and yellow squares on the port side.

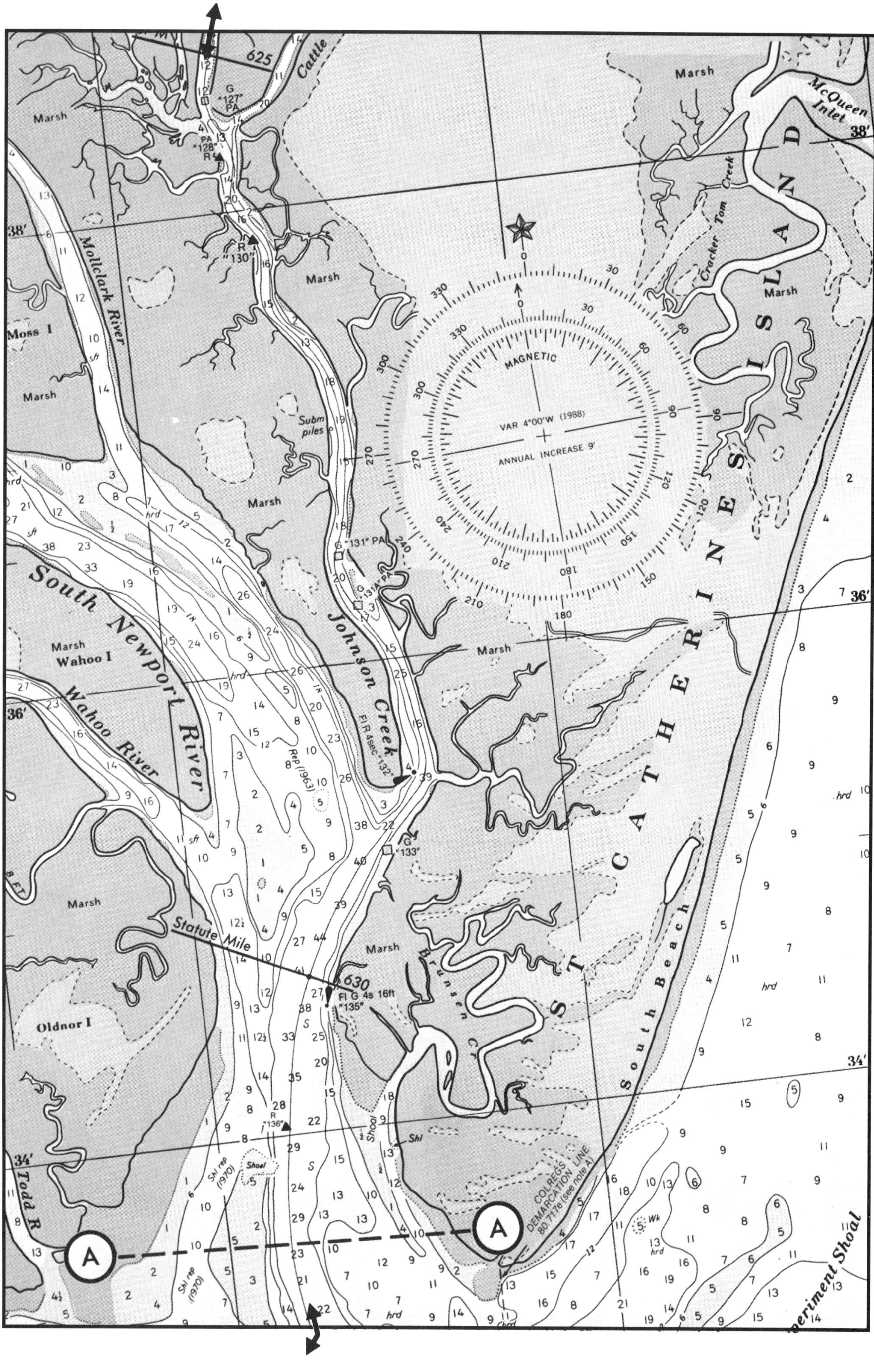
625
Cattle
Marsh
McQueen Inlet
G "127" PA
PA "128" R
R "130"
Mollclark River
Moss I
Cracker Tom Creek
ST CATHERINES ISLAND
MAGNETIC
VAR 4°00'W (1988)
ANNUAL INCREASE 9'
Subm piles
G "131" PA
G "131A" PA
South Newport River
Wahoo I
Wahoo River
Johnson Creek
Fl R 4sec "132"
Rep (1963)
G "133"
Statute Mile
630
Fl G 4s 16ft "135"
Brunsen Cr
South Beach
Oldnor I
R "136"
Shoal
Shl rep (1970)
Todd R
COLREGS DEMARCATION LINE 80.717e (see note A)
A
38'
36'
34'

Joins Page 208

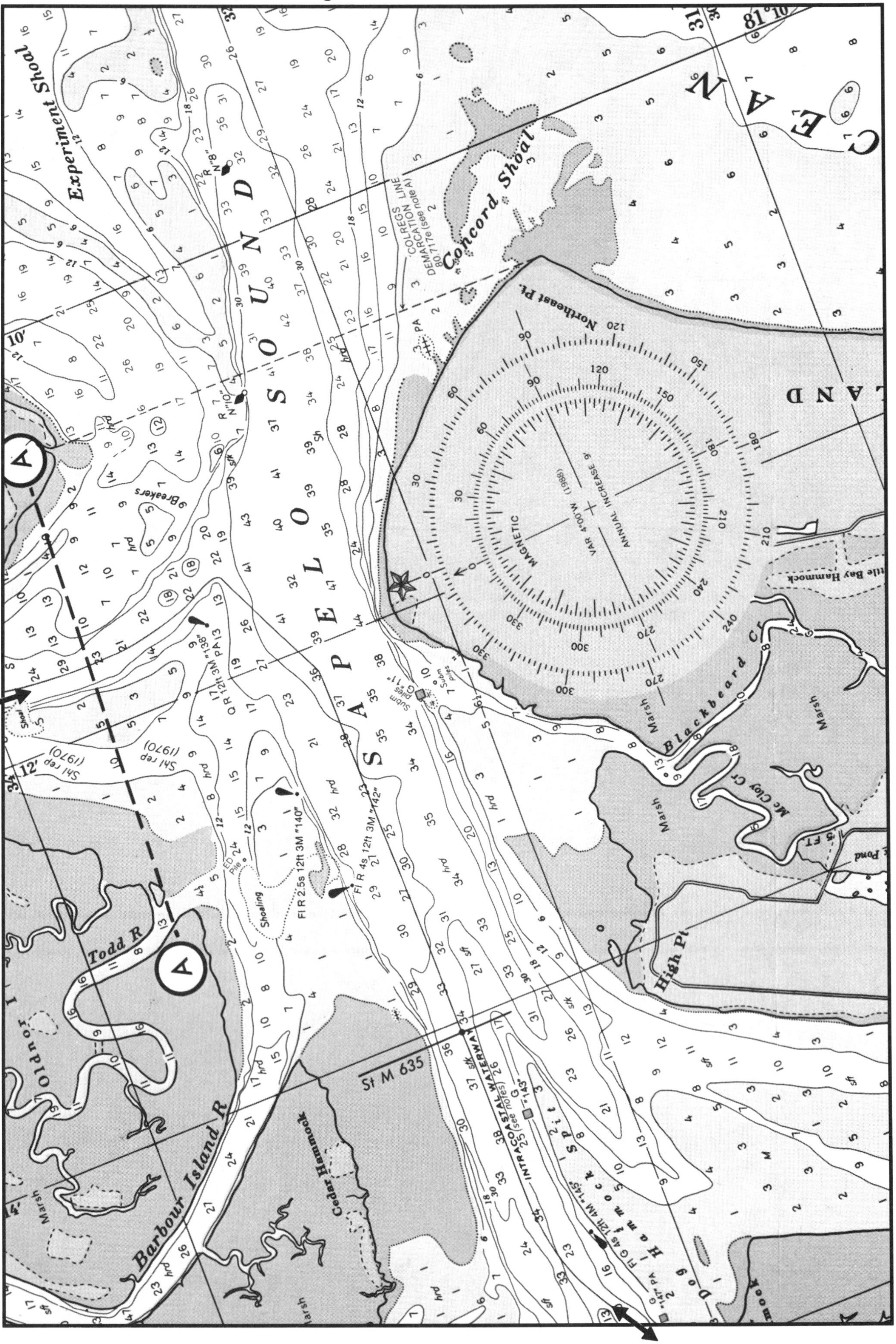


StM635

109

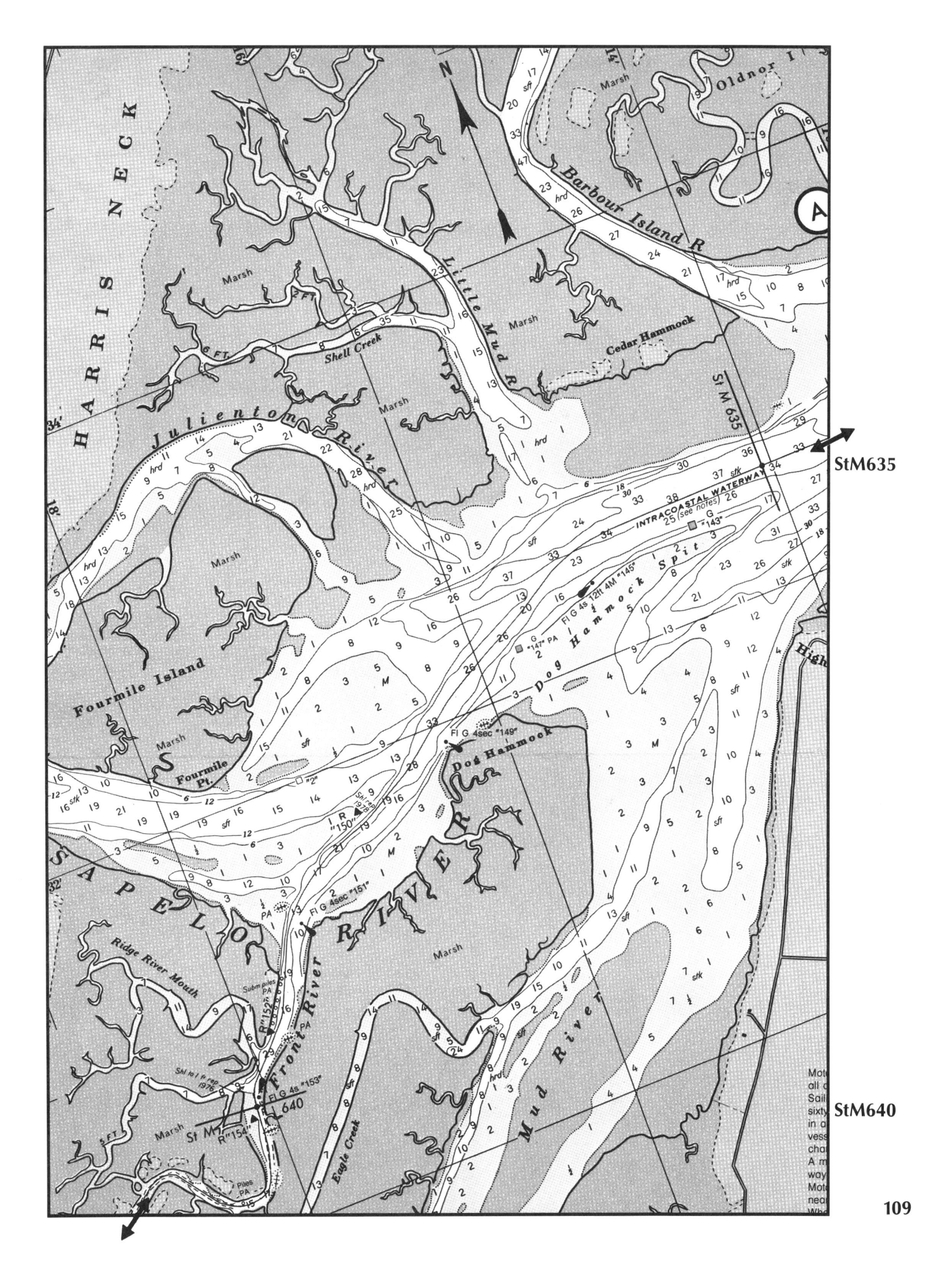

StM640

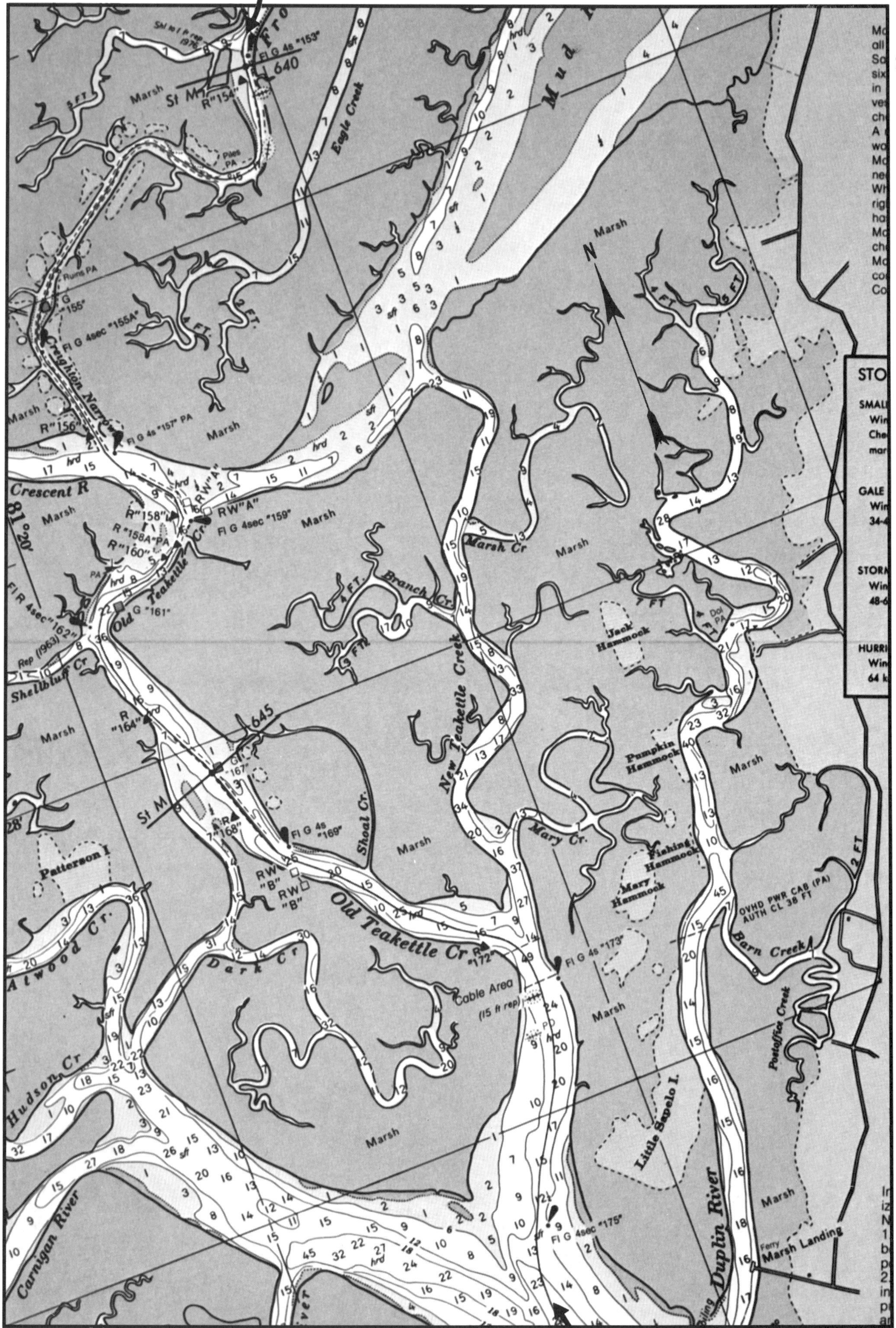


StM645

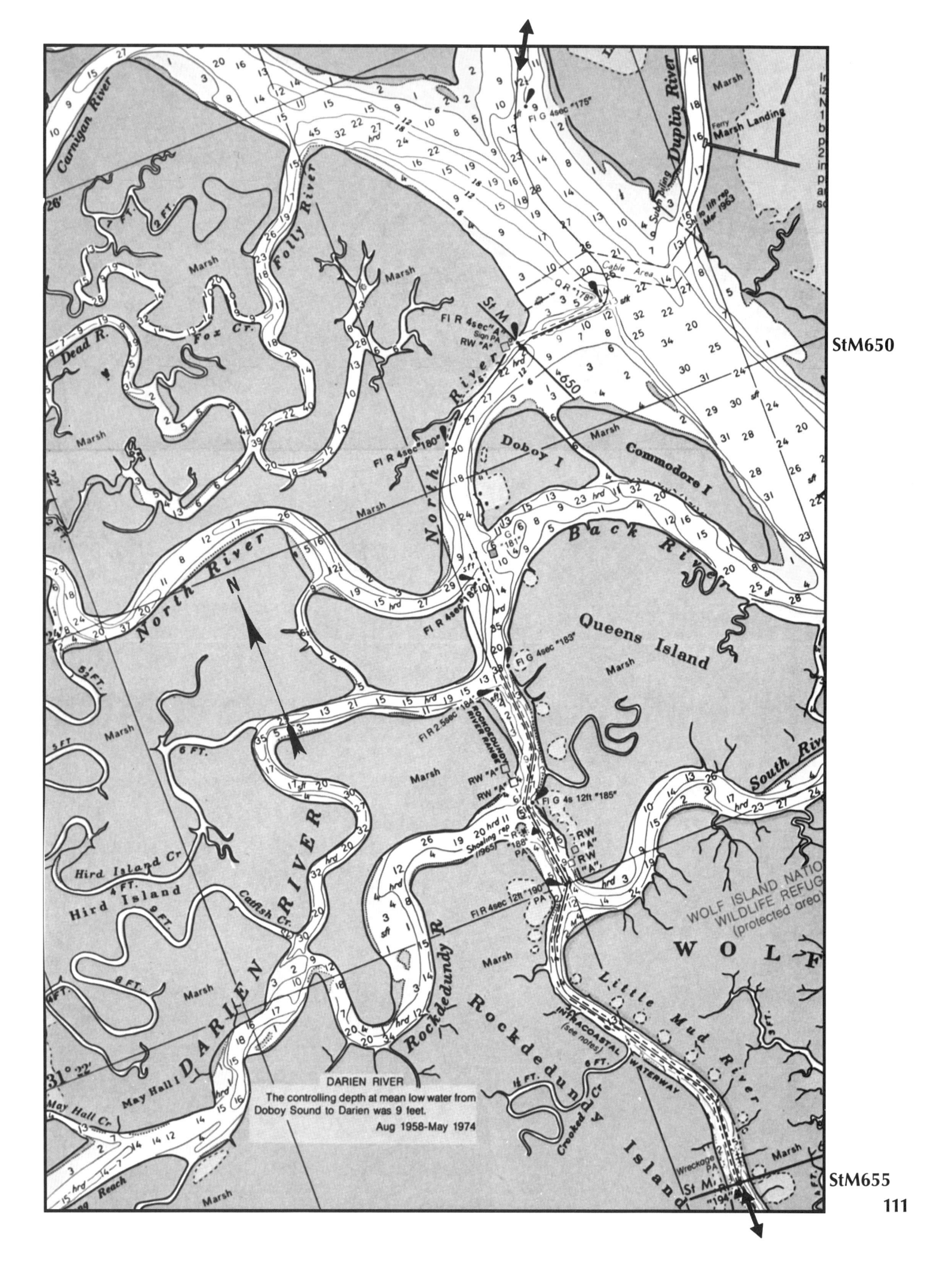

**DARIEN RIVER**
The controlling depth at mean low water from
Doboy Sound to Darien was 9 feet.
Aug 1958-May 1974

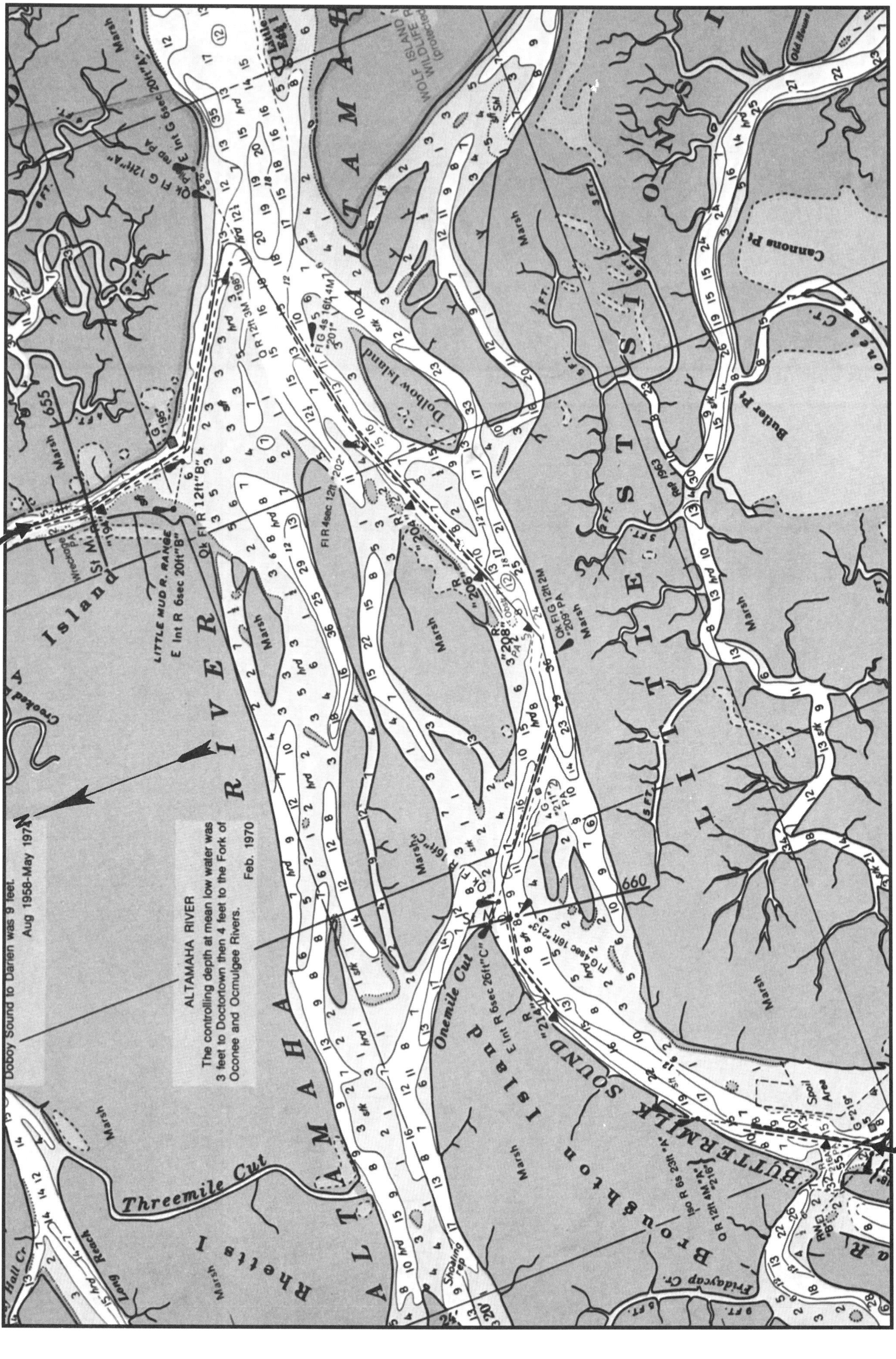


StM655

StM660

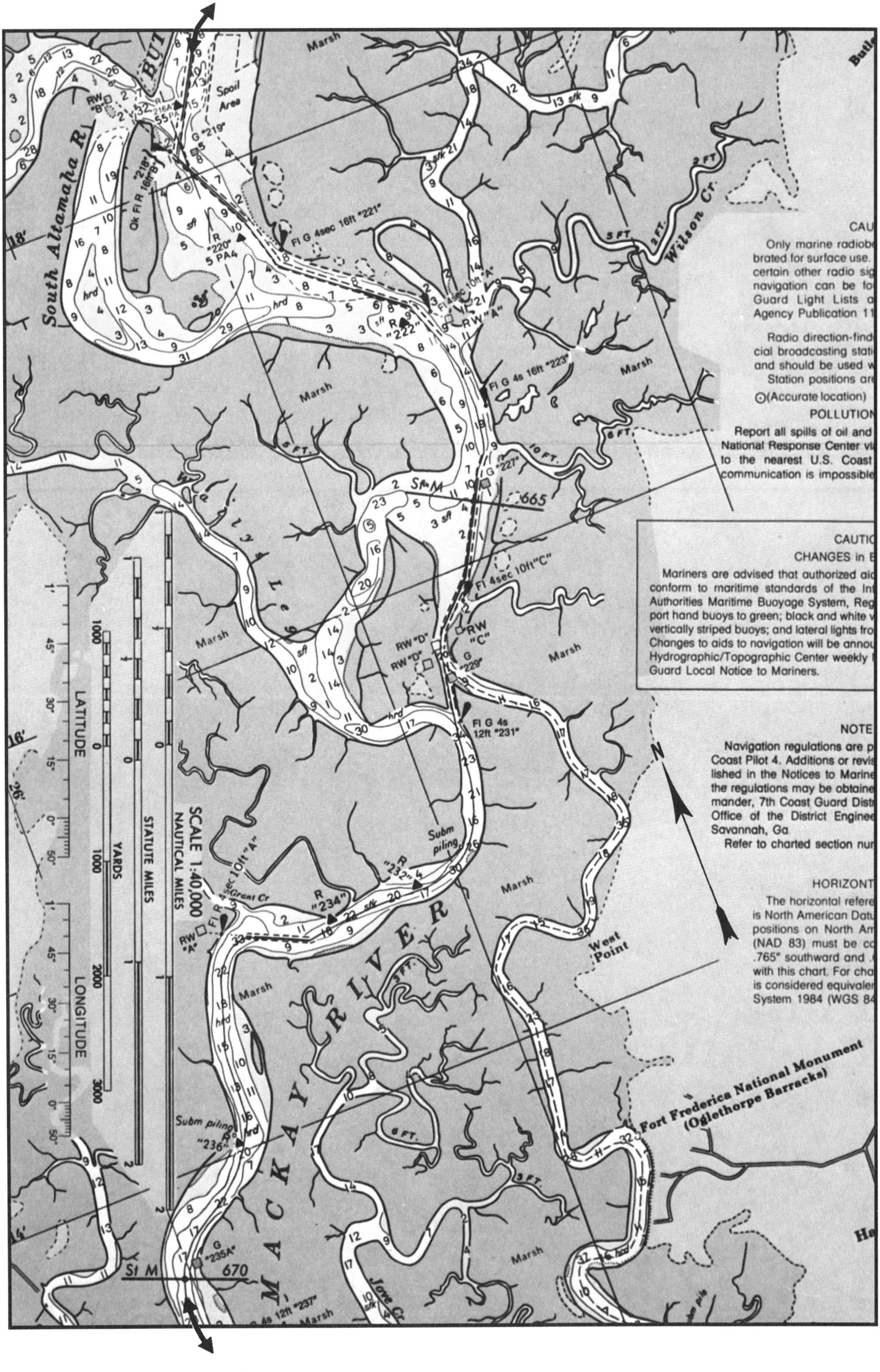


StM665

StM670

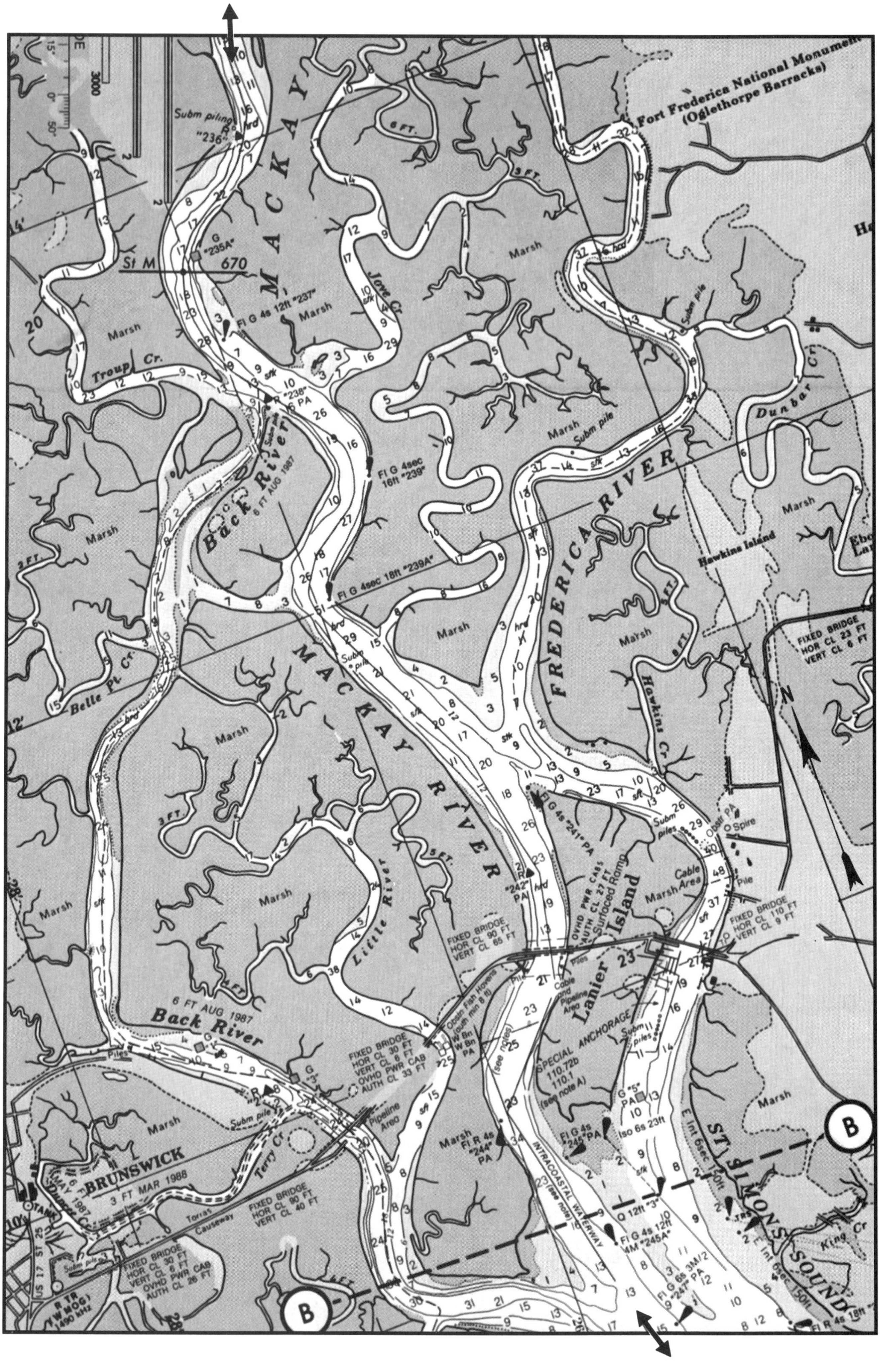


StM670

StM675

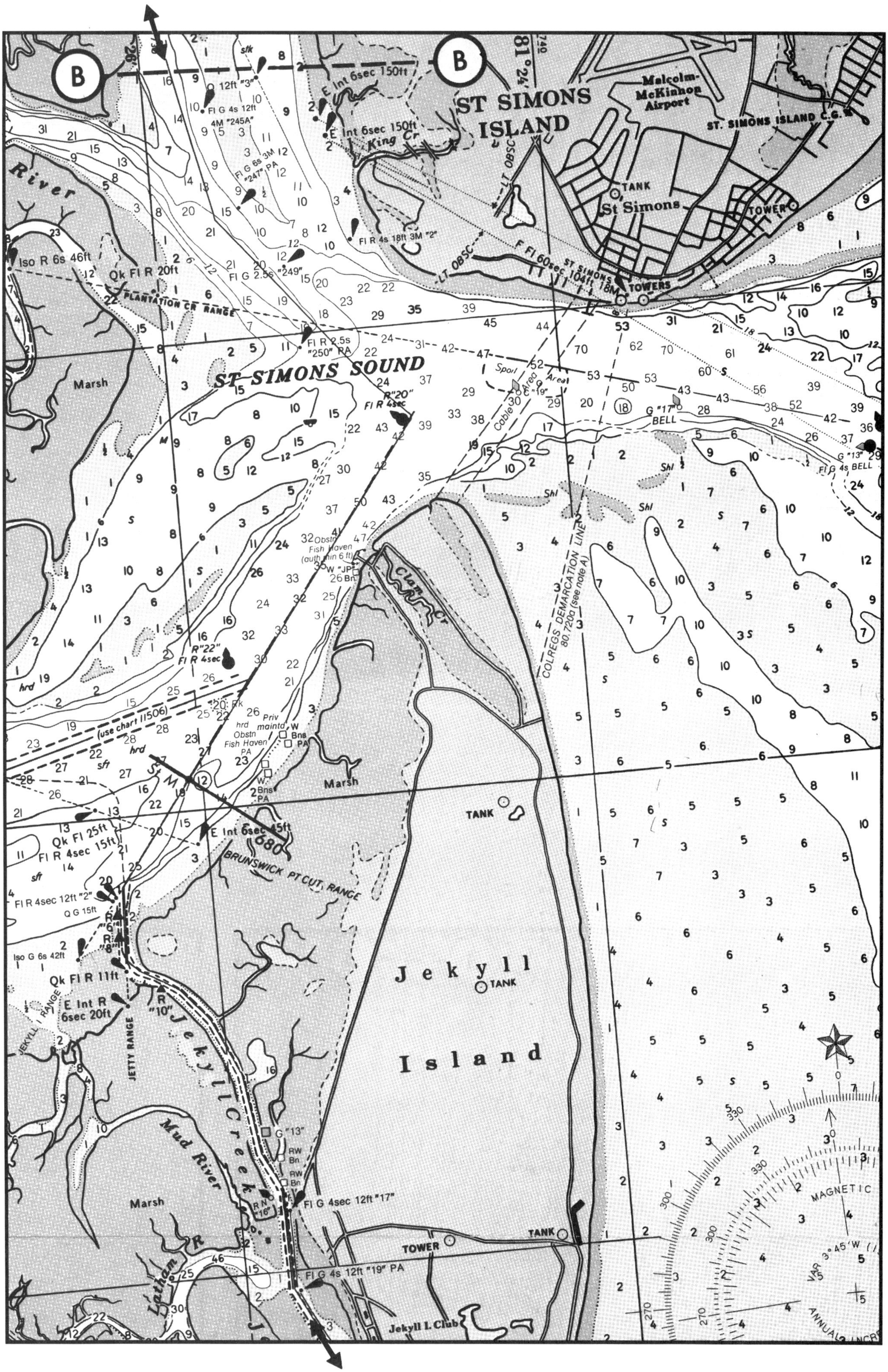


Joins Page 209

StM680

116

BR684.3

StM685

StM690

For Alternate Route Turn To Page 233

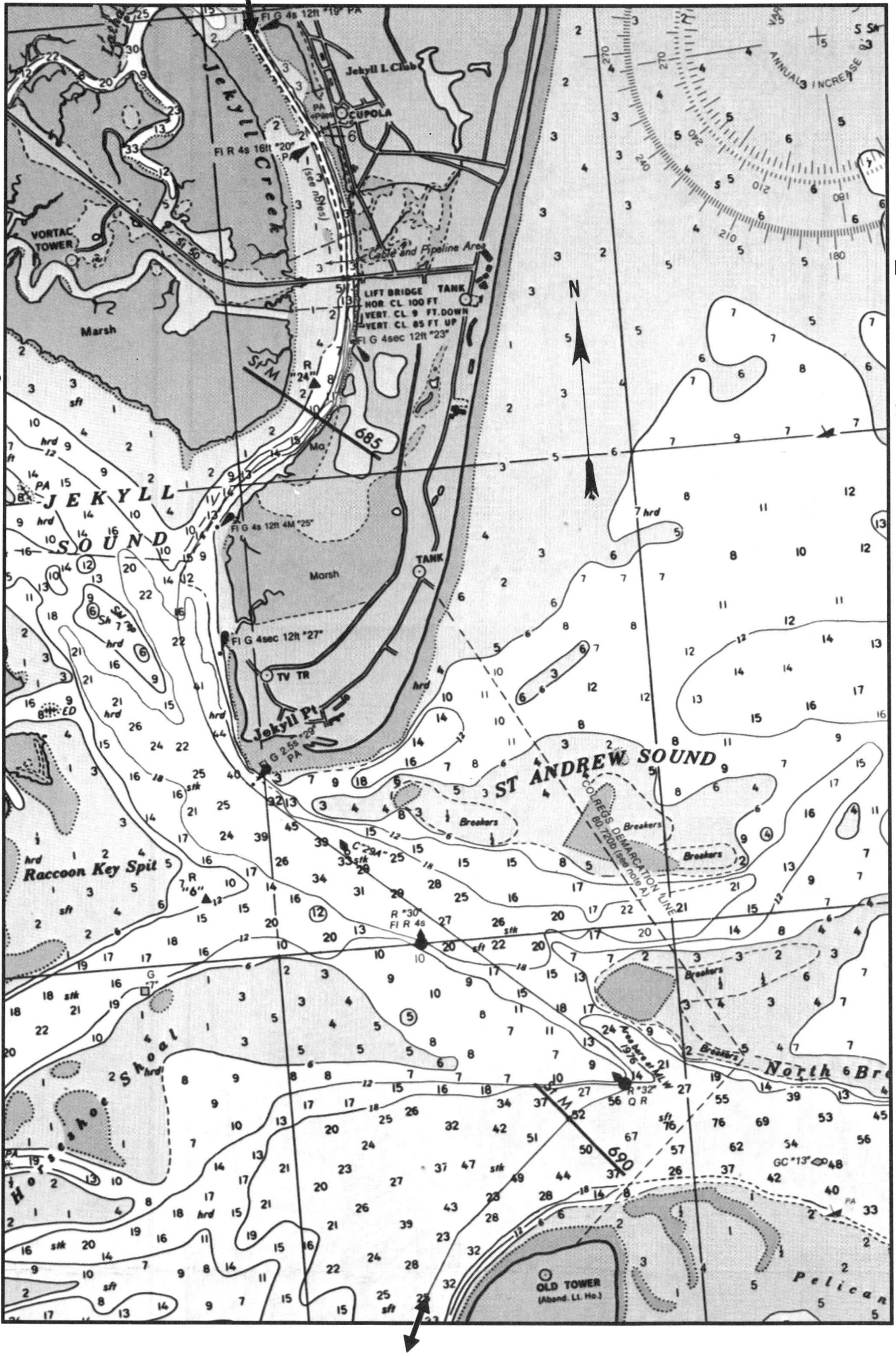

JEKYLL SOUND

ST ANDREW SOUND

Raccoon Key Spit

Horseshoe Shoal

Jekyll Creek

Jekyll I. Club

CUPOLA

VORTAC TOWER

Marsh

LIFT BRIDGE TANK
HOR. CL. 100 FT.
VERT. CL. 9 FT. DOWN
VERT. CL. 85 FT UP

Cable and Pipeline Area

TANK

TV TR

Jekyll Pt.

Breakers

COLREGS DEMARCATION LINE

North Br

Pelican

OLD TOWER
(Aband. Lt. Ho.)

Fl G 4s 12ft "19" PA

Fl R 4s 16ft "20" PA

Fl G 4sec 12ft "23"

Fl G 4s 12ft 4M "25"

Fl G 4sec 12ft "27"

R "30"
Fl R 4s

R "32"
Q R

GC "13"

StM690

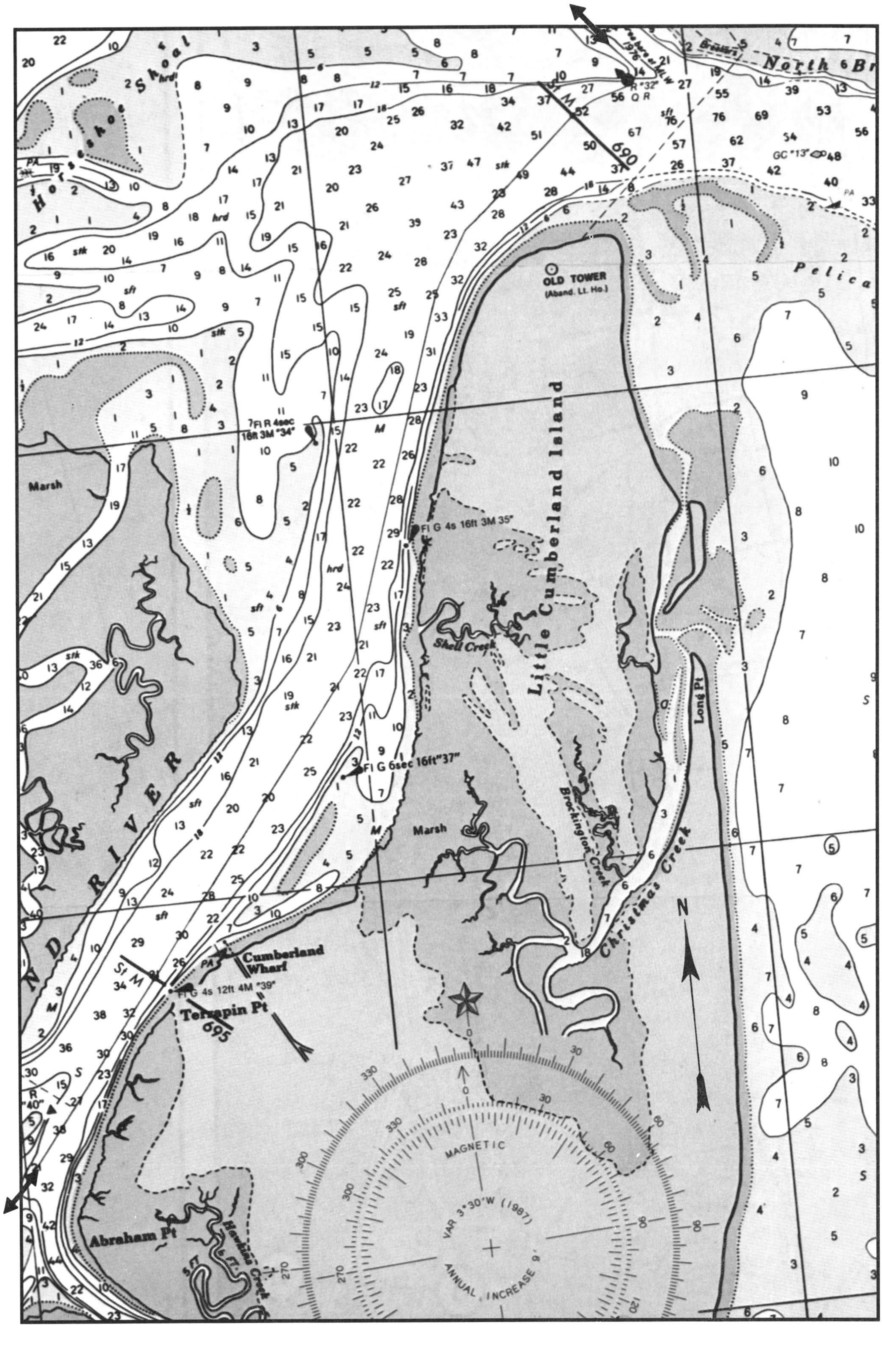


StM695

For Alternate Route Turn To Page 234

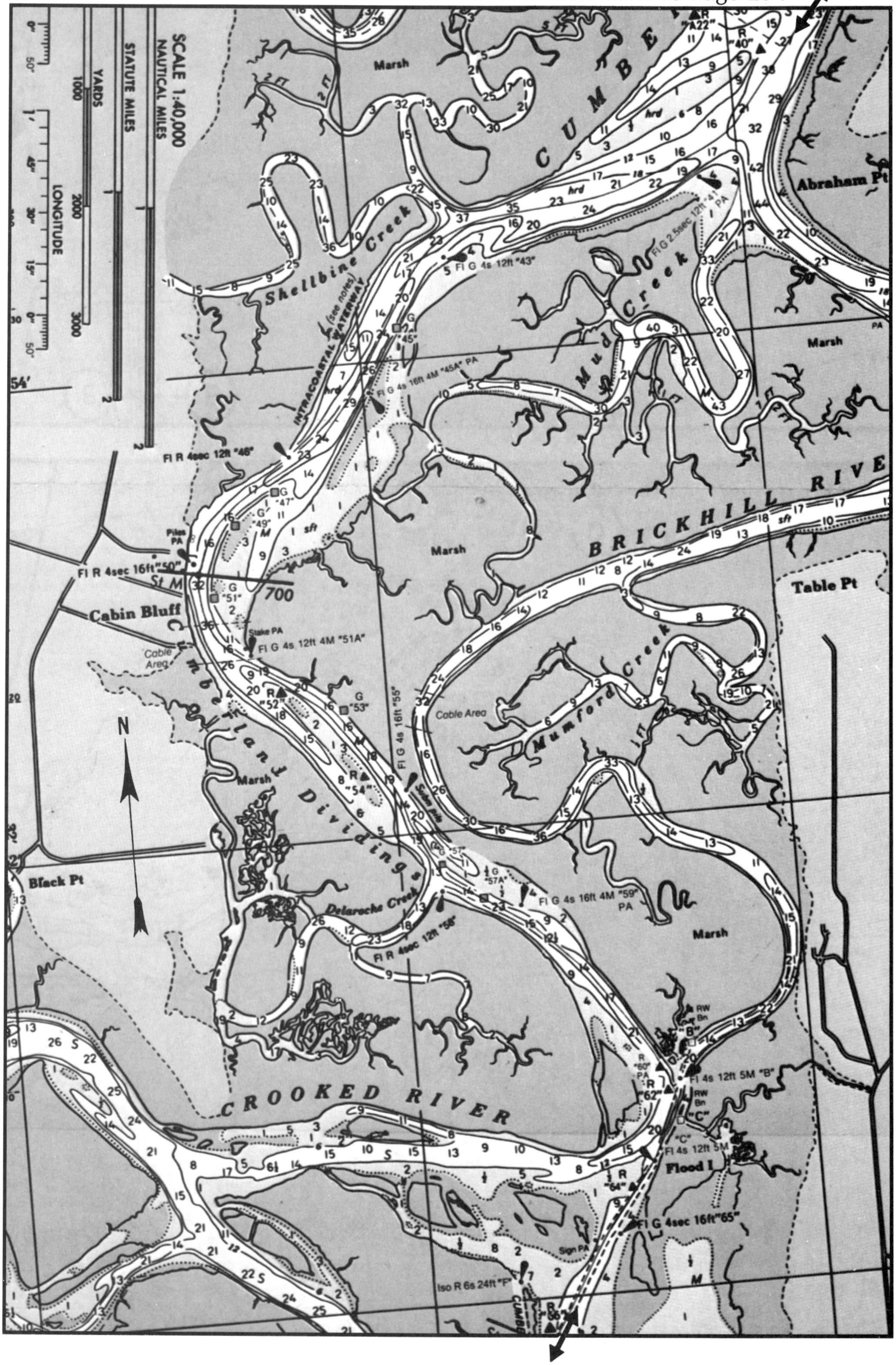


StM700

StM705

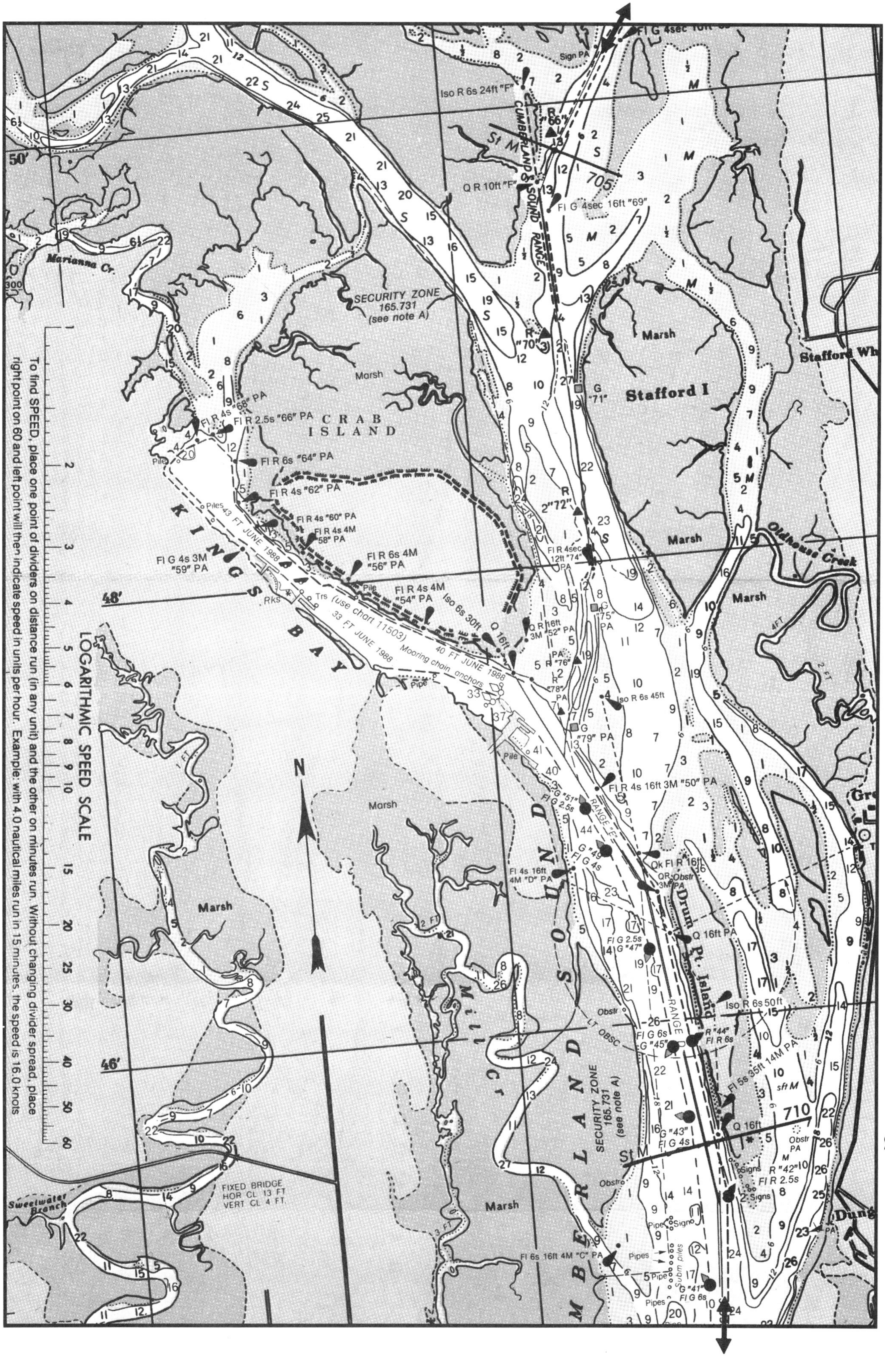


StM705

StM710

StM710

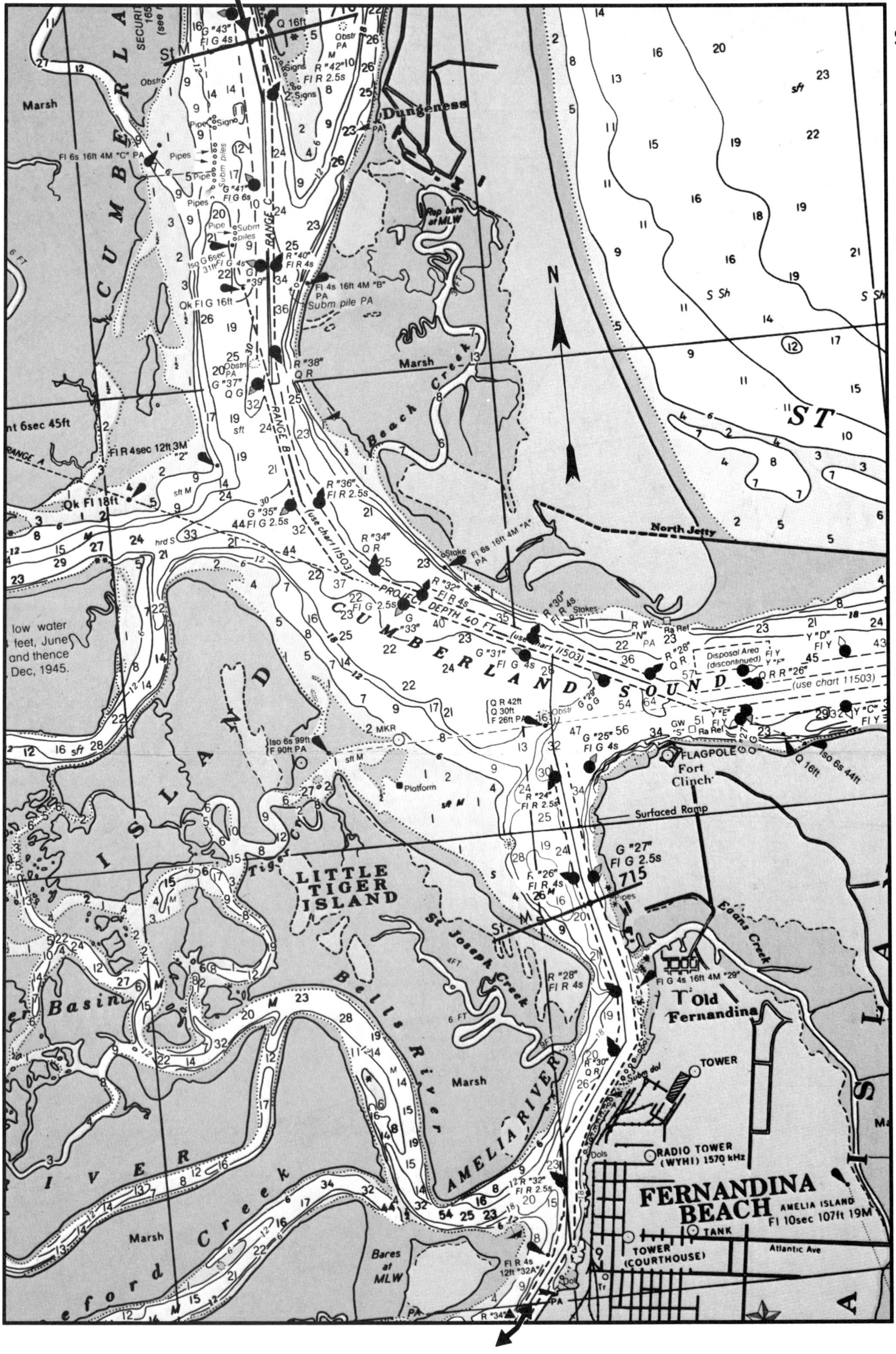


Joins Page 210

StM715

Joins Page 210

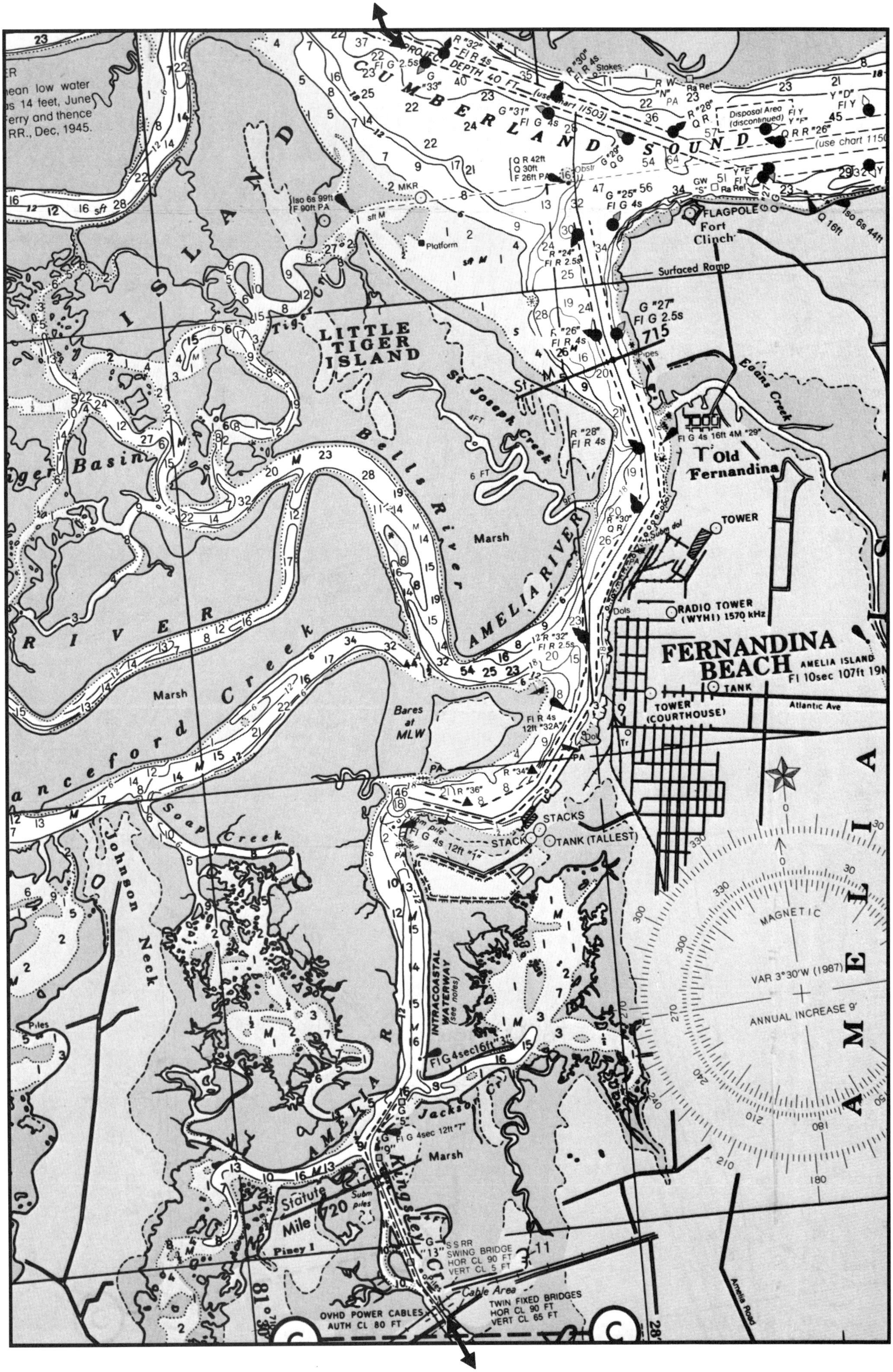


StM715

StM720

BR720.7

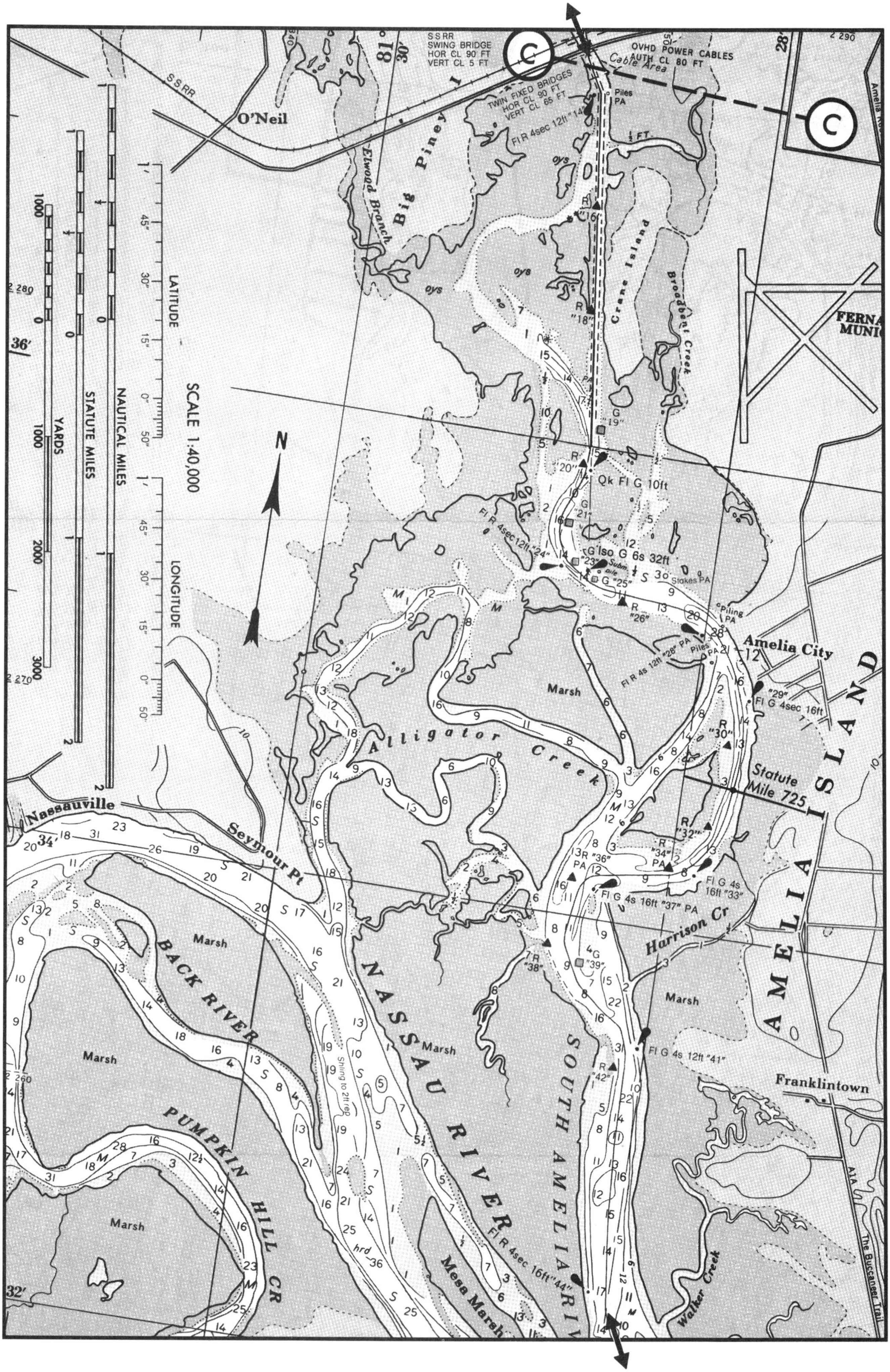
SSRR
SWING BRIDGE
HOR CL 90 FT
VERT CL 5 FT
OVHD POWER CABLES
AUTH CL 80 FT
Cable Area
TWIN FIXED BRIDGES
HOR CL 90 FT
VERT CL 65 FT
Piles PA
Fl R 4sec 12ft "14"
O'Neil
Big Piney
Elwood Branch
Crane Island
Broadbent Creek
FERNA
MUNIC
R "16"
R "18"
G "19"
R "20"
Qk Fl G 10ft
G "21"
Fl R 4sec 12ft "24"
G "23"
Iso G 6s 32ft
G "25"
Stakes PA
R "26"
Piling PA
Amelia City
Piles PA
Fl R 4s 12ft "28" PA
"29"
Fl G 4sec 16ft
R "30"
Statute Mile 725
AMELIA ISLAND
R "32"
R "34" PA
13R "36" PA
Fl G 4s 16ft "33"
Fl G 4s 16ft "37" PA
Harrison Cr
7R "38"
4G "39"
Marsh
Fl G 4s 12ft "41"
R "42"
Franklintown
A1A
The Buccaneer Trail
Walker Creek
SOUTH AMELIA RIV
Fl R 4sec 16ft "44"
Mesa Marsh
NASSAU RIVER
Shling to 2ft rep
hrd
Alligator Creek
Nassauville
Seymour Pt
BACK RIVER
PUMPKIN HILL CR
SCALE 1:40,000
LATITUDE
LONGITUDE
NAUTICAL MILES
STATUTE MILES
YARDS
N
81°
30'
28°
36'
34'
32'
oys

StM725

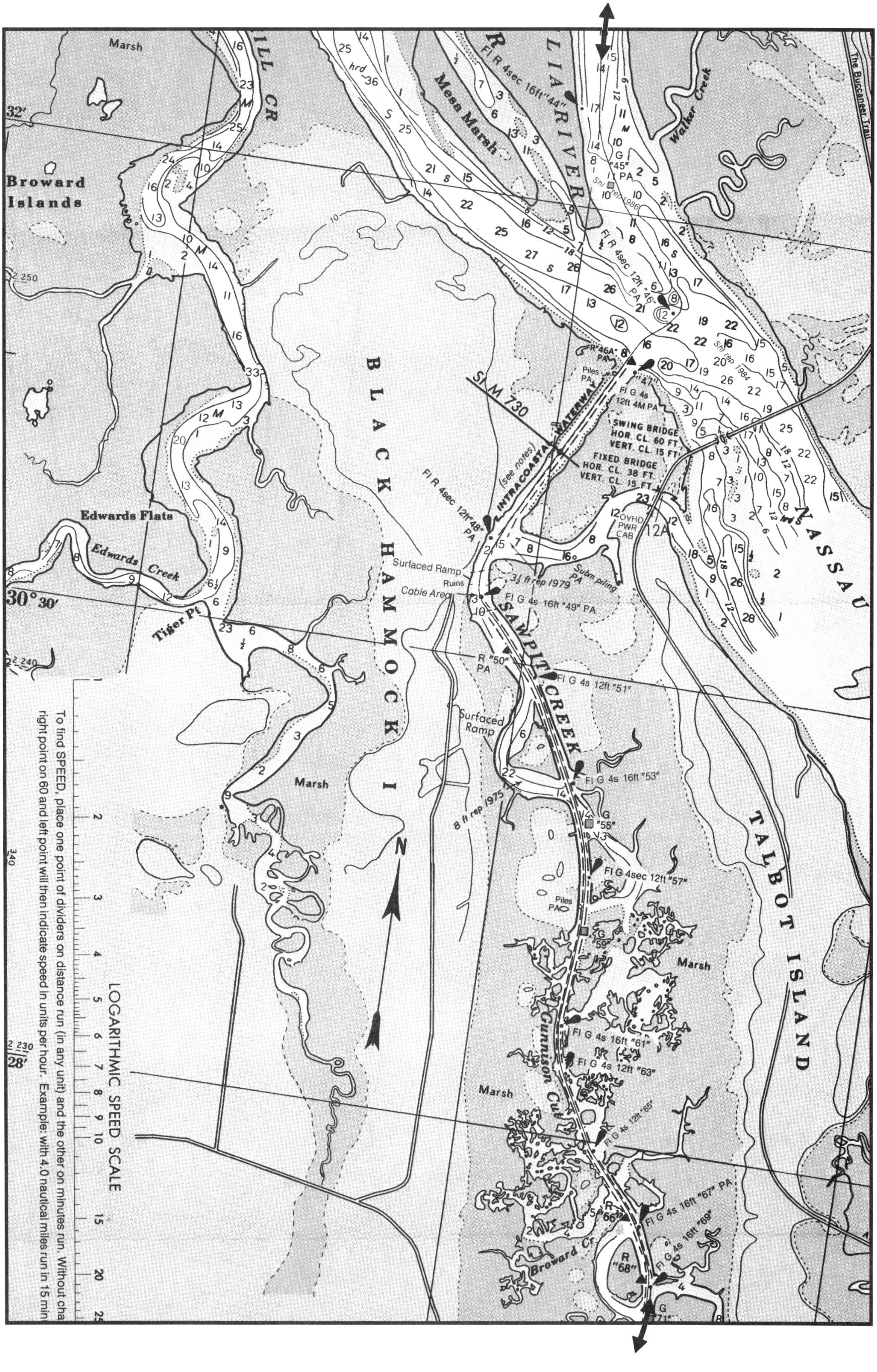
Broward Islands
Marsh
Mesa Marsh
Walker Creek
The Buccaneer Trail
BLACK HAMMOCK I
NASSAU
TALBOT ISLAND
SAWPIT CREEK
INTRACOASTAL WATERWAY
St M 730
SWING BRIDGE HOR. CL. 60 FT. VERT. CL. 15 FT.
FIXED BRIDGE HOR. CL. 38 FT. VERT. CL. 15 FT.
OVHD PWR CAB
Edwards Flats
Edwards Creek
Tiger Pt
Surfaced Ramp
Ruins
Cable Area
Subm piling PA
Piles PA
Gunnison Cut
Broward Cr
LOGARITHMIC SPEED SCALE
To find SPEED, place one point of dividers on distance run (in any unit) and the other on minutes run. Without cha
right point on 60 and left point will then indicate speed in units per hour. Example: with 4.0 nautical miles run in 15 min

StM730

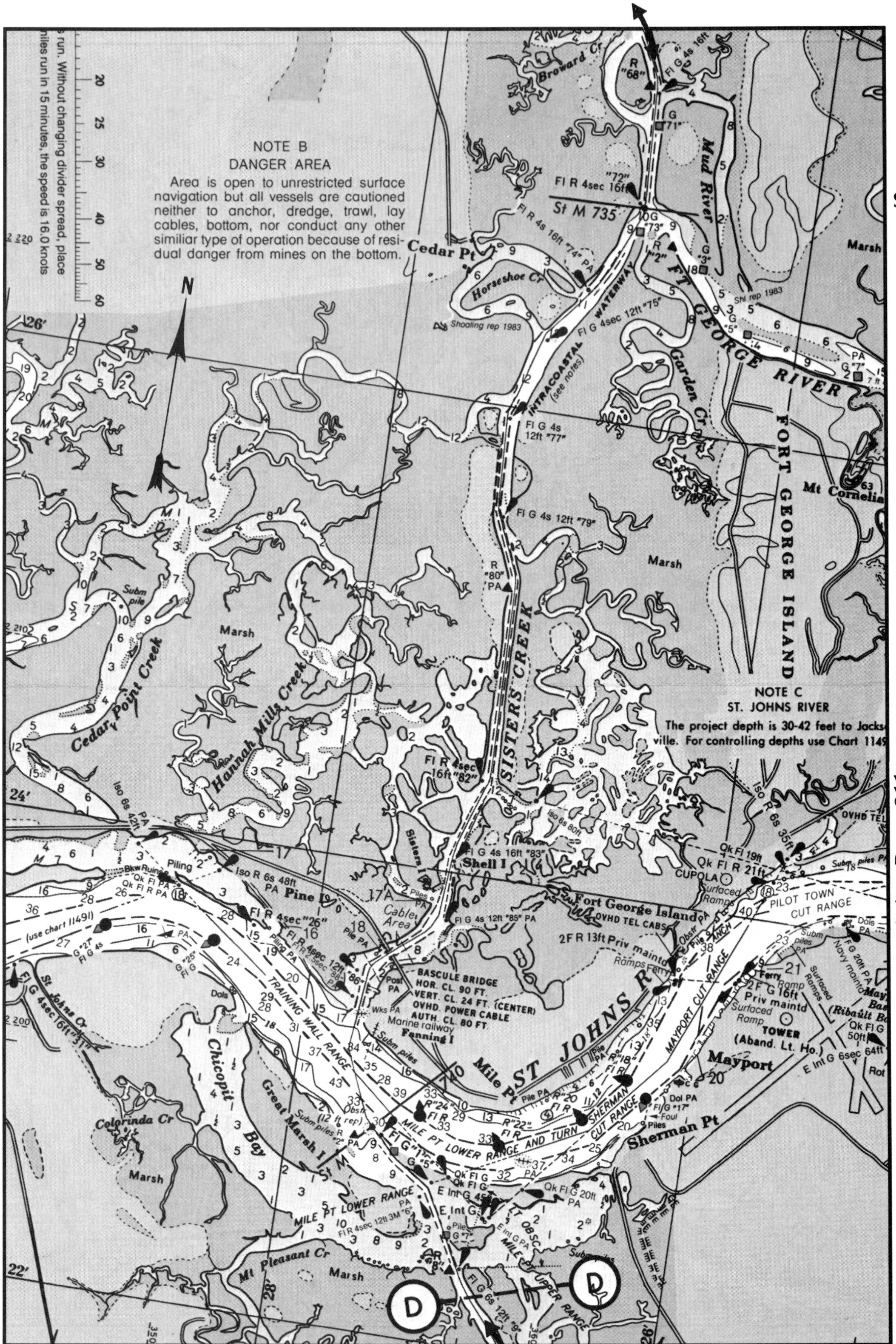


StM735

Joins Page 211

BR739.2

StM740

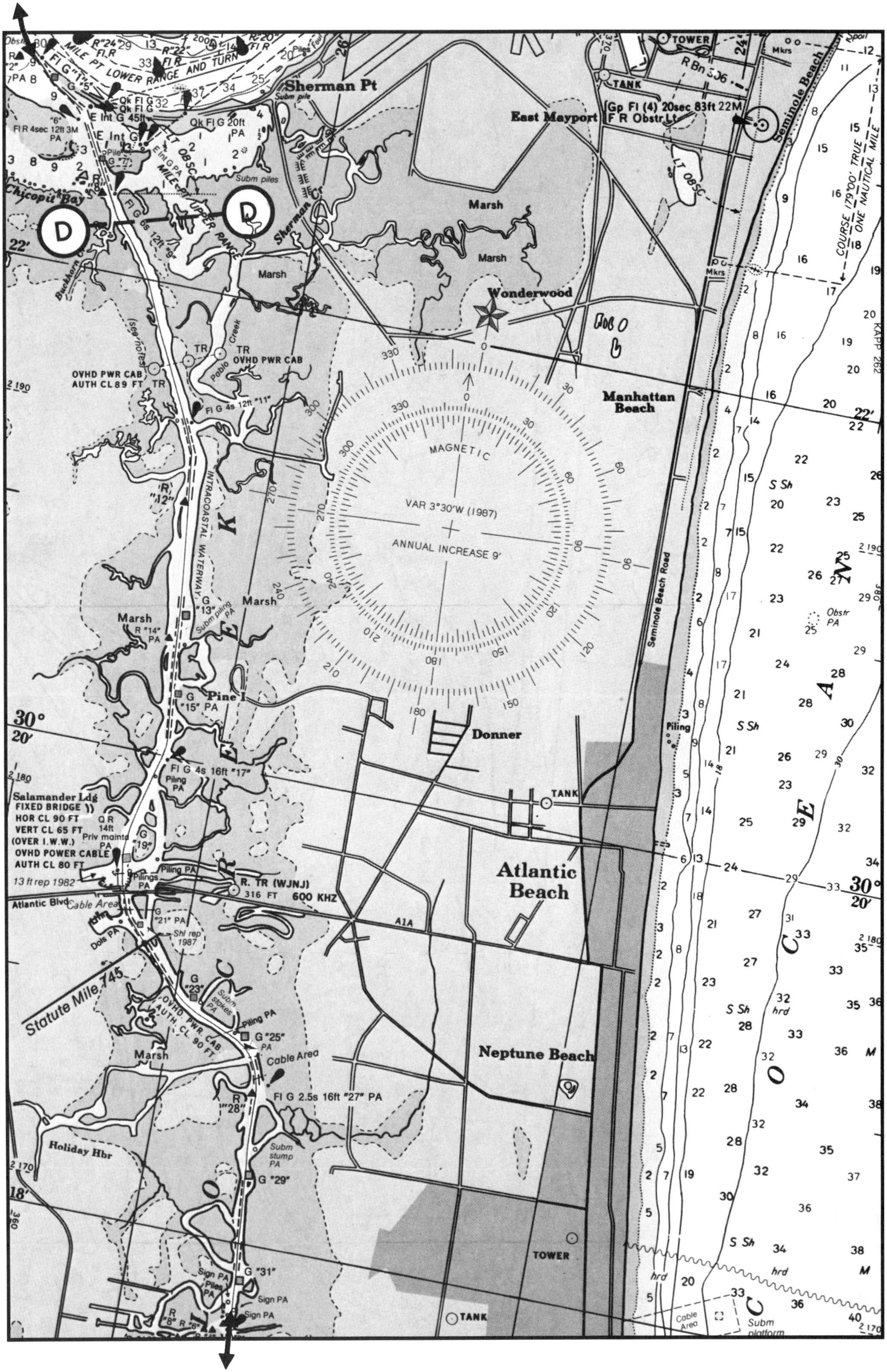
Sherman Pt
East Mayport
TOWER
TANK
Gp Fl (4) 20sec 83ft 22M
F R Obstr Lt
Seminole Beach
COURSE 179°00' TRUE
ONE NAUTICAL MILE
Chicopit Bay
MILE PT LOWER RANGE AND TURN
MILE PT UPPER RANGE
Sherman Cr
Marsh
Wonderwood
Pablo Creek
OVHD PWR CAB
AUTH CL 89 FT
Manhattan Beach
MAGNETIC
VAR 3°30'W (1987)
ANNUAL INCREASE 9'
INTRACOASTAL WATERWAY
Seminole Beach Road
Pine I
Donner
Salamander Ldg
FIXED BRIDGE
HOR CL 90 FT
VERT CL 65 FT
(OVER I.W.W.)
OVHD POWER CABLE
AUTH CL 80 FT
13 ft rep 1982
Atlantic Blvd
Cable Area
R. TR (WJNJ)
316 FT
600 KHZ
A1A
Atlantic Beach
Statute Mile 745
OVHD PWR CAB
AUTH CL 90 FT
Neptune Beach
Fl G 2.5s 16ft "27" PA
Holiday Hbr
TOWER
TANK
O C E A N
30°
20'
22'
18'

StM745

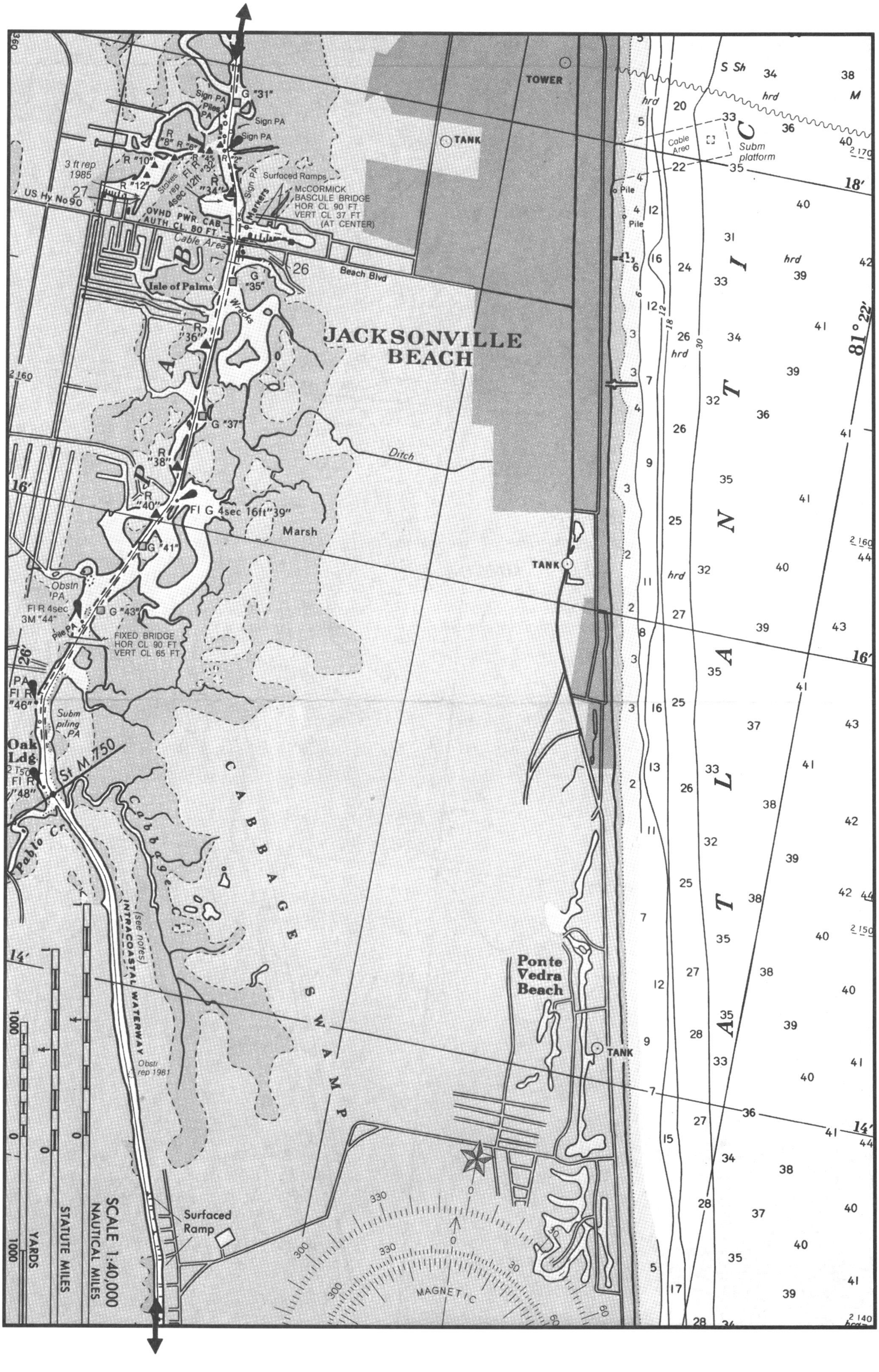

126

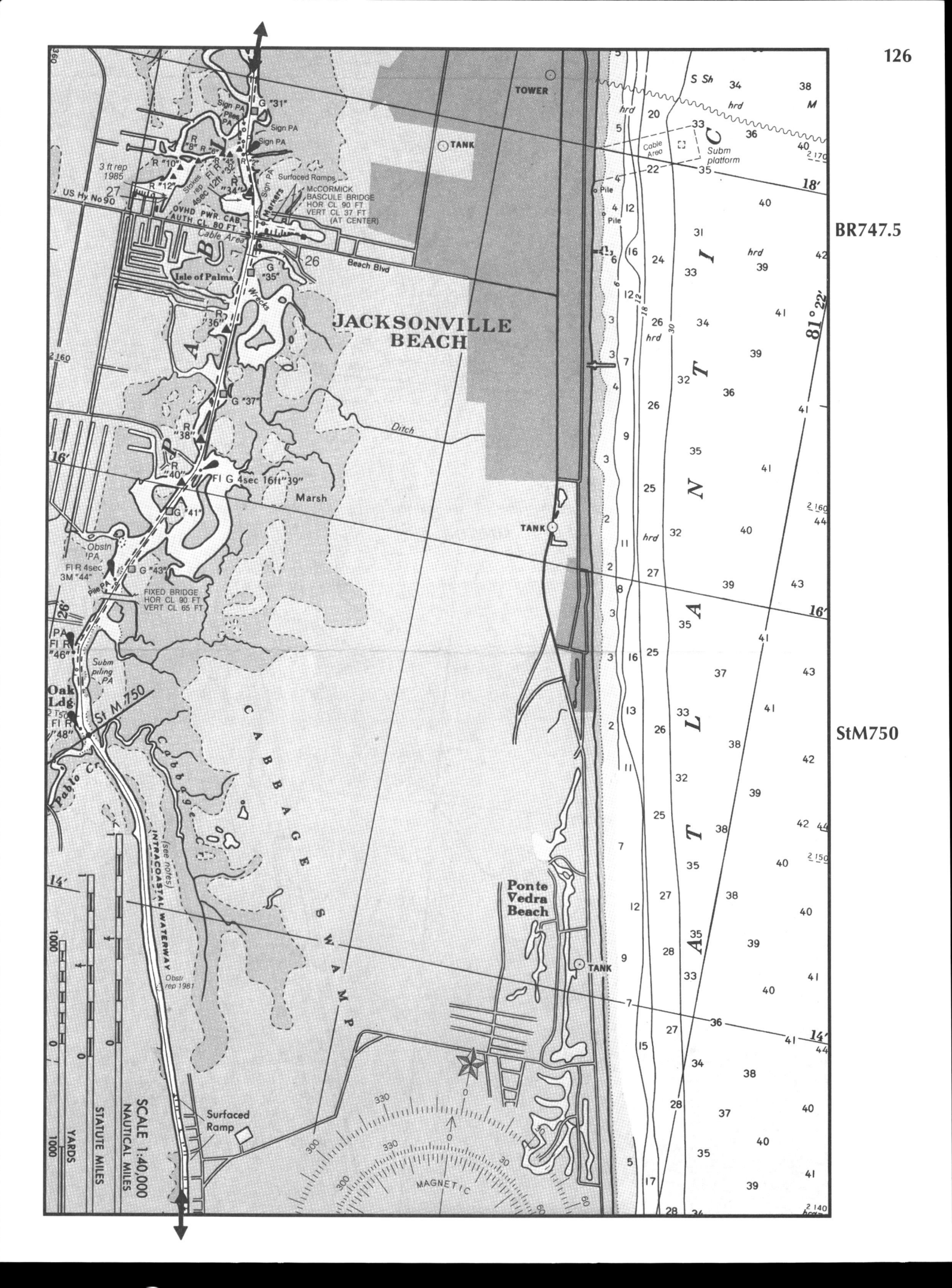

BR747.5

StM750

JACKSONVILLE
BEACH

TOWER

TANK

S Sh
hrd

Cable
Area

Subm
platform

McCORMICK
BASCULE BRIDGE
HOR CL 90 FT
VERT CL 37 FT
(AT CENTER)

Beach Blvd

G "31"

Sign PA
Piles
PA

Sign PA

Sign PA

R
"8"

R
"10"

R
"12"

3 ft rep
1985

US Hy No 90

OVHD PWR. CAB.
AUTH CL 80 FT

Cable Area

Isle of Palms

G "35"

R
"36"

Wrecks

G "37"

R
"38"

R
"40"

Fl G 4sec 16ft "39"

G "41"

Marsh

Ditch

Obstn
PA

Fl R 4sec
3M "44"

G "43"

FIXED BRIDGE
HOR CL 90 FT
VERT CL 65 FT

Pile PA

PA
Fl R
"46"

Subm
piling PA

Oak
Ldg

St M 750

Fl R
"48"

Pablo Cr.

INTRACOASTAL WATERWAY

CABBAGE SWAMP

(see notes)

Obstn
rep 1981

SCALE 1:40,000

STATUTE MILES

NAUTICAL MILES

YARDS

1000

1000

Surfaced
Ramp

Surfaced Ramps

MAGNETIC

Ponte
Vedra
Beach

TANK

TANK

ATLANTIC

18'

16'

16'

14'

14'

81° 22'

2170

2160

2160

2150

2140

127

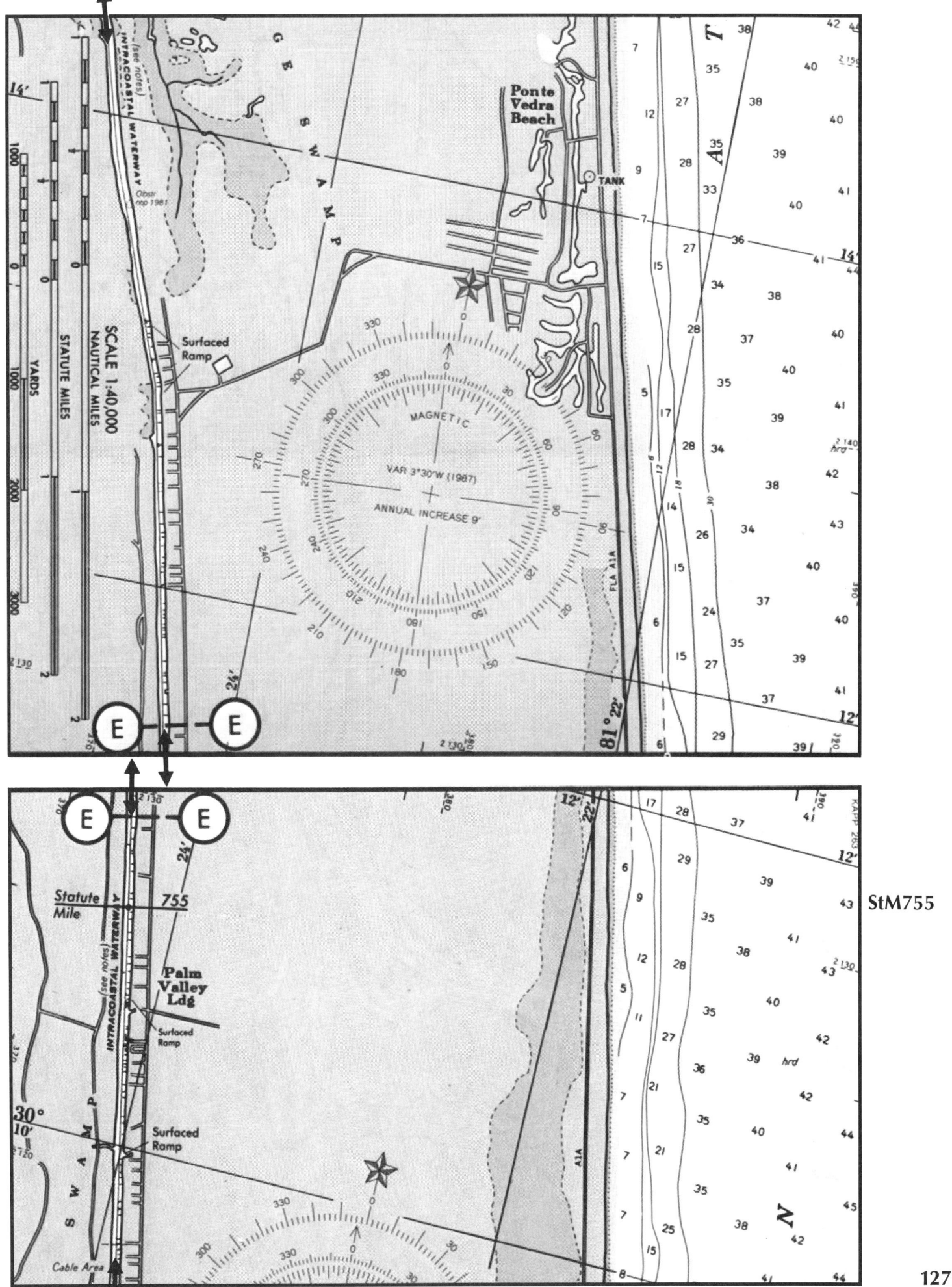

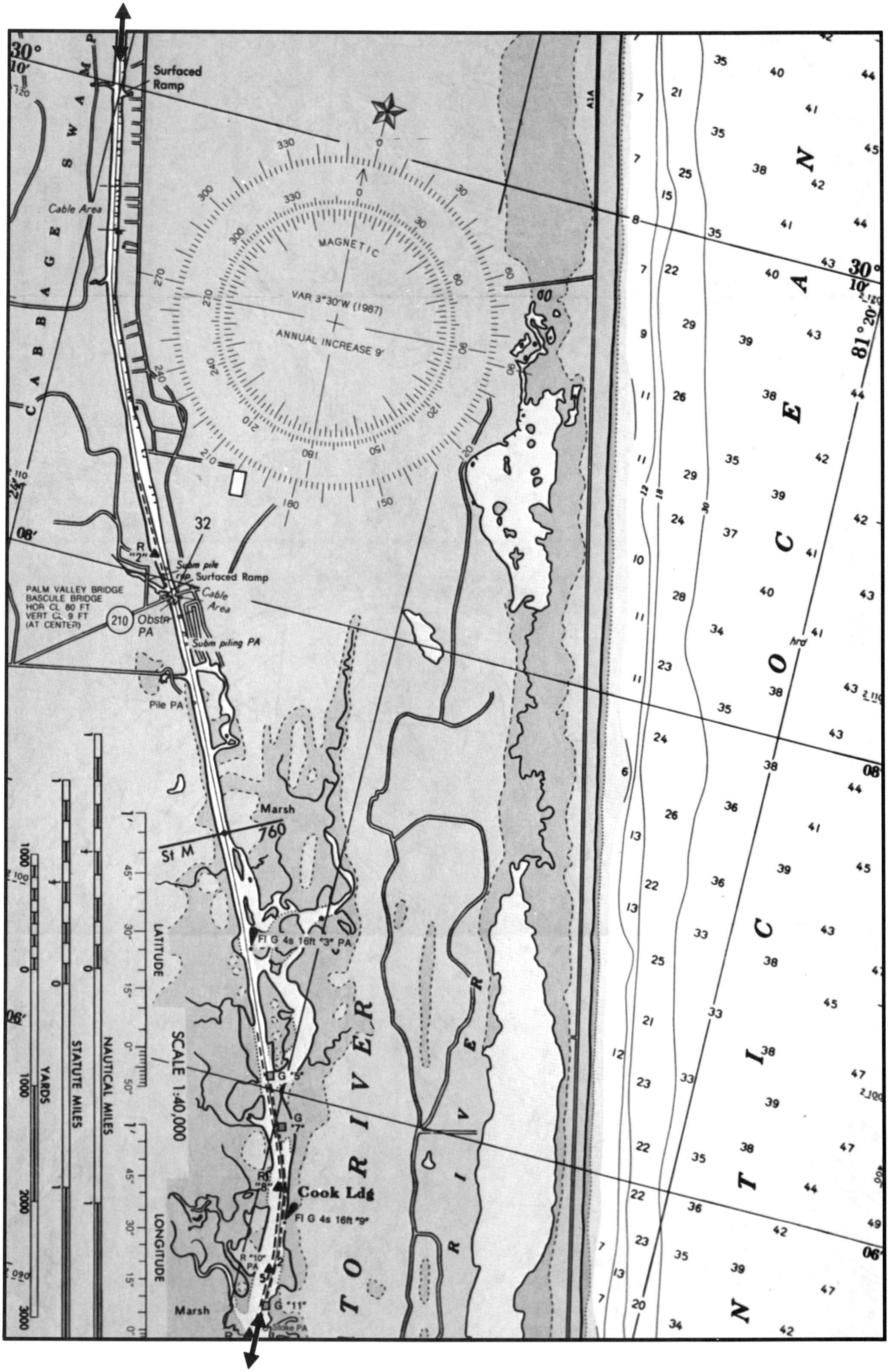


BR758.8

StM760

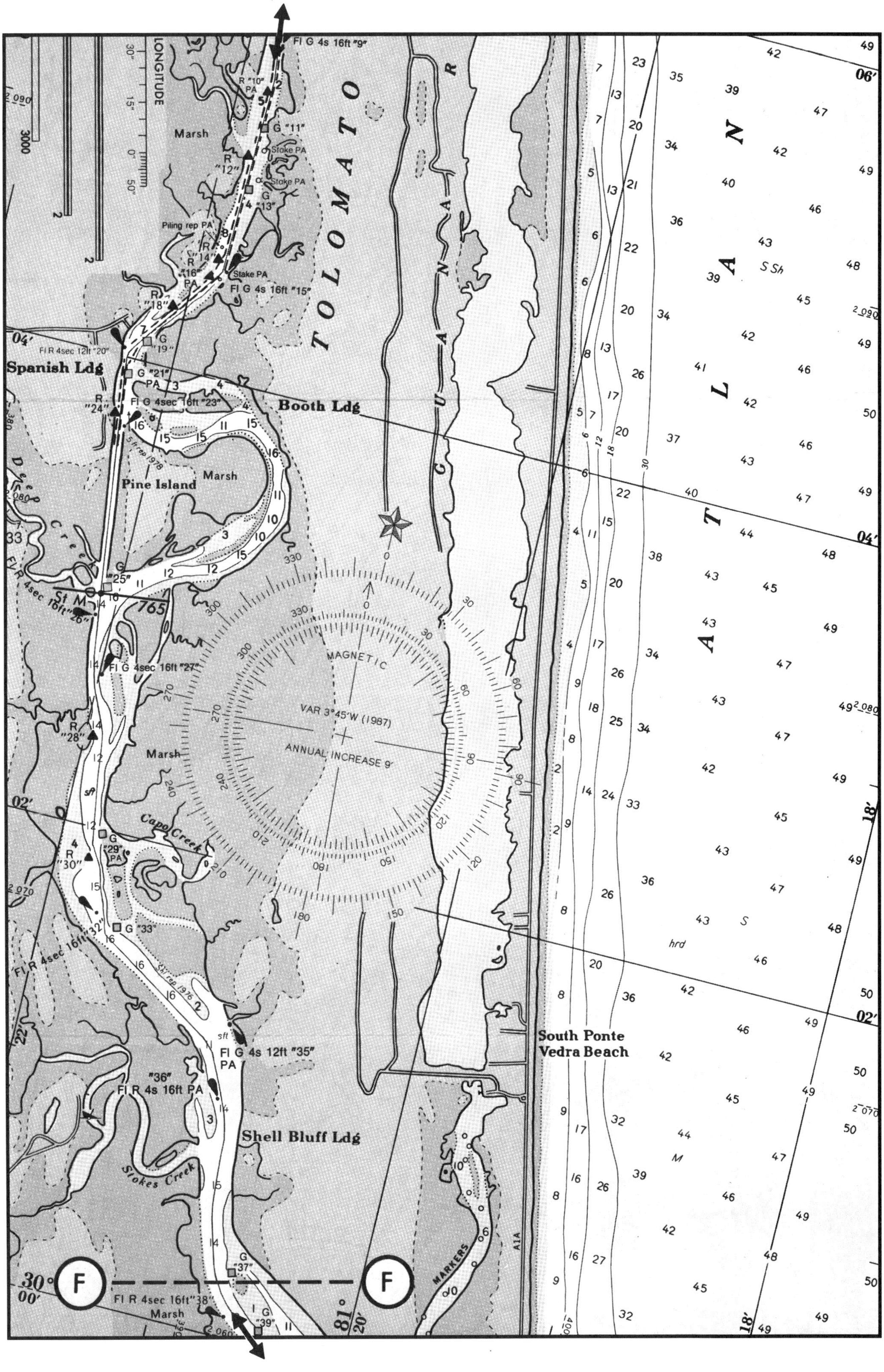

TOLOMATO R
GUANA R
ATLANTIC
Spanish Ldg
Booth Ldg
Pine Island
Marsh
Capo Creek
Stokes Creek
Shell Bluff Ldg
South Ponte Vedra Beach
MAGNETIC
VAR 3°45'W (1987)
ANNUAL INCREASE 9'
LONGITUDE
Fl G 4s 16ft "9"
Fl G 4s 16ft "15"
Fl R 4sec 12ft "20"
Fl G 4sec 16ft "23"
Fl R 4sec 16ft "26"
Fl G 4sec 16ft "27"
Fl R 4sec 16ft "32"
Fl G 4s 12ft "35" PA
"36" Fl R 4s 16ft PA
Fl R 4sec 16ft "38"
Stake PA
Piling rep PA
MARKERS
A1A
30° 00'
81° 20'
04'
02'
06'
18'
765
F
F


StM765

130

F

F

KAPP 279

81°
20'

GUANA RIVER

MARKERS

Statute
Mile

770

FI R 4sec
16ft "38"

G
"37"

G
"39"

FI G 4s 12ft "41"

D "42"
R

FI R 4sec 16ft "44"

R
"44A"

FI G 4s
16ft "45"
PA

Subm
piles

Subm pile
Pile

MARKERS

Casa Cola Creek

G
"47"

INTRACOASTAL WATERWAY
(see notes)

T O L O M A T O

FI R 4sec
16ft "48"

FI G 4s 16ft "49"

FI G 4s 16ft "51"

Marsh

R
"52"

2

FI R 4s 12ft "54"
PA

Usina Beach

Kamp

A1A

Robinson Creek

FI G 4s 12ft "55"

St M   775

Cable Area
Priv maintd R

G
"57"

TANK

FEC

81°20'

StM770

30°00'

30°
00'

2 060

2 060

S Sh

2 950

58'

2 040

2 040

S Sh

StM775

56'

58'

56'

18'

(29)

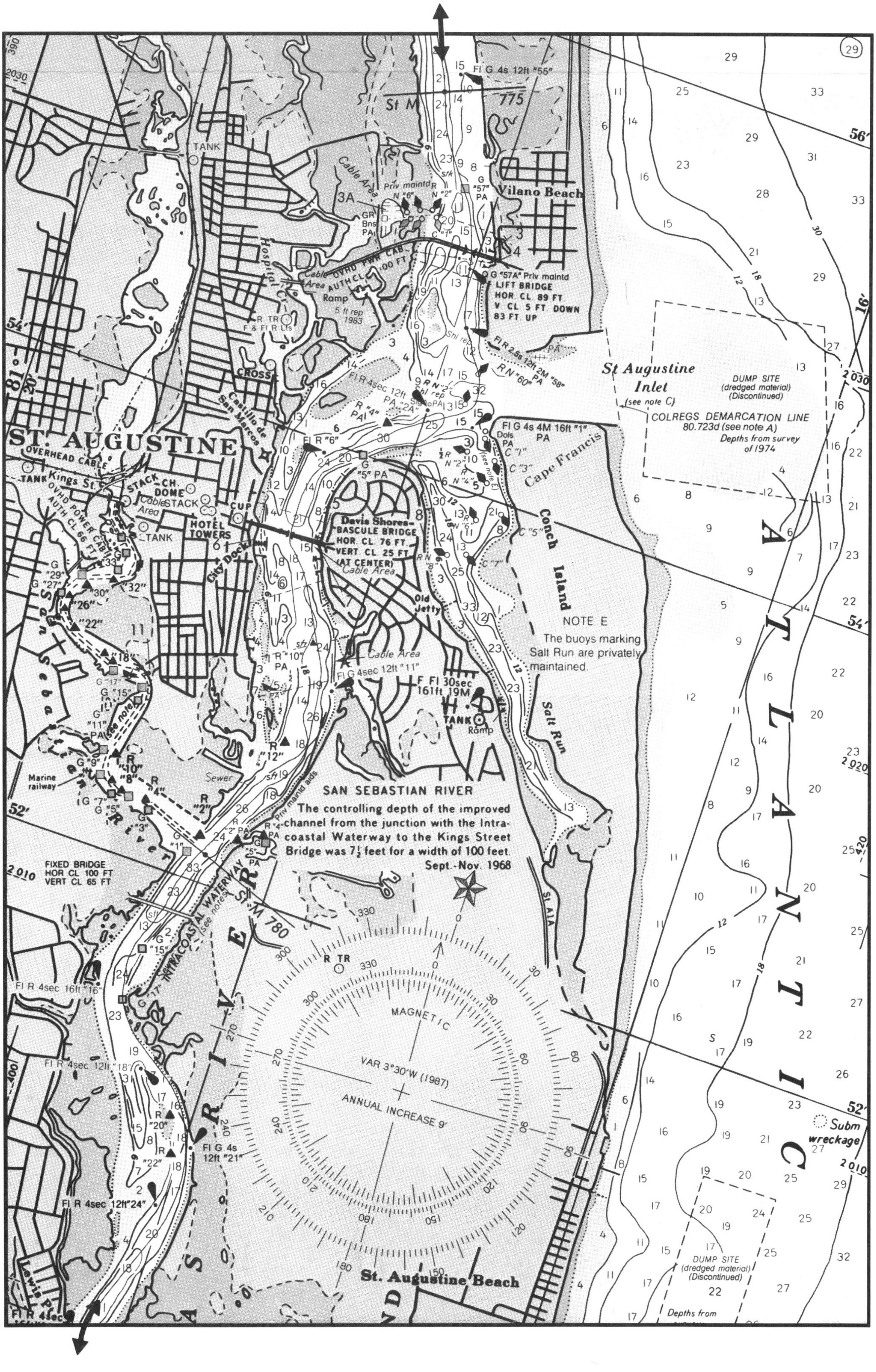


StM775

BR775.8

BR777.9

StM780

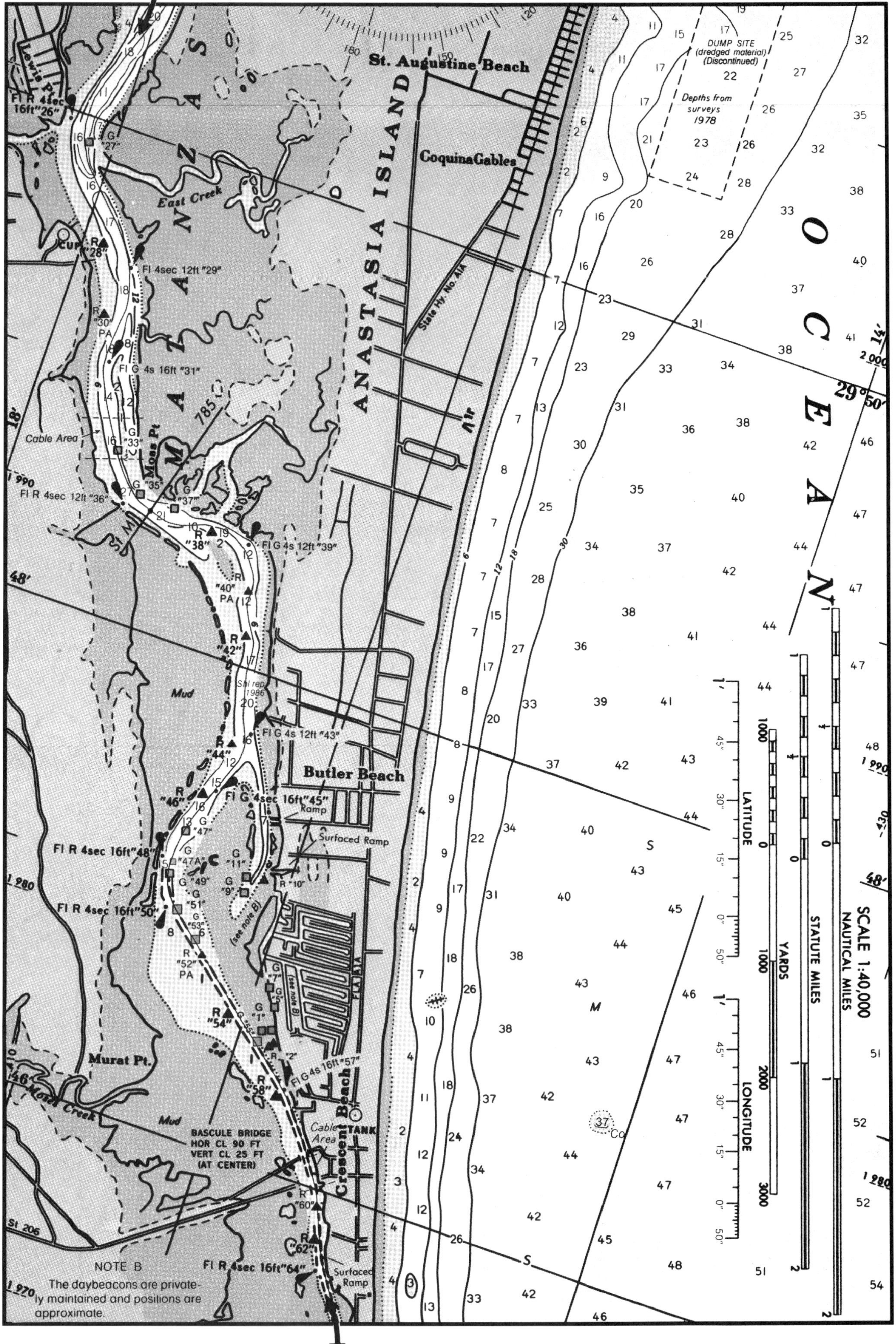


StM785

BR788.6

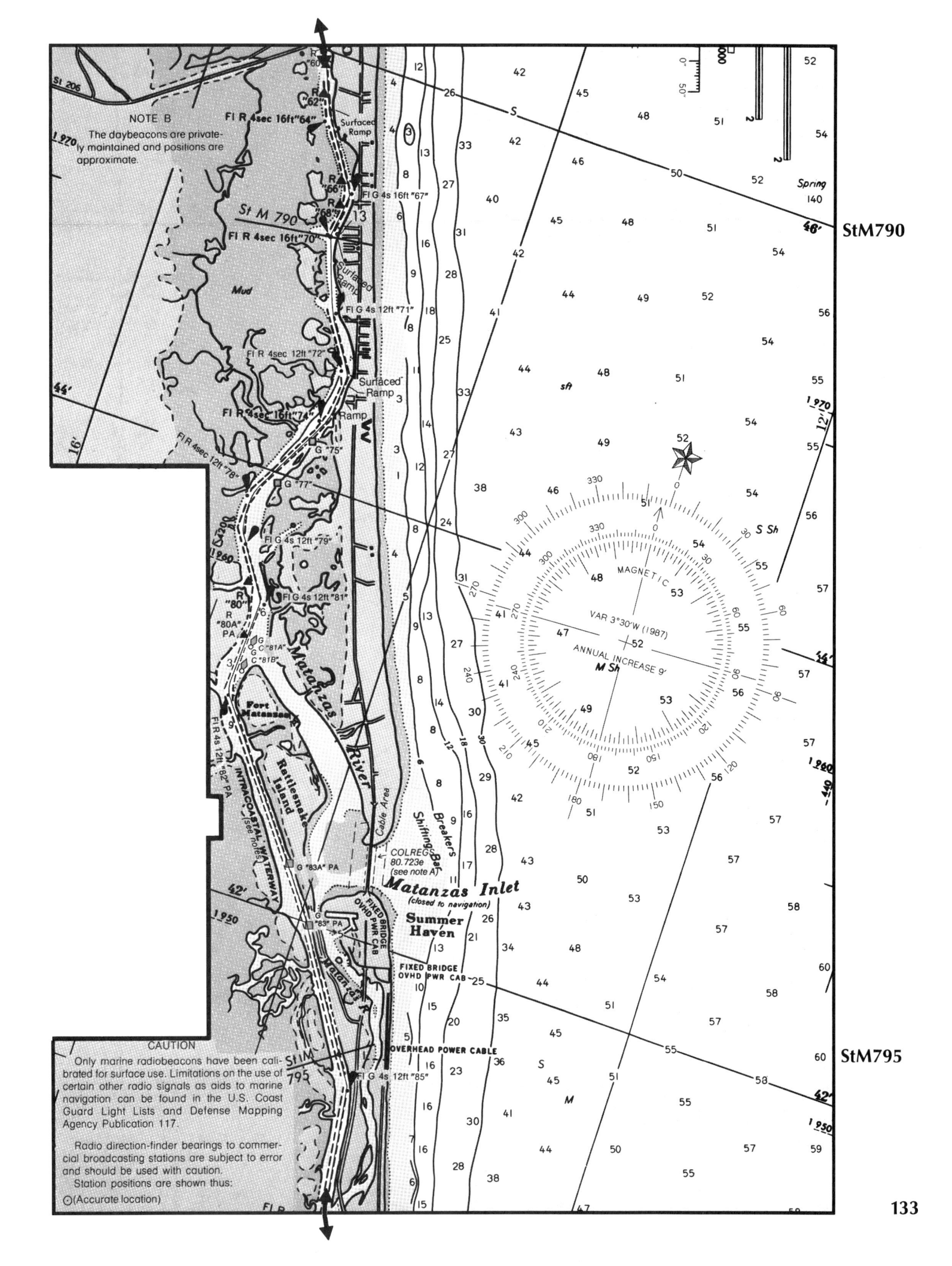

**NOTE B**
The daybeacons are privately maintained and positions are approximate.

**CAUTION**
Only marine radiobeacons have been calibrated for surface use. Limitations on the use of certain other radio signals as aids to marine navigation can be found in the U.S. Coast Guard Light Lists and Defense Mapping Agency Publication 117.

Radio direction-finder bearings to commercial broadcasting stations are subject to error and should be used with caution.
Station positions are shown thus:
⊙(Accurate location)

MAGNETIC
VAR 3°30'W (1987)
ANNUAL INCREASE 9'

Matanzas River
Fort Matanzas
Rattlesnake Island
INTRACOASTAL WATERWAY (See notes)
Cable Area
Breakers
Shifting Bar
COLREGS 80.723e (see note A)
Matanzas Inlet (closed to navigation)
Summer Haven
FIXED BRIDGE OVHD PWR CAB
OVERHEAD POWER CABLE

StM790

StM795

133

StM795

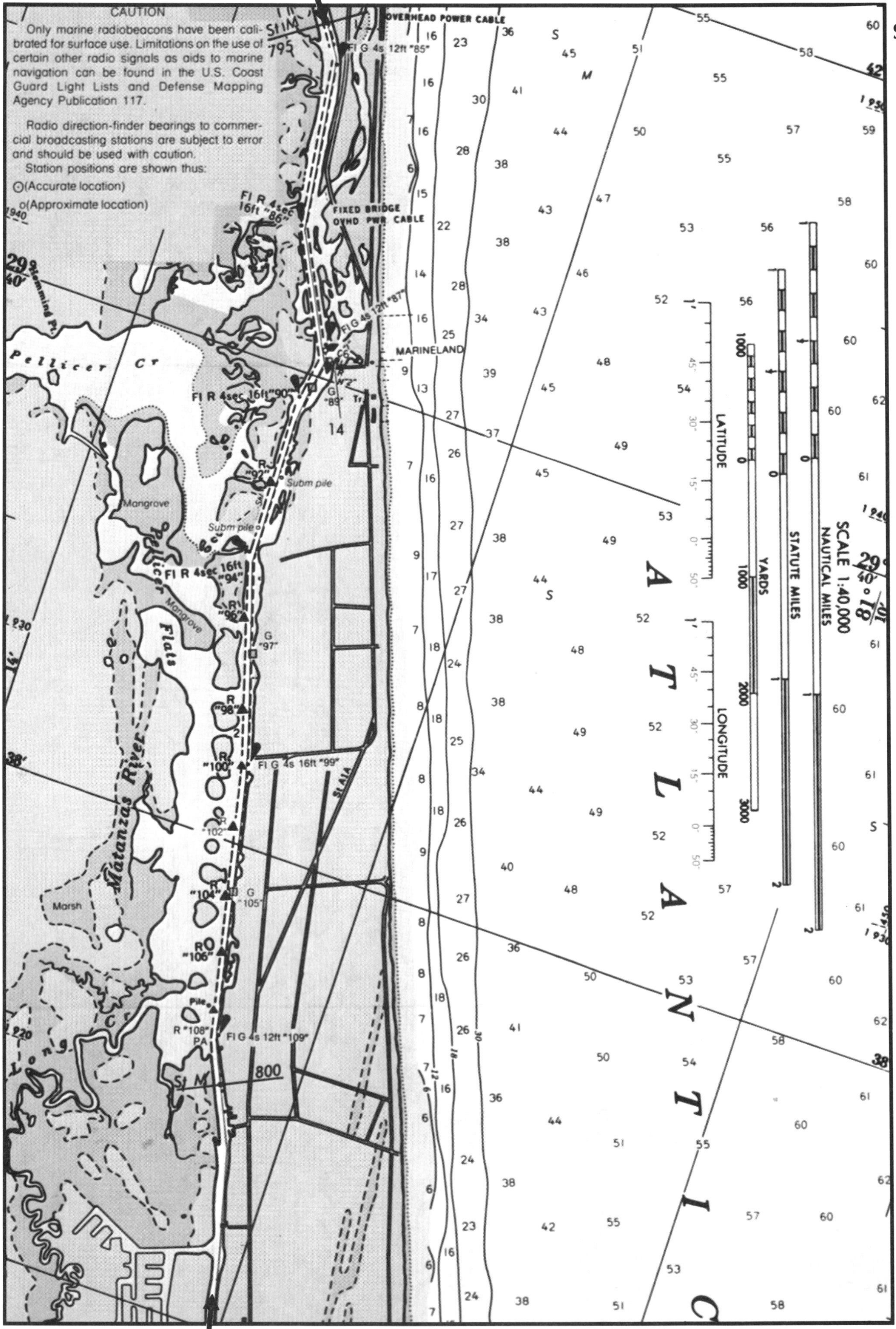


StM800

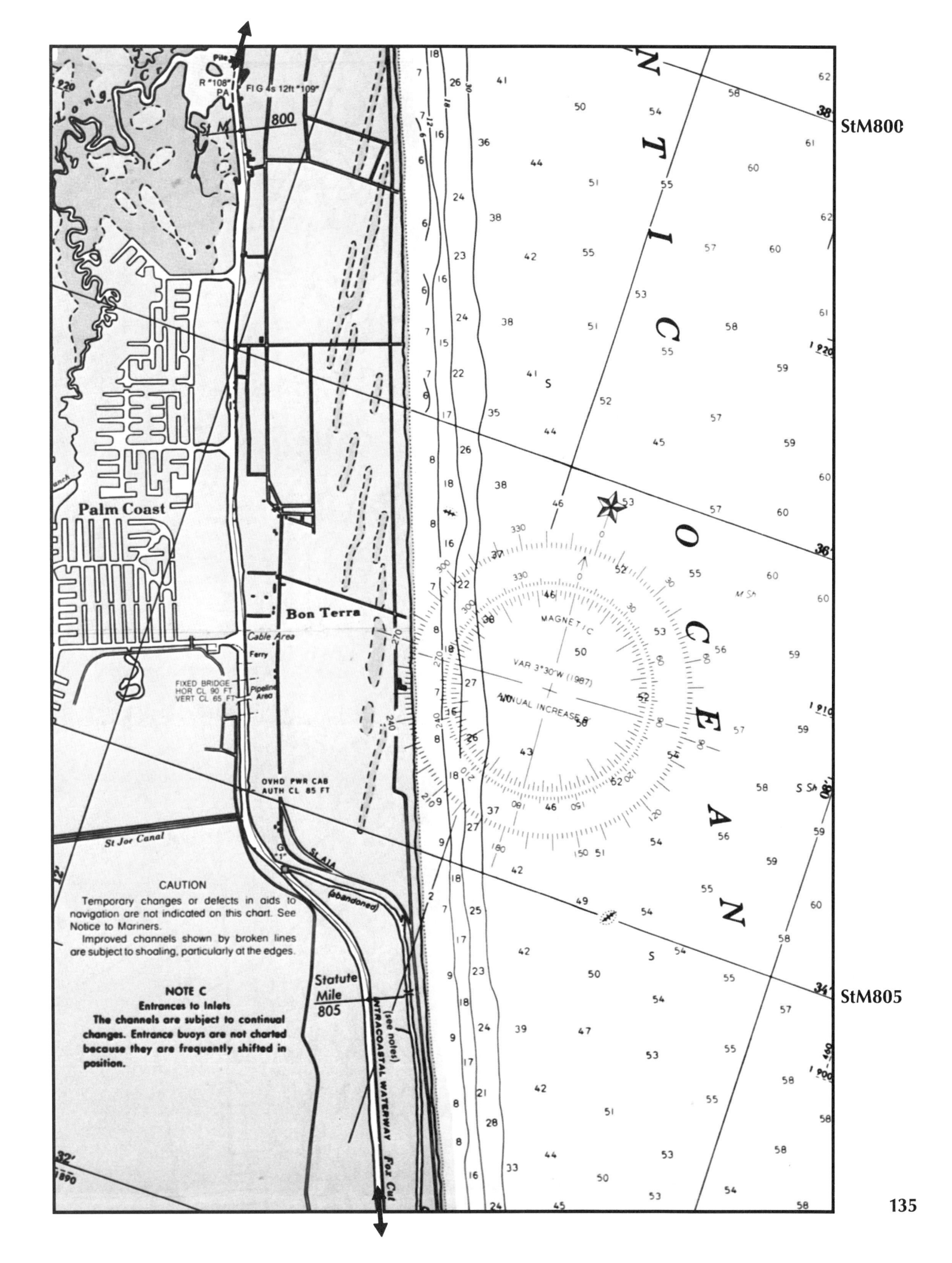

StM800

StM805

**CAUTION**
Temporary changes or defects in aids to navigation are not indicated on this chart. See Notice to Mariners.
Improved channels shown by broken lines are subject to shoaling, particularly at the edges.

**NOTE C**
**Entrances to Inlets**
The channels are subject to continual changes. Entrance buoys are not charted because they are frequently shifted in position.

Palm Coast

Bon Terra

FIXED BRIDGE
HOR CL 90 FT
VERT CL 65 FT

OVHD PWR CAB
AUTH CL 85 FT

St Joe Canal

Statute Mile 805

Fox Cut

INTRACOASTAL WATERWAY

ATLANTIC OCEAN

MAGNETIC
VAR 3°30'W (1987)
ANNUAL INCREASE 8'

136

StM805

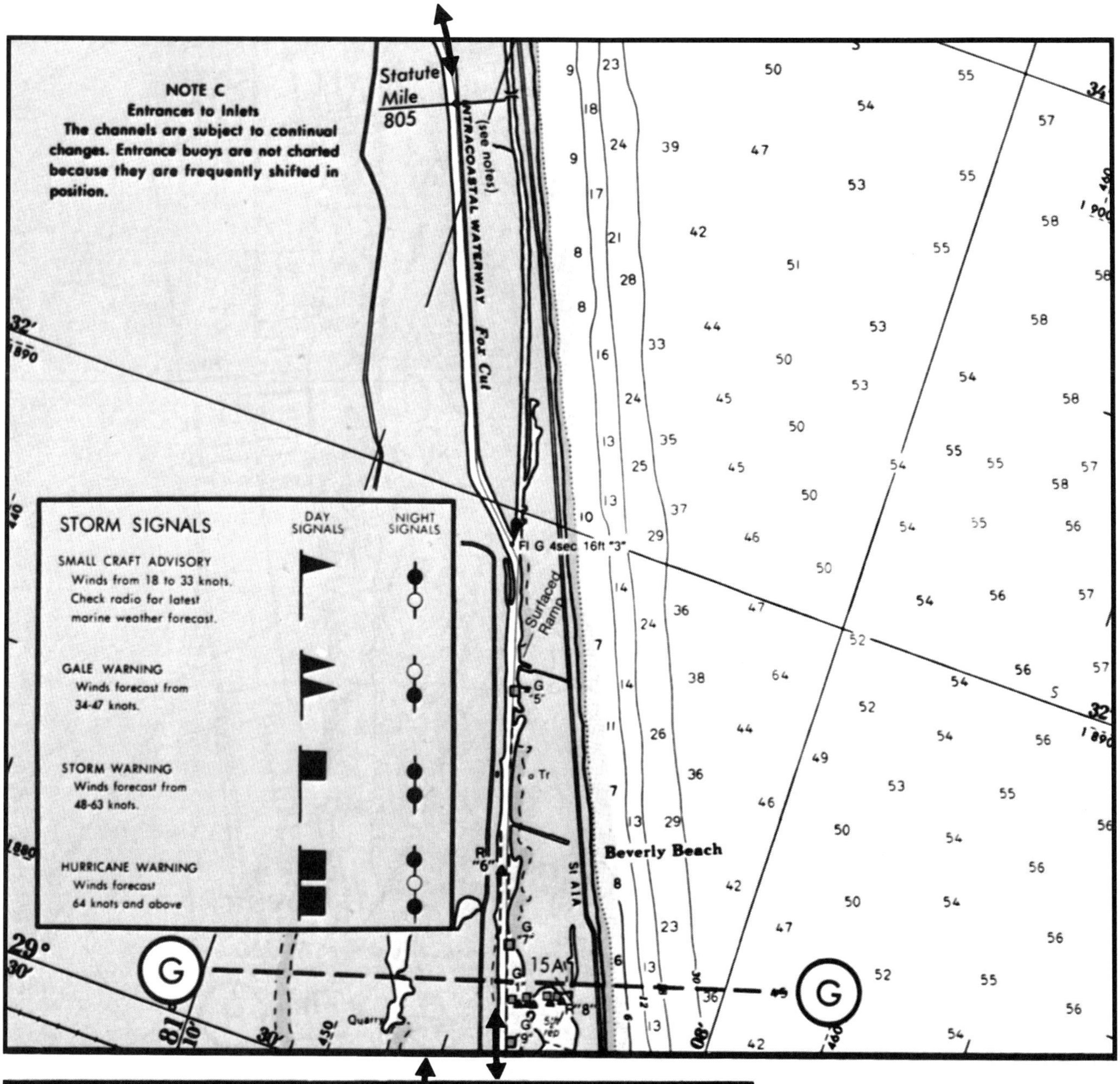

## NOTE C
### Entrances to Inlets
The channels are subject to continual changes. Entrance buoys are not charted because they are frequently shifted in position.

Statute Mile 805

INTRACOASTAL WATERWAY

Fox Cut

(see notes)

Fl G 4sec 16ft "3"

Surfaced Ramp

## STORM SIGNALS

| | DAY SIGNALS | NIGHT SIGNALS |
|---|---|---|
| **SMALL CRAFT ADVISORY** Winds from 18 to 33 knots. Check radio for latest marine weather forecast. | | |
| **GALE WARNING** Winds forecast from 34-47 knots. | | |
| **STORM WARNING** Winds forecast from 48-63 knots. | | |
| **HURRICANE WARNING** Winds forecast 64 knots and above | | |

G "5"

Tr

R "6"

Beverly Beach

St A1A

G "7"

G 15A

R "8"

G "9" 5 ft rep

KAPP 280

G "7"

15A

G

R "8"

G "9" 5 ft rep

Quarry

Cement plant

STACKS

6 ft rep 1983

Subm pile

Fl G 4s 12ft "13"

G "11"

PLANE COORDINATE GRID

Florida State Grid, east zone, is indicated by dashed ticks at 10,000 foot intervals. The last three digits are omitted.

SUPPLEMENTAL INFORMATION

Consult U.S. Coast Pilot 4 for important supplemental information.

Statute Mile 810

St 11

OVERHEAD POWER CABLES AUTHORIZED CL 85 FT

StM810

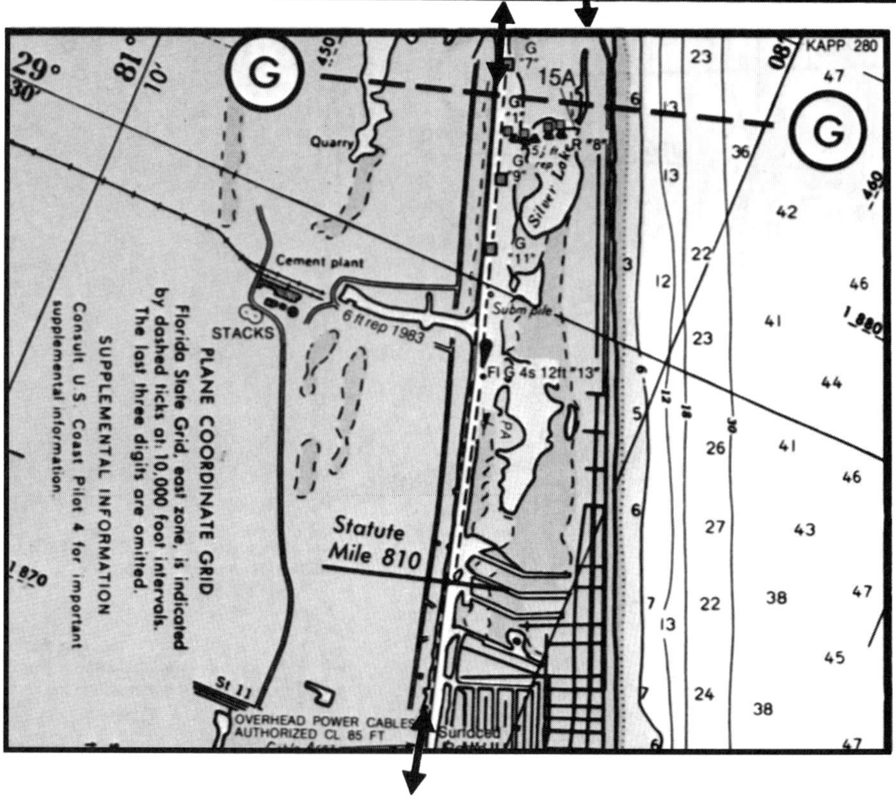

BR810.6

137

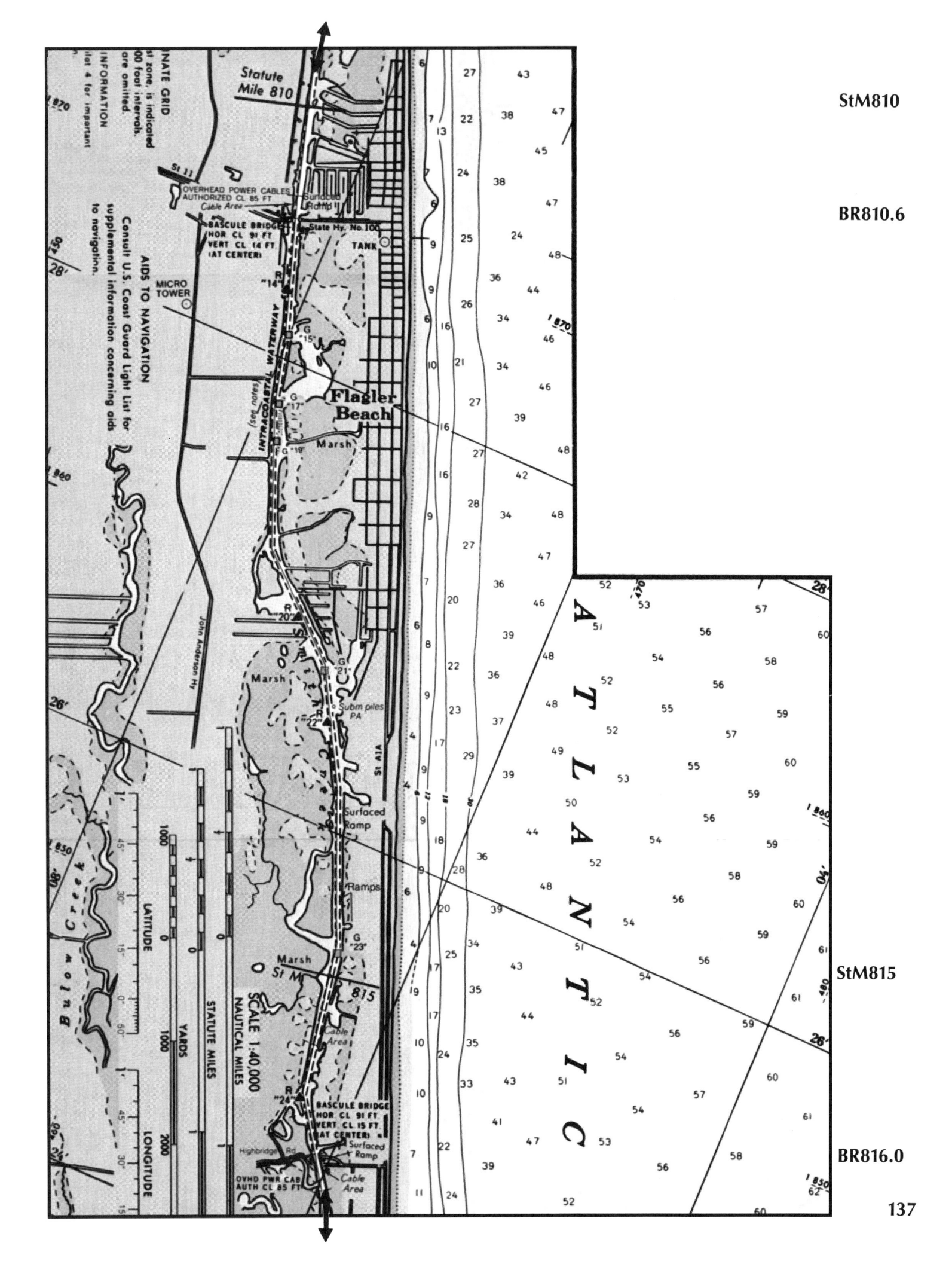

BR816.0

StM820

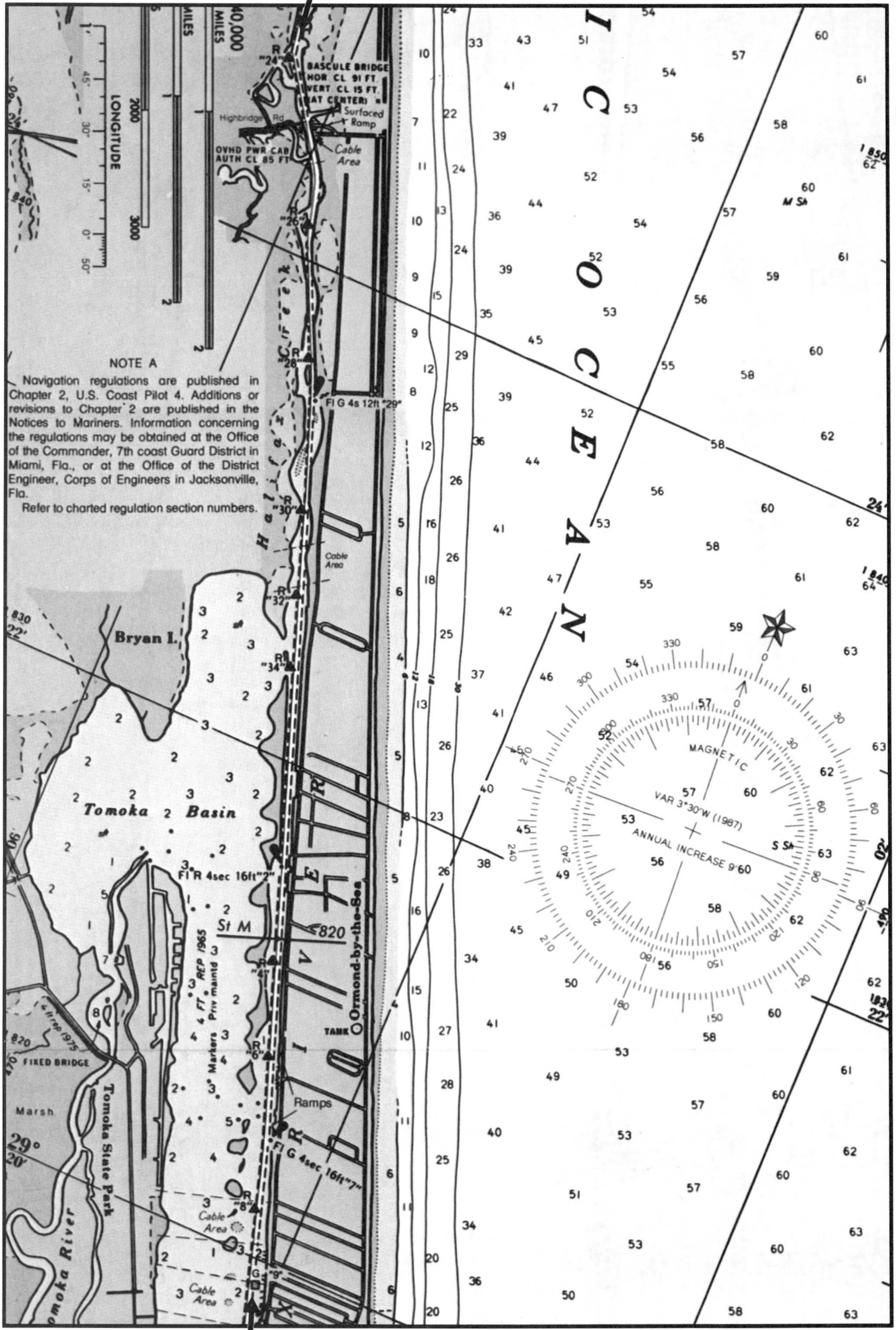

139

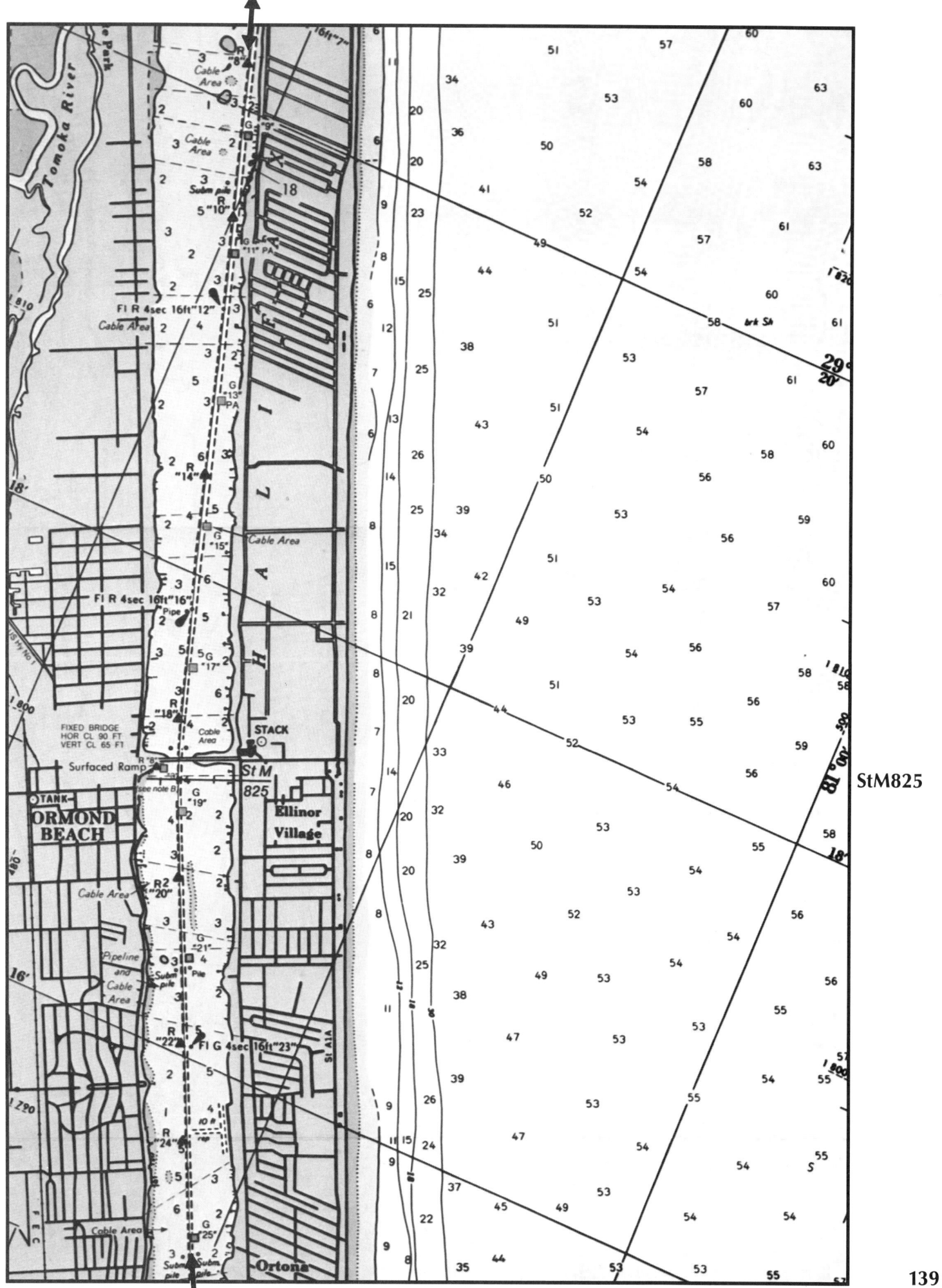

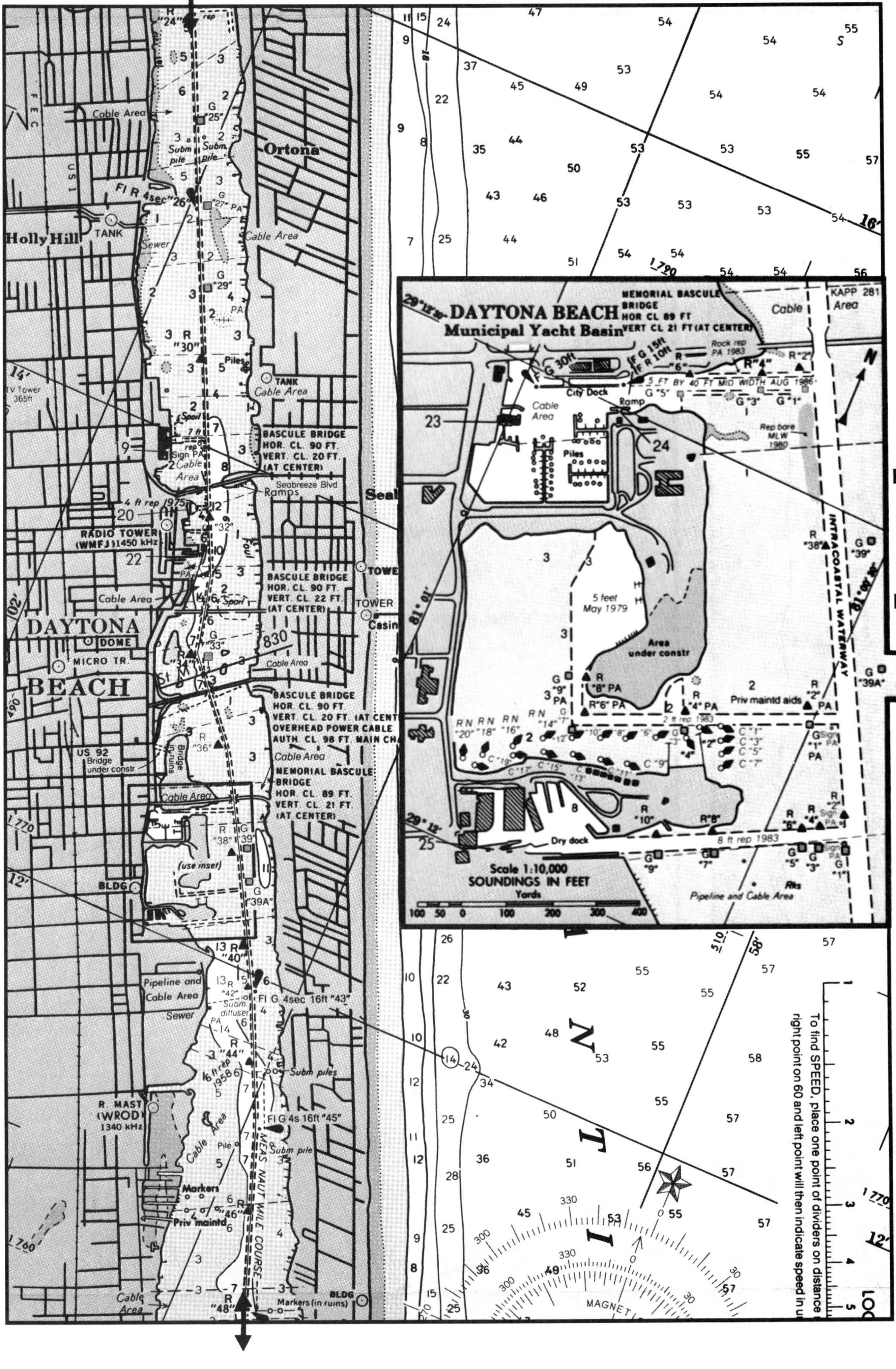

140

StM835

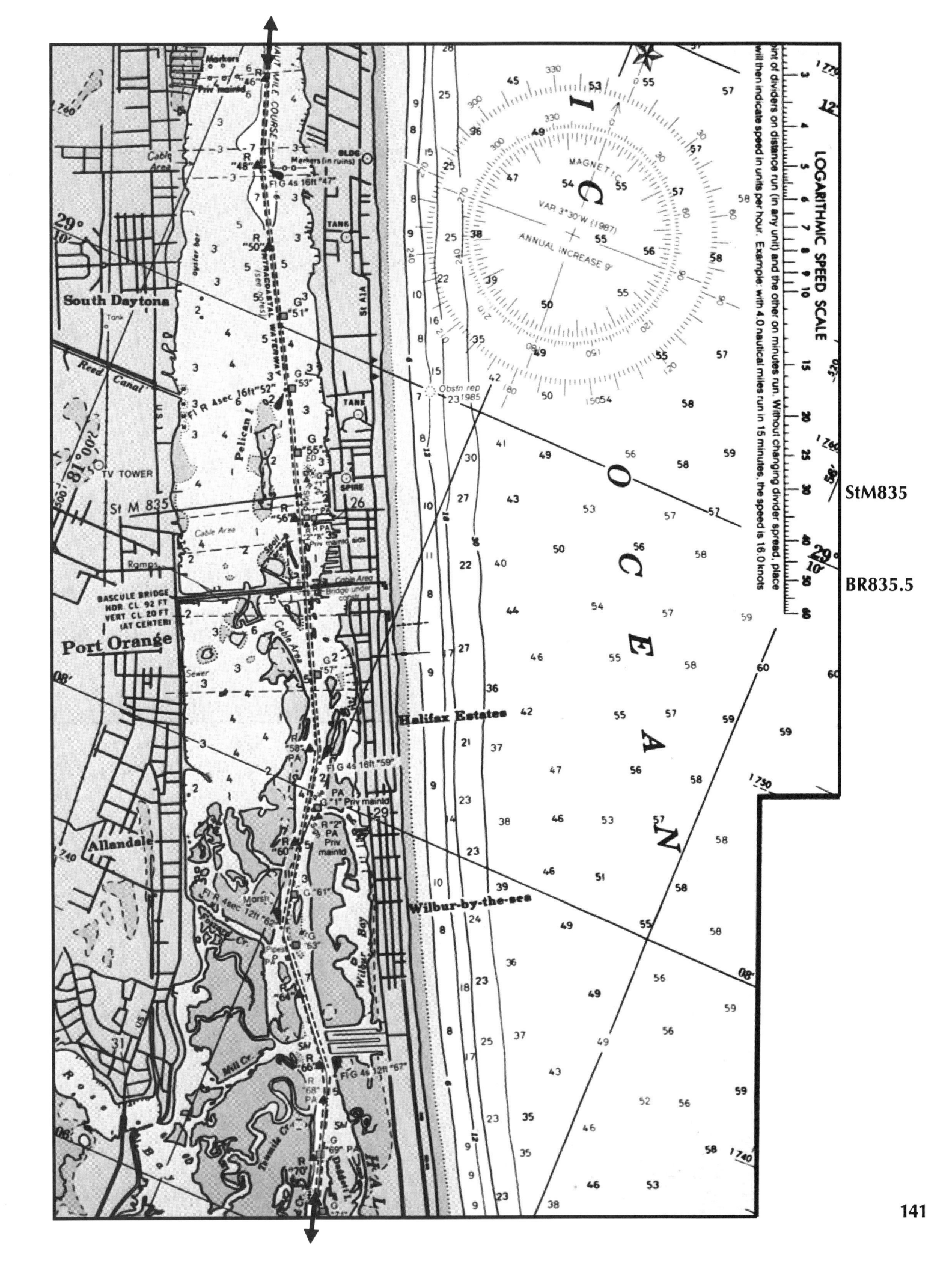

BR835.5

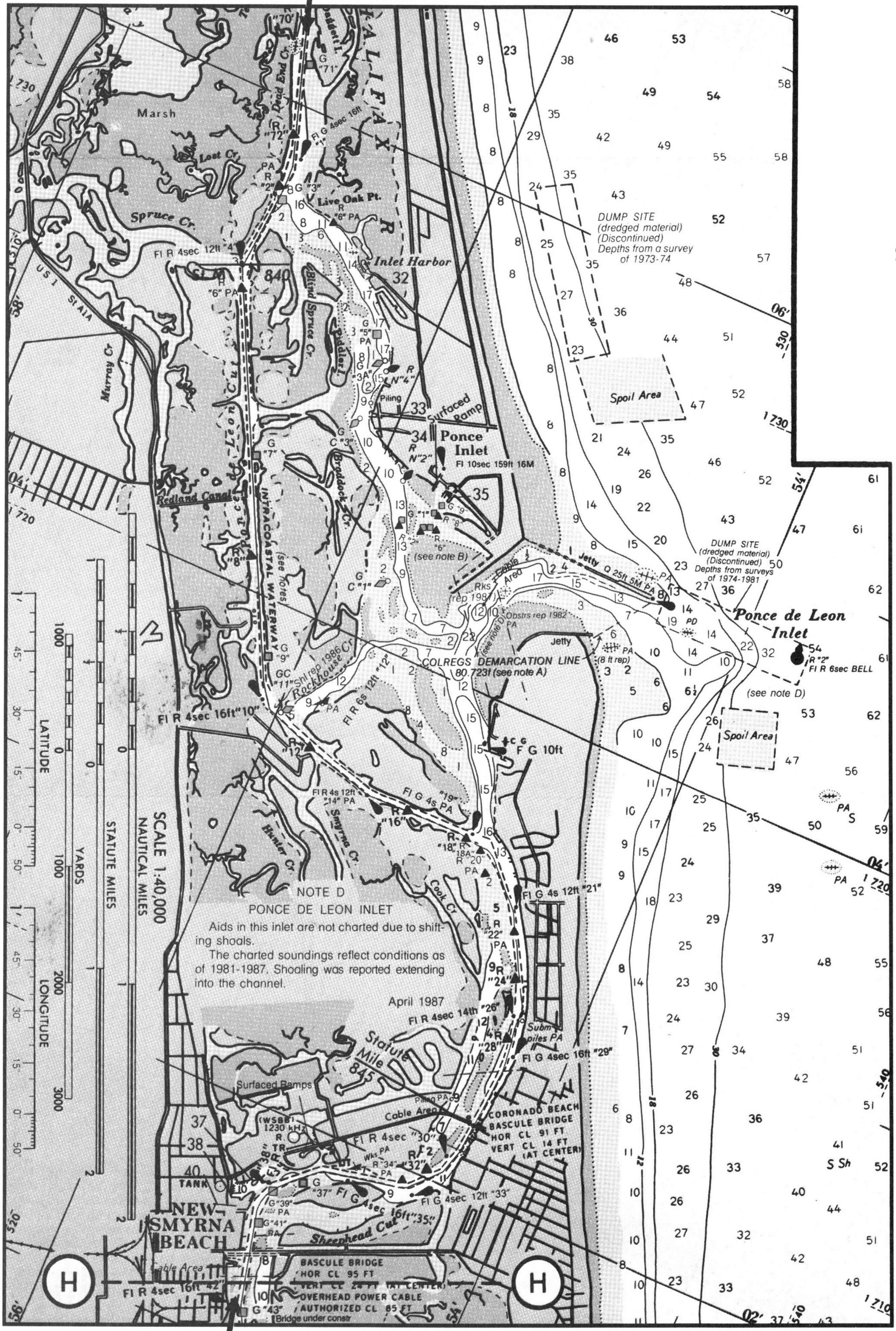
StM840
BR845.0
BR846.5
Ponce de Leon Inlet
Ponce Inlet
Fl 10sec 159ft 16M
NOTE D
PONCE DE LEON INLET
Aids in this inlet are not charted due to shifting shoals.
The charted soundings reflect conditions as of 1981-1987. Shoaling was reported extending into the channel.
April 1987
COLREGS DEMARCATION LINE
80.723f (see note A)
DUMP SITE
(dredged material)
(Discontinued)
Depths from a survey of 1973-74
Depths from surveys of 1974-1981
Spoil Area
Inlet Harbor
Live Oak Pt.
Spruce Cr.
Lost Cr.
Marsh
HALIFAX R
INTRACOASTAL WATERWAY
Redland Canal
Murray Cr.
Statute Mile 845
Surfaced Ramps
Surfaced Ramp
CORONADO BEACH
BASCULE BRIDGE
HOR CL 91 FT
VERT CL 14 FT
(AT CENTER)
BASCULE BRIDGE
HOR CL 95 FT
OVERHEAD POWER CABLE
AUTHORIZED CL 85 FT
Bridge under constr
NEW SMYRNA BEACH
Sheephead Cut
Cable Area
TANK
SCALE 1:40,000
NAUTICAL MILES
STATUTE MILES
YARDS
LATITUDE
LONGITUDE
Fl R 6sec BELL
Fl G 10ft
Jetty

BR846.5

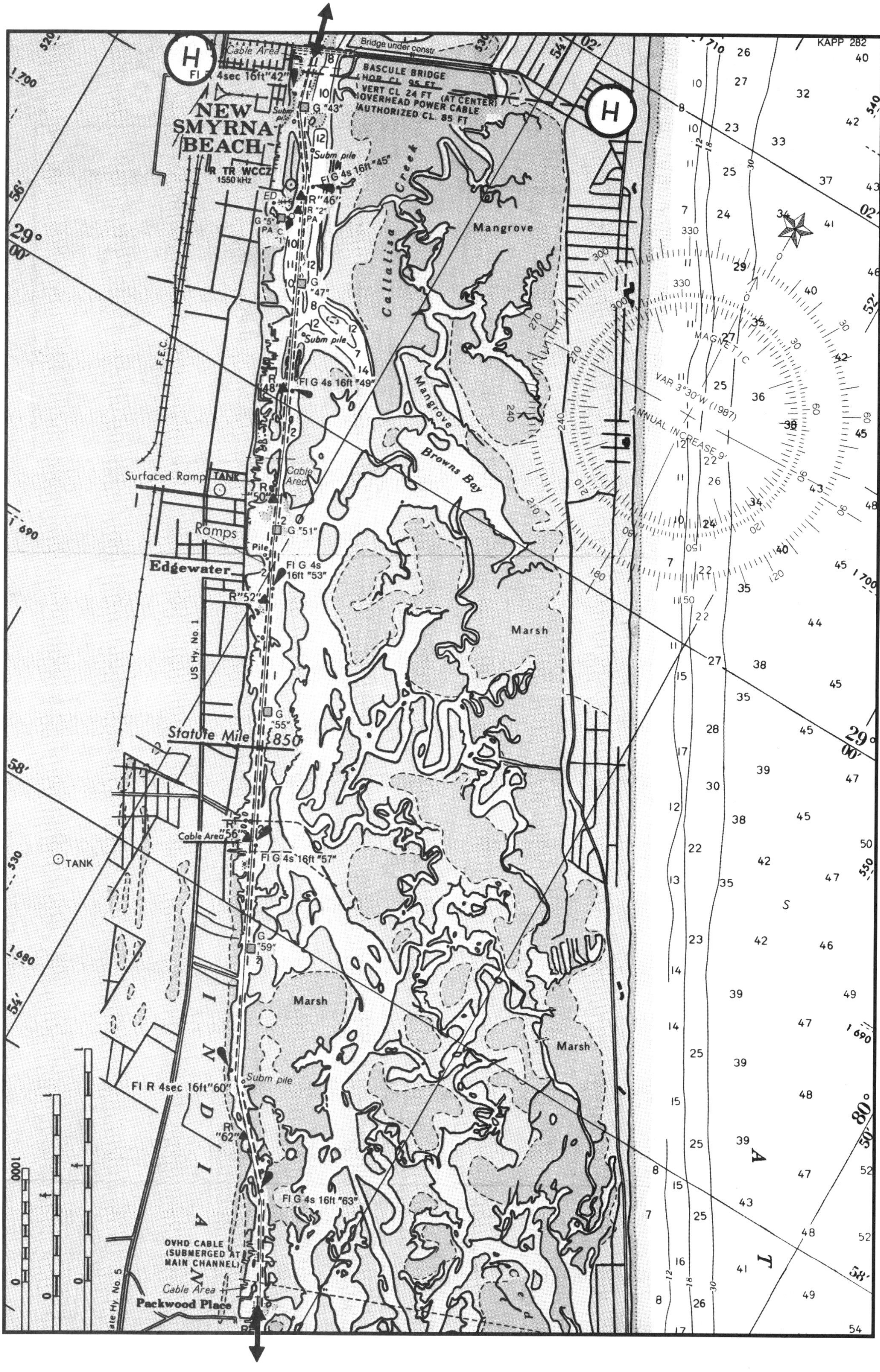


StM850

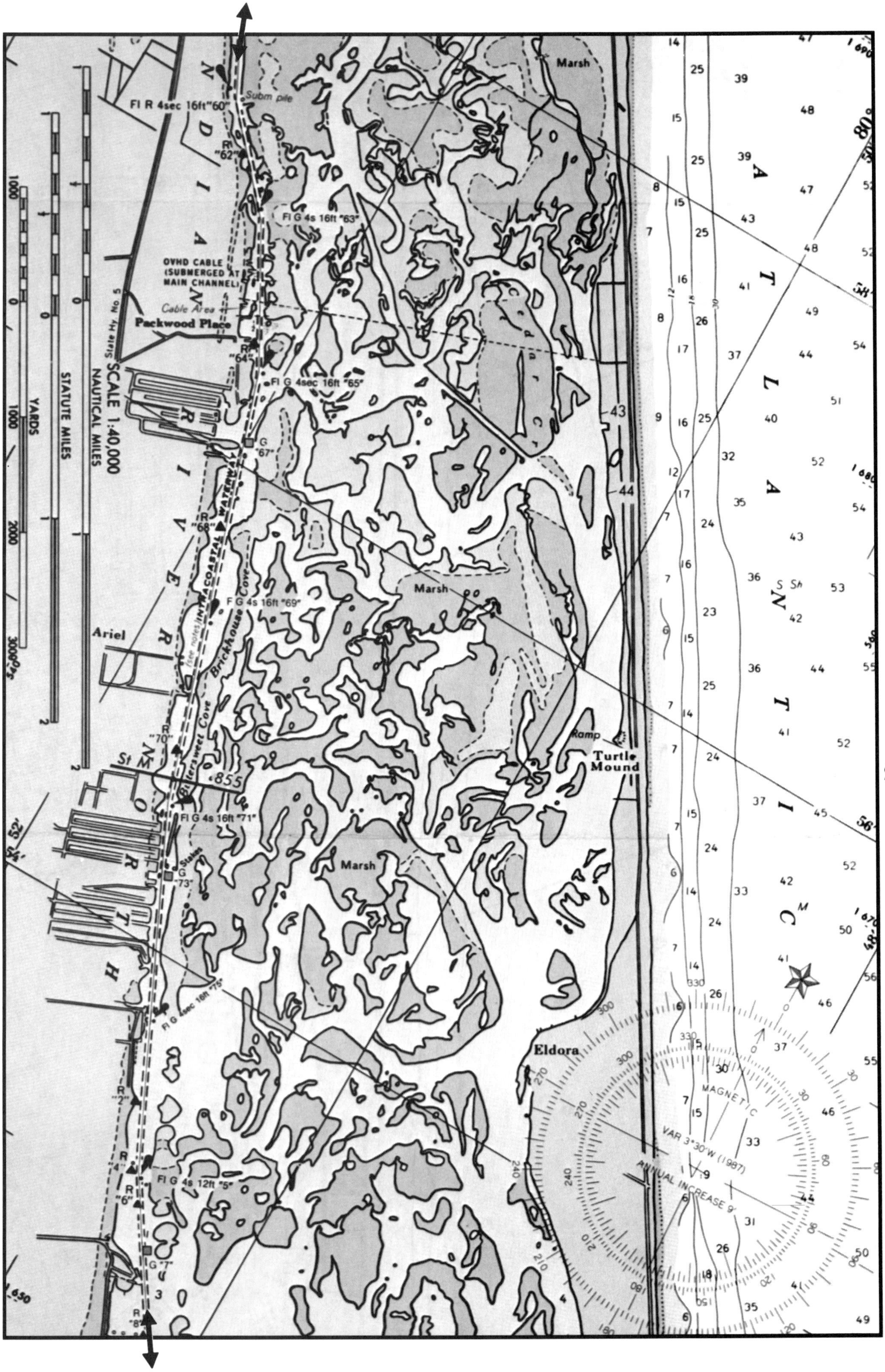
INDIAN RIVER NORTH
ATLANTIC
Marsh
Subm pile
Fl R 4sec 16ft "60"
R "62"
Fl G 4s 16ft "63"
OVHD CABLE (SUBMERGED AT MAIN CHANNEL)
Cable Area
Packwood Place
State Hy. No. 5
R "64"
Fl G 4sec 16ft "65"
SCALE 1:40,000
NAUTICAL MILES
STATUTE MILES
YARDS
G "67"
INTRACOASTAL WATERWAY
R "68"
F G 4s 16ft "69"
Brickhouse Cove
Ariel
R "70"
Bittersweet Cove
St M
855
Fl G 4s 16ft "71"
Stakes
G "73"
Fl G 4sec 16ft "75"
R "2"
R "4"
Fl G 4s 12ft "5"
R "6"
G "7"
R "8"
Ramp
Turtle Mound
Eldora
MAGNETIC
VAR 3°30'W (1987)
ANNUAL INCREASE 9'

StM855

StM860

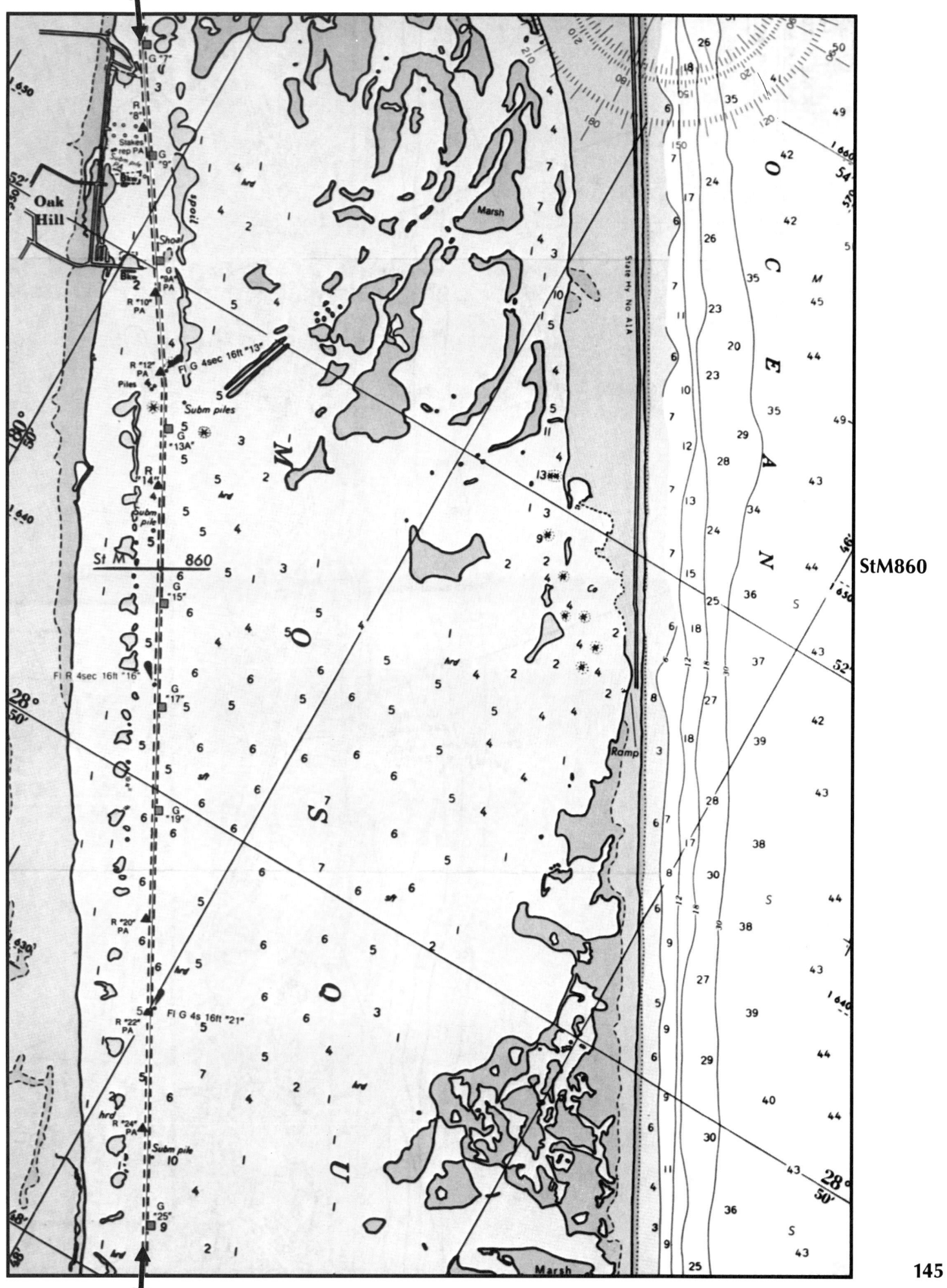

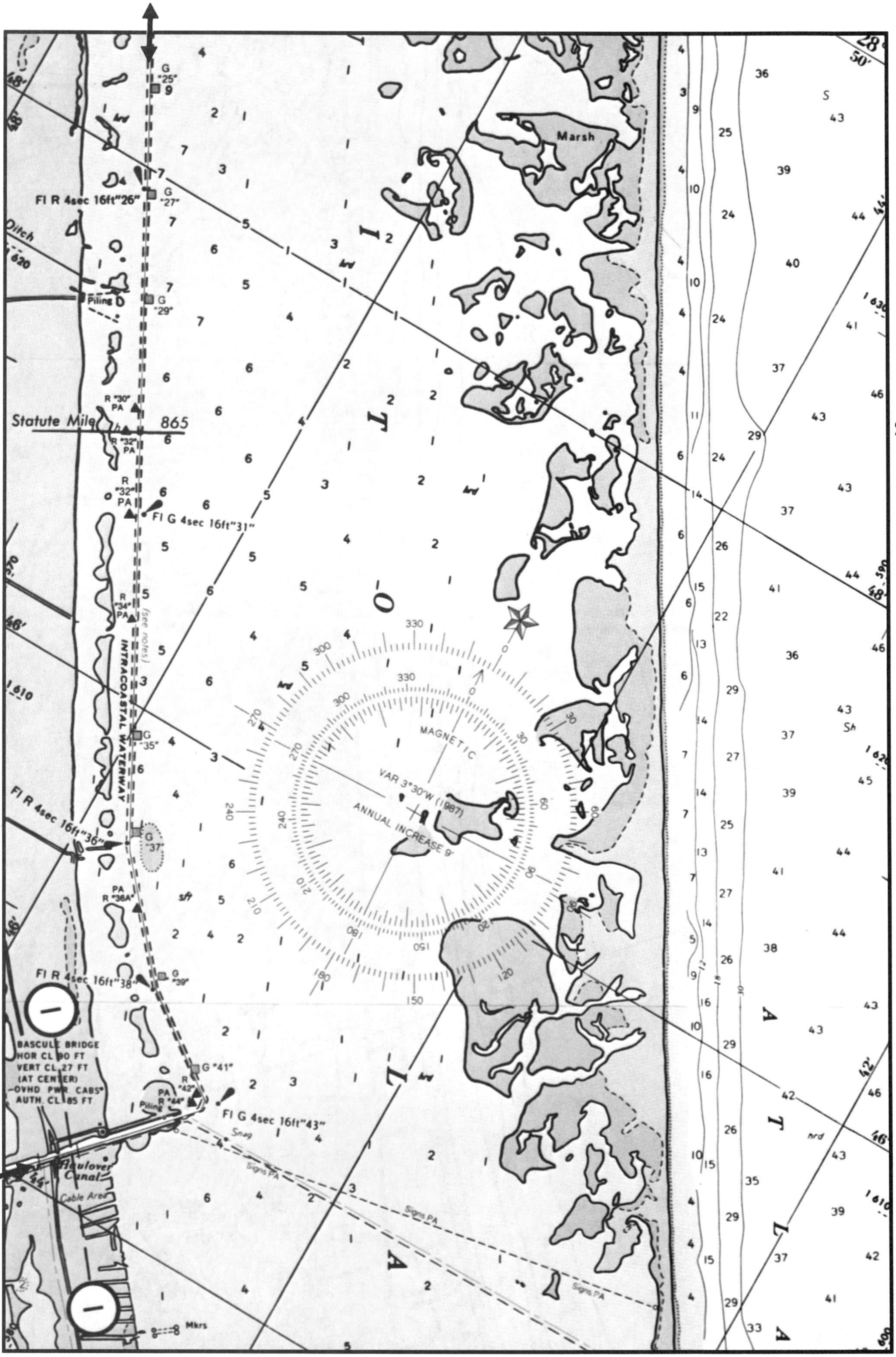


StM865

BR869.2

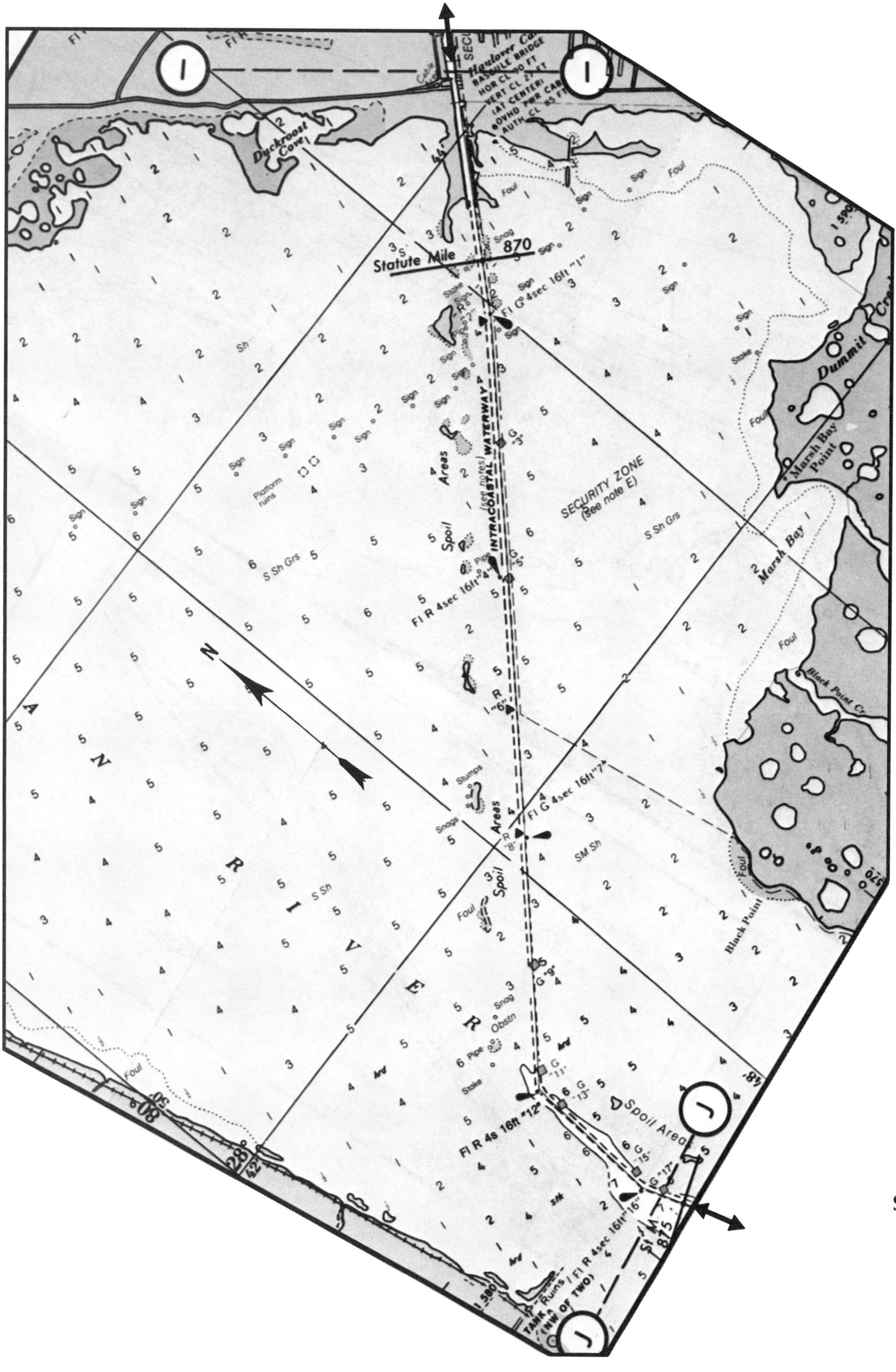


BR869.2

StM870

StM875

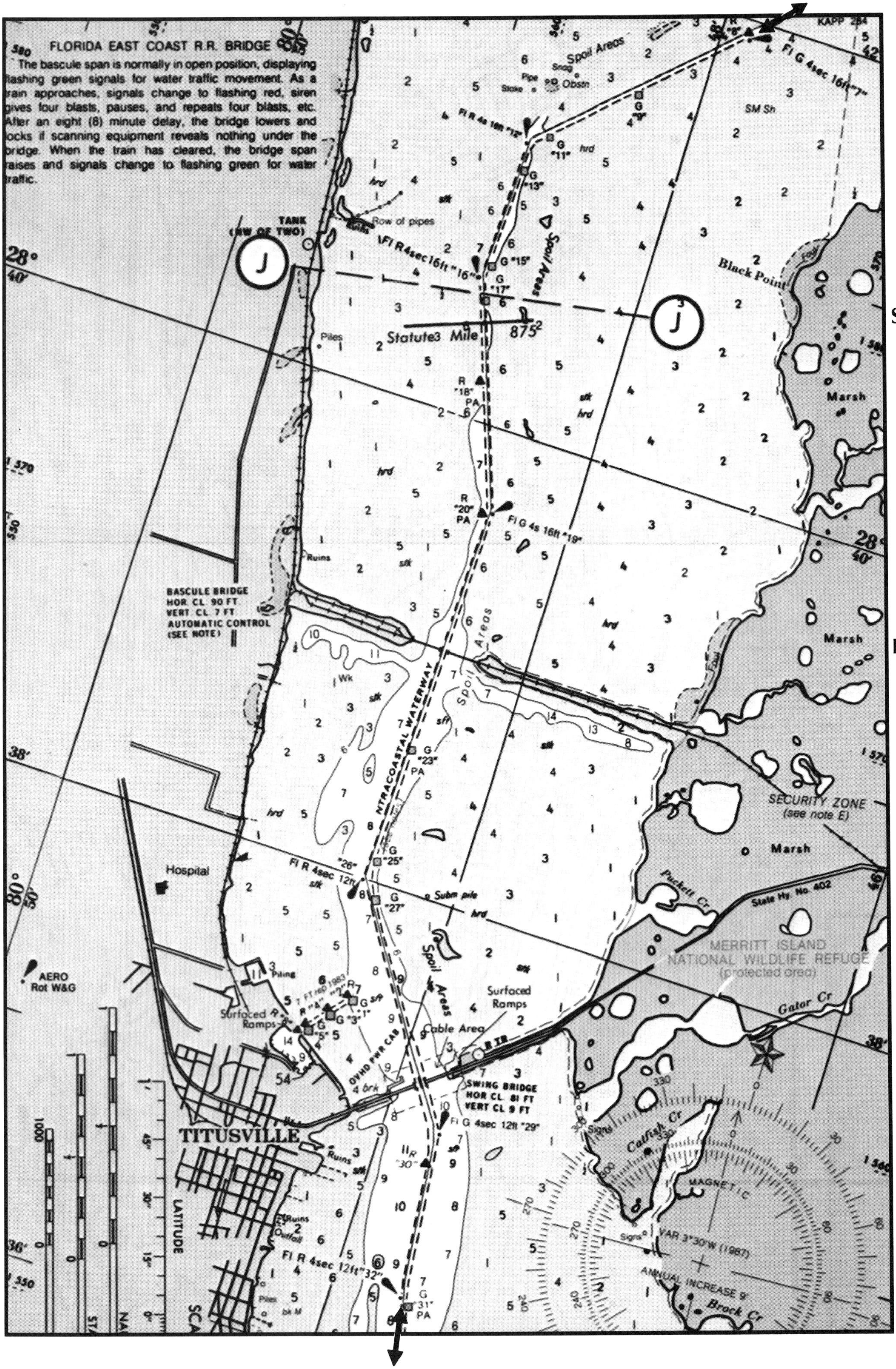

148

## FLORIDA EAST COAST R.R. BRIDGE

The bascule span is normally in open position, displaying flashing green signals for water traffic movement. As a train approaches, signals change to flashing red, siren gives four blasts, pauses, and repeats four blasts, etc. After an eight (8) minute delay, the bridge lowers and locks if scanning equipment reveals nothing under the bridge. When the train has cleared, the bridge span raises and signals change to flashing green for water traffic.

StM875

BR876.6

BR878.9

TANK (NW OF TWO)

Spoil Areas

Black Point

SM Sh

Marsh

Statute Mile 875

R "18" PA

R "20" PA

Fl G 4s 16ft "19"

BASCULE BRIDGE
HOR. CL. 90 FT.
VERT. CL. 7 FT.
AUTOMATIC CONTROL
(SEE NOTE)

INTRACOASTAL WATERWAY

Spoil Areas

Marsh

SECURITY ZONE
(see note E)

Hospital

Fl R 4sec 12ft "26"

G "23" PA

G "25"

G "27"

Subm pile

Puckett Cr

State Hy. No. 402

MERRITT ISLAND
NATIONAL WILDLIFE REFUGE
(protected area)

Gator Cr

AERO
Rot W&G

Piling

7 FT rep 1983

R "A"

G "3"

G "5"

Surfaced Ramps

OVHD PWR CAB

Surfaced Ramps

Cable Area

R T8

SWING BRIDGE
HOR. CL. 81 FT
VERT. CL. 9 FT
Fl G 4sec 12ft "29"

Signs

Catfish Cr

TITUSVILLE

Ruins

R "30"

LATITUDE

SCALE

Fl R 4sec 12ft "32"

G "31" PA

MAGNETIC

VAR 3°30'W (1987)

ANNUAL INCREASE 9'

Brock Cr

28° 40'

38'

80° 40'

36'

BR878.9

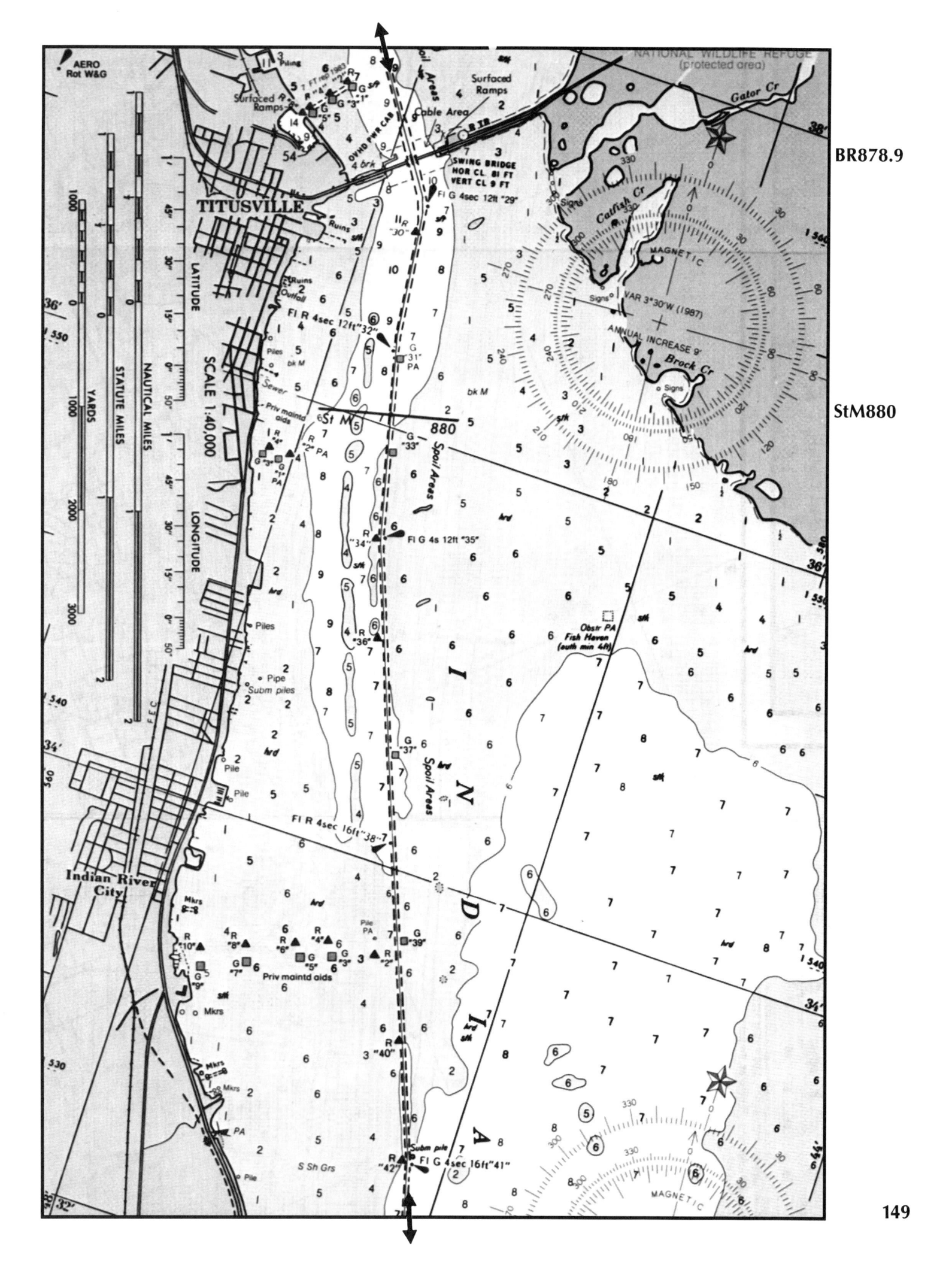

StM880

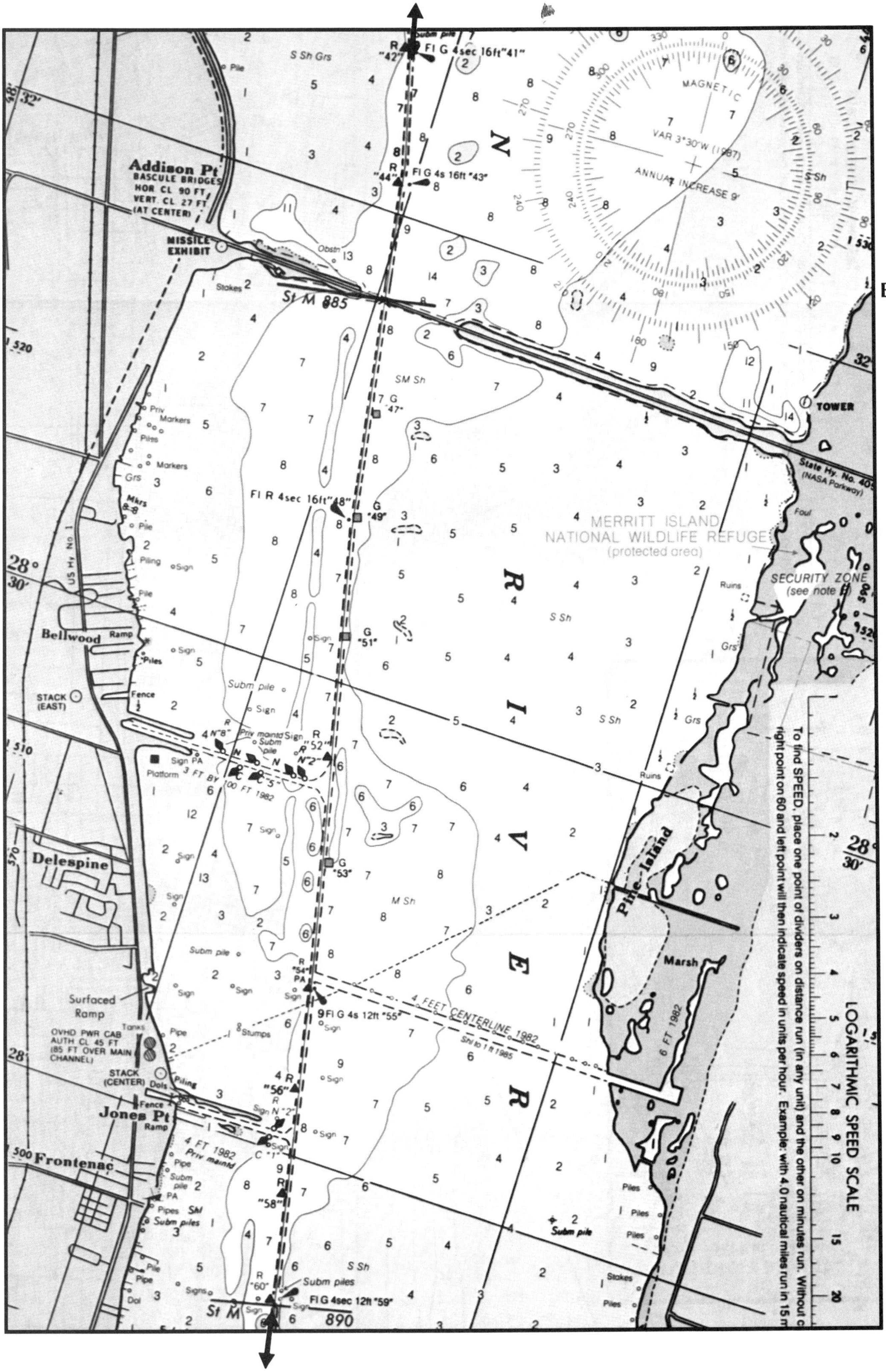


BR885.0

StM890

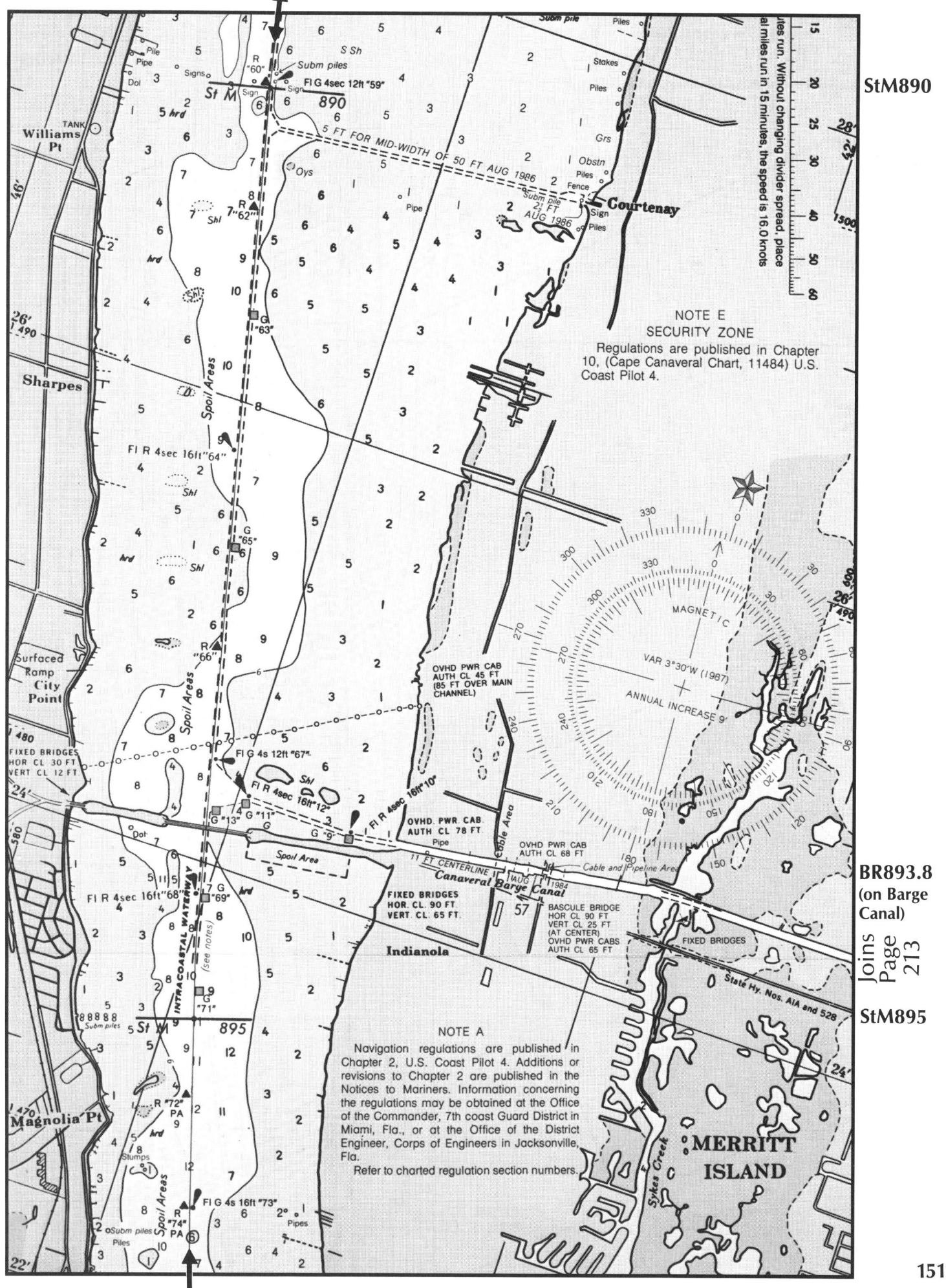

StM890

NOTE E
SECURITY ZONE
Regulations are published in Chapter 10, (Cape Canaveral Chart, 11484) U.S. Coast Pilot 4.

BR893.8
(on Barge Canal)

Joins Page 213

StM895

NOTE A
Navigation regulations are published in Chapter 2, U.S. Coast Pilot 4. Additions or revisions to Chapter 2 are published in the Notices to Mariners. Information concerning the regulations may be obtained at the Office of the Commander, 7th coast Guard District in Miami, Fla., or at the Office of the District Engineer, Corps of Engineers in Jacksonville, Fla.
Refer to charted regulation section numbers.

151

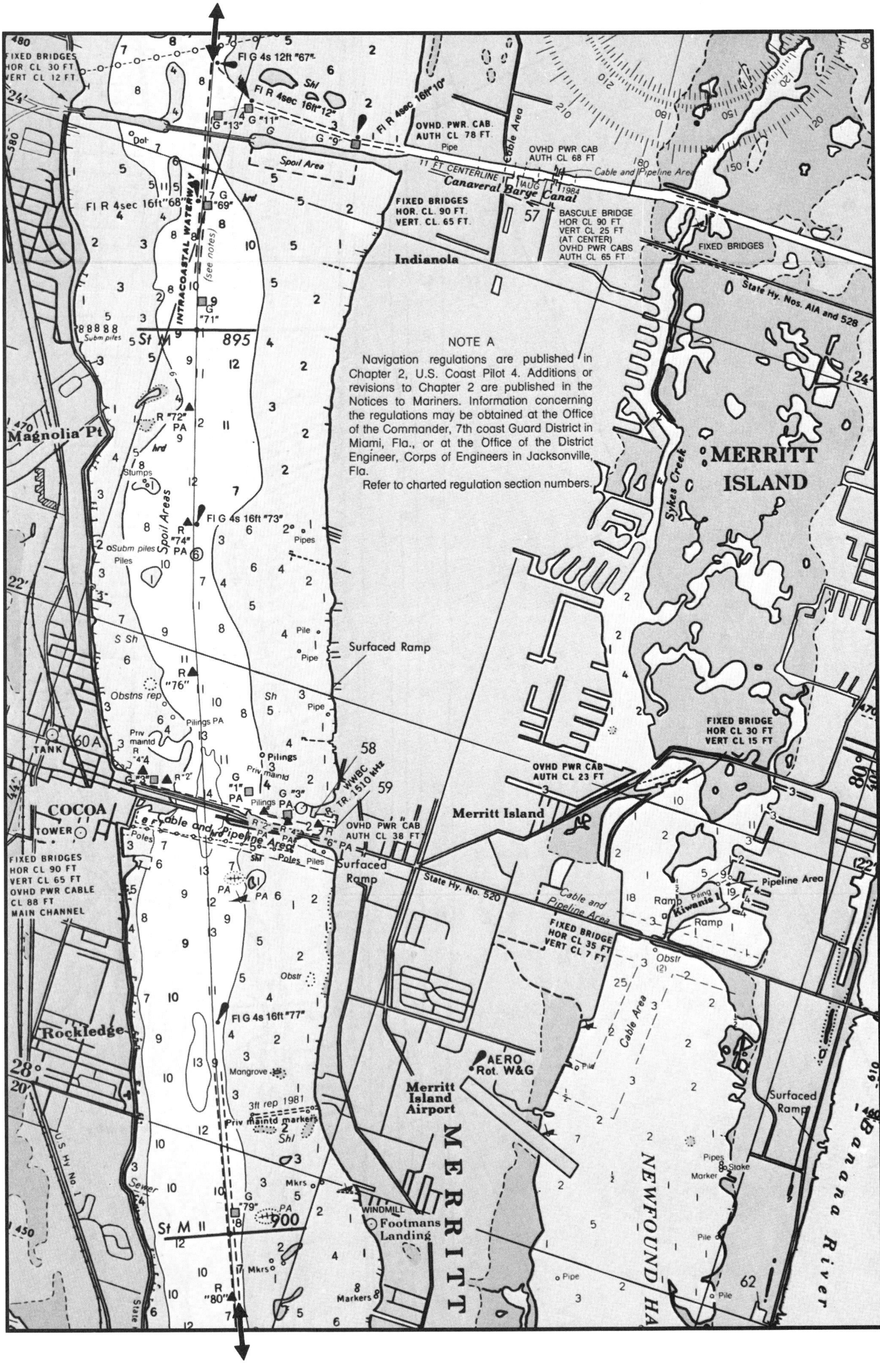


BR893.8
(on Barge
Canal)

Joins
Page
213

StM895

StM900

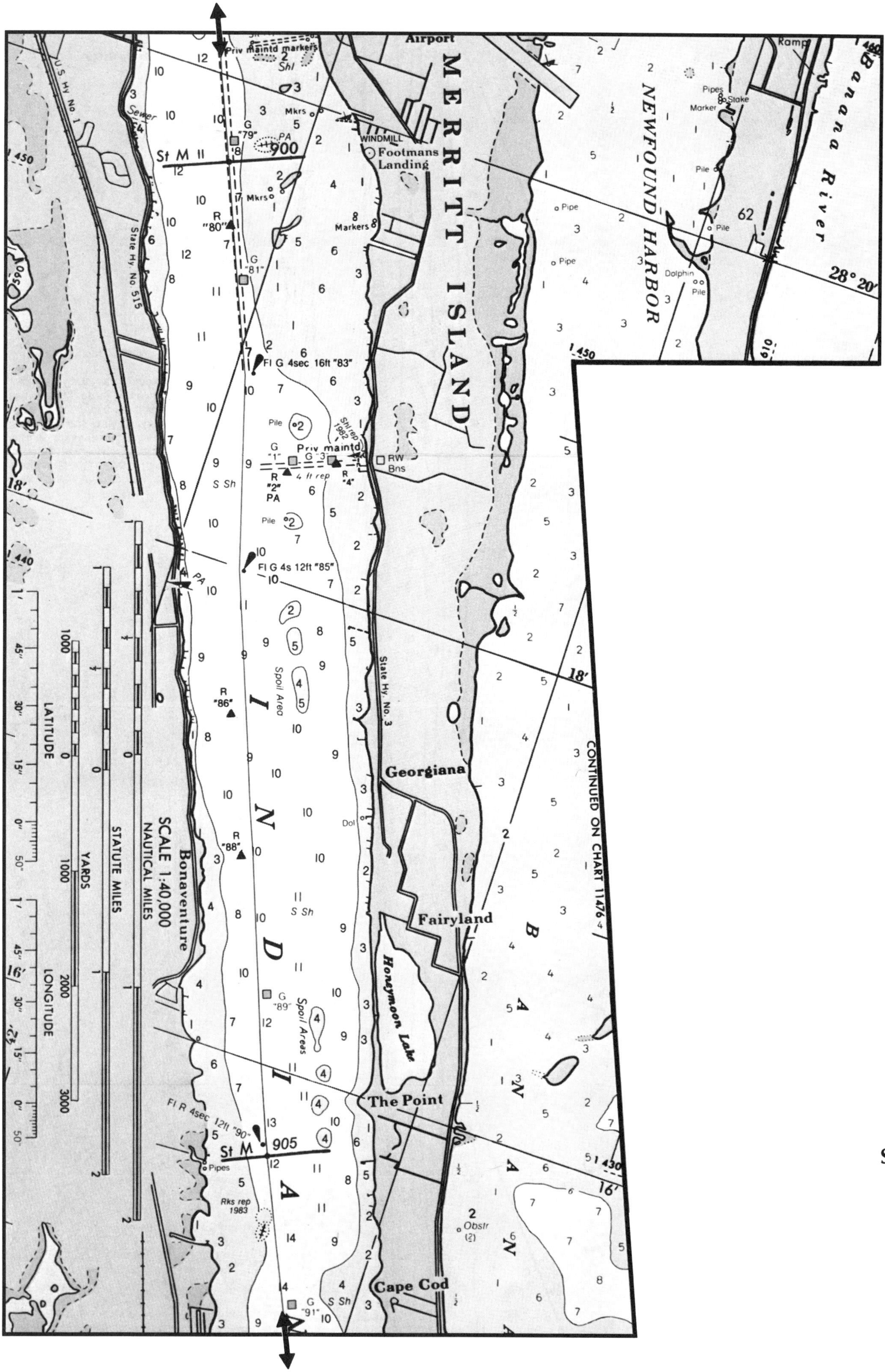


StM900

StM905

154

StM905

StM910

LONGITUDE

2000

3000

30'
15'
0'
50'

G "89"
Spoil Areas

Fl R 4sec 12ft "90"
St M 905

The Point

Rks rep 1983

Honeymoon Lake

I N T A N A R

4 3 N

1 430

16'

Cape Cod

G "91"
S Sh

2
Obstr (2)

Stakes
Pipe

Lotus

Subm pipe PA
Pipes

Pile
Pipes
Piles

R "92" PA

Pipe
Pile

Pile

R I V E R

Pineda

FEC

Pipe Subm pile PA
Pipes
Piles

Pile

R "94"

Spoil Area

1 420

6
1 420

14'

800

Plover Pt

Subm stake
Subm piles

Mangrove Pt

M Sh

NOTE B
The daybeacons are privately
maintained and positions are
approximate.

Fl G 4s 12ft "95"

Spoil Area PA

M Sh
(2 ft rep 1986)

Priv maintd
markers

1 410

R "6A"

R I V E R

Surfaced Ramp
FIXED BRIDGES
HOR CL 90 FT
VERT CL 65 FT

Spoil Area

12'
300
330
330
300
300

MAGNETIC
VAR 3°30'W (1987)
ANNUAL INCREASE 9'

FIXED BRIDGES
HOR CL 60 FT
VERT CL 43 FT

G "1" G "3" G "5"
R "6"

G "7A"

(see note B)
4 ft rep 1981

1 410

620

1 400

Statute Mile

910

Spoil Area

G "7"
R "6"

Piling

12'

Palm Shores

R "98"

K

Subm pile
Grs

G

K

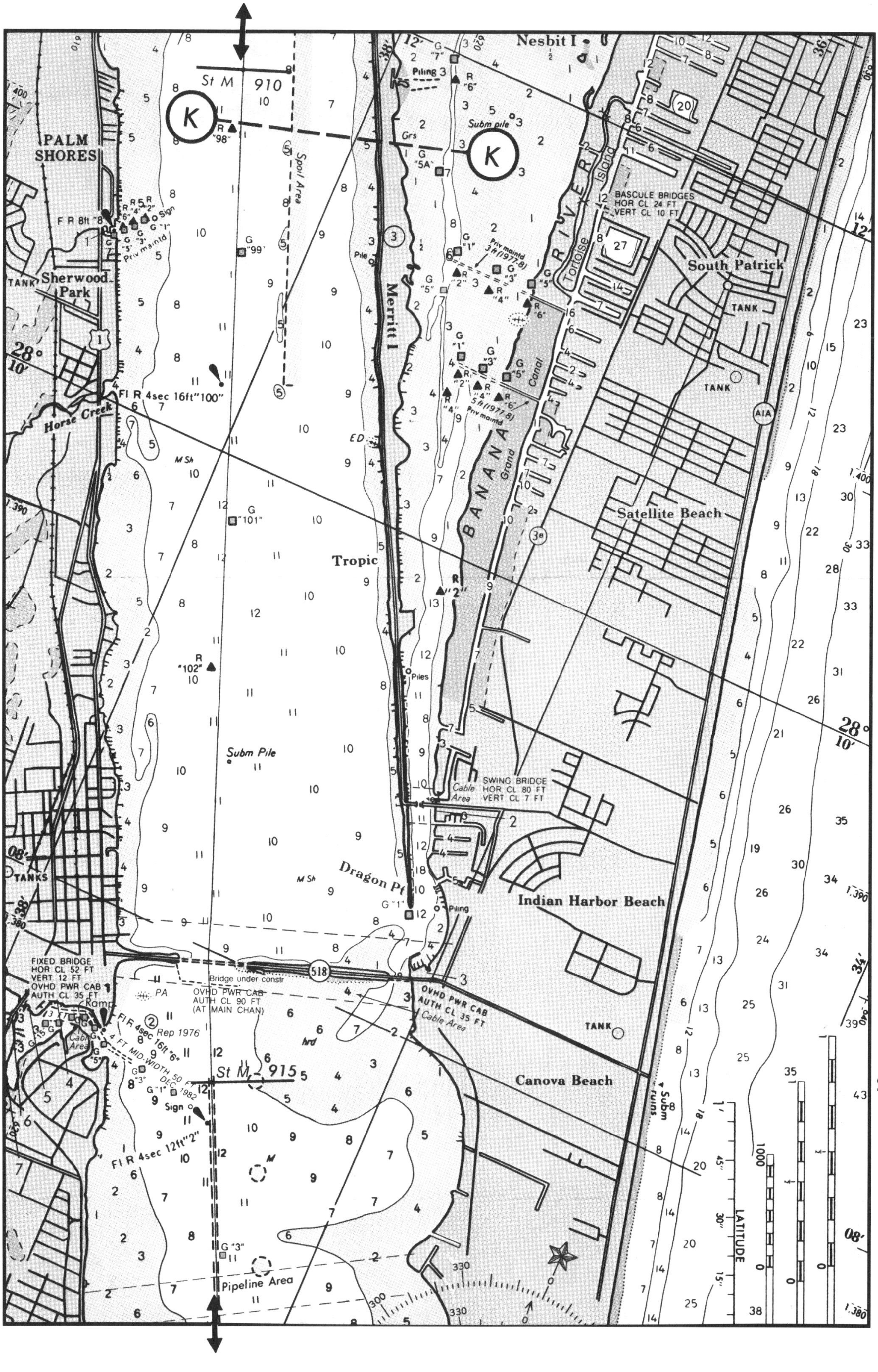


StM910

StM915

StM915

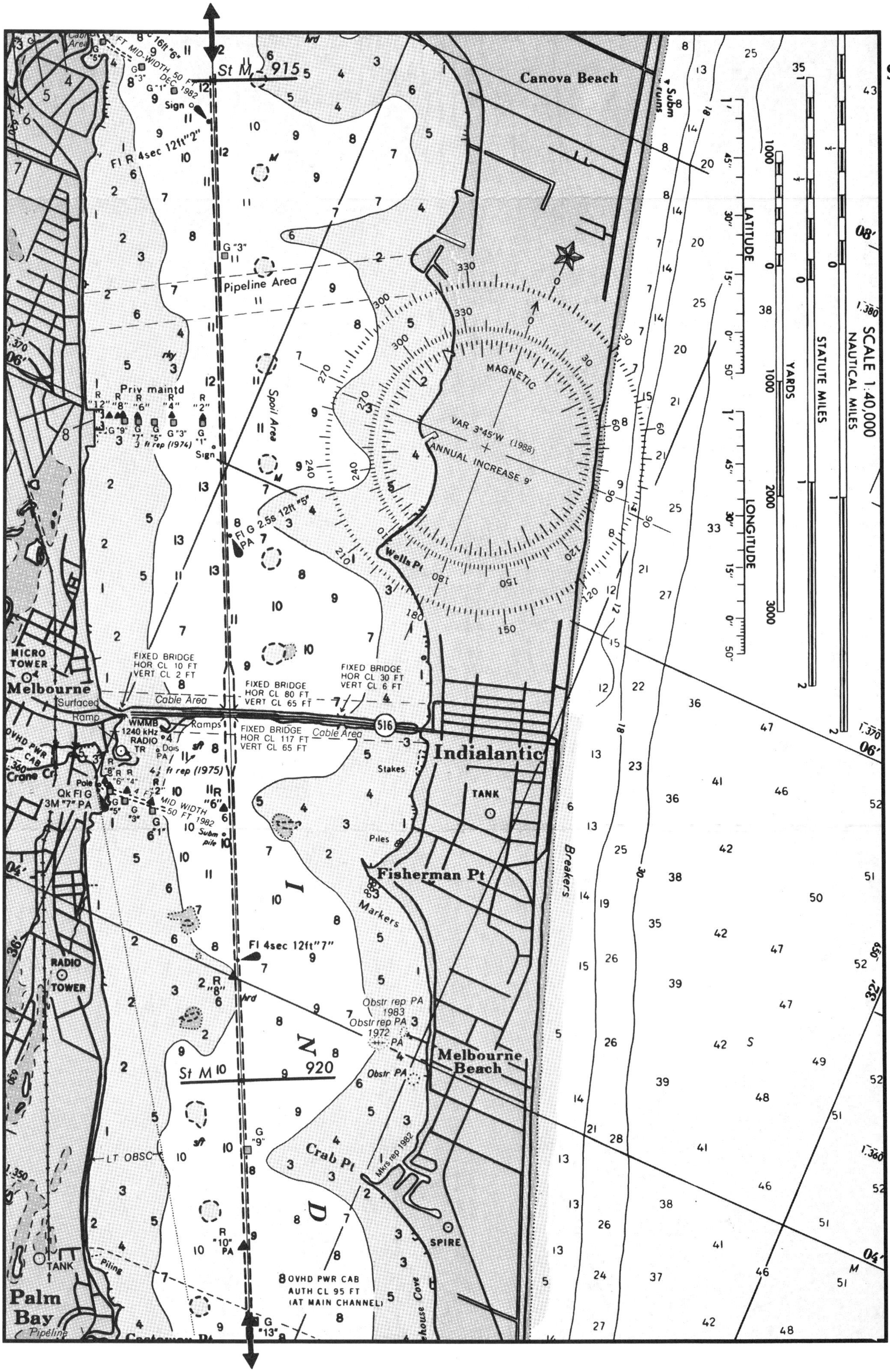


StM920

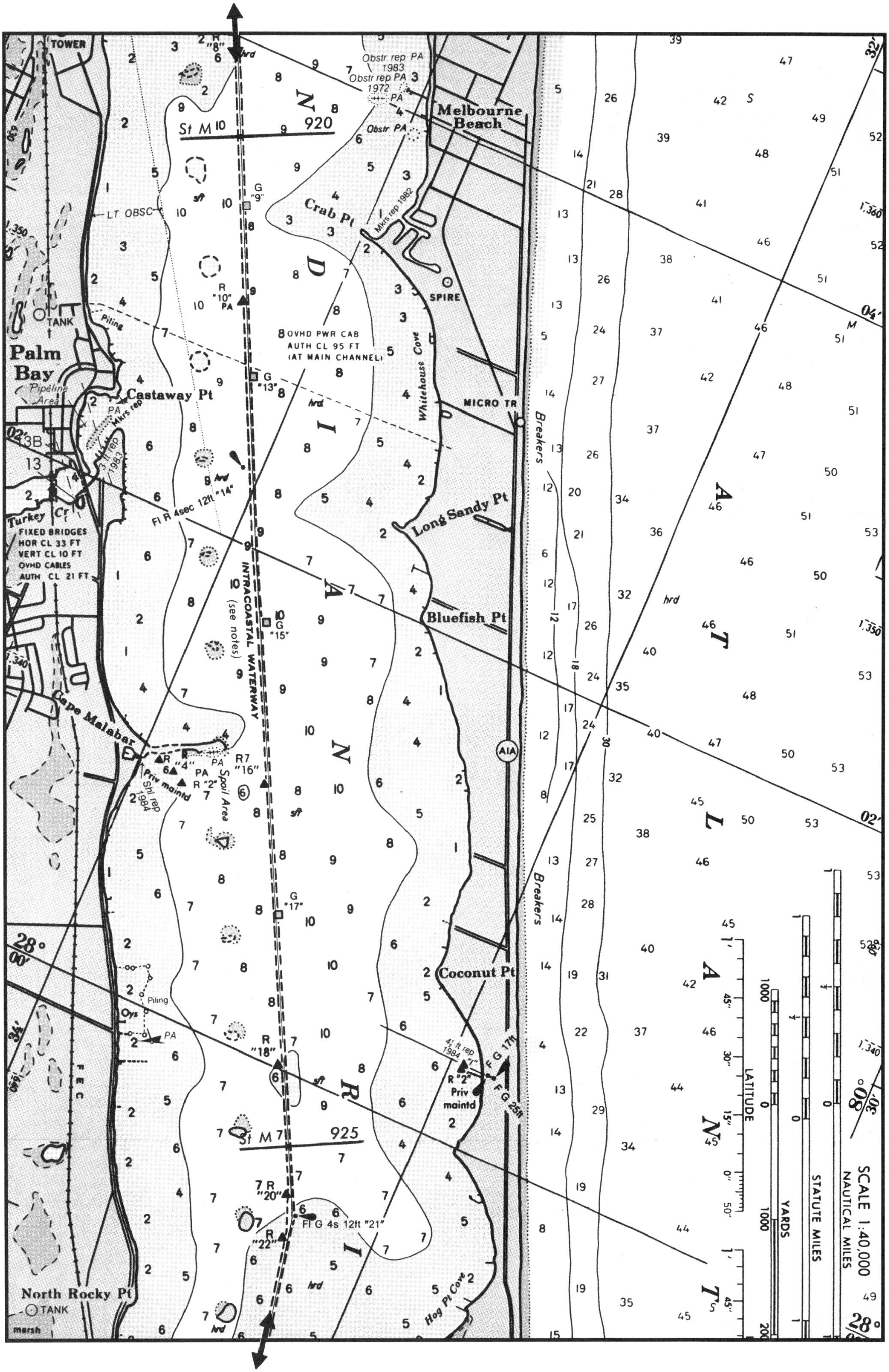


StM920

StM925

StM925

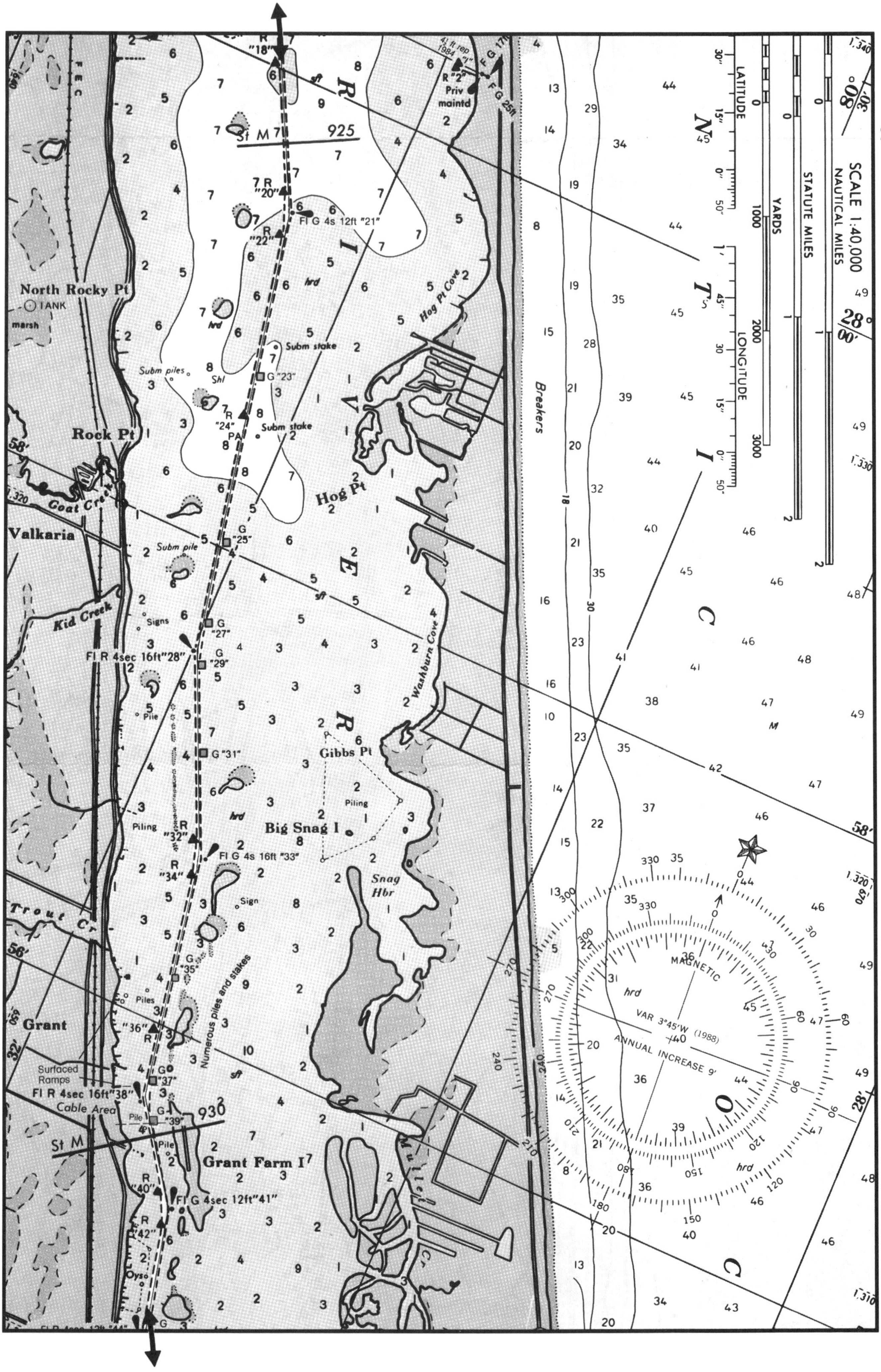


StM930

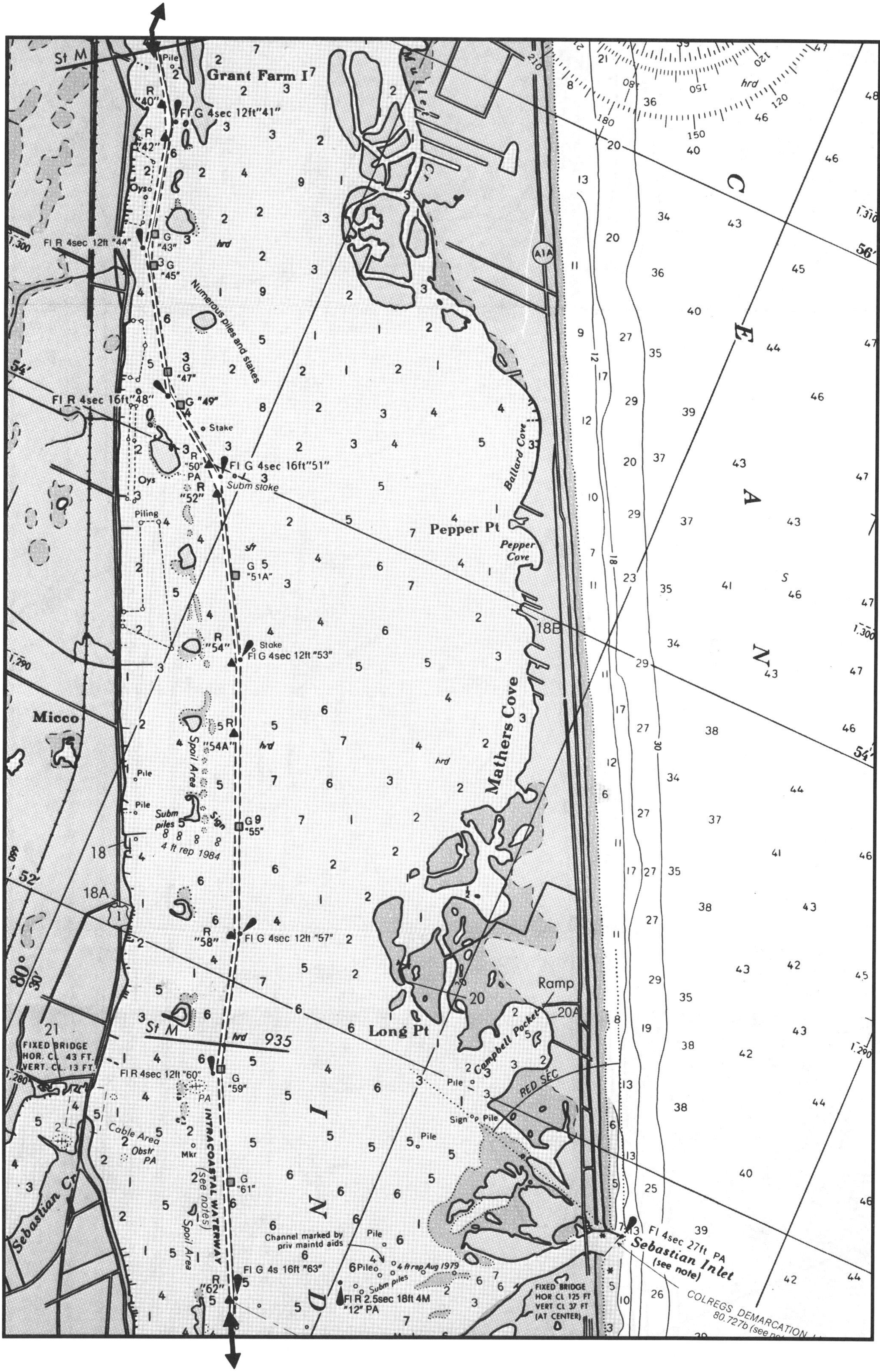
StM930
Grant Farm I
Fl G 4sec 12ft "41"
Fl R 4sec 12ft "44"
Numerous piles and stakes
Fl R 4sec 16ft "48"
Stake
Fl G 4sec 16ft "51"
Subm stake
Piling
Ballard Cove
Pepper Pt
Pepper Cove
Stake
Fl G 4sec 12ft "53"
Micco
Mathers Cove
Spoil Area
Subm piles
4 ft rep 1984
Fl G 4sec 12ft "57"
Ramp
Long Pt
Campbell Pocket
St M
935
FIXED BRIDGE
HOR. CL. 43 FT.
VERT. CL. 13 FT.
Fl R 4sec 12ft "60"
Cable Area
Obstr PA
Mkr
INTRACOASTAL WATERWAY
(see notes)
RED SEC
Sign
Pile
Sebastian Cr
Channel marked by
priv maintd aids
4 ft rep Aug 1979
Subm piles
Fl G 4s 16ft "63"
Fl R 2.5sec 18ft 4M
"12" PA
FIXED BRIDGE
HOR CL 125 FT
VERT CL 37 FT
(AT CENTER)
Fl 4sec 27ft PA
Sebastian Inlet
(see note)
COLREGS DEMARCATION
OCEAN
INDIAN
StM935

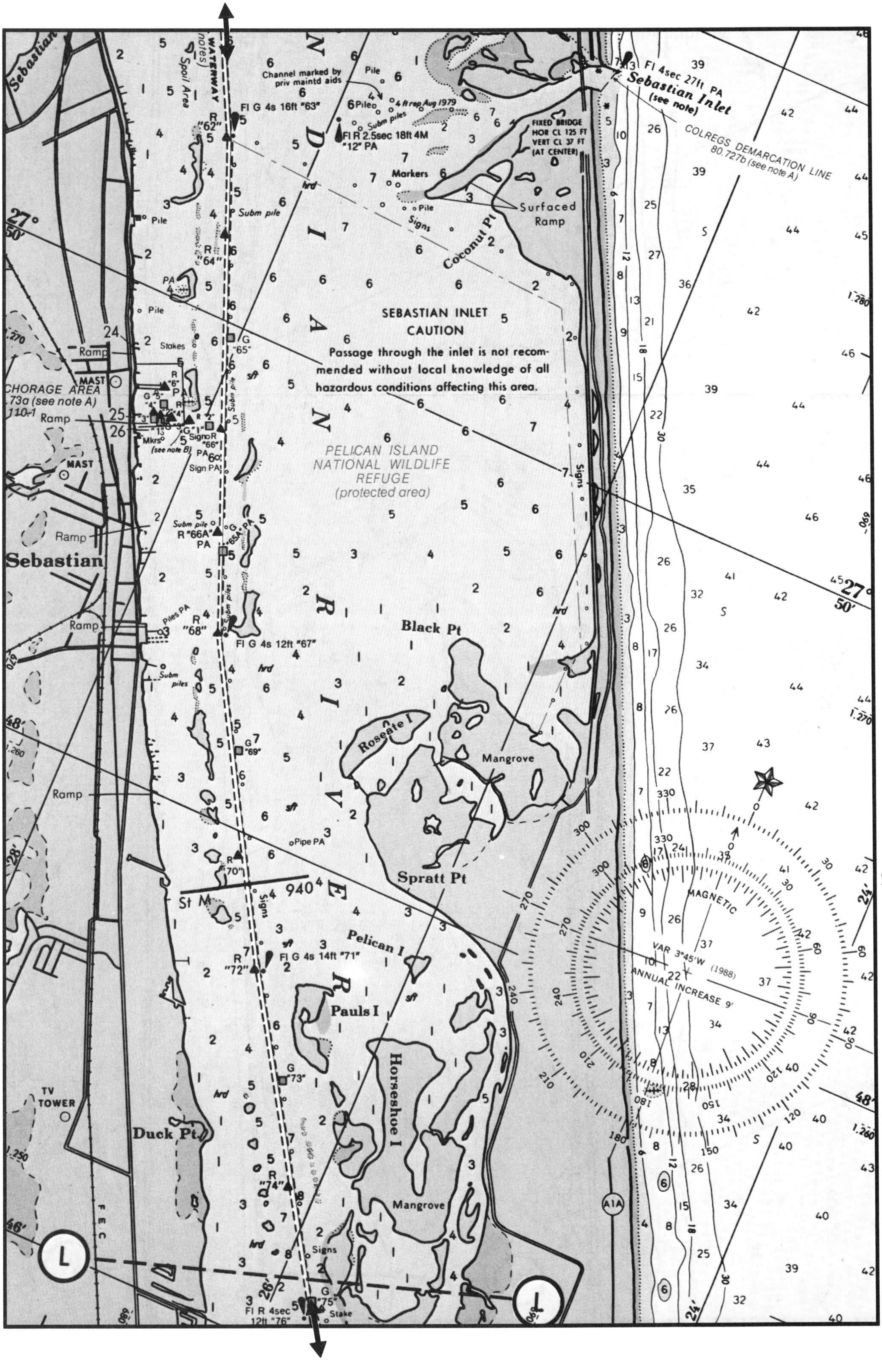
SEBASTIAN INLET
CAUTION
Passage through the inlet is not recommended without local knowledge of all hazardous conditions affecting this area.
PELICAN ISLAND NATIONAL WILDLIFE REFUGE
(protected area)
Sebastian Inlet
(see note)
Fl 4sec 27ft PA
COLREGS DEMARCATION LINE
80.727b (see note A)
FIXED BRIDGE
HOR CL 125 FT
VERT CL 37 FT
(AT CENTER)
Surfaced Ramp
Coconut Pt
Channel marked by priv maintd aids
Black Pt
Roseate I
Mangrove
Spratt Pt
Pelican I
Pauls I
Horseshoe I
Duck Pt
TV TOWER
Sebastian
MAGNETIC
VAR 3°45'W (1988)
ANNUAL INCREASE 9'
WATERWAY
Spoil Area

StM940

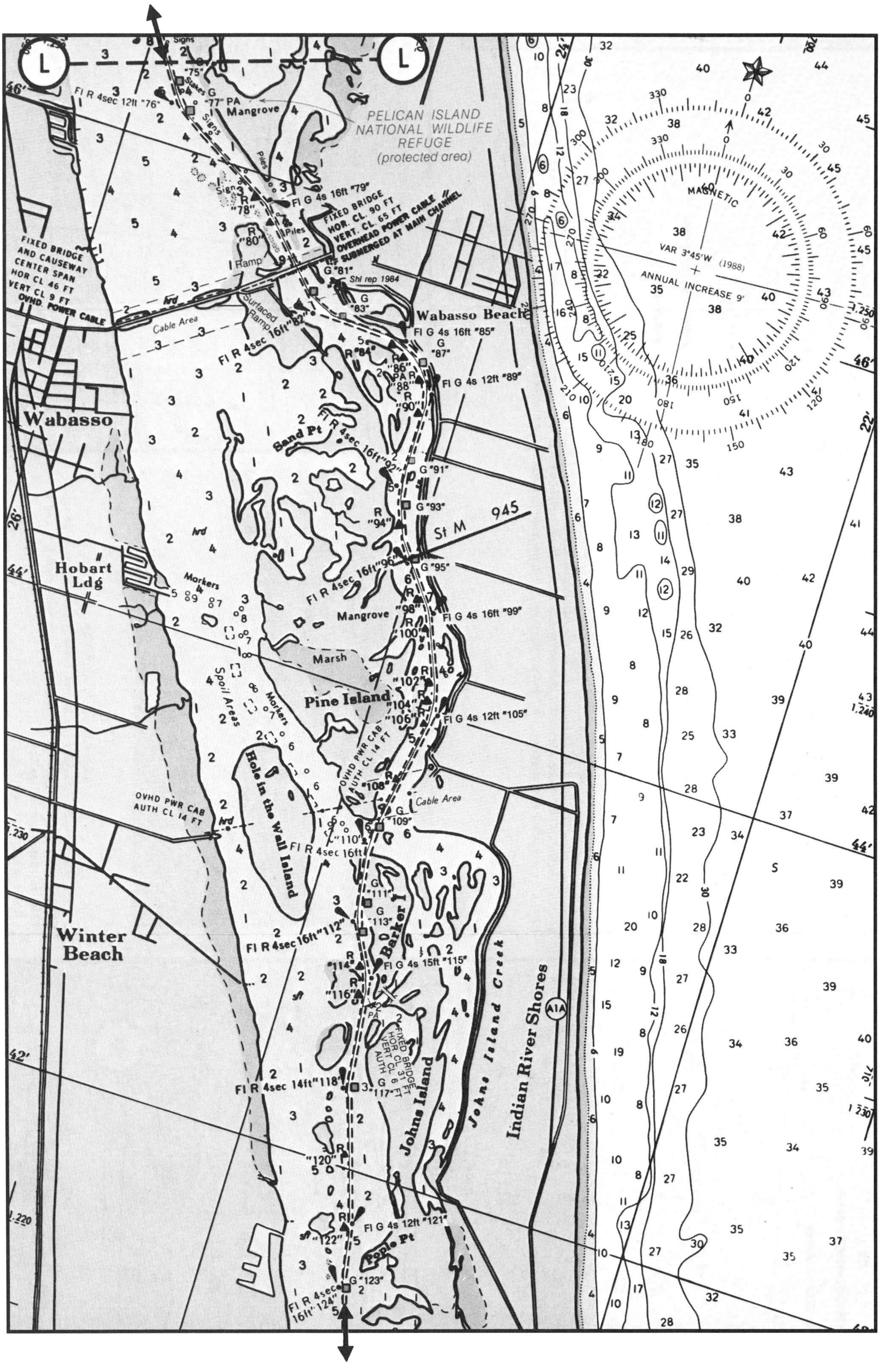
PELICAN ISLAND NATIONAL WILDLIFE REFUGE (protected area)
Mangrove
FIXED BRIDGE HOR. CL. 90 FT VERT. CL. 65 FT
OVERHEAD POWER CABLE SUBMERGED AT MAIN CHANNEL
FIXED BRIDGE AND CAUSEWAY CENTER SPAN HOR CL 46 FT VERT CL 9 FT OVHD. POWER CABLE
Cable Area
Surfaced Ramp
Ramp
Shl rep 1984
Wabasso Beach
Wabasso
Sand Pt
St M 945
Hobart Ldg
Markers
Mangrove
Marsh
Pine Island
Spoil Areas
Hole in the Wall Island
OVHD PWR CAB AUTH CL 14 FT
Cable Area
Winter Beach
Barker
FIXED BRIDGE HOR CL 31 FT VERT CL 6 FT AUTH
Johns Island
Johns Island Creek
Indian River Shores
A1A
Pople Pt
MAGNETIC
VAR 3°45'W (1988)
ANNUAL INCREASE 9'

StM945

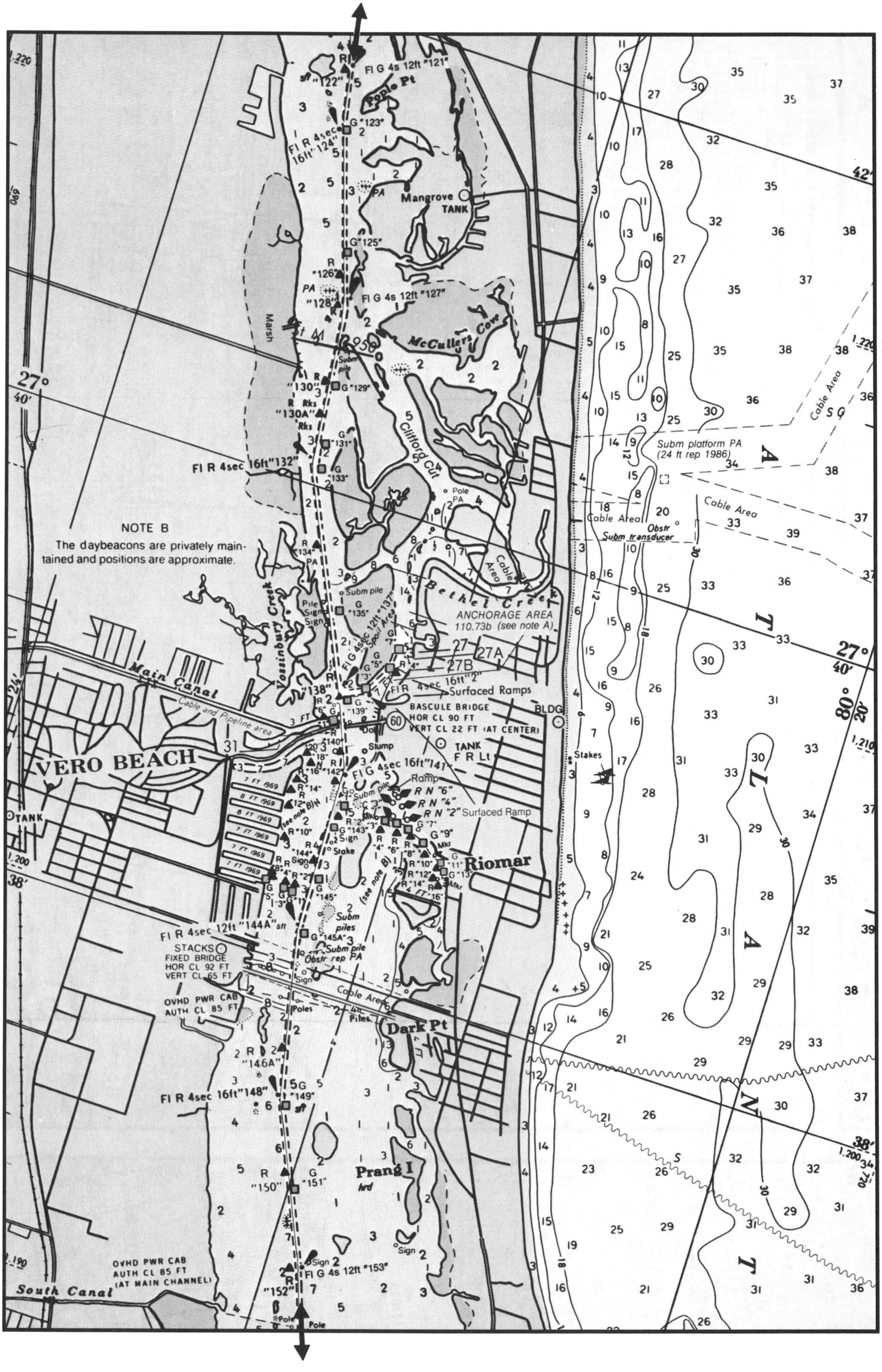


StM950

BR951.9

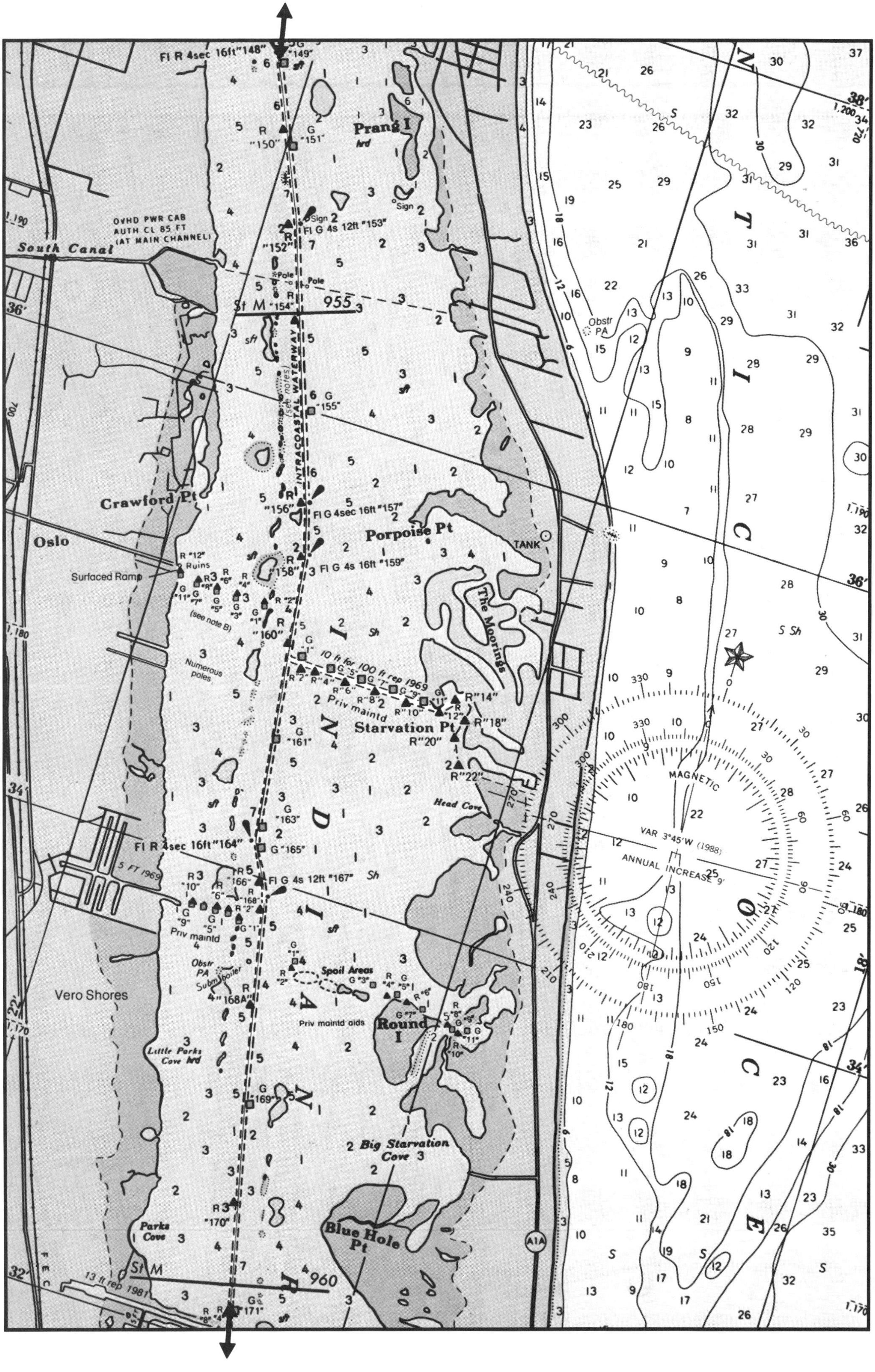

StM955

StM960

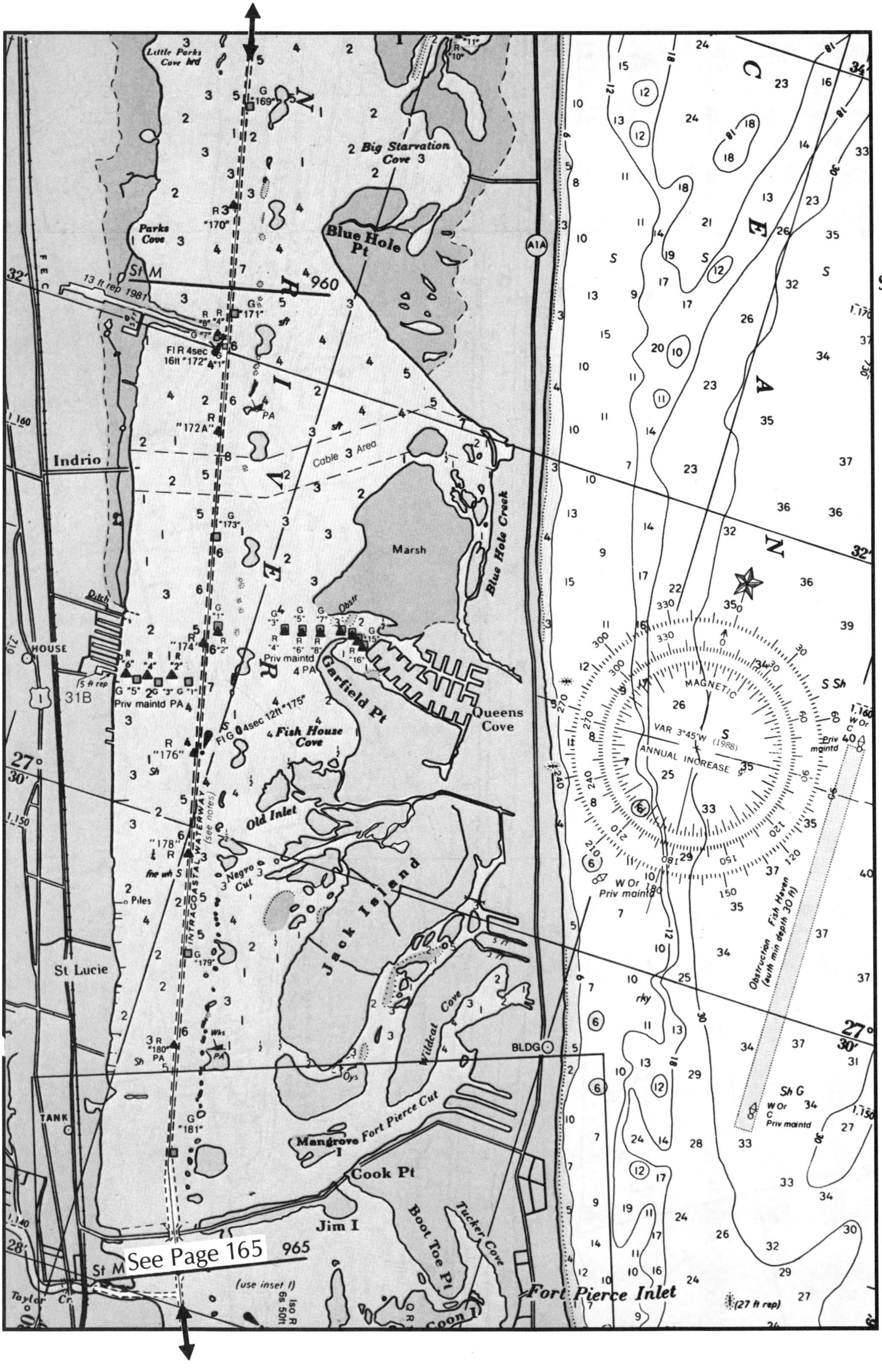


StM960

BR964.8

StM965

BR964.8

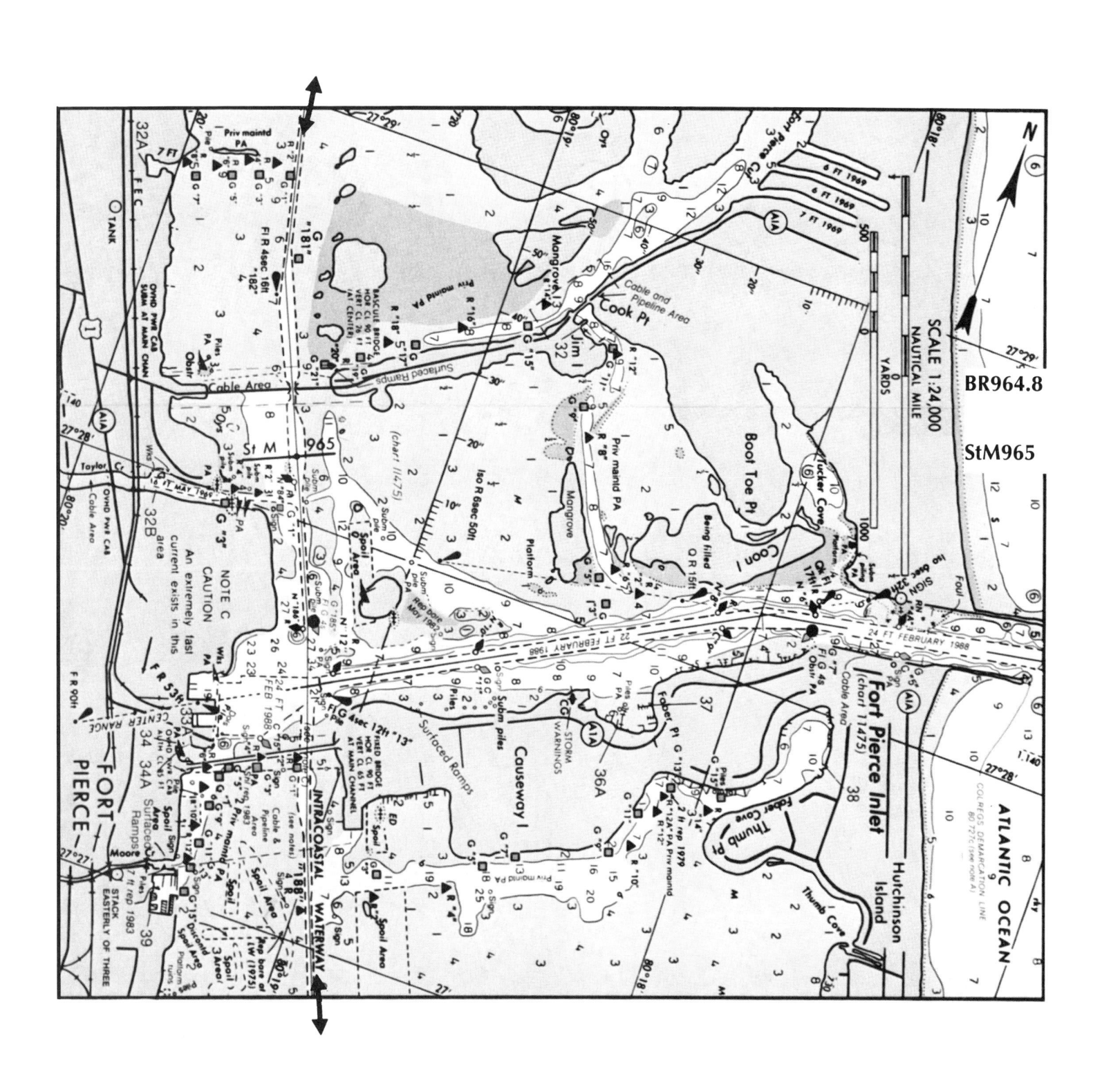

StM965

166

BR964.8

StM965

StM970

Mangrove Fort
Cook Pt
Jim I
Boot Toe Pt
Tucker Cove
Coon I
Fort Pierce Inlet
965
St M
Taylor Cr.
FORT PIERCE
(use inset I)
Iso R 6s 50ft
Q R 15ft
(27 ft rep)
N "4"
R 29
30
27
26
Fl R 4s "2"
WHISTLE
24 FT FEBRUARY 1988
(chart 11475)
G C "3"
CG
Faber Cove
STORM WARNINGS
Causeway I
Thumb Pt
COLREGS DEMARCATION LINE
80.727c (see note A)
STACK
Platform ruins
R "188"
See Page 165
Sewer
Sign
Sign
G "189"
Hook Pt
Surfaced Ramp
TANK
Jennings Cove
Sh
R "190"
M
G "191"
M
Hutchinson Island
A1A
Bear Pt
Fl R 4sec 16ft "192"
OVHD PWR CAB AUTH CL 85 FT (AT MAIN CHANNEL)
Bear Point Cove
G "193"
M
R "194"
M
G "195" 970
St M
R "196"
M
Middle Pt
Middle Cove
Shl
Shl
Shl

SCALE 1:40,000
LATITUDE
LONGITUDE
YARDS
STATUTE MILES
NAUTICAL MILES

F.E.C.

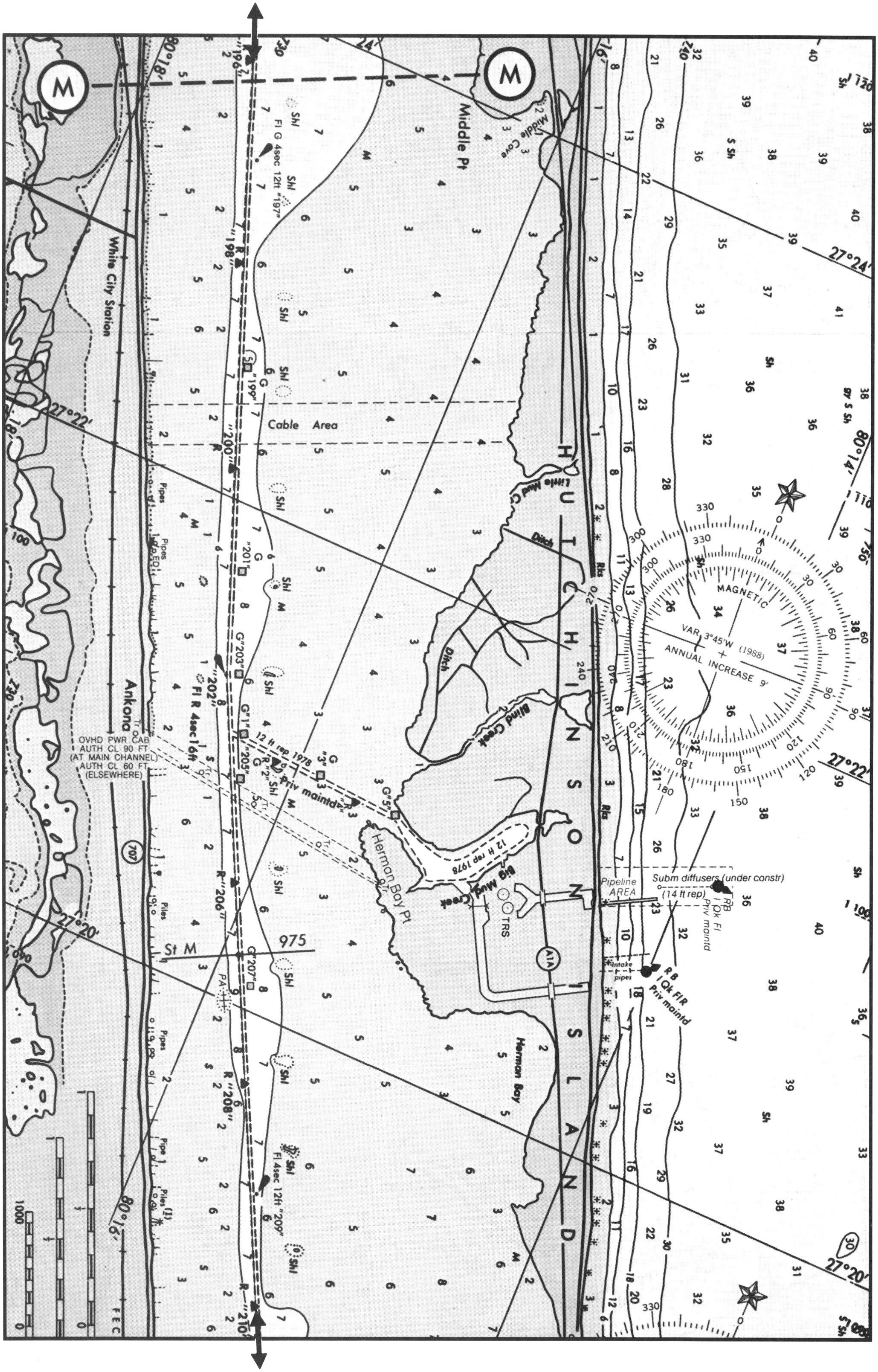
White City Station
Ankona
Middle Pt
Middle Cove
Cable Area
HUTCHINSON ISLAND
Little Mud C
Blind Creek
Big Mud Creek
Herman Bay Pt
Herman Bay
Ditch
MAGNETIC
VAR 3°45'W (1988)
ANNUAL INCREASE 9'
OVHD PWR CAB
AUTH CL 90 FT
(AT MAIN CHANNEL)
AUTH CL 60 FT
(ELSEWHERE)
Cable Area
Pipeline AREA
Subm diffusers (under constr)
(14 ft rep)
12 ft rep 1978
Priv maintd
St M 975
27°24'
27°22'
27°20'
80°18'
80°16'
80°14'

StM975

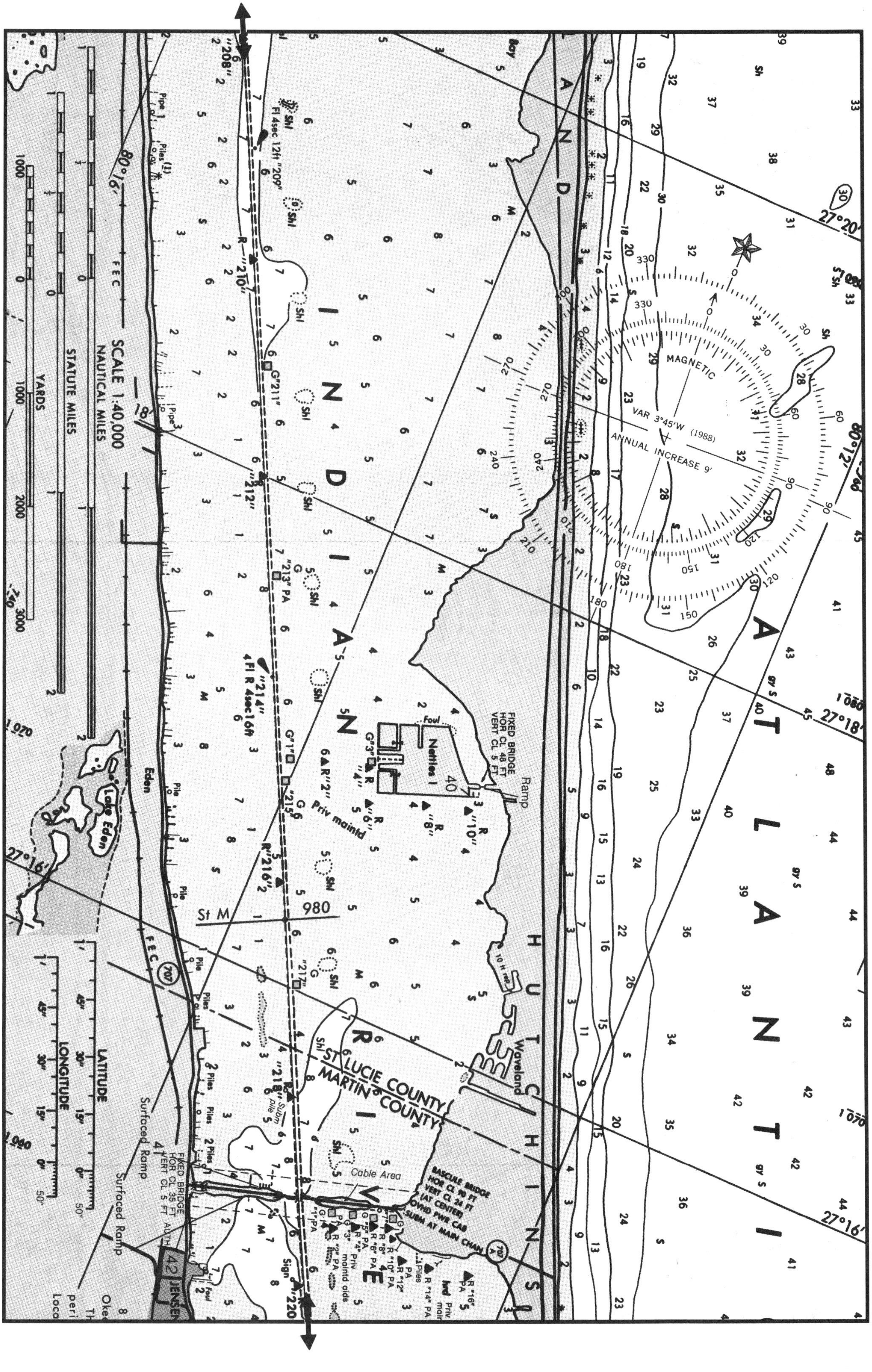


StM980

BR981.4

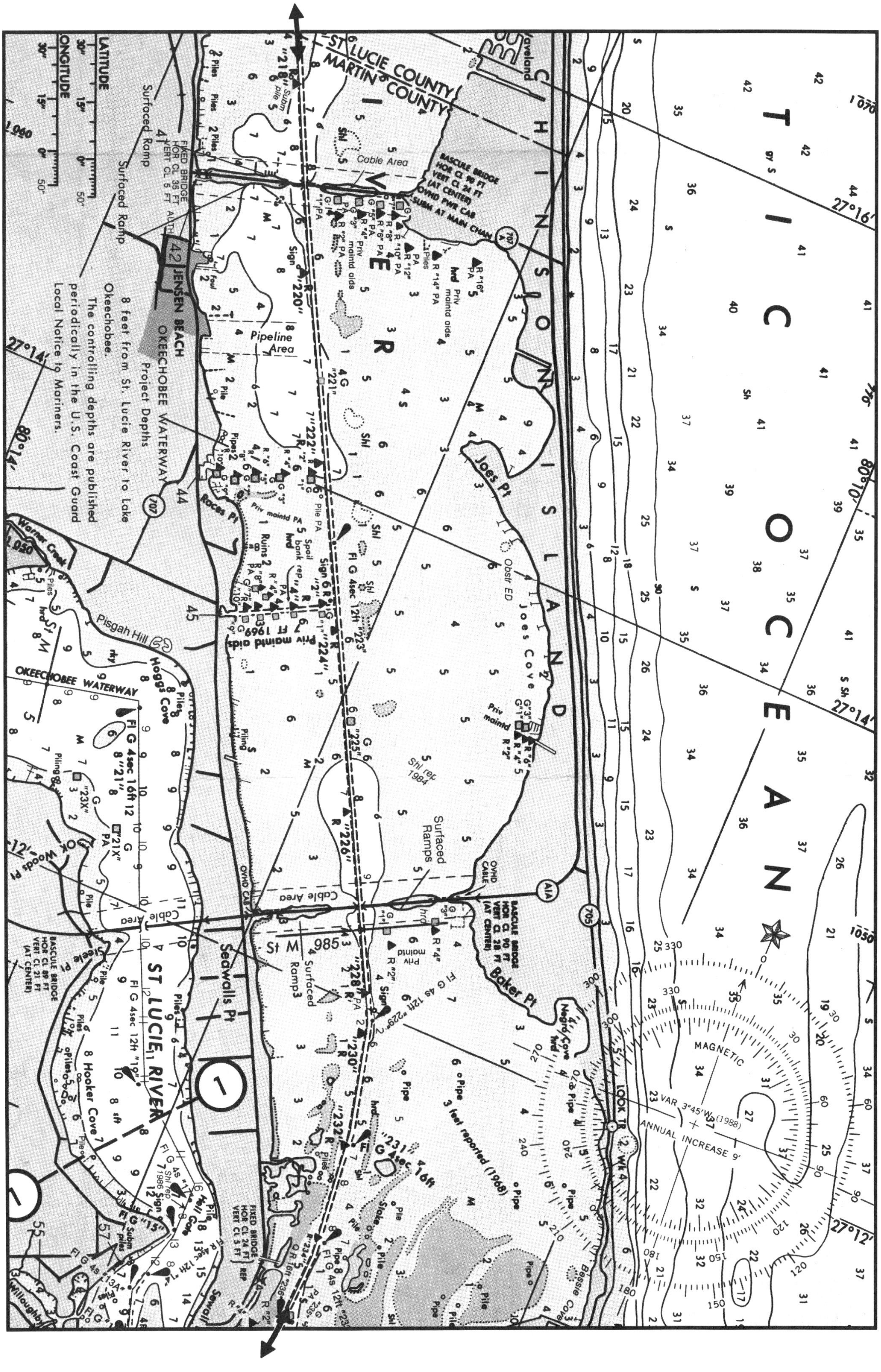


BR981.4

BR984.9
StM985

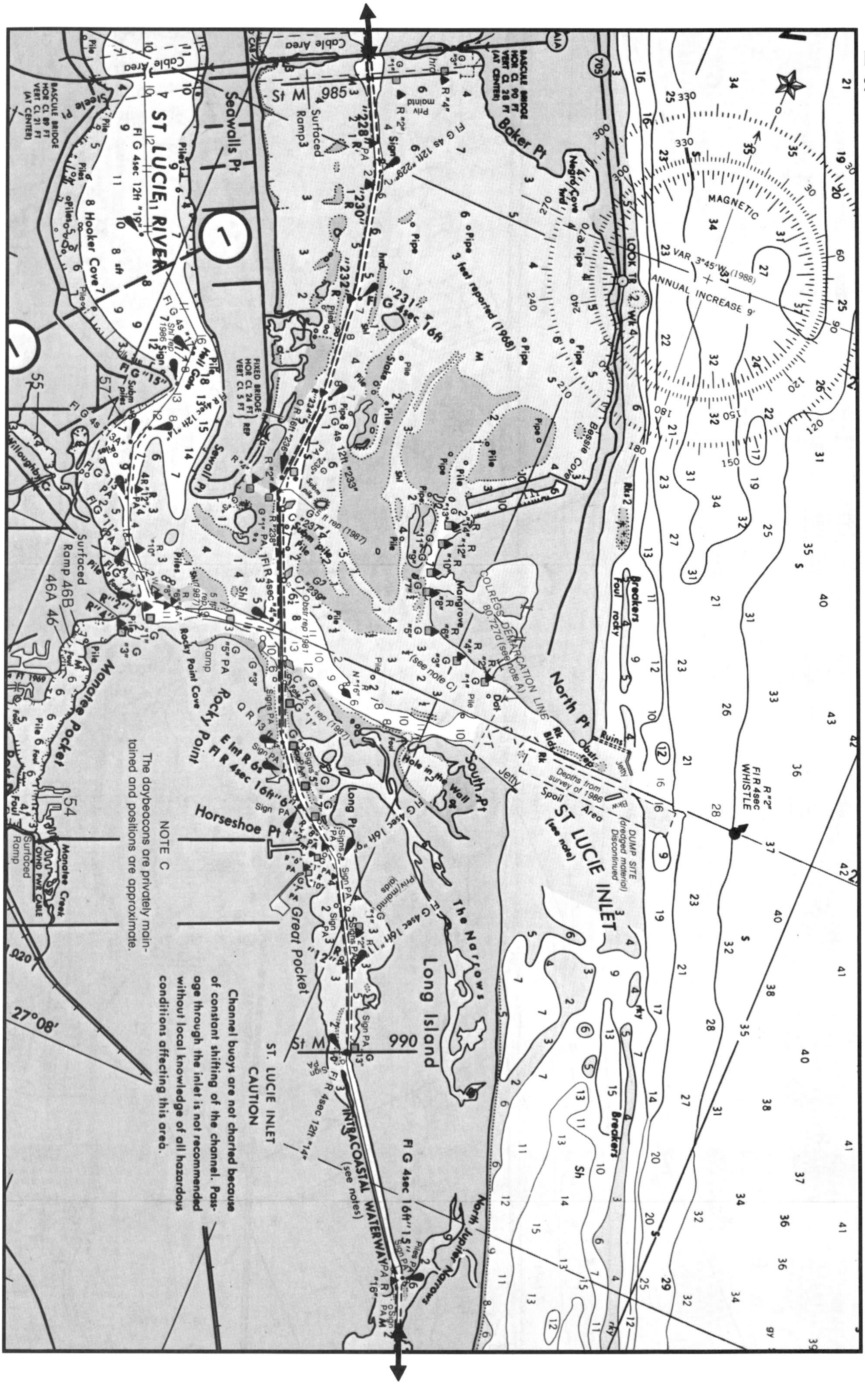
ST. LUCIE INLET
CAUTION
Channel buoys are not charted because of constant shifting of the channel. Passage through the inlet is not recommended without local knowledge of all hazardous conditions affecting this area.
NOTE C
The daybeacons are privately maintained and positions are approximate.
ST LUCIE INLET
ST LUCIE RIVER
INTRACOASTAL WATERWAY
Long Island
The Narrows
North Jupiter Narrows
Great Pocket
Horseshoe Pt
Rocky Point
Rocky Point Cove
Manatee Pocket
Manatee Creek
Sewall Pt
Seawalls Pt
Hooker Cove
Hell Gate
Baker Pt
Bessie Cove
North Pt
South Pt
Hole in the Wall
Long Pt
Mangrove
Steele Pt
Willoughby Cr
COLREGS DEMARCATION LINE 80.727d (see note A)
DUMP SITE (dredged material) Discontinued
Spoil Area
Depths from survey of 1986
Breakers
MAGNETIC
VAR 3°45'W (1988)
ANNUAL INCREASE 9'
St M 985
St M 990
27°08'
BASCULE BRIDGE HOR CL 90 FT VERT CL 28 FT (AT CENTER)
FIXED BRIDGE HOR CL 24 FT VERT CL 5 FT
BASCULE BRIDGE HOR CL 89 FT VERT CL 21 FT (AT CENTER)
Cable Area
Surfaced Ramp
R "2" Fl R 4sec WHISTLE

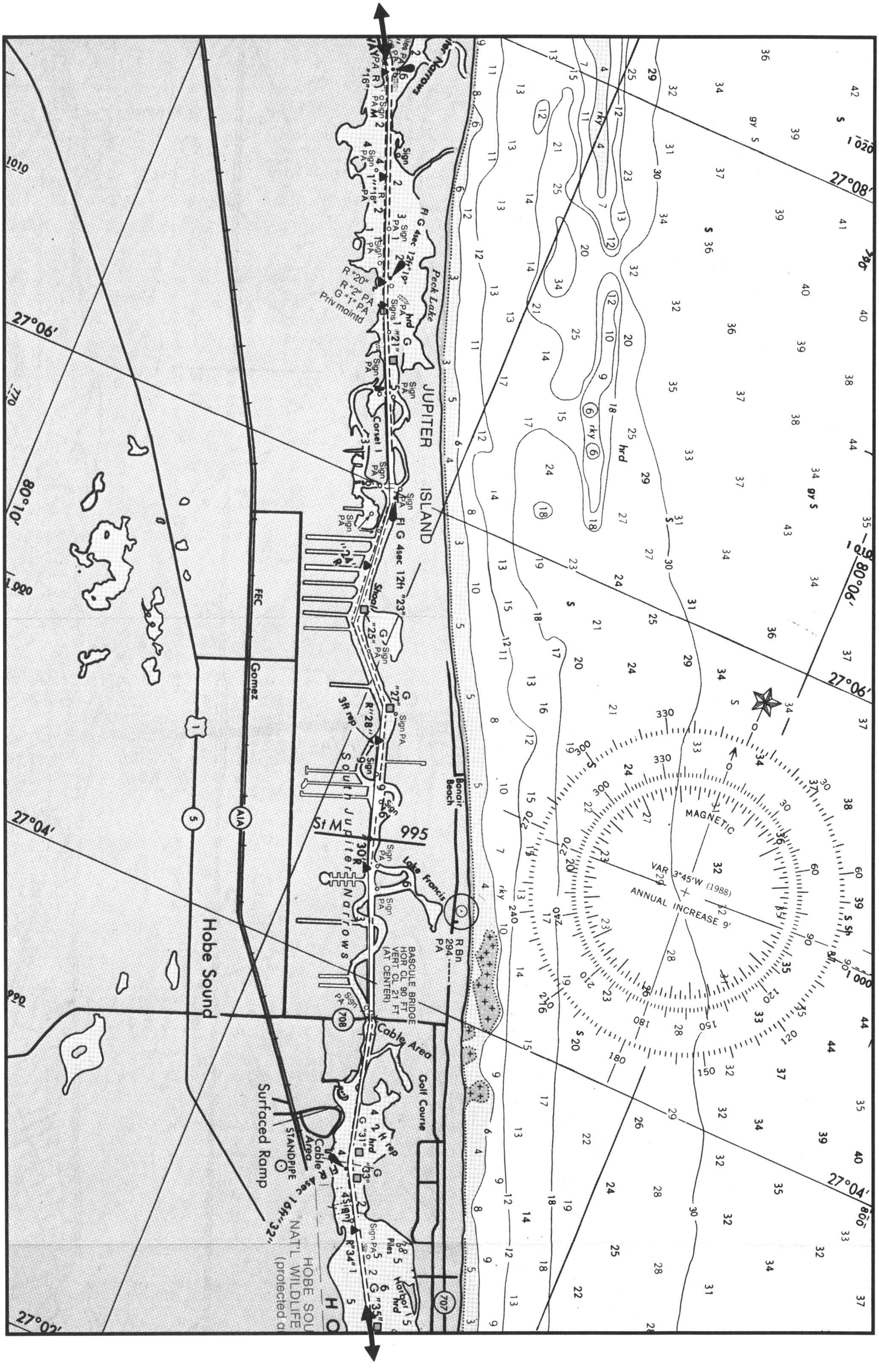


StM995

BR995.9

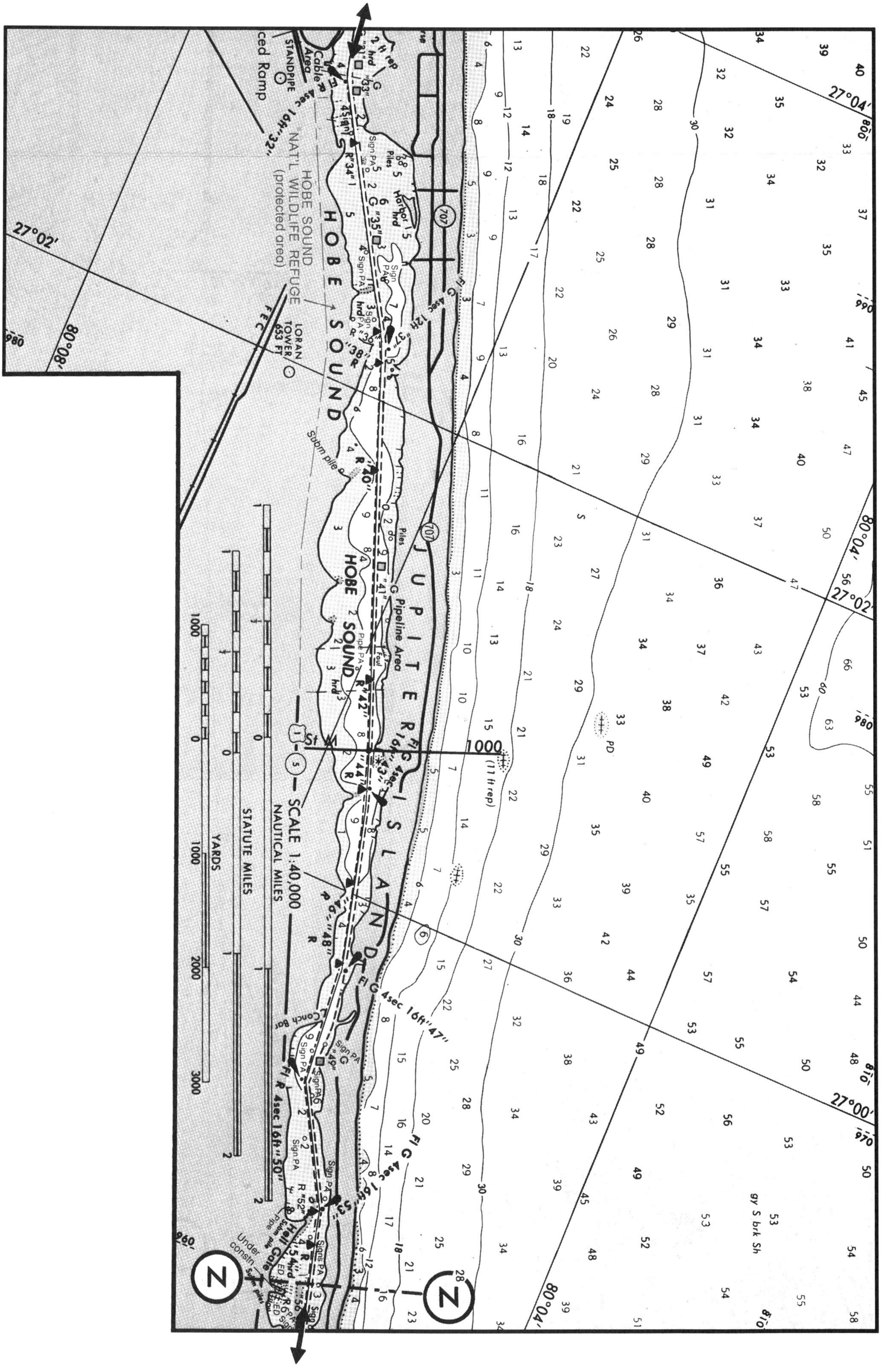
JUPITER ISLAND
HOBE SOUND
HOBE SOUND
HOBE SOUND NAT'L WILDLIFE REFUGE (protected area)
LORAN TOWER 653 FT
Pipeline Area
Conch Bar
Hell Gate
Cable Area
STANDPIPE
SCALE 1:40,000
NAUTICAL MILES
STATUTE MILES
YARDS
Fl G 4sec 16ft "53"
Fl R 4sec 16ft "50"
Fl G 4sec 16ft "47"
Fl G 4sec 16ft "43"
Fl G 4sec 12ft "37"
Fl R 4sec 16ft "32"
27°00'
27°02'
27°04'
80°04'
80°08'
gy S brk Sh
StM1000

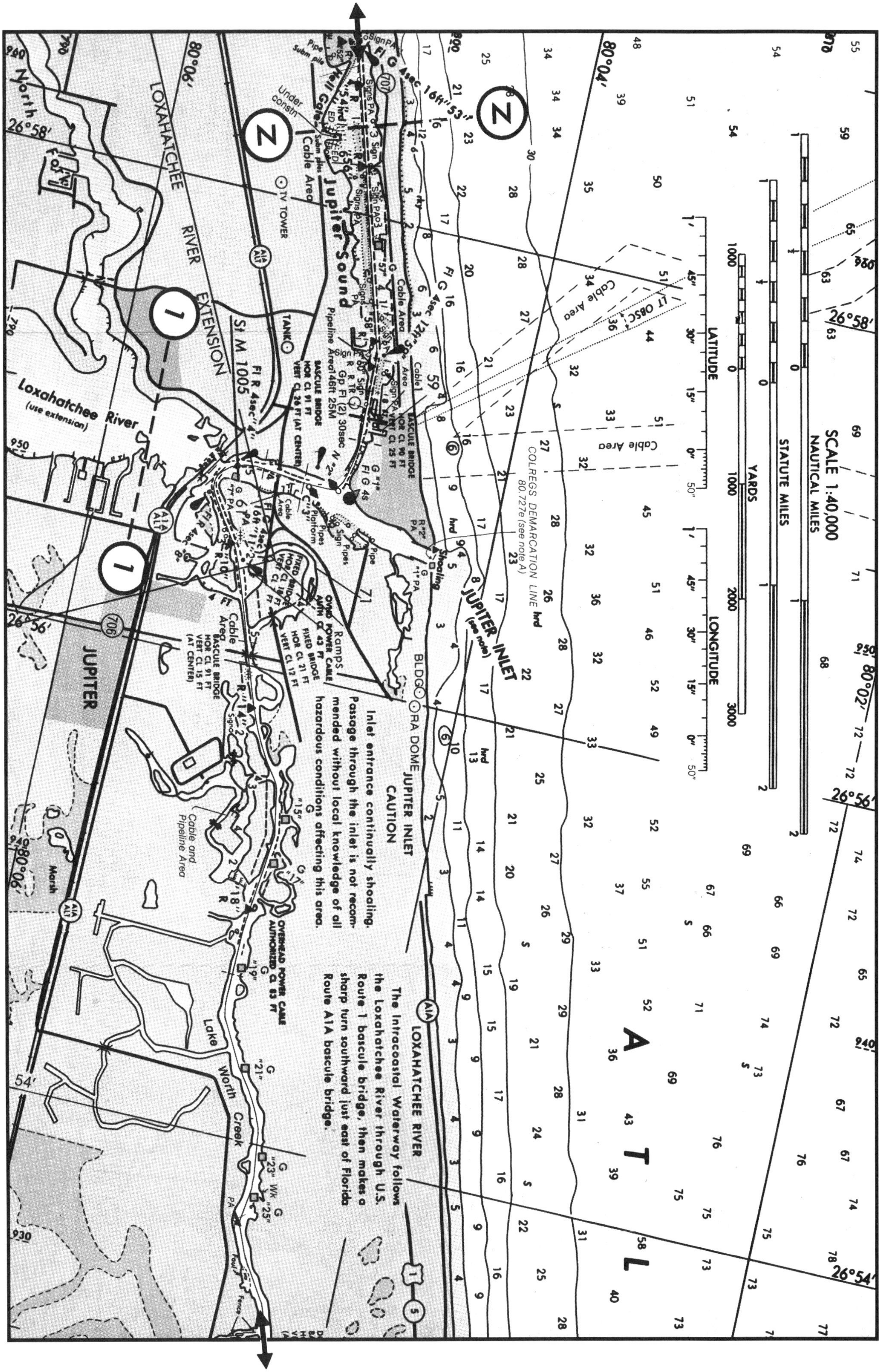


BR1004.1

BR1004.8

BR1006.2

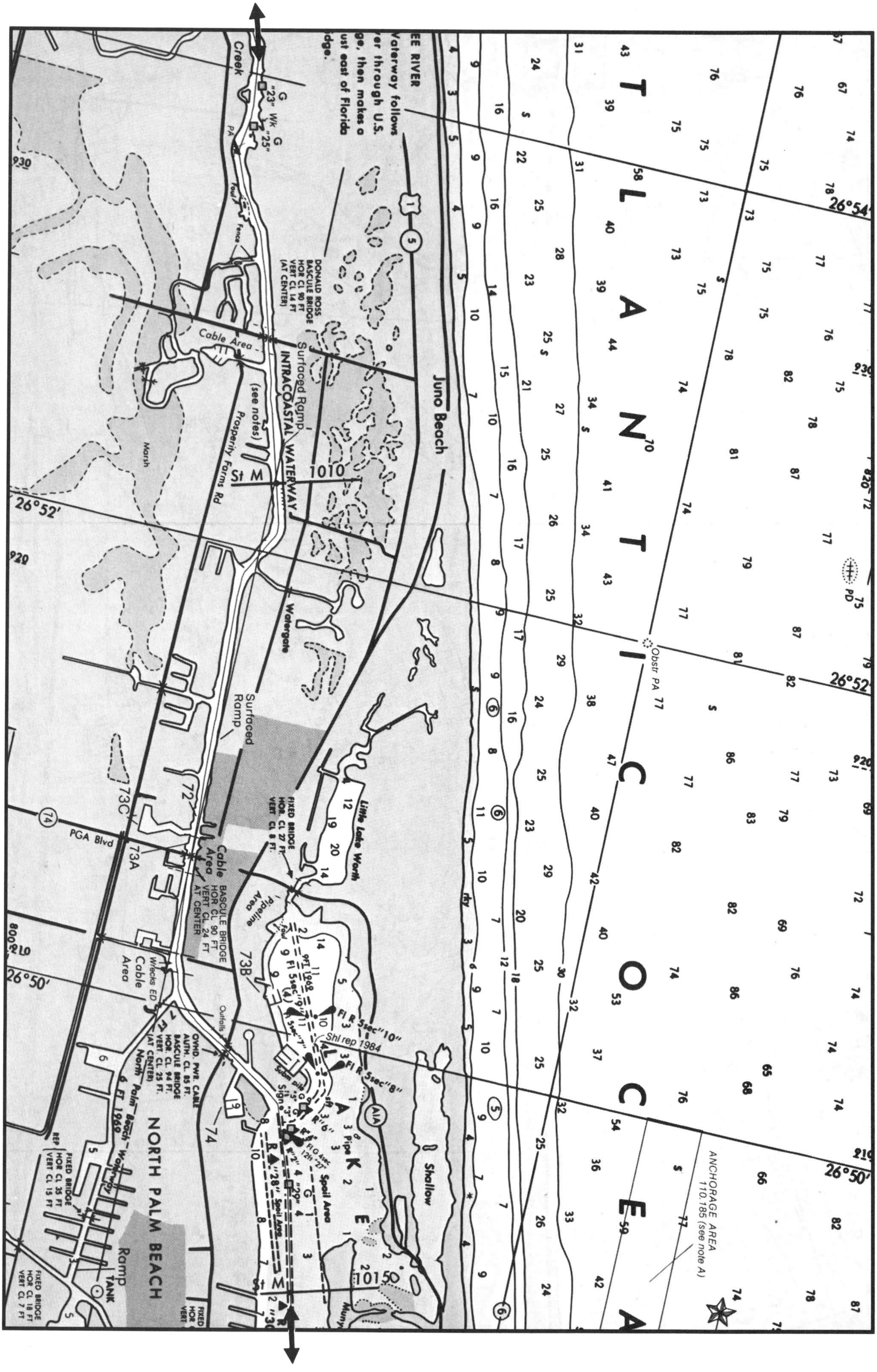


BR1009.3

StM1010

BR1012.6

BR1013.7

StM1015

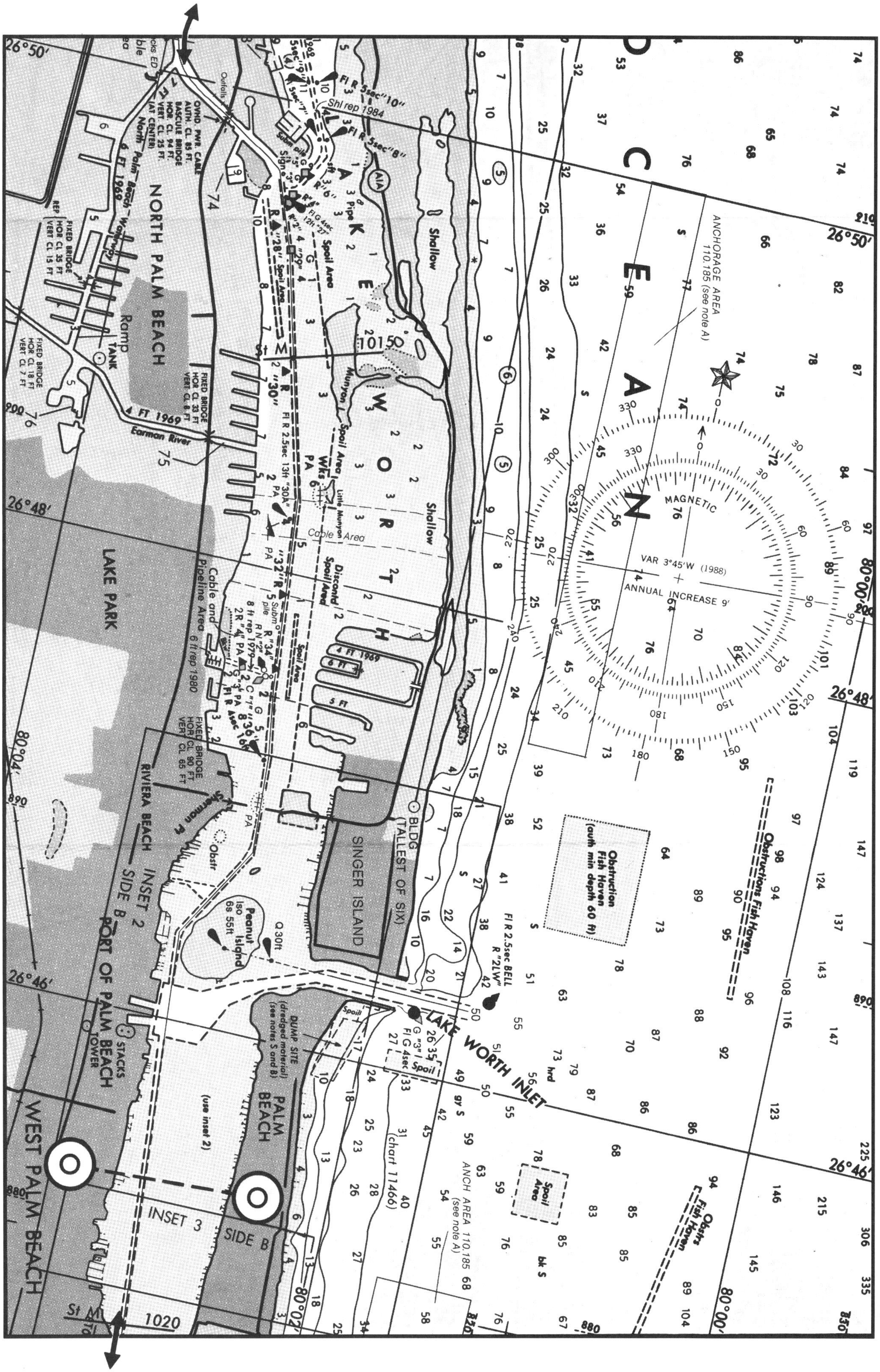


BR1013.7

StM1015

StM1020

SCALE 1:24,000

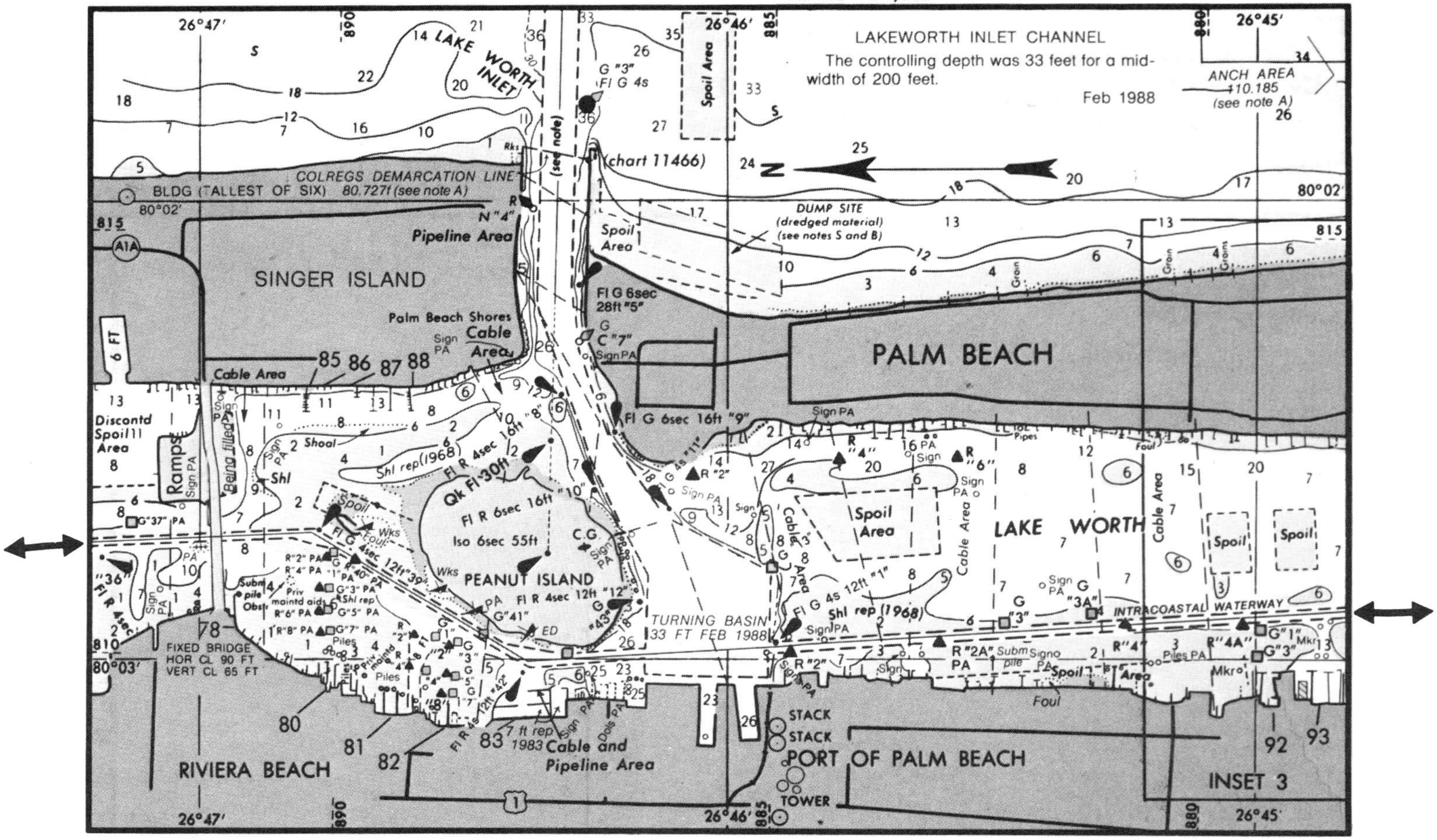

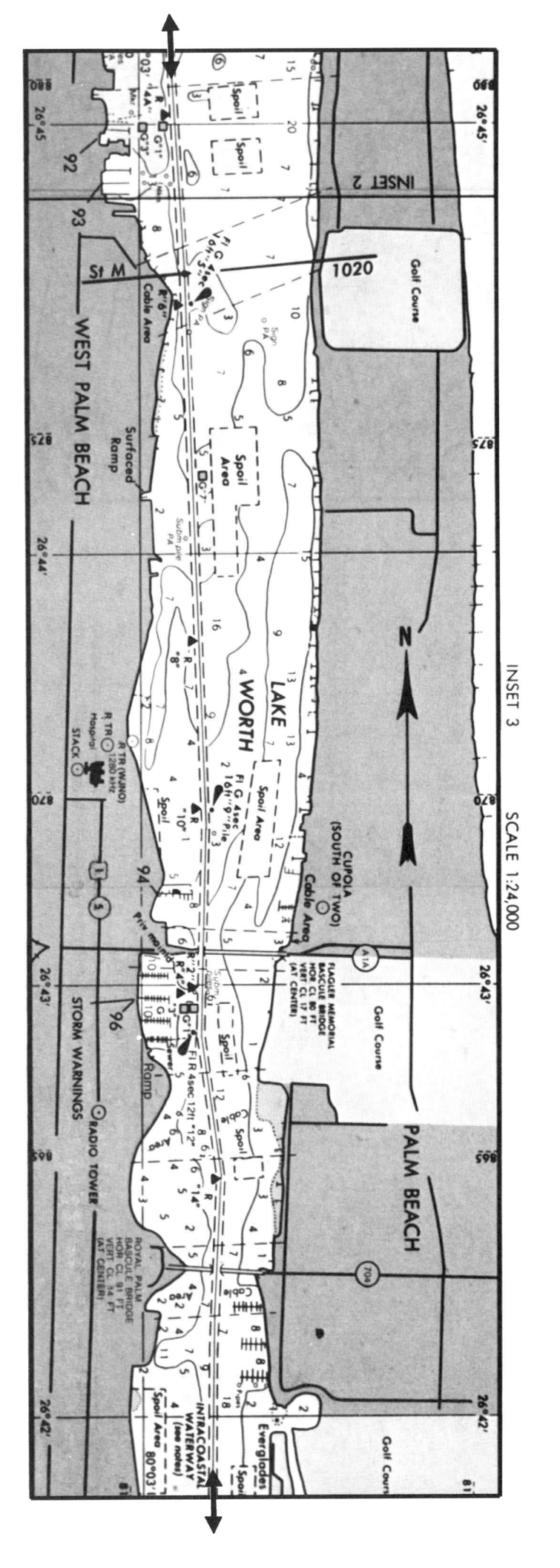

StM1020

BR1021.9

BR1022.6

177

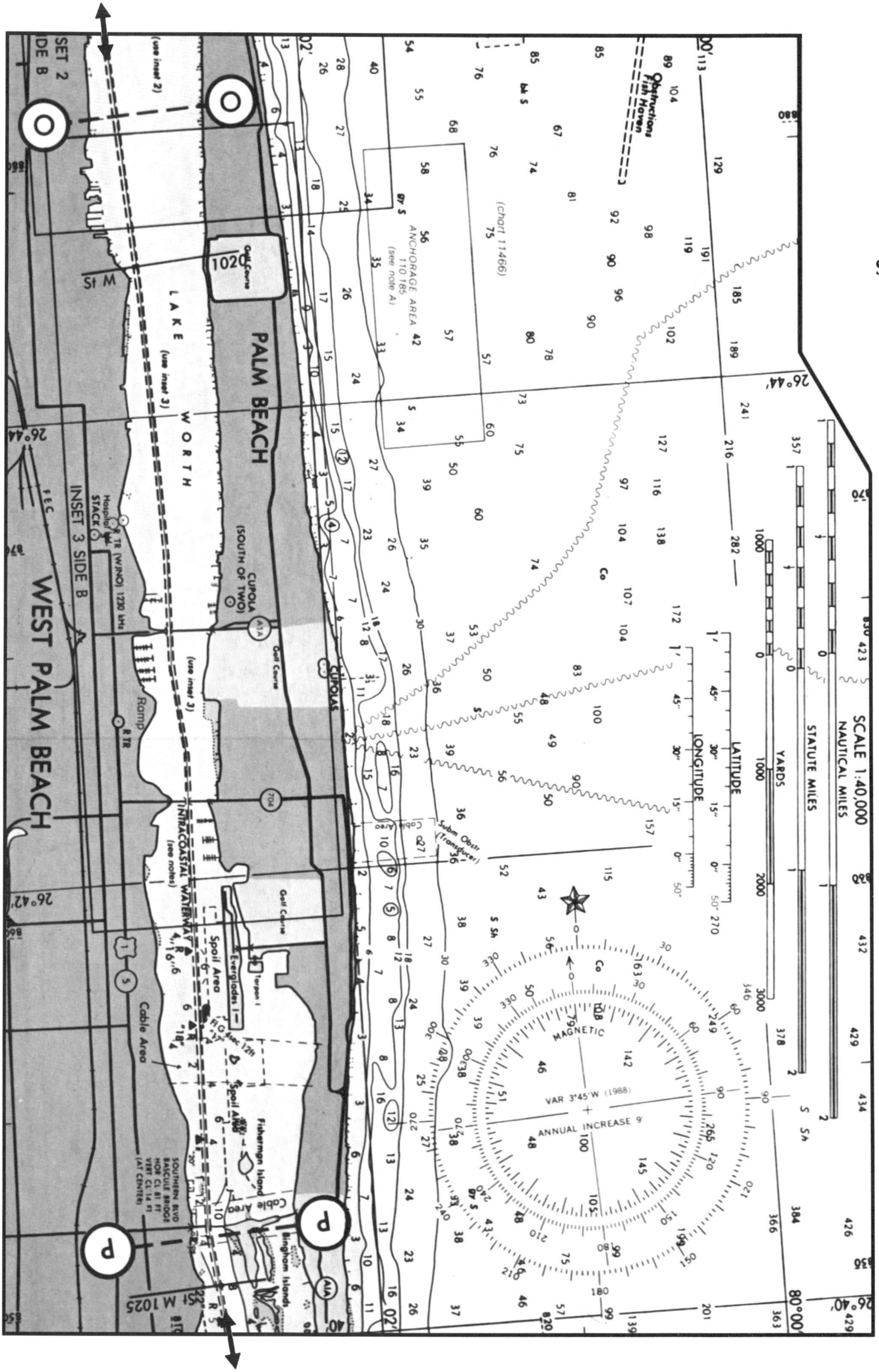

178

StM1020

BR1021.9

BR1022.6

BR1024.7

StM1025

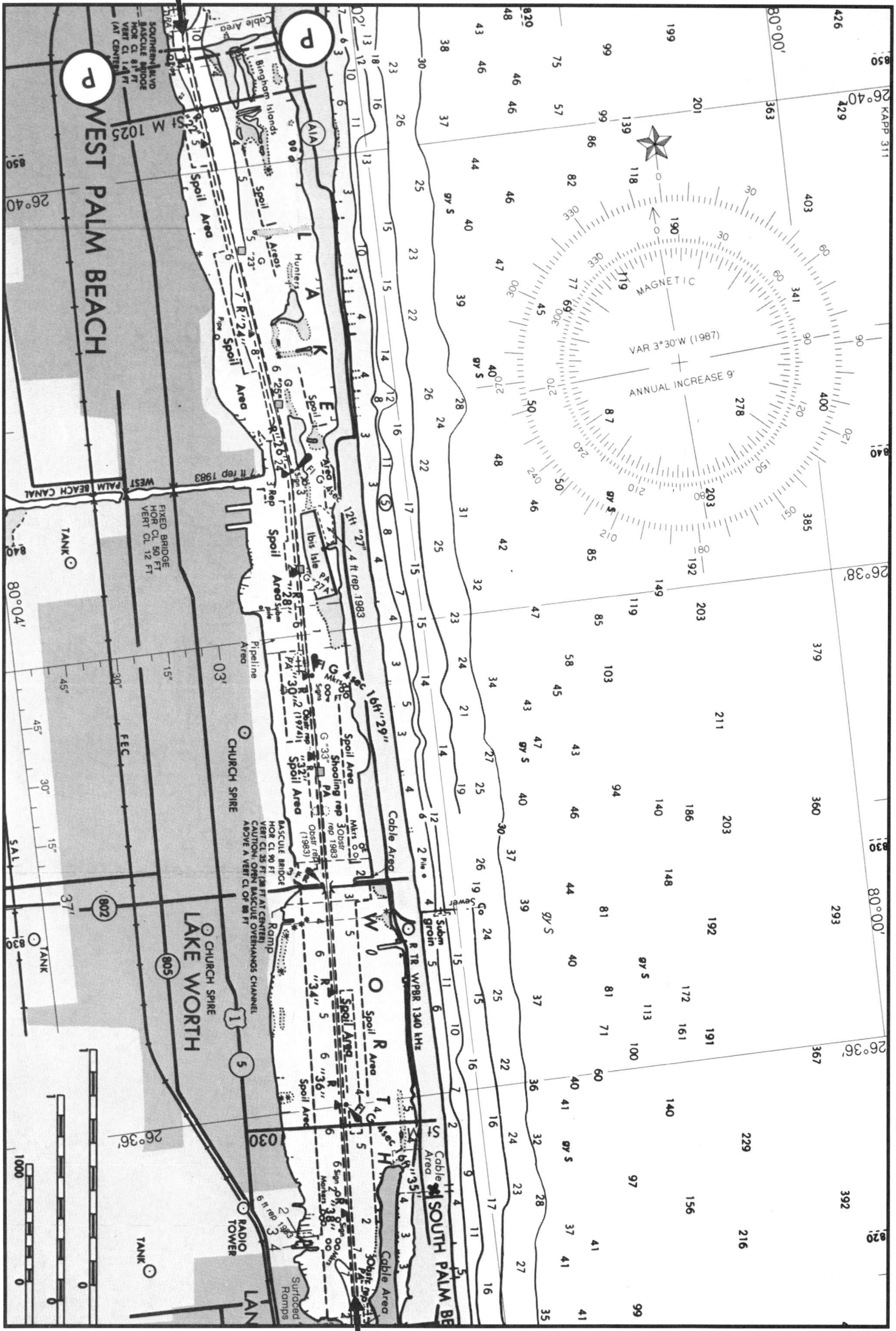


BR1024.7

StM1025

BR1028.8

StM1030

BR1031.0

StM1030 BR1031.0 BR1035.0 BR1035.8

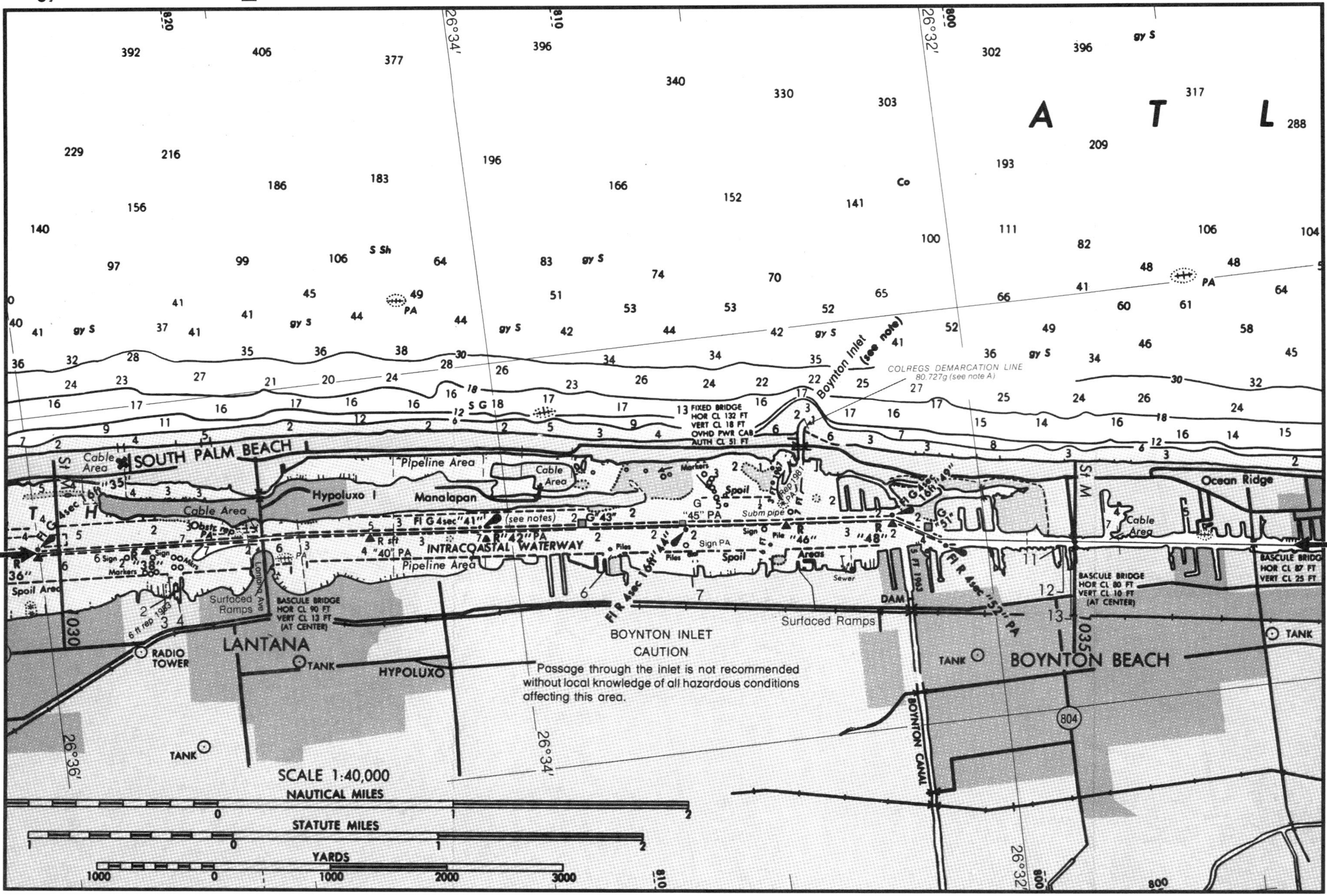

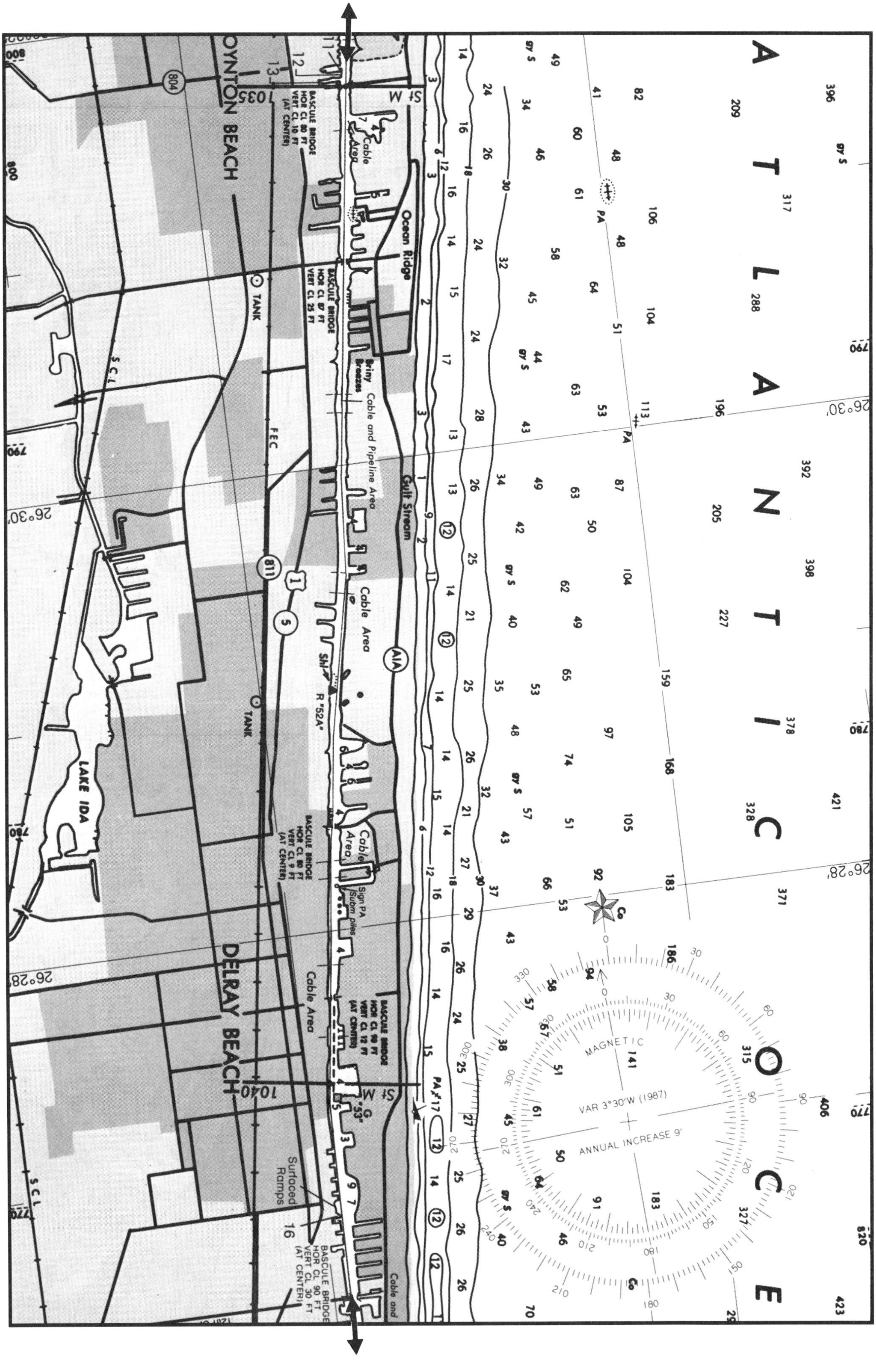


BR1035.0

BR1035.8

BR1038.7

BR1039.6

StM1040

BR1041.0

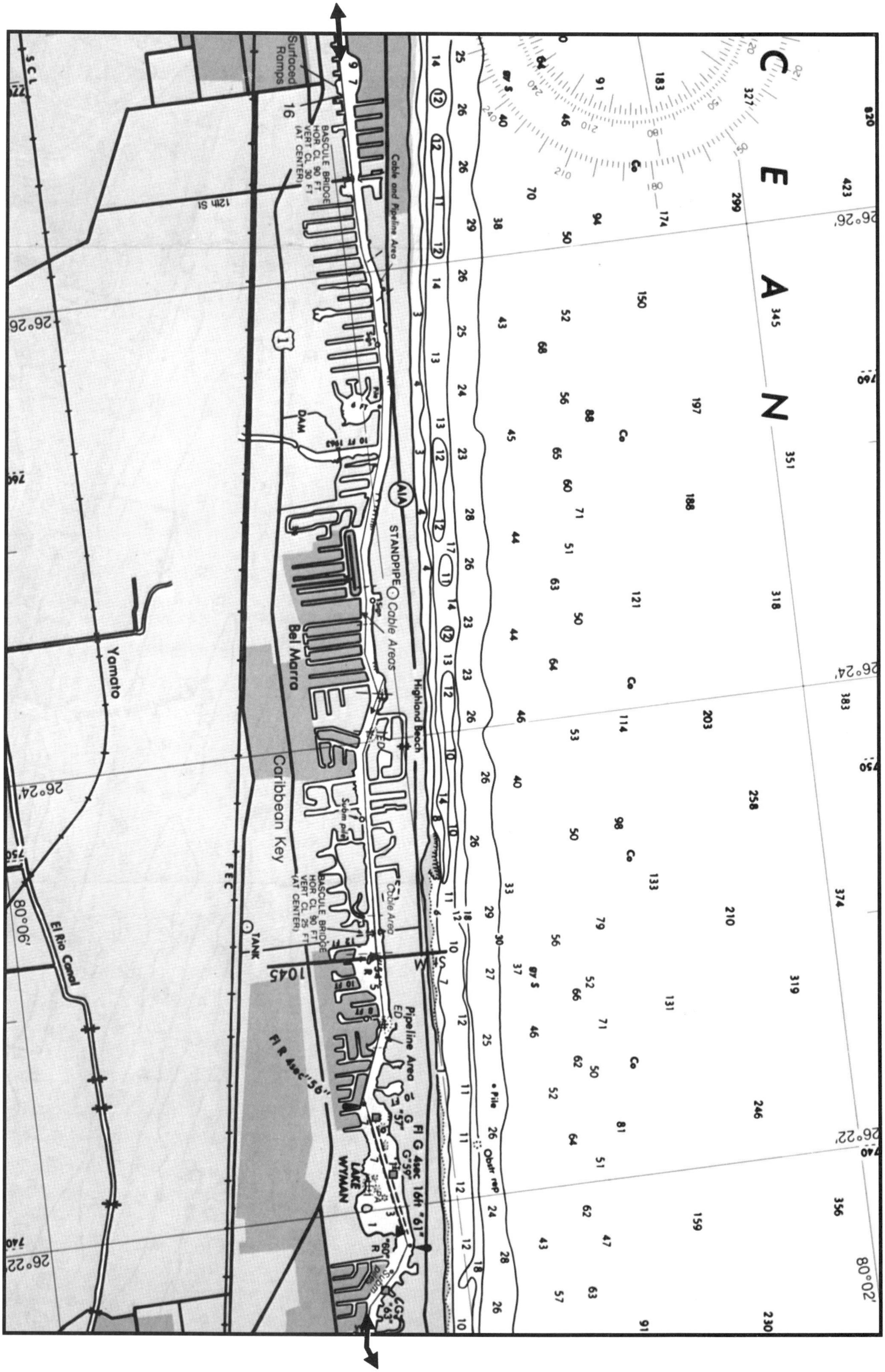


BR1041.0

BR1044.9
StM1045

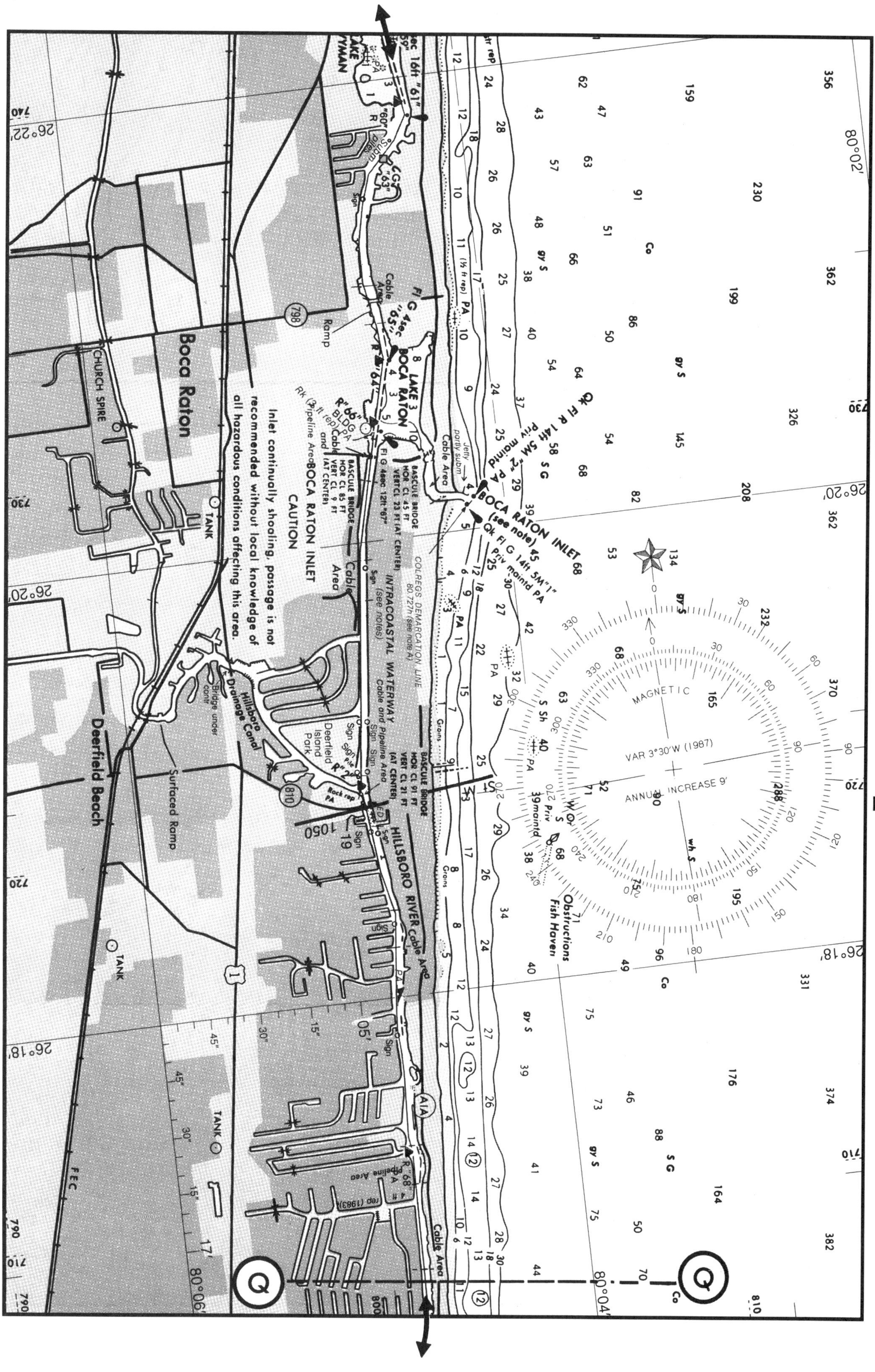


BR1047.5

BR1048.2

BR1050.0

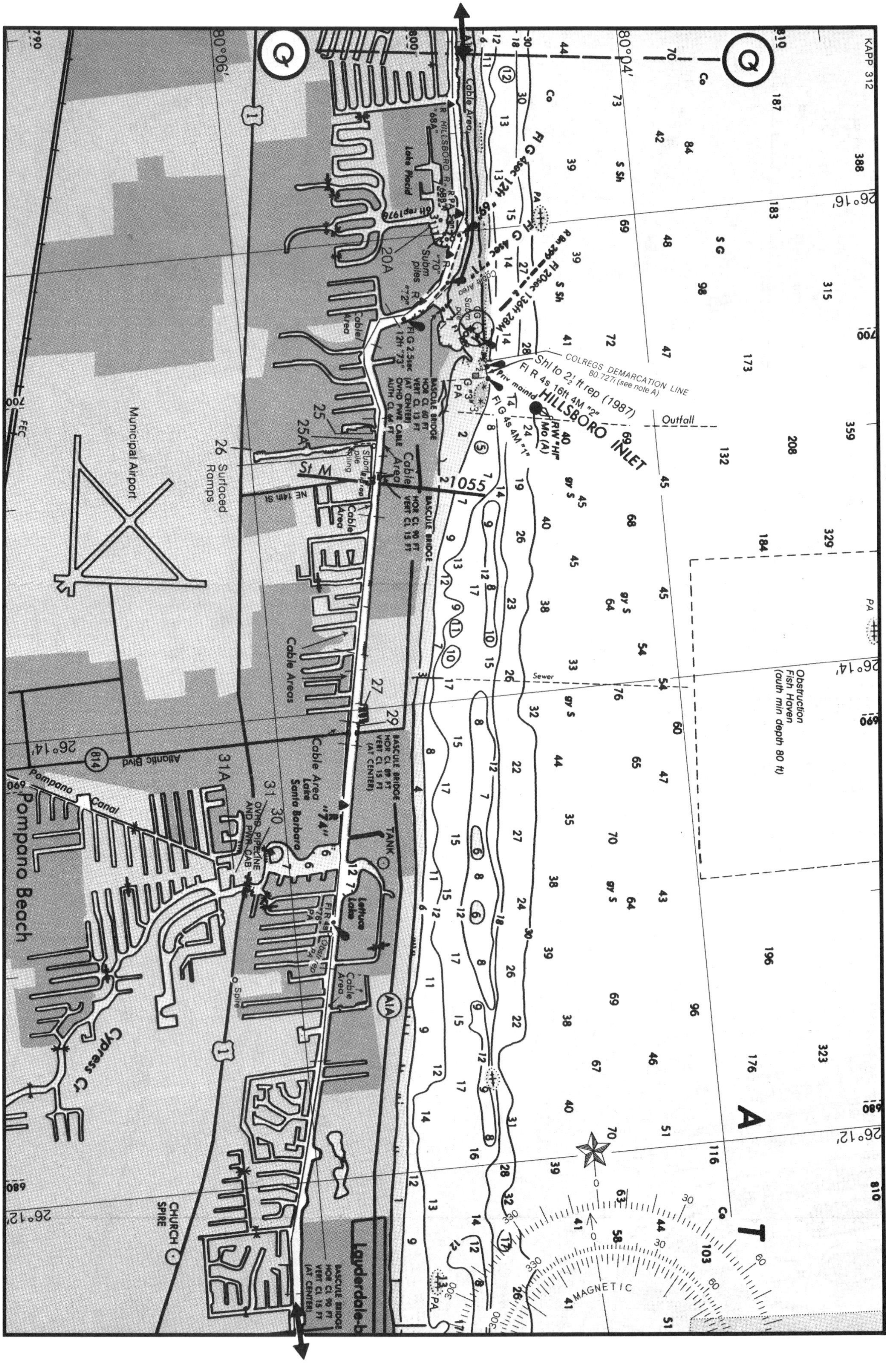


BR1055.0

BR1056.0

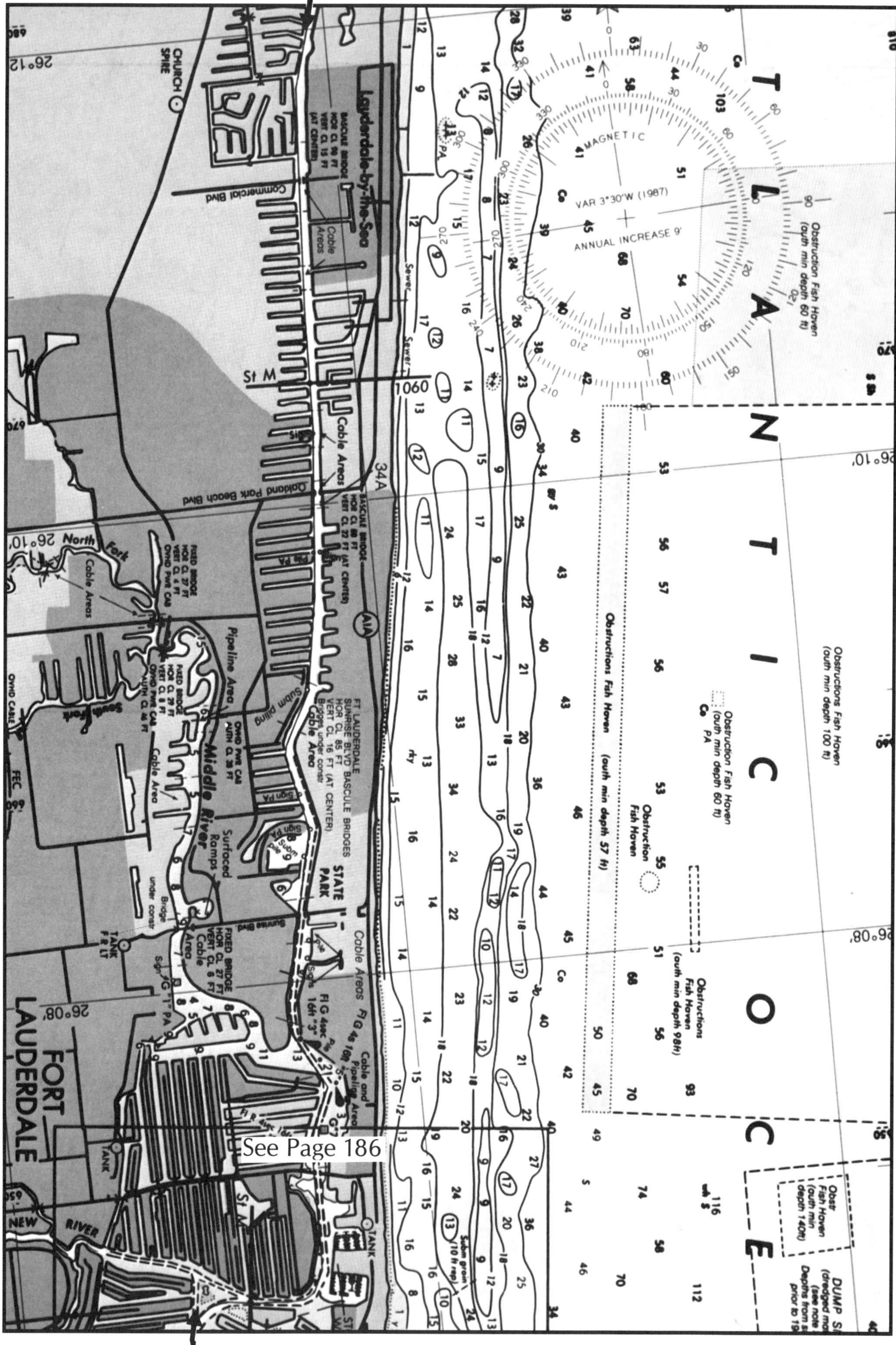


BR1059.0

StM1060

BR1060.5

BR1062.6

BR1064.0

StM1065

Joins Page 218

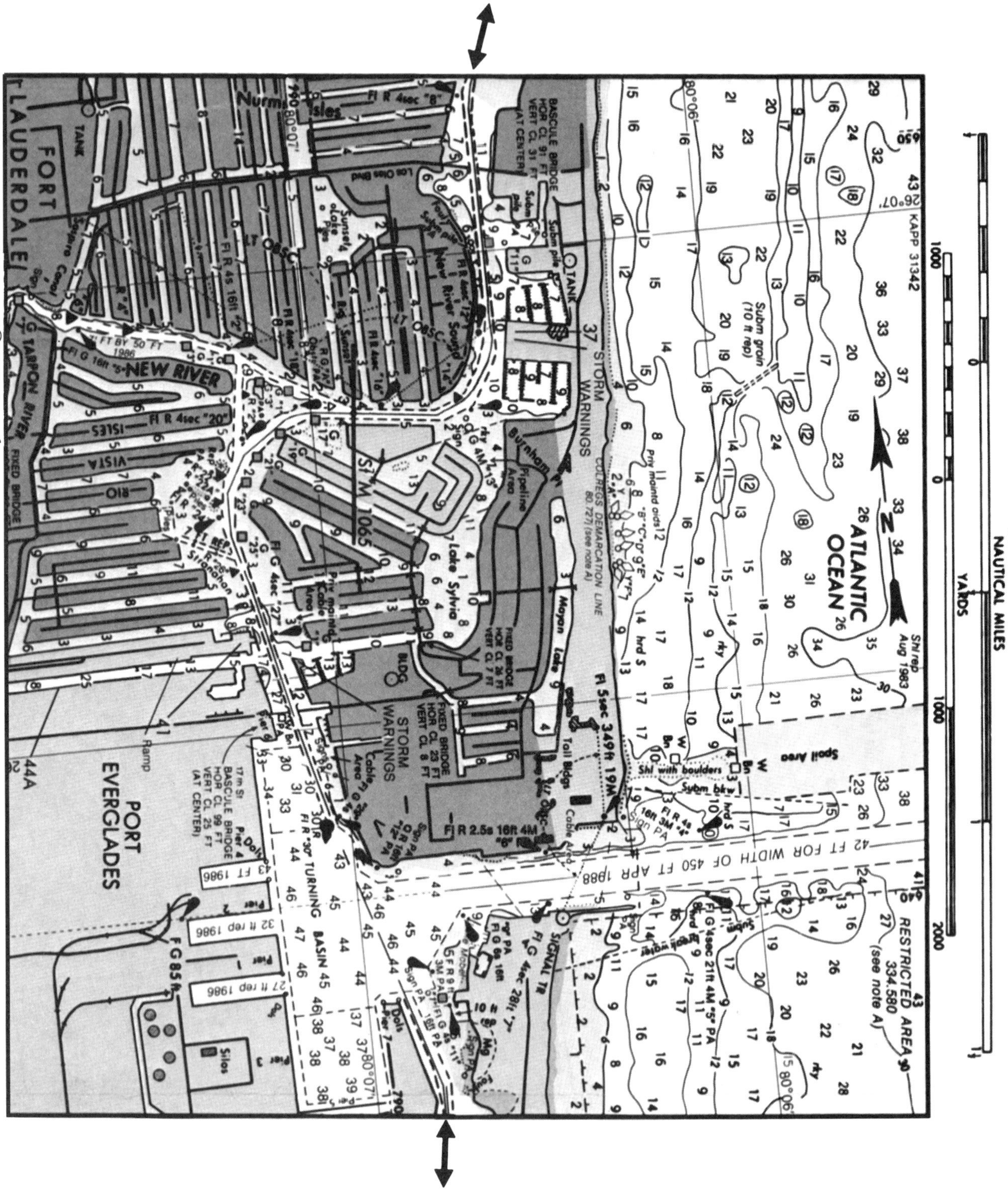


BR1064.0

StM1065

BR1065.9

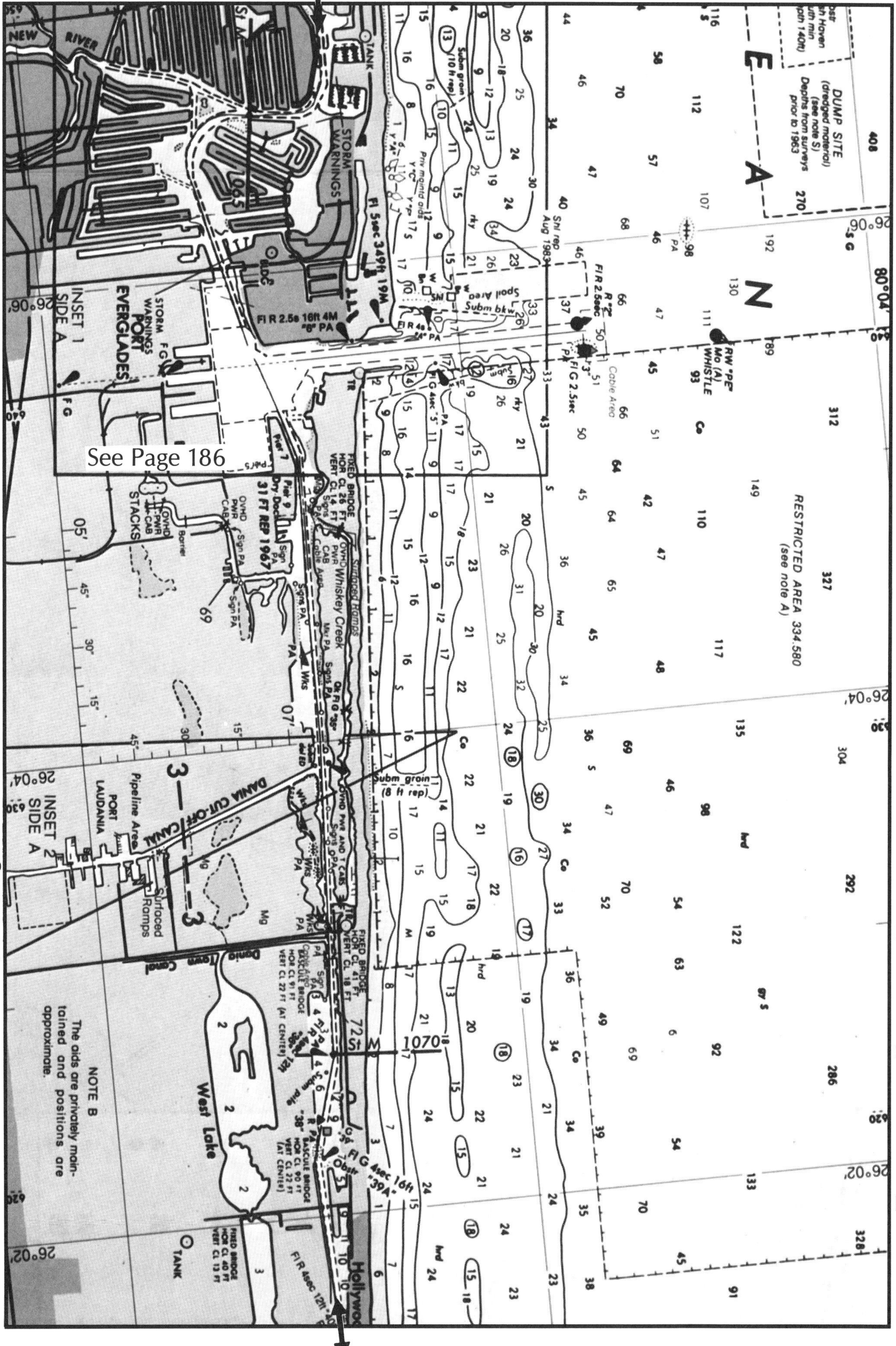


Joins Page 218

StM1065

BR1065.9

BR1069.4

StM1070

BR1070.5

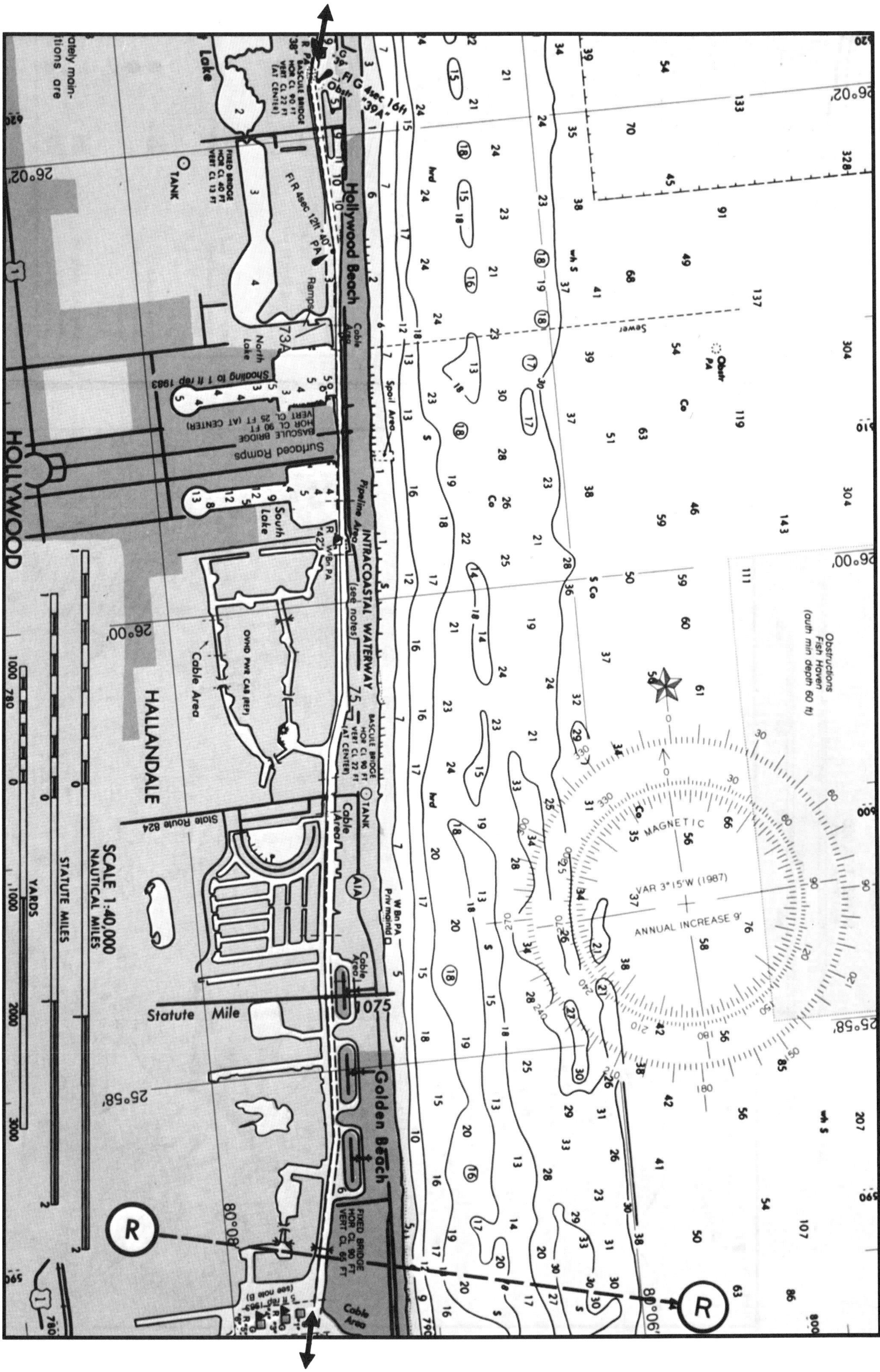


BR1070.5

BR1072.2

BR1074.0

StM1075

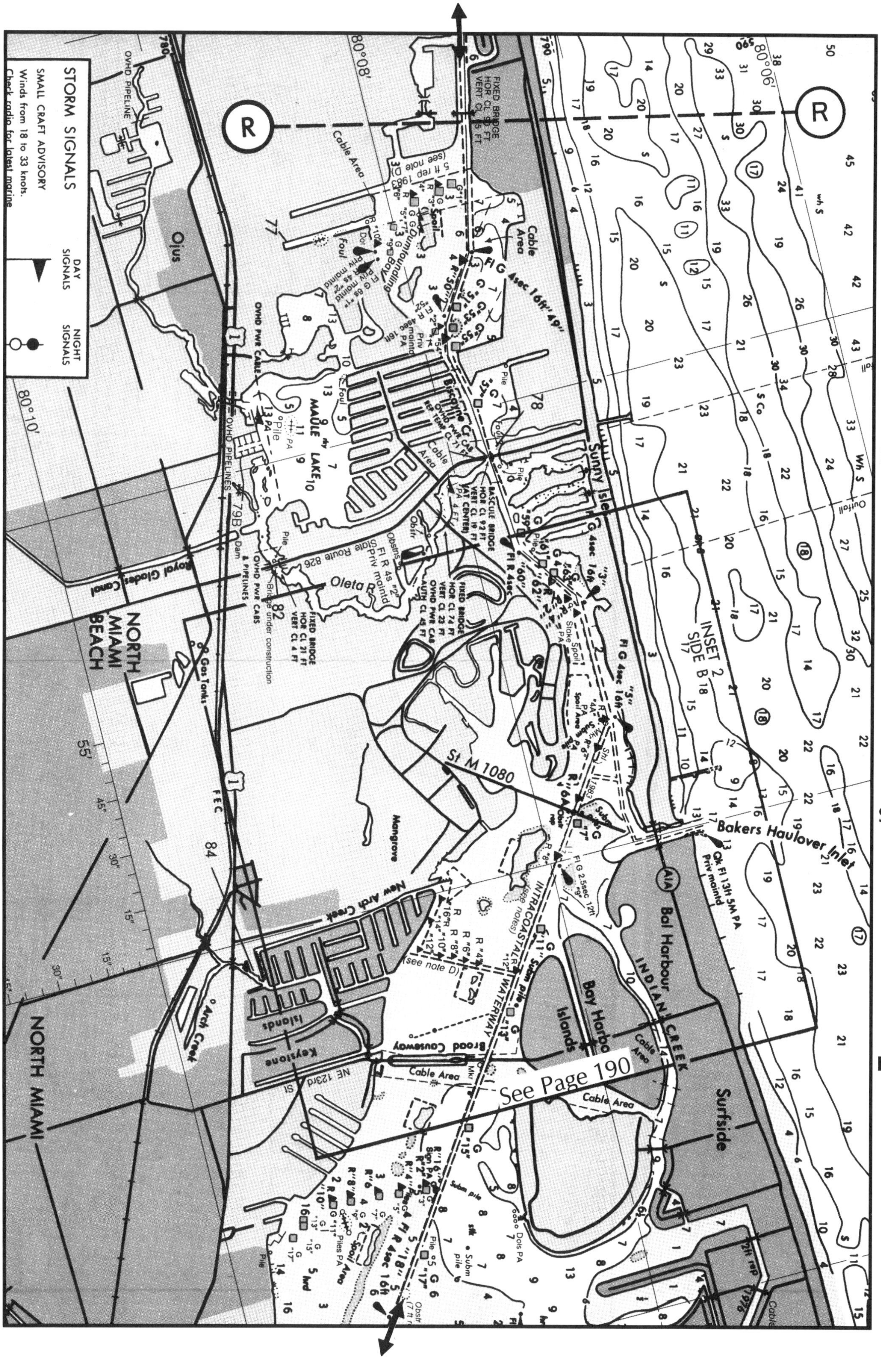


BR1078.0

StM1080

BR1081.4

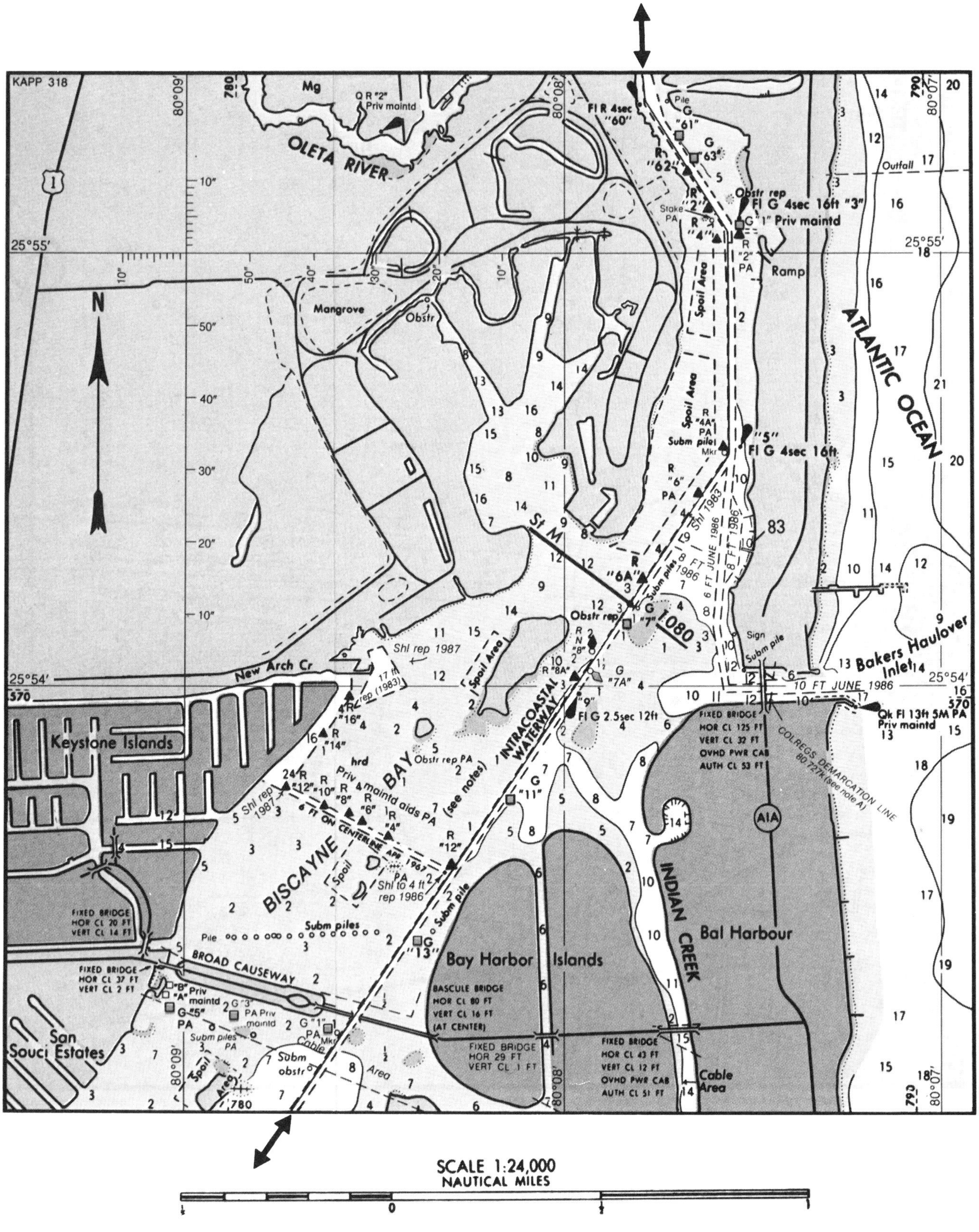


StM1080

BR1081.4

Joins Page 189

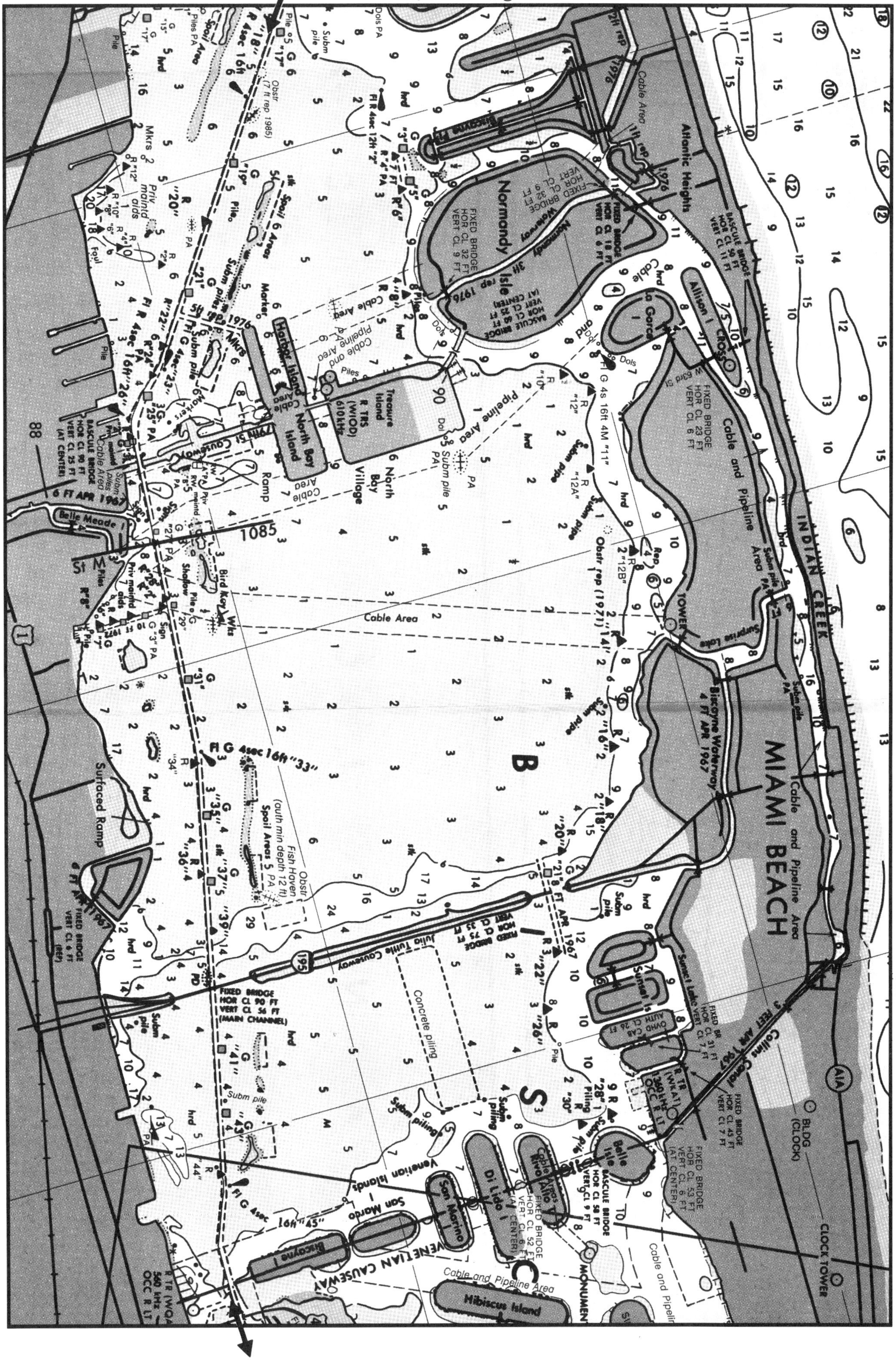


BR1084.6

StM1085

BR1087.1

BR1088.6

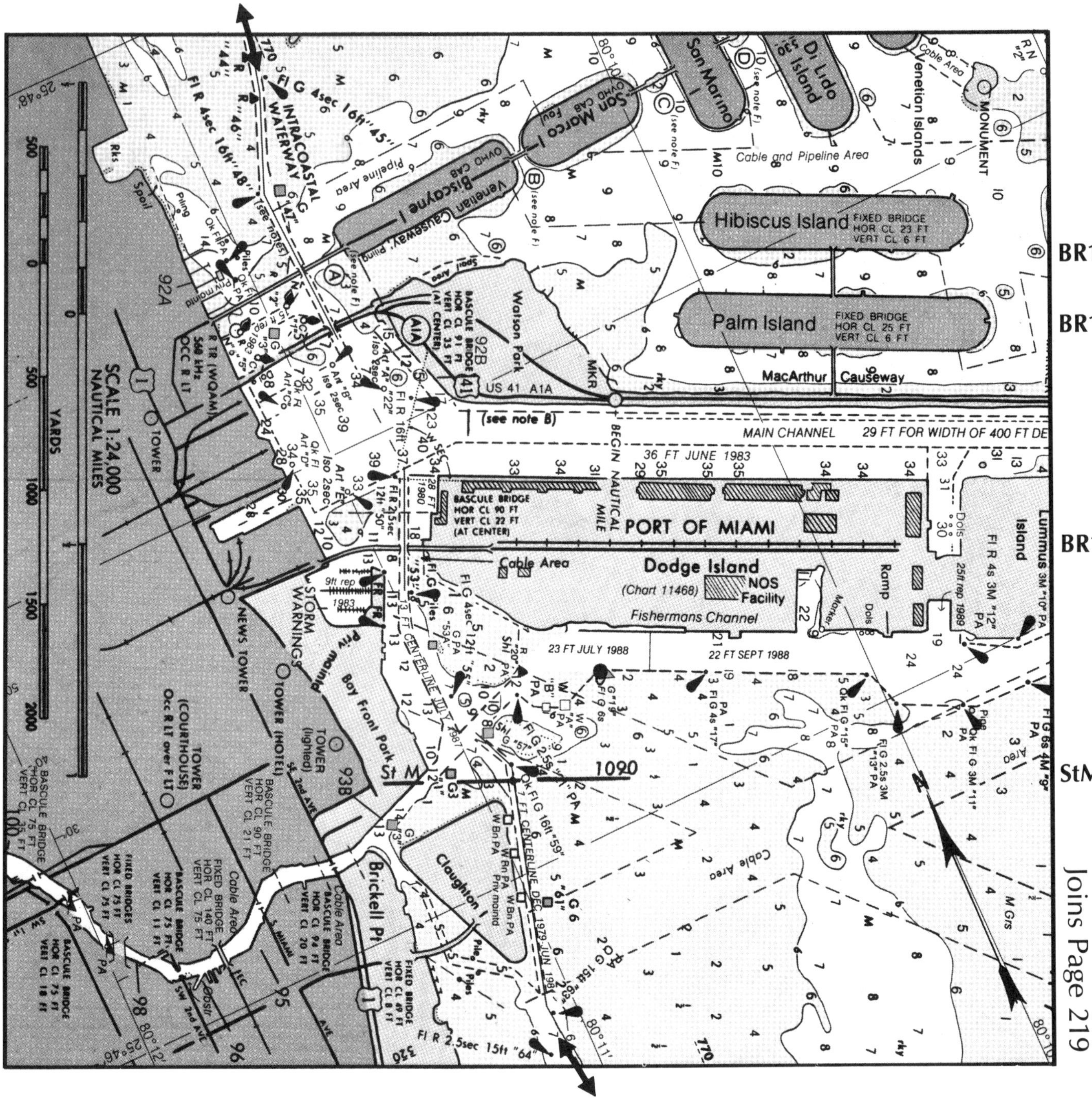

192

BR1088.6

BR1088.8

BR1089.4

StM1090

Joins Page 221

Joins Page 219

SCALE 1:24,000
NAUTICAL MILES

YARDS

INTRACOASTAL WATERWAY

Venetian Causeway

Biscayne I.

San Marco I.

San Marino

Di Lido Island

Venetian Islands

MONUMENT

Cable and Pipeline Area

Hibiscus Island — FIXED BRIDGE HOR CL 23 FT VERT CL 6 FT

Palm Island — FIXED BRIDGE HOR CL 25 FT VERT CL 6 FT

MacArthur Causeway

US 41 A1A

Watson Park

BASCULE BRIDGE HOR CL 91 FT VERT CL 33 FT (AT CENTER)

BASCULE BRIDGE HOR CL 90 FT VERT CL 22 FT (AT CENTER)

(see note B)

MAIN CHANNEL    29 FT FOR WIDTH OF 400 FT DE

36 FT JUNE 1983

BEGIN NAUTICAL MILE

PORT OF MIAMI

Dodge Island
(Chart 11468)    NOS Facility

Cable Area

Fishermans Channel

23 FT JULY 1988

22 FT SEPT 1988

Lummus Island

Ramp

STORM WARNINGS

NEWS TOWER

TOWER

TOWER (COURTHOUSE) Occ R Lt over F Lt

TOWER (HOTEL) (lighted)

Miami River

Bay Front Park

Brickell Pt

Claughton

1090

St M

BASCULE BRIDGE HOR CL 75 FT VERT CL 75 FT

FIXED BRIDGE HOR CL 75 FT VERT CL 11 FT

BASCULE BRIDGE HOR CL 75 FT

BASCULE BRIDGE HOR CL 90 FT VERT CL 21 FT

FIXED BRIDGE HOR CL 140 FT VERT CL 75 FT

BASCULE BRIDGE HOR CL 75 FT VERT CL 20 FT

FIXED BRIDGE HOR CL 49 FT VERT CL 8 FT

BASCULE BRIDGE HOR CL 75 FT VERT CL 18 FT

NOTE F
VENETIAN CAUSEWAY BRIDGES

A. — BASCULE BRIDGE
HOR CL 60 FT
VERT CL 8 FT
(AT CENTER)

B. — FIXED BRIDGE
HOR CL 51 FT
VERT CL 6 FT
(AT CENTER)

C. — FIXED BRIDGE
HOR CL 52 FT
VERT CL 6 FT
(AT CENTER)

D. — FIXED BRIDGE
HOR CL 52 FT
VERT CL 6 FT
(AT CENTER)

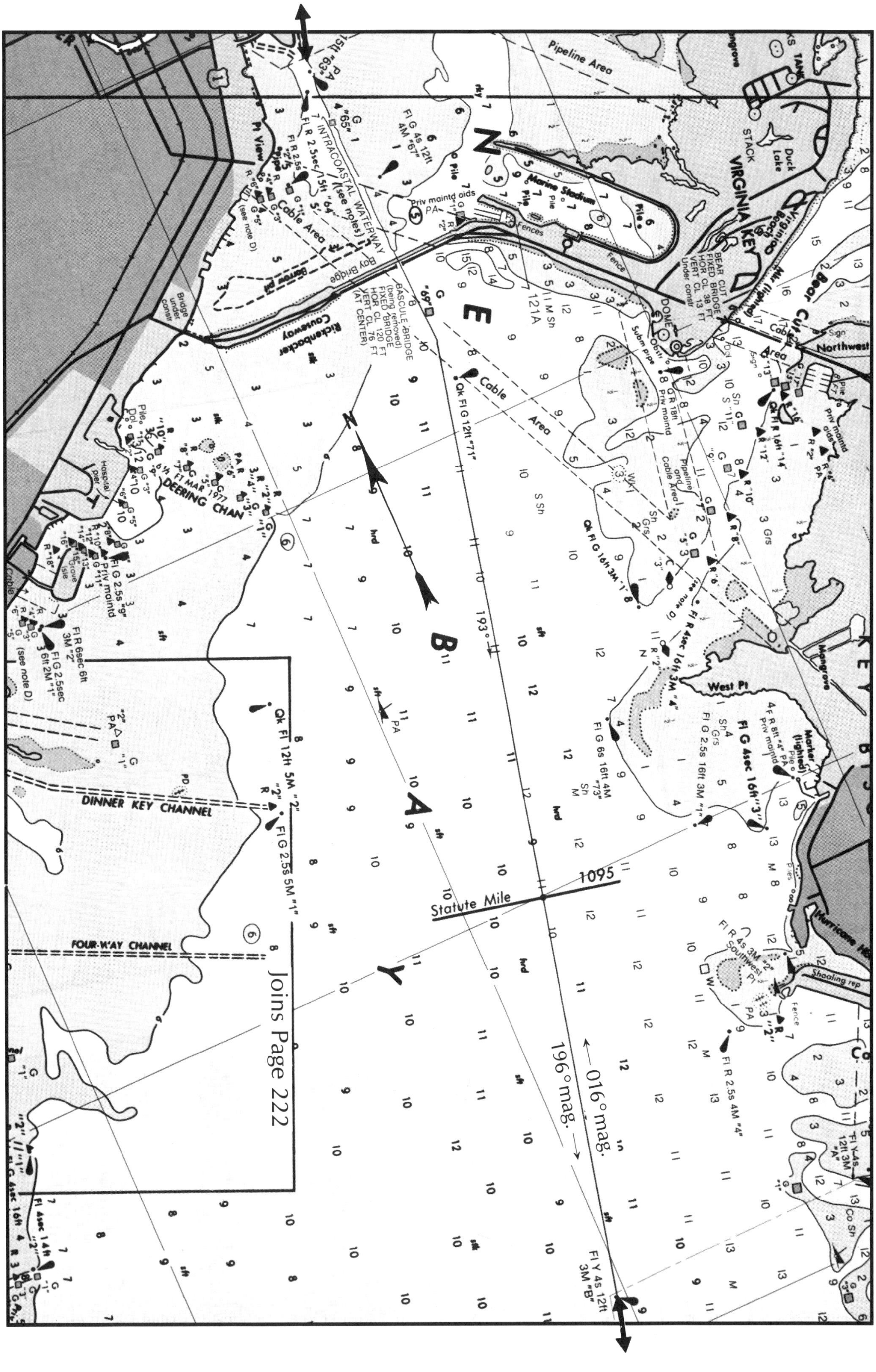
Joins Page 222
Statute Mile
1095
←016°mag.
196°mag.→
193°
VIRGINIA KEY
Bear Cut
Rickenbacker Causeway
Marine Stadium
INTRACOASTAL WATERWAY (see notes)
Pipeline Area
Cable Area
DEERING CHAN
DINNER KEY CHANNEL
FOUR-WAY CHANNEL
West Pt
Duck Lake
BEAR CUT FIXED BRIDGE HOR CL 38 FT VERT CL 13 FT Under constr
BASCULE BRIDGE (being removed) FIXED BRIDGE HOR CL 120 FT VERT CL 76 FT (AT CENTER)

StM1095

Joins Page 220

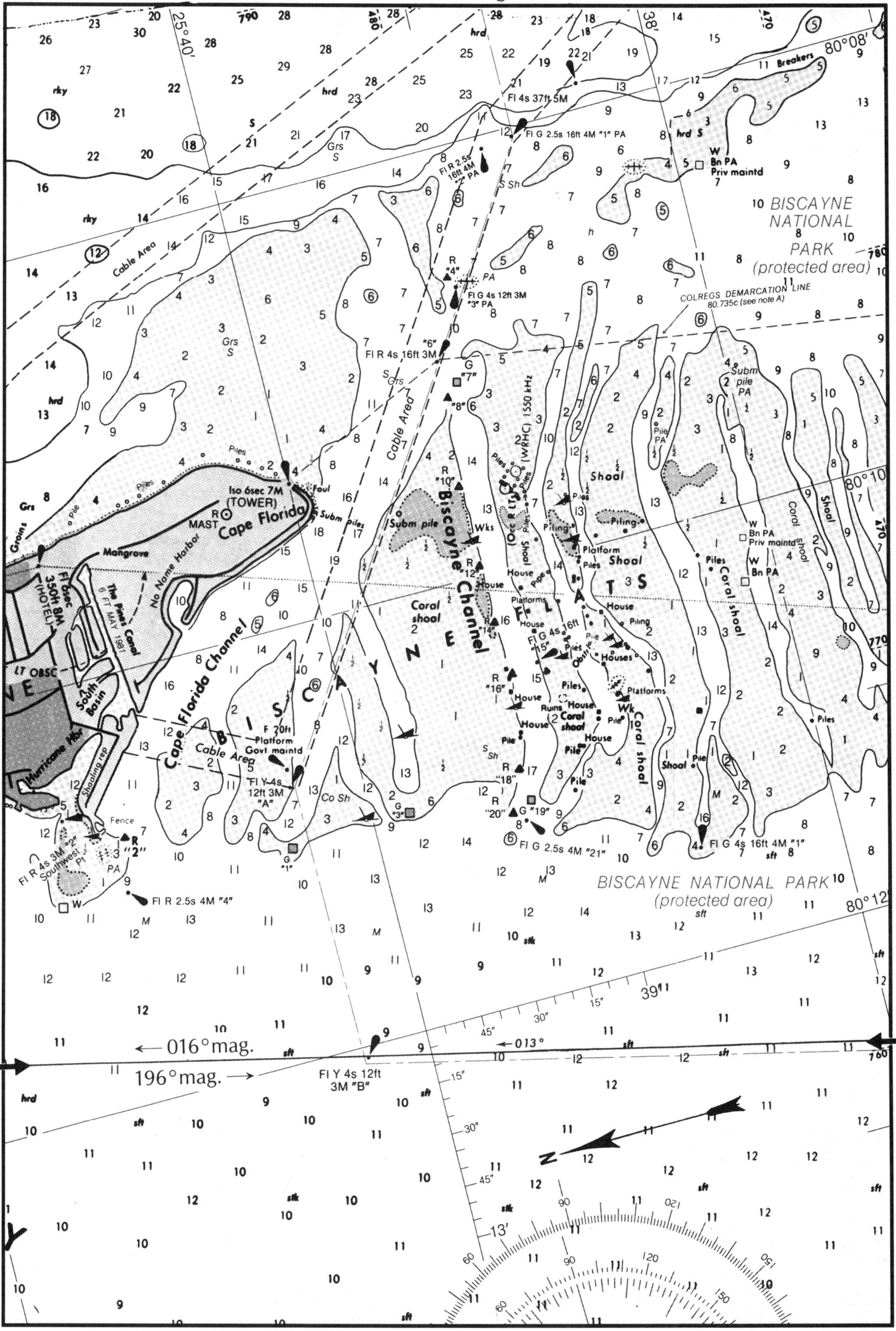

194

80°08'

BISCAYNE
NATIONAL
PARK
(protected area)

COLREGS DEMARCATION LINE
80.735c (see note A)

Breakers
Fl 4s 37ft 5M
Fl G 2.5s 16ft 4M "1" PA
W Bn PA Priv maintd
Fl R 2.5s 16ft 4M "2" PA
S Sh
Fl G 4s 12ft 3M "3" PA
R "4" PA
"6"
Fl R 4s 16ft 3M
G "7"
"8"
R "10"
Subm pile
(WRHC) 1550 kHz
Biscayne Channel
Wks
R "12"
House
House
Coral shoal
House
N E
Platforms
Fl G 4s 16ft
"14"
Piles
Obst
House
Houses
R "16"
House
Piles
House
Ruins House
Coral shoal
Wk
House
Platforms
House
Pile
Pile
R "18"
S Sh
G "3"
R "20"  G "19"
Fl G 2.5s 4M "21"
Fl G 4s 16ft 4M "1"

Subm pile PA
Pile PA
Shoal
W Bn PA Priv maintd
W Bn PA
Coral shoal
Shoal
Coral shoal
Piles
Shoal
M
Wk
770

BISCAYNE NATIONAL PARK
(protected area)

Cape Florida
Iso 6sec 7M (TOWER)
MAST R
Foul
Subm piles
No Name Harbor
Mangrove
Groins
Pile
Grs
Piles
The Pines Canal
6 FT MAY 1981
Fl 6sec 350ft 8M (HOTEL)
LT OBSC
South Basin
Hurricane Hbr
Cape Florida Channel
Shoaling rep
Fence
R "2"
PA
Fl R 4s 3M "2"
Southwest Pt
W
Fl R 2.5s 4M "4"

Cape Florida Channel
B I S C A Y N E
Cable Area
F 20ft Platform Govt maintd
Fl Y 4s 12ft 3M "A"
Co Sh
G "1"

016° mag.
196° mag.
013°
Fl Y 4s 12ft 3M "B"

80°10'

80°12'

25°40'

Cable Area

rky
rky
Grs S
Grs S
S Grs
hrd

470

760

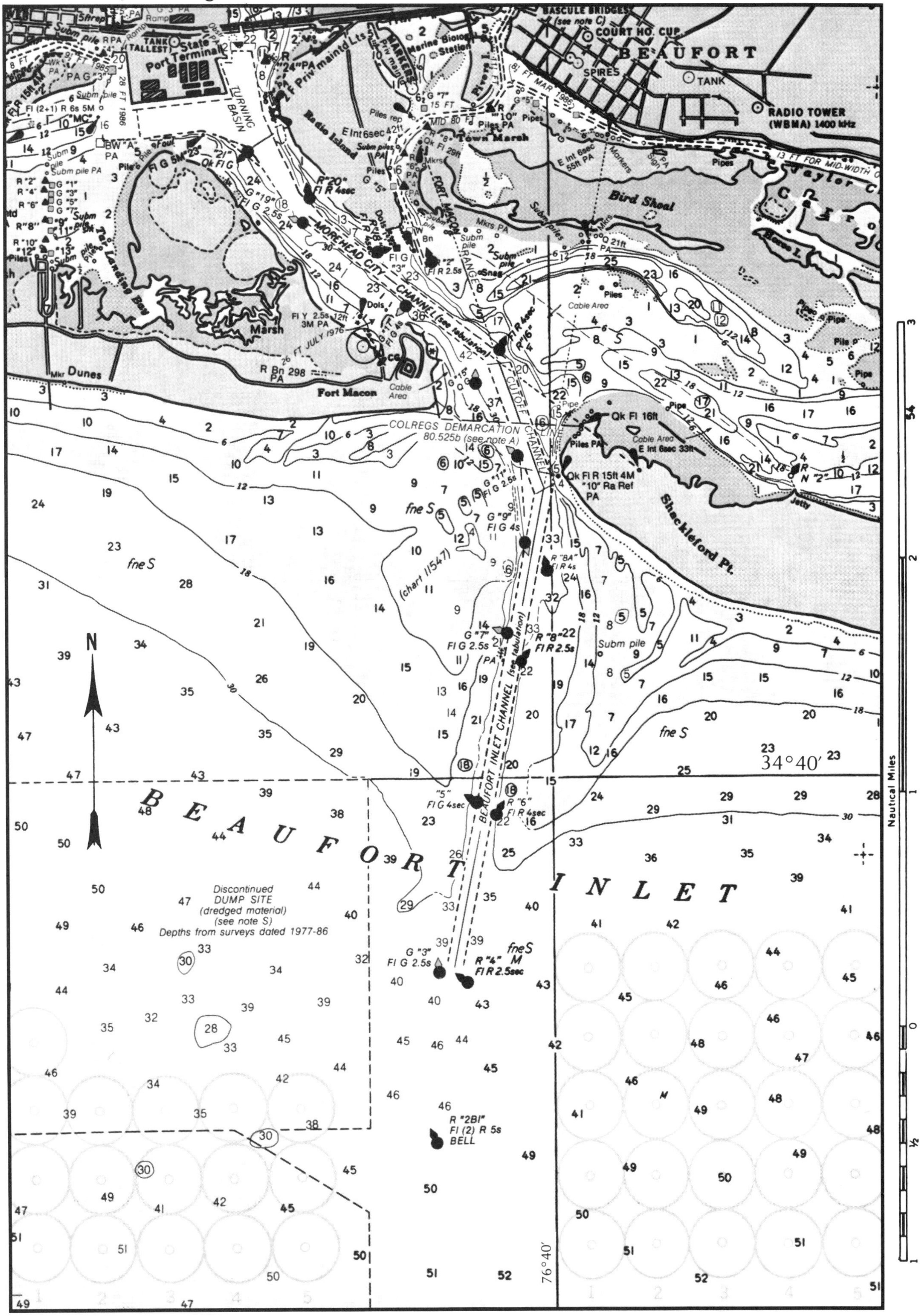
BEAUFORT
COURT HO. CUP.
SPIRES
TANK
RADIO TOWER
(WBMA) 1400 kHz
BASCULE BRIDGES
(see note C)
State Port Terminal
TANK (TALLEST)
TURNING BASIN
Radio Island
Marine Biological Station
Town Marsh
Bird Shoal
Taylor Creek
Carrot Island
Horse I.
FORT MACON RANGE
MOREHEAD CITY CHANNEL (see tabulation)
CUTOFF CHANNEL
Fort Macon
Dunes
Marsh
Tar Landing Bay
Cable Area
COLREGS DEMARCATION
80.525b (see note A)
Qk Fl 16ft
Qk Fl R 15ft 4M
"10" Ra Ref
PA
E Int 6sec 33ft
Shackleford Pt.
Jetty
(chart 11547)
fne S
Subm pile
BEAUFORT INLET CHANNEL (see tabulation)
BEAUFORT INLET
34°40′
76°40′
Discontinued
DUMP SITE
(dredged material)
(see note S)
Depths from surveys dated 1977-86
R "2BI"
Fl (2) R 5s
BELL
N
Nautical Miles

# Southport, NC

## Joins Page 56

**196**

Fl (4) 10s 169ft 19M
R Bn 298°

OAK ISLAND
COAST GUARD

Fort Caswell
See wall

TANK

Western Bar Channel

PA 10

SMITH ISLAND RANGE

G "13"
Fl G 2.5s

G "11"
Fl G 4s

Cable Area

Fl G 2.5s

Jay Bird Shoals

Q G BELL

G "9"

R "8"
Fl R 4s

Bald Hea

BALD HEAD SHOAL CHANNEL RANGE

G "7"
Fl G 4s

Platform
(lighted)

PD

Bald Head Shoal

Sand dunes

Breakers

25
R "6"
Fl R 2.5s

(see tabulation)

G "5"
Fl G 2.5s

R "4"
Fl R 4s

33°50'

"3"
Fl G 4s

MAGNETIC

R "2CF"
Fl R (2) 5s BELL

stk

VAR 7°00'W (1988)

ANNUAL INCREASE

Dump Site
(dredged material)
(see note S)
Depths from surveys
of 1974-79-80

Nautical Miles

Georgetown — Winyah Bay, SC

Joins Page 197

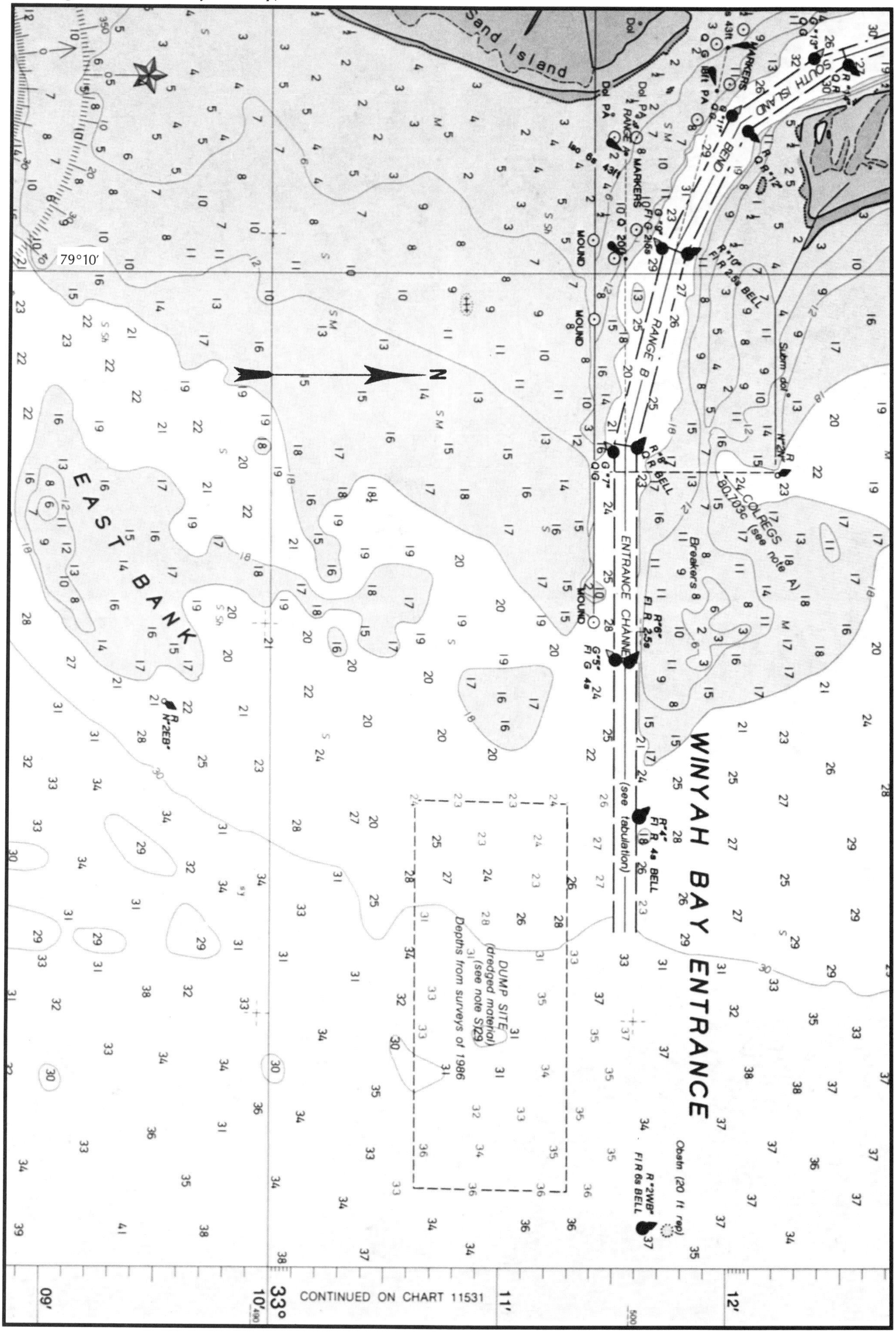

Charleston, SC

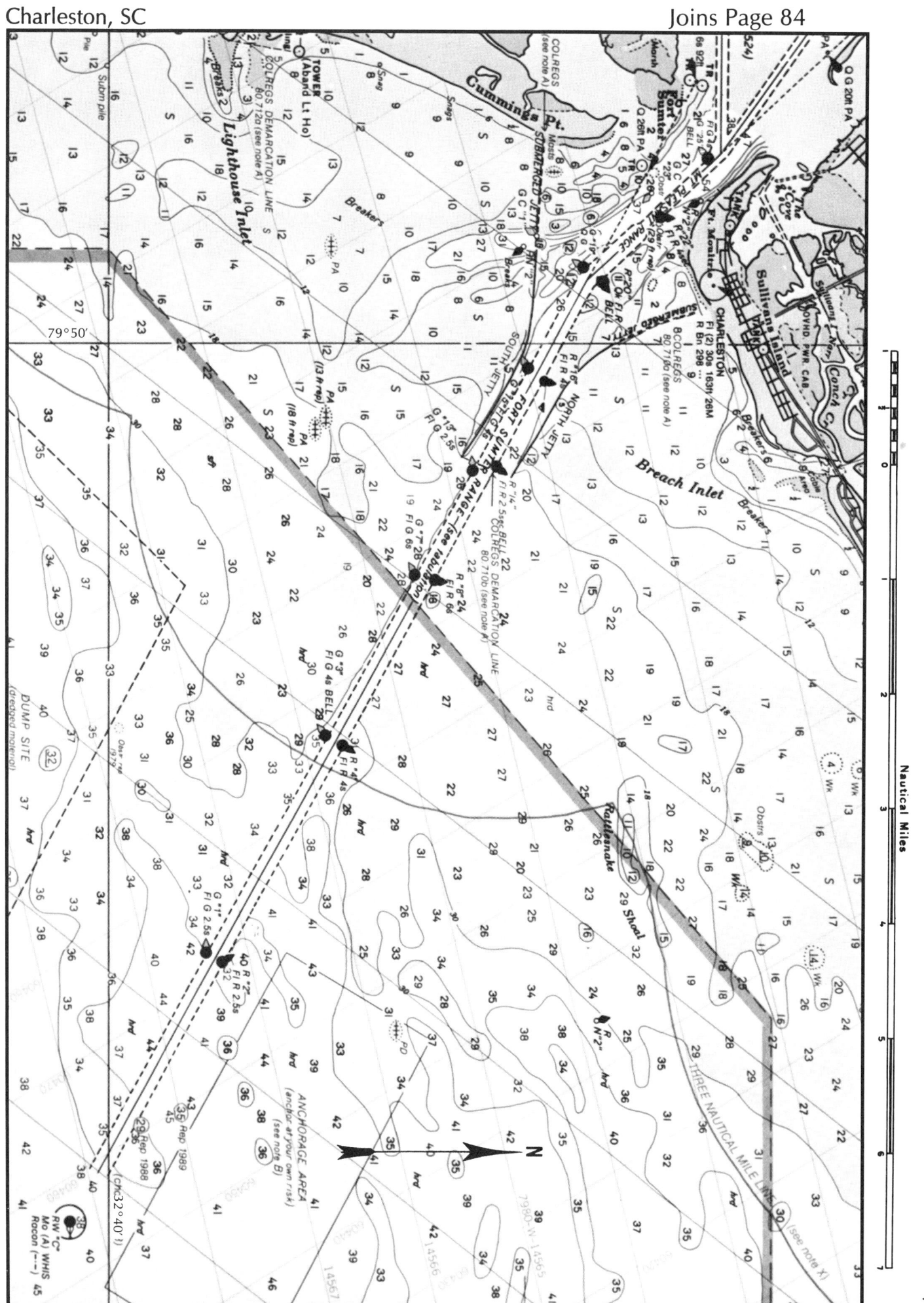

Joins Page 91

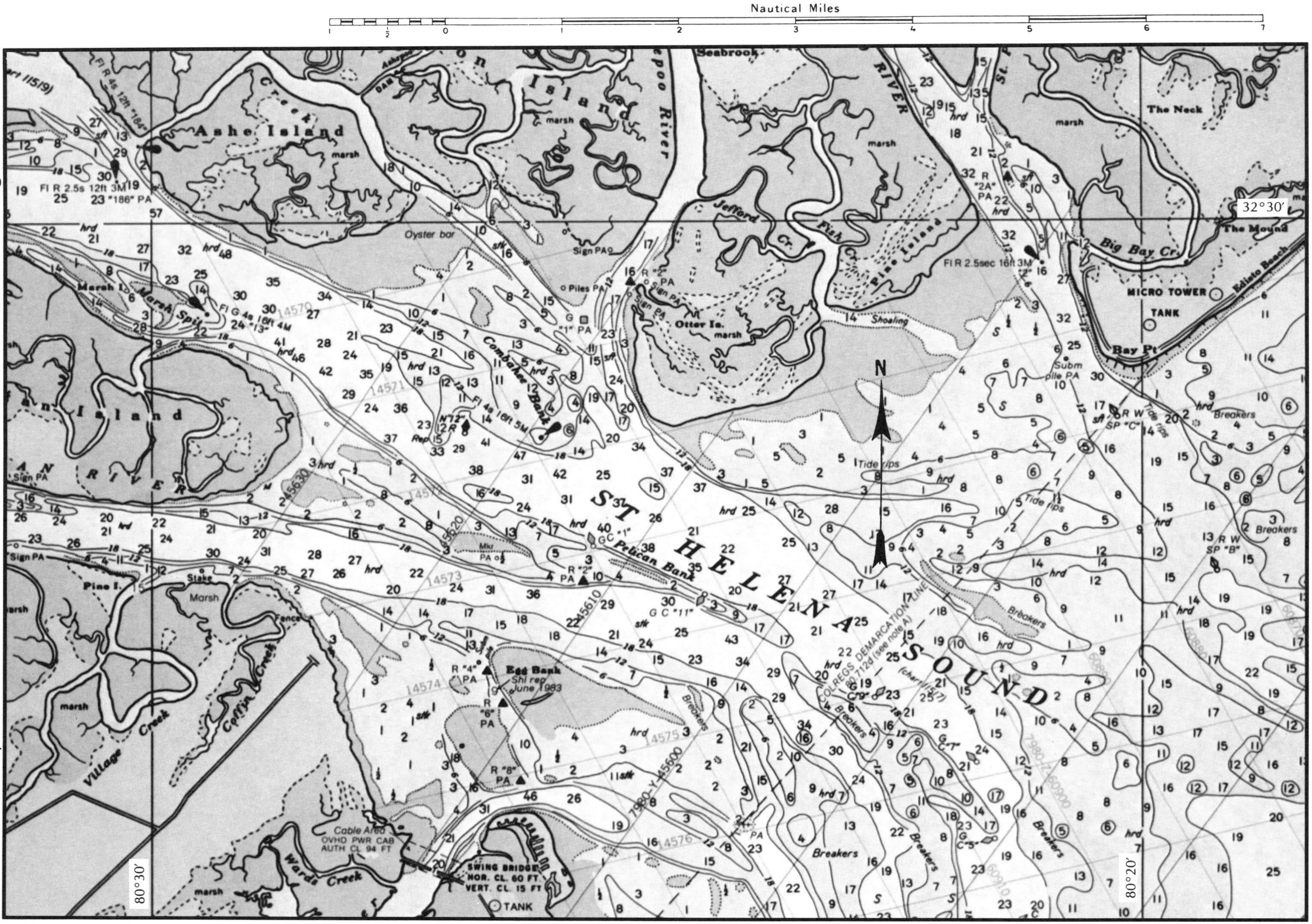




Joins Page 201

St. Helena Sound, SC

Port Royal Sound, SC

# Port Royal Sound, SC

Hilton Head, SC

Joins Page 98

204

COOPER RIVER

Bull Cr.

Broad Cr.

Marsh

Calibogue Shoal

Calibogue Cay

Lawton

Hair Py.

CALIBOGUE SOUND

Harbour Town

Priv maintd

Fl G 6s 15ft "1" PA
Q G 15ft "3" PA
Fl 2.5sec 90ft "HT"

Q R 15ft "4" PA
Q R "2" PA

4½ ft rep 1983

Marsh

TANK

ISLAND

HILTON

Sea Pines Plantation

Baynard Cove

Baynard Cove Cr.

Braddock Cove

Braddock Pt.
South Sea Pines
Dunes

Tank

Sign

Grenadier Shoal

G "5"
PA

R "4"
PA

Barrett Shoals

Priv maintd

Piling

N

Fl G 6s 16ft
(4 ft rep)
4M "3"

COLREGS DEMARCATION LINE
80.715 (see note A)

32°05′

Breakers

R
N "2"

80°50′

12

Piling

Joins Page 206

Nautical Miles

Savannah River, SC/GA

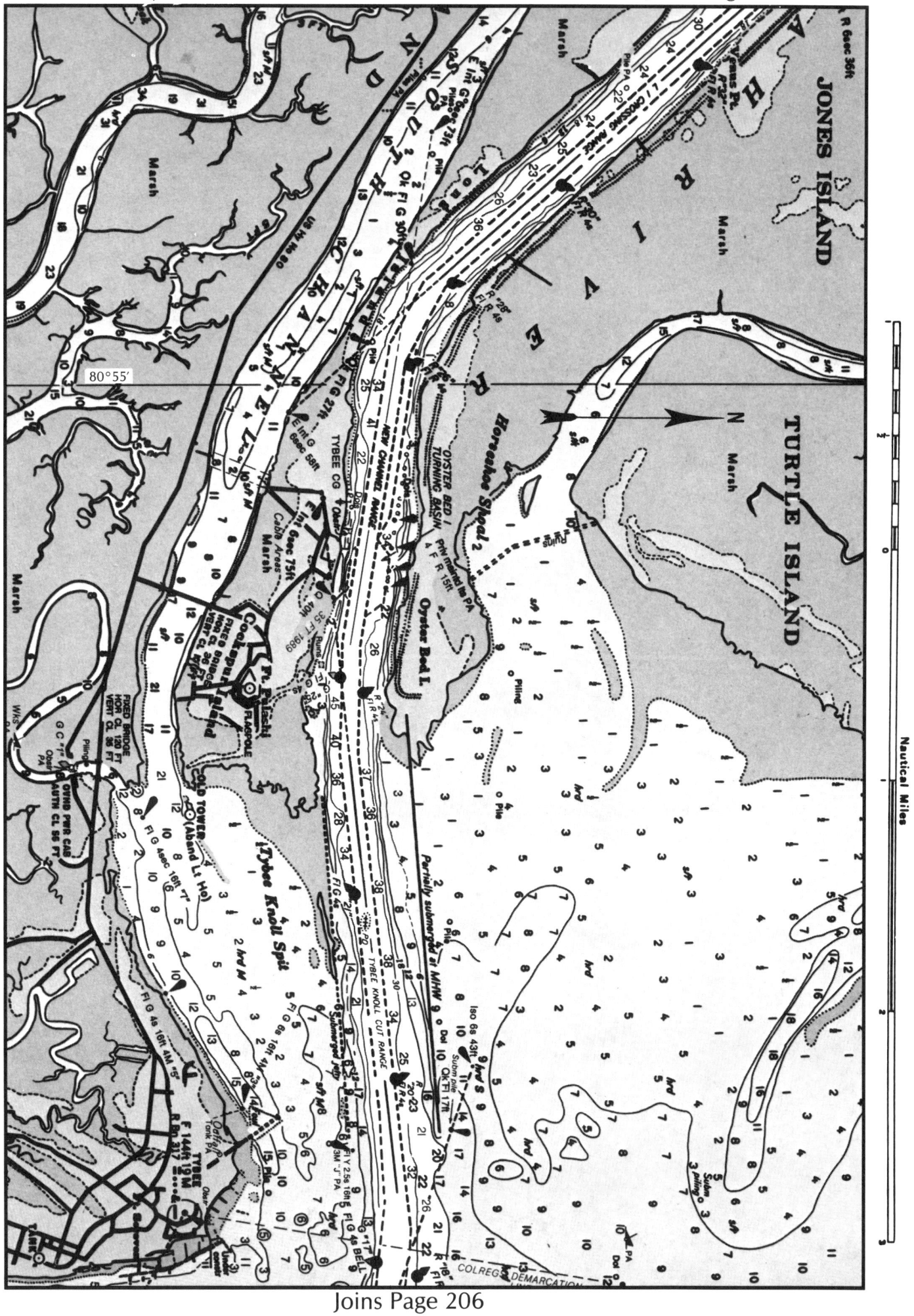

Joins Page 205



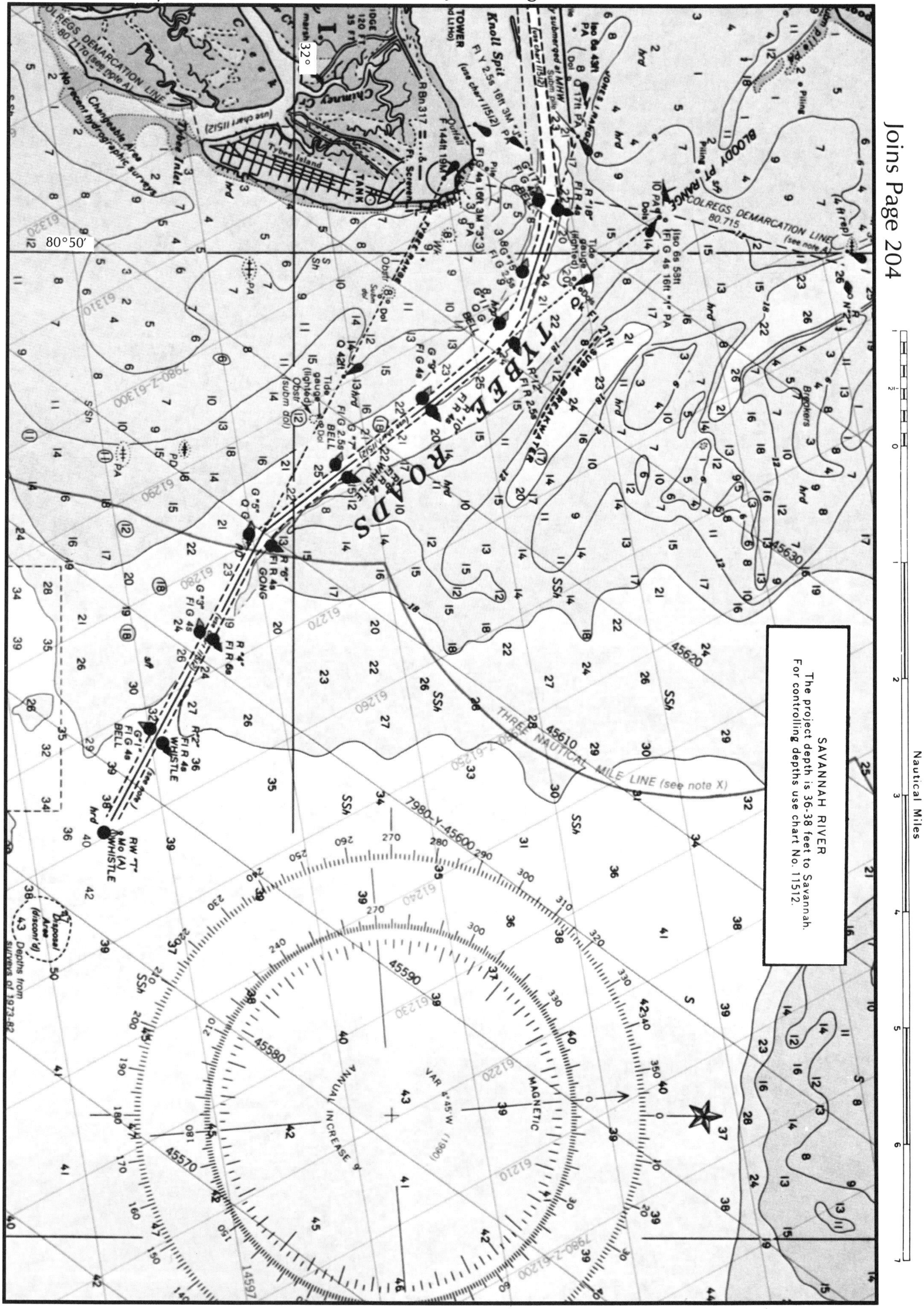


Joins Page 204

St. Catherines Sound, GA

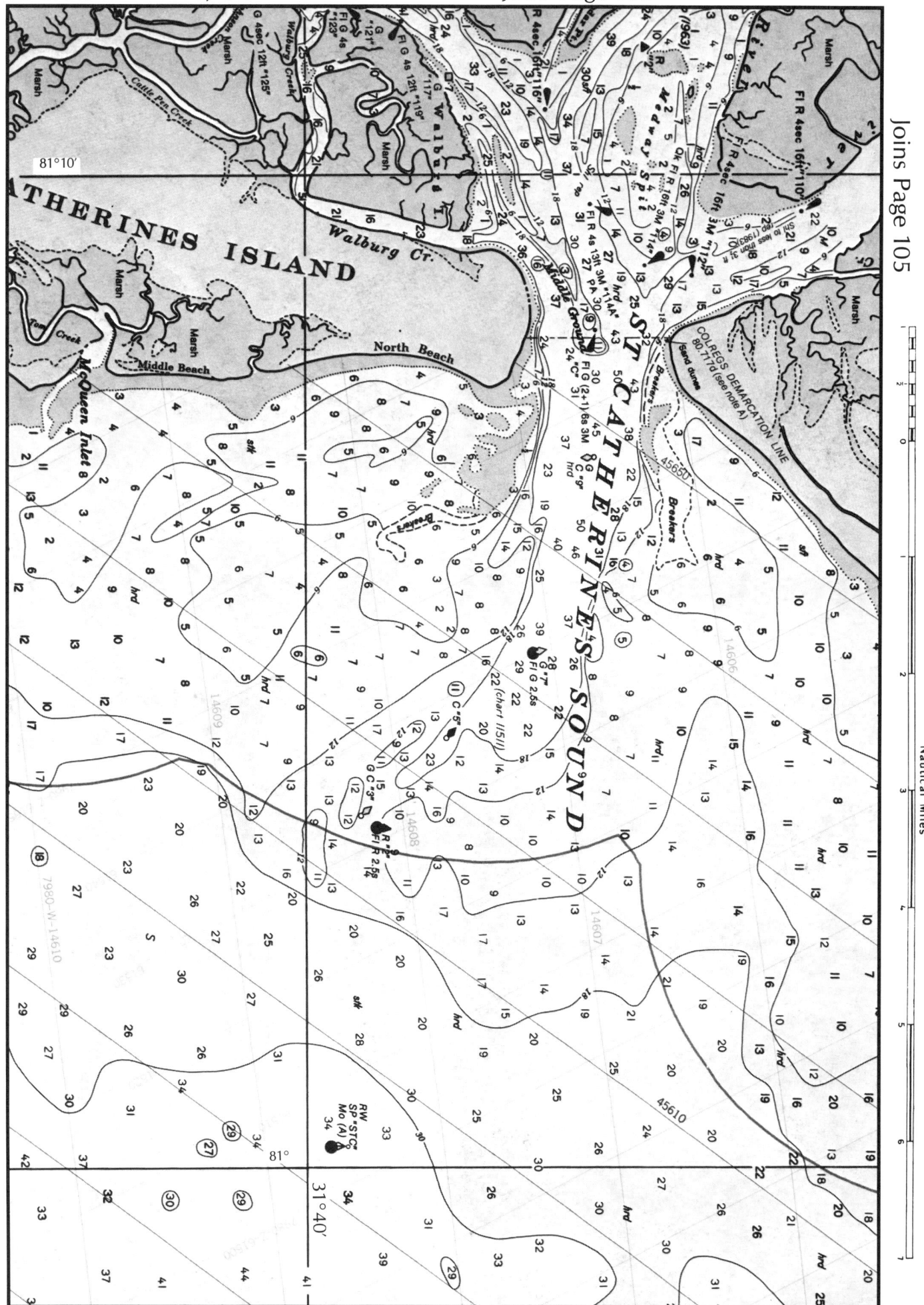

Joins Page 107

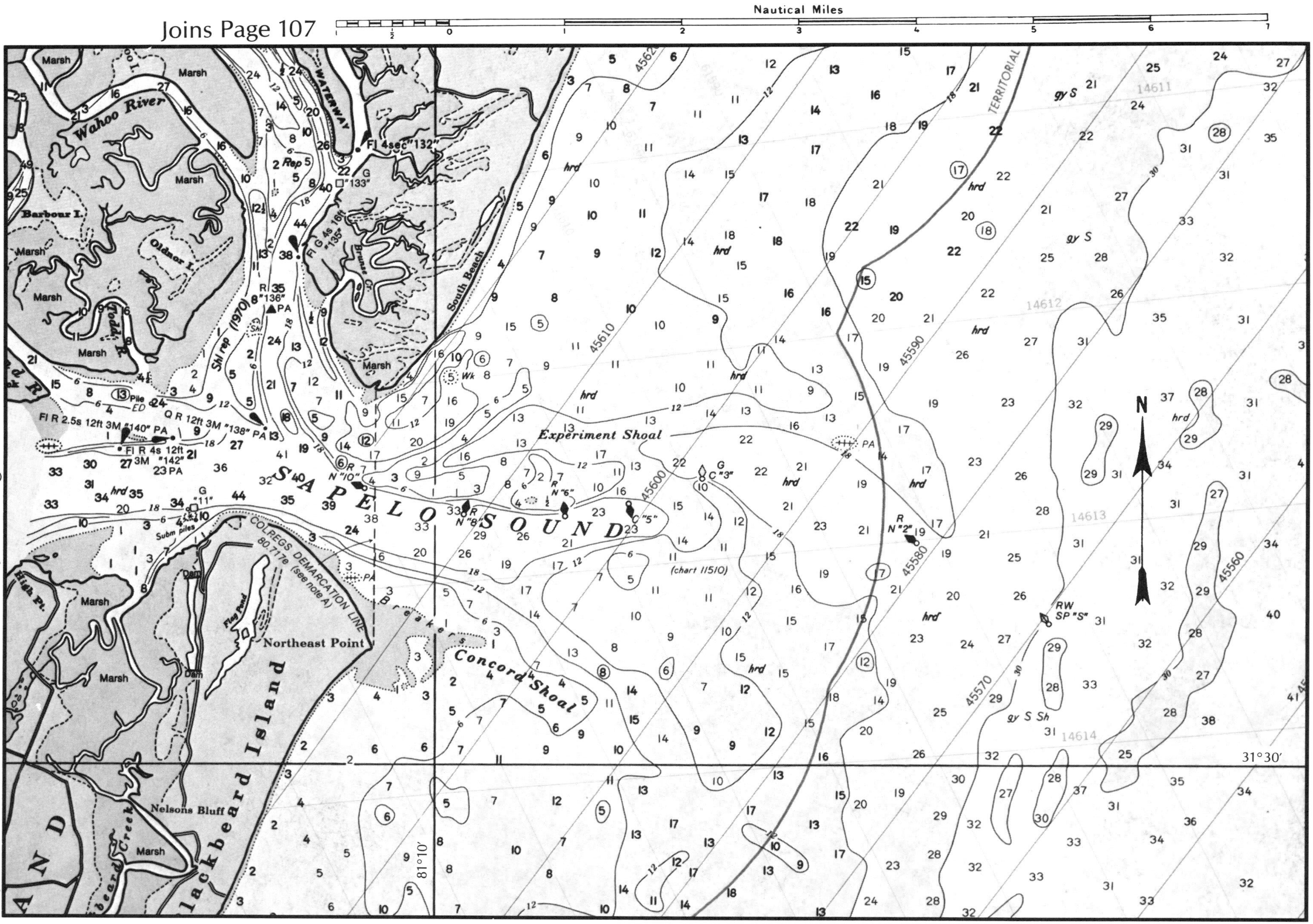


Joins Page 108

Sapelo Sound, GA

Joins Page 115

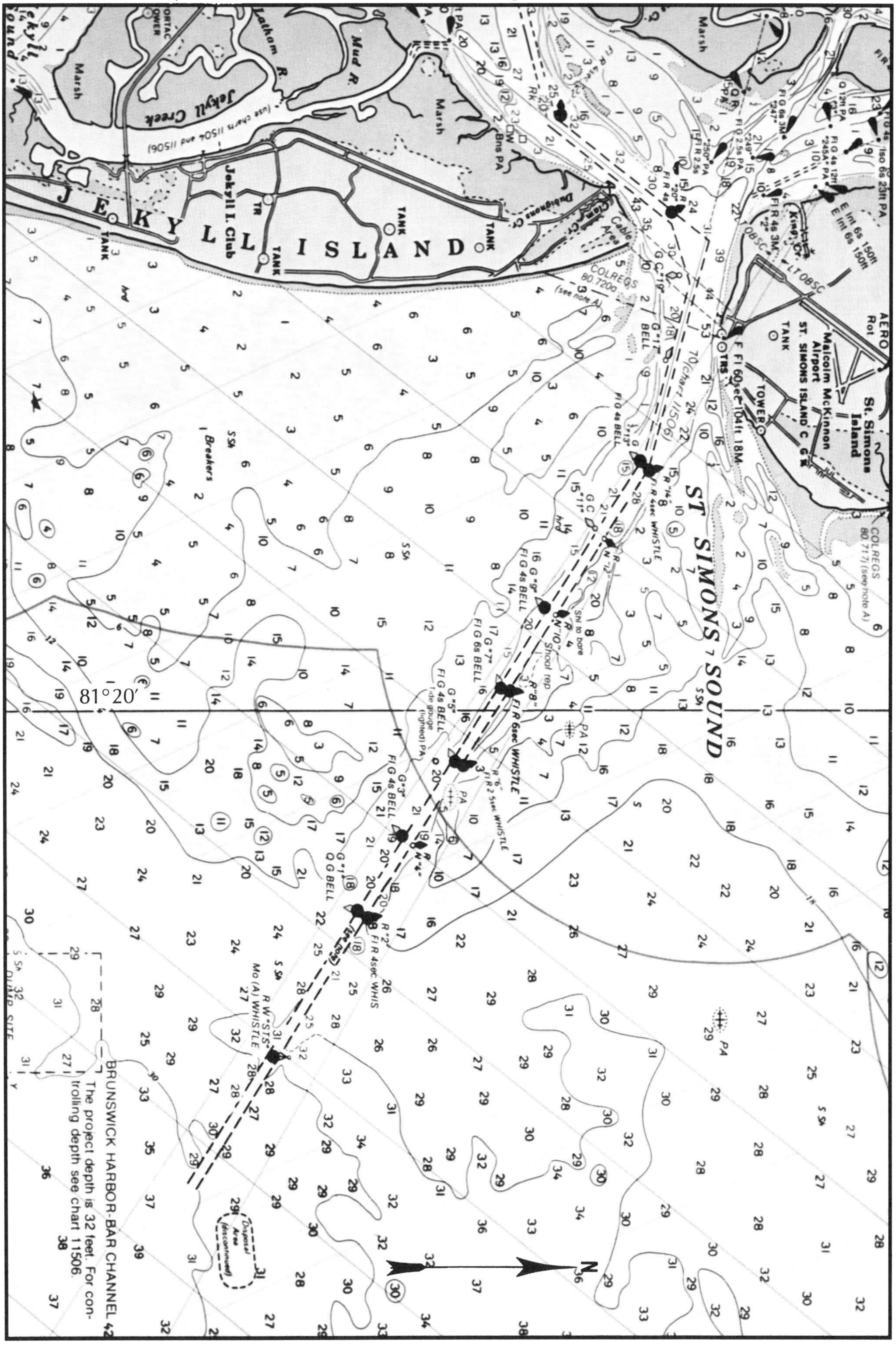


Joins Page 115

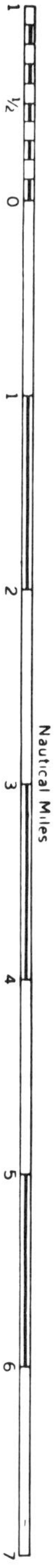

Joins Page 120



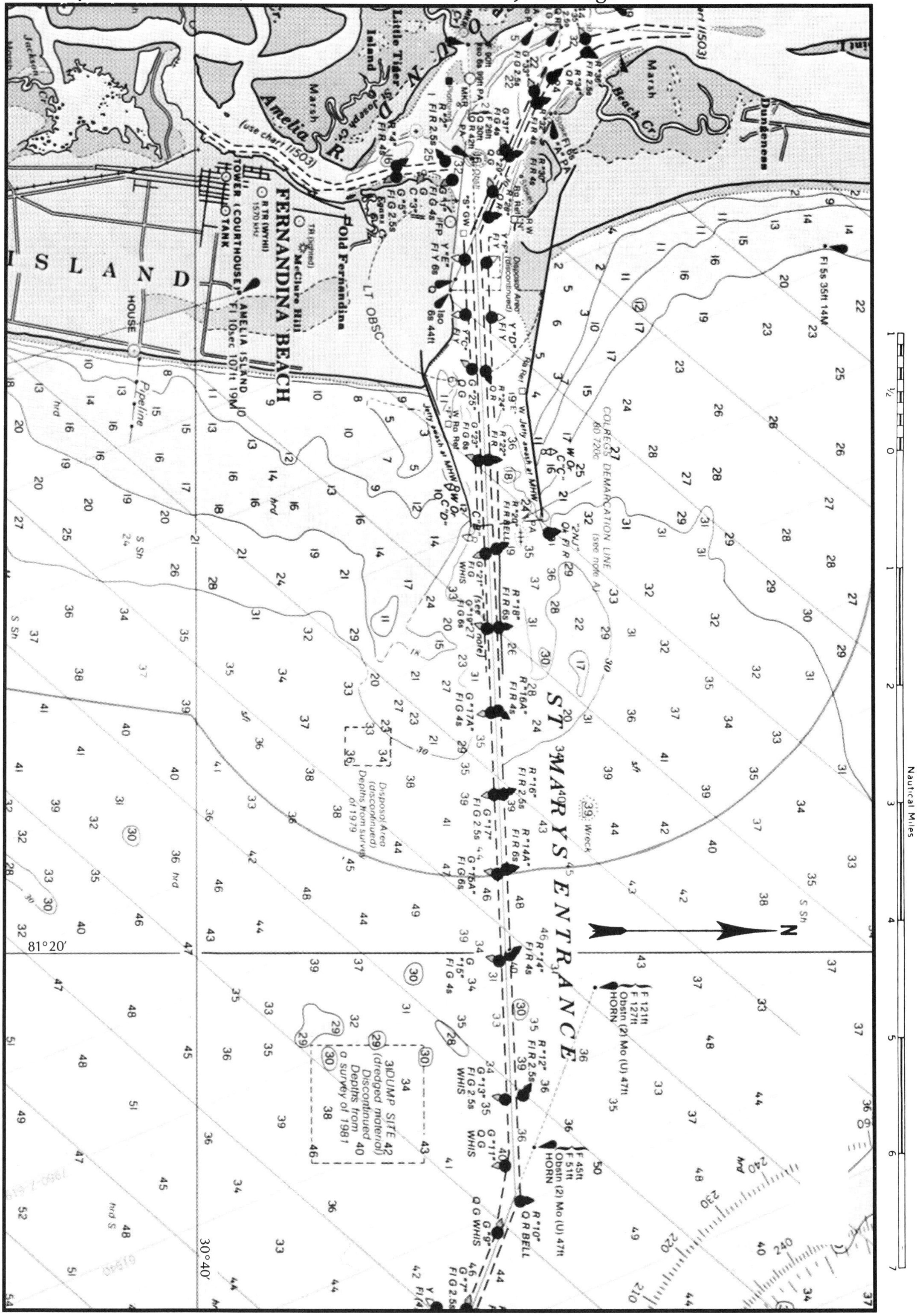

St. John River Entrance, FL

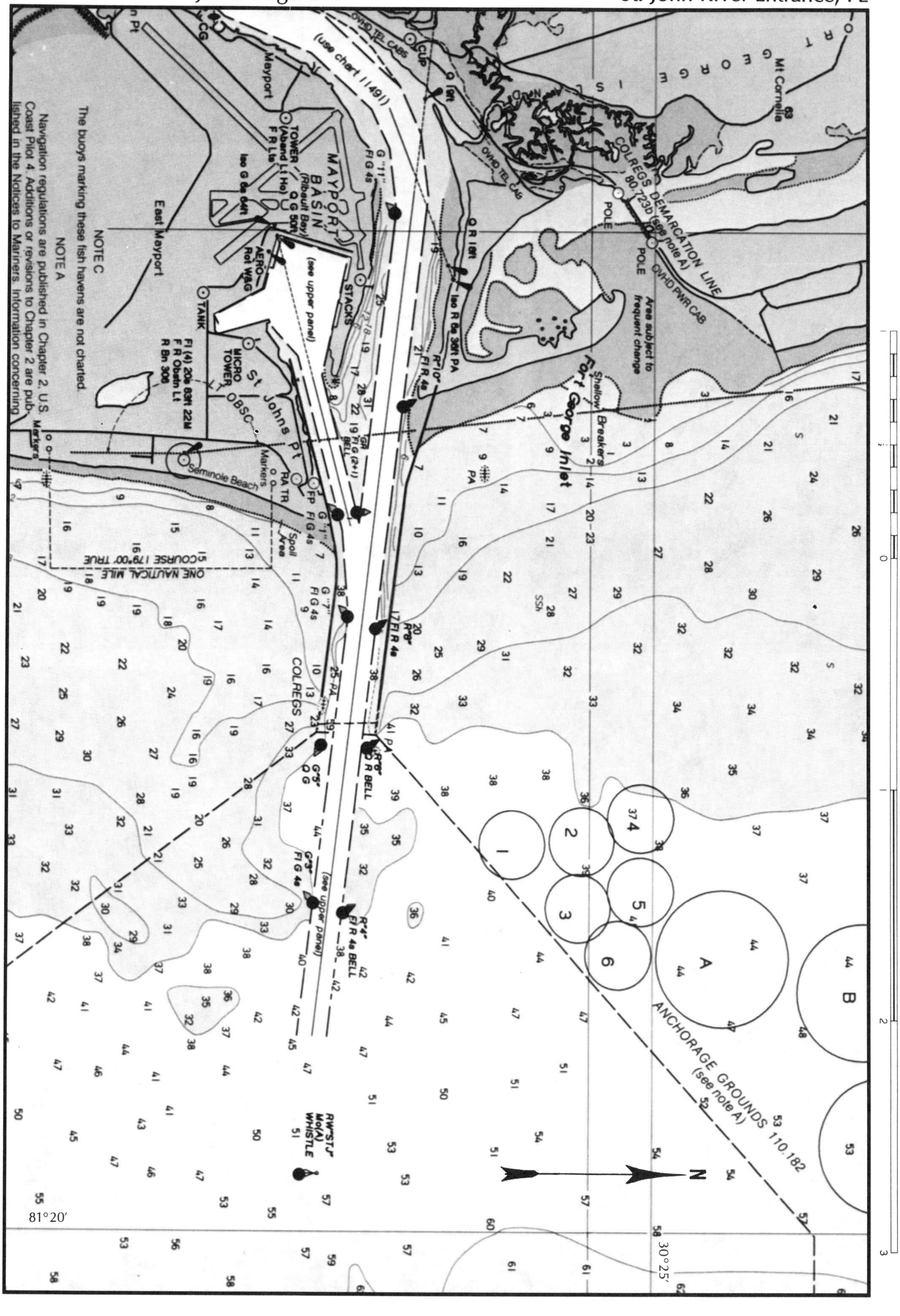
Nautical Miles
ANCHORAGE GROUNDS 110.182 (see note A)
COLREGS DEMARCATION LINE 80.723b (see note A)
Fort George Inlet
Area subject to frequent change
Breakers
Shallow
MAYPORT BASIN (Ribault Bay)
St Johns Pt
Seminole Beach
East Mayport
Mayport
Mt Cornelia
(use chart 11491)
(see upper panel)
ONE NAUTICAL MILE COURSE 179°00' TRUE
RW "STJ" Mo(A) WHISTLE
30°25'
81°20'
NOTE C
The buoys marking these fish havens are not charted.
NOTE A
Navigation regulations are published in Chapter 2, U.S. Coast Pilot 4. Additions or revisions to Chapter 2 are published in the Notices to Mariners. Information concerning

# Cape Canaveral Barge Canal, FL

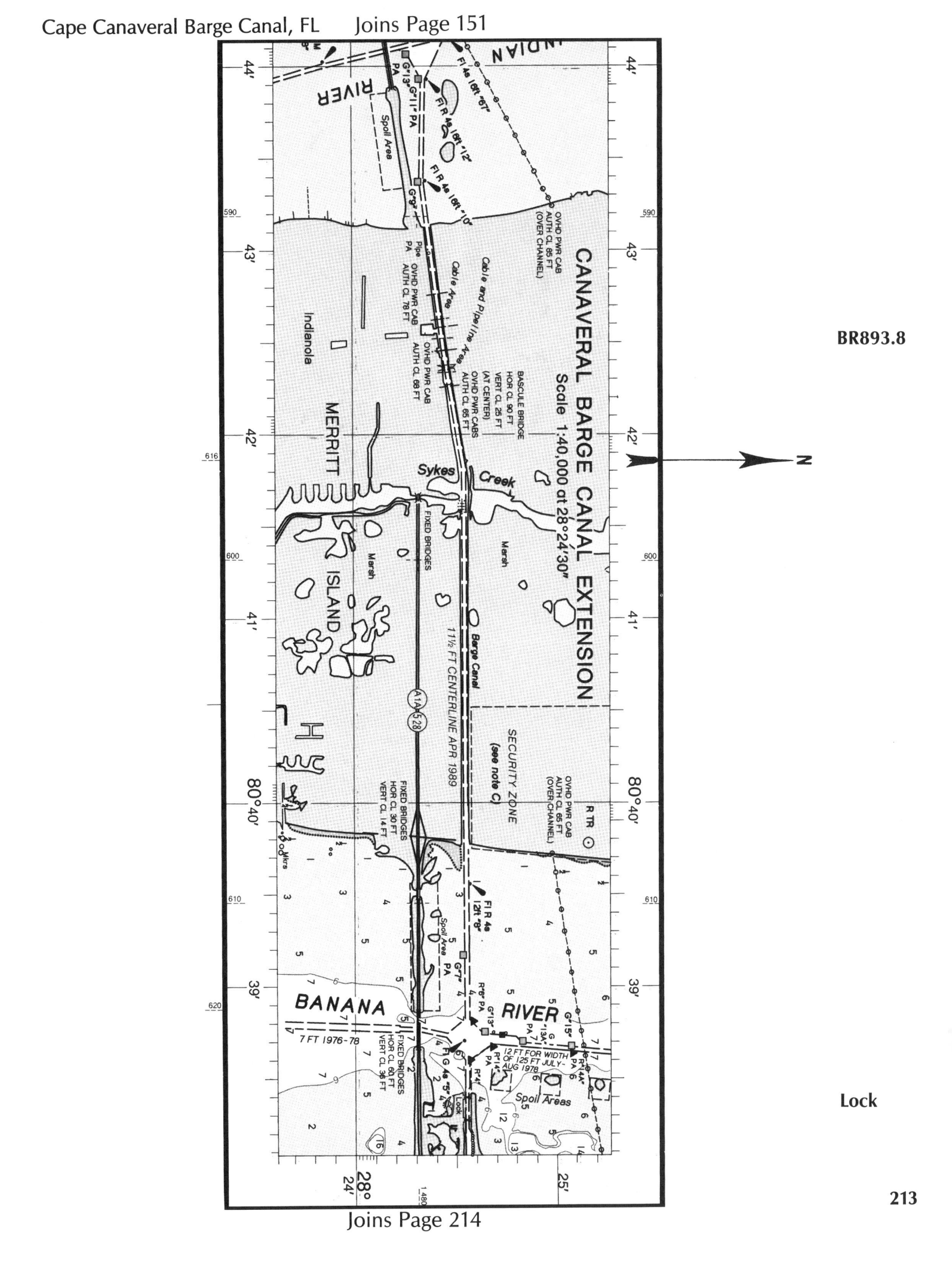

BR893.8

Lock

# Cape Canaveral Barge Canal, FL

## Joins Page 213

**214**

BARGE CHANNEL

Fl G 4s "5"

R "4" PA

R "14" PA

G "13A" PA

Dol 7

Dol

Spoil Area

Spoil Area

**Lock**

FIXED BRIDGES
HOR CL 60 FT
VERT CL 36 FT

LOCK
WIDTH 90 FT
LENGTH 600 FT

Iso G 6s 54ft

Fender

A1A

12 FT CENTERLINE APR 1989

Dolphin

OVHD PWR CAB
AUTH CL 85 FT

BASCULE BRIDGES
HOR CL 90 FT
VERT CL 25 FT
(AT CENTER)

PA

Priv maintd
Markers

**BR**

Q G 25ft

Ramp

N

Rep dredged
to 12 ft May 1983

Rep dredged to 12ft May 1983

CANAVERAL BARGE CANAL

R "2"

WEST BASIN
31 FEET APRIL 1989

12

12

15

23

27

13

Wk
(20ft rep)

9½ FT FOR MIDDLE WIDTH

OVHD PWR CAB
AUTH CL 85 FT

**CG**

Nautical Miles

0

## Joins Page 215

Joins Page 214


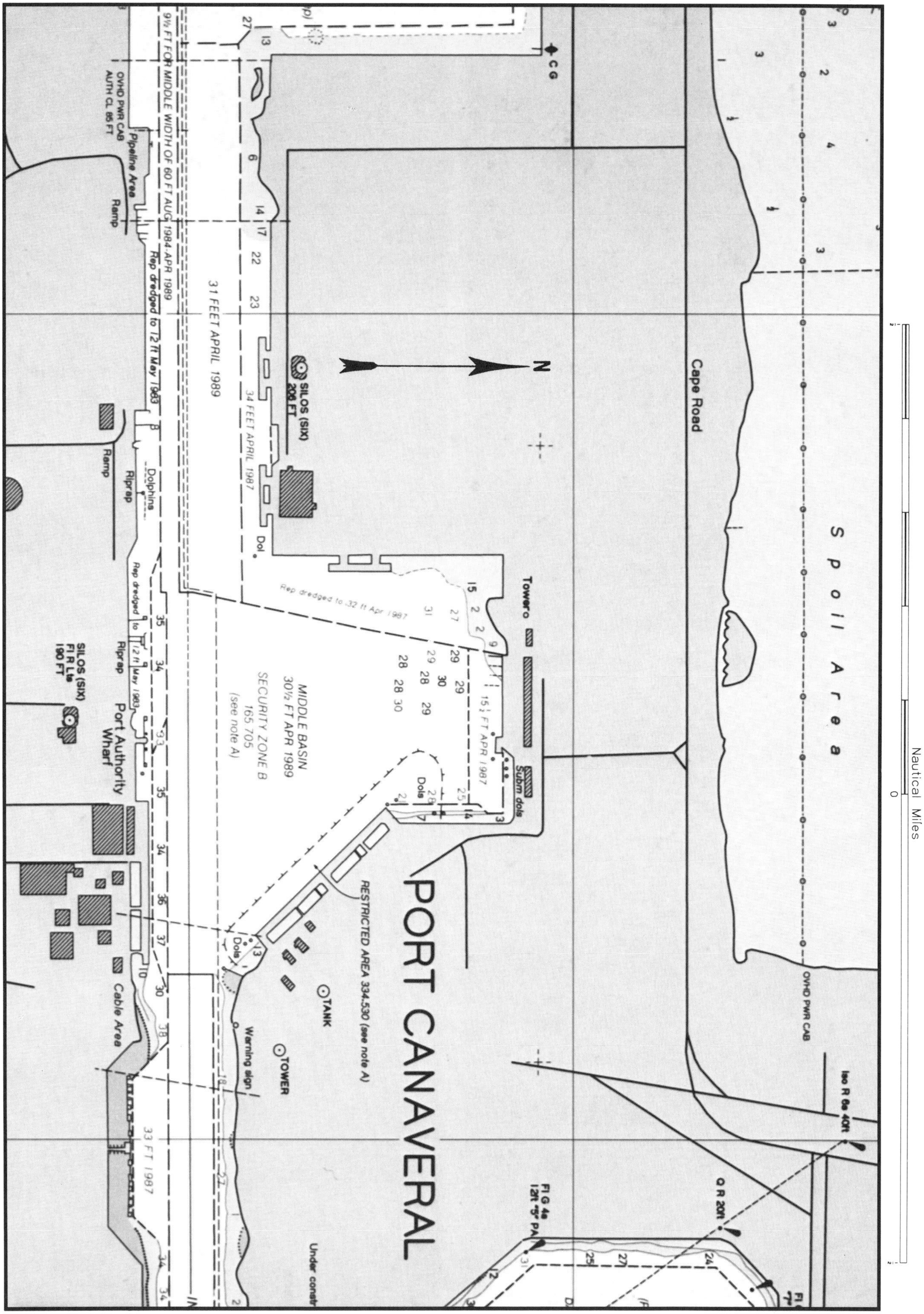


Joins Page 216

# Cape Canaveral Barge Canal, FL

## TIDAL INFORMATION

| Name | Place (LAT/LONG) | Height referred to datum of soundings (MLLW) | | | |
|---|---|---|---|---|---|
| | | Mean Higher High Water | Mean High Water | Mean Low Water | Extreme Low Water |
| | | feet | feet | feet | feet |
| Cape Canaveral | (28°26′N/80°34′W) | 3.8 | 3.7 | 0.2 | -2.0 |

# Cape Canaveral Entrance, FL — Joins Page 216

Joins Page 186



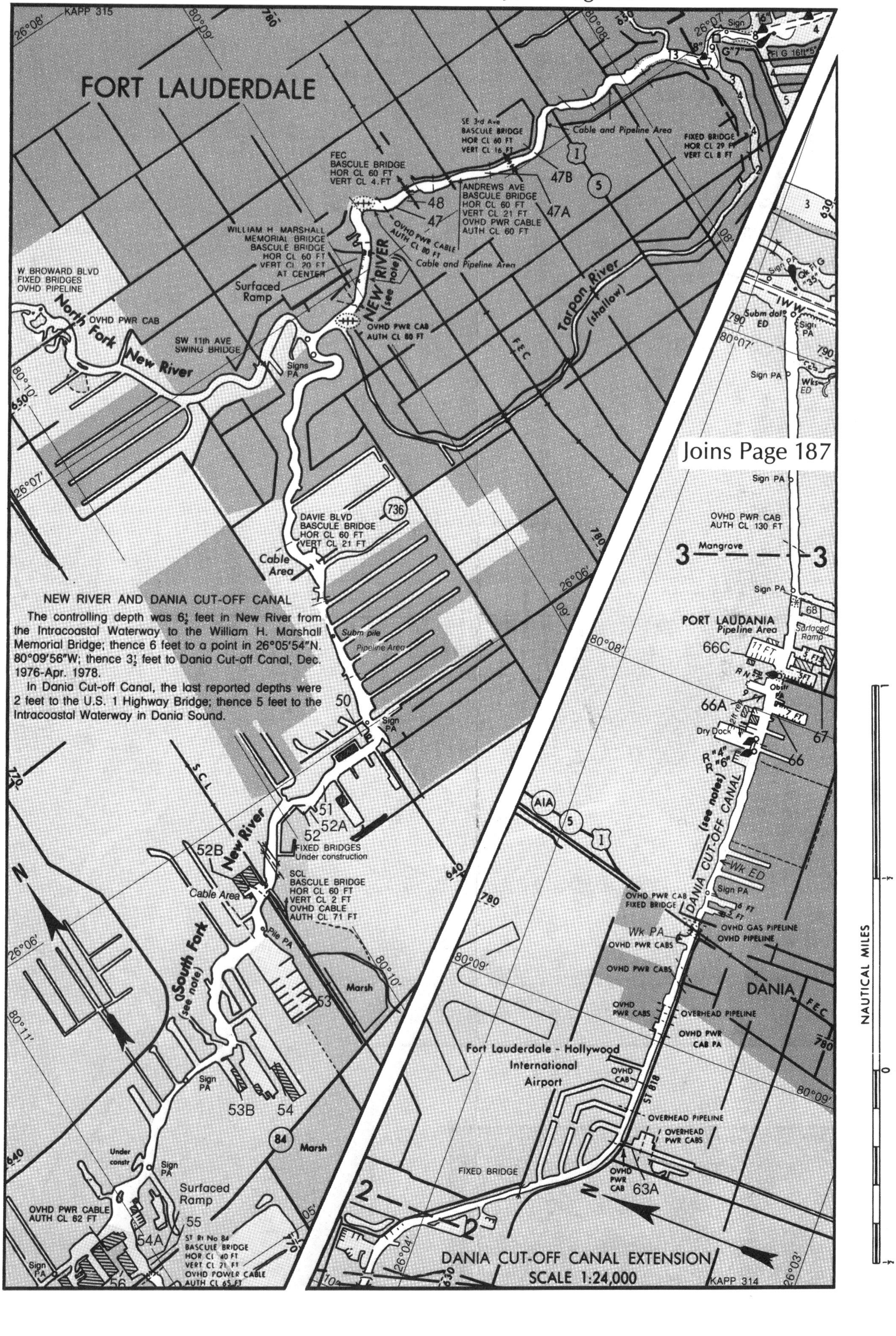

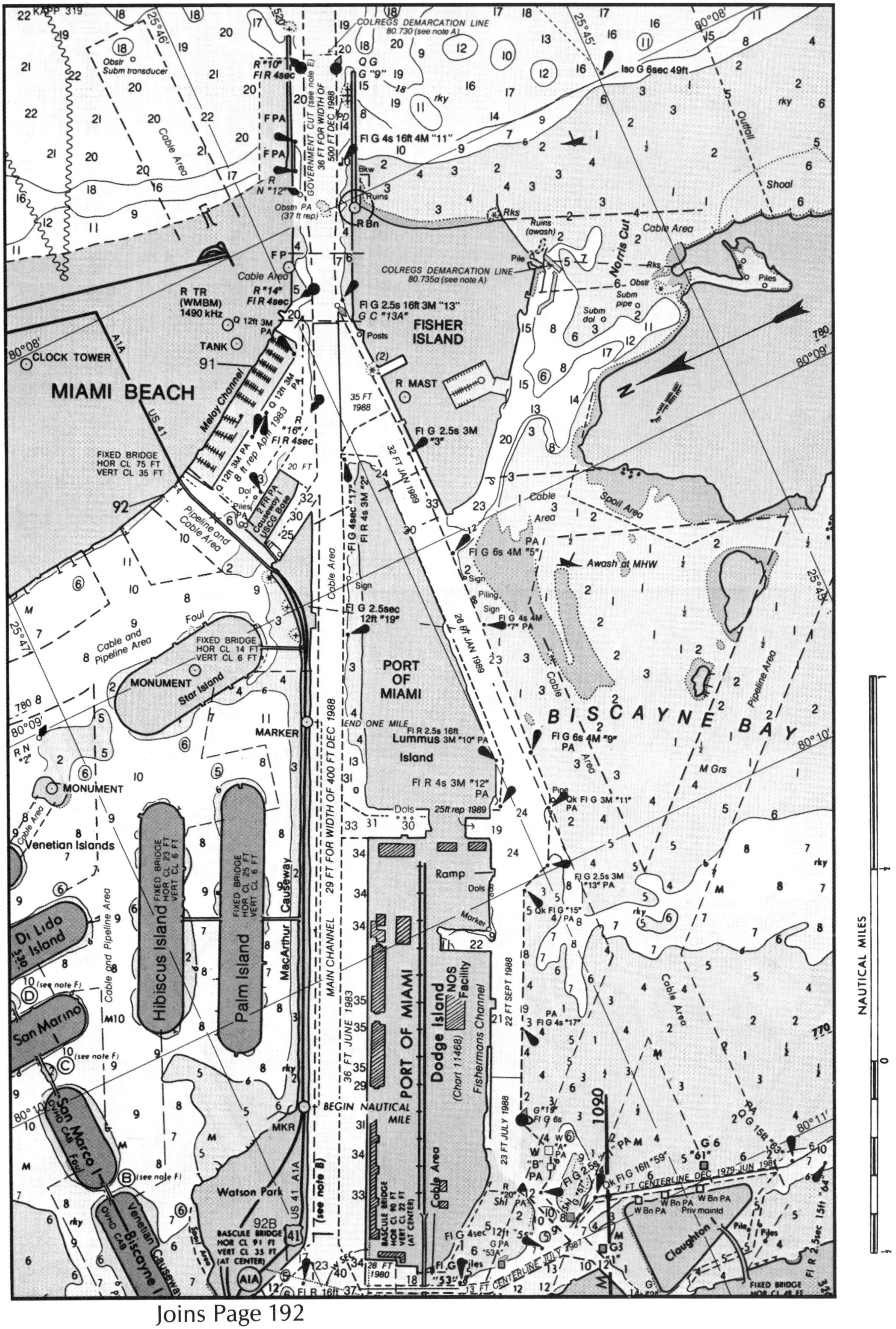
COLREGS DEMARCATION LINE
80.730 (see note A)
GOVERNMENT CUT (see note E)
36 FT FOR WIDTH OF 500 FT DEC 1988
Iso G 6sec 49ft
Fl G 4s 16ft 4M "11"
Cable Area
Norris Cut
COLREGS DEMARCATION LINE
80.735a (see note A)
R TR (WMBM) 1490 kHz
TANK
CLOCK TOWER
MIAMI BEACH
FISHER ISLAND
R MAST
Meloy Channel
Fl G 2.5s 16ft 3M "13"
Fl G 2.5s 3M "3"
FIXED BRIDGE HOR CL 75 FT VERT CL 35 FT
Pipeline and Cable Area
USCG Base
Spoil Area
Fl G 6s 4M "5"
Awash at MHW
Cable and Pipeline Area
FIXED BRIDGE HOR CL 14 FT VERT CL 6 FT
MONUMENT
Star Island
PORT OF MIAMI
Lummus Island
BISCAYNE BAY
MARKER
Venetian Islands
Di Lido Island
Hibiscus Island
FIXED BRIDGE HOR CL 23 FT VERT CL 6 FT
Palm Island
FIXED BRIDGE HOR CL 25 FT VERT CL 6 FT
MacArthur Causeway
MAIN CHANNEL 29 FT FOR WIDTH OF 400 FT DEC 1988
36 FT JUNE 1983
PORT OF MIAMI
Dodge Island
(Chart 11468)
NOS Facility
Fishermans Channel
22 FT SEPT 1988
23 FT JULY 1988
San Marino
San Marco
Biscayne
Venetian Causeway
Watson Park
BASCULE BRIDGE HOR CL 91 FT VERT CL 35 FT (AT CENTER)
BASCULE BRIDGE HOR CL 90 FT VERT CL 22 FT (AT CENTER)
BEGIN NAUTICAL MILE
END ONE MILE
Cable Area
Claughton I
7 FT CENTERLINE DEC 1979-JUN 1981
13 FT CENTERLINE JULY 1987
NAUTICAL MILES

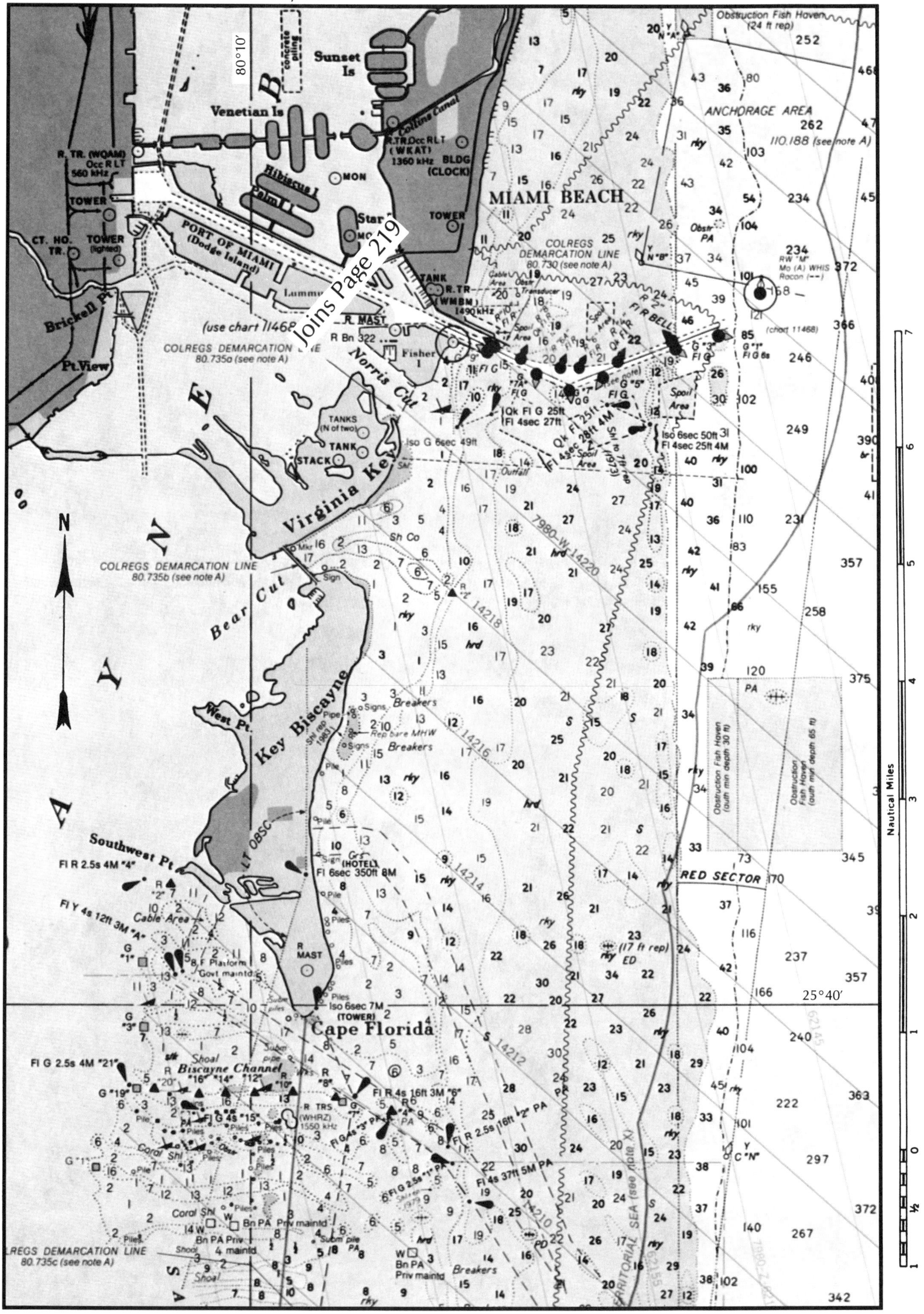

Joins Page 219

Joins Page 194

Miami River, FL　　　Joins Page 192

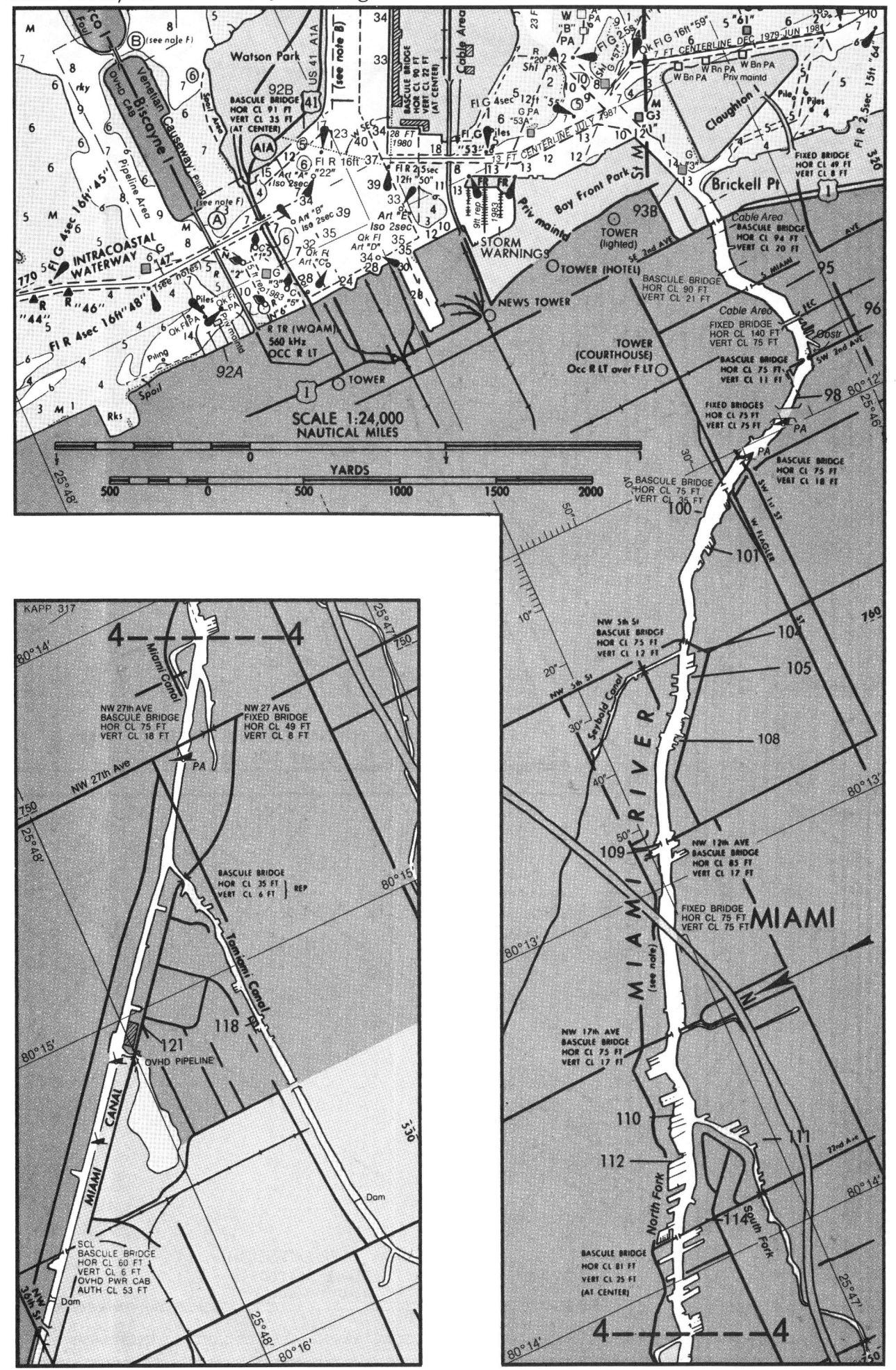

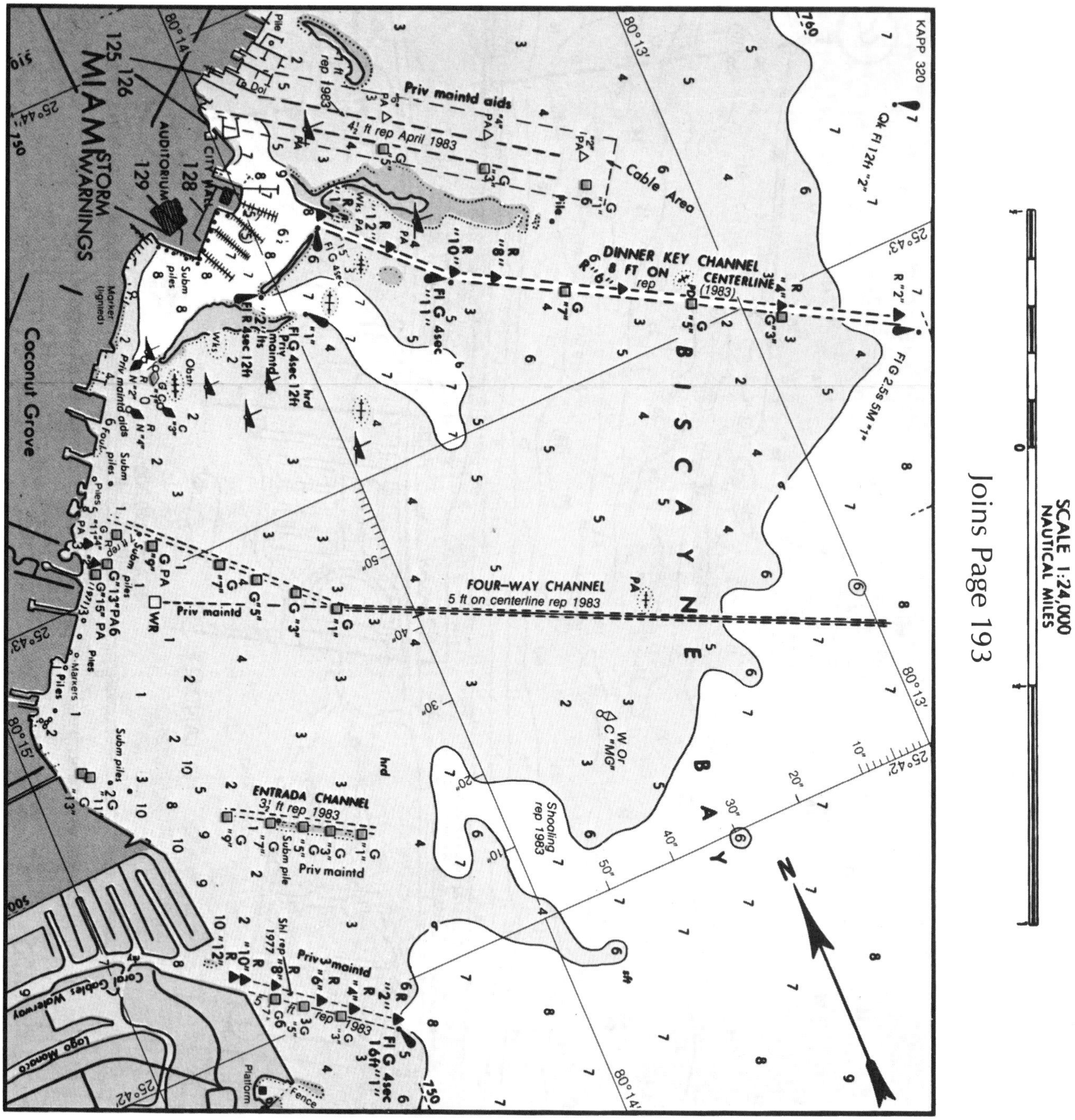


Joins Page 193

**Great Dismal Swamp Canal**

Joins Page 3

StM10

Lock10.6

BR11.1

StM15

# Great Dismal Swamp Canal (cont.)

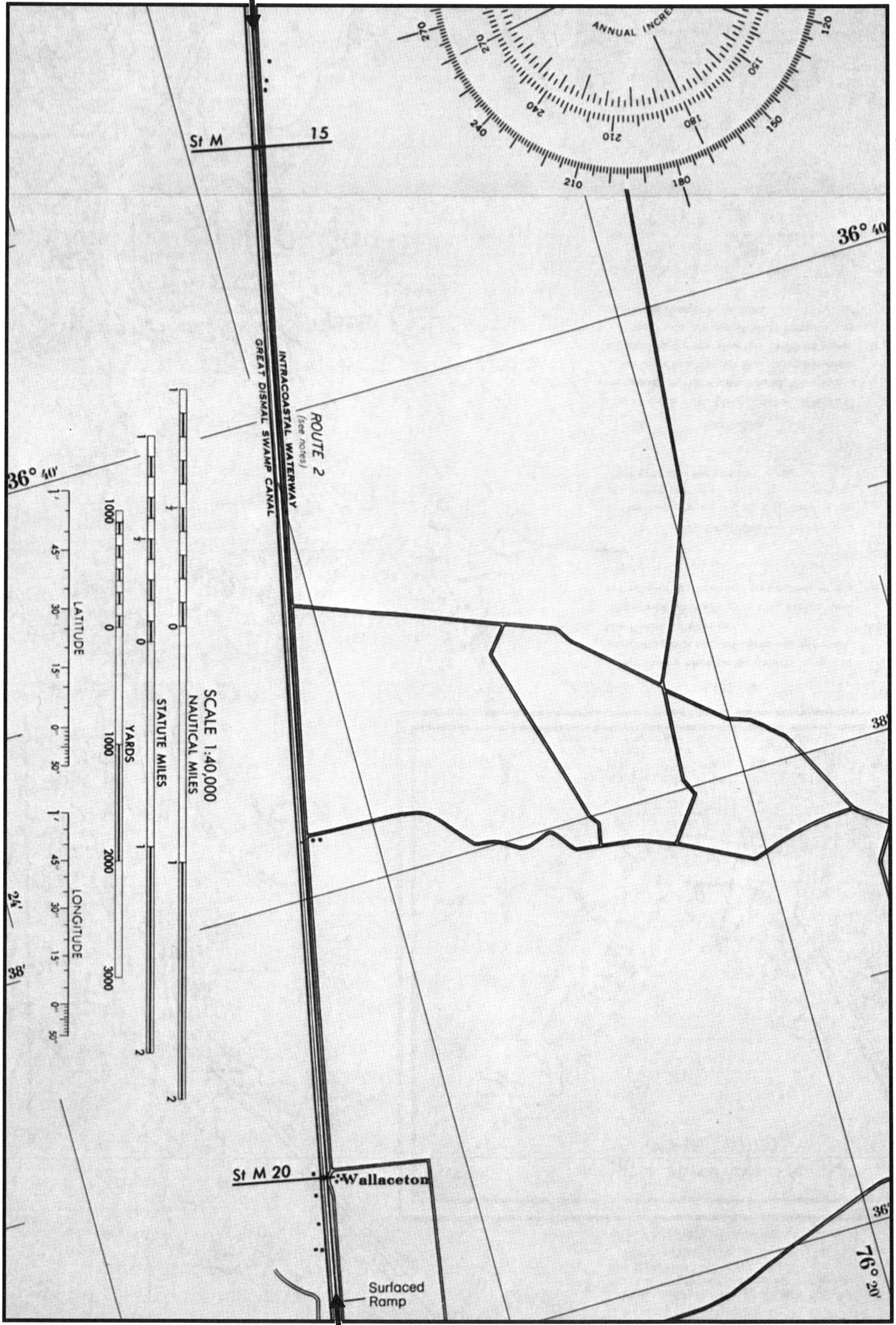

224

StM15

36° 40′

36° 40′

St M    15

INTRACOASTAL WATERWAY
GREAT DISMAL SWAMP CANAL

ROUTE 2
(see notes)

ANNUAL INCRE

270
270
240
240
210
210
180
180
150
150
120

38

SCALE 1:40,000
NAUTICAL MILES
STATUTE MILES
YARDS

LATITUDE
LONGITUDE

45″
30″
15″
0″
50′
25′
38′

1000
0
1000
2000
3000

0
1
2

St M 20

Wallaceton

StM20

36′

Surfaced
Ramp

76° 20′

# Great Dismal Swamp Canal (cont.)

StM20

St M 20 · Wallaceton

76°20'

Surfaced Ramp

⊙ TOWER ★

FEEDER DITCH

MAGNETIC
VAR 9°30'W (1990)
ANNUAL INCREASE 7'

Cypress swamp

②

VIRGINIA
NORTH CAROLINA

StM25

St M 25

225

# Great Dismal Swamp Canal (cont.)

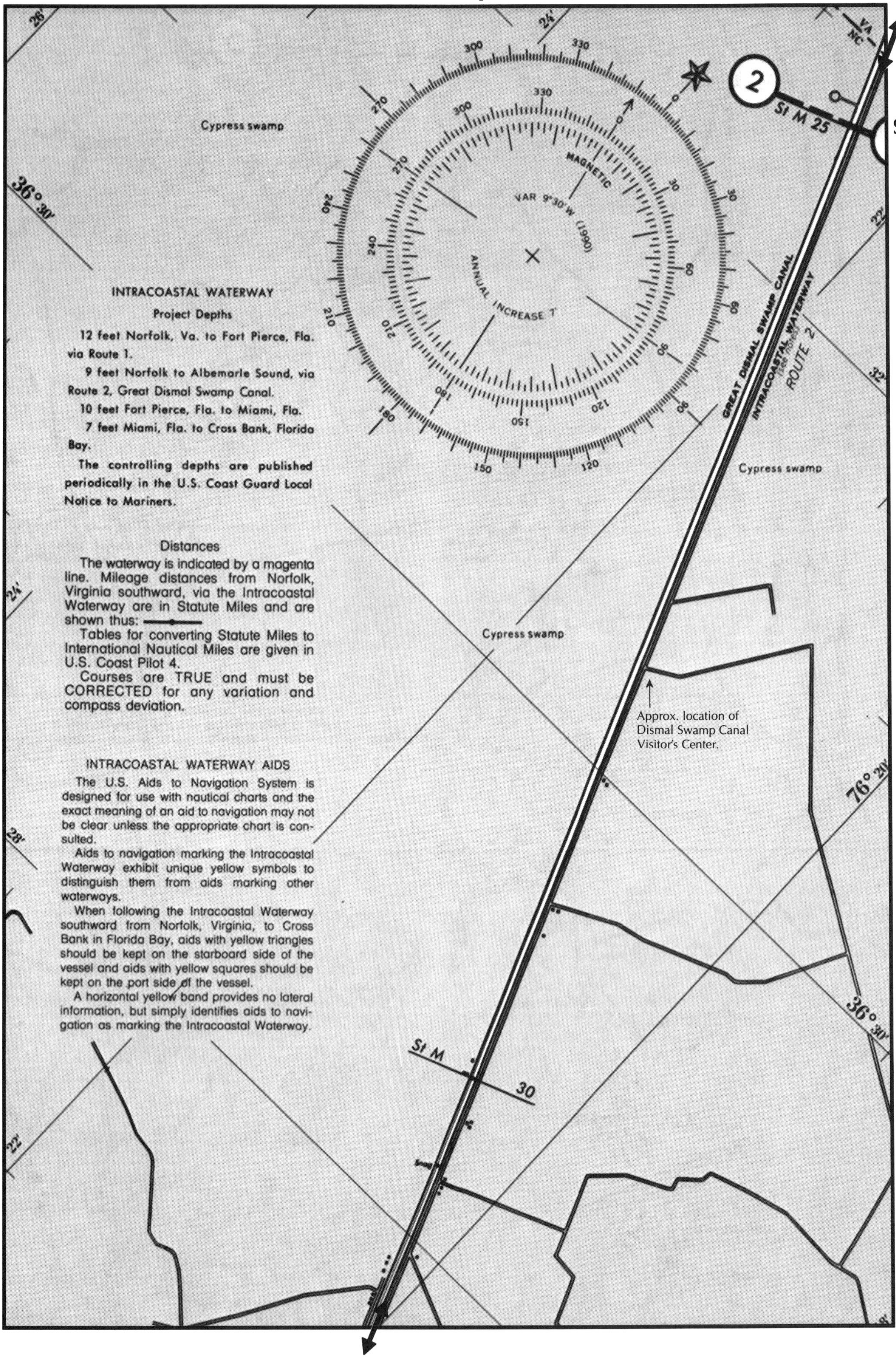

226

Cypress swamp

MAGNETIC

VAR 9°30'W (1990)

ANNUAL INCREASE 1'

StM25

2

St M 25

VA
NC

Cypress swamp

## INTRACOASTAL WATERWAY
### Project Depths

12 feet Norfolk, Va. to Fort Pierce, Fla. via Route 1.

9 feet Norfolk to Albemarle Sound, via Route 2, Great Dismal Swamp Canal.

10 feet Fort Pierce, Fla. to Miami, Fla.

7 feet Miami, Fla. to Cross Bank, Florida Bay.

The controlling depths are published periodically in the U.S. Coast Guard Local Notice to Mariners.

### Distances

The waterway is indicated by a magenta line. Mileage distances from Norfolk, Virginia southward, via the Intracoastal Waterway are in Statute Miles and are shown thus: ●━━━●

Tables for converting Statute Miles to International Nautical Miles are given in U.S. Coast Pilot 4.

Courses are TRUE and must be CORRECTED for any variation and compass deviation.

GREAT DISMAL SWAMP CANAL

INTRACOASTAL WATERWAY
(see note)

ROUTE 2

Cypress swamp

Cypress swamp

Approx. location of Dismal Swamp Canal Visitor's Center.

76° 20'

### INTRACOASTAL WATERWAY AIDS

The U.S. Aids to Navigation System is designed for use with nautical charts and the exact meaning of an aid to navigation may not be clear unless the appropriate chart is consulted.

Aids to navigation marking the Intracoastal Waterway exhibit unique yellow symbols to distinguish them from aids marking other waterways.

When following the Intracoastal Waterway southward from Norfolk, Virginia, to Cross Bank in Florida Bay, aids with yellow triangles should be kept on the starboard side of the vessel and aids with yellow squares should be kept on the port side of the vessel.

A horizontal yellow band provides no lateral information, but simply identifies aids to navigation as marking the Intracoastal Waterway.

36° 30'

St M

30

StM30

# Great Dismal Swamp Canal (cont.)

gation as marking the Intracoastal Waterway.

StM 30

Bridge under construction

**SOUTH MILLS**
SOUTH MILLS N.C. BASCULE BRIDGE
HOR. CL. 60 FT.
VERT. CL. 4 FT.
OVHD PWR & TV CAB
AUTH CL 75 FT
SOUTH MILLS LOCK
WIDTH 52 FT.
LENGTH 300 FT

StM30

BR32.6

Lock33.2

TURNERS CUT
INTRACOASTAL WATERWAY
ROUTE 2
(see notes)

St M 35

StM35

SCALE 1:40,000
NAUTICAL MILES
STATUTE MILES
YARDS
LATITUDE
LONGITUDE

### CAUTION
### CHANGES in BUOYAGE

Mariners are advised that authorized aids to navigation are being changed to conform to maritime standards of the International Association of Lighthouse Authorities Maritime Buoyage System, Region B. Significant changes are: black port hand buoys to green; black and white vertically striped buoys to red and white vertically striped buoys; and lateral lights from white to red or green as appropriate. Changes to aids to navigation will be announced in the Defense Mapping Agency Hydrographic/Topographic Center weekly Notice to Mariners and the U.S. Coast Guard Local Notice to Mariners.

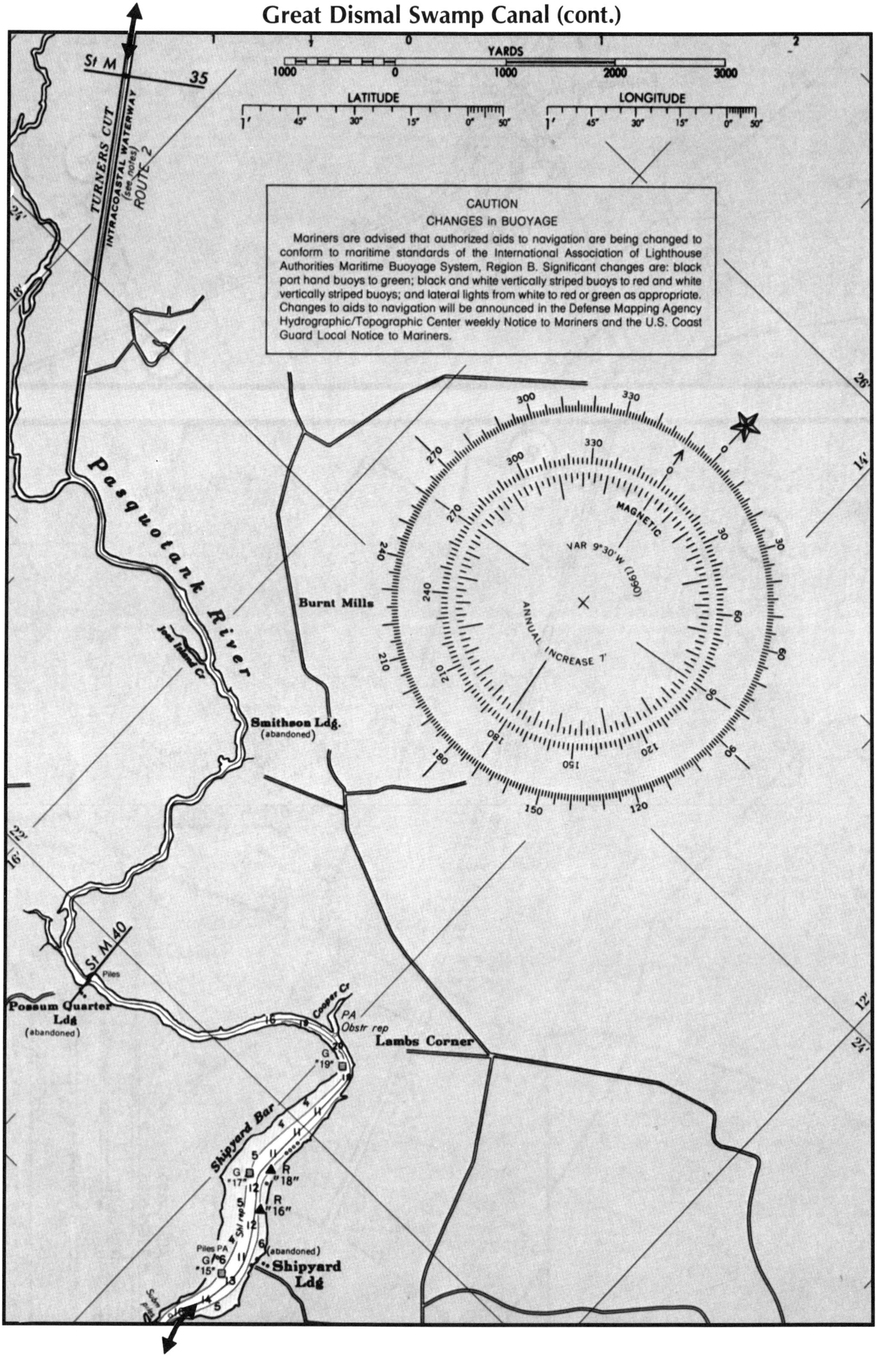

# Great Dismal Swamp Canal (cont.)

"Shipyard Ldg" (abandoned)

Shipyard Bar

Lambs Corner

Possum Quarter Ldg (abandoned)

Smithson Ldg (abandoned)

Burnt Mills

Pasquotank River

Turners Cut

INTRACOASTAL WATERWAY ROUTE 2 (see notes)

**CAUTION**
**CHANGES IN BUOYAGE**

Mariners are advised that authorized aids to navigation are being changed to conform to maritime standards of the International Association of Lighthouse Authorities Maritime Buoyage System, Region B. Significant changes are: black port hand buoys to green; black and white vertically striped buoys to red and white vertically striped buoys; and lateral lights from white to red or green as appropriate. Changes to aids to navigation will be announced in the Defense Mapping Agency Hydrographic/Topographic Center weekly Notice to Mariners and the U.S. Coast Guard Local Notice to Mariners.

VAR 9°30'W (1990)
MAGNETIC
ANNUAL INCREASE 7'

LATITUDE
LONGITUDE
YARDS

228

**Great Dismal Swamp Canal (cont.)**

# Great Dismal Swamp Canal (cont.)

230

BR50.7

StM50

BR47.7

StM55

CITY

TOWER TANK

ELIZABETH CITY BASCULE BRIDGES
HOR CL 90 FT
VERT CL 2 FT

CUP

ELEVATOR

Knobbs Cr (see note)

Pipeline Area
OVHD PWR CAB
AUTH CL 75 FT

St M 50

Machelhe I

Cable & Pipeline Area

Subm Pipe

FTG 4S 5M
19ft *gr*
Piles Piles PA

River

Obstr rep

N.S.R.R.
SWING BRIDGE
HOR CL 42 FT
VERT CL 3 FT
OVHD PWR CABLES
AUTH CL 85 FT

Sawyers Cr

Camden

Snag

center-
thence
oject.
e 1974.

Cottage Pt

Camden Causeway

158

Hospital Pt

Trees

Trees

Chapter 2,
Chapter 2
mation con-
Office of the
Portsmouth,
neer, Corps
s.

Forbes
Bay

Piles
PA

PA Piles

Qk Fl G 15ft "7"

Chantilly

Cobb Pt

3 ft rep 1975 Piles PA

2 ft rep 1974 Piles PA

INTRACOASTAL WATERWAY

ROUTE 2

(see notes)

Anson Pt

Trees
Trees

Dam

Fl R 4s 15ft "2"

G "1"

TANK

Davis
Bay

305° mag.

St M 55

Whitehall
Shores

Dam

Treasure Pt

StM55

PA
2 PA
9 Piles rep

4 ft rep
1980

AERO Rot W & G

330

Brickhouse Pt

Ditch

Fl G 4sec 15ft "5A"
PA

295½°

136¼°

146° mag.

Taylors

hrd

330

MAGNETIC

VAR 9°30'W (1990)

Qk Fl 16ft "5"

hrd

E R

NCREASE 7'

125° mag.

125¼°

# Great Dismal Swamp Canal (cont.)

# Great Dismal Swamp Canal (cont.)

232

Miles Pt

MAGNETIC

VAR 9°45'W (1990)

ANNUAL INCREASE 7'

StM65

326° mag.

317.64°

Snags

Snags

P A S Q

Subm piles

Subm piles

Subm piles

hrd

sft

Fl R 4s 3M "2"

St M 65

110°

120° mag.

INTRACOASTAL WATERWAY (see notes)

ROUTE 2

Sound Landing

N

Fl G 4s 16ft "1" PA
Ra Ref

hrd

300° mag.

PASQUOTANK RIVER
ENTRANCE
Fl 2.5sec 23ft

hrd

3

Joins Page 13

3

O U N D

sft

Obstr rep 1984
PA

W Or

Umbrella Cut Alternate Route, GA

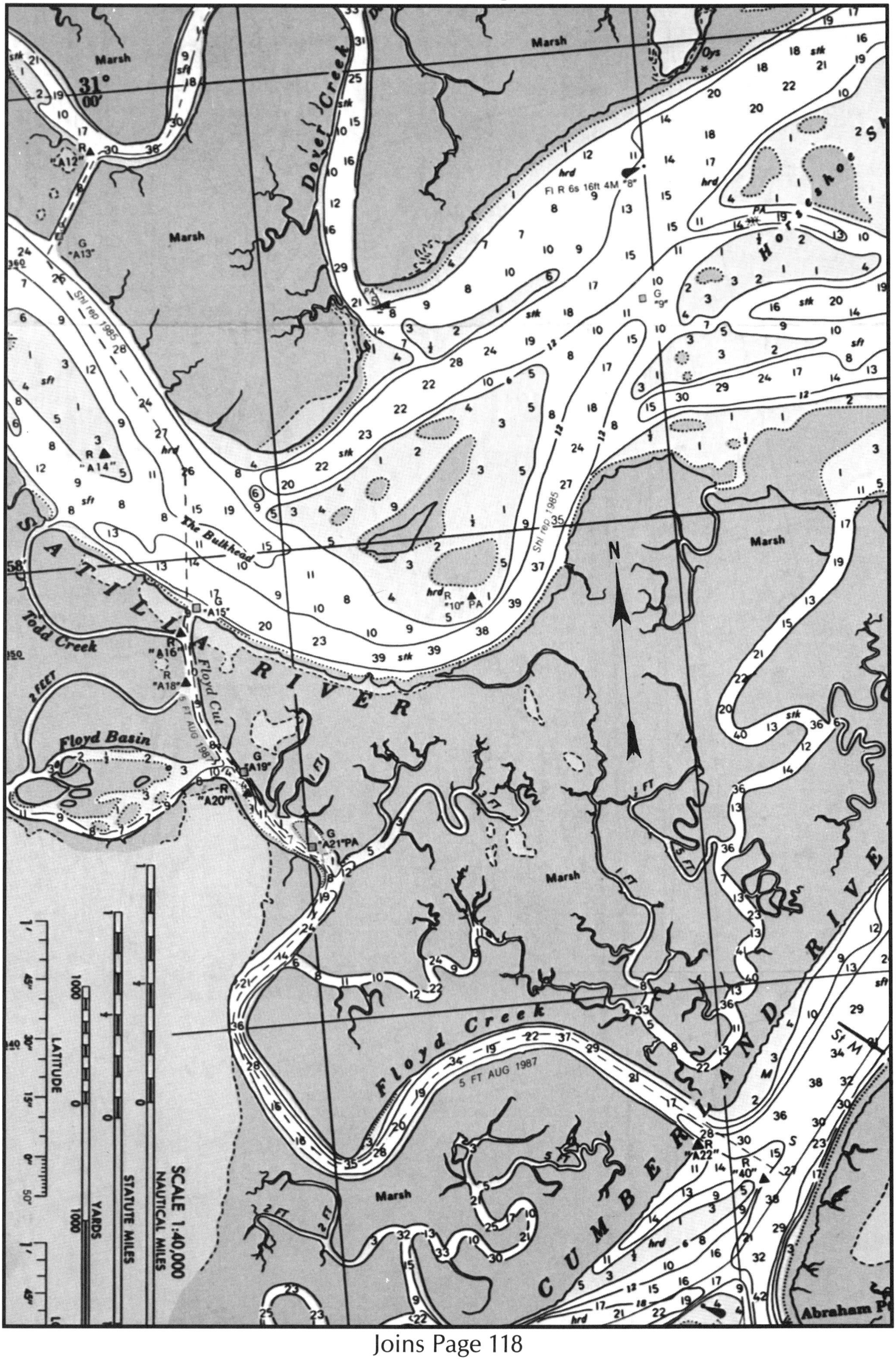

# APPENDIX A
## Bridges (Under 65 Feet) and Locks on the Intracoastal Waterway

The following list contains all of the bridges on the ICW with clearances of less than 65 feet, several new fixed bridges not yet shown on the charts, and all of the locks. Listed operating characteristics of each bridge and lock are based on the latest available data as of August 1990. Please keep in mind that these regulations change constantly to facilitate the movement of automobile, truck, and train traffic, resulting in more restrictions every year.

The statute mile label in the left column matches the label on the appropriate chart locating the bridge or lock. The next column gives the commonly used name for the structure. In your waterway travels, you will often hear several different names for a bridge. The name given here should get you a response when you call the tender on the VHF radio, Channel 13 or 16.

Other columns give the type of bridge or lock and its clearance when closed. Locks are not negotiable until the gates open and you have been given the green light to enter.

The "Restricted Period" column refers to the months of the year or days of the week (or both) during which bridge operations are regulated. Outside such restricted periods, bridges and locks should "open on demand" whenever the proper signal is given.

"Regulated Hours" are the times of the day, *during the restricted period only*, when bridge openings are limited. These restrictions, which at first glance are very confusing, make a bit more sense if you remember that in most cases they are designed to facilitate land traffic. Thus, restrictions are heaviest during rush hours and, in Florida, during the tourist seasons.

The "Comments" include observations on local currents, which side of a bridge to pass through, etc. Let's put it all together with an example:

Turn to mile 777.9 and locate the entry for the Bridge of Lions in St. Augustine, Florida. This is a bascule bridge (i.e., it opens under the influence of counterbalancing weights) with an overhead clearance of 25 feet when closed. Its openings are subject to one set of restrictions Monday through Friday, and to another on weekends and holidays. This means *some* restrictions are in effect every day. The "Regulated Hours" column tells us that on Monday through Friday from 7:00 AM to 6:00 PM it opens only on the hour and half-hour, but it won't open at all at 8:00 AM, noon, or 5:00 PM if land traffic warrants. The federal holiday and weekend openings are also limited between 7:00 AM and 6:00 PM, when it will only open on the hour and half-hour.

If you arrive at the Bridge of Lions before 7:00 AM or after 6:00 PM any day of the year, it should open at your signal. Note the comment about strong currents in the vicinity of the bridge, and stand well back until the opening is clear for your boat.

Keep in mind that the regulated hours apply *only* during the restricted periods, and a bridge should open on demand during any period not listed as restricted, and at any time of day outside regulated hours even on restricted days. Before cursing a bridge tender, please give him a call on the VHF radio to clarify the current opening situation. Occasionally, a malfunction of the bridge equipment or a special event will cause a temporary delay. We have found bridge operators extremely helpful in making all of this go smoothly.

| Statute Mile (StM) | Bridges or Locks | Type | Clearance (or lock lift) | Restricted Period | Regulated Hours (Comments) |
|---|---|---|---|---|---|
| 2.6 | Norfolk & Portsmouth Belt Line R.R. | Lift | 6' | | Opens on demand |
| 2.8 | Jordon Hwy | Lift | 15' | Mon–Fri (except hldys) | Closed 6:30–7:30am, 3:30–4:30pm |
| 3.6 | Norfolk & Western R.R. | Lift | 10' | | Usually open |
| 5.8 | Gilmerton Hwy | Bascule | 11' | | Opens on demand |
| 5.8 | Norfolk & Western R.R. | Bascule | 7' | | Opens on demand — Open together |
| | **The Great Dismal Swamp Canal Route** | | | | Restrictions may vary with water level. Call Corps of Engineers in Norfolk (804-441-3641) for latest data. |
| 10.6 | Deep Creek Lock | | approx. 12' max. | Apr 15–Oct 15 / Oct 16–Apr 14 | Opens at 8:30am, 11am, 1:30pm, 3:30pm / Opens at 8:30am, 12 noon, 3:30pm |
| 11.1 | Deep Creek Hwy | Bascule | 4' | | Opens in conjunction with the Deep Creek Lock |
| 32.6 | South Mills Hwy | Bascule | 4' | | Opens in conjunction with the South Mills Lock |
| 33.2 | South Mills Lock | | approx. 12' max. | Apr 15–Oct 15 / Oct 16–Apr 14 | Opens at 8:30am, 11am, 1:30pm, 3:30pm / Opens at 8:30am, 12 noon, 3:30pm |
| 47.7 | Norfolk Southern R.R. | Swing (hand-operated) | 3' | | Usually open |
| 50.7 | Elizabeth City Hwy Rt 158 | Bascule | 2' | | Opens on demand |
| | **Virginia Cut Route** | | | | |
| 8.1 | Millville–Norfolk & Portsmouth R.R. | Swing | 7' | | Usually open |

# Appendix A 236

| Statute Mile (StM) | Bridges or Locks | Type | Clearance (or lock lift) | Restricted Period | Regulated Hours (Comments) |
|---|---|---|---|---|---|
| 8.8 | Virginia Hwy Rt 104 | Bascule | 12' | | Opens on demand |
| 11.5 | Great Bridge Lock | | 2.7' | | Opens on demand – wait for signal |
| 12.0 | Great Bridge Hwy Rt 168 | Swing | 6' | Daily | 6am–7pm; opens on the hour |
| 13.9 | Norfolk Southern R.R. | Bascule | 7' | | Opens on demand |
| 15.2 | Virginia Hwy Rt 604 | Swing | 4' | Daily | 6am–7pm; opens on the hour and half-hour (May change as of 8/90) |
| 20.2 | North Landing Hwy | Swing | 6' | Daily | 6am–7pm; opens on the hour and half-hour |
| 28.3 | Pungo Ferry Rt 726 | Swing | 7' | | Opens on demand |
| 84.2 | Alligator River Hwy | Swing | 14' | | Opens on demand (Will not open if wind speed is over 34 knots) |
| 113.7 | Fairfield Hwy Rt 94 | Swing | 7' | Apr 1–Nov 30 | 7am–7pm; opens on the hour and half-hour (Use the south draw) |
| 125.9 | Wilkerson Hwy | Fixed | 65' authorized | | Reported up to 2 feet less than authorized clearance |
| 157.2 | Hobucken Hwy | Swing | 6' | Apr 1–Nov 30 | 7am–7pm; opens on the hour and half-hour (Use the east draw) |
| 195.8 | Core Creek Hwy | Swing | 16' | Apr 1–Nov 30 | 6am–7pm; opens on the hour and half-hour (Use the east draw) |
| 203.8 | Beaufort & Morehead R.R. | Bascule | 4' | | Usually open |

### Gallant Channel, Beaufort NC

| Statute Mile (StM) | Bridges or Locks | Type | Clearance (or lock lift) | Restricted Period | Regulated Hours (Comments) |
|---|---|---|---|---|---|
| | Gallant Channel Rt 70 Hwy | Bascule | 13' | May 1–Oct 31 | 7:30am–7:30pm; opens on the half-hour |
| | Beaufort & Morehead R.R. | Bascule | 4' | | Usually open |
| 206.7 | Atlantic Beach Hwy | Fixed | *65' | | *Replaces swing bridge |
| 240.7 | Onslow Beach Hwy | Swing | 12' | | Opens on demand (Use northwest draw) |
| 260.7 | Surf City Hwy | Swing | 12' | Daily | 7am–7pm; opens on the hour |
| 278.1 | Figure Eight Island Hwy | Swing | 20' | | Opens on demand |
| 283.1 | Wrightsville Beach Hwy | Bascule | 20' | Daily | 7am–7pm; opens on the hour |
| 323.6 | Holden Beach | Fixed | *65' | | *Replaces swing bridge |
| 337.9 | Sunset Beach Hwy | Pontoon | (no vertical clearance) | Apr 1–Oct 31 | 7am–7pm; opens on the hour (Do not pass through draw until cable is dropped) |
| 347.3 | Little River Hwy | Swing | 7' | | Opens on demand |
| 365.4 | Seaboard Coast Line R.R. | Bascule | 16' | | Opens on demand |
| 371.0 | Socastee Hwy | Swing | 11' | Apr 1–Jun 30 Oct 1–Nov 30 Mon–Fri | 7–10am; 2–6pm; opens on the hour and half-hour |
| | | | | May 1–Jun 30 Oct 1–Oct 31 wknd & hldys | 10am–2pm; opens on the hour and half-hour |
| 462.2 | Ben Sawyer Memorial Hwy Rt 703 | Swing | 31' | Mon–Fri (except hldys) | Closed 7–9am, 4–6pm |
| | | | | Wknd & hldys | 9am–7pm; opens on the hour |
| 470.8 | Wappoo Creek, James Is. Hwy Rt 171 | Bascule | 33' | Mon–Fri (except hldys) | Closed 6:30–9am, 4–6:30pm |
| | | | | Apr 1–Nov 30 wknd & hldys | 9am–7pm; opens on the hour and half-hour |
| | | | | Apr 1–Nov 30 Mon–Fri | 9am–4pm; opens on the hour and half-hour (Use caution due to strong currents in the vicinity of the bridge) |
| 479.3 | John F. Limehouse | Swing | 12' | Mar 15–Jun 15 Sep 15–Nov 15 Mon–Fri (except hldys) | 9am–4pm; opens every 20 minutes |
| | | | | Jun 16–Sep 14 Nov 16–Mar 14 Mon–Fri (except hldys) | 6:30–9am, 4–6:30pm; opens on the hour and half-hour (Caution advised when running through the bridge with a current. A slight crosscurrent is noticeable on the flood and the ebb at both approaches) |
| 501.3 | Whooping Island Hwy Rt 174 | Swing | 8' | | Opens on demand (Caution: Crosscurrents are encountered on the ebb in the west approach and the flood in the east approach) |
| 536.0 | Ladies Island Hwy | Swing | 30' | Mon–Sat (except hldys) | 7–9am, 4–6pm; opens on the hour |

| Statute Mile (StM) | Bridges or Locks | Type | Clearance (or lock lift) | Restricted Period | Regulated Hours (Comments) |
|---|---|---|---|---|---|
| | | | | Apr 1–Jun 30 Sep 1–Nov 30 Mon–Sat (except hldys) | 9am–4pm; opens every 20 minutes (Extreme caution: Crosscurrents are encountered in the approach on the flood and the ebb) |
| 579.9 | Causton Bluff Hwy | Bascule | 21' | Mon–Fri (except hldys) | 6:30–9am; 4:30–6:30pm; opens at 7am, 8am and 5:30pm |
| 592.8 | Skidaway Narrows Hwy | Bascule | 22' | | Opens on demand |
| 684.3 | Jekyll Island Hwy St. Rt. 50 | Lift | 9' | | Opens on demand |
| 720.7 | Seaboard System R.R. at Kingsley Creek | Swing | 5' | | Opens on demand (Caution: Velocities up to 2.5 knots on the flood and 3 knots on the ebb, especially with favoring winds, may be expected) |
| 739.2 | Sisters Creek Hwy | Bascule | 24' | | Opens on demand (Caution: Crosscurrents are encountered during both flood and ebb) |
| 747.5 | McCormick Rt 90 | Bascule | 37' | Apr 1–May 31 Oct 1–Nov 30 | 7–8:30am, 4:30–6pm; opens on the hour and the half-hour |
| | | | | Wknd & hldys | Noon to 6pm; opens on the hour and half-hour |
| 758.8 | Palm Valley Hwy Rt 210 | Bascule | 9' | | Opens on demand |
| 775.8 | Vilano Beach Hwy | Lift | 5' | Mar 15–Dec 15 | 7am–6pm; opens every 20 minutes |
| | | | | Wknd & hldys | 9am–sunset; opens every 20 minutes (Caution: Tidal currents run at angles to the bridge. Flood currents up to 1 knot and ebb currents up to 1.5 knots during normal weather) |
| 777.9 | Bridge of Lions at St. Augustine | Bascule | 25' | Mon–Fri (except hldys) | 7am–6pm; opens on the hour and half-hour, but may not open at 8am, 12 noon, 5pm |
| | | | | Wknd & hldys | 7am–6pm; opens on the hour and half-hour (Caution: Tidal currents, particularly ebb, run at right angles to the bridge. Flood currents are 1 knot and ebb 1.5 knots) |
| 788.6 | Crescent Beach Hwy Rt 206 | Bascule | 25' | | Opens on demand |
| 810.6 | Flagler Beach Hwy Rt 100 | Bascule | 14' | | Opens on demand |
| 816.0 | Highbridge Road | Bascule | 15' | | Opens on demand |
| 829.1 | Seabreeze Blvd at Daytona Beach | Bascule | 20' | Mon–Sat (except hldys) | 7:30–8:30am, 4:30–5:30pm, but opens at 8am and 5pm |
| 829.7 | Main Street | Bascule | 22' | | Opens on demand |
| 830.1 | Broadway | Bascule | 20' | | Opens on demand |
| 830.6 | Memorial | Bascule | 21' | Mon–Sat (except hldys) | 7:45–8:45am, 4:45–5:45pm; opens at 8:15am and 5:15pm |
| 835.5 | Port Orange | Fixed | *65' | | *Replaced bascule |
| 845.0 | Coronado Beach at New Smyrna | Bascule | 14' | Daily | 7am–6pm; opens every quarter-hour |
| 846.5 | Harris Saxon at New Smyrna Beach | Fixed | *65' | | *Replaced bascule |
| 869.2 | Haulover Canal | Bascule | 27' | | Opens on demand |
| 876.6 | Florida East Coast R.R. | Bascule | 7' | | Automatic; usually open, but closes for oncoming trains |
| 878.9 | State Rt 402 Hwy at Titusville | Swing | 9' | Mon–Fri | 6:45–7:45am, 4:15–5:45pm |
| 885.0 | NASA Parkway Rt 405 at Addison Point | Bascule | 27' | Mon–Fri (except hldys) | 6:30–8am, 3:30–5pm |
| 893.8 | **Canaveral Barge Canal** | | | | |
| | SR3 near Indianola | Bascule | 25' | Mon–Fri (except hldys) | On demand from 6am–10pm, except 6:45–7:45am & 4:15–5:45pm when it need not open |
| | | | | Daily | 10pm–6am, on signal if 3 hours' notice given |
| | Canaveral Barge Canal Lock | | 4' | Daily | In operation from 6am–9:30pm only (Await signal before entering; tie up to south wall) |
| | SR401 at Port Canaveral | Bascule | 25' | Mon–Fri (except hldys) | 6:30–8am, 3:30pm–5:15pm; need not open |
| 951.9 | Merrill Barber SR60 at Vero Beach | Bascule | 22' | Mon–Fri (except hldys) | 7:45–9am, 12 noon–1:15pm, 4–5:15pm; opens at 8:30am, 12:30 & 4:30pm |
| | | | | Dec 1–Apr 30 Mon–Fri (except hldys) | 7am–6pm; opens every 15 minutes, except as restricted above |

| Statute Mile (StM) | Bridges or Locks | Type | Clearance (or lock lift) | Restricted Period | Regulated Hours (Comments) |
|---|---|---|---|---|---|
| 964.8 | SR A1A Hwy north of Fort Pierce | Bascule | 26' | | Opens on demand |
| 981.4 | Jensen Beach SR 707A | Bascule | 24' | Dec. 1–May 1 Mon–Fri (except hldys) | 7am–6pm; opens on the hour and half-hour |
| 984.9 | Ernest Lyons SRA1A at Seawall Pt. | Bascule | 28' | Dec. 1–May 1 Mon–Fri (except hldys) | 7am–6pm; opens on the hour and half-hour |
| 995.9 | Hobe Sound Hwy Rt 708 | Bascule | 21' | | Opens on demand |
| 1004.1 | Jupiter Rt 707 Hwy | Bascule | 25' | | Opens on demand |
| 1004.8 | Jupiter Rt 1 I Iwy | Bascule | 26' | | Opens on demand |
| 1006.2 | Indiantown Rd SR 706 Hwy at Jupiter | Bascule | 15' | Nov 1–Apr 30 | 7am–6pm; opens every 20 minutes |
| 1009.3 | Donald Ross Rd at Juno Beach | Bascule | 14' | | Opens on demand |
| 1012.6 | PGA Boulevard Rt 74 Hwy | Bascule | 24' | Mon–Fri (except hldys) | 7–9am, 4–7pm; opens on the quarter- and three-quarter hour |
| | | | | Wknd & hldys | 8am–6pm; opens every 20 minutes |
| 1013.7 | Parker Bridge at North Palm Beach | Bascule | 25' | Mon–Fri (except hldys) | 7am–9am, 4pm–7pm; opens on the hour and half-hour |
| | | | | Wknd & hldys | 8am–6pm; opens every 20 minutes |
| 1021.9 | Flagler Memorial SR A1A at Palm Beach | Bascule | 17' | Nov 1–May 31 Mon–Fri (except hldys) | 8–9:30am, 4–5:45pm; opens at 8:30am & 4:45pm. 9:30am–4pm; opens on the hour and half-hour |
| 1022.6 | Royal Park/Royal Palm at West Palm Beach (SR 704) | Bascule | 14' | Nov 1–May 31 Mon–Fri (except hldys) | 8–9:30am, 3:30–5:45pm; opens at 8:45am, 4:15 & 5pm. 9:30am–3:30pm; opens on the quarter- and three-quarter hour |
| 1024.7 | Southern Blvd SR 700/80 at West Palm Beach | Bascule | 14' | Nov 1–May 31 Mon–Fri (except hldys) | 7:30–9am, 4:30–6:30pm; opens at 8:15am & 5:30pm |
| 1028.8 | Lake Worth | Bascule | 38' | | Opens on demand |
| 1031.0 | Lantana | Bascule | 13' | Dec 1–Apr 30 (wknd & hldys) | 10am–6pm; opens on the hour and the quarter-, half- and three-quarter hour |
| 1035.0 | Boynton Beach SR 804 Hwy | Bascule | 10' | | Opens on demand |
| 1035.8 | Boynton Beach/ Woolbright Rd Hwy | Bascule | 25' | | Opens on demand |
| 1038.7 | North Delray Beach, N.E. 8th St. | Bascule | 9' | Nov 1–May 31 (wknd & hldys) | 11am–6pm; opens every 15 minutes |
| 1039.6 | Atlantic Avenue (SR 806) at Delray Beach | Bascule | 12' | Nov 1–May 31 Mon–Fri | 10am–6pm; opens on the hour and half-hour |
| 1041.0 | Linton Blvd (12th St) at Delray Beach | Bascule | 30' | | Opens on demand |
| 1044.9 | Spanish River Rd | Bascule | 25' | | Opens on demand |
| 1047.5 | Palmetto Park Rd (SR 798) at North Boca Raton | Bascule | 19' | | Opens on demand |
| 1048.2 | Camino Real Hwy at South Boca Raton | Bascule | 9' | | Opens on demand (Caution: Strong currents may be encountered) |
| 1050.0 | Hillsboro Blvd (SR 810) at Deerfield Beach | Bascule | 21' | Oct 1–May 31 | 7am–6pm; opens on the hour and the quarter-, half- and three-quarter hour |
| 1055.0 | Northeast 14th St at Pompano | Bascule | 15' | Daily | 7am–6pm; opens on the quarter-hour and three-quarter hour |
| 1056.0 | Atlantic Blvd (SR 814) near Pompano Beach | Bascule | 15' | Daily | 7am–6pm; opens on the hour and half-hour |
| 1059.0 | Commercial Blvd at Lauderdale-by-the-Sea | Bascule | 15' | Nov 1–May 15 Mon–Sat | 8am–6pm; opens every quarter-hour |
| 1060.5 | Oakland Park Beach Blvd Hwy at Fort Lauderdale | Bascule | 22' | Nov 15–May 15 Mon–Fri (except hldys) | 7am–10pm; opens every 20 minutes |
| | | | | Wknds & hldys | 10am–10pm; opens every quarter-hour |
| 1062.6 | Sunrise Blvd (SR 838) at Fort Lauderdale | Bascule | 21' | Nov 15–May 15 daily | 7:15–6:15pm; opens on the quarter- and three-quarter hour |
| 1064.0 | Las Olas Blvd at Fort Lauderdale | Bascule | 31' | | Opens on demand |
| 1065.9 | Brooks Memorial/SE 17th St Cswy at Fort Lauderdale | Bascule | 25' | Daily | 7am–7pm; opens 15 minutes after the last closing (A time clock is displayed showing the number of minutes remaining before the draw is available for opening) |
| 1069.4 | Dania Beach (SR A1A) Hwy | Bascule | 22' | | Opens on demand |

| Statute Mile (StM) | Bridges or Locks | Type | Clearance (or lock lift) | Restricted Period | Regulated Hours (Comments) |
|---|---|---|---|---|---|
| 1070.5 | North Hollywood (Sheridan St) | Bascule | 22' | | Opens on demand |
| 1072.2 | Hollywood Blvd (SR 820) | Bascule | 25' | Nov 15–May 15 daily | 10am–6:00pm; opens on the hour and half-hour |
| | | | | May 16–Nov 14 wknds & hldys | 9am–7pm; opens on the hour and half-hour |
| 1074.0 | Hallandale Blvd (SR 824) Hwy | Bascule | 22' | Daily | 7:15am–6:15pm; opens on the quarter- and three-quarter hour |
| 1078.0 | N.E. 163rd St (SR 826) at Sunny Isles | Bascule | 30' | Mon–Fri | 7am–6pm; opens on the quarter- and three-quarter hour |
| | | | | Wknds & hldys | 10am–6pm; opens on the quarter- and three-quarter hour |
| 1081.4 | Broad Cswy (NE 123rd St) at Bay Harbor Island | Bascule | 16' | Daily | 8am–6pm; opens on the quarter- and three-quarter hour |
| 1084.6 | 79th St. Cswy | Bascule | 25' | | On demand |
| 1087.1 | Julia Tuttle (36th St) Cswy | Fixed | 56' | | (Caution: This is the lowest fixed bridge on the ICW) |
| 1088.6 | Venetian Cswy (West span) at Miami | Bascule | 8' | Nov 1–Apr 30 (except hldys) Mon–Fri | 7–9am, 4:30–6:30pm; opens on the hour and half-hour |
| 1088.8 | MacArthur Cswy (SR A1A) | Bascule | 35' | Nov 1–Apr 30 | 7–9am, 4:30–6:30pm; opens on the hour and half-hour |
| 1089.4 | Dodge Island R.R. & Hwy at Miami | Bascule | 22' | Mon–Sat (except hldys) | 7:15am–5:45pm; opens on the quarter- and three-quarter hour |
| | | | | Sunday | 9:15am–2:15pm; opens on the quarter- and three-quarter hour |
| | | | | Saturday | 9:20–11:10am, 12:20–2:10pm; no openings |

# APPENDIX B
## General Pilotage Notes

**1. Note A**
Navigation Regulations are published in Chapter 2, U.S. Coast Pilot 4. Additions or revisions to Chapter 2 are published in the Notices to Mariners. Information concerning the regulations may be obtained at the Office of the Commander for the appropriate Coast Guard District, or at the Office of the District Engineer, Corps of Engineers.

**2. Soundings are in feet at Mean Lower Low Water**

**3. Heights are in feet above Mean High Water**

**4. *Intracoastal Waterway Project Depths:***
- 12 feet from Norfolk, Virginia to Fort Pierce, Florida
- 10 feet from Fort Pierce, Florida to Miami, Florida
- 7 feet from Miami, Florida to Cross Bank, Florida Bay.

The controlling depths are published periodically in the U.S. Coast Guard Local Notice to Mariners.

**5. Intracoastal Waterway Aids**
Intracoastal Waterway aids are characterized by a yellow strip. Proceeding from Norfolk, Virginia to Key West, Florida:
- Aids with red reflectors are on the starboard side; green reflectors are on the port side.
- Where the Intracoastal Waterway coincides with another waterway, the dual-purpose aids have distinctive yellow triangles on the starboard side and yellow squares on the port side.

**6. *Caution***
- Temporary changes or defects in aids to navigation are not indicated on this chart. See Notice to Mariners.
- Improved channels shown by broken lines are subject to shoaling, particularly at the edges.

**7. *Caution***
Small craft should stay clear of large commercial and government vessels even if small craft have the right of way.

**8. *Pollution Reports***
Report all spills of oil and hazardous substances to the National Response Center via 800-424-8802 (toll-free) or to the nearest U.S. Coast Guard facility if telephone communication is impossible (33 CFR 153).

**9. *Warning***
The prudent mariner will not rely solely on any single aid to navigation, particularly on floating aids. See U.S. Coast Guard Light List and U.S. Coast Pilot for details.

Appendix C    240

# APPENDIX C
## Pilotage Notes for Individual Charts
The following notes contain information of importance
to the charts on the designated pages.

### For pages 53–76:

NOTE C

Entrances to Inlets

The channels are subject to continual changes. Entrance buoys are not charted because they are frequently shifted in position. Passage through the inlets is not recommended without local knowledge of all hazardous conditions affecting the areas.

### For pages 116–117:

NOTE D

CAUTION

The entrance to St. Andrew Sound is subject to frequent change. Buoys 3, 5, 7 and 9 are not charted as they are frequently shifted in position.

### For pages 115–129, 211, and 233–234:

TIDAL CURRENT DATA

| PLACE | POSITION | | MAXIMUM CURRENTS | | | |
|---|---|---|---|---|---|---|
| | | | Flood | | Ebb | |
| | Lat. | Long. | Direction (true) | Average velocity | Direction (true) | Average velocity |
| | ° ′ N. | ° ′ W. | deg. | knots | deg. | knots |
| **ST. SIMONS SOUND** | | | | | | |
| Entrance-------------------------- | 31 08 | 81 24 | 300 | 2.1 | 110 | 1.9 |
| Brunswick River, off Quarantine Dock- | 31 07 | 81 28 | 300 | 1.3 | 125 | 2.1 |
| Brunswick, off Prince Street Dock----- | 31 08 | 81 30 | 340 | 1.0 | 165 | 1.3 |
| **ST. ANDREWS SOUND** | | | | | | |
| Entrance-------------------------- | 30 59 | 81 24 | 270 | 2.1 | 105 | 2.2 |
| Jekyll Creek, south entrance---------- | 31 02 | 81 26 | 60 | 1.0 | 230 | 1.4 |
| Cumberland River, north entrance------ | 30 57 | 81 26 | 190 | 1.3 | 20 | 1.5 |
| Cabin Bluff, Cumberland River--------- | 30 53 | 81 31 | 170 | 1.3 | 355 | 1.3 |
| **CUMBERLAND SOUND** | | | | | | |
| St. Marys Entrance------------------ | 30 43 | 81 27 | 275 | 2.3 | 90 | 2.6 |
| Beach Creek ent., 0.2 mile NW. of----- | 30 44 | 81 29 | 340 | 1.5 | 165 | 2.2 |
| Stafford Island, west of-------------- | 30 49 | 81 29 | 0 | 1.3 | 180 | 1.3 |
| Old Fernandina, Amelia River---------- | 30 11 | 81 28 | 190 | 1.4 | 0 | 1.8 |
| Kingsley Creek, highway bridge-------- | 30 38 | 81 29 | 150 | 1.1 | 330 | 1.6 |
| **NASSAU SOUND** | | | | | | |
| Midsound, 1 mi. N. of Sawpit Creek ent | 30 31 | 81 27 | 310 | 1.7 | 135 | 1.7 |
| South Amelia River, off Walker Creek-- | 30 32 | 81 28 | 340 | 1.4 | 160 | 1.4 |
| Nassau River, SW. of Mesa Marsh------ | 30 32 | 81 29 | 295 | 1.5 | 130 | 1.7 |
| Ft. George River--------------------- | 30 27 | 81 27 | 335 | 0.3 | 160 | 0.9 |
| **ST. JOHNS RIVER** | | | | | | |
| ST. JOHNS RIVER ENT. (between jetties) | 30 24 | 81 23 | 275 | 1.9 | 100 | 2.3 |
| Mayport---------------------------- | 30 24 | 81 26 | 210 | 2.2 | 25 | 3.1 |
| Mile Point, southeast of-------------- | 30 23 | 81 27 | 240 | 2.7 | 75 | 2.9 |
| Pablo Creek bascule bridge----------- | 30 19 | 81 26 | 180 | *3.4 | 0 | *5.2 |
| Sisters Creek entrance (bridge)------- | 30 23 | 81 28 | 0 | 1.4 | 180 | 1.4 |

*Due to changes in the waterway this velocity is probably too large.

### For page 192:

NOTE B

The area in Miami Harbor from the turning basin to the northwest corner of Lummus Island is utilized intermittently as a seaplane operating area.

### For page 195:

TIDAL INFORMATION

| Place | Height referred to datum of soundings (MLLW) | | | |
|---|---|---|---|---|
| | Mean Higher High Water | Mean High Water | Mean Low Water | Extreme Low Water |
| | feet | feet | feet | feet |
| Core Creek Bridge | 2.3 | 2.2 | 0.1 | −3.0 |
| North River Bridge | 2.0 | 1.8 | 0.1 | −3.0 |
| Morehead City, Port Terminal | 3.6 | 3.3 | 0.2 | −3.0 |
| Beaufort, Duke Marine Lab | 3.4 | 3.2 | 0.1 | −3.0 |
| Shell Point | 1.8 | 1.7 | 0.1 | −3.0 |
| Cape Lookout | 4.2 | 3.9 | 0.2 | −3.0 |

Note-In Core Sound the tides are greatly modified by the winds, the effects of which are often greater than the tides.

(1287)

# For page 195 (cont.):

| MOREHEAD CITY HARBOR CHANNEL DEPTHS |||||||||
|---|---|---|---|---|---|---|---|---|
| CORPS OF ENGINEERS SURVEYS TO SEPT. 1987 |||||||||
| CONTROLLING DEPTHS FROM SEAWARD IN FEET AT MEAN LOW WATER (MLW) |||||||| PROJECT DIMENSIONS |
| NAME OF CHANNEL | LEFT OUTSIDE QUARTER | LEFT INSIDE QUARTER | RIGHT INSIDE QUARTER | RIGHT OUTSIDE QUARTER | DATE OF SURVEY | WIDTH (FEET) | LENGTH (NAUT. MILES) | DEPTH MLW (FEET) |
| BEAUFORT INLET CHANNEL (A) | 37.5 | 42.0 | 42.0 | 42.0 | 9-87 | 450 | 2.08 | 42 |
| CUTOFF CHANNEL | 40.0 | 40.0 | 40.0 | 28.5 | 7-86 | 600 | 0.57 | 40 |
| MOREHEAD CITY CHANNEL (B) | B37.5 | 40.0 | 40.0 | A34.0 | 3,6-87 | 400-750 | 1.43 | 40 |
| TURNING BASIN | | | | | | | | |
| EAST LEG | 38.5 | 39.5 | 38.5 | 36.5 | 1-87 | 800-1000 | | 40 |
| WEST LEG | 28.5 | 35.0 | 35.0 | 35.0 | 6-86 | 850-1450 | | 35 |

DEPTHS ARE EXPRESSED TO THE NEAREST HALF-FOOT.
A. THE WIDENER ON THE NORTH SIDE HAS A CONTROLLING DEPTH OF 36.0 FEET.
B. THE WIDENER ON THE SOUTH SIDE HAS A CONTROLLING DEPTH OF 40.0 FEET.
NOTE - CONSULT THE CORPS OF ENGINEERS FOR CHANGES SUBSEQUENT TO THE ABOVE INFORMATION

PRODUCED BY COMPUTER ASSISTED METHODS

# For page 196:

| CAPE FEAR RIVER CHANNEL DEPTHS |||||||||
|---|---|---|---|---|---|---|---|---|
| CORPS OF ENGINEERS REPORT OF JULY 1988 AND SURVEYS TO AUGUST 1988 |||||||||
| CONTROLLING DEPTHS FROM SEAWARD IN FEET AT MEAN LOWER LOW WATER (MLLW) |||||||| PROJECT DIMENSIONS |
| NAME OF CHANNEL | LEFT OUTSIDE QUARTER | LEFT INSIDE QUARTER | RIGHT INSIDE QUARTER | RIGHT OUTSIDE QUARTER | DATE OF SURVEY | WIDTH (FEET) | LENGTH (NAUT. MILES) | DEPTH MLLW (FEET) |
| BALDHEAD SHOAL | 35.0 | 37.0 | 38.0 | 36.0 | 4-88 | 500 | 3.0 | 40 |
| SMITH ISLAND | 26.0 | 36.0 | 42.0 | 38.5 | 7-88 | 500 | 1.0 | 40 |
| BALDHEAD CASWELL CHANNEL | 40.5 | 43.0 | 42.5 | 43.0 | 4-88 | 500 | 0.4 | 40 |
| SOUTHPORT CHANNEL | 41.0 | 44.0 | 44.0 | 40.0 | 4-88 | 500 | 1.0 | 40 |
| BATTERY ISLAND CHANNEL | 42.5 | 44.5 | 43.0 | 31.0 | 4-88 | 500 | 0.5 | 40 |
| LOWER SWASH | 35.0 | 38.0 | 39.5 | 35.0 | 3-88 | 400 | 1.6 | 38 |
| SNOWS MARSH | 36.0 | 36.5 | 37.5 | 34.5 | 9-87 | 400 | 3.1 | 38 |
| HORSESHOE SHOAL | 37.0 | 38.0 | 37.0 | 37.0 | 3-88 | 400 | 1.2 | 38 |
| REAVES POINT | 34.5 | 38.0 | 37.5 | 37.0 | 2-88 | 400 | 1.2 | 38 |
| LOWER MIDNIGHT | 36.5 | 38.0 | 37.5 | 37.5 | 4-88 | 400 | 1.6 | 38 |
| UPPER MIDNIGHT | 37.5 | 38.5 | 38.0 | 37.0 | 4-88 | 400 | 2.7 | 38 |
| LOWER LILLIPUT | 31.0 | 32.0 | 37.5 | 37.0 | 4-88 | 400 | 1.9 | 38 |
| UPPER LILLIPUT | 38.5 | 38.0 | 37.5 | 37.5 | 4-88 | 400 | 1.9 | 38 |
| KEG ISLAND | 37.0 | 38.0 | 37.0 | 37.0 | 5-88 | 400 | 1.4 | 38 |
| BIG ISLAND LOWER | 37.5 | 38.5 | 38.5 | 31.0 | 5-88 | 400 | 0.8 | 38 |
| BIG ISLAND UPPER | 39.0 | 39.5 | 39.5 | 30.5 | 1-88 | 400 | 0.5 | 38 |
| LOWER BRUNSWICK | 19.5 | 38.5 | 38.0 | 35.0 | 7-87 | 400 | 1.6 | 38 |
| UPPER BRUNSWICK | 21.0 | 39.0 | 39.0 | 34.0 | 7-87 | 400 | 1.0 | 38 |
| FOURTH EAST JETTY | 31.0 | 38.5 | 38.0 | 38.5 | 5-88 | 400 | 1.2 | 38 |
| BETWEEN CHANNEL | 33.5 | 40.5 | 40.0 | 38.5 | 6-88 | 550 | 0.8 | 38 |
| ANCHORAGE BASIN & APP CHANNEL | 36.0 | 38.0 | 37.0 | 32.0 | 5-88 | 450-1090 | 1.3 | 38 |
| HWY 74-76 TO BATTLESHIP | 26.5 | 35.5 | 36.0 | 34.5 | 2-88 | 300-400 | 0.6 | 32 |
| TURNING BASIN | 15.0 | 28.0 | 29.0 | 26.5 | 4-85 | 800 | - | 32 |
| BATTLESHIP TO HWY 133 | 12.0 | 26.5 | 30.5 | 20.0 | 3-88 | 300-400 | 1.1 | 32 |
| HWY 133 TO HILTON BR | 30.0 | 31.5 | 33.0 | 29.0 | 3-88 | 300-400 | 0.5 | 32 |
| THENCE TO END OF PROJECT | 20.0 | 24.5 | 21.5 | 21.0 | 1-88 | 200 | 1.2 | 25 |

NOTE - CONSULT THE CORPS OF ENGINEERS FOR CHANGES SUBSEQUENT TO THE ABOVE INFORMATION

PRODUCED BY COMPUTER ASSISTED METHODS

### TIDAL INFORMATION

| Place ||  Height referred to datum of soundings MLLW ||||
|---|---|---|---|---|
| Name | (LAT/LONG) | Mean Higher High Water | Mean High Water | Mean Low Water | Extreme Low Water |
| | | feet | feet | feet | feet |
| Bald Head | (33°52'N/78°00'W) | 4.8 | 4.5 | 0.2 | -2.0 |
| Southport | (33°55'N/78°01'W) | 4.6 | 4.3 | 0.2 | -2.0 |
| Reaves Point | (34°00'N/77°57'W) | 4.2 | 4.0 | 0.1 | -2.0 |
| Wilmington | (34°14'N/77°57'W) | 4.5 | 4.3 | 0.2 | -1.5 |

(1287)

Appendix C   242

## For pages 197–198:

TIDAL INFORMATION

| Place | | Height referred to datum of soundings MLLW | | | |
|---|---|---|---|---|---|
| Name | (LAT/LONG) | Mean Higher High Water | Mean High Water | Mean Low Water | Extreme Low Water |
| | | feet | feet | feet | feet |
| Clambank Cr, Goat I (33°20'N/79°12'W) | | 5.1 | 4.9 | 0.2 | -2.5 |
| Winyah Bay Ent (s Jetty) (33°11'N/79°09'W) | | 5.1 | 4.8 | 0.2 | -2.5 |
| Georgetown, Sampit R (33°22'N/79°17'W) | | 3.5 | 3.4 | 0.1 | -2.5 |
| North Santee R Inlet (33°08'N/79°15'W) | | 4.9 | 4.6 | 0.1 | -2.5 |
| Brown I, S Santee R (33°09'N/79°20'W) | | 4.5 | 4.2 | 0.1 | -2.5 |

(1087)

WINYAH BAY AND GEORGETOWN HARBOR

TABULATED FROM SURVEYS BY THE CORPS OF ENGINEERS - REPORTS TO MAY 15, 1984 AND SURVEYS TO JAN. 1987

| CONTROLLING DEPTHS FROM SEAWARD IN FEET AT MEAN LOWER LOW WATER (MLLW) | | | | | | PROJECT DIMENSIONS | | |
|---|---|---|---|---|---|---|---|---|
| NAME OF CHANNEL | LEFT OUTSIDE QUARTER | LEFT INSIDE QUARTER | RIGHT INSIDE QUARTER | RIGHT OUTSIDE QUARTER | DATE OF SURVEY | WIDTH (FEET) | LENGTH (NAUT. MILES) | DEPTH MLLW (FEET) |
| ENTRANCE CHANNEL | 25.7 | 27.4 | 27.5 | 19.4 | 2-86 | 600 | 2.0 | 27 |
| RANGE B | 26.4 | 30.6 | 31.0 | 28.9 | 2-86 | 600 | 0.9 | 27 |
| SOUTH ISLAND BEND | 28.6 | 29.9 | 26.6 | 22.6 | 2-86 | 600 | 1.2 | 27 |
| RANGE C | 25.6 | 26.9 | 25.5 | 26.1 | 2-86 | 400 | 1.4 | 27 |
| RANGE D | 27.8 | 27.8 | 28.1 | 24.8 | 2-86 | 400 | 1.5 | 27 |
| RANGE E | 20.7 | 25.5 | 25.5 | 24.8 | 2-84;2-86 | 300 | 4.6 | 27 |
| FRAZIER PT. BEND | 25.3 | 26.9 | 26.5 | 28.0 | 8-84 | 300-700 | 1.0 | 27 |
| RABBIT ISLAND CHANNEL | 24.5 | 24.7 | 25.2 | 25.1 | 2-84 | 300 | 1.8 | 27 |
| SAMPIT PT. CHANNEL | 28.1 | 28.1 | 28.3 | 27.4 | 10-86 | 300 | 0.7 | 27 |
| TURNING BASIN | 25.0 | 25.8 | 26.1 | 25.4 | 1-87 | 400-600 | 0.55 | 27 |

NOTE-CONSULT THE CORPS OF ENGINEERS FOR CHANGES SUBSEQUENT TO THE ABOVE INFORMATION

PRODUCED BY COMPUTER ASSISTED METHODS

## For page 199:

NOTE B

DANGER AREA

Area is open to unrestricted surface navigation but all vessels are cautioned neither to anchor, dredge, trawl, lay cables, bottom, nor conduct any other similar type of operation because of residual danger from mines on the bottom.

Anchorage in the designated area is at your own risk.

TIDAL INFORMATION

| Place | | Height referred to datum of soundings (MLLW) | | | |
|---|---|---|---|---|---|
| Name | (LAT/LONG) | Mean Higher High Water | Mean High Water | Mean Low Water | Extreme Low Water |
| | | feet | feet | feet | feet |
| Dewees Inlet | (32°50'N/79°44'W) | 5.5 | 5.2 | 0.2 | -3.5 |
| Fort Sumter | (32°45'N/79°52'W) | 5.5 | 5.2 | 0.2 | -3.5 |
| Charleston,(Customhouse Wharf) | (32°47'N/79°56'W) | 5.8 | 5.5 | 0.2 | -3.5 |
| Rockville, Bohicket Creek | (32°36'N/80°12'W) | 6.3 | 5.9 | 0.2 | -3.5 |
| Edisto Beach, Edisto Island | (32°30'N/80°18'W) | 6.4 | 6.1 | 0.2 | -3.5 |

(1189)

CHARLESTON HARBOR ENTRANCE

TABULATED FROM SURVEYS BY THE CORPS OF ENGINEERS - REPORT OF MAY 1990

| CONTROLLING DEPTHS FROM SEAWARD IN FEET AT MEAN LOWER LOW WATER (MLLW) | | | | | | PROJECT DIMENSIONS | | |
|---|---|---|---|---|---|---|---|---|
| NAME OF CHANNEL | LEFT OUTSIDE QUARTER | LEFT INSIDE QUARTER | RIGHT INSIDE QUARTER | RIGHT OUTSIDE QUARTER | DATE OF SURVEY | WIDTH (FEET) | LENGTH (NAUT. MILES) | DEPTH MLLW (FEET) |
| FORT SUMTER RANGE | 39.2 | 42.5 | 42.3 | 39.7 | 4-90 | A1000 | 9.0 | 35 |
| MOUNT PLEASANT RANGE | 40.6 | 43.0 | 45.2 | 39.5 | 10-89 | A1000-600 | 1.6 | 35 |

A. CHANNEL MAINTAINED TO A WIDTH OF 800 FEET FOR FORT SUMTER RANGE AND 800-600 FEET FOR MOUNT PLEASANT RANGE.

NOTE - CONSULT THE CORPS OF ENGINEERS FOR CHANGES SUBSEQUENT TO THE ABOVE INFORMATION

PRODUCED BY COMPUTER ASSISTED METHODS

## For pages 204–205:

**SAVANNAH RIVER CHANNEL DEPTHS**

TABULATED FROM SURVEYS BY THE CORPS OF ENGINEERS-REPORT OF OCT 1989

CONTROLLING DEPTHS FROM SEAWARD IN FEET AT MEAN LOWER LOW WATER (MLLW) — PROJECT DIMENSIONS

| NAME OF CHANNEL | LEFT OUTSIDE QUARTER | LEFT INSIDE QUARTER | RIGHT INSIDE QUARTER | RIGHT OUTSIDE QUARTER | DATE OF SURVEY | WIDTH (FEET) | LENGTH (NAUT. MILES) | DEPTH MLLW (FEET) |
|---|---|---|---|---|---|---|---|---|
| TYBEE RANGE | 39.6 | 40.2 | 40.5 | 39.4 | 10-89 | 600 | 3.3 | 40 |
| BLOODY POINT RANGE | 38.1 | 39.4 | 40.1 | 34.8 | 10-89 | 600 | 3.0 | 40 |
| JONES ISLAND RANGE | 39.6 | 41.5 | 41.6 | 40.0 | 10-89 | 600 | 1.2 | 40 |
| TYBEE KNOLL CUT RANGE | 37.0 | 37.5 | 37.4 | 34.6 | 10-89 | 500 | 2.5 | 38 |
| NEW CHANNEL RANGE (A) | 33.8 | 37.5 | 37.2 | 34.5 | 10-89 | 500 | 1.6 | 38 |
| L. I. CROSSING RANGE | 33.5 | 37.2 | 38.7 | 33.7 | 10-89 | 500 | 2.6 | 38 |
| LOWER FLATS RANGE | 37.9 | 40.2 | 40.2 | 36.3 | 10-89 | 500 | 1.3 | 38 |
| UPPER FLATS RANGE | 38.1 | 40.5 | 40.2 | 36.4 | 10-89 | 500 | 1.2 | 38 |
| THE BIGHT CHANNEL | 35.9 | 38.4 | 40.5 | 37.4 | 10-89 | 600 | 1.5 | 38 |
| FT. JACKSON RANGE | 35.7 | 37.4 | 36.7 | 34.0 | 10-89 | 500 | 0.7 | 38 |
| OGLETHORPE RANGE | 34.5 | 37.4 | 37.0 | 34.4 | 10-89 | 500 | 1.2 | 38 |
| WRECKS CHANNEL (B) | 37.7 | 37.6 | 38.9 | 35.9 | 10-89 | 500 | 1.5 | 38 |
| CITY FRONT CHANNEL | 39.3 | 40.0 | 38.0 | 36.0 | 10-89 | 400 | 1.5 | 38 |
| MARSH ISLAND CHANNEL | 36.4 | 38.7 | 38.3 | 37.5 | 10-89 | 400 | 1.7 | 38 |
| KINGS ISLAND CHANNEL (C) (D) | 37.3 | 39.6 | 37.6 | 35.6 | 10-89 | 400 | 2.1 | 38 |
| WHITEHALL CHANNEL (E) | 33.0 | 37.2 | 36.8 | 36.4 | 10-89 | 400 | 0.6 | 36 |
| PORT WENTWORTH CHANNEL (F) | 31.8 | 29.0 | 29.0 | 30.4 | 6,10-89 | 200 | 1.2 | 30 |

A. OYSTER BED I. TURNING BASIN-CONTROLLING DEPTH 38.6 FT.
B. FIG ISLAND TURNING BASIN-CONTROLLING DEPTH 31.0 FT.
C. MARSH ISLAND TURNING BASIN-CONTROLLING DEPTH 28.4 FT.
D. KINGS ISLAND TURNING BASIN-CONTROLLING DEPTH 23.5 FT.
E. ARGYLE ISLAND TURNING BASIN-CONTROLLING DEPTH 30.0 FT.
F. PORT WENTWORTH TURNING BASIN-CONTROLLING DEPTH 27.0 FT.

NOTE. AT MEAN HIGH WATER, DEPTHS ARE ABOUT 7 FEET GREATER AT LOWER END OF THE HARBOR AND 7.7 FEET GREATER AT UPPER END OF HARBOR.
NOTE - CONSULT THE CORPS OF ENGINEERS FOR CHANGES SUBSEQUENT TO THE ABOVE INFORMATION

PRODUCED BY COMPUTER ASSISTED METHODS

**TIDAL INFORMATION**

| Place | Mean Higher High Water (feet) | Mean High Water (feet) | Mean Low Water (feet) | Extreme Low Water (feet) |
|---|---|---|---|---|
| Tybee Light | 7.4 | 7.0 | 0.2 | -4.0 |
| Savannah River Ent. | 7.5 | 7.1 | 0.2 | -4.5 |
| Savannah | 8.6 | 8.1 | 0.3 | -4.5 |
| Beach Hammock | 7.5 | 7.1 | 0.2 | -4.0 |

(288)

## For pages 200–206:

**TIDAL INFORMATION**

| Place Name (LAT/LONG) | Mean Higher High Water (feet) | Mean High Water (feet) | Mean Low Water (feet) | Extreme Low Water (feet) |
|---|---|---|---|---|
| Savannah (32°05'N/81°06'W) | 8.6 | 8.1 | 0.2 | -4.5 |
| Savannah River Entrance (32°02'N/80°54'W) | 7.5 | 7.1 | 0.2 | -3.0 |
| Martins Industry (32°02'N/80°35'W) | 6.9 | 6.6 | 0.2 | -4.0 |
| Hilton Head (32°14'N/80°40'W) | 7.2 | 6.8 | 0.2 | -4.5 |
| Port Royal (32°22'N/80°41'W) | 7.8 | 7.4 | 0.2 | -4.0 |
| Beaufort (32°26'N/80°40'W) | 8.1 | 7.7 | 0.2 | -4.0 |
| Combahee Bank (32°29'N/80°26'W) | 6.7 | 6.4 | 0.2 | -4.0 |

(889)

## For pages 207–208:

**TIDAL INFORMATION**

| Place Name (LAT/LONG) | Mean Higher High Water (feet) | Mean High Water (feet) | Mean Low Water (feet) | Extreme Low Water (feet) |
|---|---|---|---|---|
| Savannah River Ent. Egg Islands, | 7.5 | 7.1 | 0.2 | -4.5 |
| Ossabaw Sound | 7.8 | 7.4 | 0.2 | -4.0 |
| Walburg Creek Ent., St. Catherines Sound | 7.7 | 7.3 | 0.2 | -3.5 |
| Blackbeard Island, Sapelo Sound | 7.5 | 7.1 | 0.2 | -3.5 |
| Sapelo Island, Doboy Sound | 7.4 | 7.0 | 0.2 | -3.5 |

(1287)

## For pages 209–210:

**TIDAL INFORMATION**

| Place Name (LAT/LONG) | Mean Higher High Water (feet) | Mean High Water (feet) | Mean Low Water (feet) | Extreme Low Water (feet) |
|---|---|---|---|---|
| Sapelo Island, Doboy Sound, GA (31°23'N/81°17'W) | 7.4 | 7.0 | 0.2 | -3.5 |
| St. Simons Light, GA (31°08'N/81°24'W) | 7.2 | 6.8 | 0.2 | -3.5 |
| Brunswick, East River, GA (31°09'N/81°30'W) | 7.9 | 7.5 | 0.2 | -3.5 |
| Jekyll Point, St. Andrew Sound, GA (31°01'N/81°26'W) | 7.2 | 6.8 | 0.2 | -3.5 |
| St. Marys Entrance, North Jetty, GA (30°43'N/81°26'W) | 6.3 | 6.0 | 0.2 | -3.5 |
| Fernandina Beach (outer coast), FL (30°38'N/81°26'W) | 6.2 | 5.9 | 0.2 | -4.0 |

(889)

Appendix C 243

Appendix C  244

# For page 212:

**TIDAL INFORMATION**

| Place | | Height referred to datum of soundings (MLLW) | | | |
|---|---|---|---|---|---|
| Name | (LAT/LONG) | Mean Higher High Water | Mean High Water | Mean Low Water | Extreme Low Water |
| | | feet | feet | feet | feet |
| South Jetty, St. Johns River | (30°24′N/81°23′W) | 5.4 | 5.1 | 0.2 | -3.0 |
| Nassau Sound | (30°31′N/81°27′W) | 5.9 | 5.6 | 0.2 | -3.0 |
| Atlantic Beach | (30°20′N/81°24′W) | 5.7 | 5.4 | 0.2 | -3.0 |

(1189)

**ST. JOHNS RIVER CHANNEL DEPTHS**

TABULATED FROM SURVEYS BY THE CORPS OF ENGINEERS-REPORT OF NOV 1987
AND SURVEYS TO FEB 1987

| CONTROLLING DEPTHS FROM SEAWARD IN FEET AT MEAN LOWER LOW WATER (MLLW) | | | | | | PROJECT DIMENSIONS | | |
|---|---|---|---|---|---|---|---|---|
| NAME OF CHANNEL | LEFT OUTSIDE QUARTER | LEFT INSIDE QUARTER | RIGHT INSIDE QUARTER | RIGHT OUTSIDE QUARTER | DATE OF SURVEY | WIDTH (FEET) | LENGTH (NAUT. MILES) | DEPTH MLLW (FEET) |
| ST. JOHNS BAR CUT RANGE, EAST SECTION | 41.7 | 41.7 | 40.4 | 32.4 | 2-87 | 800 | 2.1 | 42 |
| ST. JOHNS BAR CUT RANGE, WEST SECTION | 23.5 | 38.0 | 38.0 | 35.7 | 2-87 | 800 | 1.5 | 38 |
| PILOT TOWN CUT RANGE | 22.7 | 38.0 | 38.0 | 38.0 | 2-87 | 950 | 0.7 | 38 |

NOTES-(1) THE RANGE LIGHTS DO NOT IN EVERY INSTANCE MARK THE CENTERLINE OF THE CHANNEL.
NOTE - CONSULT THE CORPS OF ENGINEERS FOR CHANGES SUBSEQUENT TO THE ABOVE INFORMATION

PRODUCED BY COMPUTER ASSISTED METHODS

# For pages 216–217:

**PORT CANAVERAL CHANNEL DEPTHS**

TABULATED FROM SURVEYS BY THE CORPS OF ENGINEERS - REPORT OF FEB 1990
AND SURVEYS TO JAN 1990

| CONTROLLING DEPTHS FROM SEAWARD IN FEET AT MEAN LOWER LOW WATER (MLLW) | | | | | | PROJECT DIMENSIONS | | |
|---|---|---|---|---|---|---|---|---|
| NAME OF CHANNEL | LEFT OUTSIDE QUARTER | LEFT INSIDE QUARTER | RIGHT INSIDE QUARTER | RIGHT OUTSIDE QUARTER | DATE OF SURVEY | WIDTH (FEET) | LENGTH (NAUT. MILES) | DEPTH MLLW (FEET) |
| OUTER REACH | 41.6 | 42.6 | 42.6 | 42.2 | 2,3-89 | 400 | 5.5 | A44 |
| MIDDLE REACH | B39.6 | B41.0 | C37.2 | C32.9 | 1-90 | 400-300 | 0.9 | A44 |
| INNER REACH | 25.4 | 32.1 | 35.2 | 30.5 | 3,11-89 | 300 | 0.6 | A44 |

A . U.S NAVY PROJECT - EXCEEDS CORPS OF ENGINEERS PROJECT DEPTH OF 37 FEET.
B . SHOALING TO 28.4 FEET WITHIN AN AREA BOUNDED BY 28°24′32″ - 80°35′29″,
    28°24′33.8″-80°35′30.5″,28°24′33.8″-80°35′33.5″,28°24′32.2″-80°35′33.5″.
C . SHOALING TO 32.9 FEET WITHIN AN AREA BOUNDED BY 28°24′36″ - 80°34′58″,
    28°24′33.8″ - 80°35′00″, 28°24′33.8″ - 80°35′05″, 28°24′36″ - 80°35′05″.
NOTE - CONSULT THE CORPS OF ENGINEERS FOR CHANGES SUBSEQUENT TO THE ABOVE INFORMATION

PRODUCED BY COMPUTER ASSISTED METHODS

# For page 219:

### NOTE B

The area in Miami Harbor from the turning basin to the northwest corner of Lummus Island is utilized intermittently as a seaplane operating area.

### NOTE E

### CAUTION

Cross-channel current variations in Government Cut are particularly difficult to negotiate because of variances between predicted and actual currents. Caution should be exercised when entering from sea during flood tide with northeasterly winds; a strong turning torque occurs when just inside the north jetty. A similar but less serious situation occurs when leaving the port during ebb tides. Horizontal current gradients occur in the turning basin at the northwest corner of Dodge Island which may make maneuvering difficult. Ships may encounter current anomalies at the mouth of the Miami River.

# For page 220:

**TIDAL INFORMATION**

| Place | Height referred to datum of soundings (MLLW) | | | |
|---|---|---|---|---|
| | Mean Higher High Water | Mean High Water | Mean Low Water | Extreme Low Water |
| | feet | feet | feet | feet |
| Jupiter Inlet | 2.8 | 2.7 | 0.2 | -2.0 |
| Port of Palm Beach | 2.9 | 2.8 | 0.2 | -2.0 |
| Lake Worth Pier (ocean) | 3.1 | 3.0 | 0.2 | -2.0 |
| Hillsboro Inlet (inside) | 2.8 | 2.2 | 0.2 | -2.0 |
| Port Everglades | 2.9 | 2.8 | 0.2 | -2.0 |
| Miami Harbor Entrance | 2.8 | 2.7 | 0.2 | -2.0 |
| Fowey Rocks | 2.7 | 2.6 | 0.2 | -1.5 |

(1088)

# For page 221:

### MIAMI RIVER

The controlling depths were 14 feet on the centerline from the mouth to the Tamiami Canal; thence 9 feet to the dam at the 36th St. bridge.

Oct. 1986

### NOTE B

The area in Miami Harbor from the turning basin to the northwest corner of Lummus Island is utilized intermittently as a seaplane operating area.

# APPENDIX D
# Mileage Tables and Conversion Tables

## COASTWISE DISTANCES
## NORFOLK, VA., TO KEY WEST, FLA.
### (Nautical Miles)

Figure at intersection of columns opposite ports in question is the nautical mileage between the two. Example: Norfolk, Va., is 503 nautical miles from Savannah, Ga.

| | Chesapeake Bay Entrance 36°56.3'N, 75°58.6'W | Norfolk, Va. 46°50.9'N, 76°17.9'W | Diamond Shoals 35°08.0'N, 75°15.0'W | Morehead City, N.C. 34°42.8'N, 76°41.8'W | Southport, N.C. 33°54.8'N, 78°01.0'W | Wilmington, N.C. 34°14.0'N, 77°57.0'W | Georgetown, S.C. 33°21.4'N, 79°16.9'W | Charleston, S.C. 32°47.2'N, 79°55.2'W | Port Royal, S.C. 32°22.3'N, 80°41.6'W | Savannah, Ga. 32°05.0'N, 81°05.7'W | Brunswick, Ga. 31°08.0'N, 81°29.7'W | Fernandina Beach, Fla. 30°40.3'N, 81°28.0'W | Jacksonville, Fla. 30°19.2'N, 81°39.0'W | St. Augustine, Fla. 29°53.6'N, 81°18.5'W | Cape Canaveral, Fla. 28°24.6'N, 80°36.5'W | Fort Pierce, Fla. 27°27.5'N, 80°19.3'W | Stuart, Fla. 27°12.2'N, 80°15.6'W | Port of Palm Beach, Fla. 26°46.1'N, 80°03.0'W | Port Everglades, Fla. 26°05.6'N, 80°07.0'W | Miami, Fla. 25°47.0'N, 80°11.0'W | Key West, Fla. 24°33.7'N, 81°48.5'W | Straits of Florida 24°25.0'N, 83°00.0'W |
|---|---|---|---|---|---|---|---|---|---|---|---|---|---|---|---|---|---|---|---|---|---|---|
| 27 | | | | | | | | | | | | | | | | | | | | | | |
| 117 | 144 | | | | | | | | | | | | | | | | | | | | | |
| 222 | 249 | 105 | | | | | | | | | | | | | | | | | | | | |
| 315 | 342 | 198 | 133 | | | | | | | | | | | | | | | | | | | |
| 336 | 363 | 219 | 154 | 21 | | | | | | | | | | | | | | | | | | |
| 365 | 392 | 248 | 184 | 87 | 108 | | | | | | | | | | | | | | | | | |
| 402 | 429 | 285 | 220 | 130 | 151 | 79 | | | | | | | | | | | | | | | | |
| 465 | 492 | 348 | 284 | 191 | 212 | 141 | 90 | | | | | | | | | | | | | | | |
| 476 | 503 | 359 | 295 | 206 | 227 | 154 | 102 | 51 | | | | | | | | | | | | | | |
| 527 | 554 | 410 | 346 | 260 | 281 | 210 | 156 | 110 | 51 | | | | | | | | | | | | | |
| 533 | 560 | 416 | 352 | 265 | 286 | 216 | 166 | 120 | 104 | 50 | | | | | | | | | | | | |
| 557 | 584 | 440 | 377 | 294 | 315 | 247 | 197 | 152 | 115 | 82 | 53 | | | | | | | | | | | |
| 560 | 587 | 443 | 379 | 296 | 317 | 246 | 199 | 152 | 145 | 90 | 56 | | | | | | | | | | | |
| 612 | 639 | 495 | 438 | 367 | 388 | 283 | 251 | 251 | 195 | 169 | 167 | 120 | | | | | | | | | | |
| 647 | 674 | 530 | 476 | 407 | 428 | 329 | 298 | 298 | 242 | 216 | 214 | 167 | 69 | | | | | | | | | |
| 666 | 693 | 549 | 497 | 423 | 444 | 353 | 324 | 324 | 268 | 242 | 240 | 192 | 91 | 32 | | | | | | | | |
| 678 | 705 | 561 | 509 | 443 | 464 | 369 | 341 | 340 | 285 | 262 | 259 | 211 | 110 | 52 | 36 | | | | | | | |
| 720 | 747 | 603 | 550 | 485 | 506 | 407 | 383 | 382 | 327 | 304 | 301 | 253 | 152 | 94 | 78 | 46 | | | | | | |
| 743 | 770 | 626 | 573 | 508 | 529 | 434 | 406 | 405 | 350 | 327 | 324 | 276 | 175 | 117 | 101 | 68 | 27 | | | | | |
| 881 | 908 | 764 | 711 | 646 | 667 | 572 | 544 | 543 | 488 | 465 | 462 | 414 | 313 | 255 | 239 | 207 | 165 | 151 | | | | |
| 942 | 969 | 825 | 772 | 707 | 728 | 633 | 605 | 604 | 549 | 526 | 523 | 475 | 374 | 316 | 300 | 267 | 226 | 211 | 73 | | | |

Chesapeake Light (36°54.3'N, 75°42.8'W) to: Norfolk, 42 miles; Baltimore, 165 miles.
Cape Fear River entrance buoy 2CF (33°49.5'N, 78°03.7'W) to Wilmington, 28 miles.
Charleston Harbor entrance buoy 2C (32°40.7'N, 79°42.8'W) to Charleston, 12.3 miles.
Savannah Light (31°57.0'N, 80°41.0'W) to Savannah, 25 miles.
St. Johns River entrance buoy STJ (30°23.6'N, 81°19.2'W) to Jacksonville, 23 miles.
Entrance lighted whistle buoy (24°27.7'N, 81°48.1'W) to Key West, 6.3 miles.

Each distance is by shortest route that safe navigation permits between the two ports concerned. The navigator must make his own adjustments for non-direct routes selected to run with or avoid the Gulf Stream. For example, the table shows a distance of 561 miles by direct route from Diamond Shoals to Port of Palm Beach; distances via the routes shown in Chapter 3, Coast Pilot 4, are: Outer route, 572 miles; Gulf Stream route, 593 miles; Inner route, 628 miles.

Appendix D 245

# INSIDE-ROUTE DISTANCES
## FERNANDINA BEACH, FLA., TO KEY WEST, FLA.
### (Nautical and Statute Miles)

Figure at intersection of columns opposite ports in question is the nautical/statute mileage between the two. Example: St. Augustine, Fla., is 271 nautical miles (312 statute miles) from Miami, Fla.

*Nautical miles* (upper/left reading) and *Statute miles* (lower/right reading)

Ports (with coordinates), in order along the route:

- Norfolk, Va. — 36°50.9'N. 76°17.9'W.
- Fernandina Beach, Fla. — 30°40.3'N. 81°28.0'W.
- Jacksonville, Fla. — 30°19.2'N. 81°39.0'W.
- St. Augustine, Fla. — 29°53.6'N. 81°18.5'W.
- Marineland, Fla. — 29°40.1'N. 81°13.0'W.
- Daytona Beach, Fla. — 29°12.6'N. 81°00.7'W.
- New Smyrna Beach, Fla. — 29°01.7'N. 80°55.1'W.
- Titusville, Fla. — 28°37.3'N. 80°47.9'W.
- Cocoa, Fla. — 28°21.3'N. 80°43.1'W.
- Eau Gallie, Fla. — 28°07.9'N. 80°37.1'W.
- Melbourne, Fla. — 28°05.0'N. 80°35.5'W.
- Vero Beach, Fla. — 27°39.0'N. 80°22.4'W.
- Fort Pierce, Fla. — 27°27.5'N. 80°19.3'W.
- Salerno, Fla. — 27°08.8'N. 80°11.6'W.
- Stuart, Fla. — 27°12.2'N. 80°15.6'W.
- Port Mayaca, Fla. — 26°59.1'N. 80°36.8'W.
- Clewiston, Fla. — 26°45.6'N. 80°55.2'W.
- Moore Haven, Fla. — 26°50.0'N. 81°05.3'W.
- Fort Myers, Fla. — 26°38.9'N. 81°52.3'W.
- Jupiter, Fla. — 26°56.8'N. 80°05.4'W.
- Port of Palm Beach, Fla. — 26°46.1'N. 80°03.0'W.
- Fort Lauderdale, Fla. — 26°06.8'N. 80°07.2'W.
- Port Everglades, Fla. — 26°05.6'N. 80°07.0'W.
- Miami, Fla. — 25°47.0'N. 80°11.0'W.
- Tavernier, Fla. — 25°00.7'N. 80°31.3'W.
- Matecumbe Harbor, Fla. — 24°51.1'N. 80°44.5'W.
- Marathon, Fla. — 24°42.2'N. 81°06.7'W.
- Flamingo, Fla. — 25°08.5'N. 80°55.4'W.
- Key West, Fla. — 24°33.7'N. 81°48.5'W.

### Distances from Norfolk, Va. (nautical / statute miles)

| To | Nautical | Statute |
|---|---|---|
| Fernandina Beach | 623 | 717 |
| Jacksonville | 659 | 758 |
| St. Augustine | 676 | 778 |
| Marineland | 692 | 796 |
| Daytona Beach | 722 | 831 |
| New Smyrna Beach | 735 | 846 |
| Titusville | 764 | 879 |
| Cocoa | 780 | 898 |
| Eau Gallie | 795 | 915 |
| Melbourne | 798 | 918 |
| Vero Beach | 827 | 952 |
| Fort Pierce | 839 | 966 |
| Salerno | 860 | 990 |
| Stuart | 865 | 995 |
| Port Mayaca | 892 | 1026 |
| Clewiston | 915 | 1053 |
| Moore Haven | 926 | 1066 |
| Fort Myers | 975 | 1122 |
| Jupiter | 873 | 1005 |
| Port of Palm Beach | 885 | 1018 |
| Fort Lauderdale | 925 | 1064 |
| Port Everglades | 927 | 1067 |
| Miami | 947 | 1090 |
| Tavernier | 999 | 1150 |
| Matecumbe Harbor | 1017 | 1170 |
| Marathon | 1045 | 1203 |
| Flamingo | 1050 | 1208 |
| Key West | 1081 | 1244 |

### Distances from Fernandina Beach, Fla. (nautical miles)

| To | Naut. |
|---|---|
| Jacksonville | 36 |
| St. Augustine | 53 |
| Marineland | 69 |
| Daytona Beach | 99 |
| New Smyrna Beach | 113 |
| Titusville | 141 |
| Cocoa | 157 |
| Eau Gallie | 172 |
| Melbourne | 175 |
| Vero Beach | 204 |
| Fort Pierce | 216 |
| Salerno | 237 |
| Stuart | 242 |
| Port Mayaca | 269 |
| Clewiston | 292 |
| Moore Haven | 303 |
| Fort Myers | 353 |
| Jupiter | 251 |
| Port of Palm Beach | 262 |
| Fort Lauderdale | 303 |
| Port Everglades | 304 |
| Miami | 324 |
| Tavernier | 378 |
| Matecumbe Harbor | 394 |
| Marathon | 422 |
| Flamingo | 427 |
| Key West | 458 |

# INSIDE-ROUTE DISTANCES
## NORFOLK, VA., TO FERNANDINA BEACH, FLA.
### (Nautical and Statute Miles)

Figure at intersection of columns opposite ports in question is the nautical/statute mileage between the two. Example: Morehead City, N.C., is 445 nautical miles (512 statute miles) from Fernandina Beach, Fla.

*51 statute miles via Dismal Swamp Canal
*44 nautical miles via Dismal Swamp Canal

Appendix D 247

## Conversion Tables

### INTERNATIONAL NAUTICAL MILES TO STATUTE MILES
1 nautical mile   6,076.12 feet or 1,852 meters   1 statute mile = 5,280 feet or 1,609.35 meters

| Nautical miles | 0 | 1 | 2 | 3 | 4 | 5 | 6 | 7 | 8 | 9 |
|---|---|---|---|---|---|---|---|---|---|---|
| 0 | 0.000 | 1.151 | 2.302 | 3.452 | 4.603 | 5.754 | 6.905 | 8.055 | 9.206 | 10.357 |
| 10 | 11.508 | 12.659 | 13.809 | 14.960 | 16.111 | 17.262 | 18.412 | 19.563 | 20.714 | 21.865 |
| 20 | 23.016 | 24.166 | 25.317 | 26.468 | 27.619 | 28.769 | 29.920 | 31.071 | 32.222 | 33.373 |
| 30 | 34.523 | 35.674 | 36.825 | 37.976 | 39.126 | 40.277 | 41.428 | 42.579 | 43.730 | 44.880 |
| 40 | 46.031 | 47.182 | 48.333 | 49.483 | 50.634 | 51.785 | 52.936 | 54.087 | 55.237 | 56.388 |
| 50 | 57.539 | 58.690 | 59.840 | 60.991 | 62.142 | 63.293 | 64.444 | 65.594 | 66.745 | 67.896 |
| 60 | 69.047 | 70.197 | 71.348 | 72.499 | 73.650 | 74.801 | 75.951 | 77.102 | 78.253 | 79.404 |
| 70 | 80.554 | 81.705 | 82.856 | 84.007 | 85.158 | 86.308 | 87.459 | 88.610 | 89.761 | 90.911 |
| 80 | 92.062 | 93.213 | 94.364 | 95.515 | 96.665 | 97.816 | 98.967 | 100.118 | 101.268 | 102.419 |
| 90 | 103.570 | 104.721 | 105.871 | 107.022 | 108.173 | 109.324 | 110.475 | 111.625 | 112.776 | 113.927 |

### STATUTE MILES TO INTERNATONAL NAUTICAL MILES

| Statute miles | 0 | 1 | 2 | 3 | 4 | 5 | 6 | 7 | 8 | 9 |
|---|---|---|---|---|---|---|---|---|---|---|
| 0 | 0.000 | 0.869 | 1.738 | 2.607 | 3.476 | 4.345 | 5.214 | 6.083 | 6.952 | 7.821 |
| 10 | 8.690 | 9.559 | 10.428 | 11.297 | 12.166 | 13.035 | 13.904 | 14.773 | 15.642 | 16.511 |
| 20 | 17.380 | 18.249 | 19.118 | 19.986 | 20.855 | 21.724 | 22.593 | 23.462 | 24.331 | 25.200 |
| 30 | 26.069 | 26.938 | 27.807 | 28.676 | 29.545 | 30.414 | 31.283 | 32.152 | 33.021 | 33.890 |
| 40 | 34.759 | 35.628 | 36.497 | 37.366 | 38.235 | 39.104 | 39.973 | 40.842 | 41.711 | 42.580 |
| 50 | 43.449 | 44.318 | 45.187 | 46.056 | 46.925 | 47.794 | 48.663 | 49.532 | 50.401 | 51.270 |
| 60 | 52.139 | 53.008 | 53.877 | 54.746 | 55.615 | 56.484 | 57.353 | 58.222 | 59.091 | 59.959 |
| 70 | 60.828 | 61.697 | 62.566 | 63.435 | 64.304 | 65.173 | 66.042 | 66.911 | 67.780 | 68.649 |
| 80 | 69.518 | 70.387 | 71.256 | 72.125 | 72.994 | 73.863 | 74.732 | 75.601 | 76.470 | 77.339 |
| 90 | 78.208 | 79.077 | 79.946 | 80.815 | 81.684 | 82.553 | 83.422 | 84.291 | 85.160 | 86.029 |

### FEET TO METERS

| Feet | 0 | 1 | 2 | 3 | 4 | 5 | 6 | 7 | 8 | 9 |
|---|---|---|---|---|---|---|---|---|---|---|
| 0 | 0.00 | 0.30 | 0.61 | 0.91 | 1.22 | 1.52 | 1.83 | 2.13 | 2.44 | 2.74 |
| 10 | 3.05 | 3.35 | 3.66 | 3.96 | 4.27 | 4.57 | 4.88 | 5.18 | 5.49 | 5.79 |
| 20 | 6.10 | 6.40 | 6.71 | 7.01 | 7.32 | 7.62 | 7.92 | 8.23 | 8.53 | 8.84 |
| 30 | 9.14 | 9.45 | 9.75 | 10.06 | 10.36 | 10.67 | 10.97 | 11.28 | 11.58 | 11.89 |
| 40 | 12.19 | 12.50 | 12.80 | 13.11 | 13.41 | 13.72 | 14.02 | 14.33 | 14.63 | 14.93 |
| 50 | 15.24 | 15.54 | 15.85 | 16.15 | 16.46 | 16.76 | 17.07 | 17.37 | 17.68 | 17.98 |
| 60 | 18.29 | 18.59 | 18.90 | 19.20 | 19.51 | 19.81 | 20.12 | 20.42 | 20.73 | 21.03 |
| 70 | 21.34 | 21.64 | 21.95 | 22.25 | 22.55 | 22.86 | 23.16 | 23.47 | 23.77 | 24.08 |
| 80 | 24.38 | 24.69 | 24.99 | 25.30 | 25.60 | 25.91 | 26.21 | 26.52 | 26.82 | 27.13 |
| 90 | 27.43 | 27.74 | 28.04 | 28.35 | 28.65 | 28.96 | 29.26 | 29.57 | 29.87 | 30.17 |

### METERS TO FEET

| Meters | 0 | 1 | 2 | 3 | 4 | 5 | 6 | 7 | 8 | 9 |
|---|---|---|---|---|---|---|---|---|---|---|
| 0 | 0.00 | 3.28 | 6.56 | 9.84 | 13.12 | 16.40 | 19.68 | 22.97 | 26.25 | 29.53 |
| 10 | 32.81 | 36.09 | 39.37 | 42.65 | 45.93 | 49.21 | 52.49 | 55.77 | 59.06 | 62.34 |
| 20 | 65.62 | 68.90 | 72.18 | 75.46 | 78.74 | 82.02 | 85.30 | 88.58 | 91.86 | 95.14 |
| 30 | 98.42 | 101.71 | 104.99 | 108.27 | 111.55 | 114.83 | 118.11 | 121.39 | 124.67 | 127.95 |
| 40 | 131.23 | 134.51 | 137.80 | 141.08 | 144.36 | 147.64 | 150.92 | 154.20 | 157.48 | 160.76 |
| 50 | 164.04 | 167.32 | 170.60 | 173.88 | 177.16 | 180.45 | 183.73 | 187.01 | 190.29 | 193.57 |
| 60 | 196.85 | 200.13 | 203.41 | 206.69 | 209.97 | 213.25 | 216.54 | 219.82 | 223.10 | 226.38 |
| 70 | 229.66 | 232.94 | 236.22 | 239.50 | 242.78 | 246.06 | 249.34 | 252.62 | 255.90 | 259.19 |
| 80 | 262.47 | 265.75 | 269.03 | 272.31 | 275.59 | 278.87 | 282.15 | 285.43 | 288.71 | 291.99 |
| 90 | 295.28 | 298.56 | 301.84 | 305.12 | 308.40 | 311.68 | 314.96 | 318.24 | 321.52 | 324.80 |

# APPENDIX E
## NOAA Chart Cross-Reference and Notice to Mariners Information

### NOAA Chart Cross-Reference
Pages 1–12 NOAA chart #12206, 25th edition, April 28, 1990

Pages 13–31 NOAA chart #11553, 23rd edition, August 5, 1989

Pages 32–52 NOAA chart #11541, 24th edition, August 26, 1989

Pages 53–76 NOAA chart #11534, 24th edition, May 27, 1989

Pages 77–94 NOAA chart #11518, 24th edition, October 29, 1988

Pages 95–114 NOAA chart #11507, 23rd edition, January 7, 1989

Pages 115–129 NOAA chart #11489, 25th edition, January 21, 1989

Pages 130–154 NOAA chart #11485, 25th edition, May 13, 1989

Pages 155–178 NOAA chart #11472, 25th edition, March 4, 1989

Pages 179–194 NOAA chart #11467, 26th edition, August 19, 1989

Page 195 NOAA chart #11545, 53rd edition, February 13, 1988

Page 196 NOAA chart #11537, 26th edition, January 7, 1989

Pages 197–198 NOAA chart #11532, 15th edition, October 10, 1987

Page 199 NOAA chart #11521, 19th edition, June 30, 1990

Pages 200–203, 206 NOAA chart #11513, 19th edition, May 19, 1990

Pages 204–205 NOAA chart #11512, 50th edition, January 13, 1990

Pages 207–208 NOAA chart #11509, 21st edition, January 9, 1988

Pages 209–210 NOAA chart #11502, 22nd edition, November 25, 1989

Page 211 NOAA chart #11489, 25th edition, January 21, 1989

Page 212 NOAA chart #11490, 12th edition, April 21, 1990

Pages 213–216 NOAA chart #11478, 14th edition, March 24, 1990

Page 217 NOAA chart #11476, 16th edition, March 10, 1990

Pages 218–219, 221–222 NOAA chart #11467, 26th edition, August 19, 1989

Page 220 NOAA chart #11466, 26th edition, February 4, 1989

Pages 223–232 NOAA chart #12206, 24th edition, March 5, 1988

Pages 233–234 NOAA chart #11489, 25th edition, January 21, 1989

### U.S. Coast Guard Local Notices to Mariners
Local Notices to Mariners for this chartbook area may be obtained by contacting the United States Coast Guard at the following addresses.

- For Virginia and North Carolina, contact:
  U.S. Coast Guard District Commander
  Fifth Coast Guard District
  Federal Building
  431 Crawford Street
  Portsmouth, VA 23704-5004
  Phone, day — (804) 398-6486
  Phone, night — (804) 398-6231

- For South Carolina, Georgia, and Florida, contact:
  U.S. Coast Guard District Commander
  Seventh Coast Guard District
  Brickell Plaza Building
  909 SE 1st Avenue
  Miami, FL 33131-3050
  Phone, day — (305) 536-5621
  Phone, night — (305) 536-5611

# APPENDIX F
## Facilities Listings

Locations of public marine facilities are designated on the charts by large numbers with leaders. The numbers refer to the facility tabulations here. In the tidal difference column, a plus (+) or minus (−) means that tidal heights at the facility run the designated number of hours later or earlier, respectively, than tides at the reference station. Approach depths are referenced from the nearest natural or dredged channel.

### For pages 1–12 and 223–232:

Tidal reference station: HAMPTON ROADS

| NO | LOCATION | MEAN RANGE-FT. | DIFF (HRS) | APPROACH-FEET (REPORTED) | ALONGSIDE-FEET (REPORTED) | ELECTRICITY / MOORINGS-BERTHS | RAMP SURFACED-NATURAL | REPAIRS HULL-MOTOR-RADIO | MARINE RAILWAY-FEET | LIFT CAPACITY-TONS | BOAT RENTAL CANOE-ROW-MOTOR | CHARTER HOUSE-SAIL | FOOD-LODGING-CAMPING | TOILETS-SHOWERS-LAUNDRY | PUMP-OUT STATION | WINTER STORAGE WET-DRY | NAUTICAL CHART SALES | WATER-ICE | GROCERIES-HARDWARE | BAIT-TACKLE | DIESEL OIL-GASOLINE |
|---|---|---|---|---|---|---|---|---|---|---|---|---|---|---|---|---|---|---|---|---|---|
| 1 | LEE'S YT HBR | 2.6 | +¼ | 20 | 15 | B | S | HMR | | 5 | RM | | | T | | WD | C | WI | GH | BT | DG |
| 2 | WESTERN BRANCH | 2.6 | +¼ | 10 | 10 | E | | MR | | | | | | TS | | | | W | | | |
| 3 | VIRGINIA BT+YT | 2.6 | +¼ | 14 | 6 | BME | | HMR | 58 | 35 | | | F | TSL | P | | | W | H | | DG |
| 7 | TIDEWATER YACHT | 2.8 | +¼ | 8 | 8 | BME | | HMR | | 60 | | | FL | TSL | P | W | C | WI | GH | | DG |
| 8 | PIRATE COVE MAR | | | 5 | 4 | BME | S | | 50 | 20 | | | F | TS | | W | | WI | GH | BT | DG |
| 9 | ATLANTIC YT BSN | 0 | | 12 | 10 | BME | | HMR | 100 | 60 | | | | TSL | | W | C | W | H | | DG |
| 10 | MERCER'S BT HS | 0 | | | | BM | S | | | | R | | F | T | | | | WI | G | BT | G |
| 11 | LEE'S BT+TACKLE | 0 | | 4 | 4 | BME | S | | | | RM | | FC | TS | P | | | I | G | BT | G |
| 12 | W. LEIGH ANSELL | 0 | | 20 | 5 | BME | S | | | | | | F | TSL | | W | | WI | G | | DG |
| 14 | HARRISON'S MAR | 0 | | | | BME | | HM | | | | | | TS | | | | WI | GH | | DG |
| 15 | COINJOCK EXXON | 0 | | 12 | 9 | ME | | | | | | | F | TSL | | W | C | WI | GH | | DG |
| 15A | W.L. TATE | 0 | | 12 | 10 | BE | | HM | | 60 | | | | | | W | | WI | H | | |
| 19 | RIVERSIDE BOAT | 0 | | 12 | 17 | BE | | HMR | 150 | 60 | | | | TS | P | WD | | WI | H | | |
| 20 | ELIZABETH CITY | 0 | | 12 | 17 | BE | | HMR | 150 | 60 | | | | TS | | WD | | WI | | | DG |
| 21 | PELICAN MARINA | 0 | | 7 | 7 | BE | S | M | | | | | FL | TSL | | | C | WI | H | BT | DG |
| 22 | CAUSEWAY MARINA | 0 | | 6 | 3 | | S | M | | | | | | | | | C | I | H | BT | G |
| 23 | CITY MARINA | | | 4 | 4 | | S | M | | | | | | | | | | | | | G |

### For pages 13–31:

| NO | LOCATION | MEAN RANGE-FT. | DIFF (HRS) | APPROACH-FEET (REPORTED) | ALONGSIDE-FEET (REPORTED) | ELECTRICITY / MOORINGS-BERTHS | RAMP SURFACED-NATURAL | REPAIRS HULL-MOTOR-RADIO | MARINE RAILWAY-FEET | LIFT CAPACITY-TONS | BOAT RENTAL CANOE-ROW-MOTOR | CHARTER HOUSE-SAIL | FOOD-LODGING-CAMPING | TOILETS-SHOWERS-LAUNDRY | PUMP-OUT STATION | WINTER STORAGE WET-DRY | NAUTICAL CHART SALES | WATER-ICE | GROCERIES-HARDWARE | BAIT-TACKLE | DIESEL OIL-GASOLINE |
|---|---|---|---|---|---|---|---|---|---|---|---|---|---|---|---|---|---|---|---|---|---|
| 1A | PANTEGO CREEK | 0 | | 4½ | 40 | | | | | | | | | | | | C | I | H | BT | G |
| 3 | BELHAVEN MARINE | 0 | | 8 | 8 | BE | | HM | | 60 | | | FL | T | | | | WI | GH | | DG |
| 4 | RIVER FOREST | 0 | | 9 | 9 | BME | S | M | | | | | FLC | TSL | | | C | WI | GH | | DG |
| 4A | WALDROPS MARINA | | | 6 | 5 | BME | N | | | | | | C | TSL | | WD | | WD | | | |
| 5A | MASCEO DANIELS | | | 4 | 3 | | | | | | | | | | | | C | WI | GH | BT | G |
| 5C | HOPKINS MARINA | 0 | | 6 | 4 | B | S | | 33 | 40 | | | | T | | | | WI | GH | BT | G |
| 6A | HOBUCKEN MARINA | | | 5 | | E | | | | | | | FLC | TS | | | | WI | G | BT | |
| 8 | R.E. MAYO CO. | 0 | | 12 | 12 | ME | SN | | | | | | | T | | | | I | GH | BT | DG |
| 10 | PARADISE SHORES | | | 5 | 4 | BE | | | | | | | | T | | | | I | G | B | |
| 11 | ALLIGATR RVR MAR | | | 8 | 8 | BE | S | M | | | | | FC | TSL | | W | | WI | G | BT | DG |

## For pages 32–52:

| NO | LOCATION | TIDES: MEAN RANGE-FT | TIDES: DIFF (HRS) HAMPTON ROADS | DEPTH: APPROACH-FEET (REPORTED) | DEPTH: ALONGSIDE-FEET (REPORTED) | SERVICES: ELECTRICITY-MOORINGS-BERTHS (TRANSIENTS) | RAMP SURFACED-NATURAL | REPAIRS HULL-MOTOR-RADIO | MARINE RAILWAY-FEET | LIFT CAPACITY-TONS | BOAT RENTAL: CANOE-ROW-MOTOR | CHARTER-HOUSE-SAIL | FOOD-LODGING-CAMPING | TOILETS-SHOWERS-LAUNDRY / PUMP-OUT STATION | WINTER STORAGE WET-DRY | SUPPLIES: NAUTICAL CHART SALES | WATER-ICE | GROCERIES-HARDWARE | BAIT-TACKLE | DIESEL OIL-GASOLINE |
|---|---|---|---|---|---|---|---|---|---|---|---|---|---|---|---|---|---|---|---|---|
| 1 | ORIENTAL MARINA | | | 8 | 6 | B E | | M | | | | | FL | TSL | | | WI | G | | DG |
| 1A | LARRY W KEMP | | | 5 | 8 | B E | S | | | | | | F | | WD | | WI | | | DG |
| 2 | NEUSE WAYS | | | 9 | 10 | BME | S | HM | 60 | | | | FL | TSL | | | WI | GH | BT | DG |
| 3C | WHITTAKER CREEK | | | 8 | 8 | BME | | HMR | | | | C S | F | TSL | W | C | WI | H | | DG |
| 3D | SAILCRAFT INC | | | 10 | 8 | | | HMR | | 15 | | | | TS | | C | WI | H | | |
| 3F | PARADISE SHORES | | | 3 | 3 | M | S | | | | | | F C | TS | D | | WI | GH | BT | G |
| 4A | SEA GATE ASSN | | | 7 | 7 | BME | S | M | | | | | | TS | | C | WI | | B | DG |
| 6 | TOPSAIL MARINE | 2.5 | -1 | 16 | 19 | | | | | | | | F | T | | | WI | H | B | DG |
| 10 | LANE'S OUTBOARD | 2.8 | -1 | 10 | 6 | | | HM | | 30 | | | | | | | | | | |
| 10A | INLAND MARINA | 2.8 | -1 | 4 | 4 | BME | | HM | 40 | | M | HS | | | WD | | | | | |
| 11 | MOREHEAD SPORT | 2.8 | -1 | 3 | 4 | BME | S | HMR | | 30 | | | | T | WD | | WI | H | T | G |
| 11B | GREEN BAY MARINA | | | 3½ | 3½ | B E | S | | | | | | | | WD | | WI | | T | G |
| 12 | MOREHEAD CITY YT | 2.8 | -1 | 6 | 6 | B E | | | | | | | F | TSL | W | C | WI | | | DG |
| 15 | MOREHEAD GULF DK | 2.8 | -1 | 12 | 12 | B E | | | | | | | | TS | | | W | H | | DG |
| 17 | TRIPLE ESS MAR | | | 3½ | 8 | | S | | | | | | F | TS | | | WI | GH | BT | G |
| 18 | THE ANCHORAGE | 2.5 | -1 | 6 | 6 | B E | S | M | | | | | FL | TS | WD | C | WI | GH | BT | DG |
| 19A | CROWS NEST MAR | 2.5 | -1 | 4 | 5 | | S | HMR | | 10 | | | F | T | D | | WI | | BT | DG |
| 19B | ATLANTIC BEACH | | | 6 | 6 | B E | S | M | | | M | | | TSL | WD | C | WI | H | BT | DG |
| 20 | THE HARBOR MASTER | 1.5 | -½ | 5½ | 4 | BME | | H | 35 | 12 | | | | TS | WD | | W | H | | |
| 20A | 70 WEST MARINA | 1.5 | -½ | 6 | 6 | | | HMR | | 10 | | | F | T | | C | WI | GH | BT | G |
| 21 | CANNON BOAT WKS | 1.5 | -½ | 6 | 8 | B | | HM | 70 | | | | | T | W | | W | | | |
| 22 | TAYLOR BOAT WKS | 1.5 | -½ | 6 | 6 | B E | | H | 50 | | | | | | | | W | | | |
| 24 | SPOONER'S CRK YT | 1.2 | -½ | 6½ | 8 | B E | | HMR | | 60 | | | F | TSL | W | C | WI | GH | | DG |
| 24B | ISLAND HARBOR | | | 5 | 5 | BME | S | HM | | | | C S | F C | T | W | C | WI | GH | BT | DG |
| 25 | SWANSBORO YT BSN | 2.0 | -1½ | 4 | 6 | B E | | HM | | | | C | F | TS | W | | WI | GH | BT | DG |
| 26 | TOMMY'S MAR MOT | 2.0 | -1½ | 36 | 6 | BM | S | M | | | M | | F | T | D | | I | GH | BT | G |
| 27 | DUDLEY'S MARINA | 2.0 | -1½ | 7 | 6 | B E | S | HM | 65 | 4 | | C | F | TS | WD | | WI | GH | BT | DG |
| 29 | CASPER'S MARINA | 2.2 | -1½ | 12 | 8 | B E | N | HM | 40 | 20 | | | | TS | D | C | WI | H | | DG |
| 30 | MATTHEWS LANDING | 2.2 | -½ | 4 | 4 | B E | | | | | | | | | WD | | WI | | BT | G |
| 30A | SWAN POINT MAR | 3.0 | -1½ | 8 | 6 | BME | S | HMR | | 5 | | C | | TSL | WD | C | WI | GH | BT | DG |
| 30B | NEW RIVER MARINA | 3.0 | -1½ | 14 | 12 | BME | SN | HMR | | | | C | FLC | TSL | WD | C | WI | GH | BT | DG |
| 32 | THOMAS BAIT&TKL | 2.5 | -1 | 4 | 5 | E | S | | | | | | F | T | | | WI | G | BT | DG |
| 34 | IVEY LEWIS | | | 5½ | 6 | | | HM | 6 | 5 | | | | | | | WI | GH | BT | DG |
| 35 | ANNAMARINA | | | 6 | 6 | B E | S | | | | | | FL | TS | WD | C | WI | GH | BT | DG |
| 36 | BUSH'S REPAIR CTR | | | 3 | 3 | | S | M | | | | | | | D | | | H | | G |
| 37A | SCOTTS HILL MAR | | | 5 | 4 | BME | S | M | | | | | F | T P | WD | C | WI | GH | BT | DG |
| 38 | LINWOOD BELL | | | 3 | 3 | | | HM | 60 | 28 | | | | T | | | W | | | |
| 38A | JOHNSON MARINE | | | 3 | 3 | | S | HM | 25 | 3 | | | F | T | WD | | WI | GH | | G |
| 40 | SEA PATH TRANS | | | 10 | 14 | B E | | | | | | C | | TSL P | W | C | WI | G | | DG |
| 41 | WRIGHTSVILLE MAR | | | 10 | 10 | B E | | | 60 | | | | | TS | W | C | I | GH | BT | DG |
| 41B | ATLANTIC MARINE | | | 6 | 6 | BME | | HMR | 26 | 30 | | | FL | T P | WD | C | WI | GH | BT | G |
| 44 | GULF MARINA | | | 12 | 10 | B E | | | | | | | F | TS | | C | WI | H | BT | DG |
| 45 | BRADLEY CK 66 MAR | | | 6½ | 6 | BME | | HMR | | 45 | | | | TSL | | C | WI | H | | DG |
| 46 | MASONBORO BTYD | | | 7 | 7 | B E | | HM | | 19 | | | | TSL | W | | WI | H | | |

## For pages 53–76:

| NO | LOCATION | TIDES: MEAN RANGE-FT. | TIDES: DIFF (HRS) CHARLESTON | DEPTH: APPROACH-FEET (REPORTED) | DEPTH: ALONGSIDE-FEET (REPORTED) | SERVICES: ELECTRICITY-MOORINGS-BERTHS (TRANSIENTS) | RAMP SURFACED-NATURAL | REPAIRS HULL-MOTOR-RADIO | MARINE RAILWAY-FEET | LIFT CAPACITY-TONS | BOAT RENTAL: CANOE-ROW-MOTOR | CHARTER-HOUSE-SAIL | FOOD-LODGING-CAMPING | TOILETS-SHOWERS-LAUNDRY / PUMP-OUT STATION | WINTER STORAGE WET-DRY | SUPPLIES: NAUTICAL CHART SALES | WATER-ICE | GROCERIES-HARDWARE | BAIT-TACKLE | DIESEL OIL-GASOLINE |
|---|---|---|---|---|---|---|---|---|---|---|---|---|---|---|---|---|---|---|---|---|
| 2 | CAROLINA INLET | | | 6 | 5 | BME | | HMR | 45 | 2 | | | F | TS | WD | C | WI | H | BT | DG |
| 2A | SKIPPY WINNER'S | | | 8 | 13 | B E | | | | | | C | | TSL | W | | WI | GH | | D |
| 2C | PIRATE COVE MAR | | | 8 | 7 | BME | | HMR | 55 | 40 | | | F | TS | WD | C | WI | GH | BT | DG |
| 5 | SOUTHPORT MARINA | 4.1 | 0 | 8 | 8 | B E | S | HMR | | 30 | | | FL | TSL | WD | C | WI | | BT | DG |
| 7 | SPORTSMAN'S MAR | 4.0 | -¼ | 7 | 6 | BME | S | | | | | C | FL | TSL | W | | I | | BT | G |
| 7A | FAIRCLOTH'S MAR | 4.0 | -¼ | 3 | 1 | BME | N | | | | | | F | T | D | | WI | G | BT | G |
| 7C | RAY KIRBY | | | 6 | 6 | ME | S | M | 40 | | | | F | T | | | WI | GH | BT | DG |
| 8 | OCEAN ISLE MAR | | | 4 | 4½ | | S | | | | | | | T | | | WI | GH | BT | G |
| 9 | INLET VIEW MARINA | | | 12 | 6 | B E | S | HM | | 5 | M | CH | F | T | WD | C | WI | H | BT | DG |
| 10 | HUGHES MARINA | 4.6 | +½ | 5 | 5 | B E | | | | 12 | M | C | FL | | WD | C | I | | BT | DG |
| 14 | CAPT HARRY'S BAIT | 5.0 | +¼ | 3 | 3 | B | S | | | | RM | | F | T | | | WI | G | BT | G |
| 15 | LITTLE RIVER | 5.2 | +1 | 9 | 6 | B E | S | HM | | | M | C | F | TS | W | | WI | | | DG |
| 16A | BELLA MARINA | | | 8 | 4 | | | HMR | | 5 | | | F | T | D | | WI | H | BT | DG |
| 17 | PALMETTO SHORES | 5.0 | +½ | 6 | | BME | S | HMR | 36 | | | C | | TS | W | C | WI | | BT | DG |
| 17A | VEREEN'S MARINA | | | 6 | 6 | B E | | MR | | | | C | F | TS | W | C | WI | GH | BT | DG |
| 18H | ARBOURGATE VIL MAR | | | 11 | 8 | B E | | MR | | | | C S | F | TSL P | W | C | WI | GH | BT | |
| 20B | INLET PORT MAR | | | 6 | 3 | BM | S | | | | | | F | TS | W | C | WI | | BT | DG |
| 21 | HAGUE MARINA | | | 7 | 9 | B E | | HM | | | | | F | TSL | WD | C | WI | GH | | DG |
| 22 | BUCKSPORT MARINA | | | 25 | 10 | BME | SN | MR | | | | | F C | TS | W | | WI | G | BT | DG |
| 23 | WACCA WACHE MAR | | | 12 | 6 | BME | S | | | | M | | F | TS | WD | C | WI | GH | BT | DG |
| 23A | BELLE ISLE MAR | | | 9 | 7 | B E | S | HMR | | | | | FL | TSL P | W | C | WI | GH | BT | DG |
| 24 | EXXON MARINA | 3.3 | +2 | 12 | 10 | BME | | MR | | 20 | | | | T | W | C | WI | GH | | DG |
| 25 | GEORGETOWN LNDG | | | 30 | 25 | B E | | HMR | | | | C | FL | TSL P | W | C | WI | GH | BT | DG |
| 26 | GULF AUTO MARINE | 3.3 | +2 | 12 | 12 | B | | | | | | | | TSL | | | WI | GH | | DG |
| 26A | NAUTICA MARINE | 3.3 | +2 | | | | | | | | | | | T | D | C | | H | T | |
| 26B | INLET PORT MAR | | | 7 | 7 | B E | S | | | | | C | F | TS | | C | WI | GH | BT | DG |
| 26C | CEDAR HILLS | | | 2 | 2 | | N | | | | | | | T | WD | | WI | GH | BT | G |

## For pages 77–94:

| NO | LOCATION | TIDES: MEAN RANGE-FT | TIDES: DIFF (HRS) CHARLESTON | DEPTH: APPROACH-FEET(REPORTED) | DEPTH: ALONGSIDE-FEET(REPORTED) | SERVICES: ELECTRICITY-MOORINGS-BERTHS (TRANSIENTS) | SERVICES: RAMP SURFACED-NATURAL | SERVICES: REPAIRS HULL-MOTOR-RADIO | SERVICES: MARINE RAILWAY-FEET | SERVICES: LIFT CAPACITY-TONS | SERVICES: BOAT RENTAL CANOE-ROW-MOTOR | SERVICES: BOAT RENTAL CHARTER-HOUSE-SAIL | SERVICES: FOOD-LODGING-CAMPING | SERVICES: TOILETS-SHOWERS-LAUNDRY / PUMP-OUT STATION | SERVICES: WINTER STORAGE WET-DRY | SUPPLIES: NAUTICAL CHART SALES | SUPPLIES: WATER-ICE | SUPPLIES: GROCERIES-HARDWARE | SUPPLIES: BAIT-TACKLE | SUPPLIES: DIESEL OIL-GASOLINE |
|---|---|---|---|---|---|---|---|---|---|---|---|---|---|---|---|---|---|---|---|---|
| 1 | WILD DUNES YACHT | | | 10 | 10 | B E | S | M | | | | C S | FL | TSL P | WD | C | WI | GH | BT | DG |
| 1A | BREACH INLET TEX | | | 9 | 5 | B E | | M | | | | S | F | | W | | WI | G | BT | DG |
| 2A | MT PLEASANT MAR | | | 10 | 10 | | S | | | 30 | | | | | WD | | WI | | BT | DG |
| 3 | DARBY MAR+SUPLY | 5.2 | -¼ | | | | | | | | | | | S | | | | H | | |
| 3A | RIPLEY LIGHT MAR | | | 12 | 12 | BME | | HM | | | | | FL | TSL P | D | C | WI | GH | BT | DG |
| 4 | LOCKWOOD MUN MAR | 5.2 | | 8 | | B E | S | MR | | | | C | FL | TSL P | WD | C | WI | GH | T | DG |
| 4A | STONO MARINA | | | 15 | 10 | B E | | HM | | | | | F | TSL P | WD | C | WI | H | | DG |
| 4B | BUZZARD'S ROOST | | | 12 | 12 | B E | | MR | | | | | F | TSL P | W | C | WI | GH | | DG |
| 5 | B+B SEAFOOD | 5.3 | ¾ | 7 | 12 | ME | S | | | | | | | T | WD | | WI | G | BT | DG |
| 6 | DOWNTOWN MARINA | 7.4 | 1 | 20 | 15 | B E | S | HM | | | | | FL | TSL | W | C | WI | GH | | DG |
| 7 | BEAUFORT MARINA | 7.4 | +1 | 6 | 12 | B E | | HM | 65 | | | | | TSL | W | C | WI | GH | | DG |
| 8 | MARSH HARBOUR MAR | | | 8 | 8 | B E | | HM | | 50 | | C | | T | WD | | WD | | | |

## For pages 95–114:

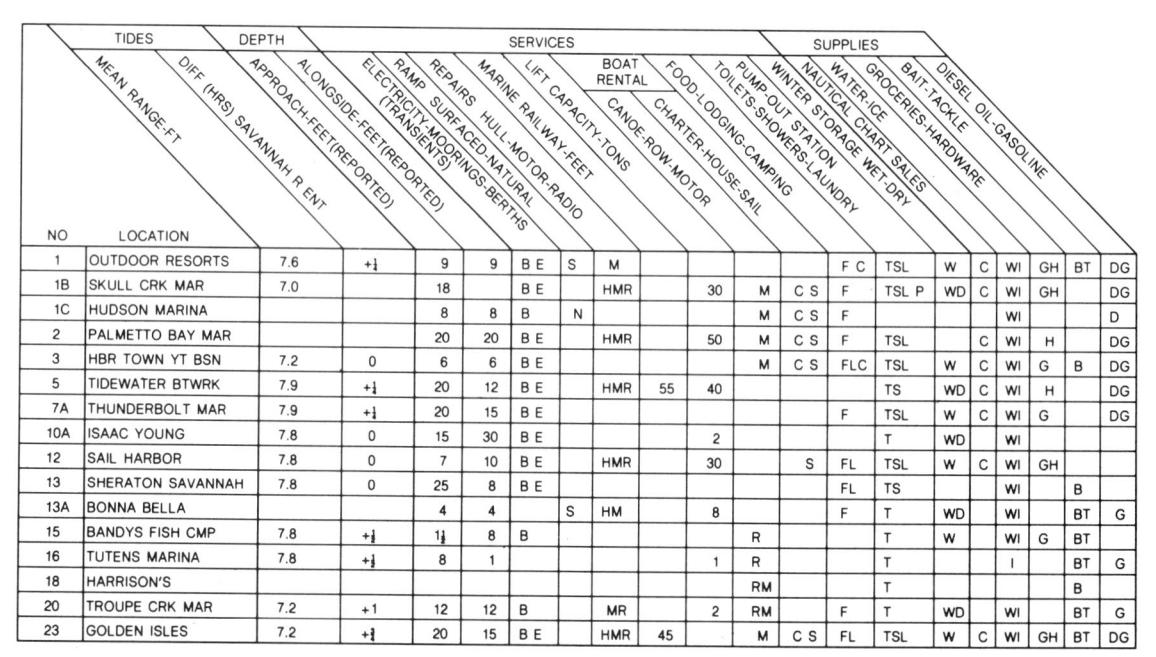

| NO | LOCATION | TIDES: MEAN RANGE-FT | TIDES: DIFF (HRS) SAVANNAH R ENT | DEPTH: APPROACH-FEET(REPORTED) | DEPTH: ALONGSIDE-FEET(REPORTED) | SERVICES: ELECTRICITY-MOORINGS-BERTHS (TRANSIENTS) | SERVICES: RAMP SURFACED-NATURAL | SERVICES: REPAIRS HULL-MOTOR-RADIO | SERVICES: MARINE RAILWAY-FEET | SERVICES: LIFT CAPACITY-TONS | SERVICES: BOAT RENTAL CANOE-ROW-MOTOR | SERVICES: BOAT RENTAL CHARTER-HOUSE-SAIL | SERVICES: FOOD-LODGING-CAMPING | SERVICES: TOILETS-SHOWERS-LAUNDRY / PUMP-OUT STATION | SERVICES: WINTER STORAGE WET-DRY | SUPPLIES: NAUTICAL CHART SALES | SUPPLIES: WATER-ICE | SUPPLIES: GROCERIES-HARDWARE | SUPPLIES: BAIT-TACKLE | SUPPLIES: DIESEL OIL-GASOLINE |
|---|---|---|---|---|---|---|---|---|---|---|---|---|---|---|---|---|---|---|---|---|
| 1 | OUTDOOR RESORTS | 7.6 | +¼ | 9 | 9 | B E | S | M | | | | | F C | TSL | W | C | WI | GH | BT | DG |
| 1B | SKULL CRK MAR | 7.0 | | 18 | | B E | | HMR | | 30 | M | C S | F | TSL P | WD | C | WI | GH | | DG |
| 1C | HUDSON MARINA | | | 8 | 8 | B | N | | | | M | C S | F | | | | WI | | | D |
| 2 | PALMETTO BAY MAR | | | 20 | 20 | B E | | HMR | | 50 | M | C S | F | TSL | | C | WI | H | | DG |
| 3 | HBR TOWN YT BSN | 7.2 | 0 | 6 | 6 | B E | | | | | M | C S | FLC | TSL | W | C | WI | G | B | DG |
| 5 | TIDEWATER BTWRK | 7.9 | +¼ | 20 | 12 | B E | | HMR | 55 | 40 | | | | TS | WD | C | WI | H | | DG |
| 7A | THUNDERBOLT MAR | 7.9 | +¼ | 20 | 15 | B E | | | | | | | F | TSL | W | C | WI | G | | DG |
| 10A | ISAAC YOUNG | 7.8 | 0 | 15 | 30 | B E | | | | 2 | | | | T | WD | | WI | | | |
| 12 | SAIL HARBOR | 7.8 | 0 | 7 | 10 | B E | | HMR | | 30 | | S | FL | TSL | W | C | WI | GH | | |
| 13 | SHERATON SAVANNAH | 7.8 | 0 | 25 | 8 | B E | | | | | | | FL | TS | | | WI | | B | |
| 13A | BONNA BELLA | | | 4 | 4 | | S | HM | | 8 | | | F | T | WD | | WI | | BT | G |
| 15 | BANDYS FISH CMP | 7.8 | +½ | 1½ | 8 | B | | | | | R | | | T | W | | WI | G | BT | |
| 16 | TUTENS MARINA | 7.8 | +½ | 8 | 1 | | | | | 1 | R | | | T | | | I | | BT | G |
| 18 | HARRISON'S | | | | | | | | | | RM | | | T | | | | | B | |
| 20 | TROUPE CRK MAR | 7.2 | +1 | 12 | 12 | B | | MR | | 2 | RM | | F | T | WD | | WI | | BT | G |
| 23 | GOLDEN ISLES | 7.2 | +¾ | 20 | 15 | B E | | HMR | 45 | | M | C S | FL | TSL | W | C | WI | GH | BT | DG |

## For pages 115–129, 211, and 233–234:

| NO | LOCATION | TIDES: MEAN RANGE-FT | TIDES: DIFF (HRS) MAYPORT | DEPTH: APPROACH-FEET(REPORTED) | DEPTH: ALONGSIDE-FEET(REPORTED) | SERVICES: ELECTRICITY-MOORINGS-BERTHS (TRANSIENTS) | SERVICES: RAMP SURFACED-NATURAL | SERVICES: REPAIRS HULL-MOTOR-RADIO | SERVICES: MARINE RAILWAY-FEET | SERVICES: LIFT CAPACITY-TONS | SERVICES: BOAT RENTAL CANOE-ROW-MOTOR | SERVICES: BOAT RENTAL CHARTER-HOUSE-SAIL | SERVICES: FOOD-LODGING-CAMPING | SERVICES: TOILETS-SHOWERS-LAUNDRY / PUMP-OUT STATION | SERVICES: WINTER STORAGE WET-DRY | SUPPLIES: NAUTICAL CHART SALES | SUPPLIES: WATER-ICE | SUPPLIES: GROCERIES-HARDWARE | SUPPLIES: BAIT-TACKLE | SUPPLIES: DIESEL OIL-GASOLINE |
|---|---|---|---|---|---|---|---|---|---|---|---|---|---|---|---|---|---|---|---|---|
| 2 | CLYDE E SMITH&SON | 7.3 | +½ | | | | | | | | | | F | | | | I | G | | DG |
| 4 | GULF OIL CORP. | 7.3 | +½ | 28 | 6 | M | | | | | | | | | | | W | | | DG |
| 5 | MAC'S BAIT | 7.2 | +¾ | 4 | | | | M | 20 | 2 | | | | T | | | WI | | B | |
| 6 | THE JEKYLL MAR | 6.6 | +¼ | 15 | 8 | BME | | | | 2 | | CH | FLC | TS | | | WI | | BT | DG |
| 9 | FERNANDINA | 6.1 | +½ | 8 | 6 | B E | S | | | | | | FL | TS | | C | WI | H | BT | DG |
| 11 | KERRY DELL | | | 8 | 12 | B E | | HM | 80 | 20 | | | | TS | WD | | W | | | DG |
| 12 | SANDBAR REST | 5.6 | +1 | 4 | 4 | E | | | | | | | F | T | | | | | | |
| 12A | NASSAU SOUND | | | 7 | 2 | | N | | | | R | | | T | | | WI | | BT | G |
| 16 | PIRATES COVE | 4.0 | +¼ | 3 | 3 | | SN | | | | | | FLC | TS P | D | | WI | | BT | |
| 17 | WHITE SHELL | 4.0 | +¼ | 0 | 0 | | | | | | | | F | T | | | WI | G | BT | |
| 17A | SISTERS CREEK | 4.0 | +¼ | 12 | 8 | B E | | HM | | 37 | | | F | TSL | WD | C | WI | GH | | DG |
| 18 | SISTERS CRK FISH | 4.0 | +¼ | 8 | 8 | BME | S | | | | | | F C | TS | | | W | | BT | |
| 20 | MONTY'S MARINA | 4.5 | 0 | 20 | 10 | B E | S | | | | | C | F | T | | | WI | | BT | DG |
| 21 | MAYPORT PUBLIC BTRP | 4.5 | 0 | 4 | 4 | | S | | | | | | | T | | | WI | | B | |
| 26 | BEACH MARINE | 2.0 | +1¾ | 10 | 10 | B E | | HMR | 35 | | C M | CH | FL | TSL P | W | C | WI | GH | BT | DG |
| 27 | JACKSONVILLE YT B | 2.0 | +1¾ | 6 | 6 | B E | | M | | 4 | | | | | WD | | I | | | G |
| 32 | PALM VALLEY BR | | | 0 | 0 | | S | | | | | | F | T | | | WI | | BT | |
| 33 | PINE IS FISH | 2.5 | | 4 | 4 | | S | | | | | | C | TS | | | WI | | BT | |

## For pages 130–154:

| NO | LOCATION | TIDES: Mean Range-Ft | TIDES: Diff (Hrs) Miami Hbr Ent | DEPTH: Approach-Feet (Reported) | DEPTH: Alongside-Feet (Reported) | SERVICES: Electricity-Moorings-Berths (Transients) | Ramp Surfaced-Natural | Repairs Hull-Motor-Radio | Marine Railway-Feet | Lift Capacity-Tons | Boat Rental Canoe-Row-Motor | Charter-House-Sail | Food-Lodging-Camping | Toilets-Showers-Laundry / Pump-Out Station | SUPPLIES: Winter Storage Wet-Dry | Nautical Chart Sales | Water-Ice | Groceries-Hardware | Bait-Tackle | Diesel Oil-Gasoline |
|---|---|---|---|---|---|---|---|---|---|---|---|---|---|---|---|---|---|---|---|---|
| 2 | USINA'S FISHING | 4.2 | +¾ | 25 | 6 | | S | M | | | M | | C | TSL | | | I | G | BT | G |
| 3 | RIVERSIDE FISH | 4.2 | +¼ | | | | | | | | M | | | | | | | | B | |
| 3A | CAMACHEE COVE | | | 8 | 8 | BME | | HMR | | 37 | M | C S | F | TSL | W | C | WI | GH | BT | DG |
| 4 | ST AUGUSTINE | 4.2 | +¼ | | | | | M | | | | | | | | | | H | T | |
| 5 | RIVER VIEW MOTEL | 4.2 | +½ | 20 | 12 | BM | | | | | | | FL | | | | WI | | | |
| 6 | MUNICIPAL MARINA | 4.2 | +½ | 20 | 14 | B E | | | | | | | | TSL P | W | | WI | | | DG |
| 7 | ANCHORAGE MOTOR | 4.2 | +½ | 18 | 4 | B E | | | | | | | L | T | | | | | | |
| 8 | BY-THE-SEA MAR | | | 7 | 8 | B E | | | | | | | FL | TS | W | | WI | | | DG |
| 11 | HARRY XYNIDES | 4.0 | +1 | 25 | 15 | ME | | HMR | 100 | | | | | | | | W | H | | D |
| 13 | DEVIL'S ELBOW | | | | | | S | | | | M | | F C | TS | | | WI | | BT | |
| 14 | MARINELAND MAR | | | 12 | 6 | B E | S | | | | | | FLC | TSL | | | WI | GH | | DG |
| 15A | FLAGLER BEACH | | | 6 | 6 | B E | | HM | 50 | 50 | | | | TS | W | C | WI | H | | DG |
| 18 | ORMOND MARINA | | | 5 | 5 | B E | S | HM | | | M | | | TS | WD | C | WI | | B | DG |
| 19 | ALOHA MARINA | | | 5 | 4 | | | HMR | 30 | 9 | | | FL | L | WD | C | WI | GH | | G |
| 20 | DIXIE QUEEN LANDING | | | 8 | 6 | B E | | | | | M | C S | F | T | W | | WI | G | | |
| 22 | ENGLISH JIM'MARINA | | | 6 | 6 | B E | | | | | M | | | TSL | W | C | WI | H | | DG |
| 23 | HALIFAX R YACHT | | | 7 | 6 | B E | | | | | | | F | TS | | | WI | | | |
| 24 | CITY OF DAYTONA | | | 7 | 7 | B E | S | | | | | | | TSL P | W | | WI | | | DG |
| 25 | DAYTONA MARINA | | | 8 | 8 | B E | | HMR | | 400 | | | F | TSL | W | C | WI | GH | | DG |
| 26 | SEVEN SEAS MAR | 0.7 | +3½ | 6½ | 10 | B E | | HM | | 30 | | | F | TSL | | C | WI | GH | | DG |
| 29 | PERRYS S PENIN | 0.7 | +3 | 5 | 5 | B E | S | | | | | C | | TS | WD | C | WI | H | BT | DG |
| 31 | BRIGADOON FISH | 0.5 | +3½ | 3 | 5 | ME | | | | | | | | T | | | WI | | BT | |

| NO | LOCATION | TIDES: Mean Range-Ft | TIDES: Diff (Hrs) Miami Hbr Ent | DEPTH: Approach-Feet (Reported) | DEPTH: Alongside-Feet (Reported) | SERVICES: Electricity-Moorings-Berths (Transients) | Ramp Surfaced-Natural | Repairs Hull-Motor-Radio | Marine Railway-Feet | Lift Capacity-Tons | Boat Rental Canoe-Row-Motor | Charter-House-Sail | Food-Lodging-Camping | Toilets-Showers-Laundry / Pump-Out Station | SUPPLIES: Winter Storage Wet-Dry | Nautical Chart Sales | Water-Ice | Groceries-Hardware | Bait-Tackle | Diesel Oil-Gasoline |
|---|---|---|---|---|---|---|---|---|---|---|---|---|---|---|---|---|---|---|---|---|
| 32 | INLET HBR FISH | 1.5 | +¾ | 12 | 12 | | S | M | | 10 | | | F | TS | WD | | WI | GH | BT | DG |
| 33 | FISHERMANS WHRF | 1.5 | +¾ | 10 | 8 | | | | | | | | F | | | | I | | | |
| 34 | TIMMONS FISH | 2.2 | +¼ | 17 | 8 | BME | | | | | | | F | | | | WI | | | D |
| 35 | LIGHTHOUSE BTYD | 2.2 | +¼ | 6 | 9 | B E | S | HM | 65 | 60 | | | FL | TSL | D | C | WI | GH | | DG |
| 37 | CAUSEWAY MARINA | 2.0 | +¾ | 10 | 6 | E | | HMR | | 3 | | | | T | WD | | WI | H | | DG |
| 38 | SEA HARVEST YHT | 2.0 | +¾ | 12 | 8 | B E | | | | | | | | TSL | | | WI | | | DG |
| 40 | RIVERSIDE MARINE | 2.0 | +¼ | 10 | 6 | | | HMR | | 10 | | | F | T | WD | C | WI | H | BT | G |
| 44 | CEDAR CREEK RCT | | | 2 | 3 | E | S | M | | | C M | | FLC | TSL | W | | WI | GH | BT | G |
| 54 | WESTLAND MARINA | | | 9 | 12 | B E | | HMR | | | | | F | TS | WD | C | WI | G | | DG |
| 57 | TINGLEYS MARINA | | | 15 | 10 | ME | S | | | | | | FLC | TSL | WD | C | WI | G | BT | DG |
| 58 | ISLAND PT YACHT | | | 5½ | 5½ | B E | | | | | | | | TS | W | | WI | | | DG |
| 59 | INDIAN COVE MAR | | | 5 | 5 | B E | | HMR | | 25 | | | | TSL | | C | WI | | | DG |
| 60A | WHITELY MARINE | | | 7 | 8 | B E | | HM | | 37 | | | | TSL | W | C | WI | H | | |
| 62 | BANANA R MARINE | | | 4½ | 6 | B E | | HM | 45 | 30 | | | | TSL | WD | C | W | H | | |

# For pages 155–178:

| NO | LOCATION | TIDES: MEAN RANGE-FT | TIDES: DIFF (HRS) MIAMI HBR ENT | DEPTH: APPROACH-FEET (REPORTED) | DEPTH: ALONGSIDE-FEET (REPORTED) | SERVICES: ELECTRICITY-MOORINGS-BERTHS (TRANSIENTS) | RAMP SURFACED-NATURAL | REPAIRS HULL-MOTOR-RADIO | MARINE RAILWAY-FEET | LIFT CAPACITY-TONS | BOAT RENTAL: CANOE-ROW-MOTOR | BOAT RENTAL: CHARTER-HOUSE-SAIL | FOOD-LODGING-CAMPING | TOILETS-SHOWERS-LAUNDRY / PUMP-OUT STATION | SUPPLIES: WINTER STORAGE WET-DRY | NAUTICAL CHART SALES | WATER-ICE | GROCERIES-HARDWARE | BAIT-TACKLE | DIESEL OIL-GASOLINE |
|---|---|---|---|---|---|---|---|---|---|---|---|---|---|---|---|---|---|---|---|---|
| 1 | DIAMOND 99 MAR | 0.0 | | 7 | 7 | BM | | | | | | C S | | TSL | W | | WI | H | B | DG |
| 2 | INDIAN HBR MAR | 0.0 | | 10 | 8 | B E | S | HMR | | 60 | | | | TSL | | C | WI | GH | T | DG |
| 3 | ANCH EAU GALLIE | 0.0 | | 6 | 8 | B E | | HM | | | | | F | TSL | WD | C | WI | GH | | DG |
| 4 | EAU GALLIE YT B | 0.0 | | 10 | 8 | B E | | HMR | 120 | 50 | | | F | TSL | W | C | WI | GH | | DG |
| 5 | HARBOR MARINA | 0.0 | | 4 | 4 | R F | | | | | | | | | W* | | W | | | |
| 6 | EAU GALLIE HAR C | 0.0 | | 4 | 4 | BME | | | | | | | L | TS | | | WI | | | |
| 7 | KEELS + WHEELS | 0.0 | | 3 | 3 | | S | HM | | | | | | | WD | C | W | H | | G |
| 8 | NOEL YACHT CEN | 0.0 | | 8 | 10 | B E | S | HMR | 33 | 7 | M | C S | | TSL | WD | C | WI | H | | DG |
| 13 | PALM BAY MARINA | | | 3 | 2 | BME | S | | | | | | FL | T L | WD | | WI | GH | BT | G |
| 13B | PELICAN HBR MAR | | | 4 | 4 | B E | | | | | | | | P | W | | | | | |
| 18 | SUMMIT LANDING | 0.0 | | 5 | 5 | B E | | HMR | 40 | | | C | F | TS | W | C | WI | GH | BT | DG |
| 18A | MINER'S MARINA | | | 6 | 4 | B | | HMR | | 3 | | | | TS | D | C | WI | H | | G |
| 18B | S MELBOURNE MAR | | | 4 | 6 | B E | S | | | 6 | M | H | FL | P | D | | I | | BT | DG |
| 20 | LONG PT REC AREA | 0.0 | 0 | 3 | 3 | | N | | | | C | | C | TSL | | | WI | G | BT | |
| 20A | S BEACH MARINA | | | 5 | 5 | BME | S | HM | | 2 | CRM | | C | T | WD | | WI | H | BT | DG |
| 21 | SEBASTIAN R MAR | 0.0 | | 3½ | 5 | B E | S | | | | | H | F | TS P | W | | WI | | BT | DG |

| NO | LOCATION | TIDES: MEAN RANGE-FT | TIDES: DIFF (HRS) MIAMI HBR ENT | DEPTH: APPROACH-FEET (REPORTED) | DEPTH: ALONGSIDE-FEET (REPORTED) | SERVICES: ELECTRICITY-MOORINGS-BERTHS (TRANSIENTS) | RAMP SURFACED-NATURAL | REPAIRS HULL-MOTOR-RADIO | MARINE RAILWAY-FEET | LIFT CAPACITY-TONS | BOAT RENTAL: CANOE-ROW-MOTOR | BOAT RENTAL: CHARTER-HOUSE-SAIL | FOOD-LODGING-CAMPING | TOILETS-SHOWERS-LAUNDRY / PUMP-OUT STATION | SUPPLIES: WINTER STORAGE WET-DRY | NAUTICAL CHART SALES | WATER-ICE | GROCERIES-HARDWARE | BAIT-TACKLE | DIESEL OIL-GASOLINE |
|---|---|---|---|---|---|---|---|---|---|---|---|---|---|---|---|---|---|---|---|---|
| 32 | LITTLE JIM FISH | | | 8 | 8 | BME | N | | | | | | F | T | | | I | | BT | G |
| 32A | RIVERSIDE MAR | | | 8 | 8 | B E | | HMR | | 60 | | | | TS | WD | C | | H | | DG |
| 32B | TAYLOR CREEK M | | | 8 | 5 | | | HMR | | 20 | M | | F | T | D | C | WI | GH | BT | DG |
| 33A | HARBOUR HOUSE | | | 4 | 5 | | | | | | | C | F | T | | | WI | | | |
| 34 | MARINA-FT PIERCE | 0.7 | +2 | 8 | 5 | B | | HM | | | | | | T | | | W | H | | |
| 34A | ST.LUCIE CO.REC DEP | T | | 5 | 5 | | S | | | | | | | | | | I | | BT | |
| 36A | FT PIERCE INLET | | | 6 | 6 | | | HM | | | | | FL | TSL P | WD | | WI | G | | |
| 37 | PELICAN YACHT C | 0.7 | +2 | 7 | 7 | BME | | | | | | | F | TSL | | | WI | | B | DG |
| 38 | COCONUT COVE APT | 0.7 | +2 | 2 | 10 | B | | | | | | | | | W | | | | | DG |
| 39 | FT PIERCE CITY | 0.7 | +2 | 8 | 8 | B E | S | | | | | | F | TSL P | W | C | WI | H | | DG |
| 40 | NETTLES IS MARINA | | | 8 | 8 | B E | | HMR | | | | | FL | TSL | W | | WI | GH | | G |
| 41 | MARTIN COUNTY R | 0.5 | +2¼ | | | | S | | | | | | | T | | | | | | |
| 42 | SNOOK NOOK BT+T | 0.5 | +2¼ | 4 | 3 | B | | | | | | | F | | | C | WI | H | BT | |
| 44 | BAILEY BOAT HBR | 0.5 | +2¼ | 5 | 5 | B E | | HM | 50 | 8 | | | F | TS | WD | C | WI | H | | |
| 45 | OUTRIGGER RESORT | 0.5 | +2¼ | 8 | 8 | B E | | | 120 | | | C | FL | TSL | | | WI | | | DG |
| 46 | MARINA CAY MAR | 0.8 | +2¼ | 8 | 7 | B E | | | | | | | | TSL P | W | | WI | | | DG |
| 46A | POCKET WATCH MAR | | | 7 | 7 | BME | | HMR | | 40 | | | | T | WD | | W | H | | DG |
| 46B | SHIPLEYS MARINA | | | 5 | 5 | BME | S | HM | | | | | | T | WD | | WI | | B | DG |
| 49 | PIRATE COVE YHT | 0.8 | +2¼ | 9 | 5 | B E | | MR | | | | | FL | TSL P | W | | WI | H | BT | DG |
| 50 | PHILS MOTOR RPR | 0.8 | +2¼ | 5 | 4 | B E | | HM | 40 | 15 | | | | TS | WD | | | | | |
| 51 | MANATEE MARINA | 0.8 | +2¼ | 5 | 3½ | BME | S | HMR | 40 | 6 | | C | FL | TSL | WD | | WI | G | | DG |
| 54 | LOWES BOATYARD | 0.8 | +2¼ | 6 | 6 | B E | | HMR | | 150 | | | | TS | WD | C | W | H | | |
| 55 | WHITICARS BTWORK | 0.5 | | 3½ | 3½ | | | HM | 50 | | | | | T | | | W | H | | DG |
| 57 | BAY HARBOR CLUB | 0.5 | | 10 | 8 | B E | | | | | | | FL | | | | | | | |

| NO | LOCATION | TIDES: MEAN RANGE-FT | TIDES: DIFF (HRS) MIAMI HBR ENT | DEPTH: APPROACH-FEET (REPORTED) | DEPTH: ALONGSIDE-FEET (REPORTED) | SERVICES: ELECTRICITY-MOORINGS-BERTHS (TRANSIENTS) | RAMP SURFACED-NATURAL | REPAIRS HULL-MOTOR-RADIO | MARINE RAILWAY-FEET | LIFT CAPACITY-TONS | BOAT RENTAL: CANOE-ROW-MOTOR | BOAT RENTAL: CHARTER-HOUSE-SAIL | FOOD-LODGING-CAMPING | TOILETS-SHOWERS-LAUNDRY / PUMP-OUT STATION | SUPPLIES: WINTER STORAGE WET-DRY | NAUTICAL CHART SALES | WATER-ICE | GROCERIES-HARDWARE | BAIT-TACKLE | DIESEL OIL-GASOLINE |
|---|---|---|---|---|---|---|---|---|---|---|---|---|---|---|---|---|---|---|---|---|
| 59 | JIB CLUB INC | 1.3 | +1¼ | 8 | 8 | B E | | | | | | C | F | TSL | | C | WI | GH | BT | DG |
| 61 | JUPITER MARINE | | | 8 | 8 | BME | | HM | | 30 | M | C | F | TSL | WD | C | WI | H | B | DG |
| 71 | ARTS OUTBOARD | | | 6 | 3 | | | HMR | 24 | 4 | | | | | WD | | | H | | |
| 72 | E&H BOAT WORKS | 0.0 | 0 | 8 | 8 | | | HMR | 75 | 70 | | | | | D | | | H | | |
| 73B | OLD PORT COVE | | | 8 | 12 | B E | | | | | | | F | TSL | WD | | WI | H | B | D |
| 73C | SOVEREL MAR HBR | | | 10 | 6 | B E | | HMR | | 30 | | C | F | TSL | WD | | WI | GH | T | DG |
| 74 | N PALM BEACH M | 0.0 | | 7 | 5 | BME | | | | | | | L | TSL | | C | W | H | | DG |
| 75 | NORTHLAKE MAR | | | 6 | 3 | | | | | | M | | | | D | | I | | | DG |
| 76 | LOTT BROS INC | 0.8 | +¾ | 5 | 3 | | | | | 2½ | | C | | T | W | C | W | H | BT | G |
| 78 | BLUE HERON DOCKS | 2.0 | +1¼ | 8 | 5 | BM | | | | | | C | | TSL | W | | WI | | BT | |
| 80 | FLORIDA MAR SER | 2.0 | +1¼ | 6 | 6 | | | HMR | 80 | 75 | | | | | | C | | | | D |
| 81 | LAKE HAVEN DOCKS | 2.0 | +1¼ | 5 | 5 | B E | | | | | | | | TS | | | WI | G | | |
| 82 | OLD SLIP MARINA | 2.0 | +1¼ | 7 | 7 | B E | | H | 45 | 25 | | | | TS | | | W | H | | |
| 83 | CITY OF RIVIERA | 2.0 | +1¼ | 6& | 7 | B E | | M | | | | C S | | TSL P | WD | | WI | | | DG |
| 85 | CANNONSPORT MAR | 2.0 | +1¼ | 14 | 20 | B E | | | | | | | | TSL | | | WI | | | DG |
| 86 | BUCCANNEER YTCB | 2.0 | +1¼ | 25 | 25 | B E | | | | | | | FL | L | W | | WI | | B | DG |
| 87 | SAILFISH MARINA | 2.0 | +1¼ | | | B E | | | | | | C S | FL | TSL | | | WI | GH | BT | DG |
| 92 | RYBOVICH+SONS | 0.8 | +1¾ | 8 | 6 | | | HMR | 70 | 40 | | | | | WD | | WI | GH | BT | G |
| 93 | SPENCER BOAT CO | 0.8 | +1¾ | 12 | 12 | B E | S | HMR | 100 | 160 | | | FL | TSL | WD | C | WI | H | | DG |
| 94 | FLAGLER MARINA | | | 10 | 10 | B E | | MR | | | | C | | TSL | W | | WI | G | B | DG |
| 96 | CHASE DEVELOPMNT | | | 9 | 10 | B E | | | | | | | | TSL | | C | WI | G | | DG |

# For pages 179–194, 218–219, and 221–222:

| NO | LOCATION | TIDES: MEAN RANGE-FT | TIDES: DIFF (HRS) MIAMI HBR ENT | DEPTH: APPROACH-FEET(REPORTED) | DEPTH: ALONGSIDE-FEET(REPORTED) | SERVICES: ELECTRICITY-MOORINGS-BERTHS (TRANSIENTS) | RAMP SURFACED-NATURAL | REPAIRS HULL-MOTOR-RADIO | MARINE RAILWAY-FEET | LIFT CAPACITY-TONS | BOAT RENTAL: CANOE-ROW-MOTOR | BOAT RENTAL: CHARTER-HOUSE-SAIL | FOOD-LODGING-CAMPING | TOILETS-SHOWERS-LAUNDRY | PUMP-OUT STATION | WINTER STORAGE WET-DRY | SUPPLIES: NAUTICAL CHART SALES | WATER-ICE | GROCERIES-HARDWARE | BAIT-TACKLE | DIESEL OIL-GASOLINE |
|---|---|---|---|---|---|---|---|---|---|---|---|---|---|---|---|---|---|---|---|---|---|
| 2 | GUNDLACHS MARINA | | | 3 | 3 | B | S | HMR | | 8 | | | F | T | | D | | WI | | | G |
| 3 | MURRELLE MARINE | | | 5 | 5 | BME | | HMR | | 35 | | | | TS | | | | I | H | | |
| 4 | LANTANA BOAT YD | | | 8 | 8 | B E | | HMR | 120 | 150 | | | | TSL | | | | WI | H | | DG |
| 6 | LAKE WORTH BOAT | | | 6 | 6 | B E | | HMR | | 70 | | | F | TS | | WD | C | WI | GH | BT | DG |
| 7 | HYPOLUXO MARINA | | | | 6 | | | HM | | 30 | | | | T | | D | | WI | H | BT | G |
| 11 | SEA MIST MARINA | | | 15 | 10 | B E | | HMR | | 4 | M | | F | TS | | WD | C | WI | GH | BT | DG |
| 12 | TWO GEORGES MAR | | | 9 | 12 | BME | | | | | | C | F | TS | | | | WI | G | BT | |
| 13 | SEA MIST MARINA | | | 6 | 7 | B E | | M | | 3 | M | | F | TS | | WD | C | WI | GH | BT | DG |
| 16 | MYCO 66, INC. | | | 10 | 6½ | B E | S | | | | | C | L | TSL | | W | C | WI | GH | BT | DG |
| 19 | COVE MARINA . | 0.0 | | 6 | 8 | B E | | HM | | 20 | | | F | TSL | | W | | WI | GH | BT | DG |
| 20A | LIGHTHOUSE POINT | 2.0 | +½ | 9 | 12 | | | HMR | 45 | 45 | | | F | TSL | | | | WI | H | BT | DG |
| 25 | MERRITT BT-ENG | | | 6 | 6 | | | HMR | 60 | 50 | | | | TS | | | C | W | H | | D |
| 25A | STARBOARD MARINA | | | 3 | 3 | | | M | | 8 | | | | | | D | | I | | | G |
| 26 | BLUE LAGOON-POMP | | | 5 | 5 | | | HMR | | 50 | | | | | | | C | | H | | G |
| 27 | SANDS HARBOR INN | | | 14 | 13 | B E | | MR | | | M | C | FL | TSL | | | | WI | GH | BT | DG |
| 29 | BASIN MARINE CTR | | | 15 | 12 | E | | M | | 1 | M | C | F | T L | | W | | WI | | BT | DG |
| 30 | CAPTAINS COVE | | | 6 | 6 | | | HMR | 40 | 30 | | | F | | | | C | WI | | | G |
| 31 | POMPANO BEACH | | | 6 | | | | HMR | | 20 | | | | | | D | | | H | | |
| 31A | CYPRESS MARINE | | | 5 | 5 | | | HM | | | | | | | | D | C | | H | | |
| 34A | MARINA MAR | | | 6 | 3 | B | | HMR | 30 | 4 | | | | T | | D | C | WI | H | | G |
| 37 | BAHIA MAR YT CTR | 2.3 | +¾ | 12 | 10 | B E | | | | | M | C | F | TSL | | W | C | WI | GH | | DG |
| 41 | LAUDERDALE MAR | 2.3 | +¾ | 10 | 10 | B E | S | HMR | | 12 | | C | | TS | P | | C | WI | | BT | DG |
| 44A | INTRACOASTAL M | 2.3 | +¾ | 15 | 4 | | | HM | | 5 | | | | T | | D | | WI | H | B | G |
| 47 | SUN POWR DIESEL | 2.4 | +¾ | 20 | 10 | B E | | MR | | | | | | T | | | | WI | | | DG |
| 47A | HATTERAS | | | 8 | 9 | BM | | HMR | 85 | 70 | | | | | | | | W | H | | |
| 47B | MUNICIPAL MARINA | | | 17 | 10 | BME | S | | | | | | FL | | | W | | | | | |
| 48 | RIVERFRONT MARINA | | | 8 | 8 | M | | HMR | | 10 | | | F | T | | D | C | WI | GH | BT | DG |
| 50 | SUMMERFIELD | | | 10 | 8 | | | HM | 65 | 50 | | | | TS | | W | | W | H | | |
| 51 | BROWARD MARINE | | | | | | | HMR | 125 | 150 | | C | | | | W | | | H | | |
| 52 | LAUDERDALE YHT | | | 7 | 7 | BME | | HMR | 100 | 100 | | | | TS | | WD | | W | H | | DG |
| 52A | LAUDERDALE S-S | | | 4 | 8 | BME | | HMR | 110 | 50 | | | | TS | | WD | C | W | H | | |
| 53 | MARINA BAY | | | 35 | 40 | B E | | | | | | | FL | TSL | | W | | WI | | | DG |
| 53B | ROLLY MARINE S | | | 9 | 12 | BME | | HMR | | 75 | | | | TSL | | WD | | W | H | T | DG |
| 54 | ANCHORAGE MAR | | | 6 | 6 | B E | | HMR | 70 | | | | | T | | W | | W | H | | |
| 54A | HOLIDAY MARINA | | | 7 | 6 | | | HMR | | | | | F | | | | C | WI | H | BT | |
| 55 | PAIGO BROS, INC | | | 9 | 8 | BME | S | HMR | | 30 | | | F | T | | WD | C | WI | H | | DG |
| 56 | BRADFORD MARINE | | | 9 | 9 | B E | | HMR | 130 | 230 | M | | | TS | | W | | W | H | | D |
| 59 | OCEAN OUTLET M | | | 3 | 2 | | S | M | | | | | F | | | WD | | I | | BT | |
| 59A | RAMGOH | | | 4 | 2 | BM | S | HM | 50 | 3 | | | | | | WD | | | H | | G |
| 60 | RUSTIC INN | | | | | | | | | | | | F | T | | | | | | | |
| 60A | CALMAC MARINA | | | 10 | 8 | ME | S | HM | 26 | 8 | M | | F | TS | | D | | WI | H | B | G |
| 61 | RAVENSWOOD MAR | | | 7 | 4 | B E | | HM | | 10 | | | | TS | | D | | | H | | |
| 63A | JANISCH MARINA | | | 5 | 6 | | | M | | 5 | | | | T | | D | | I | H | BT | G |
| 66 | ROYALE PALM | | | 10 | 10 | B E | | HMR | | 50 | | | | TSL | | | | W | H | | D |
| 66A | DERECTOR GUNNELL | | | 8 | 12 | | | HM | 140 | 350 | | | | TS | | | | WI | | | |
| 66C | PLAY BOY MARINA | | | 8 | 8 | | | H | | 70 | | | | TS | | | | I | H | | |
| 67 | HARBOUR TOWNE M | | | 7 | 7 | B E | S | HMR | 50 | 70 | | | F | TS | | W | C | WI | GH | BT | DG |
| 68 | CITY OF DANIA | | | | | | | | | | | | F | TS | | | | WI | | BT | |
| 69 | DRY MARINA | | | 12 | 2 | | SN | HMR | | | | | | T | | D | C | WI | H | B | G |
| 72 | SEA LEGS MARINA | | | 6 | 12 | ME | N | R | | | M | C S | FL | S | | W | | WI | | BT | DG |
| 73A | S S HOLLAND PARK | | | | | | S | | | | | | | T | | | | W | | | |
| 75 | GULFSTREAM WATER S | | | 20 | 10 | BME | | | | | M | C S | F | T | | W | | WI | | | |
| 77 | HI-LIFT MARINA | | | 12 | 6 | | | M | | | | | | T | | D | C | W | H | | G |
| 78 | SUNNY ISLES BOAT | 2.0 | +1 | 4 | 8 | | | | | | RM | C | | | | | | | | | |
| 79B | MAULE LAKE MAR | | | 10 | 10 | B E | | HMR | | 68 | M | C S | F | TSL | | WD | C | WI | GH | BT | DG |
| 82 | BLUE MARLIN FISH | | | 7 | 3 | | S | M | | | | | | T | | | | I | | BT | |
| 83 | HAULOVER MARINA | 2.0 | +1 | 10 | 8 | B E | S | | | | | | F | T | P | W | C | WI | GH | BT | DG |
| 84 | KEYSTONE PT MAR | 1.5 | +1¾ | 6 | 20 | B E | | HMR | | 30 | | | | T | | WD | | WI | | | DG |
| 88 | SKYWAY MARINE | 1.8 | +2 | 5 | 5 | B E | | HMR | 45 | 20 | | | | TS | | WD | | WI | GH | BT | DG |
| 90 | FLAMINGO YCHT B | 2.0 | +1¾ | 8 | 8 | BME | | M | | | M | C | FL | TSL | P | W | | WI | | | DG |
| 91 | MIAMI BEACH MAR | | | | | B E | | | | | M | C S | FL | TSL | P | W | C | WI | GH | BT | DG |
| 92 | LANGERS MARINA | 2.0 | +1¼ | 5 | 5 | | | MR | 25 | 4 | | | | T | | | | WI | H | | DG |
| 92A | BISCAYNE BAY MAR | | | 7 | 4 | B E | | HMR | | | M | C S | FL | TSL | P | | C | WI | GH | BT | DG |
| 92B | WATSON ISLAND FUEL | | | 16 | 15 | BM | S | HM | | | M | | F | TSL | | | C | WI | H | BT | DG |
| 93B | DUPONT PLAZA | | | 80 | 35 | BME | | | | | | | FL | T L | | | | WI | | | DG |
| 94 | TOMMYS BOATYARD | 2.0 | +1¾ | 14 | 5 | | | HM | 50 | 25 | | | | | | | | | | | |
| 95 | DAWSON MARINE | 2.0 | +1¾ | 20 | 7 | | | | | | | | F | T | | | | WI | G | BT | DG |
| 96 | MIAMI SHIPYARD | 2.0 | +1¾ | 15 | 15 | | | HMR | 190 | | M | CHS | | TS | | | | | | | |
| 98 | ATLANTIC MARINE | 2.0 | +1¾ | 15 | 16 | B E | | HM | | 20 | | | | T | | WD | | | | | G |
| 100 | MIAMI PIONEER C | 2.0 | +1¾ | 6 | 3 | | | | | | | | | TS | | | | W | | | |
| 101 | TONYS MARINE | 2.0 | +1¾ | 15 | 6 | BME | | HM | | 40 | | | | | | W | | | | | |
| 104 | EIGHTH AVENUE | 2.0 | +1¾ | 10 | 6 | BME | | | | | | | | TS | | | | W | | | |
| 105 | NORSEMAN SHPBDG | 2.0 | +1¾ | 4 | 5 | B E | | HMR | 65 | | | | | T | | | | W | | | |
| 108 | ANCHOR MARINE | 2.0 | +1¾ | | | | | M | | | | | | | | | | | | | |
| 109 | MERRILL STEVENS | 2.0 | +1¾ | 6 | 8 | B E | | HM | 165 | 30 | | | | TS | | WD | | WI | | | DG |
| 110 | NUTA'S BOATYARD | 2.0 | +2 | 20 | 6 | B E | | HM | | 35 | | | | TS | | | | WI | GH | | |
| 111 | ALLIED MARINE C | 2.0 | +2 | 12 | 10 | | | HMR | 135 | 300 | | | | TS | | | | | | | DG |
| 112 | HARDIE YCHT BSN | 2.0 | +2 | 13 | 10 | | | | | | | | | TS | | W | | W | | | |
| 114 | POLANDS YCHT BSN | 2.0 | +2 | 15 | 8 | B E | S | | 40 | | | | | TS | | WD | | W | H | | |
| 118 | BERTRAM YCHT YD | 2.0 | +2 | 14 | 8 | B E | | HMR | 85 | 100 | | | | T | | W | | | H | T | DG |
| 121 | JONES BOATYARD | 2.0 | +2 | 12 | 12 | B E | | H | | 200 | | | FL | TS | | W | C | WI | GH | | DG |
| 121A | MARINA BISCAYNE | | | 8 | 7 | B E | S | HM | | 7 | M | C | F | TS | P | WD | C | WI | GH | BT | DG |
| 122 | CRANDON PARK M | 2.0 | +1 | 10 | 10 | BME | S | | | 5 | | C | F | T | P | WD | | WI | | BT | DG |
| 125 | MONTY TRAINERS | 1.9 | +1½ | 7 | 7 | B E | | | | | M | | F | TSL | | | | WI | H | | |
| 126 | MERRILL STEVENS | 1.9 | +1½ | 9 | 5 | B E | | HMR | 55 | 30 | | C | | TS | | WD | | WI | H | | DG |
| 128 | DINNER KEY MAR(H) | 1.9 | +1½ | 7 | 10 | B E | S | | | | | C S | L | TSL | P | | | WI | GH | BT | |
| 129 | CASTLE HBR SLBT | 1.9 | +1½ | | | | | | | | | S | | | | | | | | | |

# INDEX

Adams Creek, NC, 34, 35
Adams Creek Canal, NC, 35
Addison Point, FL, 150
Albemarle Sound, NC, 13–16
Alligator River, NC, 16–20
Alligator River–Pungo River Canal, NC, 20–24
Altamaha River, GA, 112
Amelia City, FL, 122
Amelia River, FL, 120, 121
Ashepoo/Coosaw Cutoff, SC, 91
Ashepoo River, SC, 91
Ashley River, SC, 84, 85
Atlantic Beach, FL, 125
Atlantic Beach, NC, 38
Bakers Haulover Inlet, FL, 190
Bal Harbour, FL, 189, 190
Banana River, FL, 152–155
Bay River, NC, 30, 31
Bear River, GA, 105
Beaufort, NC, 37
Beaufort, SC, 93, 94
Beaufort Inlet, NC, 195
Beaufort River, SC, 94, 95
Belhaven, NC, 26
Berkley, VA, 2
Biscayne Bay, FL, 189–194
Biscayne Channel, FL, 194, 220
Boca Raton, FL, 183
Bogue Sound, NC, 38–41
Boynton Beach, FL, 180, 181
Boynton Inlet, Fl, 180
Bucksport, SC, 67, 68
Brickyard Creek, SC, 93
Broad Creek, NC, 11, 12
Broad Creek, NC, 32
Brunswick River, GA, 115
Buck Island, NC, 10, 11
Bull Creek, SC, 68
Bull Creek, SC, 98
Burnside River, GA, 103
Buttermilk Sound, GA, 112, 113
Calabash Creek, SC, 62
Calibogue Sound, SC, 98, 204
Camden Mill, VA, 3
Camp Lejeune, NC, 42, 43
Canaveral Barge Canal, FL, 151, 213–216
Cape Canaveral, FL, 213–217
Cape Fear River, NC, 54–56
Cape Fear River Entrance, NC, 56, 196
Cape Florida Channel, FL, 194
Carolina Beach, NC, 53, 54
Charleston, SC, 84
Charleston Harbor Entrance, SC, 199
Chesapeake, VA, 2
Cocoa, FL, 152
Coconut Grove, FL, 193, 222
Coinjock, NC, 9, 10
Cooper River, SC, 84
Cooper River, SC, 98, 99, 204
Coosaw River, SC, 91–93
Core Creek, NC, 35, 36
Creighton Narrows, GA, 110

Crescent Beach, FL, 132
Cumberland Dividings, GA, 118
Cumberland Island, GA, 117–120
Cumberland River, GA, 117–119, 234
Cumberland Sound, GA, 119, 120
Currituck, NC, 8
Currituck Sound, NC, 8
Dania, FL, 187
Dania Cut-off Canal, FL, 187, 218
Daufuskie Island, SC, 98, 99, 204
Dawho River, SC, 89
Daytona Beach, FL, 140
Deep Creek, NC, 223
Delray Beach, FL, 181, 182
Dinner Key, FL, 193, 222
Doboy Sound, GA, 111
Dover Creek, GA, 234
Dover Cut, GA, 233
Dragon Point, FL, 155
Dumfoundling Bay, FL, 189
Eastham Creek, NC, 28, 29
Elba Island Cut, GA, 100
Elizabeth City, NC, 230
Elizabeth River, VA, 1
Elliott Cut, SC, 85
Enterprise Landing, SC, 67
Estherville–Minim Creek Canal, SC, 74, 75
Factory Creek, SC, 94
Fairfield, NC, 22
Fernandina Beach, FL, 120, 121
Fields Cut, SC, 100
Fisher Island, FL, 219
Fishermans Channel, FL, 192, 219, 221
Five Fathom Creek, SC, 77, 78
Florida Passage, GA, 104
Flagler Beach, FL, 137
Floyd Creek, GA, 234
Floyd Cut, GA, 234
Fort Lauderdale, FL, 185–187
Fort Pierce, FL, 164–166
Fort Pierce Inlet, FL, 166
Fourmile Creek Canal, SC, 75, 76
Fox Cut, FL, 135, 136
Frederica River, GA, 113, 114
Front River, GA, 109, 110
Gale Creek, NC, 29, 30
Gallant Channel, NC, 37
Georgetown, SC, 72
Gilmerton, VA, 2, 3
Goose Creek, NC, 28, 29
Government Cut, FL, 219, 220
Grant, FL, 158
Great Bridge, VA, 3, 4
Great Pee Dee River, SC, 71, 72
Gunnison Cut, FL, 123
Halifax Creek, FL, 138
Halifax River, FL, 138–142
Harbor River, SC, 78
Haulover Canal, FL, 146–147
Hell Gate, GA, 103
Hillsboro Inlet, FL, 184
Hillsboro River, FL, 183

Hilton Head Island, SC, 97, 98, 204
Hobe Sound, FL, 172
Hobuken, NC, 29
Hollywood Beach, FL, 188
Hurricane Harbor, FL, 193, 194
Hutchison Island, FL, 167–170
India Creek, FL, 189–191
Indian River, FL, 147–170
Indian River North, FL, 143–144
Isle of Hope, GA, 102
Isle of Palms, SC, 82, 83
Jacksonville Beach, FL, 126
Jekyll Creek, GA, 115, 116
Jekyll Sound, GA, 116
Jensen Beach, FL, 169
Johnson Creek, GA, 106, 107
Jupiter Inlet, FL, 173
Jupiter Island, FL, 171, 173
Key Biscayne, FL, 193, 194
Kings Bay, GA, 119
Kingsley Creek, FL, 121
Lake Boca Raton, FL, 183
Lake Worth, FL, 174–180
Lake Worth Inlet, FL, 175
Lake Wyman, FL, 182
Lanier Island, GA, 114
Lantana, FL, 179, 180
Lauderdale-by-the-Sea, FL, 185
Little Alligator River, NC, 16
Little Mud River, GA, 111, 112
Little River, SC, 62
Little Satilla River, GA, 233
Lockwoods Folly, NC, 58
Mackay River, GA, 113, 114
Mantanzas Inlet, FL, 133
Mantanzas River, FL, 131–133
Manatee Pocket, FL, 170
Marineland, FL, 134
Masonboro Inlet, NC, 51, 52
Maule Lake, FL, 189
Maw Point, NC, 30, 31
May River, SC, 97, 98
McClellanville, SC, 77, 78
Melbourne, FL, 156
Miami, FL, 191–193, 219–221
Miami Beach, FL, 191, 219
Miami River, FL, 221
Millville, VA, 3
Money Island, NC, 38
Morehead City, NC, 38
Mosquito Lagoon, FL, 145, 146
Mount Pleasant, SC, 83, 84
Mud River, GA, 109, 110
Myrtle Grove Sound, NC, 52, 53
Nassau River, FL, 122, 123
Neuse River, NC, 31, 33
New River, FL, 185–187, 218
New River, NC, 44, 45
New River, SC, 99
New Smyrna Beach, FL, 142, 143
Nixon Crossroads, SC, 63
No Name Harbor, FL, 194

Norfolk, VA, 1, 2
North Edisto River, SC, 89
North Landing, VA, 5
North Miami Beach, FL, 189
North Newport River, GA, 106
North Palm Beach, FL, 175
North River, GA, 111
North River, NC, 10–12
North Santee River, SC, 75
Ogeechee, GA, 103, 104
Old Teakettle Creek, GA, 110
Onslow Beach, NC, 43, 44
Oriental, NC, 33
Ormond Beach, FL, 139
Ossabaw Island, GA, 104, 105
Pablo Creek, FL, 125, 126
Palm Bay, FL, 157
Palm Beach, FL, 175–178
Palm Coast, FL, 135
Pamlico River, NC, 27, 28
Palm Shores, FL, 155
Parris Island, SC, 95, 96
Pasquotank River, NC, 228–232
Peletier Creek, NC, 38
Pinckey Island, SC, 97
Pompano Beach, FL, 184
Ponce de Leon Inlet, FL, 142
Ponte Vedra Beach, FL, 126, 127
Port Everglades, FL, 186
Port Orange, FL, 141
Port Royal, SC, 94
Port Royal Sound, SC, 95, 96, 202, 203
Portsmouth, VA, 2
Price Creek, SC, 81
Prince Creek, SC, 68
Pungo Ferry, VA, 6
Pungo River, NC, 24–27
Ramshorn Creek, SC, 99
Riviera Beach, FL, 175

"Rock Pile," SC, 63–66
Salt Run, FL, 131
Sampit River, SC, 72
San Sebastian River, FL, 131
Sapelo Island, GA, 108–111
Sapelo River, GA, 108, 109
Sapelo Sound, GA, 108, 208
Satilla River, GA, 116, 233, 234
Savannah River, GA, 100, 205
Sawpit Creek, FL, 123
Sears Landing, NC, 47
Sebastian, FL, 160
Sebastian Inlet, FL, 159, 160
Shallot Inlet, NC, 60
Sisters Creek, FL, 124, 211
Skidaway Narrows, GA, 102
Skidaway River, GA, 102
Skull Creek, FL, 97
Smith Creek, FL, 137
Snows Cut, NC, 53, 54
Socastee, SC, 66, 67
South Amelia River, FL, 122, 123
South Edisto River, SC, 90
South Mills, NC, 227
South Newport River, GA, 107
South Santee River, SC, 76
Southport, NC, 56, 57
Spooner Creek, NC, 38, 39
St. Andrew Sound, GA, 116, 117
St. Augustine, FL, 131
St. Augustine Creek, GA, 100, 101
St. Augustine Inlet, FL, 131
St. Catherines Sound, GA, 106, 207
St. Helena Sound, SC, 200, 201
St. Johns River Entrance, FL, 211, 212
St. Lucie Inlet, FL, 170
St. Lucie River, FL, 169, 170
St. Marys River Entrance, GA, 210
St. Simons Sound, GA, 114, 115, 209

Stono River, SC, 85–87
Stump Sound, NC, 46, 47
Sunny Isles, FL, 189
Sunset Beach, NC, 61
Swansboro, NC, 41, 42
Thunderbolt, GA, 101
Titusville, FL, 148, 149
Tolomato River, FL, 128–131
Tomoka Basin, FL, 138
Topsail Beach, NC, 48
Topsail Sound, NC, 47, 48
Tybee Roads, SC, 206
Umbrella Creek, GA, 233
Umbrella Cut, GA, 233
Vernon River, GA, 103
Vero Beach, Fl, 162
Virginia Key, FL, 193
Wabasso, FL, 161
Waccamaw River, SC, 67–72
Wachesaw Landing, SC, 68–69
Wadmalaw River, SC, 87–89
Walbury Creek, GA, 106
Wallaceton, NC, 224, 225
Wappoo Creek, SC, 85
Watts Cut, SC, 90
West Landing, VA, 5
West Palm Beach, FL, 177, 178, 179
Whiskey Creek, NC, 52
White Hall Shores, NC, 230
White Point, SC, 89
Whittaker Creek, NC, 33
Wilkerson Creek, NC, 24
Wilmington River, GA, 100, 101
Winyah Bay, SC, 72–74, 197, 198
Wright Creek, NC, 27
Wright River, SC, 99, 100
Wrightsville, NC, 51